HID

Georgia

HIDDEN ®

Georgia

Including Atlanta, Savannah, Jekyll Island, and the Okefenokee

FOURTH EDITION

Marty Olmstead

Ulysses Press ®
BERKELEY, CALIFORNIA

Published by:
ULYSSES PRESS
P.O. Box 3440
Berkeley, CA 94703
www.ulyssespress.com

ISSN 1523-5297
ISBN 1-56975-497-7

Printed in Canada by Transcontinental Printing

10 9 8 7 6 5

MANAGING EDITOR: Claire Chun
EDITOR: Lily Chou
COPYEDITOR: Barbara Schultz
EDITORIAL ASSOCIATES: Leona Benten, Kathryn Brooks,
    Nicholas Denton-Brown, Sara Pflantzer
TYPESETTERS: Lisa Kester, Matt Orendorff
CARTOGRAPHY: Pease Press
HIDDEN BOOKS DESIGN: Sarah Levin
COVER DESIGN: Leslie Henriques, Sarah Levin
INDEXER: Sayre Van Young
PHOTOGRAPHY: *garden:* Georgia Department of Economic
    Development; *golfer:* photos.com
ILLUSTRATOR: Doug McCarthy

Distributed by Publishers Group West

For Harriette Haines

Acknowledgments

Year after year, my home state of Georgia proves that it is still the most hospitable place in the world. So many people helped me with tips and support that I can't thank them all in print. In addition to friends both old and new, the representatives of the Georgia Department of Industry, Trade and Tourism provided valuable information and assistance during my research.

What's Hidden?

At different points throughout this book, you'll find special listings marked with this symbol:

◀ HIDDEN

This means that you have come upon a place off the beaten tourist track, a spot that will carry you a step closer to the local people and natural environment of Georgia.

The goal of this guide is to lead you beyond the realm of everyday tourist facilities. While we include traditional sightseeing listings and popular attractions, we also offer alternative sights and adventure activities. Instead of filling this guide with reviews of standard hotels and chain restaurants, we concentrate on one-of-a-kind places and locally owned establishments.

Our authors seek out locales that are popular with residents but usually overlooked by visitors. Some are more hidden than others (and are marked accordingly), but all the listings in this book are intended to help you discover the true nature of Georgia and put you on the path of adventure.

Write to us!

If in your travels you discover a spot that captures the spirit of Georgia, or if you live in the region and have a favorite place to share, or if you just feel like expressing your views, write to us and we'll pass your note along to the author.

We can't guarantee that the author will add your personal find to the next edition, but if the writer does use the suggestion, we'll acknowledge you in the credits and send you a free copy of the new edition.

ULYSSES PRESS
P.O. Box 3440
Berkeley, CA 94703
E-mail: readermail@ulyssespress.com

Contents

Maps

OUTDOOR ADVENTURE SYMBOLS

The following symbols accompany national, state and regional park listings, as well as beach descriptions throughout the text.

	Camping			Waterskiing
	Hiking			Canoeing or Kayaking
	Biking			Boating
	Horseback Riding			Boat Ramps
	Swimming			Fishing

ONE

Georgia Wandering

Scarlett O'Hara and Rhett Butler. Martin Luther King, Jr., and James Earl Carter. Ted Turner and Ty Cobb. Bobby Jones and Herschel Walker. Erskine Caldwell, Eugenia Price, Margaret Mitchell. Lady Chablis and Little Richard. The Allman Brothers and James Brown. Pogo and Uncle Remus. These are some of the colorful characters—real and fictional, living or legends or both—to come out of the state of Georgia. They've wandered Tobacco Road, the Okefenokee Swamp, Peachtree Street and the Marshes of Glynn until, in some people's minds, fact is virtually indistinguishable from fiction. Visitors at one middle Georgia country inn have actually asked to see where Scarlett and Rhett are buried.

The largest state east of the Mississippi, Georgia has room for them all. As the 13th colony, it has a long and lively history in which Revolutionary heroes, Civil War soldiers, contemporary statesmen, writers, singers, cotton farmers and grand dames have all played important roles.

From the snow-capped peaks in the northwest corner of the state to the golden islands strung along the Atlantic coast, the topography is almost as varied as the people. Despite this diversity, many Georgians don't seem to get around much, let alone move away from home. The state has 159 counties, three times as many as, say, the much-larger California. In the rural areas, where no big cities dominate, locals refer to "over in White county," for example, as if it were the other side of the moon, when in fact you are often standing within sight of the next county.

Rural Georgia includes not only the peanut farms of the southwest but the pecan groves of the middle of the state and large chunks of the mountainous areas. Many communities seem not to have changed all that much in the past 50 years, thanks in part to heroic preservation efforts but also because of the regional tradition of letting well enough alone. Thomasville in the south, practically in Florida, and Washington, which is between Augusta and Athens, are two of the smaller cities whose award-winning preservationist efforts have resulted in block after block of homes that predate the Civil War. So far, Thomasville has made better use of these mansions as bed-and-breakfast inns, but Washington may yet rival it in terms of tourist accommodations.

Some of the most memorable places in Georgia are not even on the mainland but on the pretty islands on the other side of the Intracoastal Waterway that runs along the eastern seaboard. Among them are wonderfully named places like Jekyll, Sea Island, Sapelo and Cumberland Island, a hard-to-get-to swath of mostly undeveloped wilderness that made headlines in 1996 when the late John F. Kennedy, Jr., chose to get married there.

Then there are interesting towns like Colquitt, home of the esteemed *Swamp Gravy* revue; Plains, where former President James Carter grew up; Warm Springs, whose hot waters soothed the aches and pains of another president, Franklin D. Roosevelt; Clayton, a mountain town renowned for its folk artists; Buena Vista, where an artist named St. EOM spent his last years building a five-acre monument to his visions; Zebulon, where you can spend the night in a place called Inn Scarlett's Footsteps; and Social Circle, a good name for a town with one of the most popular restaurants in Georgia. And that's not even getting into the wackier places.

Meanwhile, Atlanta has emerged as the capital of the New South, a city that continues to grow at a dizzying pace that thrills many locals but flabbergasts pokier outsiders whose idea of a really bad day is having to drive on Atlanta's freeways. Since the 1996 Summer Olympics brought worldwide fame to the city, which is the state's capital, the place is busier than ever, with new restaurants opening every week (or so it seems) and a growing number of interesting places to stay.

The cities of Macon, Athens, Columbus and Savannah are more manageable. Situated in the heart of the state, Macon capitalizes on its convenient location with attractions such as the Georgia Music Hall of Fame and the Georgia Sports Hall of Fame. Athens, where the University of Georgia is headquartered, is home to the Georgia State Botanical Gardens, a logical legacy for the city where the country's first garden club was organized. Built on the banks of the Chattahoochee River, which runs down the western border, Columbus has several military-related attractions due to its neighbor, Fort Benning, as well as to the city's importance as a boat-building site during the Civil War. Savannah needs the least introduction of all, thanks to the international acclaim of John Berendt's *Midnight in the Garden of Good and Evil*. The book and subsequent movie made household names out of Lady Chablis and Jim Williams, the late antiques dealer whose affair set a dramatic series of events in motion.

Through this drama—as well as movies and songs—you can learn a lot about the way Georgia looks and how people talk and live. But the only way to get to know the real Georgia and the people who live there and love it is to visit.

▼▼▼▼▼▼▼▼▼▼▼▼▼▼

The Story of Georgia

GEOLOGY

With the peaks of the Blue Ridge Mountains poking up from the northern landscape near the Alabama, Tennessee and North Carolina borders and the Atlantic Ocean lapping at the shore on the east side, Georgia is blessed with more topographical diversity than most states. The swamps, creeks and rivers that intertwine with the Intracoastal Waterway make this the southern portion of what is known as the Low Country (referring to the sea-level landscape), an area shared by South Carolina.

At least half the state comprises low coastal plains, portions of which—some as far north as Albany—were once underwater. North of Macon, around Athens in the middle eastern part of the state, the land turns hilly, with fertile slopes that define the Piedmont region. Farther north are the bigger hills and then the mountains, which are divided into the Appalachian Plateau in the northwest, the Appalachian Ridge and Valley region in the far north, and part of the Blue Ridge Mountains in the northeast corner.

While the Savannah River, salty at the mouth and fresh up around Augusta, defines the state line with South Carolina, the Chattahoochee extends along the length of the western border with Alabama. Visitors arriving in Atlanta by jet can often get a bird's-eye view of just how green the state is; the approach to Hartsfield International Airport usually includes about a half hour of relatively low-altitude flight over what seems to be unadulterated forest (many lowrise homes lurk beneath the canopy of oaks and pines). More than two-thirds of Georgia is forested, including thousands of acres within the Okefenokee Swamp, which also encompasses a bit of north Florida land.

Georgia's coast is relatively young. At the peak of the last Ice Age, the beach was some 95 miles east of where it is now. Charter boat captains know the Gulf Stream is a full 75 miles offshore today, quite a trek for deep-sea fishing, yet there are plenty of fish, mollusks and crustaceans in the waterways that wend among the islets within sight of the coast.

Over thousands of years, Appalachian highland erosion, carried east by the Savannah and Altamaha rivers, formed the Coastal Plain. Wind, tides and ocean currents still shift the marshes and beach sand as well as the dunes that define both the mainland coast and the perimeters of numerous barrier islands. Though the various barrier islands have their distinctive aspects, they are more alike than different, with miles of golden marshes and sugar-sand beaches.

FLORA   With apologies to the state symbol, the peach, the botanical image most often associated with Georgia is Spanish moss. Yes, it's a dull gray with such insignificant flowers that they go unnoticed. But there it hangs, transforming the graceful branches of centuries-old oak trees into something poetic. Its etymology is complex. The French explorers referred to it in their language as "Spanish beard." The Spanish, picking up the gauntlet, called it "French hair." Leave it to the peace-loving Swedes—in this case the 18th-century botanist Carolus Linnaeus—to come up with something that means "looks like moss." Hence, the garbled result: Spanish moss. The relentless Southern humidity that wilts everything else creates ideal conditions for this epiphyte (not a parasite), which depends on trees for support, sucking in sunlight, water and carbon dioxide along with goodies washed down in rainfall to create nourishment. As something that softens the landscape, even disguising it to some extent, Spanish moss is the quintessential Southern plant.

Only special plants can survive the salty, sandy environment of the coast. Sea oats, a favorite tourist souvenir because of their pretty plumes, have been found to be crucial to dune stabilization, thanks to their root system; as a result, picking sea oats is now prohibited by law. The salt marsh, which from a distance looks uniform in height and color, is a mixture dominated by cord-grass marsh that grows in various lengths.

The cities along the coast pride themselves on their azaleas, which provide a riot of magenta and white petals in the spring. Flowering dogwood, fragrant magnolias and honeysuckle create a dreamscape for romantics with their creamy flowers and rich scents. Here, and virtually throughout the state, the fast-creeping kudzu vine is constantly claiming fenceposts and telephone poles, sometimes camouflaging entire abandoned buildings in leafy green.

Farther inland are found six native species of pine—slash, loblolly, pond, longleaf, short leaf and spruce. Other trees with a high profile in the region include live oak, laurel oak, American beech, white oak, Southern magnolia, pignut hickory, dogwood, witch hazel, fringe tree, chinkapin and pawpaw, as well as the saw palmetto most often associated with the coastal islands. Bald cypress and tupelo dominate lakes and sloughs. On higher portions of the flood plain are more tupelos in addition to oaks, hickories and maples; one of the most productive plants in this area is the switch cane, providing wildlife with tasty dinners of edible leaves. Inland, particularly in the Okefenokee Swamp, cypress, tupelo and bay trees anchor their roots in the thick peat.

> Because slash pine grows so fast, it is favored by the paper and pulp companies whose widespread plantings line many a coastal Georgia highway.

Away from the coast, ten rivers flow through the rolling Magnolia Midlands, the largest watershed east of the Mississippi. One of them, the Altamaha, is an important ecosystem that is tidal even 40 miles inland. Its floodplains create the rich soils on which farmers grow world-famous sweet Vidalia onions, millions of pounds of blueberries and other crops. Farther west, the land supports peanut farms, pecan groves and white cotton fields.

The mountains that rim the top of the state are rampant with spring wildflowers like wild ginger and chickweed, which bloom along with rhododendrons and hardy dogwood. At the highest elevations, Catawba rhododendron and mountain ash flourish on what are called rock balds (although these "rock balds" often have forested tops). Below the summit, yellow birch and bass-wood are common trees; in the lower elevations are northern hardwood forests where Goldies, marginal and intermediate, are the characteristic wood ferns.

In descending order are the cove forests, which support diverse forest habitats of tulip poplar, ash, silverbell, oaks and magnolia; hemlock and heath forests; white pine forests; slope forests—mostly a mixture of oak and hickory since the chestnuts succumbed to a blight in the 1930s; and ridge forests around the Appalachian Trail, which are mostly virgin red oak. Blueberries flourish in this environment, pleasing the grouse and bear populations in summer and fall.

FAUNA   One of the joys of a trip to Georgia's coast is the chance to see dolphins swimming and leaping in the rivers and ocean. Sometimes entire pods of them chase shrimp boats or pleasure craft, seeming to enjoy it as we might like waterskiing. They share these extensive saltwater systems with myriad species of fish, reptiles such as loggerhead turtles, and crustaceans and mollusks—the sweet blue crabs, the shrimp and the oysters found in rivers and creeks. Above soar the terns, seagulls and, especially over the marshes, graceful white egrets.

On the beach itself, clams, sand dollars and the elusive ghost crabs burrow into the sand but can be found at low tide. The only marine turtle that regularly nests on the coast is the loggerhead sea turtle, which can grow to 800 pounds. They, too, are a threatened species, protected by both state and federal law. In the blackwater rivers, anglers find game fish like redbreast, bluegill, largemouth bass and catfish. They also encounter, less happily, water snakes, alligators and the occasional cottonmouth—none of these should be approached in any way.

While raccoons, squirrels, deer, duck, quail and other relatively small creatures are common along the coast, the really big mammals such as black bears stick to their mountain habitats. Along with venomous snakes such as copperhead, coral snake, cottonmouth and three rattlesnake species—of which one is the eastern diamondback—these critters are best left alone.

HISTORY   Long before the British established the 13th colony on the bluff of the Savannah River and named it after King George II, American Indians had the beaches, forests and rivers all to themselves. It wasn't until 1540, when explorer Hernando de Soto traveled through the area, that the natives suffered sickness and death in the wake of their exposure to unfamiliar European diseases. Later came the territorial disputes and cruel greed that would result in the forced migration of thousands of the native inhabitants from the northern part of the state.

FOR THE BIRDS

Georgia is a birder's paradise: ospreys swirl above the cypress in Okefenokee; wild turkey, dove and quail scoot in the underbrush of the woods; and some 350 migratory birds use the flyway above this part of the eastern seaboard. Throughout the state you are likely to see robins, crows, ruby-throated hummingbirds, warblers, woodpeckers (one version complete with red cockade), bald eagles, wrens, thrushes, warblers and purple martins, as well as predatory hawks and owls.

Thanks to the presence of several mounds in Georgia—the major ones being Etowah, Ocmulgee and Kolomoki—plus odd structures such as the 5000-year-old eagle effigy near Eatonton, historians have discovered artifacts from as far back as 10,000 years ago. The Paleo-Indian relics date from the days when nomadic hunters roamed the region, stalking their animals of prey—not deer and foxes but more likely giant sloths and woolly mammoths. By 1000 B.C. the hunter-gatherers of the Archaic period began agricultural endeavors; shards of their pottery have been found on coastal islands and elsewhere. Some of the mounds, though mysterious in many ways, tell much about the tribes of the Woodland period, while others defy explanation. Finally, around A.D. 900, people of the Mississippian period are known to have developed formal social structures, villages and rituals as well as farming techniques considered quite advanced for the time. By the time the colonists arrived, the Cherokee, Creek, Choctaw and Chickasaw tribes were all that remained of the numerous societies that had lived here over the centuries.

COLONIAL PERIOD   General James Edward Oglethorpe and a group of colonists founded the colony of Georgia in February 1733. Armed with a charter appointing the general and 19 associates as Trustees of the 13th (and last) colony, the founders were financed by England to aid the worthy poor of the mother country, to increase trade and navigation and to strengthen the colonies—particularly, to protect Carolina against Spanish Florida. After the English had settled Charles Town in 1670, the territory south of it had become a battleground between them and the Spanish, a conflict that would last until 1763. It was a tall order but one to which Oglethorpe responded with talent and success.

After inspecting several potential sites, Oglethorpe found what he considered "a healthy Situation, about Ten Miles from the Sea." He noted that the banks of the river, on the south side, were about 40 feet high, flat at the top, leveling into high ground that extended five or six miles.

"Ships that draw Twelve Feet Water can ride within Ten Yards of the Bank. Upon the River-side, in the Centre of this Plain, I have laid out the Town."

Oglethorpe and Colonel William Bull proceeded to establish the town based on a grid pattern (still in place today), intersected with public squares that give the town a distinct flavor and influence its social life.

More colonists arrived, many of them poor people who were unsuccessful in England but were considered good prospects for success in the colony. Scottish and Irish immigrants followed and by the mid-19th century, Germans as well. Fears of conflicts with the Spanish eventually slowed the rapid pace of settlement, although upriver, in places like Augusta, people felt safe enough to build homes and start their new lives.

As for the American Indians, the local Yamacraw people followed the lead of Tomo-chi-chi, whose auspicious meeting with Oglethorpe led to his granting the colonists permission to settle at the spot chosen by Oglethorpe. Thus Savannah was spared—as it was spared during subsequent times of turmoil—from the warfare that hindered the establishment of other American colonies.

Oglethorpe opposed the practice of slavery that was countenanced in the name of economic development in other colonies—after all, this was to be a haven for the oppressed—but 16 years after Georgia was founded, the rule against owning slaves was repealed. Likewise, the dream of "no rum" faded as well, and alcohol was allowed in the colony.

Meanwhile, the military advanced down the coast, having built Fort Jackson near Savannah. The barrier islands were fortified against the Spanish and French who fought for rights to the region continually. The British prevailed in the Battle of Bloody Marsh on St. Simons Island, a 1742 ambush that turned the tide of invasion. Eventually the Spanish abandoned their attempts to take over the fertile Georgia coast.

In 1776, Georgia joined other colonies in announcing independence from Britain, but by 1779, Savannah and every other major town in Georgia fell to the crown. Even after the British departed, the colonists took decades to recover from the destruction. Eli Whitney's invention of the cotton gin in 1793 helped jumpstart the economy by encouraging a boom in production that led to the phrase "King Cotton." It also destined the slaves to backbreaking labor while the planter class improved its lot in terms of education, culture and the social graces. It should be noted, however, that the vast majority of Georgia farms produced cotton and other crops without slave labor; the minority that held slaves were over 1000 acres. In the antebellum period there were also anomalies, such as former slaves who had earned their freedom and lived in Savannah and other cities as well as a handful of African Americans who owned slaves themselves.

Another group, the Cherokee, fared worse than the slaves in many ways: they were doomed by the discovery of gold on their lands in north Georgia. An advanced and highly organized nation, the Cherokee were headquartered in New Echota, not far from Atlanta. They printed a newspaper, were the first to develop a syllabary and chartered a constitution along the lines of the U.S. Constitution. Yet they were treated as interlopers once a white man found gold in 1829. Untold thousands of prospectors participated in the country's first real gold rush, which was centered in Dahlonega. Within the decade, President Andrew Jackson sided with the white Georgians who had essentially outlawed Cherokee land ownership. The native groups were rounded up and deported westward on the fatal march forever known as the Trail of Tears.

CIVIL WAR The worldwide phenomenon known as *Gone With the Wind* didn't so much exaggerate the ravages of the Civil War as it did dramatize them in ways that people who've read the book or seen the movie—most likely, both—"remember" the war in a certain way. Some of those ways—the notion that most Southerners held slaves, first of all, and secondly that they were willing to die for the right to own them—were invalid premises.

But if Georgia's dependence on agriculture was its salvation in the mid-1800s, it was the state's undoing by 1861 when the national debate over abolition peaked. Without slaves, the necessary field work couldn't be done profitably. Non-slaveholding Southerners were, by and large, determined to assert the state's right to govern itself. And so the war broke out in nearby Charleston and hundreds of thousands of men died because of it.

The face of Georgia is still scarred from the War between the States, not only at the wonderfully preserved battleground sites such as Chickamauga (where the second-bloodiest fight in the entire war took place) and the chilling cemetery at the Andersonville prison site, but also in the empty spaces. The town of Old Clinton, for example, was once a boom town, home to thousands, and for all intents and purposes would have become a major metropolitan hub had it not been for the Union troops who turned into a nigh ghost town. Today the town is among more than 200 significant Civil War sites; hundreds of other places, such as Atlanta's Cyclorama, will also interest history buffs.

Gone With the Wind illustrated General William Tecumseh Sherman's torching of Atlanta, in which he decimated 4000 buildings, leaving the city in ruins after it finally surrendered in September 1864. From there, he set out with 60,000 troops on the famous March to the Sea. They were enormously successful in this campaign of burning and looting, yet for various and sundry

A NEW START

Companies like Coca-Cola and CNN have changed the face of Atlanta—the capital not only of Georgia but of the entire New South—by creating a burgeoning economic base. Delta Air Lines, Lockheed, United Parcel Service and other major firms have made the most of the city's unparalleled location for cashing in on the renaissance of the Deep South economy. Atlanta and the rest of the state had survived the torment of defeat and reconstruction wrought by "carpetbaggers."

reasons spared such towns as Madison and, most importantly, the fantastic architectural heritage of Savannah. Instead of burning the lovely coastal dowager, he delivered it as a Christmas present to President Lincoln.

RECONSTRUCTION TO THE PRESENT   Savannah, spared the torch, continued to cling to tradition in its relatively isolated coastal location. Atlanta, by contrast, had to rebuild from the ground up. The opportunity to remake itself in a new image—after all, the city had only been 25 years old when Sherman came to town—was not lost on the citizens. Maybe there's something special in the Chattahoochee River waters, but the Atlanta sense of can-do and an in-your-face civic boosterism must have gotten its start then, sowing the seeds for the all-out effort a century and a half later to win its long-shot bid to host the 1996 Summer Olympics.

By the 1930s, Georgia had many reasons to be proud. Atlanta's Bobby Jones won the grand slam in golf. Margaret Mitchell's *Gone With the Wind* became a publishing phenomenon. Delta Air Lines and Eastern Airlines started servicing Atlanta. The biggest blemish on the face of the state was its reluctance to embrace racial equality. The birth of Martin Luther King, Jr., in Atlanta in 1929 would eventually alter the history of the Equal Rights struggle; Jimmy Carter, the peanut farmer from Plains, would finally make it as the first Georgian into the White House a little more than two decades later.

Now Georgia has entered the big time in terms of visitors. Tourism in Savannah is the envy of cities half its size. The Olympics gave a boost to regional pride and let the world see how far it had come, not only in civic sophistication but in racial tolerance as well. Atlanta and Savannah support sizable gay communities, perhaps surprising in cities so far deep in the Bible Belt. Following are summaries of what you can see in Georgia today.

Where to Go   You could start, like General Oglethorpe, by exploring Savannah. Now world-famous because of "The Book"— as *Midnight in the Garden of Good and Evil* is known locally—Savannah has actually been a popular tourist destination for decades. It's not the quirky characters who draw most visitors, but the two-and-a-half-square-mile historic district with block after block of 18th- and 19th-century buildings. Spared General Sherman's torch during the Civil War, these exquisite structures infuse the entire city with an ambience of graciousness and a sense of history. When the South suffered financial ruin after the War, and then when cotton lost its throne as King, there was no money for urban renewal on a grand scale. Citizens rallied when significant structures were threatened with demolition; the work of Historic Savannah inspired other people to save and restore their own homes. There are numerous tours of these and other attractions offered throughout the year. Farther afield are the quiet Tybee Island and scenic waterways, from the Savannah River to the Atlantic Ocean, that make the area ideal for outdoor activities.

Southeast Georgia includes the rest of the 100-mile coastline and the **Golden Isles**. Moss-draped oaks, golden marsh, blue waterways and plentiful seabirds (and seafood) add up to a picture-perfect paradise. You can visit Sapelo Island, now owned by the descendants of slaves; the state parks and the former Millionaire's Club at Jekyll Island; and the untamed beauty of Cumberland Island, accessible only by ferry. Inland is the incredible Okefenokee Swamp, where alligators slither in the tannin-rich waters beneath the cypress trees. Farther inland are small towns and farmlands boasting unique attractions, such as the museum in Fitzgerald that honors both the blue (Union) and the gray (Confederate) troops.

The mountains are chilly, especially at night, in the mid-spring and mid-fall; some lodgings in this region close in the dead of winter.

Southwest and West Central Georgia is still dotted with quail plantations and the Victorian homes erected by Northern snowbirds who flocked to this area, particularly to Thomasville, in the early 1900s. In the corner, Lake Seminole offers the best bass fishing in the state. There's more fishing at George T. Bagby State Park, near Fort Gaines, where you can see relics from the days when this was a frontier outpost. Nearby are the Kolomoki Mounds, the ancient series of intriguing structures dating back thousands of years. This is also the land of presidents, from Jimmy Carter, born and raised in Plains, to Franklin D. Roosevelt, who bathed in the healing waters of Warm Springs near his winter retreat.

There's no question that **Atlanta** is the capital not only of Georgia but of the entire New South. A self-made city built on the ashes of Civil War battles, Atlanta has come into its own, with world-class restaurants, major-league sports facilities and an international airport that serves the corporate headquarters of such famous names as CNN and Coca-Cola. It's a city of neighborhoods: the funky streets of Sweet Auburn, where Martin Luther King, Jr., grew up and preached; the graceful boulevards of Buckhead; the colorful shops and restaurants of Virginia-Highlands; the farflung satellite communities of Roswell and Marietta to the north. A visit to Atlanta challenges the very concept of the "sleepy old South."

The Mountains of north Georgia stretch from Alabama to North Carolina. This is where the Appalachian Trail begins, in the forests well north of Atlanta. Whitewater canoeing, hiking and exploring the back roads and folk-art galleries are among the diversions in this part of the state. History is alive in these hills, from the largest military park in the country (Chickamauga) to various Indian sites.

Two sites dear to the heart of hundreds of thousands of Georgians—the University of Georgia and the Augusta National Golf Club, where the legendary Masters is played each spring— are located in **East Central Georgia.** Athens is a lively college town, whose nightclubs spawned such major rock groups as the B-52's and R.E.M. Augusta is more sedate, a river town proud of its cotton heritage and its unique museum devoted to Southern art. The amazingly preserved and restored antebellum homes of Washington make this one of the best towns in the state for admirers of 18th- and 19th-century architecture. Within the city limits are five historic districts, two national landmarks and 21 properties listed on the National Register of Historic Places.

All of Georgia tends to be humid, even Atlanta, which is in the Piedmont region. Atlanta and parts north receive an occasional dusting—or more—of snow, but all in all the state has a mild climate.

Some of the prettiest and best-preserved antebellum homes and towns can be visited in **Middle Georgia.** Most of Madison, for instance, is on the National Register of Historic Places; Milledgeville, formerly the state capital, is a close second in terms of stately houses. Macon, at the center of the state, celebrates its musical roots—and those of the entire state—with a knockout of a music hall of fame starring such regional talents as Otis Redding, Little Richard, Gladys Knight and the Allman Brothers. South of Macon is a series of small towns where peaches and camellias grace the landscape.

When to Go

SEASONS

Georgia's climate is considered mild, but that's just on the average. Winters in the mountains and even as far south as Atlanta can be quite cold, with many nights below freezing. Winters are much more temperate in the southern part of the state, which shares many climatic factors with northern Florida. About every 20 years it snows briefly on the coast around Savannah. Although winters are so mild that people have to wait a month or two to wear the sweaters they received as holiday gifts, the humidity can subtract a few degrees.

Spring is balmy all around; azaleas and magnolias scent the air and the heavy heat of summer is months away. It rains like clockwork on the coast during many summer afternoons on the coast, though sometimes the showers are quite brief. A major rainstorm can make driving almost impossible.

Summertime can be very hot everywhere but at the beaches and in the mountains. This is the time to find a cottage near a body of water. Sea breezes keep temperatures down, and the ocean—though warm in summer—feels cooler than the air. Though most hotels and motels are air-conditioned, permanent beach residents often rely instead on light winds that usually keep afternoon temperatures from reaching the high 90s. Nights are warm without exception.

Autumn is a beautiful time in the mountains, where hiking trails are quite crowded on crisp days. This time of year brings good deals to the beach towns because the weather is mostly clear and often almost balmy until around Thanksgiving. Places like Savannah are as popular in October as they are in April and May, now that visitors have caught on to the climate.

The biggest downside to late summer and early fall in the coastal region is, of course, the threat of hurricanes. Tropical storms are more likely, however; heavy downpours during full moons are likely to flood roadways, particularly those along the intracoastal waterway.

CALENDAR OF EVENTS

Georgians have a lot to celebrate, starting with spring weather. Cherry blossoms and stately homes both open in the spring and several events coincide with these happenings. The state's many agricultural products, livestock and crafts also get their own calendar dates. Then there are sporting events, such as The Masters' Golf Tournament, and quirky homespun festivals that are worthwhile to include in your Georgia wanderings.

JANUARY

January, being the coldest month of the year in Georgia (in some places, in fact, the only cold month), is not a popular time for fairs and festivals. (Or perhaps it's because most people party so much during the holidays that they're too exhausted to produce an event, using the month, instead, to rest.)

Atlanta   For ten days surrounding the national holiday marked by Martin Luther King, Jr.'s birthday on January 15, **King Week** offers a full roster of cultural arts and entertainment as well as speeches and interfaith services.

FEBRUARY

Savannah   The **Black Heritage Festival** fills the first two weeks of the month with art exhibits, dance performances, theater, lectures and musical concerts at Savannah State University. Old Fort Jackson is the site of a major **Civil War re-enactment** in the middle of the month, complete with cannon firings, nautical music, sea shanties and displays of sailors' art.

Atlanta   The largest juried gardening and horticultural show in the region, the **Southeastern Flower Show** blossoms for five days in the middle of the month in midtown Atlanta, with four acres of exhibition space.

Middle Georgia   The **Georgia National Rodeo** takes place the last two weeks of the month in Perry at the Georgia National Fairgrounds & Agricenter, where rodeos are the main attraction and the livestock and horse shows are free.

MARCH **Savannah** A highlight of every spring is the annual **Savannah Tour of Homes & Gardens** late this month. Self-guided walking tours make the rounds of private homes and gardens; each stop is different in terms of age and style but all feature 18th- and 19th-century buildings. Acclaimed as one of the top events in the country every year, **St. Patrick's Day** festivities commence on the 13th and culminate with a grand parade on the last day, with countless parties before, during and after, including live music in the City Market square.

Golden Isles & Southeast Georgia There's nothing like Fitzgerald's **Rattlesnake Roundup** in the middle of the month. In addition to arts-and-crafts displays, there are rattlesnake demonstrations, dancing, music and food. For over a quarter of a century, the **Jekyll Island Garden Club Tour of Homes and Flower Show** has been the loveliest event held in the Historic District of this golden isle.

Middle Georgia Macon's ten-day **Cherry Blossom Festival** attracts thousands of people in the middle of the month to appreciate the stunning sight of more than 265,000 Yoshino cherry trees blooming downtown, along with 500 events including concerts, exhibits and parades.

APRIL **Golden Isles & Southeast Georgia** Celebrating one of Georgia's world-famous crops, the **Vidalia Onion Festival** is a four-day event late in the month. Cooking demonstrations show how to cook with the world's sweetest onion, while street dancers, rodeo performers, a parade, a carnival and an air show provide entertainment. In honor of the funny and politically astute comic-strip alligator, **PogoFest** features a parade, a barbecue, a cartooning award, arts, crafts, entertainment and children's activities. Traditional acoustic Appalachian and bluegrass music, jam sessions, concerts, Appalachian crafts, a live theater production of "Foxfire" and children's activities take place during the **Bear on the Square Mountain Music and Folk Art Festival** in downtown Dahlonega the last weekend of the month.

Southwest and West Central Georgia Different musicians and artists perform each year at Bainbridge's River Town Days Festival in the middle of the month. There's an antiques and collectibles show, a 5K run, entertainment for the kids and a night-time street dance.

Atlanta **Inman Park Spring Festival & Tour of Homes** gives visitors a close-up view of Atlanta's first planned suburb, including many examples of early-20th-century architecture. In addition, there are art exhibitions and a dance festival.

East Central Georgia Exhibitors from all over the country bring their classic wooden speedboats, many dating from the 1920s to the 1960s, to the **Lake Hartwell Antique Boat Festival**. Golf aficionados flock to Augusta in droves for the seven-day **Masters Tournament** early in the month.

Middle Georgia   Early April is the **Hawkinsville Harness Horse Festival and Spring Celebration,** known as one of the biggest and best public parties in the state. During the third week of the month, the **Pan African Festival at the Tubman Museum** in Macon celebrates the Pan African culture and its contributions to America. Featured activities include a parade of masquerades, Caribbean steel bands, reggae, African music, dancers, film, children's activities and cultural demonstrations.

Southwest and West Central Georgia   The Chehaw National Indian Festival, which happens on the middle weekend of the month, is one of the ten largest American Indian performing-arts and cultural festivals in the country, with tribes coming from as far away as South America to perform in dance teams and other events.

MAY

Atlanta   The Taste of the South at Stone Mountain offers a wonderful opportunity to taste some of the classic delectables favored in this part of the country. From Georgia's own Brunswick stew and Vidalia onion creations to specialties from Louisiana and Texas, your taste buds will never be the same. The **Atlanta Jazz Festival** is an all-month, mostly alfresco series of concerts throughout the city, culminating in back-to-back performances by major artists over Memorial Day weekend in Piedmont Park.

East Central Georgia   Southworks Arts Festival takes place late in the month in Watkinsville and includes two days of musical entertainment, Southern gourmet foods, a market of arts and crafts, and a regional juried art exhibition.

The Mountains   The **Prater's Mill Fair** is known far and wide as one of the top festivals for handmade crafts and folk art in the entire southeast. The 1855 mill is located ten miles northeast of Dalton. (The fair repeats in mid-October.)

Golden Isles & Southeast Georgia   The Jekyll Island Musical Theatre Festival starts late this month and runs through July at an amphitheater open to the soft sea breezes.

JUNE

Southwest and West Central Georgia   Newnan, known as the "City of Homes" because of its five historic districts, generally manages to be in full boom at this time of year for the **Magnolia Blossom Festival** on the first weekend of June. Local artists, craftspeople, food vendors, entertainers and merchants all get into the act.

Atlanta   Telling stories is a major part of life in the Deep South, and this time-worn tradition is celebrated in June at the **Roswell Storytelling Festival** on the outskirts of Atlanta.

The Mountains   Cloggers, fiddlers and other musicians converge on Dahlonega every fall for a traditional **Bluegrass Festival**.

Middle Georgia   The famous fuzzy fruit is honored early this month at the **Georgia Peach Festival** in Fort Valley known for producing the world's largest peach cobbler.

JULY

Golden Isles & Southeast Georgia   The annual **Sunshine Festival** is an island-wide party on St. Simons Island for the first few days of the month, featuring rides (Ferris wheel and rollercoaster), arts-and-crafts exhibits, military displays and food from top restaurants, capped by fireworks on July 4th.

Atlanta   The **Fantastic Fourth Celebration** is a three-day wing-ding at Stone Mountain Park, where bursts of light illuminate the sky from both the base and the top of the mountain; entertainment includes a lasershow extravaganza. The Georgia History Center hosts an annual **Civil War Encampment** for two days mid-month, featuring Federal and Confederate soldiers, tents, campfires, cavalry, music, artillery and drills.

Middle Georgia   The hot days of summer inspired the **Watermelon Festival** in Cordele, which calls itself the Watermelon Capital of the World. There are fireworks, a parade, dancing, gospel singing, and entertainment, including all kinds of watermelon-related contests.

AUGUST

Golden Isles & Southeast Georgia   St. Simons Island holds a **Sea Island Festival** honoring the African-based Geechee culture with music, food and crafts.

Atlanta   Just outside the capital, the **Vineyard Fest** at Chateau Elan Winery & Resort spells the end of summer with a grand finale to its summer concert series and all-day festivities with hot-air balloons, music, food and wine, games and tastings.

The Mountains   The first three weekends of the month comprise the **Rock City Fairy Tale Festival** on Lookout Mountain, a perfect location for gnomes and fairies.

SEPTEMBER

Golden Isles & Southeast Georgia   The small town of Kingsland hosts an annual **Labor Day Weekend Catfish Festival** with all kinds of food (catfish as one of the treats, of course), a parade and children's entertainment.

Southwest and West Central Georgia   Of course the town of Plains, Jimmy Carter's birthplace, would have to have a **Peanut Festival**, which shows you everything you need to know about the lowly legume and the many ways to eat them.

The Mountains   A watermelon-eating contest—in conjunction with a seed-spitting contest—is part of the hilarity at the **Banks County Festival** in early September. Festivities include a parade, a cake walk, arts-and-crafts displays, food booths and more in the town of Homer.

Savannah   Greek dancing and food highlight the three-day Savannah Greek Festival.

OCTOBER

Golden Isles & Southeast Georgia   The **Okefenokee Festival** in Folkston is headquartered in a restored train depot on Main Street and features a bike race, handmade arts and crafts, food, entertainment and a parade. The **Cotton Harvest Festival and Fly In** in Hazlehurst offers a cotton-pickin' good time with arts, crafts, children's entertainment, a fun run and great food.

Southwest and West Central Georgia   Plantation-home tours, primitive folk-art displays, an antique show and a children's plowing contest are highlights of the annual **Mule Day Heritage Festival** at Callaway Plantation near Pine Mountain.

The Mountains   Red Delicious, Golden Delicious, Winesaps, Fujis, Mutsus and Granny Smiths are just some of the varieties you can sample at **Apple Day** in Ellijay, actually two mid-month weekends that celebrate one of the town's top-two products (the other being barbecue). The **Georgia Marble Festival** is a unique opportunity to check out marble sculpture and fine arts, crafts and theatrical productions in Jasper, located in the heart of the state's marble country. With its Teutonic ambience, Helen is the perfect place for a blow-out **Oktoberfest**, complete with polka music, the best of wursts and full beer steins for all. Dahlonega relives the **Gold Rush Days** during a full weekend of panning for gold and gemstones and a look back at the glory days of 1838.

Middle Georgia   You don't have to love barbecue to love the **Big Pig Jig**, but it helps. There's more to this early October event in Vienna than cooking and eating, though: there are pig-judging contests and much more at what's been called the Redneck Mardi Gras. The **Georgia National Fair** in Perry also early this month focuses on agrarian life with livestock exhibits, free entertainment, fine arts, a petting zoo, fireworks, a flower show, baking competitions, antique tractors and cars, food and big-name concerts.

Savannah   The first Saturday of every month, River Street hosts an **Arts & Crafts Festival** on the banks of the Savannah River with food, art and entertainment.

NOVEMBER

The Mountains   The **Toccoa Harvest Festival** is a weekend of old-time demonstrations, country crafts, a quilt and art show, antiques and entertainment as well as children's activities.

The holidays are festive throughout the state, particularly at Callaway Gardens and in Savannah as well as the capital city. Even in small towns you'll find Main Street dressed up for the season with garlands and special street lights.

DECEMBER

Atlanta   A special family-oriented event during the holidays, the **Candlelight Tours** take people through the 1928 Swan House and 1845 Tullie Smith Farm at the Atlanta History Center.

The Mountains   From before Thanksgiving until early January, Rock City's **Enchanted Garden of Lights** creates a twinkling fairy-tale accenting the natural beauty of the gardens.

Southwest and West Central   In the middle of the month, the **Holiday Tour of Homes** in Pine Mountain features select homes, inns and churches in the area.

Before You Go

VISITORS CENTERS

The **Georgia Department of Industry, Trade and Tourism** publishes a free comprehensive booklet, "Georgia on My Mind," on the state's attractions, including some sporting opportunities and lodging choices (campsites, too) but no restaurants. It lists the addresses and telephone numbers for state parks and local visitors bureaus. You may also order free state road maps from them. ~ 285 Peachtree Center Avenue Northeast, Suite 1000, Atlanta, GA 30303-1230; 404-656-3545, 800-847-4842, fax 404-651-9063; www.georgia.org.

There is a **Georgia State Welcome Center** north of Savannah that dispenses information and oodles of brochures on Savannah and the rest of coastal Georgia. ~ Off Route 95. In the southern part of the state, the **Welcome Center** near Valdosta has computerized connections to regional lodging and campgrounds. ~ Off Route 75 between Exits 1 and 2. In addition, most towns have a chamber of commerce or visitor information center (see individual chapters). As a general rule, these tourist information centers are not open on weekends.

PACKING

What you should pack depends on when you travel to Georgia and, to a lesser extent, where. While jackets for men and dresses for women are rarely part of the dress code, you'll never be out of place in them on city streets or in restaurants. In small towns and in the countryside, jeans and sneakers are perfectly acceptable. In cities, you'll feel more comfortable in khakis and walking shoes for touring, though you will doubtless see people in skimpy shorts and T-shirts. Except for formal events such as the Masters or major art exhibits or other cultural programs in the big cities, attire is generally quite casual throughout the state.

In winter, sweaters, jackets and even mittens are a good idea for the mountain areas. Even as far south as Savannah, January and February can be very cold months. Spring mornings and late autumn days can be crisp everywhere.

In the summer, you won't need any cover up in the outdoors except in the mountains, where nights are cold in spring and cool even in summer. However, the heat forces many museums, stores and restaurants to crank up the air conditioning so, with that in mind, take some kind of wrap. There is no truly dry season in Georgia; this goes double for summer, when brief afternoon showers are common and downpours are always a possibility. Take a windbreaker, raincoat and/or umbrella to be on the safe side.

The beaches are very, very casual for the most part. On St. Simons Island or Sea Island and in the city of Savannah, people dress up much more than they do on, say, Tybee or Jekyll islands. The sun can be brutal from June well into September; serious sunscreen and a hat or cap will be necessary everywhere south of Macon. If you think you might go out to a barrier island or into the Okefenokee Swamp, you will rue the day you forgot to pack industrial-strength bug repellent. Spring evenings usually bring an onslaught of "no see-ums," nearly invisible bugs that are harmless but quite irritating.

In the area of dress, as in so many things, Atlanta is a world unto itself. In this sense, the capital city has more in common with New York than with the rest of the state. People dress very well, especially for evenings out. This means a skirt or dress for ladies, a coat and tie for gentlemen. You're unlikely to see blue jeans in any nice restaurant except in well-known casual neighborhoods such as Virginia-Highland.

Bring a camera to capture the charming and historic scenes you're guaranteed to encounter.

LODGING

Eighteenth-century homes, Victorian mansions, island estates, restored farmhouses, lakeside cottages, cabins in the woods, seaside motels and historic hotels offer something for Georgia travelers of every taste and budget. They are the colorful alternatives to the plentiful—and mostly less expensive—chain motels and hotels found near interstates and in country towns as well as big cities.

The towns and cities with antebellum homes that survived the ravages of the Civil War have the most potential for transforming the old buildings into charming inns with the patina of

WHEELIN' AND DEALIN'

To make the most of your stay, it's wise to shop around for lodging bargains. One region's peak season may be another's off period. Deals are next to impossible on spring weekends, particularly St. Patrick's Day in Savannah, the Masters golf tournament in Augusta, the Cherry Blossom Festival in Macon and so forth. Now that Georgia has been discovered by so many travelers, October competes with May for the most popular month of the year. However, along the coast, October through December are usually mild months and bargains are a real possibility. Similarly, late February to mid-March is an iffy period where you might luck out with fabulous weather anywhere in the state. Or not, of course.

history and the pampering of modern conveniences. In this arena, no place comes close to Savannah, although smaller locales such as Madison and even tinier towns have a wealth of old homes that have been converted and welcome overnight guests. In the past few years, Savannah innkeepers have realized the gold mine on which they sit and charge accordingly. Yet if price is a consideration, one only has to book accommodations on the outer rim of the Historic District, where rooms are less expensive but the breakfasts and hospitality are equally good.

In terms of lodging, Atlanta is an anomaly. Since the capital city suffered massive destruction in the Civil War, antebellum homes here are few and far between. However, it's a mystery why this cosmopolitan city has such a paucity of individual inns. There are some great hotels, but relatively few are independent and able to offer the kind of unique ambience that makes overnight stays memorable. Still, more inns have opened in recent years and there are a number of extremely nice bed-and-breakfast spots north of the Perimeter Road such as Marietta and Roswell.

Then, of course, there are places where the accommodations are part of the experience, inns where you can absorb the atmosphere of the locale in a unique way. One such place is the Greyfield Inn, the only commercial lodging on Cumberland Island. Not far away is Little St. Simons, a private island with chic/rustic accommodations; on nearby Jekyll, spending the night at the Jekyll Island Club Hotel puts you on familiar footing with the millionaires who lived here in their own club in the late 1800s. Another is Melhana Plantation, in the heart of quail-hunting south Georgia. In every part of the state you can find a small lodge or hotel— the Hotel Warm Springs Bed and Breakfast, Glen-Ella Springs Inn in Clarkesville, the Tarrer Inn on the square in Colquitt—that personify the surrounding town. Other unusual accommodations can be found in the middle of nowhere, such as Inn Scarlett's Footsteps in Zebulon, the Old Town Plantation in Louisville, and the Colemans Lake Resort on its own lake.

Rates for accommodations vary tremendously around the state. In some small towns, a night in an antebellum home with a full Southern breakfast is likely to cost half what something similar would cost in Savannah or Atlanta. For the sake of consistency, we have one price range for each of four categories statewide, based on double occupancy, high-season rates. You may notice that most of the accommodations listed in Savannah's Historic District, for example, are deluxe or ultra-deluxe. The hundreds of thousands of dollars it costs to buy and restore an old home in this area, and then furnish it with period antiques, results in high prices for visitors.

Budget lodgings are priced at less than $60 for two; rooms are clean and comfortable but lack any frills. *Moderate*-priced hotels are $60 to $90, a rate that usually includes a larger room, plusher furniture and at least a continental breakfast. *Deluxe*-priced accommodations run between $90 and $125 for a homey B&B or a double in a resort. For *ultra-deluxe* lodging, the price is more than $125 a night, which means you will get a full breakfast and lots of pampering. Outside of Atlanta and Savannah's Historic District, Georgia has few lodgings in the top range unless you book a suite at a major hotel. At ultra-deluxe inns, you may well find a concierge, for example, who can do all the things a regular hotel concierge can do, from booking theater tickets to remembering how you like your eggs cooked and whether you prefer pralines or mints on your pillow each night.

> Wherever you go, the price of a meal will likely include all the iced tea you can drink. Be sure to ask if it's sweet tea or not; if you don't want it sweet, you should make the request when you place your order.

DINING

There are lots of similarities in restaurant menus all over Georgia, but you will find regional differences in terms of availability, pricing, sophistication and popularity.

The bountiful coast and freshwater mountain streams supply seafood and trout; the rich farmlands of inland Georgia are known for peaches, Vidalia onions, peanuts and many other fruits and vegetables. To this mix, add the Southern sweet tooth that gives us lemon meringue pie; the African-American heritage behind hushpuppies, collard greens with ham hocks, and "chitlins"—slang for chitterlings, which are fried pork rinds—as well as other treats; and the home cooks who popularized the biscuits, grits and ham available in every coffee shop from Tennessee to Florida.

Ten years ago, cities such as Savannah had only a handful of fine restaurants such as Elizabeth on 37th. At the other end of the spectrum, inexpensive barbecue houses and seafood emporiums continued to flourish, offering fresh food at family-friendly prices. However, most places were midrange, from the classics such as the Pirates' House and Johnny Harris' to the memorable places along River Street and to the not-so-memorable ones in the shopping malls; ethnic spots were limited to one tired old Chinese place downtown and an Italian joint off Victory Drive. Now Southern cuisine is something to be proud of and visitors will find a bevy of eateries from which to choose. Macon is following the same pattern of growth; every few months a new eatery seems to appear.

Atlanta is the undisputed queen of cuisine, though. With excellent restaurants opening at a mind-boggling rate, the capital supports an incredible number of restaurants of every stripe. Ethnic options are more plentiful here than anywhere else in the state; you can find Vietnamese, Korean, Thai and other Asian restaurants along with French and Italian, which seems to be the most

Text continued on page 24.

Comfort Food

The first thing a Georgia host is apt to ask a visitor is "Would you like a little something to eat?" The exception is in Savannah, where the first question is, "What can I fix you to drink?" In any event, you won't have to worry about going hungry or getting thirsty anywhere in the state.

At 99 percent of the places that serve breakfast, you'll be served a cup of coffee practically before you sit down. (If you don't say something, it's likely to be followed by orange juice.) You can order something else—in urban areas, café latte or cranberry juice are more common—but then you'll have to make the grits decision. Go for it! There's almost always a pot of grits simmering on the stove. Add some butter, salt and pepper and *voilà*—you have Southern-style polenta. The stronger among us may get red-eye gravy on those grits, but by and large tomatoes are a little too much first thing in the morning. Biscuits are light and crunchy and should be smeared with honey or preserves usually already on the table.

By lunchtime, coffee is replaced by iced tea. If you don't like yours sweet, say so. More and more places offer a choice for visitors who would like to avoid the sugar and keep all their teeth. Absolutely the best places for your midday meal—often called dinner, particularly on Sunday, as opposed to supper—are the family-style restaurants where people are seated at large tables and either served or invited to help themselves to the buffet. The Blue Willow Inn in Social Circle is the most famous in the state, but almost every region has a place like it within driving distance. Anything made with the famously sweet Vidalia onions, perfect Georgia pecans or those well-known peanuts from Plains is bound to be good. In any event, expect fried chicken, country ham, sweet potatoes, green beans, collard or turnip greens, mashed potatoes, some kind of fish and, if you're lucky, squash casserole. Once in a while you can even get a delicacy like okra or she-crab soup.

If you're in Savannah, you'll want to offer your guests a glass (preferably in the shape of a boot, the way some Savannahians serve it on Robert E. Lee's birthday) of **Chatham Artillery Punch**. Here is one variation:

    1 pound tea
    3 gallons Catawba wine
    1 gallon rum
    1 gallon brandy
    1 gallon rye whiskey
    1 gallon gin
    2 gallons cold water
    5 pounds brown sugar
    2 quarts maraschino cherries
    3 dozen oranges, juiced
    3 dozen lemons, juiced
    champagne or carbonated water

Steep the tea in the cold water overnight. The next day, strain the leaves out and add the orange and lemon juice, sugar, cherries and liquors.

You will need one or two large crocks for what is now about 10 gallons of liquid. Cover lightly and allow to ferment for 2 to 6 weeks. To serve, mix 1 gallon of the stock with one quart champagne. Pour over ice in a punch bowl and serve. (The taste is mild but the effect is dynamite.)

popular cuisine of all. Atlantans love to dine out, so visitors should be delighted with the choices available. Some of the top restaurants are, oddly enough, in shopping centers and office buildings. Most likely, it's the result of a fast-moving populace; few people have the time to drive a long distance for dinner and instead demand convenience along with high quality.

Georgia's colorful country towns, and even some small cities, support an array of restaurants housed in old homes or other restored buildings, where bountiful buffets are the order of the day. The Blue Willow in Social Circle is the benchmark: on Sunday, people drive from deep in the surrounding countryside to feast and socialize. Usually these are a one-price-fits-all bargain, where you either go through the buffet line or, less common, are served family style at communal or private tables. These settings provide wonderful opportunities to visit with the locals and learn more about what's going on around town.

As with accommodations, the cost of meals in the state varies widely. Most places are in the middle range; the few places that charge in the $20 range for an entrée are relatively rare and tend to be fairly priced for what you get. In every corner of the state, you can find a budget meal for less than $9, although at that price it's apt to be either breakfast, barbecue or a blue-plate special; many places listed as moderate will often have something in the budget category on the menu as well. *Budget* restaurants are frequently barbecue or home-cooking places that offer quick service and good value for your dining dollar; entrées are under $9. *Moderate*-priced meals are in the $9 to $15 range for a dinner entrée; the surroundings are more pleasant and you'll get a lot more than you would expect for the same price in the Northeast or on the West Coast. *Deluxe* meals have entrées from $15 to $20, and at *ultra-deluxe* establishments, most of the entrées are going to cost more than $20. Deluxe and ultra-deluxe restaurants are, of course, the cream of the crop; they usually offer a wine list, an elegant ambience that's likely to have some historical significance, and a highly trained staff eager to make sure your visit is pleasurable on all counts. Restaurants listed serve lunch and dinner unless otherwise noted.

LIQUOR LAWS

Liquor is sold throughout the state, but the laws vary from county to county and sometimes from city to city. The legal age for purchasing and consuming alcohol in Georgia is 21; proper photo ID must be shown at time of purchase if requested. People under the legal age cannot enter nightclubs that do not serve food. No alcoholic beverage can be taken away from a bar or restaurant, nor carried or consumed in an open container in a car or on public property. On Sunday, liquor may be sold at restaurants and private clubs, but only after noon. Some jurisdictions prohibit any alcohol sales on Sunday. Closing time for most bars in big cities like Atlanta is 2 a.m.

Most of Georgia—including Atlanta—is very family-oriented. **TRAVELING**
The smaller towns and cities are casual; well-behaved children **WITH**
are welcome in restaurants, hotels and inns. Some of the top-tier **CHILDREN**
inns are probably not the best places for toddlers, who aren't
likely to appreciate the formality, much less the fine furnishings.

Georgia's state parks are well-suited to families, with extra
beds and fold-out sofas usually available. It's always good to inquire in advance about special needs. The moun-
tains offer many diversions, such as Rock City and
hiking trails. Resort complexes such as Callaway
Gardens also have special attractions for the young
set. The beaches and islands are ideal for all ages; life
is completely casual and the sand and surf provide
endless free entertainment. National Science Center's
Fort Discovery in Augusta and Oatland Island Education Center are wonderful places for family outings.

> Suggestions for entertain-
> ing children in the Metro
> Atlanta area are printed
> weekly in a special
> page within the Mon-
> day Living section of
> the *Atlanta Journal-
> Constitution*.

Boating, crabbing, fishing, biking (on completely flat
roads) and ferry rides are delightful diversions for everyone, from
toddlers on up. A word of caution: though alligators lie mostly
hidden under water, they are extremely large and very fast creatures. Never leave your kids alone on the ground near a source
of water and be doubly cautious at night, since the animals are
more active after dark.

Atlanta has several museums that kids will love, as well as
outdoor attractions such as the Atlanta History Center, the Zoo
and, of course, Stone Mountain. If you plan to drive a lot in the
capital, though, you'll want to have plenty of things for the children to do in the car.

Once you're away from the big cities, you'll find most stores
are closed after dark and on Sunday morning, so stock up with
enough supplies to tide you over.

Book reservations in advance, making sure that the places you
stay accept children—many bed and breakfasts do not. If you need
a crib or extra cot, arrange for it ahead of time. A travel agent
can be of help here, as well as with almost all other travel plans.

If you are traveling by air, try to reserve bulkhead seats where
there is plenty of room. Take along extras you may need, such as
diapers, changes of clothing, snacks and toys, or small games.
When traveling by car, be sure to take along the extras, too. Make
sure you have plenty of water and juices to drink; dehydration
can be a subtle problem.

A first-aid kit is a must for any trip. Along with adhesive ban-
dages, antiseptic cream and something to stop itching, include
any medicines your child's pediatrician might recommend to

treat allergies (particularly if you visit in spring), colds, diarrhea or any chronic problems your child may have.

WOMEN TRAVELING ALONE

Traveling solo grants an independence and freedom different from that of traveling with a partner, but single travelers are more vulnerable to crime and should take additional precautions.

It is better not to let strangers know you are traveling alone or where you are staying or planning to travel. It's unwise to hitchhike and probably best to avoid inexpensive accommodations on the outskirts of town; the money saved does not outweigh the risk. Bed and breakfasts, youth hostels and YWCAs are generally your safest bet for lodging, and they also foster an environment ideal for bonding with fellow travelers.

Travelers 62 and older get discounts on the Georgia ParkPass (required to park at all state parks) as well as on tent/RV sites.

The more rural areas are somewhat safer, but at the same time, women traveling alone are considered something of an anomaly outside the big cities. It's best to avoid accommodations at motels in industrial areas or other places where there is no real neighborhood after dark. When requesting reservations at hotels and motels, ask for rooms near the elevator or facing a central courtyard rather than find yourself in a remote location.

Keep all valuables well-hidden and clutch cameras and purses. Avoid late-night treks or strolls through undesirable parts of town, but if you find yourself in this situation, continue walking with a confident air until you reach a safe haven. A fierce scowl never hurts.

These hints should by no means deter you from seeking out adventure. Wherever you go, stay alert, use your common sense and trust your instincts. If you are hassled or threatened in some way, never be afraid to yell for assistance. It's also a good idea to carry change for a phone call and to know a number to call in case of emergency. Grady Memorial Hospital has a **Rape Crisis Center** in Atlanta. ~ 404-616-4861. For more hints, get a copy of *Safety and Security for Women Who Travel* (Travelers' Tales).

GAY & LESBIAN TRAVELERS

Atlanta and Savannah are the best places for gay and lesbian travelers in Georgia. The oldest gay and lesbian information line in the state is **Savannah's First City Network**. You can get recorded information on clubs and events. ~ 912-236-2489. Athens has a lively entertainment scene, especially for its size. Elsewhere, the scene is less sophisticated. Rural Georgia is largely conservative, however, and while the hospitality is consistent, gay and lesbian travelers will find few, if any, particularly gay-friendly inns or restaurants outside the cities. Midtown Atlanta boasts the largest percentage of gay residents in the state; there are gay-friendly hotels, restaurants, night clubs, bookstores and newspapers.

Southern Voice publishes news and features of interest to gays and lesbians. ~ 1076 Sonolite Road, Atlanta, GA 30306; 404-876-1819; www.southernvoice.com. Please see Chapter Five for details about Atlanta's gay and lesbian services.

The AARP offers membership to anyone over 50. Benefits of AARP membership include travel discounts with a number of firms. ~ 601 E Street NW, Washington, DC 20049; 800-424-3410; www. aarp.org, e-mail member@aarp.org.

SENIOR TRAVELERS

Elderhostel offers reasonably priced, all-inclusive educational programs in a variety of locations throughout the year. ~ 11 Avenue de Lafayette, Boston, MA 02111; 877-426-8056, fax 617-426-0701; www.elderhostel.org, e-mail registration@elder hostel.org.

Be extra careful about health matters. In addition to the medications you ordinarily use, it's a good idea to bring along the prescriptions for obtaining more. Consider carrying a medical record with you—including your medical history and current medical status as well as your doctor's name, telephone number and address. Make sure that your insurance covers you while away from home.

Atlanta is the most convenient city in the state, with countless barrier-free buildings and ample public transportation, particularly MARTA. Hartsfield International Airport is the most accessible airport in the state and better than many around the country. There you can find car-rental agencies that offer lift-equipped vans. For information, the Mayor's Office of Constituent Services has a Disability Coordinator at 404-330-6026.

DISABLED TRAVELERS

Of special interest to travelers with disabilities is Warm Springs in west central Georgia, where President Franklin D. Roosevelt retreated to enjoy physical therapy in the mineral baths. Most state parks and historic sites are equipped to deal with most special needs.

Providing helpful information for disabled travelers are the **Society for Accessible Travel & Hospitality** at 347 5th Avenue, Suite 610, New York, NY 10016, 212-447-7284, fax 212-725-8253, www.sath.org; and the **MossRehab ResourceNet** at Moss-Rehab Hospital, 1200 West Tabor Road, Philadelphia, PA 19141, 215-456-9600, www.mossresourcenet.org.

Travelin' Talk, a network of people and organizations, provides assistance as well. ~ P.O. Box 1796, Wheat Ridge, CO 80034; 303-232-2979; www.travelintalk.net. **Access Able Travel Source** has worldwide information online. ~ 303-232-2979; www. access-able.com.

Be sure to check in advance when making room reservations. Some hotels feature facilities for those in wheelchairs.

FOREIGN TRAVELERS

Passports and Visas   Most foreign visitors need a passport and tourist visa to enter the United States. Contact your nearest United States embassy or consulate well in advance to obtain a visa and to check on any other entry requirements.

Customs Requirements   Foreign travelers are allowed to carry in the following: 200 cigarettes (1 carton), 50 cigars or 2 kilograms (4.4 pounds) of smoking tobacco; one liter of alcohol for personal use only (you must be 21 years of age to bring in alcohol); and US$100 worth of duty-free gifts that can include an additional quantity of 100 cigars. You may bring in any amount of currency, but must fill out a form if you bring in over US$10,000. Carry any prescription drugs in clearly marked containers. (You may have to produce a written prescription or doctor's statement for the custom's officer.) Meat or meat products, seeds, plants, fruits and narcotics are not allowed to be brought into the United States. Contact the **United States Customs Service** for further information. ~ 1300 Pennsylvania Avenue NW, Washington, DC 20229; 202-927-6724; www.customs.treas.gov.

Driving   If you plan to rent a car, an international driver's license should be obtained before arriving in the United States. Some car rental agencies require both a foreign license and an international driver's license. Many also require a lessee to be at least 25 years of age; all require a major credit card. Seat belts are mandatory for the driver and all passengers. Children under the age of 6 or 60 pounds should be in the back seat in approved child safety restraints.

Currency   United States money is based on the dollar. Bills come in denominations of $1, $2, $5, $10, $20, $50 and $100. Every dollar is divided into 100 cents. Coins are the penny (1 cent), nickel (5 cents), dime (10 cents) and quarter (25 cents). Half-dollar and dollar coins are rarely used. You may not use foreign currency to purchase goods and services in the United States. Consider buying traveler's checks in dollar amounts. You may also use credit cards affiliated with an American company such as Interbank, Barclay Card and American Express.

Electricity and Electronics   Electric outlets use currents of 110 volts, 60 cycles. To operate appliances made for other electrical systems, you need a transformer or other adapter. Travelers who use laptop computers for telecommunication should be aware that modem configurations for U.S. telephone systems may be different from their European counterparts. Similarly, the U.S. format for videotapes is different from that in Europe; National Park Service visitors centers and other stores that sell souvenir videos often have them available in European format on request.

Weights and Measures   The United States uses the English system of weights and measures. American units and their metric equivalents are: 1 inch = 2.5 centimeters; 1 foot (12 inches) = 0.3 meter; 1 yard (3 feet) = 0.9 meter; 1 mile (5280 feet) = 1.6 kilometers; 1 ounce = 28 grams; 1 pound (16 ounces) = 0.45 kilogram; 1 quart (liquid) = 0.9 liter.

Outdoor Adventures

From whitewater rafting to golfing to catching crabs on a lazy creek, Georgia offers sports and nature opportunities galore. Georgia's mountains are famous for canoeing and, in the far north, whitewater rafting. These activities offer a chance for an upclose look at the scenery—and the cold water—and are usually offered through outdoor adventure outfits who steer you to the good places. The creeks and sounds along the coast are excellent for canoeing and kayaking, respectively.

CAMPING

You can make the most of the Georgia outdoors by camping overnight in myriad settings and configurations. Many state parks offer tent and RV camping; a number, such as Providence Canyon, have backcountry sites where you can hike in and have the place to yourself. For the most part, tent and RV sites are equipped with water and electricity. To make camping reservations at any state park, contact 800-864-7275; www.gastateparks.org.

A wonderful online resource that details all of Georgia's state parks and historic sites is www.dnr.state.ga.us.

Private campgrounds are a common feature in the mountain region; often they double as fish camps, near rivers or lakes where you can angle to your heart's content. Some of these, and all the state parks, are listed in *Georgia on My Mind*, available from the **Georgia Department of Industry, Trade and Tourism**. ~ 285 Peachtree Center Avenue Northeast, Suite 1000, Atlanta, GA 30303-1230; 404-656-3545, 800-847-4842, fax 404-651-9063; www.georgia.org. Or contact the **Georgia Department of Natural Resources** for a free brochure. Closed Saturday and Sunday. ~ 770-389-7275, 800-864-7275.

If you park within a state park, you'll need to display a Georgia ParkPass (except on Wednesday, when parking is free), sold at all parks and historic sites. You can also get one by calling 800-864-7275.

WATER SAFETY

Except during tropical storms or, of course, hurricanes (the season runs from July through November), the surf along Georgia's coast is fairly tame. Incoming tides often bring irresistible opportunities for body surfing but the real surfing potential poses no threat to California's reputation. Swimming, boating and fishing are safe in clear weather, though you shouldn't depart the beach or marina without life preservers for everyone on board. Despite the calm waters, squalls can appear suddenly during the summer and doom even experienced boaters to a rainy night spent huddling under the bow. If you think you might go off-shore, inform the dock of your plans and take along charts and emergency equipment.

Wherever you swim, don't do it alone. Follow the instructions of the lifeguard or, if none is on duty, check the various flags on the beach. If the flag is red, do not go in the water. Low tide can be especially deceptive because sandbars tempt swimmers and walkers too far offshore; the incoming tide brings too fast a current to make it back to shore. Never take your eyes off a child who is near water, no matter how calm conditions may appear.

If you plan to kayak or canoe, be sure to learn about the tides and the river and their hazards before you go. Survey the situation firsthand and find experts to give you their opinions. Submerged boulders, waterfalls, wildlife and other potential dangers are often not apparent to the untrained eye.

FISHING & CRABBING

Anglers over 16 years must have a recreational fishing license for crabbing and saltwater fishing, which you can do from beaches, docks and even some bridges. Crabbing is best done from docks, though some people use poles, nets and baskets to forage beside the jetties and rocks at low tide. If you're a nonresident over 16 years, you will also need a license for freshwater fishing in Georgia's lakes and streams. Licenses are available at bait-and-tackle shops, marinas, and hardware and sporting-goods stores; you can also purchase them online at www.permit.com or by calling 888-748-6887.

HIKING

Hiking trails abound in north Georgia; however, mountain-bike trails are few and far between at this time. North Georgia anchors the southern end of the Appalachian Trail, where you can hike a short distance or all the way to New England. Providence Canyon and other state parks harbor extensive trail systems. The 100-mile coast allows few opportunities for wilderness hiking other than on some of the islands such as Cumberland. The beaches are hard-packed in most places; the public has access to all but the privately owned islands.

TWO

Savannah

"If you haven't seen Savannah, you haven't see the South" was a popular slogan of civic boosters back in the '60s and '70s. As dated as the phrase may sound, it was true then and it's true now. Savannah has a colorful history and a citizenry bent on preserving the best of the past. It has an unmistakable lady-like charm that distinguishes it from, say, fast-paced Atlanta; it has an architectural heritage only Charleston and New Orleans can rival in this part of the world; it has salt water and Old World manners and a wealth of things to do. The downtown area, where the vast majority of antebellum buildings are located, is compact enough to be toured in a day or two. But the city's leisurely pace is contagious. After all, one doesn't gulp down a mint julep.

Today, this historic city, founded on the bluff of the Savannah River 18 miles from the Atlantic Ocean, has more going for it now than ever. With millions of visitors lavishing their attention (and their travel budgets) on this city of some 131,000, Savannah has at last capitalized on its unique history. Elegant homes once threatened with collapse or abandonment are now prized for their design and craftsmanship; they stand shoulder to shoulder in a two-and-a-half-square-mile National Historic District that is among the largest such parcels in the country. The downtown shopping area has been revitalized, new shops and restaurants are opening at a rapid clip, and dozens of exquisite bed-and-breakfast inns can hardly find a room for all the travelers who want to come during the prime spring and fall seasons.

Savannah's most famous—and perhaps only unwelcome—visitor was General William Tecumseh Sherman. He arrived here, flush with the success of the scorched-earth campaign he had waged from Atlanta and almost to the sea, in the winter of 1864. Shortly after his arrival on December 22, he fired off the now-famous telegram to Abraham Lincoln:

"To His Excellency President Lincoln . . .
Dear Sir:
I beg to present you as a Christmas Gift, the City of Savannah with 150 heavy guns and plenty of ammunition and also about 25,000 bales of cotton."
—W. T. Sherman Maj. Genl.

Perhaps Sherman was swayed by all those guns and so much cotton. Or perhaps he was entranced by the city. Then, as now, Savannah enchanted visitors with 18th- and early-19th-century mansions, nearly two dozen landscaped squares, graceful churches, Spanish moss and well-mannered citizens. Sherman was, after all, staying at the Green-Meldrim House, one of the prettiest mansions in town (now an Episcopalian parish house open to public).

It is chilling to think how close the city came to losing its heritage a century later in the name of urban development. One historic square was destroyed to make room for a parking garage and it wasn't until the 1950s, when a wrecking ball was practically ready to swing on one of the most historical mansions, that citizens banded together to stop the destruction. The Historic Savannah Foundation—along with individual homeowners—has done a magnificent job of saving and restoring hundreds of significant structures.

Savannah's story began in 1733, when the colony of Georgia was founded here. In England in the 1720s, according to historian Kenneth Coleman, two unrelated concerns began to coalesce into the concept of a Georgia colony. For one, the well-established South Carolina colony was exposed on its southern flank not only to potential incursions of Spaniards from Florida but also to a loss of trade thanks to the aggressive French, a newer but in some ways more imminent threat. Meanwhile, General James Edward Oglethorpe and other British philanthropists became increasingly intent on establishing a colony that would welcome the "worthy poor" of England. In due course a substantial group of some 100 colonists was assembled and, at the expense of a group of Trustees, set sail on the frigate *Ann* in 1732, bound for Charles Town (Charleston, S.C.). The *Ann* arrived on January 13, 1733, and the next day Oglethorpe sailed south to scout the ideal site for a settlement. This area he claimed to have found in short order; he sent an insightful description of it, which is included in Coleman's excellent book, *Colonial Georgia—A History,* to the Trustees the following week:

"I fixed upon a healthy Situation, about Ten Miles from the Sea. The River here forms an Half-moon; along the South side of which the Banks are about Forty Feet high, and on the Top a Flat, which they call a Bluff. The plain High ground extends into the Country Five or Six Miles, and along the River-side about a mile. . . ."

The peaceful progress of the new colony was assured almost entirely by the cooperation of Chief Tomo-chi-chi of the Yamacraw Indians who lived up the river. Oglethorpe began laying out the nascent town in a pattern of squares interspersed with parks, most of which were named after people prominent in the colony's development or historical events such as battles. (One was named for Nathanael Greene, a Rhode Island native whose leadership in helping free Georgia from British occupation was rewarded with ownership of a nearby plantation. Later, Mulberry Grove was the site of most of Eli Whitney's work in developing the first

Text continued on page 36.

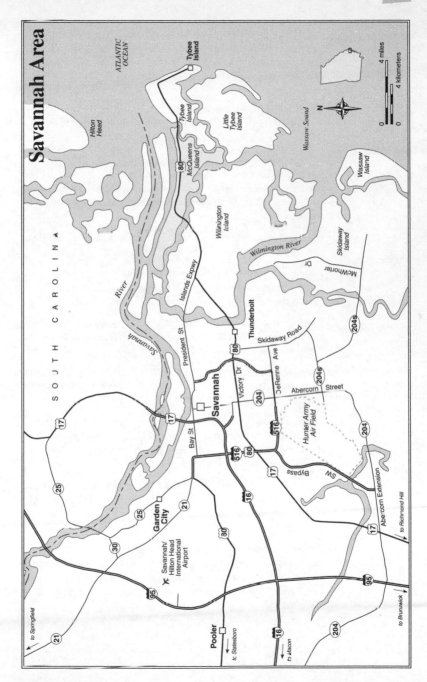

Savannah Area

ATLANTIC OCEAN

Tybee Island

Tybee Island

Little Tybee Island

McQueens Island

Hilton Head

Wassaw Sound

Wassaw Island

Skidaway Island

McWhorter Dr

Wilmington Island

Wilmington River

SOUTH CAROLINA

Savannah River

River

Islands Expwy

President St

Thunderbolt

Skidaway Road

80

204s

Victory Dr

DeRenne Ave

204

204s

Abercorn Street

Savannah

Bay St

17

Hunter Army Air Field

204

516

516

80

SW Bypass

17

16

25

Garden City

21

30

516

Abercorn Extension

17

to Richmond Hill

25

Savannah/ Hilton Head International Airport

80

95

to Brunswick

21

to Springfield

95

to Statesboro

Pooler

16

to Macon

204

0   4 miles

0   4 kilometers

N

Two-day Getaway

Savannah

Day 1
- Check into a bed and breakfast in the Forsyth Park area, which is less congested than the Historic District neighborhood. Start your day with breakfast at **Clary's Café** (page 60), where the order of the day is anything with grits.

- To get cracking on Savannah's many historic locales, stroll (or drive) north on Abercorn Street to Lafayette Square. On the west side of the square is the **Andrew Low House** (page 47), available for tours.

- Located just across Harris Street is the **Cathedral of St. John the Baptist** (page 47), easily recognizable by its twin spires.

- Search out important gravestones, including that of Constitution-signer Button Gwinnett, at the **Colonial Park Cemetery** (page 47), on the far side of Liberty Street.

- Travel north on Abercorn Street to Oglethorpe Square, where you can tour the William Jay–designed **Owens-Thomas House and Museum** (page 43), one of the two top house museums in town.

- Afterwards, be sure to visit the nearby **Isaiah Davenport House** (page 43), just a couple of blocks north at State and Habersham streets.

- Amble (if you're on foot; otherwise, drive around it) south through Columbus Square and turn left onto York Street. Your nose will no doubt detect **Wall's Bar-B-Que** (page 58) before you do—treat yourself to a tasty, soulful lunch of spicy pork.

- Work off that potato salad with an outing near the water. Head east on President Street until you reach **Fort Jackson** (page 71), where military re-enactments are regular events during the summer months.

- Return to town and rest up for dinner (hopefully you've made reservations) at one of the hot spots in the City Market area such as **Bistro Savannah** (page 58), which specializes in regional cuisine. Finish up the evening with a late drag show at **Club One** (page 62).

Day 2
- Linger over breakfast at your inn before heading out for a day in the open air. Head east on Victory Drive across the Wilmington River and the Bull River bridges to reach **Fort Pulaski** (page 72) on Cockspur Island. Walk around the grounds of the fort that was built on a strategic bank of the Savannah River.

- Press on towards the beaches, crossing Lazaretto Creek as you approach Tybee Island and then heading towards the lighthouse you'll see ahead on the left. Climb to the top of the **Tybee Island Lighthouse** (page 72) for a bird's-eye view of the island before touring the excellent **Tybee Island Museum** (page 74).

- Refuel with lunch outdoors at the **North Beach Grill** (page 79), practically next door to the museum.

- Once you're suitably refreshed, take a walk along the beach here, or drive to the south end of the island and park on one of the cross streets for a longer beach walk.

- Start heading back to town, but as you leave the final bridge, the Wilmington Bridge, bear right and follow the signs to the intriguing waterfront **Bonaventure Cemetery** (page 66).

- Your stomach's likely growling by now. Pick from an array of Low Country cuisine choices at family-friendly prices at the **Pirates' House** (page 56).

cotton gin.) Twenty-one of these squares remain, gracing the city with leafy walk-ways studded with benches and usually a monument or two.

Savannah's architectural glory was nearly destroyed by fire, once in 1796 and to a lesser extent in 1820, after wealthy cotton merchants had contracted English architect William Jay to build grand mansions for them. One of the best examples of Jay's work still in existence is the Owens-Thomas House, now a museum.

Savannah claims many distinctions beyond being the first capital of the 13th colony. It had the first Jewish congregation in the South, the first agricultural ex-perimental garden in North America, the first Sunday school in America, the first Negro Baptist congregation in the country, America's first golf course, and the first steamship to cross an ocean, the SS *Savannah*.

The old homes, the riverfront, the neighboring islands and Southern hospital-ity have been drawing visitors since the beginning, but nothing prepared Savan-nahians for the onslaught of tourists following the 1994 publication of *Midnight in the Garden of Good and Evil*. Basing a largely true plot on a killing executed by a high-profile antiques dealer, author John Berendt spun a tale that managed to incorporate history, gossip and local color into a spellbinder that remained on the *New York Times'* bestseller list for four years. Despite some jabs at Savannah's beloved eccentrics and the revelation of society secrets, most Savannahians seem to consider Berendt a Yankee who will always be welcome.

But there is far more to Savannah than moss and mayhem. Rivers and creeks meander through the marshy islands to the east and south of the city; new homes continue to go up on the south side and on the largely residential islands. Savannah was chosen for the yacht-racing events of the 1996 Summer Olympics, shining the spotlight on the myriad water-related activities, from sailing to dolphin watch-ing, that are available in the area.

These waterways provide welcome respite during Savannah's summertime heat blasts. Many days top 90° between June and September; sometimes it rains briefly every afternoon for a week, which cools things off but creates high humidity. On the other hand, even in winter temperatures hit freezing only about 32 times. The average winter temperature is 50°; in spring, 66°; in summer, 80°; in autumn, 68°. The climate is termed semitropical, with an average annual rainfall of just under 50 inches. Visitors learn to follow the example of the locals and slow down—a lot—when it's hot.

Historic Savannah

The Savannah River was the lifeblood of the city in the beginning, from the day General James Oglethorpe sailed across the Atlantic and up the Savannah River in 1733. Now, more than a century after cotton was king, tourists are the ones who are fueling the city coffers. The greatest concentration of attractions is along the river bluff and in the two-and-a-half-square-mile National Historic Landmark district. The district, which is laid out in an easy-to-grasp gridwork, can be covered on foot in a couple of days, absorbed in narrated tours, appreciated in on-and-off-again trolley tours, in horse-drawn carriages or, as a last resort, via private automobile. Note that many downtown streets are one way and that the driver on the right yields at the squares. The boundaries are the Savannah River on the north, East Broad Street on the east, Gaston Street on the south and Martin Luther King Jr. Boulevard (formerly West Broad Street) on the west. Some residents, borrowing a concept from New York's SoHo district, use the term "N.O.G.S." in reference to those lucky enough to live "north of Gaston Street."

In touring, remember that some attractions are closed on Sunday or Monday, and many are closed on Sunday mornings.

River Street runs below the bluff next to the currents of water that mark Savannah's northern limits. It runs from Barnard Street eight blocks east to where it loops up to connect with Bay Street. This is where boats in the late 18th and 19th century unloaded their cargo, which was stored in warehouses that now house restaurants and shops at water level.

SIGHTS

There is a tiny outpost of visitor information in the heart of tourist country, down by the river at the **River Street Hospitality Center.** ~ 1 River Street; 912-651-6662.

The **Olympic Cauldron sculpture** punctuates the east end of River Street, a legacy of the 1996 Summer Games. The 17-foot structure, which contained the Olympic flame during the Games—the sailing events were held in Savannah—was made by blacksmith Ivan Bailey, whose work can be seen elsewhere on railings and fountains throughout the historic district. ~ River Street.

Nearby is a small remnant of old **Fort Wayne**, marked by a retaining wall built by the city when Bay Street was extended. The fort was built during the Revolutionary War and later named for General Anthony Wayne in 1784. ~ River Street.

When you emerge onto Bay Street from River Street via a winding cobblestone ramp, look catticorner for one of Savannah's prime destinations. The **Pirates' House** belongs on your must-see list, whether or not you like seafood and hushpuppies. (Don't worry about distracting the patrons; if there's any place that expects tourists, this is it.) Built in 1794 as a seamen's tavern when

AUTHOR FAVORITE

I am moved almost to tears whenever I look at the **Waving Girl** and think about her story. The lonely figure, accompanied by her faithful dog, stands stock still near the east end of River Street. This poignant statue commemorates Florence Martus, who maintained a vigil here between 1887 and 1931, waving a white cloth by day and a lantern by night in greeting to the ships as they passed the lighthouse on Cockspur Island. ~ River Street.

this neighborhood was a welcome haven for sailors from all over the world, this family restaurant harbors numerous nooks and crannies (some of which secret old pirates or skeletons) within its peg-beamed rooms. Nautical displays, the occasional pirate at the bottom of a well, local artworks and just plain curiosities make this warren of rooms a diversion the kids will also love. ~ 20 East Broad Street; 912-233-5757.

Behind the Pirates' House parking lot is **Trustees' Garden Village,** site of the first economic garden in the country. It was started in 1733 by the founders of the colony and blossomed into a ten-acre agricultural experiment station with indigo, olives, flax, hemp, mulberry trees and other plants and herbs collected from around the world. Its most notable successes were the seedlings that helped begin Georgia's peach and cotton crops. The garden was subdivided in the 1750s into its current state. ~ East Broad Street off East Bay Street.

Returning west on Bay Street, and you will soon see little **Emmet Park,** named for the Irish patriot and orator Robert Emmet. It's a delightful place to rest on a bench and catch some shade, while enjoying the river view. Within the narrow park is the Harbor Light, placed 77 feet above the river in 1852 to guide ships with beams emitted from its cast-iron beacon. Judging by the number of vessels scuttled by the British in 1779 buried deep in the water, the threat of shipwreck was very real. ~ Bay Street.

On your right as you continue west are rows of tall, narrow buildings, mostly cheek by jowl.

Factors Walk (also called Factors Way) was a 19th-century meetingplace and the center of commerce for cotton merchants. Originally, cotton brokers had their offices on the upper side; warehouses occupied the lower portion along River Street. Bridgeways strung along the bluff connect these buildings. Below them, cobblestones, brought over as ballast in ships, pave the ramps that lead from Bay Street down to the river. Shops, restaurants, offices and apartments have long claimed the brokers' offices of yore along the blocks between Bull and Lincoln streets.

The 1887 **Old Cotton Exchange** was once the pulse of commerce during Savannah's heyday as the foremost cotton port in the world. ~ 100 East Bay Street.

A few steps west on East Bay Street, the original **City Exchange Bell** hangs in a replica of the cupola of the old City Exchange, which dates from 1799. Look for it on the river side between Abercorn and Drayton streets.

On Yamacraw Bluff, the grand building with the cupola is **City Hall,** built in 1905 on the site of the old City Exchange. The two-level domed Renaissance Revival building faces the spot where, on May 22, 1819, the first ocean-crossing steamship—the SS

Savannah—sailed. Closed Saturday and Sunday. ~ At Bull and Bay streets; 912-651-6790 or 912-651-6400.

Just beyond it is **Oglethorpe's Bench,** commemorating the site where the general pitched his tent on February 12, 1733.

Cross Bay Street and on your left is the former **U.S. Customs House,** easily identifiable by the six marble columns that distinguish this Greek Revival structure. Built in 1852 by John Norris,

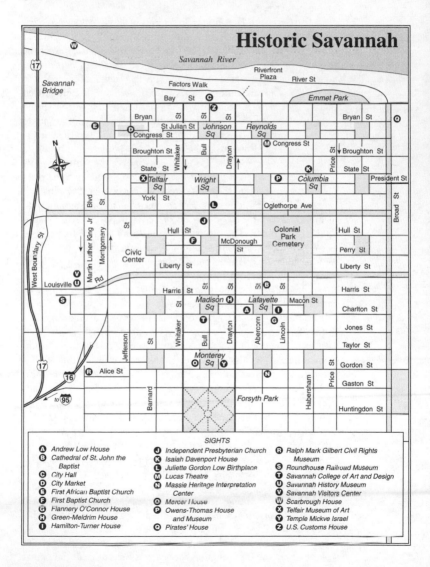

Historic Savannah

SIGHTS

- **A** Andrew Low House
- **B** Cathedral of St. John the Baptist
- **C** City Hall
- **D** City Market
- **E** First African Baptist Church
- **F** First Baptist Church
- **G** Flannery O'Connor House
- **H** Green-Meldrim House
- **I** Hamilton-Turner House
- **J** Independent Presbyterian Church
- **K** Isaiah Davenport House
- **L** Juliette Gordon Low Birthplace
- **M** Lucas Theatre
- **N** Massie Heritage Interpretation Center
- **O** Mercer House
- **P** Owens-Thomas House and Museum
- **Q** Pirates' House
- **R** Ralph Mark Gilbert Civil Rights Museum
- **S** Roundhouse Railroad Museum
- **T** Savannah College of Art and Design
- **U** Savannah History Museum
- **V** Savannah Visitors Center
- **W** Scarbrough House
- **X** Telfair Museum of Art
- **Y** Temple Mickve Israel
- **Z** U.S. Customs House

it is fronted by a row of columns said to weigh 15 tons each. ~
1 East Bay Street.

One block south, Bull Street runs into (and around) **Johnson
Square**. An obelisk in the park honors Revolutionary War hero
Nathanael Greene. You may recognize it from a number of movie
scenes, but more importantly it was the first of the six squares
laid out by General Oglethorpe. ~ Bounded by Bull, Bryan and
Congress streets.

Turn left onto East Bryan Street and walk two blocks to **Reynolds Square**, named for Captain John Reynolds, a governor of
Georgia. On your right will be **The Olde Pink House**, one of the
easiest landmarks to spot in Savannah. The formal
Georgian mansion—the last remaining from the
18th century—does indeed have a pale pink stucco
exterior that looks especially fetching in the spring
when the azaleas across the street in Reynolds Square
produce blossoms to match. Built in 1771 as the Habersham House (for Madeira trader James Habersham, a
pre-Independence Georgia governor), the house got its
nickname when the soft local bricks bled through the plas-
tered walls, staining the white stucco exterior a lasting blushing
pink. The exquisitely painted rooms (mustard, eggplant and
similarly delectable colors) are decorated with portraits and mahogany furnishings. The heavy cast-iron doors leading to vaults—
now wine cellars accommodating the restaurant's vintages—were
added when the Planters Bank of Georgia took over the house in
1811. ~ 23 Abercorn Street; 912-232-4286.

The demolition of the original City Market sparked the beginnings of Savannah's restoration effort.

Like so many of Savannah's distinctive structures before it,
the 1921 **Lucas Theatre** off Reynolds Square was threatened with
demolition by the latter half of the 20th century. Unlike so many
other Southern movie palaces of its era, the Lucas' exterior was
not decorated with Egyptian or Arabian motifs, but in the traditional Italian Renaissance style. Thanks to a multi-million-dollar
restoration project completed in 2000, the 30,000-square-foot,
1250-seat theater and many of its architectural features, including a 40-foot-wide ceiling dome, intricately detailed plasterwork
and extensive gold leaf, look good as new. Touring productions,
concerts, dramas, musicals and the occasional film rotate on the
marquee. Free self-guided tours are available daily from 9 a.m.
to 4 p.m. ~ 32 Abercorn Street; 912-234-3200, fax 912-232-1832;
www.lucastheatre.com.

Head back across the square towards the Pink House and
turn left onto St. Julian Street, the next corner. In a block you will
see **Christ Episcopal Church** on your left. The church itself was
founded in 1733, but this isn't the original building: two prede-
cessors were destroyed. Aside from its claim to be the precise
place where the first religious service was held in Georgia, Christ

Church is known for its Revere Bell, one of a very few in the southeastern U.S. and one of only about 130 in the country. Closed Monday, Tuesday, Thursday and Saturday. ~ 28 Bull Street; 912-232-4131.

Continue through (or around) Johnson Square, jog right one block and continue west on West Bryan Street. If you go left onto Jefferson Street, you will run into the four-block-long **City Market**. Flanked by stores and restaurants, this restored area now competes with River Street for the after-dark action. ~ Bounded by Congress and Bryan streets and by Franklin Square and a parking lot built on the site of the original market.

When you reach Montgomery Street, look for one of the most significant African-American sites in Savannah. The **First African Baptist Church** is the oldest black church in North America. Begun in 1773 by George Leile, a former slave who became ordained as the church's first pastor, the church claims other points of pride. It has the state's oldest pipe organ, oak pews that seat 1600, four-brick-deep walls, stained-glass windows dating from 1885 and the honor of having the country's first Sunday school—but the most memorable features are the holes in the floor. They were intended to provide ventilation for the basement, which is believed to have served as a waystation on the Underground Railroad in the 19th century. Tours by appointment only. ~ 23 Montgomery Street; 912-233-6597.

Continuing on West Bryan Street to Martin Luther King Jr. Boulevard, turn left and walk a couple of blocks to the **Scarbrough House**. This, along with the Davenport and Richardson/Owens-Thomas houses, is one of the doyennes of Savannah restoration. (Granted, the original third story was removed during the work, which took place in the 1970s well after the work on the Davenport home.) Although not as ornate or impressive as the other two, the Scarbrough home is the last great house on the western rim of the historic district; in this location, it looks almost naked, with no great square to command, only a couple of trees in front on either side. William and Julia Scarbrough had nearly completed construction when President James Monroe came through the city on his Southern tour and attended a reception in the new home. He was impressed with this further example of William Jay's architecture. Like his Telfair mansion, this one was altered later in the century, most notably by the addition of the attic story that is no longer there. Inside, four Doric columns support a balcony around a two-storied gallery hall; a barrel-vaulted ceiling is visible thanks to an atrium skylight. The Scarbrough House became a public building before being rescued and restored in the 1970s. For a long time it served as the first public school for African-American students. It now houses the **Ships of the Sea Maritime Museum**, with exhibits on Savannah's maritime history. Closed Monday. Admission. ~ 41 Martin Luther King Jr. Boulevard; 912-232-1511; www.shipsofthesea.org.

From here, head back east on West Congress to Barnard Street, then go right two blocks to **Telfair Square**. To the right, on West State Street, is the **Telfair Museum of Art**. Built in the early 1800s, the mansion (along with the art and furnishings) was bequeathed by Mary Telfair (the last member of the family) to the Savannah Historical Society and became the first house in the city to be designated a museum. The oldest art museum in the South, it houses a permanent collection of paintings, prints, sculptures and decorative arts encompassing American impressionism, Ash Can Realists and European works. Of special interest is the Regency architecture—William Jay's hand at work again—with an exterior punctuated by a rectangular porch topped by a semicircular window. The most important period rooms here are the Octagon and Dining rooms, where the decorative arts collection is displayed. Admission. ~ 121 Barnard Street; 912-232-1177; www.telfair.org.

Loop around Telfair Square to West President Street, heading east. As you come upon Wright Square, two blocks away, the old **U.S. Post Office** will be on your right. A mixture of several architectural styles, it was erected in 1898 of Georgia marble.

The large boulder in **Wright Square** marks the grave of Yamacraw Indian Chief Tomo-chi-chi, who welcomed General Oglethorpe and the colonists. Named for Sir James Wright, Georgia's third and last Colonial governor, the square also has a monument honoring William Washington Gordon, an early mayor of Savannah who established the Central of Georgia Railroad. ~ On Bull Street between State and York streets.

On the far side of the square is the **Old Chatham County Courthouse**. The first one was built in 1736; the present structure was erected in 1889, although the business of the courts has moved to a newer complex on Martin Luther King Jr. Boulevard.

North of Wright Square is State Street. Head east towards **Oglethorpe Square**. On your right is a stately, dusty-pink man-

SAVANNAH'S SQUARES

The pride of Savannahians and the bane of out-of-town drivers, the city's 20 remaining squares inarguably provide much of its charm. They also force a leisurely pace, as drivers negotiate them by turning right no matter which side you approach the square. All the squares are traversed by wide walkways and furnished with benches; most are planted with oaks, azaleas and other trees and shrubs. They are arranged along the major north–south streets in the Historic District.

sion with quite a pedigree. The English architect William Jay was the architect for a number of Savannah's prize historic homes, perhaps including the Wayne-Gordon House (now known as the Juliette Gordon Low Birthplace). But he was definitely the architect of the truly extraordinary Richard Richardson House, now famous as the **Owens-Thomas House and Museum**. Richardson, a banker and cotton merchant whose wife was related through marriage to Jay, commissioned the architect, then only 25 years old. Jay probably sent the design from England, arriving in Savannah in 1817 after construction had begun. This Regency villa was Jay's first local design and is an absolute must for fans of history and architecture. The elegant stucco exterior, the Classical Revival entrance and the elaborately ornate interior, replete with Greek design elements such as key patterns on the upper walls, showcase Jay's genius. An intricate central staircase, an arched bridge linking the front upstairs hall to the back, several false doors to give the illusion of balance and the foundation made of tabby—equal parts oyster shell, lime and sand—are all explained in an excellent guided tour of the site, which was restored in the early 1950s. Replacing the old stable yard, a parterre-style walled garden in the rear separates the home from the carriage house, which now contains a shop. Admission. ~ 124 Abercorn Street; 912-233-9743; www.telfair.org.

East of the museum a couple of blocks is **Columbia Square**. A fountain from Wormsloe Historic Site on Isle of Hope sits in the center of the square. At the corner of State Street and Habersham is a stately two-story brick house. The **Isaiah Davenport House**, more than any other museum, symbolizes Savannah's colossal restoration efforts. Davenport came to Savannah from Rhode Island and began building his home on Columbia Square in 1818, after he was elected an alderman. The exterior of the house reflects both the post-Revolutionary prosperity and the Georgian style as interpreted in Savannah, which had only 20 years earlier expanded east and west beyond the original six squares laid out by Oglethorpe. By 1955, the house had deteriorated into a tenement that was about to be torn down in order to salvage the building parts. Rallying to save the historic structure, a group of concerned citizens formed the **Historic Savannah Foundation**, which established its offices here after restoring and finishing the project. Regular tours are offered, detailing the period furnishings, portraits, architecture and other details. Admission. ~ 324 East State Street; 912-235-8097; www.davenportsavga.com.

From the house, loop around Columbia Square and go south on Habersham Street across Oglethorpe Avenue.

Oglethorpe Avenue, formerly South Broad Street, served as a burial ground for Jewish colonists. Two lanes on either side are

Text continued on page 46.

Traipsing through the Garden of Good and Evil

After years on the bestselling hardback lists, John Berendt's story of an antiques dealer and the lover he killed was finally published in paperback in 1999. The few people who hadn't already flipped through the pages of *Midnight in the Garden of Good and Evil* now have another chance to become acquainted with Lady Chablis, Mandy, Joe Odom, Luther Driggers, Uga and the rest of the cast.

Fans of the book have helped create a cottage industry in Savannah around "The Book" and its scenes. From coffee mugs to tins of Byrd's Cookies, you can commemorate the book's characters in dozens of ways. The best way, though, is to take a tour of the places mentioned in the book. Guided tours are available (in fact, good luck escaping mention of "The Book" no matter what tour you take) or you can tool around yourself and hit some of the following high spots. Most are not open to the public, but you are welcome where noted.

Start at the scene of the crime: **Mercer House**. This mansion, a pinkish Italianate house on the southwest corner of Monterey Square, was completed after the Civil War. It is such a draw that tour buses are prohibited from parking in front of it and even discouraged from slowing down. This is a residential neighborhood, after all. It was here that antiques dealer Jim Williams threw his famous parties, and if you didn't get invited to his Christmas holiday soirees, you weren't on his A-list. Eventually, Williams shot and killed his lover, Danny Hansford, here, setting in motion the chain of events that would make them both almost as famous as Scarlett and Rhett. ~ 429 Bull Street.

Also on Monterey Square is the **Temple Mickve Israel**, which has a view of Mercer House, where Williams obnoxiously hung a Nazi flag. ~ 20 East Gordon Street.

A walk south on Bull Street leads to West Gordon Street; turn right to reach **Serena Dawes' House**. Serena was quite a character in the book, a woman patterned after a 1930s beauty who married well and entertained even better a group of people that included Luther

Driggers, the man said to possess enough poison to bring down the city of Savannah. ~ 17 West Gordon Street.

Return to Bull Street and look for the **home of Lee Adler**, Williams' nemesis (at least according to the book). ~ 425 Bull Street.

Continue south to the **Armstrong House**, where Jim Williams lived before latching onto the Mercer mansion. This building used to be part of Armstrong College; behind it are the offices of Jim Williams' attorney, Sonny Seiler, who played himself in the movie and is famed hereabouts as the guardian of UGA, the University of Georgia Bulldog mascot. ~ 447 Bull Street.

Turn right onto West Gaston Street, cross Whitaker Street and turn south to reach **Forsyth Parkside Apartments**, where John Berendt lived for a while on the fourth floor. ~ Whitaker at Gwinnett streets.

Head over to Abercorn Street to visit **Clary's Café**, the former pharmacy and simple lunch counter that supplied Berendt with town gossip. It was the scene of several episodes in the book. Order some grits. ~ 404 Abercorn Street; 912-233-0402.

A few blocks down Abercorn Street, facing Lafayette Square, the **Hamilton-Turner House** was the home of Joe Odom's girlfriend "Mandy." Surrounded by elegant antiques, it is now a bed-and-breakfast inn. ~ 330 Abercorn Street; 912-233-1833.

Nightlife played a big role in *Midnight* so you should check out **Club One**, near East Bay Street, where you can see female impersonators and, on occasion, Lady Chablis herself. ~ 1 Jefferson Street; 912-232-0200.

The other nightspot in the book was **Hannah's East**, on the second story of the Pirates' House. Emma Kelly played piano here for years, having gotten her singing start at the urging of songwriter Johnny Mercer. Sadly, Hannah's East is now closed though the Pirates' House is still open for business. ~ 20 East Broad Street; 912-233-2225.

No *Midnight* tour would be complete without a stop at the **Bona-venture Cemetery**, located by the Wilmington River in Thunderbolt. If you do visit, bear in mind this is a real cemetery, not a movie set, and consider the feelings of people who come here to pay their respects to friends and family. And forget about a midnight visit; the gates are locked at sunset.

divided by a strip of greenery, planted with shrubs and trees. On the north side of Oglethorpe before you cross Bull Street is the house where the Girl Scout movement began. Almost any time you visit the **Juliette Gordon Low Birthplace**, you're likely to come across a group of touring Girl Scouts, some of the 3.5 million girls around the world who belong to the organization founded here in 1915 by Mrs. Low. The **Wayne-Gordon House** itself is fascinating, a Regency-style townhouse constructed between 1818 and 1821 for then-mayor James M. Wayne, who went on to become a Supreme Court Justice. Wayne sold the house to a niece in 1831 and it remained in the extended family until 1953, long after Juliette—nicknamed Daisy—grew up, married William Mackay Low and moved. A spirited woman, Daisy was likely subdued somewhat due to increasing deafness—though not at all above exaggerating her ailment when it suited her. After meeting Sir Robert Baden-Powell, founder of the Boy Scouts, she became enthusiastic about the British Girl Guides. Ultimately, Low became the first president of the organization. Many of her works of art and portraits of her adorn the family home, which has been restored to the period of 1886. Closed Wednesday. Admission. ~ 10 East Oglethorpe Avenue; 912-233-4501; www.girl scouts.org/birthplace.

Savannah's earliest buildings were all alike: one-story structures made of wood—plentiful in the surrounding forests—with a simple design that was perpetuated into the 1800s.

Catticorner from the Low home is the **Independent Presbyterian Church**. Woodrow Wilson was married here in 1885 to Ellen Axson, the pastor's granddaughter. The church itself was founded in 1755; the original building burned down four years after the Wilson wedding, but its 1890 replacement is thought to be a copy of the original, designed by John Holden Greene of Rhode Island in 1816. A domed ceiling, filtered light and an elevated mahogany pulpit create an elegant sanctuary. ~ 25 West Oglethorpe Avenue; 912-236-3346.

A block farther south on Bull Street is **Chippewa Square**. A bronze statue honoring James Oglethorpe stands in this square, which was laid out in 1813 to commemorate the bravery of Americans in the Battle of Chippewa during the War of 1812. ~ Bull Street between Hull and Perry streets.

The **First Baptist Church** dominates the west side of Chippewa Square. Organized in 1800, the church moved into this building in 1883 and was one of the few churches on the entire eastern seaboard that offered regular services throughout the Civil War. Its ministers included the founder of Mercer University in Macon. ~ 223 Bull Street; 912-234-2671.

On the east side of Chippewa Square, East McDonough Street leads past the old **Savannah Theatre**, believed to be the oldest continuously operating theater site in the country. Because of fires, though, little remains of the structure designed in 1818 by William Jay. ~ 222 Bull Street; 912-233-7764; www.savan nahtheatre.com.

Continuing east, McDonough Street runs into **Colonial Park Cemetery**, a peaceful place to stretch your legs and take in a bit of history, maybe even mystery. Burials began in this park-like setting, studded with trees, in 1750—making this the second-oldest cemetery in town—and ended a century later. Button Gwinnett, a Georgia signer of the Declaration of Independence, is believed to be buried here, as are luminaries such as Edward Green Malbone, the miniature painter. (It's not a good idea to go here alone at night, unless you're in a tour group.) ~ The cemetery is bordered by Abercorn Street and Oglethorpe Avenue; 912-651-6843.

From here you can see the double spires of the **Cathedral of St. John the Baptist** to the south. Follow Abercorn Street across Liberty Street and it will be on your left. The most recognizable landmark in town, this inspiring Gothic structure is not the original, though it was built to look like the one built in 1876 and destroyed by fire in 1896. Stunning stained glass (much of it from Austria), an Italian marble altar and the Coat of Arms of Pope John XXIII distinguish the interior. It is the oldest Roman Catholic church in Georgia; its parish was organized in the late 18th century. Closed Saturday. ~ 223 East Harris Street; 912-233-4709.

Lafayette Square was named after the Marquis de Lafayette, who visited Savannah in 1825 and addressed the crowd from the balcony of the Hamilton-Turner House on the east side. ~ On Abercorn Street between Harris and Charlton streets.

To visit the **Andrew Low House**, either walk one block south or continue down Abercorn Street and circle Lafayette Square to the corner of East Macon Street. Andrew Low, an English merchant, built this house in 1849 on the site of an old crenelated jailhouse. It was his son, William Mackay Low, who married Juliette Magill Gordon, who later founded the Girl Scouts. The home is furnished with period pieces including old silver donated by friends and members of the National Society of the Colonial Dames of America. Closed Thursday. Admission. ~ 329 Abercorn Street; 912-233-6854; www.andrewlowhouse.com.

Cross the square to the corner of East Charlton Street to view the **Hamilton-Turner Inn**. This Second Empire mansion was built by a former mayor in the 1870s. The home, with distinctive features such as a mansard roof and cast-iron balconies, was threatened with demolition, but the Historic Savannah Foundation intervened. It's on the tourist route because it's where "Mandy," one of the prominent characters in *Midnight*, lived. A local couple bought it in the mid-1990s and, after a massive renovation, opened it as a bed-and-breakfast inn. ~ 330 Abercorn Street; 912-233-1833, 888-448-8849; www.hamilton-turnerinn.com.

Across the street is the birthplace of an author associated more with places like Milledgeville. However, the **Flannery O'Connor House** commemorates the woman who wrote *Wise Blood* and *The Violent Bear It Away*; O'Connor was born here in 1925 and died in 1964. During the fall and early spring, literary events are often held at the former family home, which fans have filled with photographs and memorabilia. Closed Monday through Friday and mornings. ~ 207 East Charlton Street; 912-233-6014.

Go north two blocks to Harris Street and head west for three blocks to **Madison Square**, named for James Madison. Laid out in 1837, it memorializes Sargeant William Jasper, hero of the 1779 Siege of Savannah, with a monument. ~ Bull Street between Harris and Charlton streets.

On the far side of Madison Square is a pair of historic buildings. The **Green-Meldrim House** is now the parish house for the adjacent Episcopal church. It's much more famous, however, for having served as General William Tecumseh Sherman's headquarters during his occupation of Savannah during the Civil War. In a city with almost as much wrought iron as New Orleans, this building has arguably the most beautiful and elaborate workmanship. It was designed for cotton merchant Charles Green by John S. Norris, who also built the Mercer House on Monterey Square; later it was occupied by Judge Peter Meldrim, a former mayor. Oriel windows allow light in from three sides; black walnut floors, Gothic carving and marble mantels make this a popular gathering place after church services. Closed Sunday and Monday. Admission. ~ 1 West Macon Street; 912-233-3845.

Adjacent to the parish house, **St. John's Episcopal Church** faces Madison Square, as it has since 1853. Its regal Gothic Revival design is topped by spires reaching for the sky; the peals of the church chimes can be heard for blocks around. Inside this ornate church, the nave has a background of gold fleur de lis on a red field. ~ 1 West Macon Street; 912-232-1251.

On the southwest corner of the square, the former **Scottish Rite Temple** now houses a tea room/restaurant called the Gryphon Tea Room. For decades it was home to Solomon's drugstore, and much of the Victorian decor, including old drug displays and a black-and-white-tiled floor, is still on display. ~ 337 Bull Street; 912-525-5880.

Across Bull Street, the old Guards Armory building has found new life as part of the **Savannah College of Art and Design** (SCAD). Designed by William G. Preston and built in 1893, it was home to the Savannah Volunteer Guards, Georgia's oldest military unit. The college, established in 1978, offers undergraduate and graduate degrees in architecture and fine arts. More than 4000 students from all 50 states and more than 80 countries matriculate here and have had a notable impact on the neighborhood—cafés and other establishments catering to a younger crowd have opened for business. In all, the campus occupies over one million square feet in 40 buildings throughout the Historic and Victorian districts. ~ 345 Bull Street; 912-238-2383, 800-869-7223.

The students at the Savannah College of Art and Design display their work in 11 on-campus galleries, which also exhibit works by artists ranging from Tony Curtis to Squeaky Carnwath.

From Madison Square, go a block north to Liberty Street and head west past the Civic Center to Martin Luther King Jr. Boulevard. To the right across the street is the **Savannah Visitors Center**, located in an 1860 railroad station. As Savannah's popularity has grown, the center has expanded to supply visitors with every available brochure, map, coupon and helpful suggestion possible. It also sells foreign currency and has travelers'-check cashing services. ~ 301 Martin Luther King Jr. Boulevard; 912-944-0455; www.savcvb.com.

Located next door to the Savannah Visitors Center, the **Savannah History Museum** traces the history of the city and, to some extent, the history of its visitors. From the model of the SS *Savannah*—the first steamship to cross the Atlantic, in 1819—to display cases housing Revolutionary soldier mannequins and other military and civilian developments, the museum is an interesting quilt of details and artifacts such as a cotton gin. Of special interest is an 1890 Central of Georgia steam locomotive, part of a large exhibit detailing the rise (1883) and decline (1963) of the railroad that once used this very building as its passenger terminal. There's also a section on "Savannah at Sea," along with tourist icons ranging from the so-called *Forrest Gump* bench to some of the authentic monuments for which the city is renowned. Admission. ~ 303 Martin Luther King Jr. Boulevard; 912-238-1779; www.chsgeorgia.org.

A block to the south, the **Roundhouse Railroad Museum** makes an interesting add-on to the museum tour. That is, if you are really, really into trains. Construction here began in 1845; 13 of the original structures remain in varying conditions, including the massive roundhouse and operational turntable and a 125-foot-tall brick smokestack. The shops (or repair facilities) here comprise the oldest antebellum railroad repair shops still in existence in the United States. There are exhibits of locomotives, machinery and rolling stock. Admission. ~ 601 West Harris Street; 912-651-6823; www.chsgeorgia.org.

Continue south on Martin Luther King Jr. Boulevard one block past the interstate turn-off and look to the left. From video footage of local and national African-American leaders to exhibits on the way the "white ladies" dressed and acted in the department stores of the 1940s and '50s, the **Ralph Mark Gilbert Civil Rights Museum** apparently regards much of Southern culture as fair game for analysis. Which is appropriate, for the progress of African Americans toward emancipation and legal equality is best viewed in the context of the prevailing and largely oppressive society. A growing number of exhibits educate residents and visitors alike about the struggle for civil rights. Closed Sunday. Admission. ~ 460 Martin Luther King Jr. Boulevard; 912-231-8900; www.sa vannahcivilrightsmuseum.com.

From here, go north one block and turn east on West Gordon Street to **Monterey Square**, which commemorates the Battle of Monterey during the Mexican War. The monument here honors Count Casimir Pulaski, a Polish nobleman and the highest rank-ing officer killed in the American Revolution. On your left will be a peachy-pink residence now infamous for a homicide. The 1871 **Mercer House** was designed by John S. Norris and is notable for its ironwork, including eight cast-iron balconies. Though named for Confederate General Hugh Mercer, great-grandfather of Sa-vannah songwriter Johnny Mercer, no one in that family ever lived in the house. In 1970, an antique dealer named Jim Williams bought the house and restored it, but Williams will be remem-bered more for having killed his companion, Danny Hansford, thus giving author John Berendt the centerpiece of *Midnight in the Garden of Good and Evil*. The Mercer House is a private res-idence, not open for tours, but is such a draw for fans of the book that tour buses are forbidden even to pause in front of it. ~ 429 Bull Street.

On the far side of Monterey Square is the home of the oldest Jewish congregation in Georgia and the last purely Gothic Re-vival synagogue in the United States. The 1876 **Temple Mickve Israel** was begun with a group of mostly Spanish-Portuguese Jews who brought with them a Sephar Torah still possessed by the temple today. No tours Saturday or Sunday. ~ 20 East Gor-don Street; 912-233-1547.

A block east at the corner of Gordon and Abercorn streets, **Wesley Monumental United Methodist Church** is a classic Gothic Revival that commemorates the founders of Methodism in 1868 by John and Charles Wesley. The sanctuary, which dates to the late 1800s, features stunning stained-glass windows, including the outstanding Wesley Window across from the pulpit. ~ 429 Aber-corn Street.

Continuing on East Gordon Street and crossing Abercorn, you will see the **Massie Heritage Interpretation Center**. To get an image of how compact and walkable downtown Savannah is, check out the scale model of the city, maps, plans and architec-tural displays. A Heritage classroom gives children hands-on in-

struction about the particulars of Colonial life. Closed Saturday
and Sunday. ~ 207 East Gordon Street; 912-651-7022.

As befitting a city with so many fine 19th-century mansions (and
some even older), Savannah has a wealth of exquisite inns. There
are a couple of big hotels in this area, but virtually no motels.
The inns are impossibly busy during May, June, October, the major
home tours and around St. Patrick's Day, so you should call far
in advance. You can find some chain lodging on the west side of
the Historic District, where rates are more affordable.

LODGING

Historic Reservations can simplify your search for accommodations in a charming inn, bed and breakfast, or private
home. There is a two-night minimum. ~ 217 East Huntingdon
Street; 912-236-6080, 800-582-3823, fax 912-236-0127; www.
savannahinns.com.

The romance of the waterfront is a big draw at the **River Street
Inn,** one of the few inns around with views of marshes, seabirds and
passing boats. The original ballastone structure was built in 1817
as a cotton warehouse; in 1853, it expanded upwards three floors,
which is where most of the inn's 86 rooms are located. Some have
balconies offering unsurpassed close-ups of the fireworks that accompany many River Street fairs. Polished hardwood floors, large
writing desks and a mix of period antiques and reproductions
evoke the heyday of the cotton merchants. Full breakfast and
evening wine included. ~ 115 East River Street; 912-234-6400,
800-253-4229; www.riverstreetinn.com. DELUXE TO ULTRA-DELUXE.

Right on historic Factors Walk, the **Olde Harbour Inn** is ideal
for a longer stay, especially if you plan to spend much time on
River Street. The three-story 1892 structure, once a warehouse

AUTHOR FAVORITE

I'm not the only traveler to consider the plush accommodations at the
Ballastone Inn the top-of-the-line. When actor Kevin Spacey was filming
Midnight in the Garden of Good and Evil, he stayed in the dramatic China Trade
Suite. In fact, the innkeepers say he liked the antique cherrywood four-
poster bed so much they had an antique dealer ship another one to him.
Most guests, however, are content to leave the furnishings behind. All 16
rooms and suites are luxuriously outfitted, as befits an inn with a long
history that includes stints as a family home, a boardinghouse and even
a bordello. The inn's amenities are numerous, but guests who still need
something may avail themselves of a 24-hour concierge. Full breakfast
included. ~ 14 East Oglethorpe Avenue; 912-236-1484, 800-822-4553;
www.ballastoneinn.com, e-mail innkeeper@ballastoneinn.com.
ULTRA-DELUXE.

for oil, has 24 riverview suites with fully equipped kitchens. Guest rooms are furnished with 19th-century-style reproductions and a pastel color scheme. Look for the snappy green awnings facing Factors Walk. Complimentary continental breakfast and evening cordials are included. ~ 508 East Factors Walk; 912-234-4100, 800-553-6533, fax 912-233-5979; www.oldeharbourinn.com, e-mail innkeeper@oldeharbourinn.com. ULTRA-DELUXE.

If you like some of the amenities of a B&B but prefer coffee in the privacy of your own room, check out the **East Bay Inn**. Four-poster queen-size beds and other 18th-century period reproduction furniture distinguish all 28 rooms, some of which have brick walls. Continental breakfast is served in the café, Skyler's, on the ground floor. ~ 225 East Bay Street; 912-238-1225, 800-500-1225; www.eastbayinn.com. ULTRA-DELUXE.

Housed in a landmark plantation-style building, **Planters Inn** graces Reynolds Square, where blooming azaleas and horse-drawn carriages set a classic Lowcountry mood. The 60 individually decorated rooms all boast period furnishings and four-poster rice beds as well as private baths. The Parkview Room's stone balcony overlooks the tree-lined square, while the Fireplace Queen Room is perfect for a cool evening. Guests can watch the sun come up over the sloping rooftops of Savannah homes as they enjoy complimentary continental breakfast in the penthouse suite. In the evening, a complimentary wine-and-cheese gathering in the lobby, frequently accompanied by piano music, creates a pleasant atmosphere to share stories with other guests after a long day of exploring. ~ 29 Abercorn Street; 912-232-5678, 800-554-1187; www.plantersinnsavannah.com, e-mail innkeeper@plantersinnsa vannah.com. ULTRA-DELUXE.

Original windows, pine wood floors and clawfoot tubs suggest the status of the **Marshall House** as a National Landmark building (circa 1851). A $12 million restoration in 1999 resulted in 65 guest rooms and three suites. Not surprisingly, the most popular accommodations are the seven on the second floor that open onto a wrought-iron veranda, complete with rocking chairs and ceiling fans. Continental breakfast included. ~ 123 East Broughton Street; 912-644-7896, 800-589-6304, fax 912-234-3334; www.marshallhouse.com. ULTRA-DELUXE.

Comprising two Federal-style townhouses built in 1855, **The Presidents' Quarters** has 16 rooms and two suites with reproduction furnishings and understated color schemes. All the rooms in this four-story inn have a link with former presidents—at the very least, printed and framed biographies of their namesakes, including the James E. Carter Suite, which has some of the more interesting memorabilia. All rooms have working fireplaces, cable TVs and refrigerators. It's a neat and tidy place, with a lovely brick courtyard for relaxing between outings and having coffee or afternoon wine. ~ 225 East President Street; 912-233-1600, 800-233-1776, fax 912-238-0849; www.presidentsquarters.com, e-mail info@presidentsquarters.com. DELUXE TO ULTRA-DELUXE.

The **17Hundred90 Inn** is better known for its restaurant than for its 14 rooms, but the accommodations have a certain charm. Fortunately, several of them have been updated with fresh color schemes and must-have fireplaces. The decor is a mix of antiques and artwork and the occasional four-poster. Most of them look like small bachelor apartments, but considering the place is two centuries old, what would you expect? If you like natural light, be sure to demand not to be put in one of the rooms that lack windows. The three-story inn claims to be the only full-service bed and breakfast in town; certainly it's the only one with a full restaurant and bar on the ground floor. ~ 307 East President Street; 912-233-1600, 800-487-1790, fax 912-236-7123; www.17hundred90.com, e-mail innkeeper@17hundred90.com. DELUXE TO ULTRA-DELUXE.

The **Foley House Inn** is the picture of refinement in a gracious 1858 townhouse on Chippewa Square, featuring 19 rooms in adjacent buildings. Travelers who appreciate painstaking attention to detail should be impressed with the restoration efforts here, where period antiques and oriental rugs whisper elegance. The main house accommodations have a Victorian theme while those in the carriage house are more country in style. If you want to spread out for a while, book the luxurious Essex Suite, which is practically a flat. Full breakfast is included. ~ 14 West Hull Street; 912-232-6622, 800-647-3708, fax 912-231-1218; www.foleyinn.com, e-mail foleyinn@aol.com. ULTRA-DELUXE.

The chandelier in the parlor of the Foley House Inn is right from the set of *Gone with the Wind*.

Should you see an unfamiliar figure in your room at the **William Kehoe House**, don't worry: management hasn't given your room away. More likely, it's a ghost some visitors claim to have encountered in this historic property. Built in 1892 in the Renaissance Revival style for William Kehoe, who founded Kehoe Iron Works in 1874, the four-story structure has a fascinating exterior that is festooned with columns, egg and dart molding and rosettes. The interior decor is a little less fussy, featuring antique linens, fancy window treatments and quality reproductions of works such as Monet's "Lilies." Some rooms, such as the Marlowe, are extra-large; others have private verandas. The main house has two suites and ten rooms; another three are found in a 1992 townhouse in the courtyard. Amenities include privileges to the Downtown Athletic Club as well as a full breakfast. ~ 123

Habersham Street; 912-232-1020, 800-820-1020, fax 912-231-0208; www.williamkehoehouse.com. ULTRA-DELUXE.

You could stay at the 1847 **Eliza Thompson House** two dozen times and never get the same room twice. With 13 accommodations in the carriage house and 12 in the main house, it is a maze of choices—one of the most unusual inns in town. A spacious courtyard, lined with brick and adorned with black wrought iron, is accessible from all the rooms. The second-floor carriage house rooms tend to have rose-colored walls, demi-canopied beds, French doors, leather tufted chairs, small oil paintings and even smaller baths (or so it seems). The main house rooms are larger and more elegant. Continental breakfast is included. ~ 5 West Jones Street; 912-236-3620, 800-348-9378, fax 912-238-1920; www.elizathompsonhouse.com, e-mail inn keeper@elizathompsonhouse.com. DELUXE TO ULTRA-DELUXE.

The Gastonian comprises two 1868 Regency Italianate mansions connected by an elevated walkway. Including the carriage house, the elegant inn has 17 rooms and suites of varying size and decor; all have gas fireplaces that are very welcome amenities when Savannah nights turn chilly. The accommodations have so many distinctive features that no two are quite alike beyond the antiques. The enormous Caracalla Suite in the Hunter House was created from the original first-floor double parlor and, at 40 feet, is long enough to accommodate two fireplaces plus a king canopy rice bed with a view of the whirlpool tub. The Garden Suite takes up the ground floor, opening onto a brick patio with a fountain. The building is topped by the penthouse suite, complete with kitchenette and separate bathroom. An inn this size has a sufficient staff to offer guests the option of requesting breakfast served in their quarters, outside, in the dining room or in the country kitchen that's a good place for mingling with other

---

STAYING AFTER MIDNIGHT

If you read *Midnight in the Garden of Good and Evil*, you may be familiar with the house that is now the **Hamilton-Turner Inn**—it's where "Mandy" lived. Native Savannahians have transformed the Second French Empire mansion—built as the 1875 home of jeweler Samuel Hamilton—into a luxurious retreat furnished with museum-quality Empire, Eastlake and Renaissance Revival antiques. One of the most elegant of the city's inns, this will give you an idea of what the good life was like at the end of the 19th century. Full breakfast included. ~ 330 Abercorn Street; 912-233-1833, 888-448-8849, fax 912-233-9800; www.hamilton-turnerinn.com. ULTRA-DELUXE.

travelers. ~ 220 East Gaston Street; 912-232-2869, 800-322-6603, fax 912-232-0701; www.gastonian.com. ULTRA-DELUXE.

The **Dresser Palmer House** has been operating as a small B&B since the early 1990s, offering accommodations in 15 rooms and one suite in a 19th-century Italianate townhouse on the perimeter of the Historic District. A former working gallery, the inn uses rich colors and unusual antiques to set the tone. One room has parlor doors that open into the bath as well as walk-through windows leading to a private balcony. ~ 211 East Gaston Street; 912-288-3294, 800-671-0716, fax 912-238-4064; www.dresserpalmerhouse.com. DELUXE TO ULTRA-DELUXE.

DINING

Seafood stars on most Savannah menus. Flounder, shrimp, oyster and crab are particularly delectable in this part of the world. Fifteen years ago, it was a challenge to find fish that wasn't breaded and fried; now there's a choice of all kinds of cooking styles. The biggest cluster of chic restaurants is in the City Market area, but some of the finer places are spread throughout the district.

The **Shrimp Factory** is typical River Street—another bar with exposed stone walls, beamed ceilings and an ultra-casual atmosphere. It is one of the few places in the county, though, that serves Chatham Artillery Punch, a potent concoction not meant for the designated driver. Inside, red-and-white awnings add up to a kind of Disneyland take on what a seaside shrimp shack should look like. A big plus here is the historic photographs that line the entryway. As billed, you'll find lots of shrimp dishes here, as well as deviled crab, shrimp-and-crab jambalaya and flounder. ~ 313 East River Street; 912-238-4229. DELUXE.

On a warm day, **Spanky's** is an oasis of coolness on crowded River Street. Stone walls, a glistening wood bar and brick pilings suit its location. Diners congregate in the bar or take one step up into a dining room where they nosh on pizzas, chicken kabobs, pasta, hamburgers, shrimp, steak and sandwiches. Popular with the younger set, Spanky's is the place to head when you just want to eat, not necessarily dine. ~ 317 East River Street; 912-236-3009. BUDGET TO MODERATE.

Fried calamari is rare in these parts but you can find the delicacy at the **Olympia Café**. The big fat Greek menu features steaks, seafood and pasta as well as classics like moussaka and kabobs and, for vegetarians, spanikopita (spinach-cheese pie) and dolmas (stuffed grape leaves). ~ 5 East River Street; 912-233-3131. BUDGET TO DELUXE.

For pub fare and dishes like shepherd's pie, a lively, informal choice is **Kevin Barry's Irish Pub and Restaurant**, which is definitely more pub than restaurant. Unless you're a diehard party animal, though, don't even think of going near this place during the mid-March St. Patrick's Day madness. ~ 117 West River Street; 912-233-9626. BUDGET.

HIDDEN ▶ A bit more gracious than its neighbors along the waterfront, **River House Seafood** has the brick and stone walls left over from its days as a cotton warehouse. Known for fish and shrimp—prepared simply or all gussied up—this restaurant also features major-league steaks, a combination that draws in a regular local crowd as well as tourists. Breakfast, lunch and dinner are served. ~ 125 West River Street; 912-234-1900. MODERATE TO DELUXE.

A living link to Savannah's English heritage, **Churchill's Pub** celebrates British pub culture with standards like shepherd's pie, roast beef with Yorkshire pudding, Toad in the Hole (pudding with bangers, or sausages) and fish and chips. There are also some New World options, including steak and seafood. Housed in an 1853 building, the restaurant has an impressive bar that was hand-carved in England in the 1860s; you may recognize it from scenes in Clint Eastwood's movie, *Midnight in the Garden of Good and Evil*. ~ 9 Drayton Street; 912-232-8501. MODERATE TO DELUXE.

Green walls, white trim and bare wood floors create a chic setting for the ultra-contemporary cuisine at **45 Bistro**. The changing menu is ambitious, with dishes such as grilled hearts of romaine with garlic croutons, shaved parmesan and caesar dressing; a crisp lasagna of jumbo sea scallops, wilted spinach, mascarpone cheese and a spicy tomato ragu; veal *osso buco* with stewed baby carrots, Red Bliss potatoes and celery root in natural *jus*; and Black Angus filet, seared *au poivre* with gorgonzola gratinéed *pomme frites*, fresh arugula, and a tarragon roasted garlic. ~ 123 East Broughton Street; 912-234-3111. DELUXE TO ULTRA-DELUXE.

AUTHOR FAVORITE

As a child, I liked to scare myself looking at the "dungeons" at the **Pirates' House**. This longtime favorite is the ideal family restaurant, not only for the food—there's lots of it and, if you order right, it's not terribly expensive—but because of the down-home fun. Legend has it that in the bad ol' days, when the restaurant was a seamen's inn, some sailors would be drugged in the tavern and shanghaied (ergo the pirates in the name) into maritime service. A classic lunch or light dinner here is an individual iron pot of seafood gumbo, piping hot and redolent of tomatoes, consumed with housemade cornbread and a salad with divinely crunchy croutons. (The kitchen also makes legendary hushpuppies.) Usually there's a buffet option, and chicken and beef are available in addition to seafood. ~ 20 East Broad Street; 912-233-5757. MODERATE TO DELUXE.

In the 1950s, a bar called the Pirate's Cove was the watering hole of choice for Savannah's movers and shakers. As the world turns, the chic **45 South** took over and transformed the place in 1987; it's been on the Top Five list ever since. There aren't many restaurants in Savannah that serve haute cuisine, and this one does it well. Upscale appetizers like grilled quail, scallops, crab cakes or duck spring rolls could make a meal in and of themselves. Or you can go whole hog with pork tenderloin with wild rice, a rack of venison, or breast of duck with ginger beets in a port-wine reduction. Dinner only. Closed Sunday. ~ 20 East Broad Street; 912-233-1881. ULTRA-DELUXE.

Glossy tomato-red walls, high ceilings with exposed beams and a couple of mini dining areas flanking the central piano bar add up to a dramatic setting at **Suzabelle's**. In a space formerly occupied by one of Savannah's oldest Irish pubs, the restaurant opened on St. Patrick's Day, 2001. Typical menu items include grilled shrimp and scallops served on grits with crunchy okra, roasted duck with blackberry sauce, veal gorgonzola, vegetables provençal and grilled ribeye. Closed Monday. ~ 102 East Broad Street; 912-790-7888; www.suzabelles-savannah.com. DELUXE TO ULTRA-DELUXE.

For old-fashioned soul food and other treats, try tiny **Nita's Place**. Squash casserole is a Savannah favorite, but you'll find lots of other vegetables and several meat dishes on a menu based on African-American cooking. No dinner. ~ 129 East Broughton Street; 912-238-8233. BUDGET TO MODERATE.

The Monkey Bar/Fusion, a combination lounge and restaurant, occupies an open and airy space with bamboo-textured walls. The food has a pan-Asian touch with dishes like Singapore garlic shrimp, Five Spice duck and pork tenderloin with tempura asparagus. And where else could you possibly find lobster and crab ravioli with shrimp and black-eyed peas in a seafood sauce. Closed Sunday and Monday. ~ 8 East Broughton Street; 912-232-0755; www.fusion-monkeybar.com. MODERATE TO DELUXE.

The glass walls of the old Lerner's store allow natural light to stream into **Il Pasticcio**, a lively corner restaurant that was the first to venture onto Broughton Street back when people still had their doubts that downtown could come back to life. Pastas, veal and seafood get the Italian treatment at this glossy establishment, the dressiest place for dinner in this part of town. It's one of the few places to find risotto, let alone gorgonzola-encrusted filet mignon. Dinner only. ~ 2 East Broughton Street; 912-231-8888. MODERATE TO DELUXE.

Dining at **The Olde Pink House** makes some people feel like they're living large in the 18th century. This stately Georgian mansion has several dining rooms on two floors, plus the Planters

Tavern in the basement, where light dishes and piano music are served with panache. The upstairs rooms afford a better view of Reynolds Square, where in springtime the pink azalea blossoms almost match the pink stucco exterior. Inside, the four most formal rooms are painted in the deep yellow, purple, pink and green used when the house was built in 1771 for trader James Habersham. Elaborate Southern cuisine lives up to the ambiance— scored flounder in apricot-shallot sauce, pan-seared scallops and other seafood along with duck, lamb and beef dishes. Even if you're just ordering something like shrimp with country ham and grits cake in a creamy cheese sauce, take the opportunity to dress up in finery befitting the setting. Dinner only. ~ 23 Abercorn Street; 912-232-4286. DELUXE TO ULTRA-DELUXE.

With original brick walls and stone floors, the **17Hundred90** restaurant has a nearly subterranean feel. For decades, it's been a standard choice for locals, who just call it 1790—which refers to the date when the foundation was laid, not to the address. Housed in the city's oldest inn, it is a romantic destination lit by candlelight and, on cool nights, flames from two big stone fireplaces. 1790 is known for both Southern and Continental cuisine, and major entrées of veal, lamb, steaks and local seafood. The oysters Rockefeller and crab bisque are not to be missed, nor is the pecan-encrusted grouper. No lunch on Saturday or Sunday. ~ 307 East President Street; 912-236-7122, 800-487-1790. DELUXE TO ULTRA-DELUXE.

HIDDEN ►   **Wall's Bar-B-Que** is a postage stamp–size purveyor of killer 'cue. Located in an alley bounded by Houston, York and Oglethorpe streets, it is the place for chicken and pork, deviled crab, red rice and sweet potato pie. A sign says it can seat 20, but just barely, on chairs and benches. Most folks consider this a downhome take-out joint. Closed Sunday through Wednesday. ~ 515 York Street; 912-232-9754. BUDGET.

The **Sapphire Grill**'s a sophisticated dinner spot located in a three-story Savannah gray brick structure. The first-floor bar has a dining area, backed by brick walls; things are quieter upstairs, where lemon-yellow walls evoke a romantic mood. The food is a match of cutting-edge cuisine and mostly regional ingredients: benne-crusted black grouper, grilled pork chops on collard greens, and specials such as confit of organic suckling pig with truffle. There is also a chef's testing table. Dinner only. ~ 110 West Congress Street; 912-443-9962; www.sapphiregrill.com. DELUXE TO ULTRA-DELUXE.

Regional art hung on Savannah gray brick walls competes with imaginative regional cuisine for your attention at **Bistro Savannah**, but really it's no contest. The cutting-edge menu at this City Market restaurant highlights shrimp, scallops, flounder, sea bass, tuna and other waterborne delicacies. Things get pretty exotic, with daily specials that involve pan-seared tuna with ginger-soy reduction and herb-encrusted Chilean sea bass with lime vinaigrette. This is called Fresh Market cuisine and it's an enticing introduction to ingredients such as sweet Vidalia onions. You're unlikely to find a bouillabaisse of coastal seafood with handmade saffron linguine anyplace else in the region. Brick-red walls and wicker chairs add warmth to an otherwise minimalist interior in this renovated late-19th-century mercantile building. Dinner only. ~ 309 West Congress Street; 912-233-6266. DELUXE TO ULTRA-DELUXE.

The line snakes down the street in front of **The Lady & Sons** during the lunch hour. Probably everybody who works downtown knows about Paula Hiers Deen, who published a cookbook revealing the restaurant's popular recipes. A Georgia native, she dishes up cheese biscuits, hoecakes, collard greens, fried chicken, crab cakes and crab stew. If you haven't tried true Southern cooking, this would be the ideal place to begin; in the buffet line, you can try lots of different things. For those who just can't get into grits, there are other things on the menu, such as The Lady's special baked spaghetti. No dinner on Sunday. ~ 311 West Congress Street; 912-233-2600. BUDGET TO MODERATE.

Roots, Glory, The Gingerbread Man and *Forrest Gump*, along with *Midnight in the Garden of Good and Evil*, were all filmed in Savannah.

Garibaldi's Café was one of the first restaurants to open in the City Market neighborhood and heralded a renaissance in the way Savannahians dine. The menu is a contemporary marriage of northern Italian cuisine and southeastern U.S. ingredients, meaning pastas, seafood and interestingly sauced fish, such as crisp flounder with apricot sauce and grouper with crab and asiago cheese sauce. The wine list is one of the best in town. Dinner only. ~ 315 West Congress Street; 912-232-7118. DELUXE.

If you can stop yourself from filling up on the renowned bread, you'll probably find a lot to like at **Belford's Seafood and Steak**. It's a pretty, spacious restaurant that opens out onto the City Market plaza, where you can have lunch outdoors in good weather. The menu lists starters such as crab cakes and a vegetable Napoleon and main dishes like sautéed shrimp with greens and grits, grouper Provençal, Black Angus filet and top sirloin, plus nightly specials and Sunday brunch. It's been one of the most successful places to open since City Market became a reality. ~ 313 West St. Julian Street; 912-233-2626. DELUXE.

In a former garage, **SoHo South Café** doubles as a gallery with painting, sculpture and mixed media on display. At lunchtime, find a nook of your own and order quiche, soup, homemade meatloaf, roast vegetables with goat cheese, smoked salmon and dessert. Dinner entrées range from crab-stuffed shrimp to grilled lamb chops. ~ 12 West Liberty Street; 912-233-1633. BUDGET TO DELUXE.

Keep an eye out for the bright-red phone booth right off the streets of London. That's the sign of the **Six Pence Pub**, a British outpost with a cozy atmosphere and a hammered tin ceiling. English dishes are offered on day-by-day specials: shepherd's pie on Monday, bangers and mash on Saturday. There are lots of American-style sandwiches and salads, too, along with the daily ploughman's lunch, which every Anglophile will know includes soup, salad, crusty French bread and a hunk of cheese. ~ 245 Bull Street; 912-233-3156. BUDGET.

The **Gryphon Tea Room** is a standout in a city full of unusual restaurants. Named for the Gryphon clock, it has a skylight, Tiffany lamps, a black-and-white tile floor, mahogany paneling, oriental rugs and the original apothecary drawers from the drugstore that functioned here in the early 1900s. Less successful are the tiny marble tabletops that belong in an upscale night club, but at least they are good for tête-à-têtes. Owned and operated by the Savannah Academy of Art and Design (SCAD), it uses students as waitstaff and serves no alcohol. That said, it's a lot more than a tea room, though tea with pastries, scones and sandwiches is available at breakfast and from 4 to 6 p.m. Various soups, such as one with tortellini and vegetables, augment a long list of salads, including hearty ones like chicken or red potato. There are also combo plates, such as soup and spanikopita, the delightful Greek spinach wrapped in phyllo dough. Closed Sunday. ~ 337 Bull Street; 912-525-5880. BUDGET.

Nobody goes to **Mrs. Wilkes Boarding House** on the spur of the moment. You want to prepare yourself for an occasion that will tempt you to eat way, way too much food. Since no reservations are accepted, you will probably have to wait in line with everyone else. The folks you don't meet in line you'll meet inside at one of the family-style tables. The fare changes slightly, but expect fried chicken, baked ham, a zillion vegetables, hot rolls or biscuits and the like no matter when you go. Closed Sunday. ~ 107 West Jones Street; 912-232-5997. MODERATE.

Sooner or later, you've got to go to **Clary's Café**, which began as an adjunct to a neighborhood pharmacy, in business since 1903. After it was made famous in "The Book," the café expanded to take over the entire corner building. Natives still meet here on a regular basis for simple breakfasts of grits, bacon, biscuits and eggs, and some truly mediocre coffee, despite the swarms of tourists who inevitably appear. They must be the ones who order steaks, seafood omelets, waffles, and lox and bagels. ~ 404 Abercorn Street; 912-233-0402. BUDGET TO MODERATE.

SHOPPING   From the T-shirts, mugs and candy that dominate River Street stores to elegant boutiques and galleries, shoppers will find something in every price range in downtown Savannah. Antiques are available, too, at widely varying levels of price and quality. Even in high-density tourist areas, you'll find many stores closed on Sunday morning.

Antique nautical gifts, Civil War artifacts, ship wheels and Southern gourmet condiments share space at **True Grits**. ~ 107 East River Street; 912-234-8006.

A cooperative of more than two dozen regional craftspeople, **Gallery 209** has been selling sculpture, paintings, stained glass, photography, wood engravings and fiber art for a quarter of a century. ~ 209 East River Street; 912-236-4583.

Candies and cookies from your childhood vie to keep up your blood sugar at the **Savannah Candy Kitchen**. ~ 225 East River Street; 912-233-8411.

Souvenirs—some of them junky, some not—and regional food products are the specialties at the **Pirates' House Gift Shop**. ~ 20 East Broad Street; 912-233-5757.

Ray Ellis has painted the riverfront, street scenes and other aspects of Savannah life; his works hang in many a local living room. Watercolors, oils and bronzes and limited- and open-edition prints are all displayed for sale at **Ray Ellis Gallery**. Closed Sunday. ~ 205 West Congress Street; 912-234-3537, 800-752-4865.

In the rear of **The Tinder Box** is a mini-lounge where shoppers are welcome to light up some of the merchandise, including cigars and fine pipe tobacco, sold here along with smoking accoutrements. ~ 244 Bull Street; 912-232-2650.

The coolest boutique in downtown Savannah is **Gaucho**, which has dresses, jewelry, hats and all kinds of light women's clothing ideal for hot weather. ~ 250 Bull Street; 912-232-7414.

Women who prefer their dresses flowery but not frumpy will like the merchandise at **Chutzpah and Panache**, which also carries a good stock of handprinted wearables. ~ 251 Bull Street; 912-234-5007.

AUTHOR FAVORITE

Nothing makes me more homesick than one of the evocative coastal scenes photographed by the late Jack Leigh. This Savannah native gained worldwide fame when the photograph he took at Bonaventure Cemetery appeared on the cover of Midnight in the Garden of Good and Evil. This is just one of thousands of images at **Jack Leigh Gallery**. Everyone wishes they'd bought Leigh's stunning works when they were cheap but he is so talented that they may yet appreciate further. He has published several books of photographs on his own, mostly evocative collections of regional scenery. ~ 132 East Oglethorpe Avenue; 912-234-6449.

E. Shaver's is one of the best downtown bookstores, especially if you're into art and architecture. There are also plenty of best-sellers and local history tomes. ~ 320 Bull Street; 912-234-7257.

European pine, pottery, Turkish carpets and other distinctive accessories decorate **Anatolia** on Wright Square. ~ 7 West York Street; 912-447-5006.

More than 60 dealers supply three floors of antiques and collectibles at **Alexandra's Antique Gallery**, where the top floor is now a gallery featuring local artists. Vintage clothing and pottery are stocked, as well as period and deco furniture, china and crystal. ~ 320 East Broughton Street; 912-233-3999.

The stylish baskets and cool linens at **One Fish Two Fish** would be easy enough to ship home, but you might have to settle for window shopping when it comes to the china and light furniture. ~ 401 Whitaker Street; 912-447-4600.

The Checkered Moon Gallery, located in an 1850s carriage house, has functional art, wall pieces, furniture and jewelry. ~ 422 Whitaker Street; 912-233-5132.

Ellis and Company is a charming shop in a reconfigured carriage house, where lamps, frames, dishes, pillows and other gifts and home accessories have been carefully selected. ~ 15 East Harris Street; 912-236-0111.

Antique maps, prints and books are sold out of a townhouse by a couple who are among the most knowledgeable locals about regional history (and "The Book"). **V. & J. Duncan's** motto is: "The past makes a great present." ~ 12 East Taylor Street; 912-232-0338.

Most of the gifts and souvenirs in **"The Book Gift Shop and Midnight Museum"** on Calhoun Square relate to *Midnight in the Garden of Good and Evil*, but there are also some books and women's apparel. The "museum" part is very modest. ~ 127 East Gordon Street; 912-233-3867.

NIGHTLIFE   The 1950s, a time famous for its harmonizing pop groups and post-war cultural changes, is memorialized on stage Wednesday through Sunday nights and Saturday and Sunday afternoons at the **Savannah Theatre** in the form of "Jukebox Journey." Admission. ~ East MacDonough Street at Bull Street; 912-233-7764; www.savannahtheatre.com.

The ladies of the D.A.R. must have gone into orbit when watching transvestites dance and sing became a major Savannah tourist attraction. Chalk it up to the charms of Lady Chablis, the best-known of them all, who performs occasionally at **Club One**. When the Lady is not available, the stage is taken over by up to half-a-dozen practitioners of the genre. Cover. ~ 1 Jefferson Street; 912-232-0200; www.clubone-online.com.

The Monkey Bar/Fusion has live music—mostly R&B— Wednesday, Friday and Saturday nights. The bar is open from 4 p.m. Closed Sunday and Monday. ~ 8 East Broughton Street; 912-232-0755.

A house band plays on Wednesday; other groups perform Thursday through Saturday nights at **Savannah Blues**. Cover. ~ 411 West Congress Street; 912-447-5044.

Live bands rock **Malone's** Wednesday and Friday through Monday nights, mostly with classics. ~ 27 Bryant Street; 912-234-3059.

Beyond the Historic District

Savannah's Victorian District is the stepsister to the plethora of lovingly rehabilitated historic homes north of Gaston Street. The restoration effort in the blocks south of Gaston—in the neighborhood of Forsyth Park down to 37th Street—has been spotty, particularly on the west side. On the far side of Victory Drive is the early-20th-century residential area known as Ardsley Park, where many old families have homes and there are almost no shops or restaurants. Newer development has expanded out to and beyond DeRenne Avenue. Major malls and chain motels and restaurants are the rule once you get out to Abercorn Extension.

SIGHTS

Springtime in **Forsyth Park** is a glorious extravaganza of pink and white azaleas, but even during the rest of the year, families bring their kids here to feed the squirrels. (Vendors wander about selling boiled peanuts for this purpose, but some folks find the peanuts too good to share.) Shaded by oaks and magnolias, walkways crisscross the 30-acre park and its extension, bounded by Gaston Street on the north, Drayton Street on the east, Park Avenue on the south and Whitaker Street on the west. Despite its beauty, this is no place to wander after dark. As soon as the sun comes up, though, dozens of people can be seen on their constitutional walks or runs around the perimeter, which is about one and a half miles. The crowning glory of the park, which was laid out in 1851, is the elaborate white fountain near the center, a backdrop for countless souvenir photographs over the years with its female figure flanked by statues of men that are half-fish. ~ Bull Street at Gaston Street; 912-351-3841.

> The lovely Fragrant Garden for the Blind at Forsyth Park was fashioned from an old dummy fort in the middle of the park.

Across Whitaker Street from the northwest corner of Forsyth Park, the **Georgia Historical Society** houses thousands of documents and other materials documenting Georgia's past, including artifacts such as a compass and snuff box that belonged to Georgia founder James Oglethorpe. It is also the repository of one of only seven original drafts of the U.S. Constitution. Among the more intriguing papers are minutes from the first meeting of the

Georgia Medical Society and family letters, including one Garnett Andrews wrote about Eli Whitney's new cotton gin. The society, founded in 1839 and headquartered in the Hodgson House, also co-publishes (with the University of Georgia) the excellent *Georgia Historical Quarterly*. Closed Sunday and Monday. ~ 501 Whitaker Street; 912-651-2125, library 912-651-2128; www.georgiahistory.com.

From the park, head east several blocks on Gaston Street and go right on Price Street, which is one way. Take the first left onto Huntingdon Street. **King-Tisdell Cottage** is a modest 1896 structure by Victorian standards—except for its original gingerbread ornamentation—but an important museum, preserving the history of African Americans in Savannah and especially on the nearby coastal islands. The house is furnished with early-20th-century pieces accessorized with African art. The museum is named for local black citizens Eugene and Sarah King and Mrs. King's second husband, Robert Tisdell. By appointment only. Admission. ~ 514 East Huntingdon Street; 912-234-8000.

Two "hidden" attractions require a complex detour to the west side of town. Return to Price Street and turn left, travel about eight blocks and turn right on Anderson Street. Continue to the **HIDDEN** ▶ end to **Laurel Grove Cemetery**. The North Cemetery is the final resting place of some 610 Confederate soldiers, including generals Francis Bartow and Moxley Sorrel. Also here is the grave of Girl Scout founder Juliette Gordon Low. It's worth a visit at least to see the fabulous ornamental ironwork and inscriptions on the markers of lesser-known citizens. The South Cemetery was dedicated in 1852 for the burial of "free persons of color" and slaves. Laurel Grove is free and open to the public; tours can be arranged. ~ 602 West Anderson Street (North) and 2101 Kullock Street (South); 912-651-6772.

Exiting the Anderson Street entrance to Laurel Grove, turn right on Ogeechee Avenue and look for signs to Route 16 on the right. Take Route 16 to Route 95, turn north. Take Exit 18 onto Route 80, then look to the left in less than a block's length. The **HIDDEN** ▶ spiffy **Mighty Eighth Air Force Heritage Museum** is a spit-polished operation that houses videos, photographs, maps and other artifacts, such as posters and uniforms, that tell the story of the Mighty Eighth from World War II into the post-war era. Dramatic footage of Hitler, German troop activity and other pieces of history make it worth going out of your way to see. There are special sections, including one on African Americans in aviation, an exhibit about the Tuskegee airmen and another on prisoners of war. Whether or not you are a history or military buff, you will probably find the exhibits educational and very well done. Admission. ~ 175 Bourne Avenue, Pooler, off Route 16 and Route 80; 912-748-8888; www.mightyeighth.org.

From here, return to Route 95 heading south and take Exit 16 onto Abercorn Extension. This becomes Abercorn Street. After you pass the big shopping malls, take a right at a traffic light onto DeRenne Avenue and go about three long blocks to Paulsen Street.

Turn left and continue south for about a mile to Washington Avenue. For a detour through the pretty residential area of **Ardsley Park**, turn left. The street you are on has two lanes in either direction and is shaded by oaks and flanked with huge residences. Continue to the dead end at Bull Street and go right. In two blocks, take a right on 45th Street, which will take you past several blocks of spacious homes, including some that might be called villas, most of them built in the prosperous years prior to the Depression. This street (as well as 44th and 46th streets), home to some of Savannah's oldest money, circles a park that is part of Chatham Crescent, and then three more blocks to Paulsen Street. Go left

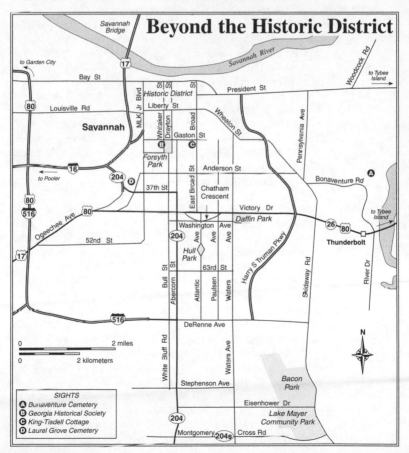

two blocks then right on Victory Drive. Turn right on this four-lane, palm-lined boulevard. As you approach the Wilmington River, you enter the town of Thunderbolt (for more about Thunderbolt, see "Islands and Waterways" later in this chapter). At the last traffic light before the bridge, turn left and immediately take the left fork to continue on River Road for two blocks, when the name changes to Bonaventure Boulevard. Savannah's most famous cemetery is less than a mile from Victory Drive. (The cemetery is also accessible from the Historic District via Skidaway Road.)

HIDDEN ►   No matter which route you take, the drive to the riverfront **Bonaventure Cemetery** sets the stage for Southern gothic drama. This area was settled in the 1760s by an English colonel who named his plantation for the Italian phrase *buono ventura* (good fortune). It's unfortunate that the final resting place of so many Savannahians has become a popular tourist attraction, but as long as visitors are respectful of the rights of others, the tours will continue. The massive stone archway ushers you into a wonderland of oaks and moss and hundreds of azaleas that dazzle the eye in early spring. Single lanes have been semi-packed over the years but remain unpaved, encouraging a leisurely pace. Real people entombed here include Savannah-born poet Conrad Aiken and composer Johnny Mercer, as well as the protagonists of *Midnight in the Garden of Good and Evil*, Jim Williams and Danny Hansford. One of the most famous "residents" of the cemetery, the so-called Bird Girl who graced the cover of *Midnight in the Garden of Good and Evil*, has long since been removed by its owners. ~ 330 Bonaventure Road; 912-651-6843.

LODGING   Several old residences in the Victorian District, immediately south of Gaston Street, have been converted to bed-and-breakfast inns. South of Park Avenue, however, there is virtually no lodging until you reach the bevy of chain motels near Abercorn Street and Eisenhower Drive.

When the **Mansion on Forsyth Park** opened in 2005, it instantly raised the bar on Savannah hotels. Other hotels offer some of its services and several bed-and-breakfast inns offer comparable guest room decor, but until the Kessler Collection (a mini-chain of deluxe properties) transformed an 1888 National Historic Landmark mansion into a 126-suite hotel, it was impossible to find so many amenities in one place: a restaurant, two lounges, a courtyard pool, high-speed internet access, 24-hour concierge, a butler floor, a fitness center, a full-service spa, business center services and 10,000 square feet of meeting space, including a grand ballroom. Oh—and a cooking school as well. ~ 700 Drayton Street; 912-238-5158, 888-711-5114; www.mansion

onforsythpark.com, e-mail info@mansiononforsythpark.com. ULTRA-DELUXE.

The decor at **The Olde Georgian Inn** is as idiosyncratic as its name. Forget the Olde Savannah paint and stuffy old furniture. This place has a lot of pizzazz. The walls are white or exposed brick; the floors are mostly bare; the furnishings, contemporary. In Phyllis's Room, for instance, there's a four-poster bed with a simple white chenille coverlet. On display throughout this 1890s Victorian are artifacts from the innkeepers' travels as well as fascinating odds and ends retrieved from beneath the house during the six-year renovation and the honeymoon cottage out back. Two of the four rooms share a bath and some pets are accepted at this refreshingly different place. Full breakfast is included. ~ 212 West Hall Street; 912-236-2911, 800-835-6831. MODERATE TO ULTRA-DELUXE.

You can sit in wicker chairs on the front porch of **The Confederate House** and watch the goings-on across the street in Forsyth Park or, if you prefer privacy, settle in the back garden with a cup of coffee. The three rooms, all named for Confederate heroes, are pretty but fairly modest compared to the grand appointments in the ground-floor public spaces. Full breakfast included. ~ 808 Drayton Street; 912-234-9779, 800-975-7457; www.theconfederatehouse.com, e-mail cwilliams252@comcast. net. ULTRA-DELUXE.

The **Azalea Inn** is more casual than most downtown inns. The place looks lived in, for one thing. Velvet chairs, lace curtains, oriental fans and other touches establish a Victorian look that extends throughout the nine rooms, two of which are in a carriage house. There is also a small swimming pool, very unusual for a Savannah inn. ~ 217 East Huntingdon Street; 912-236-2707, 800-582-3823, fax 912-236-0127; www.azaleainn.com, e-mail info@azaleainn.com. ULTRA-DELUXE.

◆◆

OPEN TO THE PUBLIC

In 1885, when Rufus Ezekiel Lester was mayor of Savannah, he had an Italianate Victorian built for his residence. A former Confederate soldier, Lester went on to the state legislature and then the U.S. Congress. His home is now **The Senator's Gate**, with four bedrooms decorated in period and reproduction pieces, all with whirlpool baths. Both the accommodations and the public spaces look more authentically Savannahian than those in most B&Bs. There is also a non-hosted two-story carriage house available for up to four people. Two-night minimum. Full breakfast included. ~ 226 East Hall Street; 912-233-6398; www.thesena torsgate.com, e-mail thesenatorsgate@aol.com. ULTRA-DELUXE.

DINING   Fine dining is a spotty affair outside of the Historic District, though there are some gems and several inexpensive places to eat. Just don't expect to see a wine list outside of the deluxe establishments.

700 Drayton Restaurant features a mix of Continental and "new world urban" cuisine typified by dishes such as pan-seared scallops with creamed leeks and caviar, roasted Colorado rack of lamb, sautéed flounder and grilled filet mignon. The sophisticated ambience is established with black flooring and floor-length, gauzy white drapes that define each seating arrangement. Opened in 2005 in the Mansion on Forsyth Park, it serves three meals a day. ~ 700 Drayton Street; 912-721-5002. DELUXE TO ULTRA-DELUXE.

Across from the southern edge of Forsyth Park, **Brighter Day Natural Foods Market** is a mecca for Savannahians who swear by vitamins and herbs. It is also probably the only place in town to get organic sandwiches, salads and juices. No dinner. ~ 1102 Bull Street; 912-236-4703. BUDGET.

If you like Johnny Harris' barbecue sauce, you can buy bottles of it at the restaurant or at local supermarkets.

To understand what Elizabeth Terry has done for regional cuisine, you have to be familiar with basic Southern foods. Terry put her restaurant on the national culinary map with dishes like black-eyed pea patty with greens and curry cream, fried grits and black-eyed pea relish with shrimp, country ham and red-eye gravy or goat cheese and red-pepper sauce, and shrimp with green onion and cream sauce in pastry. If you were to have only one meal in Savannah, and can possibly afford it, **Elizabeth on 37th** should be your choice. Typical main courses—if they can be called typical—include rack of lamb with okra and tomatoes, beef tenderloin with Madeira sauce, mustard-glazed salmon and, always, a vegetarian entrée such as roasted shiitake and oyster mushrooms, black-eyed-pea-and-carrot ragôut and truffle oil–celery relish. Dinner only. ~ 105 East 37th Street; 912-236-5547. ULTRA-DELUXE.

Clary's on Habersham is an offshoot of the Historic District restaurant, Clary's Café, that was made famous in *Midnight in the Garden of Good and Evil*. Located in the Habersham Shopping Center, it is a fabulous place for breakfast and a good place for lunch, especially salads and sandwiches. ~ 4430 Habersham Street; 912-351-0302. BUDGET TO MODERATE.

Mr. B's Hickory House features home-style cooking at breakfast, lunch and dinner. On one hand, it's just another coffee shop, with nothing distinctive about the decor or service. On the other hand, it's quite dependable and portions are generous. No dinner on Sunday. ~ 4318 Waters Avenue; 912-354-2122. BUDGET TO MODERATE.

Anything with eggplant or crab is recommended at **Wang's II Chinese Restaurant**, a cavernous yet elegant spot located between

Eisenhower Drive and Mall Boulevard. Moo shu pork and chicken and scallops Hunan style are among the chef's many specialties, which cost about half as much at lunch as at dinner. ~ 7601 Waters Avenue; 912-355-0321. MODERATE.

One of the few real interesting places on the southside is the **Toucan Cafe**. It's a little bit like a Central American rainforest—colorful toucans everywhere and lots of purple and green (though the name wasn't actually derived from the bird but from the owner's thought that "one can't but two can"). The menu is low-key international, ranging from Jamaican dishes to some Thai selections, as well as quesadillas and, according to some loyal fans, the best hamburgers and french fries in town. Vegetarians will find plenty to like here above and beyond bean sprouts. Closed Sunday and Monday. ~ 531 Stephenson Avenue; 912-352-2233. BUDGET TO MODERATE.

Generations of Savannahians grew up on **Johnny Harris'** barbecue sauce, best enjoyed in the casual back kitchen room where the spicy red stuff would spill out of a pork sandwich and it wouldn't matter. Others remember learning to dance with their fathers on the more formal evenings in the circular main dining room rimmed with wooden booths. In other words, it's so classic you can't imagine Savannah without it. The food? It's actually good, though once you range beyond barbecue and seafood it's no better than half a dozen other places in town. The ambiance? Unbeatable. Look for the dozens of cars parked under the oak trees out front. Be sure to try the Brunswick stew, a spicy concoction of meat and red sauce. Closed Sunday. ~ 1651 Victory Drive; 912-354-7810. BUDGET TO DELUXE.

SHOPPING

There are a couple of nice stores around Ardsley Park and in the Habersham Shopping Center, but not much else until you get out to the Abercorn Extension, where the chain stores are located.

The Cottage Shop occupies the maze-like ground floor of an actual cottage that is crammed full of table settings, linens, china and elegant presents for newborns. It's almost impossible not to leave with at least a little something, perhaps a candlestick or a pair of bookends. ~ 2422 Abercorn Street; 912-233-3820.

J.D. Weed and Co. is owned and operated by an old Savannah family and offers elegant antiques with a solid pedigree. ~ 102 West Victory Drive; 912-234-8540.

Major department stores and over 100 specialty shops, along with restaurants and fast-food outlets, are within the enclosed **Oglethorpe Mall**. ~ 7804 Abercorn Extension; 912-354-7038.

Savannah Mall is anchored by several national chain stores and fast-food places. ~ 14045 Abercorn Street; 912-927-7467.

Famous for decades for its benne wafers and benne bits (made with sesame seeds), the Byrd Cookie Company hit the jackpot when it began putting sweet cookies like lime coolers in pretty tins with special tops such as a reproduction of the cover of *Midnight in the Garden of Good and Evil*. The **Byrd Marketplace** stocks all these products and more, and lays out free samples of a wide variety of them, along with condiments, tabletop accessories and more. Closed Saturday. ~ 6700 Waters Avenue; 912-355-1716.

PARKS   Savannah is dotted with parks of all sizes. Few have swimming pools or tennis courts but a few have "spray pools" for cooling off on a hot day. For a full list of what's available, contact the Savannah Leisure Services Bureau at 912-351-3827.

FORSYTH PARK This 75-acre landscaped park, with its photogenic white fountain and Confederate monument, is best for strolling and lazing on benches while feeding the squirrels boiled peanuts. Its most unusual feature, however, is the **Fragrant Garden for the Blind**. Lighted tennis and basketball courts are in the extension on the south end of the park, with a one-mile jogging course and a playing field. ~ Bounded by Gaston, Whitaker, Gwinnett and Drayton streets; 912-351-3841.

BACON PARK Three interlinked nine-hole golf courses are the centerpieces of this 1021-acre park on the south side of town. There are also archery fields, baseball/soccer/football fields, tennis courts, a lighted driving range and a putting green, as well as a clubhouse. ~ Skidaway Road and Bacon Park Drive; 912-351-3837.

HULL PARK This is a tidy three acres in a nice residential neighborhood. With a "spray pool," picnic area, playground and playing field, it's a lovely place to retreat for an al fresco lunch and perhaps a game of Frisbee. ~ 55th Street at Atlantic Avenue; 912-351-3837.

DAFFIN PARK A total of 77 acres in a very convenient location make this the top athletic park in midtown. There are facilities for softball, basketball, soccer and volleyball in addition to a playground. For children only, fishing is allowed in the four-acre lake. Some of the tennis courts are clay; the hard courts can be lit at night. Daffin is also home to Grayson Stadium, home of the Sand Gnats, the city's minor-league baseball team. ~ 1301 East Victory Drive; 912-351-3837.

LAKE MAYER COMMUNITY PARK On the south side of the city, this 75-acre park is centered around a 35-acre lake populated by bream, bass, catfish and crappie; all you need is a license and a fishing pole. Facilities include tennis courts, a jogging track with fitness stations, basketball courts, a baseball diamond, a condition course for people using wheelchairs and picnic pavilions that can be reserved for large groups. It's open until 11 p.m. in summer so people can take advantage of the coolest part of the evening. ~ Montgomery Crossroad and Sallie Mood Drive; 912-652-6786.

Savannah is linked to the oceanfront beach by a series of mostly two-lane bridges spanning the rivers and creeks that divide

Islands and Waterways

the islands of the Intracoastal Waterway. Once it crosses the Wilmington River en route to Whitemarsh, Talahi, Wilmington and Tybee islands, Victory Drive becomes Route 80 (what everyone calls the Tybee Road) again; it's banked by palm trees and oleander shrubs, whose roots help secure the road during flood tides. Besides two forts and the drive itself, there are few attractions before you reach the farthest island, Tybee Island. A fort, lighthouse and museum make it worth the half-hour drive from downtown Savannah, whether or not you plan to spend the night. Many places curtail their hours in the winter months so it's a good idea to call ahead if you're traveling during cold weather.

There are two routes east from the city of Savannah to the islands, one via Victory Drive/Route 80, the other via the President Street Extension to the Islands Expressway, which joins Route 80 on Wilmington Island. The latter offers a couple of extra attractions so a good solution is to take one route east and the other back.

You can reach **Fort Jackson** from Bonaventure Cemetery by going straight out of the cemetery gates onto Bonaventure Road, bearing right at the intersection with Skidaway Road and turning right on Pennsylvania Avenue and then right on the President Street Extension, which becomes the Islands Expressway. The entrance to the fort is via Woodcock Road, the second road on the left. (From the Historic District, the fort is about three miles. Go to East Broad Street and then turn east on President Street until you pass Pennsylvania Avenue, which will be on your right.) The oldest standing military fortification in the state, Fort Jackson stands on the site of a battery erected by patriot forces during the Revolutionary War. It is an ideal location, since all boats bound for the harbor in Savannah must pass it, and surrounding marshes deter attack by foot soldiers. Long after the battery was evacuated in the wake of a malaria outbreak, Fort Jackson was established on the spot. The museum is housed in the inner fort, which is open on self-guided tours. Special demonstrations utilizing cannons are given most days from mid-June to mid-August. (There's no fear of malaria, but mosquitoes can still be a problem in humid weather here.) Closed Monday. Admission. ~ 1 Fort Jackson Road; 912-232-3945.

SIGHTS

Fort Jackson was established in time to serve during both the War of 1812 and the Civil War.

Exit Fort Jackson, turning left onto the Islands Expressway. In about a mile, as you approach the first bridge, you can see a sign on the right for the **Oatland Island Education Center**, just a short drive away. Here you can see an island in an approximate

◄ HIDDEN

natural state, although the area was settled and even farmed for cotton at one time. The center, with its animals, exhibits, walking trails and natural-history programs, is extremely popular with students and teachers. Bobcats, foxes, deer, bears, wolves, bison, alligators and panthers—species native to the area—are restricted to natural enclosures and can be seen along the nature trail. There is also a barnyard where visitors get to see and feed farm animals, and a couple of log cabins intended to evoke pioneer days. Admission. ~ 711 Sandtown Road; 912-897-3773.

Return to the Islands Expressway and turn right to continue east; the road soon connects to Route 80, which takes you to Tybee Island, about 15 miles from Oatland Island.

The other route, Victory Drive/Route 80, passes near Bonaventure Cemetery on its way to Tybee Island.

Whichever route you take, as you approach the Lazaretto Creek Bridge (the last one before Tybee Island), turn left at the signs for the **Fort Pulaski National Monument**. Now this is a fort, complete with moat and drawbridge. Located on Cockspur Island, which, like Fort Jackson, is at a critical defensive position for guarding the harbor entrance, this beautifully restored installation was built between 1829 and 1847 and named for the Revolutionary War hero Count Casimir Pulaski. Its outer walls are more than seven feet thick, thought to be a certain deterrent to artillery attack, but the first soldiers here—a force of two, in 1861—were assigned to maintenance, not defense. On January 3, however, Governor Joseph Brown ordered the Georgia Militia to garrison the fort, and after the state seceded on January 19, the fort was transferred to the Confederate States of America. By November, when the Federal Army and Navy forces attacked nearby forts in South Carolina, the Confederates abandoned Tybee Island and left Fort Pulaski as Savannah's sole means of defense. The Union Army installed cannons with rifled barrels on Tybee and shortly demanded the fort's surrender. After resisting initially, Confederate Colonel Charles Olmstead assessed the artillery damage to the fort and waved the white flag. There's more to the story, which visitors can hear on excellent tours and through interpretive displays. Admission. ~ Route 80; 912-786-5787; www.nps.gov/fopu.

The **Tybee Island Lighthouse** can be seen from as far away as Fort Pulaski, and from the top of it, visitors get a 360-degree view of the island and beyond, from Hilton Head to Little Tybee and further. To reach it, cross the bridge and continue to Campbell Avenue. Turn left for two blocks and then jog left on Van Horn Street before taking a quick right on Meddin Drive, which will take you to the parking lot, where you can leave the car in metered spaces in front of the museum across the street. Visitors can take the 150 stairs to the top, although the spiral staircase is a tough climb on hot days. Candle lantern tours are occasionally

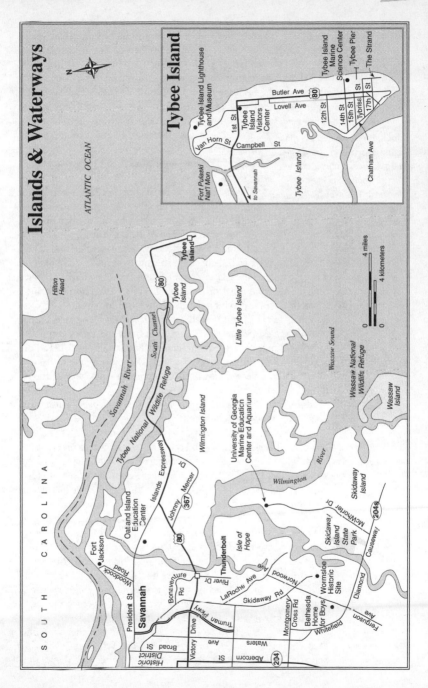

Islands & Waterways

Tybee Island

given on summer nights. Though this black-and-white structure is only about a century old, a lighthouse has been in place here since 1736. Admission. ~ 30 Meddin Drive, Tybee Island; 912-786-5801; www.tybeelighthouse.org.

About a mile after you cross the Lazaretto Creek Bridge onto Tybee Island, you'll see the **Tybee Island Visitors Center** on your right. You can ask questions and pick up brochures about accommodations and attractions. There's also a map, but it's not that you'll need it much on this small island. ~ 802 1st Street (Route 80), Tybee Island; 912-786-5444, 800-868-2322; www.tybeevisit.com.

Noble Jones named his plantation Wormsloe, either for the silk worm connotation or for the association with the Welsh word for "dragon's lair."

The Spanish explored Tybee in 1520, when Lucas Vasquez de Ayllon laid claim to it as part of his country's "La Florida," which stretched from the Bahamas all the way to Nova Scotia. The French followed, looking for sassafras roots (then believed to be a miracle cure). Then there were the pirates, the English and eventually the soldiers, who considered the island extremely important to Savannah's security. These and other historical facts are revealed and explained through the many exhibits at the **Tybee Island Museum**. It wasn't until after the Civil War that Tybee developed as a resort area, providing a desperately needed respite from the suffocating heat of some summer days in the city of Savannah. In 1885, Fort Screven, where the museum is located, was built on the north end of the island, and remains of those structures can be seen today, though mostly only from afar. Closed Tuesday. Admission. ~ Meddin Street (across from the lighthouse), Tybee Island; 912-786-5801; www.tybeelighthouse.org.

Fort Screven was built in 1885 to protect Savannah from seafaring attackers—military and otherwise. It occupies much of the north end of the island and its history is told in displays at the Tybee Island Museum located within the confines of the old fort. After it was decommissioned, private citizens began buying up the land, houses and old barracks. The finest homes can be seen, but not toured, on what is known as **Officer's Row**, a string of enormous clapboard houses situated on a slight knoll between Van Horn Street and the ocean. There is "no there, there" now; wind and salt air have taken their toll on most of the fortifications that, for the most part, lie in pieces like some giant's Legos. Kids have always enjoyed playing on and in these decaying structures, many of them offering wonderful views of the ocean, but signs are posted to stay out. ~ Van Horn Street, Tybee Island.

Beachcombers who wonder exactly what it is they've found at low tide need venture no farther than the **Tybee Island Marine Science Center**. If it's a shell or a skeleton, chances are they'll find

HIDDEN ►

a labeled specimen on display, be it a ghost crab, cockle shell or the disk-shaped keyhole urchin commonly known as a sand dollar. Also of interest are a touch tank and a cutaway of a sea-turtle egg nest. But there are very few fish. The center also offers field trips. Closed Saturday and Sunday in winter. ~ 1510 Strand Avenue, adjacent to the 14th Street parking lot north of the Tybrisa pier; 912-786-5917; www.tybeemsc.org.

Return to Savannah via Route 80; when you get off the Wilmington River Bridge, turn left onto River Road. For about a half mile along the water, in the shade of giant oaks cloaked in Spanish moss, you can see pleasure craft as well as the picturesque **shrimp boats** when they are docked here.

Return to Route 80 (Victory Drive) and continue west to a major intersection where you will turn left onto Skidaway Road. This narrow two-lane road leads through some commercial areas before reaching the marshlands as you approach the **Isle of Hope**, where the grandest of the old estates can be found on the far side of the Skidaway Narrows. The state-operated **Wormsloe Historic Site** is approached via a one-and-a-half-mile-long driveway of crushed oyster shells flanked with oak trees planted in the early 1890s. The first fortified house was built here around 1740 by Noble Jones, a colonist who came with General James Oglethorpe from England in 1733. Jones was among those encouraged to establish silk as a major source of income for the colonists. Jones, who practiced medicine, also experimented with plant propagation, developing a huge century plant and cultivating pomegranates, figs and apricots, among other fruit trees. Today, his descendants retain some 65 acres of the property, including an 1828 house (not open to the public). Visitors can, however, tour the museum, watch a video about Georgia's founding, view artifacts excavated on the grounds and walk to the tabby ruins of Noble Jones's manor house and the nearby cemetery. Closed Monday. ~ 7601 Skidaway Road; 912-353-3023; www.wormsloe.org.

Turn left out of the Wormsloe plantation onto Ferguson Avenue and continue south for just over two miles to an entranceway on the left that at first glance looks like another plantation. Here, too, is an avenue of oaks, planted on what was intended to be a colony for debtors. Few of the colonists who came to Georgia were debtors or convicts, but as it turns out an exceptionally high mortality rate here in the 18th century left many orphans. So it was that the **Bethesda Home for Boys** was founded in 1740, the oldest continuously operated home for boys in the country. Its present campus, 500 acres on Isle of Hope, was established in 1850. Here, the Cunningham Historical Center houses records relating to Bethesda's history back to the days before it was even established by the Reverend George Whitefield. Closed Saturday and Sunday. ~ 9520 Ferguson Avenue; 912-351-2040.

◄ HIDDEN

After touring Bethesda, return to Ferguson Avenue and continue south one block before taking a left onto the Diamond Causeway, which crosses what was known as Back River before Savannahian Johnny Mercer wrote "Moon River" and the waterway was renamed. Once on Skidaway Island, follow the Diamond Causeway about a mile and bear left on McWhorter Drive, which becomes Modena Island Road after four miles as it approaches the Skidaway Institute of Oceanography. The **University of Georgia Marine Education Center and Aquarium** here has more than tanks with little fish swimming around. There is an exhibit on Gray's Reef Marine Sanctuary (which is not far offshore), turtle shells and dozens of species like snook, spotted sea trout, black sea bass, pompano and others you may have seen only on menus. If you look closely you may see hermit crabs and slipper lobsters. Try the touch tank for a real feel of ocean life and study the display tracing native marine life over a span of some 12,000 years. Closed Sunday. Admission. ~ 30 Ocean Science Circle; 912-598-2496.

HIDDEN ▶

LODGING

Accommodations on Tybee Island range from low-rent motels to charming B&Bs, with a slew of decent chain motels in between. Few have pools, but on such a narrow island, you're never more than a couple of blocks from water. Rates at most places take a big dive in winter, for good reason. Several outfits can arrange stays in homes and condominiums.

HIDDEN ▶

The **Lighthouse Inn** is more country than beachy, with residential-style furnishings, hardwood floors and small refrigerators in all three rooms. Except for a few chilly winter months, guests are welcome to enjoy their complimentary continental breakfast on one of the cozy porches overlooking the garden. The owners, long-time Tybee residents, are exceptionally hospitable and knowledgeable about local activities. Full breakfast is included. ~ 16 Meddin Drive, Tybee Island; 912-786-0901, 866-786-0901; www.tybee bb.com, e-mail info@tybeebb.com. DELUXE TO ULTRA-DELUXE.

HIDDEN ▶

A short walk from the beach, the **Tybee Island Inn** was built around the turn of the 20th century as part of Fort Screven's hospital complex. Framed by live oak and palm trees, it has large screened porches (one with a hot tub), high ceilings and original pine flooring. The accommodations are distinguished by items such as an iron bedframe and a teak bunkbed. One of the three suites adjoins an extra bedroom. Full breakfast and sweets at night are included. ~ 24 Van Horn Street, Tybee Island; 912-786-9255, 866-892-4667, fax 912-786-0396; www.tybeeislandinn. com, e-mail info@tybeeislandinn.com. DELUXE TO ULTRA-DELUXE.

The **DeSoto Beach Hotel**, which had faded into near-oblivion over the decades, has been reborn with 36 new rooms decked out in amenities like microwaves and refrigerators. The four-story

hotel is right on the beach, as is the swimming pool and sundeck.
~ 212 Butler Avenue, Tybee Island; 912-786-4541, 877-786-4542,
fax 912-786-4543; www.desotobeachhotel.com. DELUXE TO
ULTRA-DELUXE.

The rooms at the three-story brick **Hunter House** (circa 1910)
aren't beachy at all, but a couple of them are quite nice, especially
the art deco–style suite on the ground floor. Size and comfort level
vary widely, though, so if you want a room with a view, ask when
you arrange accommodations at this for-
mer apartment house. A second-floor wrap-
around porch makes a nice place for continental breakfast or cocktails before dinner in
the inn's second-floor restaurant. ~ 1701 Butler
Avenue, Tybee Island; 912-786-7515; www.hun
terhouseinn.com. DELUXE.

> The origin of the name Tybee re-
> mains open to interpretation, but
> most historians trace it to the
> American Euchee Indian word
> for "salt," naturally one of the
> resources widely available
> on the island.

With 240 rooms and suites divided into three
parts (two of them four stories tall), the **Ocean
Plaza Beach Resort** is hands-down the island's
largest hotel. It's also one of the very few places offering a view of the sea. The oceanfront rooms have balconies and
there are two pools (unless you have children, don't stay near
these unless you have earplugs) but that's about it for "resort,"
unless you count the ocean-view Dolphin Reef Restaurant. ~
Ocean Front at 15th Street, Tybee Island; 912-786-7777, 800-
215-6370, fax 912-786-4531; www.oceanplaza.com. MODERATE
TO DELUXE.

Another waterfront motel is the **Sundowner Ocean Front
Inn**, a two-story inn next to the Tybrisa Pavilion, which can be
a noisy location. Some rooms have the same view as the more
expensive places; these have small balconies facing the water. King
and double rooms are modestly decorated in pastels and floral
bedcoverings; some are equipped with microwaves and refrigerators. There's also a pool. ~ 1609 Strand Avenue, Tybee Island;
912-786-4532. DELUXE TO ULTRA-DELUXE.

The **17th Street Inn** is many people's dream of the perfect
beach house. Once you see it, you have to wonder why no one
opened a place like this before 1997. A standard two-story beach
house has been converted into four units: two up and two down
(with four more units in the rear); the second story is best. Two
rooms have a wonderful private porch ideal for whiling away long
afternoons or snoozing after swimming at the beach less than a
block away. All rooms are furnished with dressing rooms and
kitchens. (This property also rents an off-site oceanview condominium.) Continental breakfast included. ~ 12 17th Street, Tybee
Island; 912-786-0607, 888-909-0607; www.tybeeinn.com, e-mail
tybeeinn@aol.com. DELUXE TO ULTRA-DELUXE.

◄ HIDDEN

DINING

Most island and waterfront restaurants, unlike those in Savannah proper, stay open on Sunday. You won't find many fast-food joints, but many places are inexpensive. Only a few offer much besides seafood, and they tend to be the pricier choices.

HIDDEN ►

On the north side of Route 80 east of the Wilmington River is a maze of dirt roads that eventually leads to **Desposito's**. Here on the Isle of Armstrong just a few yards from the source, diners in the know feast on fantastic seafood in the most casual spot in southeastern Georgia. If you order boiled shrimp, your server will cover your table with newspapers onto which you can dump the discarded shells. Oysters, snow crab and other denizens of the deep are served in the bar, too, but why bother when you can sit on the screened porch? ~ Macceo Drive; 912-897-9963. BUDGET.

HIDDEN ►

In 2003, **Loggerheads** opened in a prime location on the banks of Lazaretto Creek. In fact, the shrimp boats unload right here at the dock, meaning this casual restaurant has first crack at these sweet shellfish that are prepared in several ways. Flounder, scallops, oysters and blackboard specials (such as five-spice pork tenderloin) round out the offerings. As for the name, it was inspired by Lonesome George, a turtle who hangs out at the dock and pokes his head up on cue at sunset. ~ 1 East Route 80, Tybee Island; 912-786-8500. MODERATE TO DELUXE.

HIDDEN ►

The Crab Shack is the quintessential beach restaurant. Overlooking a tidal creek, this sprawling in-and-outdoor restaurant is totally casual. Platters of boiled shrimp and oysters, excellent deviled crabs and other island specialties are the main attraction. It's a great place for families who don't have to worry about the kids squirming or even wandering around; the place is way off the main drag. And you can spend hours just gazing out over the marsh, looking for egrets, seagulls, fish or even the moon. Most out-of-towners laugh when they see how the tables are cleared at The Crab Shack. When you've finished shelling and consuming your shrimp or whatever, you just push everything towards a big hole in the center of the table and it disappears. Did we mention casual? ~ 40-A Estill Hammock Road (off Route 80 east of the Lazaretto Creek Bridge), Tybee Island; 912-786-9857. BUDGET TO MODERATE.

George's of Tybee introduced the concept of chic dining to the island when it opened in 1998. People who'd spent all their summers peeling shrimp in their shorts couldn't believe it. In a small but elegantly decorated building, its contemporary art and dramatic brick-red walls are set off by heart-pine floors. The menu is what's known as New American cuisine with a Southern flair. Translation: grilled rack of lamb with couscous and chutney, braised mustard greens and a bourbon essence; sautéed black grouper over ragôut of Tasso ham and lima beans with Vidalia onion purée and sweet-corn vinaigrette; plus some Asian-influenced dishes such as yellowfin tuna, pan-seared and served with jalapeño-ginger rice cake with wasabi aioli. Closed Monday. ~ 1105 East Route 80, Tybee Island; 912-786-9730. DELUXE TO ULTRA-DELUXE.

As you'd imagine, the **Sundae Café & Deli** has a host of frozen goodies, including hand-dipped ice cream. On weekdays, ◄ HIDDEN they serve a budget-priced lunch special along with sandwiches, salads, and a full deli selection. Dinner is another matter: lump crab cakes, pistachio-crusted tuna, and a napoleon of portobello mushroom with fried green tomatoes accompanied by sweet potato soufflé. Closed Sunday. ~ Route 80 at Jones Avenue, Tybee Island; 912-786-7694. MODERATE TO DELUXE.

The Sugar Shack Restaurant might technically be a restaurant since it does serve food, but you'd feel overdressed if you came here during the day wearing shoes. But what looks like just another fast-food joint actually has really good shrimp sandwiches and hamburgers, and the soft-serve ice cream and milk shakes are divine on a hot day. The Sugar Shack also serves dinner platters from the grill—New York strip, grilled pork chops—plus baked ham and fried oysters. Two more things operate in its favor: it opens at 7 a.m. and serves cold beer all day. ~ 201 1st Street at Butler Avenue, Tybee Island; 912-786-4482. BUDGET TO MODERATE.

MacElwee's Seafood House claims to be the oldest seafood restaurant on Tybee, but that doesn't stop it from serving hand-cut Black Angus steaks, too. The specialties here are beer-battered and fried seafood dishes; in the "r" months, ask for local oysters. The decor includes a nod to seafaring, but that's about it. Closed Sunday. ~ 101 Route 80/Butler Avenue, Tybee Island; 912-786-4259. MODERATE TO DELUXE.

AUTHOR FAVORITE

Almost invisible beside the ruined foundations of Fort Screven, the **North Beach Grill** was the first hip place to eat on Tybee Island. No one else had thought of the natural combination of seaside location and Caribbean cuisine and it was a hit from the very beginning. The lunchtime menu is limited but at night there are major seafood entrées as well as some Southern food, vegetarian dishes and burgers. Go on a nice night when you can sit on the covered patio and catch the sea breeze because the decor inside is nil. If you're not already on island time when you get to North Beach, you will be by the time you leave. Closed Monday through Wednesday in winter. ~ 41-A Meddin Drive (across from Tybee Lighthouse), Tybee Island; 912-786-9003. MODERATE TO DELUXE.

A vision of lime green with accents of coral and blue against white plantation shutters and white ceiling fans, the 60-seat **Grille Beachside** looks like a restaurant in the Caribbean. The menu pays homage to the ocean (practically at its doorstep) with scallops and shrimp, but pork, chicken and even veal play heavy roles as well. The tables on the covered patio are less formal. ~ At the Beachside Colony, 404 Butler Avenue, Tybee Island; 912-786-4745. BUDGET TO ULTRA-DELUXE.

Even though people will tell you Tybee is unpretentious, the **Breakfast Club** seems to be pushing it. Old-timers prefer this place to fancier digs, perhaps because it's authentic. The grits are good, the bacon plentiful and the coffee terrible (so order orange juice). If you don't know anybody, sit at the counter and you soon will. No dinner. ~ 1500 Butler Avenue, Tybee Island; 912-786-5984. BUDGET.

Hunter House is one of Tybee's oldest dinner houses. Dining is upstairs in one of several small dining areas. The emphasis is on seafood prepared roasted, grilled or broiled. The house special is a pot roast dinner served with potatoes and vegetables. Closed Monday in winter. ~ 1701 Butler Avenue, Tybee Island; 912-786-7615. DELUXE TO ULTRA-DELUXE.

The Friday and Saturday country cooking and seafood buffet at **Cap'n Chris Restaurant** make this large establishment a good deal, particularly for families. À la carte dishes include fried chicken, boiled shrimp, deviled crab, sandwiches and so forth. If you're planning a long day at the beach, the weekend breakfast buffet is also a good deal. ~ Butler Avenue at 15th Street, Tybee Island; 912-786-4516. BUDGET TO MODERATE.

Locals swear that the outside tables at **AJ's Dockside Restaurant** offer the best sunset-watching on the whole island—and it's hard to disagree with them. The view across the back river is clearly the main attraction here, but AJ's also serves good hamburgers and a variety of seafood (steamed oysters, crab stew, and shrimp and grits, for starters) in a relaxed atmosphere. No lunch on weekdays. ~ 1315 Chatham Avenue, Tybee Island; 912-786-9533. MODERATE.

SHOPPING   With few exceptions, Tybee is not a shopper's paradise, but if you're in the market for a kid's pail and sand shovel, woven beach mats or T-shirts, you're in luck.

Forgot your novel? **The Casual Reader** is the only bookstore on Tybee. It also rents DVDs. ~ 1213 Route 80, Tybee Island; 912-786-7655.

The **Tybee Island Marine Science Center Gift Shop** is upstairs at the museum building and sells souvenirs like shells and note cards. ~ Adjacent to the 14th Street parking lot north of the Tybrisa pier; 912-786-5917.

T.S. Chu's has been a Tybee landmark since it opened more than half a century ago by the same Chinese-American family that runs it today. It's a huge corner store that lives up to its motto, "If it's something you use, you can find it at Chu's." The front portion has mostly beach clothes—some of them nice but most of them cheap and fun—from coverups to hats to sandals. The middle section has all manner of useful odds and ends: kitchenware, beach mats and so on. The rear is where you'll find most of the souvenirs: terrifically tacky lamps made from shells and many, many frivolous knickknacks. Chu's is a great place to dawdle if a sudden thunderstorm clouds the beach for half an hour or, less likely, an afternoon. ~ 6 Tybrisa Street, Tybee Island; 912-786-4561.

> When strolling Skidaway Island State Park's nature trails, watch out for fiddler crabs, best spotted at low tide.

The **Atlantic Beacon Gallery** displays the paintings, prints, photographs, ceramics and other works by members of the Tybee Arts Association. This is the place to buy affordable pieces you will want to keep long after the sunburn fades. ~ 1606 Butler Avenue, Tybee Island; 912-786-9386.

Forgot your bathing suit? Big hat? You can stock up at the **American Beachwear Company**. ~ 18 Tybrisa Street, Tybee Island; 912-786-8383.

NIGHTLIFE

The **Atlantic Star** offers day and evening gambling cruises for a modest fee (not counting what you spend in the casino). ~ Lazaretto Creek Marina, Tybee Island; 912-786-7827.

Loggerheads, a dockside restaurant, features acoustic jam bands and blues music Thursday through Sunday nights, usually without a cover. ~ 1 East Route 80, Tybee Island; 912-786-8500.

PARKS

SKIDAWAY ISLAND STATE PARK 🚶 ⛰ 🚤 🎣 Bordering Skidaway Narrows, part of the Intracoastal Waterway, this 533-acre park has both salt and fresh water, thanks to estuaries that flow through the marshes. Live oak, cabbage palmetto and longleaf pine stud most of the island, where visitors can walk on two nature trails, keeping an eye out for deer, raccoons and shorebirds. There are also observation towers that provide an overview. Park rangers offer periodic nature programs to acquaint visitors with the flora and fauna here. Amenities include a junior Olympic swimming pool, picnic shelters, laundry facilities, a group shelter and a playground. Day-use fee, $2. ~ 52 Diamond Causeway, Skidaway Island; 912-598-2300.

▲ There are 88 tent, trailer and RV sites; $24 per night for RVs, $22 per night for tents.

▼▼▼▼▼▼▼▼▼▼▼▼▼▼▼
Outdoor Adventures

Savannah's moderate climate encourages outdoor activities throughout the year. The humidity makes hot days feel hotter and cold days feel colder, so the ideal times for serious biking or hiking are in spring and fall and/or in the early morning and evening.

FISHING

You need a Georgia license to fish in fresh water, but not in salt water. With so much sea trout, flounder, tarpon, red drum (spottail bass) and catfish in the abundant salt waters, however, you can skip getting a license. You have your choice of shore fishing (such as at Tybee), pier fishing, or going out in a boat to fish in the rivers or even offshore. For the latter, allow about two hours to get to Snapper Banks and another hour to reach the warm Gulf Stream from Wilmington Island. Then, of course, you have the same trip back so count on an all-day excursion, often departing before dawn.

There are lots of fishing piers in the area, including ones at the **Back River** (Chatham Avenue, Tybee Island), **Lazaretto Creek** (Tybee Island) and the **Tybee Island Pier and Pavilion** (north of Tybrisa Street). A centrally located place to find bait is at **Adams Bait House**. ~ 2812 River Street, Thunderbolt; 912-352-7878.

BOAT CHARTERS

If you charter a boat or sign on for a sightseeing excursion, be sure to take a hat, sunscreen, food, drinks and bug repellent, and wear deck shoes.

Whether you're looking for in-shore or deep-sea fishing, **Lazaretto Creek Marina** can send you out in its 42-foot boat, from a four-hour excursion to an all-day outing, to the Gulf Stream. They also run sightseeing, sunset and dolphin cruises. ~ On Lazaretto Creek (take the first right immediately after you cross the Lazaretto Creek Bridge onto Tybee Island); 912-786-5848, 800-242-0166; www.tybeedolphins.com.

Salty Dawgs Charters and Tours takes sightseeing and fishing trips as well as sunset cruises and outings to other barrier islands—all aboard a 21-foot boat. ~ P.O. Box 1366, Tybee Island; 912-786-5435.

Tybee Island Charters is available for deep-sea fishing, in-shore fishing and sightseeing tours—including looking for dolphins. ~ Tybee Island; 912-786-4801; www.fishtybee.com.

For tours of the back rivers, uninhabited islands and golden marshes along Georgia's northern coast, check out **Back River Adventures**. ~ 912-786-8847; www.backriveradventures.com.

SAILING

The rivers and tidal creeks around Savannah are ideal for sailing. It's tougher going once you get to the ocean or anywhere out of sight of land.

Sail Harbor Marina teaches basic sailing skills as well as coastal piloting. As the official Olympic yachting marina, it was home base for the participants, who did the actual racing out in Wassaw Sound. You can also arrange for skippered or bareboat charters here at the facility on Turner Creek. ~ 618 Wilmington Island Road; 912-897-2896.

Lake Mayer, on Savannah's southside, is a good place for children or beginners to hone their skills without having to cope with tidal action. The **Savannah Sailing Center** has single-session and program rates for all ages. ~ Montgomery Crossroad at Sallie Mood Drive; 912-231-9996.

Savannah is a major city on the Intracoastal Waterway that stretches the length of the eastern seaboard. The Savannah River, not considered a recreational river, marks the city boundaries on the north; across the water is South Carolina. For boating and fishing, head to the marinas at Thunderbolt, which is on the Wilmington River, the largest in the area. There are also marinas at Isle of Hope and Lazaretto Creek, which is the easternmost creek, on the west side of Tybee Island. Lazaretto is a small river and, like the Wilmington, good for canoeing, kayaking and sailing.

CANOEING & KAYAKING

Sea Kayak Georgia offers guided tours of surrounding waterways. They also offer instruction as well as extended outings to the barrier islands for camping or overnight stays at bed and breakfasts. Sea Kayak also runs a small lodging facility on Tybee. ~ 1102 Butler Avenue (Route 80), Tybee Island; 912-786-8732, 888-529-2542; www.seakayakgeorgia.com.

Coastal Georgia's flat landscape, studded with pine and palm trees and intersected with waterways of all sizes, combines with its mild climate to create an outstanding setting for golf courses.

GOLF

There are three courses at **Bacon Park**, and they are interlinked so you can play 27 holes without repeating yourself. The ninth hole at the Live Oak Course is the longest in the park at 581 yards (par 5) with a canal crossing the fairway; another canal crosses the eighth on the Magnolia Course. The shortest course, at 3256 yards, is Cypress, with water on seven holes. There's a pro shop, self-service snack bar, driving range and practice green. ~ Shorty Cooper Drive; 912-354-2625.

The Savannah Golf Club is America's first golf course, established in 1794. The links are not open to the public.

The **Henderson Golf Club** is a links-style course, with challenging dog legs and lots of water and woods. The hardest hole is No. 4, a par-three that gives even veterans a hard time; the 18-hole course is par-71. You can get lessons and rent carts. There's a full bar and grill on the premises. ~ 1 Al Henderson Drive, 912-920-4653.

On the grounds of the Union Camp Corporation, the **Mary Calder Golf Course** is open to the public. The par for nine holes is 35; no carts are rented after 5 p.m. at this course on the outskirts of town. ~ West Lathrop Avenue; 912-238-7100.

The golf course at the **Wilmington Island Club** on Wilmington Island was designed by Donald Ross and opened in 1927, when the property was centered in the charming eight-story General Oglethorpe Hotel. Several owners later, the par-72 course is planted with Tifton and bermuda grass. ~ 612 Wilmington Island Road; 912-897-1615.

Off Dean Forest Road in the general vicinity of the airport is the Rees Jones–designed **Southbridge Golf Club** course. The setting is lovely, with Georgia pines and wetlands and an antebellum-style clubhouse. There's also a driving range and putting green. ~ 415 Southbridge Boulevard; 912-651-5455.

TENNIS   Tennis is extremely popular in Savannah, though between May and October you may find it advisable to play early in the morning or evening because of the heat and sun.

Many municipal and county parks have courts. At the **Daffin Park Tennis Courts**, six of the nine courts are clay (there is a fee for these); only the hard courts are lighted at night. ~ 1001 East Victory Drive; 912-351-3851.

The biggest tennis center is the **Bacon Park Tennis Complex** on the south side of town, where 16 lighted hard courts are surrounded by woods. Fee. ~ 6262 Skidaway Road; 912-351-3850.

There are also four courts that can be lit for night play in the **Forsyth Park Extension**. ~ Park Avenue between Whitaker and Drayton streets; 912-351-3852.

SWIMMING   The **Chatham County Aquatic Center** has a 50-meter pool and a six-lane, 25-yard warm-up pool. The center has changing rooms, a pro shop and a concession stand. ~ 7240 Sallie Mood Drive; 912-351-6556.

The waves on the front beach at **Tybee Island** are excellent for body surfing on an incoming tide. Once you reach the southern part of the island, however, you'll find signs warning of danger. Although you could walk to a sandbar off this shore at low tide,

AUTHOR FAVORITE

I've come across dolphins while swimming in the calmer waters of the **Back River**, off Chatham Avenue. If you like swimming without the waves, you can reach this beach by crossing the island or looping around the south end by walking along the sand. The channel attracts motorboats and other watercraft bound for fishing or excursions to nearby Little Tybee Island, so it's best to confine your swimming close to shore.

the fast-moving water cuts off any hope of return and people drown out there almost every summer. Safe swimming can be found at Fort Screven and the main beach. There are lifeguards on the weekends on the main beach.

Savannah and the islands are gloriously flat, except for one bump over a railroad track on Anderson Street. Biking hasn't caught on here in a big way; it's certainly not recommended in the Historic District unless you are out for a leisurely pedal. For more aerobic stuff, the Diamond Causeway on Skidaway Island is wide, flat and not too heavily trafficked.

BIKING

Heading toward Tybee Island on Route 80 (Victory Drive), you can get onto the **McQueen's Island Trail**, which provides six miles for hiking and biking between Bull River and Fort Pulaski. Other bike route ideas are available from the city Department of Leisure Services. ~ 912-351-3837.

Biking is fun on Tybee Island, especially if you want to explore Fort Screven or the back roads of the south end of the island, which is as flat as a pancake; do not even think about biking on the narrow two-lane road that runs from the city to the ocean.
Bike Rentals   Instead of getting salt spray on your own wheels, try **Jaime Sundance Bicycle Shop**, the only rental outfit on Tybee Island. Closed Monday. ~ Tybee Island; 912-786-9469.

All distances for hiking trails are one way unless otherwise noted.

HIKING

Savannah's flat landscape allows for hiking just about anywhere, though no matter how far you walk or hike you won't be able to get much of a view. One exception is the nature trail on Oatland Island. The **Oatland Island Education Center** contains one and a half miles of trails that lead past enclosures for animals such as tigers and foxes. The trails are pretty rough, with roots, limbs and branches that can impede progress. There are benches along the route, which can be divided into shorter portions. Pick up a free trail map in the center office. Admission.

Two easy trails offer four miles of hiking at **Skidaway Island State Park**. The **Sandpiper Trail** (1 mile) starts behind the visitors center and runs along the salt marsh, inhabited by fiddler crabs that often dart about. It leads to an island hammock where you may see deer, raccoons, opossums and maybe wild hogs among the saw palmettos and live oaks. Interpretive markers along the **Big Ferry Nature Trail** (3 miles) explain the wetland areas, where the remains of old stills can be seen in slow decay. At the end loop of the figure-eight trail are Civil War earthworks. Maps are available at the visitors center.

On the south side of Savannah, **Lake Mayer Community Park** has a one-and-a-half-mile trail within its 75 acres.

Transparation

▼▼▼▼▼▼▼▼▼▼▼▼▼

Transportation

CAR

Route 16 enters Savannah from the direction of Macon (which is the driving route you would be on coming from Atlanta); exits take you to midtown or the Historic District. **Route 95** runs north–south on the west side of Savannah, intersecting with **Route 80** on the north side and Route 16 on the south side; it is about ten miles from the intersection of Route 16 and Route 95. Savannah is also accessible from the north via **Route 17A**, which crosses the Savannah River from South Carolina, entering the city just west of downtown. To reach Tybee Island, take Route 80 east, known within the city limits as Victory Drive.

Major north–south arteries within the city are **Abercorn Street**, which is two-way but dotted with squares, as well as **Drayton** (one-way north) and **Whitaker** (one-way south) streets. To reach the south side of the city from downtown, take Abercorn Street until it turns into Abercorn Extension. Downtown Savannah was laid out in a grid pattern and is easy to negotiate. From the Savannah River all the way to DeRenne Avenue, house numbers are the same between parallel north–south streets, so that the 100 block of 45th Street and the 100 block of 69th Street, for example, are both between Habersham and Abercorn streets.

AIR

The **Savannah/Hilton Head International Airport** is 16 miles west of downtown off Route 95 north of Route 16. The most frequent flights are the one-hour-or-less runs between Savannah and Atlanta. The Savannah area is served by AirTran, American Eagle, Continental Express, Delta, Northwest, United Express and US Airways. ~ www.savannahairport.com.

Airport Express runs 15-passenger vans to hotels, businesses and residences, and offers group rates. ~ 912-964-0060.

TRAIN

Amtrak (800-872-7245; www.amtrak.com) provides rail passenger service from Savannah up and down the eastern seaboard. ~ 2611 Seaboard Coast Line Drive, Savannah; 912-234-2611.

BUS

Greyhound Bus Lines (800-231-2222; www.greyhound.com) serves Savannah with several daily departures to areas north and south, and to Atlanta. ~ 610 Oglethorpe Avenue; 912-232-2135.

CAR RENTALS

Alamo Rent A Car (800-327-9633), **Avis Rent A Car** (800-230-4898), **Budget Car & Truck Rental** (800-527-0700), **Dollar Rent A Car** (912-964-9001), **Hertz Rent A Car** (800-654-3131), **National Car Rental** (800-227-7368) and **Thrifty Car Rental** (800-367-2277) all have outlets at the Savannah/Hilton Head International Airport.

In the Historic District, cars can be rented daily or weekly from **Savannah Car and Van Rental** Monday through Friday. ~ 236 Drayton Street; 912-233-6554. In addition, **Economy Rent A Car** has an office on the south side of town. ~ 3 Posey Street; 912-352-3444.

PUBLIC TRANSIT

Chatham Area Transit (CAT) runs 20 routes, most of them disabled-accessible, in Savannah and around Chatham County. The complimentary CAT Shuttle circulates in the Historic District, connecting to most CAT bus routes. Route and schedule information is also available at the website. ~ 912-233-5767; www.catchacat.org.

The best way to get an introduction to the Historic District is to begin with a ride on the inexpensive trolleys that slowly roll around the squares and up and down the streets. You have a choice of several; the three described here allow on-off privileges so you can hop off if you want to explore a particular sight and catch the next one. The best are the **Old Town Trolley Tours** that give 90-minute excursions accompanied by narration. The orange-and-green trolleys run seven days a week, departing every 30 minutes from the Visitors Center. ~ 912-233-0083.

Gray Line offers another option, using red open-air trolleys and air-conditioned minibuses. They offer the official daily tours of the Historic Savannah Foundation. ~ 912-234-8687; www.graylineofsavannah.com.

Old Savannah Tours uses small buses as well as trolleys and has AAA, AARP and group rates. They specialize in tours of the beaches, forts and "The Book." ~ 234 Martin Luther King Jr. Boulevard; 912-234-8128, 800-517-9007; www.oldsavannahtours.com, e-mail oldsavtour@aol.com.

TAXIS

Most people visiting the Historic District will have no need for a taxi after they arrive because the area is so compact and inexpensive trolleys so readily available. Once in the greater metropolitan area, especially the islands, you will need a cab or a car. One of the few places taxis can be found easily is at the airport. Otherwise, you should phone for one because you will almost never be able to catch one on the spur of the moment.

Yellow Cab is available around the clock and, with advance notice, discounts airport trips. ~ 912-236-1133.

With advance reservations, you can book airport transport through **Toucan Taxi and Shuttle Services.** ~ 912-233-3700.

THREE

Golden Isles and Southeast Georgia

The Golden Isles—some private, some public, some wild and some tamed by the twin skills of developers and real estate agents—march down the coast of Georgia in regal procession, with names like Ossabaw, St. Catherine's, Sapelo and Jekyll announcing their mixed Indian-Spanish-English heritage.

It may surprise some visitors to learn that Georgia's entire Atlantic coastline is only about 100 miles long; its abundance of different sights, history and activities make this short distance seem much longer. Despite all these features, the towns along the Intracoastal Waterway are not overdeveloped—at least not to people accustomed to true urban density. Inland, the hard-sand beaches give way to the mushy peat bogs of the Okefenokee Swamp, where alligators swim in waters protected by the U.S. government. Inland farther still are farm towns and places that proudly maintain their Southern traditions, including one town notable for encouraging the peaceful retirement of both Union and Confederate soldiers.

With the moss, the shrimp boats and the sandy beaches of the barrier islands, all blessed with moderate temperatures, coastal Georgia is a romantic slice of heaven. After all, the late John F. Kennedy, Jr., who ostensibly could have chosen any place in the world for his wedding in 1996, wound up tying the knot on remote Cumberland Island off the coast of the southeasternmost tip of the state.

Yet for all the charms of the region often called the Golden Isles, the beginning of its settlement by the Europeans was hard-fought and often bloody. The closer the English moved towards Spanish-occupied Florida, the more tense relations became—not only in the colonies but also between London and Madrid. Fort King George was built in the Darien area in 1721 and garrisoned by British soldiers. Fourteen years later, General James Oglethorpe stepped up his vigilance against the Spanish and encouraged Highland Scots to settle nearby lands along the Altamaha River. By 1736, Oglethorpe had built Fort Frederica on St. Simons Island; four years later, he led his troops into the Battle of Bloody Marsh, a successful conflict that determined, once and for all, the English possession of the sea islands and—it is not an exaggeration to say—the future of the rest of the continent.

Many of the plantations that had grown rice or cotton in the marshy terrain of the Golden Isles were burned by General Sherman's forces during the Civil War. Slaves who had worked these lands settled on the islands, subsisting on fishing and modest agricultural projects; their descendants are still here, notably on Sapelo Island. St. Simons, after the destruction of Fort Frederica, languished until its rediscovery as a tourist destination early in this century. Jekyll Island was revived around the turn of the century by wealthy northern industrialists who founded the Jekyll Island Beach Club in the late 1880s. Eventually, club members sold the island to the state of Georgia. Sea Island is the ritziest of the lot, with prized homes lining the waterfront and golf courses.

To the south, St. Marys, the second-oldest city in the United States, received a shot in the arm when the Kings Bay nuclear submarine base opened nearby. More recently, it has gained fame as the gateway to Cumberland Island; its quaint downtown is on the National Register of Historic Places.

Inland, what was once ocean floor is now the mushy bottom of the Okefenokee Swamp, made world-famous by Walt Kelly in his newspaper comic strip, "Pogo." In addition to Waycross, Valdosta and Tifton, the largest cities in the inland southeast, a host of small towns—some memorable, some forgettable in terms of history or culture—exist without much impact from tourists. There are no crowds, no lines, no theme parks—just a quiet life, albeit with unusual attractions scattered throughout the region.

North Coast

The area due south of Savannah still has farms, but most of the plantations in this area have long since disappeared. Henry Ford and his wife, Clara, spent part of their winters here in the late 1920s, but their property, too, is no longer open to the public. However, less-famous retirees and others have discovered the delights of the climate and the slow way of life along this part of the coast.

There are no real cities between Savannah and Brunswick, farther south. The coast highway, Route 17, is the main artery, although many of the neat places to visit are accessible only by smaller roads. None of the offshore islands in this stretch can be reached by car, but the public is welcome to take guided ferry trips to Sapelo Island.

SIGHTS

Too bad there's no bridge between Skidaway and Ossabaw islands; it would simplify the drive south (but since the latter is a Heritage Preserve, there's no housing there anyway). Travelers must go inland to Route 17 to reach **Richmond Hill**.

Henry Ford's former estate is currently in private hands, but remnants of his legacy are evident. An example is the Henry Ford Kindergarten, which Mr. and Mrs. Ford opened because the town made no provision for preschool. Now the **Richmond Hill Historical Society and Museum**, it has displays from the colonial days through the Revolutionary and Civil wars and the period after Henry and Clara Ford decided to build a riverfront house as their winter home in 1925. The Fords bought a lot of property and established, among other things, a botanic society that produced 365 different types of soybeans. One of the projects that Ford, along with Thomas Edison and Harvey Firestone, conducted was producing rayon from gum trees. This was spun into a pair of socks for Ford; these very socks are among the memorabilia on view in this modest white cottage. ~ Route 144 and Timber Trail Road, Richmond Hill; 912-756-3697; www.rich mondhillcvb.org.

From Richmond Hill, follow Route 144 east and follow the signs to **Fort McAllister State Historic Park**. This is an extremely well-preserved earthwork fortification, which the Confederates built in an attempt to protect Savannah from Union forces. The larger and stronger masonry structures such as Fort Pulaski were too expensive to build, but their earthier counterparts did have advanced features such as bomb shelters and a "hot shot" gun, which fired cannonballs that had been heated in a furnace in an attempt to set the enemy's wooden ships on fire. Of the seven naval attacks on Fort McAllister, the biggest battle was in 1863, and in all that time the only casualties were the fort's commander, Major John Gallie, and its mascot, Tom Cat. Finally, General William T. Sherman fought what would be the last battle of his March to the Sea here in December 1864. The fort eventually was bought by Henry Ford, who restored much of it. Today, Fort McAllister looks the way it did in 1865. You can tour the grounds, which are shaded by oaks and have views of the salt marsh, and visit the museum with its Civil War artifacts. Admission. ~ 3894 Fort McAllister Road, Richmond Hill; 912-727-2339.

Leaving Fort McAllister, drive west to Route 95 and continue south one exit to the town of **Midway**, which lies along Route 17. This town is a pale memory now, having been settled in 1754 by Puritans from Massachusetts, descendants of the English colony that came over in 1630. Two of Georgia's three signers of the Declaration of Independence came from Midway: Lyman Hall, one of the transplanted New Englanders, and Button Gwinnett. You can see the tiny **Midway Congregational Church** here, established in 1792. It may have served as a meeting place for locals who felt strongly about the independence movement; the last official meeting here was in 1865. Open to the public, the church is a popular site for weddings and other special events. Looking at the slave gallery and the high pulpit, and walking through the cemetery, will give you a glimpse of colonial life. The old burial grounds are rich with old grave markers, made eerier by oaks and moss. Revolutionary War hero General James Screven is buried here, as is General Daniel Stewart, a patriot perhaps better known as the great-grandfather of Theodore Roosevelt. ~ Route 17, Midway; 912-884-5837.

Next door in a raised 18th-century cottage is the small **Midway Museum,** which contains furniture and artifacts such as documents from the colonial period through the Civil War. If you are interested in a tour of the church and cemetery, this is the place to inquire. Call for hours. Closed Monday. Admission. ~ Route 17, Midway; 912-884-5837.

At the intersection of Route 17 and Route 84/38, head east across Route 95 and continue for four and a half miles to a unique living-history center: **Seabrook Village,** derived from an African-American settlement that flourished at the turn of the 20th century. Descended from former slaves set free after the Civil War, the community built the one-room Seabrook School, which educated local children from around 1895 until it was closed in 1940. When it was threatened with demolition in 1990, a local biracial group geared up to save it. The effort did not stop there. Several buildings on the 104-acre site have also been restored and are used to educate visitors about a long-gone way of life. It is one of the best places on this part of the coast to see—and feel—a bit

◄ *HIDDEN*

Golden Isles & Southeast Georgia

Text continued on page 94.

Three-day Weekend

Down the Colonial Coast

If you stick to the two-lane roads while driving south from Savannah, you'll enter another part of the Colonial Coast and be rewarded with moss-laden oak trees, the scent of salt water and a pace of life rarely encountered on the Eastern Seaboard. Here are old plantations—some wasted away to boards and some maintained or restored as historical sites—and more seafood restaurants than you can visit in a week.

Day 1
- Follow Route 17 through **Richmond Hill**, where relics span the decades between settlement days and the early 1900s (when motor baron Henry Ford lived here) at the **Richmond Hill Historical Society and Museum** (page 89).

- Detour onto Route 144 for a visit to **Fort McAllister State Historic Park** (page 90), an extremely well-preserved earthwork fortification constructed by Confederate troops to protect Savannah from the Union Army.

- Return to Richmond Hill and continue south across Route 95 to the little town of **Midway**, where the tiny **Midway Congregational Church** (page 90) was established in 1792. Feast on deviled crab and fried oysters at **Holton's Seafood Restaurant** (page 98) before heading east on Route 84/38.

- You'll want to devote at least an hour to touring **Seabrook Village** (page 91), a living-history center derived from an African-American settlement that flourished at the end of the 19th century.

- Spend the night in a restored barn in nearby **Melon Bluff** (page 95).

Day 2
- After a leisurely breakfast at Melon Bluff, pack the hats, sunblock and a picnic lunch and head south on Route 95 to Eulonia, then east on Route 99 to **Meridian**. Allow about an hour to reach this waterfront town from Melon Bluff.

- Catch the ferry to **Sapelo Island** (page 94), where you can spend the morning visiting the community of **Hog Hammock** (page 96) and touring the **Reynolds Mansion** (page 96).

- Pick up Route 17 again and continue south to **Darien**, where you can spend an hour or two exploring **Fort King George** (page 94), built in the early 1700s and now a state historic site with a small museum on local history.

- Check into the **Open Gates Bed & Breakfast** (page 97) before heading out to supper. You'll find a great blend of Southern cooking and fresh seafood at the waterfront **Skipper's Fish Camp, Restaurant and Oyster Bar** (page 98).

Day 3
- Fill up on breakfast at the B&B before resuming your southward route, this time heading to the **Hofwyl-Broadfield Plantation** (page 99). You can tour the farmhouse dating from the days when this place grew acres of rice. Check out the fine silver collection in the small nearby museum.

- Follow your nose to the ocean, sticking to Route 17 until veering off onto the **St. Simons Island** causeway just north of Brunswick, about half an hour south of the plantation. Turn into the Golden Isles Marina for an alfresco lunch at **Steamers Restaurant and Raw Bar** (page 97), where you can pick something from the raw bar or order Southern-style fish or shellfish.

- Head for the busiest part of St. Simons Island, **Mallery Street**. Spend an hour or two shopping here or take a trolley tour of the island. Drive, if you have at least an hour of energy left, out to **Fort Frederica** (page 102), one of the best attractions on the island.

- Check in to the **Queen's Court** (page 108) around the corner from Mallery Street and freshen up before heading out for the evening.

- A nice spot for dinner is nearby **P.G. Archibald's** (page 113), a charming extended cottage with a huge menu.

- Make reservations for a show at the **Ritz Theatre** (page 103) in downtown Brunswick, or remain on Mallery Street, where you can find joints offering rock, blues or jazz music until late in the evening.

of history that began when the freed African Americans were allotted "one mule and 40 acres." In addition to self-guided tours and one-hour guided tours each afternoon, full three-hour tours with costumed guides are available for groups who make arrangements ahead of time. Closed Sunday and Monday. Admission. ~ 660 Trade Hill Road, Midway; 912-884-7008; www.seabrook village.org.

There is a most unusual island that welcomes visitors, but the only access is via the Sapelo Queen ferry. To get there, take the exit to Eulonia (off Route 95 or on Route 17), where you will take Route 99 southeast for about ten miles to **Meridian**. Ferries regularly depart the dock on Landing Road for the scenic voyage to **Sapelo Island**. The half-hour ride prepares you for a trip to another place and a different culture, now eclipsed on other islands that have long since been carved up into resorts. Now known as the **Sapelo Island National Estuarine Research Reserve**, it was occupied by the Guale Indians some 3000 years ago and more recently by Creek Indians, who used it as a private hunting and fishing preserve. The English bought it in 1760 and passed it on to the hands of Frenchmen. It was then bought by Thomas Spalding, a well-to-do trader known as one of the first to plant the prized sea-island cotton; he and his wife designed and built a house on the south end of the island. Eventually, land that had grown cotton and rice became little more than hunting fields for visiting rich people drawn by the ducks known to frequent this part of the flyway. Detroit motor magnate Howard Coffin—who also founded Sea Island's Cloister Hotel—owned the island for a while, before R. J. Reynolds (son of the North Carolina tobacco baron) took it over in 1936, and built a mansion used today for retreats and conferences. ~ 912-437-3224.

HIDDEN ►

The **Sapelo Island Lighthouse** restoration was completed in 1998. The 80-foot brick tower was built almost 180 years ago by the Federal government to help guide ships to the emerging port at Darien. Steps—73 of them—made of Georgia pine spiral to the top. A 10-by-10 brick fuel storage building houses an exhibit center with artifacts and photographs of the area. The lighthouse has been non-operational since 1905.

Unless you're traveling by boat, you will have to return to the mainland to continue south. The shortest route is to continue south on Route 99 from Meridian seven miles to **Darien**.

You can pick up maps for a driving tour of Darien at the **Darien-McIntosh County Chamber of Commerce/Welcome Center** overlooking the Darien River. Closed Sunday. ~ 105 Fort King George Drive, Darien; 912-437-6684, 888-849-5448; www. mcintoshcounty.com.

For all the hoopla about Savannah's history, it's interesting to learn that **Fort King George** was built 12 years before Oglethorpe arrived in America. It was the first of a series of fortifications the English constructed to blunt French expansion on the continent. Housing soldiers who defended against threats of Spanish and Indian attacks (not to mention heat, boredom and giant mosquitoes that carried yellow fever), the fort was abandoned before Oglethorpe brought Scottish Highlanders to settle Darien in 1736. Today visitors can tour this state historic site, inspect the reconstructed versions of the cypress blockhouse and visit a small museum on local history. Closed Monday. Admission. ~ Route 17, Darien; 912-437-4770.

LODGING

Some very unusual accommodations are available in this area, though they are few and far between. Chain motels cluster around the interstate, so to find individual properties you have to stray off the beaten path. In some instances, way off.

You won't find anything else on the Georgia coast quite like **Melon Bluff**. In all, the property includes 3000 acres, parts of which were roamed by American Indians until the Europeans be-

 HIDDEN

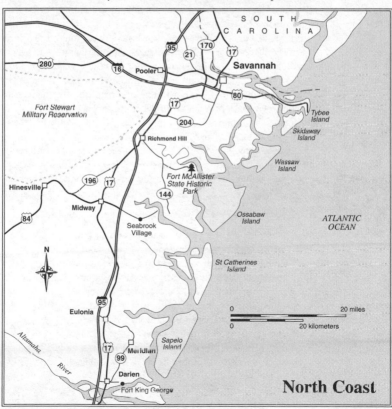

North Coast

gan arriving in 1526. The English followed the Spanish, and in the early part of the 18th century, plantations sprang up in the area, among them Melon Bluff Plantation. The current owners are managing Melon Bluff as a timber resource (the plantation contains all forest species native to the coast). Cedar, pine, sycamore, wax myrtle, sweet gum, cherry, hickory and bay ring the marshes, where many species of birds—osprey, quail, pelicans, owls, hawks and wild turkeys—live at least part of the year. Here among the trails, woods and lakes is the two-story Palmyra Barn, once the center of 1930s farm life; it has enough bedrooms to make it ideal for a retreat. Kennels and horse stalls are available, as is overnight dockage for private boats coming off the Intracoastal Waterway at St. Catherine's Sound. ~ 2999 Islands Highway, Midway; 912-884-5779, 888-246-8188, fax 912-884-3046; www.melonbluff.com, e-mail melonbluff@clds.net. DELUXE TO ULTRA-DELUXE.

If you want to spend the night but don't want to camp out on Sapelo Island, one of your options is **The Weekender**. You have a choice of one-, two- or three-bedroom accommodations in a very modest but undeniably charming setting. Each bedroom has a double bed and at least some kind of view, although the apartment is only one-story. The proprietors will pick you up at the ferry and take you back, and you can rent bicycles to cruise around the island. They provide linens and cooking utensils (microwave and toaster, too, in a shared kitchen); if you don't want to tote in your own food, inquire about getting fed when you make reservations. ~ Hog Hammock Community, Sapelo Island; 912-485-2277. BUDGET.

People traveling in large groups—families or conference groups—can arrange to stay at the huge **Reynolds Mansion**, where there's a 16-person, two-night minimum and a charge per person

AUTHOR FAVORITE

Having spent a lot of time on developed islands such as Tybee and St. Simons, I was fascinated with the lack of development on Sapelo Island. Here, beautiful oyster-shell paths and pristine woodlands surround **Hog Hammock**, a community of people descended from Spalding's slaves. Their story and much more is narrated on full- or half-day tours, which include stops at the visitors center and B.J.'s Confectionery, where you can buy snacks and cold drinks. While it is possible to tour the island independently, visitors who plan to spend the night with a roof over their heads would do well to plan ahead. Closed Monday. ~ Sapelo Island Visitors Center, Route 1, Box 1500, Darien, GA 31305; 912-437-3224.

per night. The interior is impressive, with Spanish-Mediterranean touches, an indoor pool and tropical murals dating from the days R. J. Reynolds owned the place (until his death in 1964). Be advised that public tours are conducted regularly so you won't be entirely isolated. Three meals a day are included in the room rate. ~ P.O. Box 15, Sapelo Island, GA 31327; 912-485-2299, fax 912-485-2140. ULTRA-DELUXE.

Non-chain lodging is limited around Darien, but **Open Gates Bed & Breakfast** is one exception. Facing Vernon Square, the modest 1876 Victorian has five high-ceilinged bedrooms decorated with antiques, such as a four-poster "cannonball" bed. One is in a separate structure, the old poker room; the large Island Room is on the ground floor; three others share a bath on the second floor. A pool, porches and a garden complete the ensemble. Full breakfast is included. ~ Vernon Square, Darien; phone/fax 912-437-6985; www.opengatesbnb.com, e-mail kelly@opengatesbnb.com. MODERATE TO DELUXE.

Darien's timber barons and leading merchants erected many an elaborate home around Vernon Square. In 2005, one, a Victorian house built around 1870, was converted into **Alexander's Historic Inn**. Three suites are decorated with antiques; the ground-floor Paris suite opens onto a porch. In fact, the front of the inn is graced with a double veranda where guests can relax in a swing hung from the rafters. Full breakfast is included, as is a complimentary lunch or high tea at J. M. Gale's Tearoom next door. ~ 306 Fort King George Street, Darien; 912-437-3430; www.alexandershistoricinn.com, e-mail alexanders4467@aol.com. DELUXE TO ULTRA-DELUXE.

On the Georgia coast, you can eat a fresh boiled crab with your hands or, at the other extreme, dine on *foie gras* and filet mignon served by waiters in uniform. There are few big Southern buffets available in this region (you'll have to go inland for that), but the seafood is fresh, plentiful and mostly affordable.

DINING

A big dining room with lots of Asian art distinguishes the **Beijing House III Restaurant and Lounge**. Like a lot of Chinese restaurants in the Deep South, this one's in a shopping center, but so what? That's usually an indication of reasonable prices, such as a three-course meal for $9 with a choice of ten entrées. If you're tired of the fried treatment so much local seafood receives, try the shrimp in Szechuan sauce or tossed together with cashew nuts or snow pea pods. Or opt for the numerous beef, pork or poultry dishes. A special low-price lunch and a lunchtime buffet is served every day but Saturday. ~ Ford Plaza Shopping Center, Richmond Hill; 912-756-3218. BUDGET TO MODERATE.

Steamers Restaurant and Raw Bar is the place to get your seafood fix while you're briefly out of the sight of water. Broiled shrimp and scallops, flounder, deviled egg and various combinations are a good bet, since these orders come with side dishes. But there's also pasta, baby back ribs and Low Country Boil at this place, located about one and a half miles from the Exit 14 off Route 95. Dinner only. ~ 2518 Route 17S, Richmond Hill; 912-756-3979. MODERATE TO DELUXE.

Some of the moderate-to-deluxe restaurants offer Twilight Specials, meaning you can dine—sometimes from a restricted menu—at lowered prices before the busy evening hours.

No doubt many drivers whiz past **Holton's Seafood Restaurant** in search of fast-food joints down the road. Too bad, because they are missing out on some extraordinarily tasty seafood: flounder, shrimp, scallops (boiled, broiled, fried), fried oysters and deviled crab. It's a bare-bones place but not unattractive—the kind of neat and clean family-style joint you used to find on minor highways throughout the South. Full dinners come with lots of extras. ~ 13711 Route 84 (at Route 95 and Oglethorpe Highway, Exit 76), Midway; 912-884-9151. MODERATE TO DELUXE.

HIDDEN ►

The best place to eat in Darien is at **Skipper's Fish Camp, Restaurant and Oyster Bar.** The menu is a seafood lover's dream—don't miss the local shrimp and oysters or, for that matter, the hushpuppies—but also features smoked ribs, ribeye and a peach cobbler served hot and smothered in rich vanilla ice cream. Opened in 2003 right on the Darien River, Skipper's is something of an idealized fish camp with spiffy wood walls and brick floors. ~ 85 Screven Street, Darien; 912-437-3474; www.skippersfish camp.com. BUDGET TO MODERATE.

SHOPPING   The North Coast is not exactly a shopping mecca. Along the interstate, you can find souvenirs—many of them tacky to the point of amusing—as well as regional snacks made with peanuts and pecans, but it's best to save your shopping dollars until you get to the southern part of the coast.

For one-stop shopping, head to **Georgia Islands Factory Shoppes**, where you'll find more than 50 designer and brand-name stores, including Bass (912-437-2788); Coach (912-437-3141); Liz Claiborne (912-437-3151); Mikasa (912-437-3170); Polo Ralph Lauren (912-437-2837); and Rockport (912-437-3170). ~ 1 Magnolia Bluff Way, Darien; 912-437-8360; 888-545-7224.

NIGHTLIFE   This part of the coast consists of small communities, some no larger than hammocks, and what nightlife there is tends to be in a private home or in a small lounge. For after-dark action, head down to St. Simons Island or Jekyll Island, just a short drive away.

FORT MCALLISTER STATE HISTORIC PARK 🏃 ⚓ 🚤 ⛵ This
scenic spot, where you can sit in the shade of old oak trees and
watch the river roll by, is a good place to learn about regional
military history while enjoying a foray into the great outdoors.
There is a nature trail near the river of this 1724-acre parcel,
where the fort was built as part of the coastal defense system.
There are picnic sites here as well as a museum featuring Civil
War artifacts and educational programs. Fishing is allowed on
the riverbanks. ~ 3984 Fort McAllister Road, ten miles east of
Route 95; 912-727-2339.

▲ There are 65 tent/RV sites; $17 to $19 per night. Reservations: 800-864-7275.

Development was long in coming to the North Coast
of Georgia between Savannah and Darien, but there's
been plenty of it on the South Coast. The islands of St.
Simons and Jekyll offer a bevy of lodging, dining, shopping and
entertainment options, along with plenty of beaches and waterways for recreation. Yet the area has a history similar to that of
the northern coast and you can find intriguing places to explore
on the islands, including Fort Frederica on St. Simons and the old
millionaire's enclave on Jekyll.

South Coast

When you leave Darien on Route 17/99, you will cross the Altamaha River where it enters Altamaha Sound. In about five more
miles, just before Route 17 bears to the east, you will come upon
signs leading to one of the few plantations around here open to
the public.

The great plantations that once ruled this area are, for the most
part, long gone. But there are legacies still to be viewed, along
with military sites and beautiful historic mansions, not to mention gorgeous beaches and scenic waterways. As you go through
this region, you will probably notice that many islands and at least
one town that would seem to be possessive (such as St. Simons
Island) are spelled without an apostrophe; it's a longstanding local
custom, now part of the official nomenclature.

One of the few extant plantations, let alone one open to the
public, the **Hofwyl-Broadfield Plantation** still has its antebellum
home furnished with antiques. Don't expect to see a replica of
Tara; it is a modest house by Hollywood standards. The Civil War,
as well as hurricanes and the disappearance of plentiful labor, led
to the decline of the rice empire. In 1915, descendants of early
owners William Brailsford and his son-in-law, James M. Troup,
converted the property into a dairy, which eventually shut down
in 1942. Subsequently, Ophelia Troup Dent willed the plantation
to the state in 1973. Live oaks shade the pathways lined with

SIGHTS

◀ HIDDEN

magnolias and camellias and you can walk to the marsh where the rice was grown and harvested. The impressive museum nearby has collections of fine silver and a slideshow about plantation life. Closed Monday. Admission. ~ 5556 Route 17 North, Brunswick; 912-264-7333.

To reach St. Simons, Brunswick and points south, return to the highway and take the Route 17 split south. On Route 17, known locally as Glynn Avenue, continue just past L Street and look for the signs to the island via the Torras Parkway. On the right is the **Brunswick-Golden Isles Visitors Bureau**, where you can get tons of maps and brochures not only about Brunswick but also about all the nearby islands. A short tourism video and a weather satellite monitor are available for viewing daily. ~ 2000 Glynn Avenue, Route 17 at Torras Parkway; 912-265-0260, 800-933-2627; www.brunswick-georgia.com.

St. Simons, which is larger than its neighbors, is also the most populous. It has plenty of lodging, many restaurants and more shops than you will manage to visit. Not surprisingly, there is also more traffic. Once past the tollbooth, turn right on Kings Way and again on Retreat Avenue. **Retreat Plantation** is now ensconced within the Sea Island Golf Club. Little is visible of the antebellum plantation, known for its fine sea-island cotton, but you can see the ruins of a slave hospital and a number of grave sites. The slave hospital, which dates to the 1700s, was originally two stories; made of tabby, it's been shored up somewhat. The clubhouse now sits on the site of the plantation's barn.

HIDDEN ►

Return to Kings Way and continue to Mallery Street, a neighborhood known as The Village. To the right is the fishing pier and the **Old Casino Building**, which houses the **St. Simons Visitors Center**. Open daily from 9 a.m. to 5 p.m., it is the place to find out about the regularly scheduled **trolley-car tours** that leave from the nearby parking lot. ~ 530-B Beachview Drive, St. Simons Island; 912-638-9014.

Steps away from the Visitors Center is the **St. Simons Island Lighthouse Museum**. The original lighthouse was built of tabby (cheaper than brick) and got its first keeper in 1810. The 75-foot octagonal pyramid was destroyed in 1862 by Confederates who didn't want the Federal troops to have such a useful navigational aid. The second, 104-foot lighthouse dates to 1872 and has a 129-step spiral staircase and an adjacent keeper's house, both designed by noted Georgia architect Charles Cluskey. The Victorian keeper's dwelling, furnished with period antiques, seems to be part of the lighthouse at first glance; it has excellent displays on both floors. The Coastal Georgia Historical Society maintains the museum and lighthouse, while the Coast Guard is in charge of making sure the light is operational. Admission. ~ 101 12th Street, St. Simons; 912-638-4666; www.saintsimonslighthouse.org.

After the museum, continue heading east and then north on Ocean Boulevard past **Massengale Park**, which has several miles of public beachfront. Take the next left and then quickly turn right onto Demere Road. In a few hundred yards you will see the signs for **Bloody Marsh Battle Site**. Here a monument denotes the 1742 Battle of Bloody Marsh, where the Spaniards made their final, failed attempt to expand their holdings north of Florida. ~ Demere Road, St. Simons Island.

Continue east on Demere Road until the major intersection with Frederica Road, the main—actually the only—boulevard that runs the length of the island. Take a right at the next major intersection onto Sea Island Road if you want to see the famous **Cloister resort**, the only thing on the island aside from private homes. The Cloister is more or less the clubhouse for the part-time and full-time residents here. This 1928 Spanish-Mediterranean enclave does accept guests, at either condominium buildings or in private homes. But even nonguests are welcome to drive along

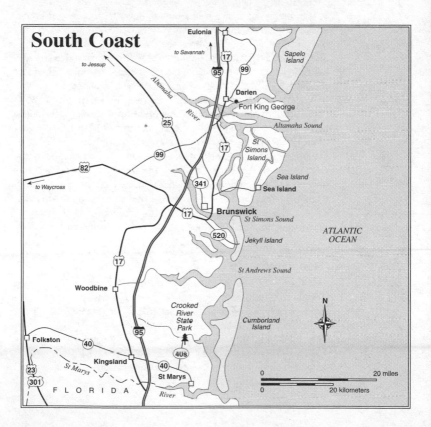

South Coast

Sea Island Drive and gawk at the hundreds of mansions, which the owners coyly refer to as cottages.

Returning to Frederica Road, continue north until the road turns left. If you bear right onto **Lawrence Road,** which runs about seven miles to its terminus at the Hampton River Club Marina, you can see road markers describing the plantations that once graced this area. Retracing your steps, go back to the intersection with Frederica Road and turn right (east); in less than a mile you will come upon more of the island's attractions.

Along Frederica Road is the small **Christ Church** that served the fortified village. In 1736, brothers John and Charles Wesley held services on the site. The sanctuary dates from 1886 and, while pretty, is not as moving as a tour through the adjacent cemetery. Among the notables buried here is the prolific St. Simons author Eugenia Price, who wrote dozens of top-selling novels, including *Savannah* and *Where Shadows Go.* Closed mornings. ~ 6329 Frederica Road, St. Simons Island; 912-638-8683; www.christ churchfrederica.org.

On the site of a once-flourishing military town, the **Fort Frederica National Monument** today is but a pale reminder of life in the mid-1700s. In 1736, three years after General James Oglethorpe founded Savannah, he and several dozen men started building this town, named for King George's son, Frederick. The fort was built, like others in the region, before the town to secure it from possible attack by the Spanish in Florida, and naturally it was constructed on the riverbank. A historic film is shown every half-hour. Admission. ~ Frederica Road, St. Simons Island; 912-638-3639; www.nps.gov/fofr.

Return to Frederica Road, heading south to Sea Island Road, where you will take a right. Near the river are two interesting historical sites, both located on what is known as Gascoigne Point. (Captain James Gascoign brought the first settlers to Frederica in 1736.) The **ruins of the slave cabins** (the Point later became Hamilton Plantation) are open to the public, along with a small

AUTHOR FAVORITE

I've always loved the poetry of Sidney Lanier, who is synonymous with the **Marshes of Glynn.** En route to St. Simons you'll pass the spot the Georgia poet made famous, a stretch of swampy grasses that is home to egrets and other waterfowl. A toll bridge across the river is the only land route to St. Simons; once on the island, you can continue to Sea Island or, if you have reservations, to Little St. Simons, a private island north of St. Simons that is accessible only by private launch.

museum, at **Epworth-by-the-Sea,** which was named for the English birthplace of John and Charles Wesley, who came to the colony to minister to the needs of the settlers. The Methodist Conference Center also has lodging and a restaurant. John Wesley returned to England to found the Methodist church, while brother John is known as the author of hundreds of hymns. ~ Off Sea Island Drive, St. Simons Island; 912-638-8688; www.epworthby thesea.org.

Just south of Epworth, **Gascoigne Bluff** is where live oak timbers were milled in the late 1700s to build the USS *Constitution,* known as "Old Ironsides." A century later, timbers here were cut for the building of the Brooklyn Bridge.

To visit **Brunswick,** cross the causeway, turn south on Route 17 and then right onto Gloucester Street, which cuts through downtown to Union Street. Turn right and in another block you will see the old Glynn County **Courthouse.** Dating from 1907, it is flanked not only by the usual live oaks dripping with moss but also by imported varieties including Chinese pistachio. The current courthouse is immediately to the north. ~ At the intersection of Union and G streets, Brunswick.

Jog east on G Street for two short blocks, then turn right (north) onto Newcastle Street for about a mile and a half. On the left you will see **Selden Park,** a 35-acre public park that stands on the site of Selden Normal & Industrial Institute (1903–1933), known for its pioneering efforts in educating local African Americans. ~ Newcastle Street near 1st Street, Brunswick.

Head south from Selden Park on Newcastle Street. **Historic Downtown Brunswick** has made some progress in historic preservation but still has a way to go. ~ Bounded by Bay, Union, London and G streets.

One of the most delightful buildings here is the **Ritz Theatre.** Built in 1898 as a 477-seat opera house, it began showing movies in 1927. It was closed for years, then reopened in 1983 and was renovated in early 2001. Now it is the home to nearly 100 events a year, including plays and musical performances. It's worth a peek, if only to pick up brochures or ask questions at the information station in the lobby. The information center is closed Sunday and Monday. ~ 1530 Newcastle Street, Brunswick; 912-262-6934; www.goldenislesarts.org.

Continue south on Newcastle Street and turn right on Gloucester, which intersects with Bay Street. In this area you can get a look at the **shrimp docks** and **Brunswick Landing Marina.** The picturesque shrimp boats, with their nets ready for harvesting shellfish, can be seen from Bay Street (Route 34) between Gloucester and Prince streets. Here, too, you can see the big ocean-bound freighters from all over the world.

Mary L. Ross Waterfront Park is home to the Liberty Ship Memorial Plaza, an outdoor musical playscape, a stage pavilion, an amphitheater and the Brunswick Harbor Market. (See "Shopping" for more information.) It's a great location for watching the sun set across the marsh. ~ Bay and Gloucester streets.

Head south on Bay Street. At Prince Street, turn left and head five blocks to Albany Street. At this intersection stands the beloved **Lovers' Oak**. It's been standing for 900 years and, according to American Indian lore, provided a place for secluded rendezvous with its sprawling, strong limbs. ~ Prince and Albany streets.

Brunswick's **Old Town National Register District**, laid out in a grid pattern, contains squares lined with turn-of-the-20th-century homes. ~ The district is bounded, more or less, by H Street, Newcastle Street, 1st Avenue and Martin Luther King Jr. Boulevard.

The **Mahoney-McGarvey House**, opposite the courthouse, is a fine example of Carpenter Gothic architecture. ~ 1709 Reynolds Street.

From Old Town, return to Gloucester Street to reach Route 17. A couple of blocks south on your left is **Overlook Park**, which affords stunning views of the river and marsh. Many people—some famous, notably Sidney Lanier—are quite taken with the scenery. It was under the **Lanier Oak** here that he was inspired to write *The Marshes of Glynn*. ~ Route 17.

Almost across the road, the **Mary Miller Doll Museum** is housed in a tiny white structure not far from the visitors bureau on Glynn Avenue (Route 17). Some 4000 dolls from 90 countries are showcased here, along with dollhouses and other displays for doll fanciers. Closed Saturday and Sunday. Admission. ~ 206–211 Gloucester Street, Brunswick; 912-267-7569.

South of the Brunswick-Golden Isles Visitors Bureau, Route 17 continues until it veers west; signs point towards the interstate. Take a left onto the Jekyll Island Causeway (Route 520), a long road over the marshes that leads to this barrier island, which was once owned by the state but has been self-sufficient since 1958.

Jekyll Island, the smallest of the lot, was named Ospo by the American Indians; General James Oglethorpe renamed it Jekyll after one of the backers of the colony. One of the general's top officers quickly established a plantation to produce the ingredients for beer to supply the troops at Frederica. The Spanish destroyed the plantation, which Horton rebuilt; it eventually passed into the hands of the duBignon family of France.

Other than the pristine beaches, there are few attractions on Jekyll Island. But the ones that exist are quite unusual. After you reach the island, continue straight until you reach Beachview Drive, then go left to Shell Road and left again. Take a right on Stable Road and you will arrive shortly at the **National Historic**

District Visitors Center, where you can see a video about the island's history and buy tram tickets for a tour of the district. If you prefer, you can tour on your own on foot. ~ 100 Stable Road; 912-635-4036; www.jekyllisland.com.

Many of the 33 original buildings are the "cottages" of wealthy snowbirds (with names like Pulitzer, Tiffany, Astor and Vanderbilt) who found the beauty, charm and easy access of this coastal retreat a peaceful antidote to the stress of raking in fortunes. The architecture varies widely; some are Shingle style, almost cottages, while others, such as the Crane mansion, are laid out in formal Italian Renaissance Revival style. (Several decades ago, some of these homes were available for overnight use but that practice has now ceased.) A few of these mansions have been restored and refurnished, and the structures are impressive; you can really imagine what it was like to live in such coddled luxury, as these families did from around 1888 to 1942.

Faith Chapel, which dates from 1904, boasts stained-glass windows by Louis Tiffany and D. Maitland Armstrong. Closed mornings. ~ Jekyll Island; 912-635-4036.

On the grounds of what is also called the Millionaire's District are some specialty shops and restaurants that were erected as service structures. The Mistletoe and Goodyear cottages have art and other traveling exhibits.

The former clubhouse has been converted to the regal **Jekyll Island Club Hotel**, the largest and prettiest hotel on the island. Admission for guided tours, offered Monday through Thursday at 2 p.m. ~ 912-635-2600.

Victoria's Carriages provides narrated carriage-drawn tours of the island, including daytime rides from the visitors center and evening rides (except Wednesday) from the Jekyll Island Club Hotel, as well as special excursions. Closed Sunday. ~ Museum Visitors Center, Stable Road; 912-635-9500.

If you continue north on Stable Road, it will join Riverview Drive. In a little over two miles, take the left fork and you will come across the **Horton Brewery**, or what was once the brewery. Directly north is the old **duBignon family cemetery**. It was John Eugene duBignon and his brother-in-law who conceived of the notion of selling Jekyll Island as a hunting retreat to the members of a club in New York City.

Return to the fork and go left if you want to see the ruins of the **Horton House**, the family's plantation home. The structure was built in 1746 as a two-story residence.

Leaving these sad old remains, bear left and head back south along Beachview Drive, which affords a view of Jekyll Island Beach, a virtually uninterrupted stretch of hard-packed beige sand. The **Jekyll Island Convention and Visitors Bureau**, situated in the convention center, is open weekdays to provide maps and other regional information. ~ 1 Beachview Drive; 912-635-4155.

To reach **St. Marys** and Cumberland Island from Jekyll Island, return across the causeway, hook up with Route 17 for a couple of miles and continue south on Route 95 until you see the exit for St. Marys (Route 40). Beside the St. Marys River, this is the southernmost town in coastal Georgia and the jumping-off point for excursions to the Cumberland Island National Seashore. The **St. Marys Welcome Center** will provide information on the area. ~ 406 Osborne Street, St. Marys; 912-882-4000, 800-868-8687, fax 912-882-5506; www.stmaryswelcome.com.

> Whether you are sleeping indoors or at a campsite on Cumberland Island, you will need plenty of sunscreen, water and insect repellent.

Across the street is **Orange Hall**, a three-story Greek Revival antebellum mansion where you can take a self-guided tour. Admission. ~ 303 Osborne Street, St. Marys; 912-576-3644.

The blocks closest to the river were included on the National Register of Historic Places back in 1976 and are easy to tour on foot. (It's best to park in a public lot since the town carefully monitors the parking limitations in the slots near the ferry docks.)

HIDDEN ► Part of the original 1788 city plan, the **Oak Grove Cemetery** has gravestones dating back to 1801. Soldiers from every U.S. war from that time on are buried here. One section has markers written in French, indicating the graves of Acadian settlers who came here from Nova Scotia in 1775. ~ Spur 40 west of Osborne Street, St. Marys.

From the American Indians to the African Americans to the Carnegie family and other 19th- and 20th-century inhabitants, exhibits at the **Cumberland Island National Seashore Museum** illustrate the lives of the people of Cumberland Island. More expansive displays are expected as more artifacts are transferred from the island to this former bank building on the mainland. Closed mornings. ~ 129 Osborne Street, St. Marys; 912-882-4336 ext. 229, 888-817-3421; www.nps.gov/cuis.

Almost directly across from the St. Marys River docks is a small museum. Submerged in a former movie theater, the **Submarine Museum** is the answer for people who are fascinated by submarines but terrified at the idea of actually riding in one. Many accoutrements from real submarines are featured here, including a working periscope that just begs to be toyed with. Models of submarines and torpedoes, films, World War II diving suits, photographs, a hands-on computer program about the Submarine Force and other exhibits tracing the history of this vessel are also on display. Closed Sunday morning and Monday. Admission. ~ 108 St. Marys Street West, St. Marys; 912-882-2782; www.stmaryssubmuseum.com.

Cumberland Island, home to the Timucuan Indians for more than 4000 years, was taken over by the Spanish in 1566. In 1736, General James Oglethorpe renamed the island, which had been called Wissoe ("sassafras") by the Indians. The English built two forts, one at either end of the island, and a hunting lodge, which they named Dungeness. Eventually, the island figured in the lives of both Nathanael Greene, who purchased a hunk of it for the oak wood, and General Light-Horse Harry Lee, another Revolutionary War hero, who died here. Greene's widow remarried and built her own four-story tabby home, which she, too, named Dungeness. Though the mansion burned, the Dungeness property was bought by Thomas Carnegie, who built himself a mansion and named it—right you are—Dungeness. Carnegie's widow acquired more and more land and her son, George, built her a mansion, **Plum Orchard** (open the second and fourth Sundays of each month). Eventually, this 1898 Georgian Revival–style mansion was donated to the National Park Foundation in 1971 and the following year, thanks to other contributions, the island became one of the country's first national seashores.

The National Park Service manages Cumberland Island and all public transit to and from it. Its offices on St. Marys Street are a gold mine of information on coastal Georgia and also the outlet for tickets, maps and other information about the **Cumberland Island National Seashore**. ~ 877-860-6787.

Ferry reservations are required for campers as well as day-trippers. However, in good weather you will want to be assured a seat on the boat, which makes two daily roundtrips (45 minutes each way) from St. Marys during the winter (except on Tuesday and Wednesday) and a third in high season. If you have no reservations and there is space, you might get aboard on a stand-by basis. (Reservations can be made up to six months in advance Monday through Friday.) Full-day (eight-hour) tours include the boat trip.

There are two disembarkation points at the Cumberland Island National Seashore and there are no services on the island unless you have reservations at the Greyfield Inn. Once on the island, visitors explore live oak forests, visit historical sites such as Plum Orchard and stroll some 17 miles of undeveloped beaches where the only footprints they see may be their own. The beaches are separated from the meadows and shrub thickets by a system of foredunes. Live oak trees stretch beyond the back dunes, which protect the trees from the corrosive salt spray. Pine trees tower over mixed hardwood forests in the central and northern sections of the island. Saltwater marshes grace the western side of Cumberland. Ferry fee. ~ P.O. Box 806, St. Marys, GA 31558; 912-882-4335, 888-817-3421, fax 912-673-7747.

The southern Golden Isles area offers a wide spectrum of accommodations, ranging from secluded mansions to beach motels. Except for Jekyll Island, you won't find many chain motels once

LODGING

you get away from Route 95. There are a number of motels along Route 17, but most are not recommended.

Around the corner from the hub of the Village, **Queen's Court** is a sweet place out of another era, or so it seems. It's comfortable, friendly and a short two blocks from the beach. One- and two-story buildings surround a small, landscaped pool area set in the shade of oaks. Some rooms are semi-suites with efficiency kitchens. ~ 437 Kings Way, St. Simons Island; 912-638-8459. MODERATE.

Conveniently located close to the beach, the 34 rooms and suites at the **Saint Simons Inn by the Lighthouse** are on the second, third and fourth floors above a ground floor devoted to parking. They are understated but have a tropical floral motif, blond furniture, refrigerators and microwaves. ~ 609 Beachview Drive, St. Simons Island; 912-638-1101; www.stsimonsinn.com. MODERATE TO DELUXE.

The **Sea Gate Inn** is a two-part affair, with rooms in the beachfront Ocean House as well as in poolside units across the street. Between the two, you have choices of standard rooms—nicer than most motels, with a bit of a Caribbean flavor—or efficiencies or one- or two-bedroom suites. Sea Gate is intersected by Ocean Boulevard, but it's convenient to both the Village and the beaches farther away from town. ~ 1014 Ocean Boulevard, St. Simons Island; 912-638-8661, 800-562-8812, fax 912-638-4932; www.seagateinn.com, e-mail sgate2@bellsouth.net. DELUXE TO ULTRA-DELUXE.

The red-roofed **King and Prince Beach & Golf Resort** has been a honeymooners' favorite for decades. There's something definitely romantic about it, particularly at night, when you can take off your shoes and stroll along the beach after dinner. Some rooms are a tad dark but spacious; villas are also available. This is one of the few Golden Isles hotels that faces the beach directly, and it has all the accoutrements you'd expect of a major hotel including an indoor pool and jacuzzi. ~ 201 Arnold Road, St. Simons Island; 912-638-3631, 800-342-0212, fax 912-634-7699; www.kingandprince.com. DELUXE TO ULTRA-DELUXE.

The **Sea Palms Golf & Tennis Resort** exemplifies the successful island resort-conference complex. Visitors approach the center of Sea Palms via a winding residential street; the succession of three-story lodging is slightly separated from the conference center where the pool and restaurant are located. A typical suite has two balconies overlooking the marsh; one is screened for those shoulder-season no-see-um nights, when cocktail hour can be sabotaged by invisible nipping insects. Renovated in 2001, guest rooms and suites boast South Seas island decor. The balconies are arranged for maximum privacy so you can fix a cup of coffee in the full kitchen and watch the sun rise over the marsh in your pajamas. Executive and deluxe rooms feature such extras as sun rooms. ~ 5445 Frederica Road, St. Simons Island; 912-638-3351, 800-841-6268, fax 912-634-8029; www.seapalms.com, e-mail seapalmsresort@bellsouth.net. MODERATE TO DELUXE.

WatersHill Bed & Breakfast is the very picture of Southern hospitality, a two-and-a-half-story residence with a gracious front porch overlooking a garden hemmed in by a white picket fence. All five guest rooms—including an extra-large one in what was probably once an attic and a ground-floor one with a private porch—are named after members of the owners' families. Decor varies widely, from country French to art deco, and incorporates antiques from different periods. Breakfast is served in the lavishly ornate dining room. ~ 728 Union Street, Brunswick; 912-264-4262, fax 912-265-6326; www.watershill.com, e-mail mathugh@mindspring.com. MODERATE TO DELUXE.

The Cloister has reigned supreme on Sea Island since 1928. Tile roofs and lush landscaping imbue the resort with a Mediterranean mood, typical of the work of designer Addison Mizner, better known for his resorts in Palm Beach, Florida. This is where dignitaries such as presidents—not just of corporations but of countries—come to get away from it all. Five miles of clean beach serve as a playground for the rich and their friends. Some 10,000 protected acres coddle 54 holes of golf, numerous tennis courts, a spa, a skeet-shooting range, riding stables and a pair of restaurants. In all, more than 250 rooms, all renovated in 2004, are available in the main building, River House, and guest and beach houses. Most of them are decorated like upscale condominiums. In the **Ocean Houses** are 56 one-, two- and three-bedroom suites as well as parlors where families and small groups

---

AUTHOR FAVORITE

I think of **Villas by the Sea Hotel & Conference Center** as The Cloister for the masses. Here, several two- and three-story villas are arranged on 17 landscaped acres with direct beach access. The one-, two- and three-bedroom accommodations have large living and dining areas, private patio or balcony and a full kitchen, making it a good choice for long stays or for families with kids. There's also a children's playground and plenty of games and planned activities for families during the season. (Rates are cheaper by the week.) You can rent bikes and pedal around the island (you may want a bike just to reach your room). ~ 1175 North Beachview Drive, Jekyll Island; 912-635-2521, 800-841-6262, fax 912-635-2569; www.jekyllislandga.com. ULTRA-DELUXE.

can gather. All meals are included. ~ 100 1st Street, Sea Island; 912-638-3611, 800-732-4752; www.cloister.com. ULTRA-DELUXE.

HIDDEN ▶

When the world is too much, savvy travelers know the antidote: **The Lodge on Little St. Simons Island.** Here, less than a 15-minute boat ride from the marina at the north end of St. Simons, guests rough it as if they were millionaires. Guest accommodations (for a maximum of 30 people) at this private, 10,000-acre island include rustic cabins as well as some fairly formal rooms in the Helen House, for example, where three separate bedrooms have hardwood floors, delicate furnishings and a shared kitchen. Meals are included and shared in the big dining room in the lodge. There's a pool and a host of water activities—not to mention the guided nature walks. You would need more than one walk to see half the creatures, although you are virtually assured of sea birds, fallow deer and an alligator or two. Some nights everyone is hauled out to the beach in the back of a truck for a Low Country Boil. If you want to do some beach swimming, you can walk or bike out; there are no improvements at the beach, and you just might have it to yourself. All meals are included. Two-night minimum. ~ Little St. Simons Island; 912-638-7472, 888-733-5774, fax 912-634-1811; www.littlestsimonsisland.com, e-mail lssi@mindspring.com. ULTRA-DELUXE.

The **Jekyll Island Club Hotel** is the grande dame of hostelries on this piece of paradise. Headquartered in the remodeled clubhouse that was part of the original Jekyll Island Club at the turn of the 20th century, this ought to give you an idea of what the members' "cottages" look like. The rooms' decor is residential in style; some have deep dusty pink walls, plantation shutters, an armoire with a TV set and room for clothes, tastefully striped bed covers and not a whole lot of extra space. Two of the old "Millionaire's Cottages" are available for private groups including families and businesses. Crane Cottage, built in 1917 in the Italian Renaissance style, has 13 rooms in the original configuration but with modern amenities. The nearby Cherokee Cottage, an older style inspired by Italian villas built in 1904, has 11 rooms. ~ 371 Riverview Drive, Jekyll Island; 912-635-2600, 800-535-9547, fax 912-635-2818; www.jekyllclub.com, e-mail jiclub@technonet.com. DELUXE TO ULTRA-DELUXE.

The majority of the 38 rooms, suites and efficiencies at the **Beachview Club** do, as the name suggests, have water views. The decor depends on the accommodation. The efficiencies are like nice motel rooms while the suites look more like fine second homes. The two-story hotel has a heated pool, hot tub and beachfront location. ~ 721 North Beachview Drive, Jekyll Island; 912-635-2256, 800-299-2228; www.beachclub.com, e-mail info@beachclub.com. DELUXE TO ULTRA-DELUXE.

Original wide pine floors, high ceilings and sizable rooms are the calling cards at **Goodbread House Bed & Breakfast Inn**. The decor varies from room to room, in style as well as beauty, but they all afford the pleasure of sleeping in a house that was built around 1870. A second-floor balcony allows guests to watch the strollers along the main drag. Full breakfast is included. ~ 209 Osborne Street, St. Marys; 912-882-7490; www.goodbreadhouse.com, e-mail info@good breadhouse.com. DELUXE.

> Built in 1872 by Captain William T. Spencer, collector of customs for the port, the Spencer House Inn gained distinction as the first hotel in the area.

The 14-room **Spencer House Inn Bed & Breakfast** opened its doors for business in 1872 and still provides accommodations to area visitors—with a few updates, of course, such as air conditioning, TV with HBO and an elevator to the second and third floors. No two rooms are quite alike, but the idea is the same: big beds, heart-pine floors with antique area rugs, a mix of antiques and reproductions, high ceilings and original moldings. Decor is simple, as befits this distinguished Greek Revival home on the National Register of Historic Places. Three verandas are furnished with large cypress rockers for taking the salt air. ~ 200 Osborne Street, St. Marys; 912-882-1872, 888-840-1872, fax 912-882-9427; www.spencerhouseinn.com, e-mail info@spencerhouseinn.com. DELUXE TO ULTRA-DELUXE.

A longtime hotel and boardinghouse, the 1916 **Riverview Hotel** has 18 rooms. Several rooms have views of Cumberland Island, which offsets the old furnishings and slightly banged-up walls. The upstairs parlor opens onto a veranda with plastic Adirondack-style chairs and a wooden porch swing. Continental breakfast is included. ~ 105 Osborne Street, St. Marys; 912-882-3242; www.riverviewhotelstmarys.com, e-mail info@riverview hotelstmarys.com. BUDGET TO MODERATE.

The lovely **Belle Tara Inn** has eight individually decorated rooms with descriptive names such as the Tropical Room and the Nautical Room. And nothing says romantic like the heart-shaped red jacuzzi in the Lover's Hideaway Room. On the grounds there's a large outdoor hot tub, more than four acres for wandering, and a goldfish pond. Full breakfast is included. ~ 300 West Conyers Street, St. Marys; 912-882-4199, 877-749-5974; www.belletara.com, e-mail belletara@tds.net. MODERATE TO ULTRA-DELUXE.

Just north of town, **Cumberland Kings Bay Lodge** is an ultra-nice motel, a two-story taupe and green affair between downtown St. Marys and the Crooked River State Park. Mini-suites have kitchenettes; there's a small grocery store on site. It's one of the few places in the area with a pool and the only one that will consider taking small pets (for an additional charge). ~ 603 Sand Bar Drive, St. Marys; 912-882-8900, 800-831-6664, fax 912-882-8908; www.cumberlandkbl.com. BUDGET.

◄ HIDDEN

HIDDEN ►   **Crooked River State Park** has 11 cottages for rent—most of them quite sizable—including a spacious screened porch plus a fireplace for chilly winter nights. Both the two- and three-bedroom options have two full-size double beds per bedroom; eight people are allowed in the smaller ones and twelve in the larger. These simple but well-kept accommodations are fully equipped (except for coffee filters and dishwashing liquid) and would make an ideal family retreat. There's a 400-acre lake right in the park where you can fish for supper; there's a fee for non-guests to swim in the pool. ~ 6222 Charlie Smith, Sr. Highway, St. Marys; 912-882-5256. MODERATE TO DELUXE.

HIDDEN ►   The **Greyfield Inn** is the ultimate in more ways than one. It's the southernmost coastal inn in Georgia and the hardest to reach. And many would say it's the most wonderful. Well, why not? It's the only game in town—in fact, there is no town. Greyfield is the sole spot on Cumberland Island where you can spend the night with a roof over your head. It is a vision: a stately mansion surrounded by oak trees and a truly fabulous front porch furnished with swings and other comfy places to sit that seem to beg for an afternoon nap. Built in 1900 by Thomas Carnegie for his daughter, the three-story inn sits amid 200 private acres; guests can arrange to visit on the public ferry or via private launch. The elegant guest rooms evoke a turn-of-the-20th-century aesthetic, with ceiling fans and ocean breezes providing natural air conditioning. Bikes are available to guests who wish to pedal down the long sandy lane to the beach; the inn will even fix a picnic lunch. All meals are included. ~ Grand Avenue, Cumberland Island; 904-261-6408, 888-243-9238; www.greyfieldinn.com, e-mail seashore @greyfieldinn.com. ULTRA-DELUXE.

DINING   The low-key **Sand Castle Café and Grill** is the place locals depend on for consistently good food at everyday, affordable prices. Breakfast choices include a buffet or à la carte choices, from the usual fare to smoked salmon with cream cheese or

AUTHOR FAVORITE

Fond as I am of enjoying a river view with my evening cocktail, I was thrilled to find **Latitude 31** at the end of a pier near the Jekyll Island Club Hotel. Overlooking the marsh and the Intracoastal Waterway, this restaurant has plenty of water-view tables. There's a raw bar outside and a long menu of seafood and pasta inside. This is probably the most relaxing place to dine on the entire island. Closed Monday. ~ 1 Pier Road, Jekyll Island; 912-635-3800. MODERATE TO DELUXE.

Cajun po'boy (poetic license allows this to be a two-egg omelet with peppers and onions on a hoagie roll with Cajun sauce). Lunch is a matter of soups, salads, sandwiches and specialties like crab cakes and a seafood platter. No dinner. Closed Tuesday. ~ 117 Mallery Street, St. Simons Island; 912-638-8883. BUDGET.

One of the few places in the Golden Isles where you'll see meat-loaf and chicken-fried steak is at **Barbara Jean's Restaurant and Bar**. This small eatery has a few booths, with old island photographs and cheery lime-green walls for decor. Turkey, pork chops, crab cakes, catfish, salmon and steak come with vegetables. ~ 214 Mallery Street, St. Simons Island; 912-634-6500. BUDGET TO DELUXE.

Cheery blue-and-white-checked cloths atop round tables surrounded by Bentwood chairs give an upbeat feeling to **Dressner's Village Café**. Sit by the windows, where only nice Swiss lace café curtains block the view of the street. This is a good place for a late, leisurely breakfast. Of all the local haunts in the Village, Dressner's has the heaviest food: bratwurst, Philly-style steak, Reuben and grilled ham sandwiches and, of course, hamburgers. There is some lighter fare, notably pita sandwiches. ~ 223 Mallery Street, St. Simons Island; 912-634-1217, fax 912-634-1198. BUDGET.

Green and tropical with a glassy blue-teal bar, the **Georgia Sea Grill** has an upscale Key West feeling. Three demi-rooms bear white walls, turquoise ceilings and small ceiling fans—a nice backdrop for yummy things like a sea-shell salad of pasta with shrimp and scallops, sandwiches and lots of grilled seafood. Closed Monday. Reservations are recommended. ~ 310-B Mallery Street, St. Simons Island; 912-638-1197. MODERATE TO ULTRA-DELUXE.

J. Mac's Island Restaurant and Jazz Bar presents gourmet versions of traditional seafood, such as blackened sea scallops and grilled Atlantic salmon. Pottery displayed along a brick wall and undistinguished lace curtains seem like skimpy decor at these prices, but you don't often get to order pecan/honey-glazed pork loin with andouille sausage. Closed Tuesday. ~ 407 Mallery Street, St. Simons Island; 912-634-0403. DELUXE TO ULTRA-DELUXE.

The Fourth of May Cafe and Deli is a corner hangout for the young and healthy crowd. Well, mostly. Fried seafood is available but more common are things like cold cucumber salad, grilled salmon, and salad plates. It's very popular as a takeout joint. Daily potluck specials range from meatloaf to jambalaya to pot roast and are an exceptional bargain. ~ 444 Ocean Boulevard, St. Simons Island; 912-638-5444, fax 912-638-5470. BUDGET.

◀ HIDDEN

The maze of rooms, cozy nooks and a courtyard that comprises **P.G. Archibald's** makes this cottage-like restaurant the most charming in town. There's a big bar and a large waiting area (which ought to be a clue), and a motley assortment of ducks and old oars that, somehow, works. The food is a huge sampling of meat, pasta and seafood dishes, including oysters prepared 15 ways. Closed Sunday. ~ 440 Kings Way, St. Simons Island; 912-638-3030. DELUXE TO ULTRA-DELUXE.

St. Simons could use more bakery/sandwich shops like **Sweet Mama's**. If you get past the cases of chocolate chip cookies, lemon squares, Key lime pie and killer brownies, you can choose a made-to-order sandwich such as ham, turkey or BLT or some salads along the same lines. On a hot day, perhaps a sorbet breeze or milkshake? Plastic chairs, red-and-white-checked linoleum floors and proximity to the beaches at the King and Prince Beach & Golf Resort are the other features. No dinner, but open evenings for dessert. ~ 1201 Ocean Boulevard, St. Simons Island; 912-638-9011. Second location (closed Sunday): 1627 Frederica Ranch in the Longview Shopping Center; 912-634-6022. BUDGET.

A giant wooden fish heralds **Crabdaddy's Seafood Grill**, a made-to-look-ramshackle building on the southeast part of the island. The restaurant, which shares a parking lot with Crab-happy (not to be confused with The Crab Trap), lives up to its billing. You can get mackerel and grouper here, along with crab (soup, cake, etc.) and the usual coastal selections every night of the week. Most items are available grilled or blackened. ~ 1217 Ocean Boulevard, St. Simons Island; 912-634-1120. DELUXE.

For a quick midday bite, the **Wine & Cheese Cellar** is one to remember. All kinds of salads, burgers and sandwiches (some grilled) plus specials like a cheese board are available to eat here or take out. Closed Sunday. ~ 211 Redfern Village, St. Simons Island; 912-638-2465. BUDGET.

You might expect a great big golf and conference resort like Sea Palms to field at least one major-league restaurant but in fact

BRUNSWICK STEW

Just as various places quibble over where the martini was invented, towns in Virginia and North Carolina claim to be the birthplace of a savory concoction called Brunswick stew. Brunswick, Georgia, gets my vote, although for all historians know, its origins may lie with American Indians, who may have been making a stew of wild game long before colonists arrived. Traditionally served alongside barbecue or seafood, a proper Brunswick stew should have chicken, beef, pork, onions and tomatoes, all flavored with Tabasco and Worchestershire sauce, among other seasonings. Variations include adding beans, creamed corn, English peas, potatoes and/or okra. The end result, however, is always a thick and spicy stew near and dear to the hearts of Southerners.

they are barely in the minors. **The Putter's Club** is a handsome room with a mix of rattan and upholstered chairs, serving salads, soups and "sandwedges" like BLT or shrimp salad, or entrées like steak, fish, shrimp or pasta. It's convenient after a round of golf and there are big TV sets tuned to sporting events ~ 5445 Frederica Road, St. Simons Island; 912-638-3351. MODERATE TO DELUXE.

For the last, oh, half-century or so, **Bennie's Red Barn** has been not only a landmark but also a popular restaurant. What brings in the regulars is the steak, an oasis of beef on an island predicated on catch of the day. Ribeye, T-bone, New York strip . . . the gang's all here. The rest of your dinner party can have their pick of chicken, pork, lamb and bushels of seafood (boiled, fried). House specialties include Brunswick stew, pecan pie and Key lime pie. ~ 5514 Frederica Road, St. Simons Island; 912-638-2844, fax 912-634-2440. MODERATE TO DELUXE.

The **Main Dining Room** at The Cloister is stately but not haughty, with beamed ceilings and a lovely fireplace, which probably doesn't see a lot of use. To enjoy the American cuisine with French flair, gentlemen are required to wear a coat and tie at dinner. The menu rotates every week but always includes at least one cold plate, which is nice during the toasty summer months. The restaurant also has an award-winning wine list. ~ 100 1st Street, Sea Island; 912-638-5111. ULTRA-DELUXE.

P.G. Archibald's (kinfolk to the branch on St. Simons) is a spacious, gracious restaurant on the ground floor of the old Royal Hotel, where coral-colored walls rise to meet a tin ceiling painted white. Offerings include grilled salmon and other seafood, plus chicken, steak and surf-and-turf combos. Lunch brings a buffet or a blue-plate special. Closed Sunday. ~ 1618 Newcastle Street, Brunswick; 912-262-1402, fax 912-638-5770. DELUXE.

Cargo Portside Grill made a big splash when it opened in 2000 in downtown Brunswick to serve fresh coastal fare from this and other ports. In addition to the regular menu, which features classics such as award-winning crab cakes, Cargo offers weekly chicken and seafood specials. Typical of the latter is the Charleston sauté with shrimp, ham and Cajun spices served over jalapeño grits with fresh okra. Closed Sunday and Monday. ~ 1425 Newcastle Street, Brunswick; 912-267-7330, fax 912-554-8783. DELUXE TO ULTRA-DELUXE.

For down-home cooking in a no-nonsense setting, a good bet is **Mack's Bar-B-Que Place**. It's near the visitors center and the St. Simons causeway and, while it is in no way, shape or form fancy, the people are friendly and the 'cue is hot. Closed Sunday. ~ 2809 Route 17 (Glynn Avenue), Brunswick; phone/fax 912-264-0605. BUDGET.

Café Solterra in the Jekyll Island Club Hotel is a neat little find. Not much more than a deli, it has a good cross-section of food you can eat there or take out: pizza, soup, salad, smoked turkey or salami sandwiches and special combos like the Pulitzer (salad and ham) or the Vanderbilt (corned beef and sauerkraut), named after the famous families who used to summer here. ~ 371 Riverview Drive, Jekyll Island; 912-635-2600, fax 912-635-2818. BUDGET TO MODERATE.

Where is Grandma when you need her? The Jekyll Island Club Hotel's **Grand Dining Room** is almost a parody of the refined restaurant, and more than a little stuffy. But it is pretty, with shell-pink walls, white columns, plantation shutters and strategically placed potted palms. In this posh ambiance, enjoy veal Française, duck breast or tournedos of beef with lobster ragôut. Reservations are recommended, especially for Sunday brunch. ~ 371 Riverview Drive, Jekyll Island; 912-635-2600. ULTRA-DELUXE.

In the Jekyll Island Historic Landmark District, Crane Cottage's **Courtyard at Crane** blends a Deep South setting with wines from Northern California and entrées inspired by the Mediterranean, including a shrimp salad, vegetable and cheese platters, pastas, rotisserie chicken and duck and mushroom focaccia. Closed Thursday through Saturday. ~ 371 Riverview Drive, Jekyll Island; 912-635-2600. DELUXE TO ULTRA-DELUXE.

The Dining Room at Villas by the Sea covers the bases with crab cakes, flounder, baby back ribs, teriyaki chicken breast and hearty dinner-plate specials, one for every night of the week. ~ 1175 North Beachview Drive, Jekyll Island; 912-635-2521. DELUXE TO ULTRA-DELUXE.

Blackbeard's Restaurant has a killer oceanfront location, with both covered and uncovered decks for soaking up the scenery. Inside is just one big room with brick tile floors (the patio flooring is real brick) and tons of windows. It's even up on an itsy-bitsy knoll, the better to catch any prevailing zephyrs. If this doesn't put you in the mood for catch of the day, what could? ~ 200 North Beachview Drive, Jekyll Island; 912-635-3522. MODERATE TO DELUXE.

Zachry's Restaurant, located directly across the street from the beach, is a stopgap measure for those moments you don't want to bother with hotel dining. A shrimp-salad sandwich and a cold beer can really hit the spot on a hot day. This strip-mall eatery also has other salads, sandwiches, a bunch of side orders like hot wings, and a full seafood entrée menu with local catches like sea trout and scallops. ~ Jekyll Island Shopping Center, 44 Beachview Drive, Jekyll Island; 912-635-3128. MODERATE TO DELUXE.

Outside of the Jekyll Island Club area, there aren't many decent restaurants on the island; most places to eat are in motels. An exception is the affable **SeaJay's Waterfront Café & Pub.** A lovely deck shaded by oak trees surrounds the single-story gray

HIDDEN ▶

clapboard building. Here you can cool off with a frozen Rum Runner, a beer or a Coke and decide if you want barbecued pork, grilled chicken or seafood of some sort. The menu is short but appealing. This would be a swell place to order what's called a Low Country Boil, a medley of shrimp, smoked sausage, corn on the cob and potatoes, often served buffet-style. ~ 1 Harbor Road, Jekyll Island; 912-635-3200. MODERATE TO DELUXE.

Though **Pauly's** has traces of the Mediterranean on its menu—gulf shrimp and linguine and fettuccini carbonara—the menu leans more to American favorites like salmon, chicken and grilled ribeye. On balmy evenings the place to sit is beneath the market umbrellas on the white-rock patio. There's also seating inside in a small room with paisley wallpaper and a wall display of wine bottles. ~ 102 Osborne Street, St. Marys; 912-882-3944. BUDGET TO MODERATE.

Seagle's has eked out space on the ground floor of the River-view Hotel. In one large and one small room, diners select from a nearly all-seafood menu. It's some of the best eating in these parts, especially if you like shrimp, oysters and grouper. Even though the mayor and every other big shot in town eats here, it's okay to wear shorts. There's an adjacent cocktail lounge. No dinner Tuesday or Wednesday and no lunch on Saturday. ~ 105 Osborne Street, St. Marys; 912-882-4187. MODERATE.

With its porch facing the river and the Cumberland Island ferry dock, **Trolley's** has the best location in town. Watch the river roll by as you munch on crawfish tails, a shrimp basket or a full dinner of steak or chicken. Trolley's also offers many sandwiches, salads and finger food, served either outside or near the bar flanked by green and maroon walls with wood panel wainscoting. ~ 104 West St. Marys Street, St. Marys; 912-882-1525. MODERATE TO DELUXE.

Lang's Marina Restaurant is in a gray-blue clapboard structure right on the St. Marys River. A local institution, it has an upscale menu with dishes like scallops linguine, chicken cacciatore and steak Oscar. Most dishes come with vegetables and/or salads. No dinner on Tuesday. Closed Sunday and Monday. ~

CATCH OF THE DAY

Crabbing, a great way to sample these local delicacies, is allowed from the piers, docks and bridges of the Golden Isles. You can get crab traps from hardware, tackle or department stores and use chicken parts for bait.
If you're over 16 years of age, you'll need a recreational fishing license (see "Fishing & Crabbing" in Chapter One for more details).

307 West St. Marys Street, St. Marys; 912-882-4432. MODERATE TO ULTRA-DELUXE.

SHOPPING   The shopping in and around the Golden Isles is as distinct as each island. By far, the greatest selection is on St. Simons, your best bet for fine clothing and antiques. Otherwise, the biggest stocks are in beachwear and souvenirs, with a few book emporia for good measure.

Within the lowrise complex known collectively as **The Shops at Redfern Village** are several special merchants, including the charming **Wild Birds Unlimited** (912-638-1422), which has just about everything for the garden, from bird seed to garden tools. Fine men's clothing and accessories are well stocked at **Thos. P. Dent Clothier, Inc.** (closed Sunday; 912-638-3118), just in case you were thinking of having dinner at The Cloister. ~ Frederica Road at Redfern Drive, St. Simons Island.

Several antique stores and galleries are spread along **Frederica Road**, many of them conveniently clustered with other nice shops, but a couple stand out. English, French, American and primitive furniture and accessories, including rugs and jewelry, distinguish **Blythe Island Antiques**. ~ 1610 Frederica Road, St. Simons Island; 912-634-1610. Regional art is the specialty at **The Palmer Gallery**. Closed Sunday and Monday. ~ 3415 Frederica Road, St. Simons Island; 912-634-0045, 888-821-0059. The selection at **Left Bank Art Gallery** is extensive, ranging from southern coastal landscapes to French, American and Russian paintings. Closed Sunday and Monday, except by appointment. ~ 3600 Frederica Road, St. Simons Island; 912-638-3017, 800-336-9469.

The **Gallery on Newcastle**, a renovated 1888 funeral home, has an impressively extensive collection of art from southeastern artists. The proprietor's own work is also displayed, as well as some antiques and other pieces from Asia and Latin America. Closed Sunday and Monday. ~ 1626 Newcastle Street, Brunswick; 912-554-0056; www.thegalleryonnewcastle.com.

Brunswick is a great town for antique browsing, with the occasional exciting find. Here are some poking-around options, all of which are closed Sunday: **Brown's Antiques**, 1328 Newcastle Street, 912-265-6099; **Downtown Antiques & Collectibles Mall**,

AUTHOR FAVORITE

I always find something decorative I just have to buy (for friends, of course) at **The Tabby House**. This adorable shop is long on taste but still manages to stock many affordable gifts and home and garden accessories. The only drawback is that it's closed on Sunday. ~ 105 Retreat Avenue, St. Simons Island; 912-638-2257.

1208 Gloucester Street, 912-264-2322; **Fizzwhistle Antiques &** **Used Bookshop**, 4738 New Jesup Highway, 912-261-1125; and **Rags & Riches Miniatures and Antique Marketplace**, 1503 Gloucester Street, 912-261-0771.

For a farmer's market experience, head to the **Brunswick Harbor Market** in Mary Ross Waterfront Park. From 7 a.m. to 7 p.m. Tuesday, Thursday and Saturday, you can find hand-picked fruits, vegetables and nuts, as well as homemade goodies like sauces, syrups, cakes and pies. ~ Bay and Gloucester streets, Brunswick.

The best one-stop shopping for beach stuff is the **Jekyll Island Shopping Center**. Here you'll find **The Sand Pail** (912-635-2327), which has T-shirts, souvenirs and bathing suits. More T-shirts, beach supplies and hardware items are available at **Maxwell's Variety and True Value Hardware Store** (912-635-2205). ~ Beach-view Drive, Jekyll Island.

The other commercial hub lies within the confines of the Jekyll Historic District. **Bianca's Boutique** (912-635-2911) is inside the Jekyll Island Club Hotel, with accessories and gifts for women. ~ 371 Riverview Drive, Jekyll Island; 912-635-2600.

Travelers who want to learn more about the region's natural history can pick up books as well as art and other gifts at **Nature's Cottage**. ~ 21 Pier Road, Jekyll Island; 912-635-3933.

The best source on the island for regional specialty food items, gourmet coffees and teas and gifts baskets is **The Commissary**, which also has fresh baked goods. ~ 24 Pier Road, Jekyll Island; 912-635-2878.

Rare books and other treasures, including maps, prints and small antiques are the main draw at **Jekyll Books and Antiques Inc.** in the old infirmary building. ~ 101 Old Plantation Road, Jekyll Island; 912-635-3077.

The **Cumberland Emporium**'s clientele includes antique deal-ers, interior designers and collectors, who come for the furniture, dishes, art, and hard-to-classify oddities amassed from all over the Southeast. ~ 714 Osborne Street, St. Marys; 912-510-6662.

You could spend half a day browsing at **Blue Goose Country Collectibles**, which peddles artwork, lace curtains, pottery, can-dles, Georgia State plates, cat collectibles and regional foods, for starters. Closed Sunday. ~ 126 Osborne Street, St. Marys; 912-673-6828.

Good luck leaving **Old Town Crafts** without buying some-thing, even if rubber stamping isn't your craft of choice. There are thousands of stamp selections, along with beads, paper, clay and other craft supplies. The owner is happy to demonstrate some stamping techniques for you, and, in this case, it really is as easy as it looks. ~ 101 East Weed Street, St. Marys; 912-882-9000, 877-313-6745; www.oldtowncrafts.com.

NIGHTLIFE   There are no big venues for touring acts on any of the islands; nightlife ranges from deejay music in island motels to jazz, blues and rock at some of the clubs. Most live music happens on the weekends, but there are midweek shows at selected places. A good place to check out life after dark is along St. Simons' Mallery Street.

The **Sand Trap** is a comfortable sports bar tuned in to the latest game. ~ 303 Mallery Street, St. Simons Island; 912-638-0245.

Rafters Blues Club features live entertainment Wednesday through Saturday. Closed Sunday. Occasional cover. ~ 315½ Mallery Street, St. Simons Island; 912-634-9755.

Ziggy Mahony's, adjacent to Bennie's Red Barn, is *the* place to be for a variety of music Thursday through Saturday. Wednesday is karaoke night. Closed Sunday through Tuesday. Cover on Friday and Saturday. ~ 5514 Frederica Road, St. Simons Island; 912-634-0999.

The **Ritz Theatre** presents dozens of plays and musicals each year in a historic, 477-seat building in the heart of Brunswick's downtown district. ~ 1530 Newcastle Street, Brunswick; 912-262-6934; www.goldenislesarts.org.

Casino action and musical shows are the main draws aboard the **Emerald Princess**, a 186-foot ship that offers cruises on Friday and Saturday nights and during the day on Saturdays and Sundays. ~ Brunswick Landing Marina, 1701 Newcastle Street, Brunswick; 912-265-3558, 800-842-0115.

On Thursday, Friday and Saturday nights, there's live music at **SeaJay's**, in a delightful location on the water not far from the bridge. ~ 1 Harbor Drive, Jekyll Island; 912-635-3200.

The **Tiki Hut** in the Jekyll Inn has live music Friday through Sunday. ~ 975 North Beachview Drive; Jekyll Island; 912-635-2531.

BEACHES & PARKS   **NEPTUNE PARK**   Located at the foot of Mallery Street, this is a beachfront park with ample picnic facilities. It doesn't take much equipment to go crabbing or fishing off the pier here. There's a children's playground and a miniature golf course. The widest part of the beach is at East Beach, which, thanks to tidal action, has been growing in recent years. There's no swimming allowed, but you can fish off the pier. ~ Mallery Street, St. Simons Island; 912-265-0620.

MASSENGALE PARK   This is a pretty swath of land with no real improvements, but the waves here are the best on the island for bodysurfing. Restrooms are the only facilities. ~ Ocean Boulevard, St. Simons Island.

JEKYLL ISLAND BEACH   This island has more than nine miles of hard-packed sand beaches. There's a bath house about

midpoint, near the Convention Center. Bodysurfing is a popular
activity here. Picnic facilities can be found at Clam Creek Picnic
Area on the north end of the island and at the
South Dunes Picnic Area on the other end. There
are also restrooms. ~ Beachview Drive, Jekyll Island.

CROOKED RIVER STATE PARK 𓀀 🏊 🚤 ⛳ With
a 400-acre lake and the ruins of an 1825 sugar mill to
explore, this enclave on the banks of the Crooked River
offers plenty for families to do. Picnic sites and restrooms
are provided for daytrippers. There's a pool (closed Labor
Day to Memorial Day; admission), a miniature golf course and a
short nature trail; you can also rent bikes. Day-use fee, $2. ~
6222 Charlie Smith Highway, St. Marys; 912-882-5256.

The McIntosh Sugar
Works mill at Crooked
River State Park was
used as a starch
factory during
the Civil War.

▲ There are 62 tent/RV sites ($20 to $22 per night) and 11
cabins ($85 to $110 per night). Reservations: 800-864-7275.

Okefenokee Swamp Area

Nothing on the coast prepares first-time
visitors for the scenery of the Okefenokee Swamp. Instead of live oaks and
moss, there are cypress and pine trees. Parts of the surrounding
landscape look quite desolate, but once you enter this vast and
mysterious terrain, your eyes become accustomed to its unique
beauty. Most of the towns that sit on various edges of the swamp
are small, with the exception of Waycross. Aside from the entrances to the Okefenokee, few attractions in this area are open on
Sunday mornings.

SIGHTS

From St. Marys, return to Route 40 heading west, cross the freeway and pass through Kingsland en route to Folkston. The **Okefenokee Chamber of Commerce,** housed in an old train depot,
has maps and information for travelers. While you're there, take
time to tour the **Folkston Railroad Depot.** Built in 1903, it is now
a museum housing all manner of railroad artifacts. At the Depot,
the Folkston Funnel Train Viewing Platform has become a mag-
net for train spotters. More than 60 trains pass through town
every day. The Depot museum and chamber are both closed Saturday and Sunday. ~ 202 West Main Street, Folkston; 912-496-
2536; www.folkston.com, e-mail folkston@planttel.net.

You can get a preview of the Okefenokee Swamp at the
Okefenokee Education and Research Center. Here, interactive
exhibits in Discovery Hall showcase the region's natural, historical and cultural heritage. Call for hours. ~ 500 Kingsland Drive,
Folkston; 912-496-7116.

Follow Route 121 southwest eight miles to the East Entrance
of the **Okefenokee National Wildlife Refuge and Wilderness Area**.
In all, there are nearly 354,000 acres of wilderness here in a

438,000-acre depression that was at one time the ocean floor. These wetlands have been preserved since 1937, having been inhabited by man since about 2500 B.C. Research on the swamp's earliest denizens is scarce, but there are Indian mounds. The name Okefenokee is derived from the white man's interpretation of the Indian phrase, "Land of Trembling Earth." The "trembling" comes from the peat bogs; you can walk on them, but not without causing nearby shrubs and trees to shake.

After the Seminoles were driven out in the mid-19th century, the Suwannee Canal Company bought about 238,000 acres here from the state of Georgia and began building an 11.5-mile canal. The idea was to log cypress, but when the canal company went belly-up, it sold its land to the Hebard Cypress Company, which completed a railroad into the western edge of the swamp. From 1909 to 1927, some 31 million board feet of lumber were taken out. A decade later, the wildlife refuge was established.

Today the Okefenokee is home to 234 species of birds, 50 species of mammals, 64 species of reptiles and 37 species of amphibians. It is one of the oldest and best-preserved freshwater areas in the country.

The **East Entrance** provides access to a four-and-a-half-mile wildlife observation drive, four and a half miles of hiking trails, two observation towers, two photo blinds, a 4000-foot boardwalk into the swamp and the **Chesser Island Homestead**, which is furnished as it was when the Chessers lived here in the 1920s and '30s. Visitors are also welcome to bicycle along the paths. You can camp with a permit; a Georgia license is required for freshwater fishing.

A three-mile approach road from this entrance leads to the **Visitors Center**, where you'll find a store, an interpretive center and a ticket outlet for boat rides into the wildlife refuge. Flatbottom boats are used for these hour-long excursions, since they draw little water and the canal used for the tours is only a few feet (nine at the most) deep. Before you set out, load up on sunscreen, insect repellent and bottled water since the boat carries only people and chairs. It is covered by a canopy; on sunny days, try to grab a middle seat to avoid over-exposure. Admission. ~ 912-496-7836; okefenokee.fws.gov.

You can rent a canoe or motorboat on your own, but if you don't know what you're doing, it's not a great idea. The swamp is home to somewhere between 10,000 and 15,000 alligators. In short, don't stand up in the canoe. Moreover, the guides on the flat boat can point out sites of interest and teach you how to spot alligators. Since the water is stained an inky black by the tannins produced by the trunks of the cypress trees, it's not as easy as you might think. Easier to spot are the turtles, especially the dangerous snapping variety; almost impossible to spy are the darting lizards such as the legless glass lizard (which looks like a snake) and the skinks, which quickly leave their tail behind if they get nabbed.

The manmade **Suwanee Canal** leads to views of large expanses—the Chesser, Grand and Mizell prairies. These lakes harbor gator holes and offer some of the region's best freshwater sport fishing. It's home to the Florida sandhill crane and other species abundant in these open areas. Admission. ~ East Entrance, Route 121, eight miles southwest of Folkston (mailing address: Okefenokee National Wildlife Refuge, Route 2, Box 3330, Folkston, GA 31537); 912-496-7836; okefenokee.fws.gov.

When you depart the East Entrance, turn left (northeast) and follow Route 121 for eight miles back into Folkston. From Folkston, it is about an hour's drive to **Waycross** via Route 23.

Before you reach the city, look for signs to Route 177, which runs southward five miles to the **Okefenokee Swamp Park**. Unlike the wilderness area, which is managed by the U.S. Fish and Wildlife Service, this attraction is commercial but nonetheless interesting. This, the **North Entrance** to the Okefenokee, is far less rustic than the eastern one. Neat boardwalks lead to animal exhibits, including a serpentarium (where there are four reptile shows a day), deer and bear observatories, alligators, otters and other swamp creatures and a collection of turtles. The boardwalk extends to a 90-foot observation tower; nearby is the dock for the boat and one-and-a-third-mile tram tours of the park. It costs ex-

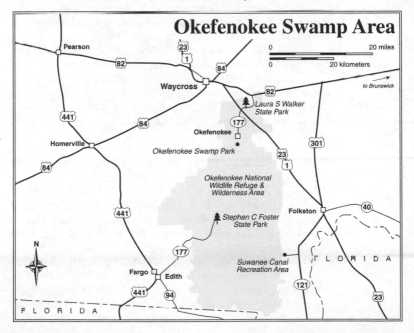

Okefenokee Swamp Area

tra to take one of the tram or water tours of varying lengths. One
of them includes a visit to the **Pioneer Island Homestead**, where
you can see cane and grist mills and other aspects of the pioneer
lifestyle in these parts. Admission. ~ Route 1 South, Waycross;
912-283-0583; www.okeswamp.com.

Exiting the park, turn north (left) on Route 1 and continue
to the intersection with Route 82; turn left (west) onto this highway to Gilmore Street, go left again and at the convergence with
HIDDEN ► Swamp Road, take another left. Swamp Road leads to **Obediah's
Okefenok**, yet another swamp-based attraction. With his father,
Isaac, Obediah Barber was one of the first white men to settle on
the north rim of the Okefenokee Swamp. A lover of nature with
a knack for zoological and botanical lore, Obediah managed to
father 20 children with two wives despite being kept busy fend-
ing off black bears. Today, all is peaceful at his former settlement,
where a boardwalk allows birdwatchers and other outdoors enthusiasts a chance to explore. There are also some animals in
captivity, assorted cabins and other sites you can see on a self-
guided tour. From time to time, Obediah's Okefenok offers living-
history programs. Admission. ~ 5115 Swamp Road, Waycross;
912-287-0090; www.okefenokeeswamp.com.

On the far side of Waycross, you can learn a little more about
the region at two different sites. From Okefenok, return via Swamp
Road and Gilmore Street until you reach Route 82, running west
towards Tifton. Turn left onto the highway until you reach Augusta Avenue, which is over a mile west of downtown Waycross.
Exit and head north.

After Augusta Avenue crosses Albany Avenue, you will come
HIDDEN ► to the **Okefenokee Heritage Center**. This combination local history and art museum houses a steam locomotive, an 1870s house,
a 1900s print shop and an exhibit on Ware County's African-
American heritage. Closed Sunday and Monday. Admission. ~
1460 North Augusta Avenue, Waycross; 912-285-4260; www.
okeheritage.org.

HIDDEN ► Next door, **Southern Forest World** is the kind of place where
kids like to play and adults don't mind learning a thing or two.
The timber companies support this museum, which in turn gently propagandizes "proper forest management." The kids can walk
inside a mammoth Loblolly pine and listen to a talking tree while
their parents see exhibits on forest management and various
kinds of woods. Together, they can all gape at the mummified dog
inside a tree. Closed Sunday and Monday, and mornings. Admission. ~ 1440 North Augusta Avenue, Waycross; 912-285-4056.

After touring the world of forests, retrace your route heading
south on Augusta Avenue all the way to Route 84 and turn right
towards Valdosta. In about 27 miles you will reach Homerville,
where you turn south onto Route 441 to Fargo. Less than a mile

south of Fargo, take a left onto Route 177, which leads to the **Southern Entrance** of the Okefenokee National Wildlife Refuge at **Stephen C. Foster State Park**. (The route out of Fargo will take you into Florida if you miss the turn-off, which is not well-marked.) This is a different part of the swamp but with many of the same critters, notably the alligators, turtles, mammals and birds. There is a small office here next to the parking lot where you can get maps and sign up for boat rentals (motor or canoe) or a guided boat tour. If you're not familiar with the flora and fauna hereabouts, check out the interpretive museum. It has displays on animals as well as botanical curiosities such as the pitcher plants, which flourish in boggy, acidic soil where few nutrients are available to the roots. How do they do it? Their "throats" collect water and nutrients from above by "swallowing" insects, digesting them with a narcotic that kills them so that the bacteria then decompose into enzymes that convert them to nitrogen. Here, too, you can see that the snowy egret has golden slippers that allows it to shuffle up to its prey. It's amazing to learn these regal creatures were once hunted so their feathers could be used as hat plumes. Some 25 miles of waterways are accessible from this entrance, which is 18 miles northeast of Fargo. Admission. ~ Route 177, Fargo; 912-637-5274.

LODGING

Across the highway from the East Entrance to Okefenokee, the **Okefenokee Pastimes Campground** has five one-room log cabins for rent. Each is furnished with a double bed and a set of bunks, a desk, chairs and a mini-refrigerator and all are equipped with heat, air conditioning and small screened porches. Overnight

AUTHOR FAVORITE

After a day of touring around the swamp, I was invigorated by the fresh, sparkling accommodations at **The Inn at Folkston**. This bungalow has four guest rooms and a pair of very knowledgeable innkeepers who can tell you where to go in the area. That is, if you ever get out of the wicker porch furniture. Each of the four rooms has its own theme—thus, the Lighthouse Room is done in blue and yellow and has a Persian carpet on heartpine floors; the Oriental Room is decorated in gray, white and brick red. Though this inn has more amenities than most bed and breakfasts, there are no TVs or phones in the rooms. There is a six-person hot tub. Rates include the requisite breakfast, as well as evening wine and cheese. ~ 509 West Main Street, Folkston; phone/fax 912-496-6256, 888-509-6246; www.innatfolkston.com, e-mail info@innatfolkston.com. DELUXE TO ULTRA-DELUXE.

guests have to use the campground bathhouse but the location can't be beat. There's a tiny store on the premises for basics and ice cream. Pets are allowed. The property is closed on Wednesday and during the hottest part of the summer, reopening in late August. ~ Route 121, eight miles south of Folkston; phone/fax 912-496-4472; www.okefenokee.com. BUDGET.

They may not have heat or air conditioning, but the four eight-person cabins at **Laura S. Walker State Park** do have electricity. Guests must bring everything themselves, even pots and sheets. In addition, a staff house that accommodates 14 can be rented; it has indoor plumbing. You can also arrange to rent the kitchen on a separate basis; it has all you need to fix a meal for 150. ~ 5653 Laura Walker Road, Waycross; 912-287-4900. BUDGET.

There's not much on the road from Homerville to Fargo, so the **Helmstead Bed & Breakfast** is easy to spot. A two-story brick home, it has four upstairs guest rooms (one without a private bath) and a lovely garden and swimming pool in the back. Full breakfast is included (choose either the "Artery Clogger" or "Healthy Choice"). ~ 1 Fargo Road (Route 441S), Homerville; 912-487-2222. BUDGET.

The nine cottages at **Stephen C. Foster State Park** are the only real lodging available at any of the entrances to the Okefenokee Swamp. They are located near the park offices. Simply decorated, each is fully equipped with linens and kitchen appliances. Each sleeps up to eight people. ~ Route 177; 912-637-5274, 800-864-7275. MODERATE.

DINING

The good news is you won't have to wear a tie to dinner in this part of Georgia. If there's any bad news, you'll have a hard time finding ethnic dishes or a variety of salads. Most places are very family-friendly and a lot of them serve enough food on one plate to feed a small family.

Whitfield's Neighborhood Café occupies a former home on a downtown corner. Look for a white brick building with a green awning. Dining is in a series of areas, one with a fireplace and another on a covered porch. Elegant appetizers (scampi, onion soup au gratin) can be followed by tenderloin filet or other meat dishes, seafood, pastas or chicken. Even at these prices, dinner entrées come with rice or potatoes, a vegetable, fresh baked breads and a salad. A lighter tavern menu is served nightly as well, with salads and sandwiches. Closed Sunday. ~ 514 Mary Street, Waycross; 912-285-9027. MODERATE TO DELUXE.

HIDDEN ►

The exact spices added to the vinegar-tomato base at **Richard's** are hard to pin down. Since it buys the sauce from a producer in Homerville, it's not a full-on barbecue joint. Inside, you'll find grilled pork chops, several chicken and steak dinners and a rack of ribs, which you eat at Formica tables surrounded by funky local art and bare floors. The place closes at 7 p.m., so if you want 'cue for dinner, you'll have to eat early. Closed Sunday. ~ 103 West Plant Avenue, Homerville; 912-487-5822. BUDGET.

Who can resist a motto like "Puttin the Hog on the Log since 1936!" That one belongs to **Jimbo's Log Kitchen**, a place where you can get Brunswick stew, grilled or fried chicken or steak plates, barbecue plates, salads, sandwiches and heavy-duty appetizers, including fried dill pickles. It's not unheard of for people to drive all the way from Waycross just for lunch here. The buffet is the best deal in a restaurant full of bargains. It's plain, it's friendly and it puts real bacon on the baked potatoes. No Sunday dinner. ~ 600 West Dame Avenue (Route 84W), Homerville; 912-487-2142. BUDGET TO MODERATE.

◄ HIDDEN

SHOPPING

The enchantingly named **Swamp Gas Gallery** is a surprise, given its boondocks location. It has pottery, sculpture, photography, jewelry, woodcarving and handmade paper, among other arts and crafts. The gallery is closed Wednesday and during the hottest part of the summer. ~ Okefenokee Pastimes, Route 121, eight miles south of Folkston; 912-496-4472; www.okefenokee.com.

The shop at the **Okefenokee Swamp Park Visitors Center** has the usual postcards and souvenirs, but also many items relating to "Pogo," the late, beloved comic strip created by Walt Kelly. ~ Route 1 South, Waycross; 912-283-0583.

PARKS

OKEFENOKEE NATIONAL WILDLIFE REFUGE 🚶 🚲 🛶
Covering about 619 square miles, this enormous swamp area offers travelers a rare glimpse at a most unusual landscape. Cypress trees, ospreys, alligators and other exotic creatures abound in these protected acres, a total of 234 species of birds, 64 species of

AUTHOR FAVORITE

I found it plenty exciting to tour the Okefenokee on a flat-bed tour boat, but for a closer look, you can rent a canoe at the concession at the East Entrance. You can pick up a map, but the simplest and safest route is to go directly down the straight, wide **Suwanee Canal** that runs 11 miles into the swamp. You'll see turtles, egrets and probably alligators and small fish as you paddle between the narrow creek banks. Admission. ~ East Entrance, Route 121, eight miles southwest of Folkston; 912-496-3331; okefenokee.fws.gov.

Text continued on page 130.

Georgia's Fearsome Gators

Of all the earth's creatures, perhaps only the Great White Shark evokes more fear than the alligator. After all, the male of the species averages some 11 to 12 feet in length and between 400 and 500 pounds in weight. Add to that their fearsome appearance: a thick skin that appears scaled like a snake's but are actually bony protective plates called scutes. Back before the white man infiltrated the swamps, the American Indians are said to have believed that alligators had special powers, including an immunity to the venom of poisonous snakes. That myth has its basis in truth: It would be the rare snake whose fangs would be so strong and long that they could penetrate the alligator's thick skin. If they could, the alligator, like most other creatures, would be poisoned by the venom.

It is conceivable that you could visit the Okefenokee Swamp without seeing one of these prehistoric-looking reptiles, just as, technically, you could visit New York City without seeing any tall buildings. Nocturnal by nature, they hunt at night, and spend the daytime hours lounging on the riverbanks, at the surface of the water with their snouts and eyes protruding above the water line, or, in exceptionally hot water, in holes. If you are out on a dock or in a boat at night, you can find alligators by moving around a working flashlight until you come across a pair of bright yellow eyes at the surface of the water. Alligators hibernate in cold weather, often from October to March.

Of course, how cold is it going to get in south Georgia for any length of time?

You can spot alligators in ponds and sluggish streams throughout southeast Georgia. Towards the middle of the state, they are frequently seen cruising right in the middle of a river, though never in whitewater. Baby alligators are brown or black and sport transverse bands of yellow across their backs that fade as they age. A mature one is black. The young ones forage for crustaceans, bugs on or near the surface of the water, frogs and what fish they can outwit. Just like humans, they eat bigger and bigger things as they grow up. Since their cone-shaped teeth are not suitable for cutting prey but holding onto it, the animals tend to swallow their prey whole. They may take it underwater and drown it or they may shake the prey back and forth until it breaks into more bite-size pieces. Alligators have been known to poach small animals as well as the occasional cow, but not human beings—unless provoked. No one is positive exactly what an alligator might consider provocation, but holding out your hand with food in it comes to mind.

Male alligators roam their own territory, which may overlap with that of several females, giving him a number of potential mates. Both male and female have been known to bellow, announcing their presence and avail-ability—doubtless a chilling sound if you're out in the swamp. Another courtship behavior is head-slapping, wherein the animals whack their heads on the water, producing an echo that tells other creatures of their location. A sort of reptilian radar, if you will. In the summer, impregnated females build a nest of mud and rotting grass, leaves and other vegetative matter. Using their feet, snouts and tail, they pack the nest in a mound that may be as high as three feet and as wide as six. When she is ready to deliver, she digs a hole in the top of the mound and deposits 20 to 60 eggs. The heat from the rotting vegetation acts as an incubator, hatching the eggs. The mother guards her young from predators for the first nine or ten weeks, so poking around the underbrush is not a good idea on a hot summer day.

If you run into an alligator, you probably won't want to stop and ponder its relationship to the crocodile or how to tell them apart. Alligators have broader, blunter snouts and when they close their jaws, all the teeth are concealed, whereas the crocodile leaves the fourth bottom tooth exposed.

Both are fast enough to catch you—that is, unless you run in a zigzag pattern. Long, weighty reptiles are notoriously clumsy in the curves.

reptiles, 50 species of mammals, 37 species of amphibians and 39 species of fish. There are three entrances to the park; boat rentals are available at the West and East entrances. The only lodging within the park is in Stephen Foster State Park on the west side, near Fargo. Day-use fee for east and west entrance, $5 per vehicle; fee for north entrance, $12 minimum. ~ The east entrance is off Route 2 near Folkston, 912-496-7836; the north entrance is at the commercial Okefenokee Swamp Park, eight miles south of Waycross, 912-283-0583; the west entrance, via Stephen C. Foster State Park, is on Route 177, 17 miles east of Fargo, 912-637-5274; okefenokee.fws.gov.

LAURA S. WALKER STATE PARK A 120-acre lake forms the centerpiece of this park (one of the few state parks to be named for a woman) to the north of the Okefenokee National Wildlife Refuge. The wildlife is abundant here, as well; a good place for spotting woodpeckers, gopher tortoises and alligators is along Big Creek Nature Trail. There's a pool for swimming (closed Monday and Labor Day through April; admission) and an 18-hole golf course. Canoe and boat rentals are available. ~ 5653 Laura Walker Road, Waycross; 912-287-4900.

▲ There are 44 tent/RV sites; $17 to $21 per night. There are four budget-priced cabins that sleep eight. Reservations: 800-864-7275.

STEPHEN C. FOSTER STATE PARK The southern entrance to the Okefenokee, this park is named for the man who wrote "The Old Folks at Home," a song best known for the refrain, "way down upon the Suwanee River." Technically, it's only 80 acres but it opens onto the massive Okefenokee National Wildlife Refuge and Wilderness Area. This is the only place to rent cottages within the swamp; it's also the most remote, a place where alligators outnumber the human inhabitants of the surrounding county. You can rent canoes and motorboats on your own or arrange a one-and-a-half-hour guided tour; it's best to call in advance for a schedule. An interpretive museum has displays on the swamp's ecosystem and the prolific wildlife in the area. As for alligators? It goes without saying. Day-use fee, $5. ~ Route 177, 18 miles northeast of Fargo; 912-637-5274.

▲ There are 66 tent/RV sites; $17 to $22 per night. You'll also find nine cottages; $70 to $90 per night. Reservations: 800-864-7275.

Inland Georgia

Inland Georgia seems to be another planet entirely after you've seen the oaks, moss, shrimp boats and sandy beaches of the coast. The southeast corner of Georgia is among the least-traveled portions of the state, except for the Okefenokee Swamp, which has almost as many tourists as alligators. Scattered within this huge area, however, are Civil War sites and some offbeat small towns.

Waycross is the biggest town between the coast and Route 75, where Tifton and Valdosta are large cities by comparison. Once you get away from the swamp, the attractions tend to be smaller in scope. If you like exploring, this is very rewarding country. The landscape is flat, intersected with numerous small roads that often require backtracking or looping to get into and out of the towns. There are some meaningful relics of the Civil War, especially in Fitzgerald and Irwinville, but nothing on the order of a military park. Visiting these back-roads villages is an experience in small-town virtues; people take their time and by and large are happy to share it with visitors.

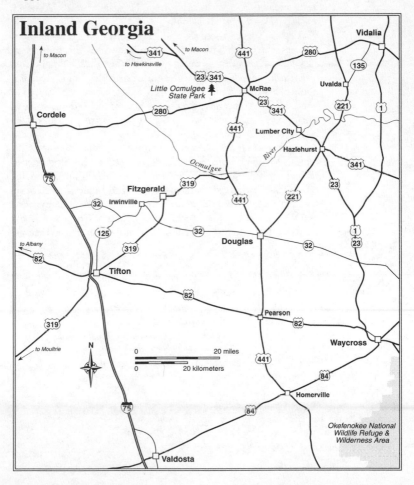

Inland Georgia

SIGHTS
When you leave Stephen C. Foster State Park, return to Homerville and continue north on Route 441 to Douglas. Here, take Route 221 north to **Hazlehurst**, a classically country sleepy town in the middle of, approximately, nowhere. Visitors are greeted at the **Hazlehurst–Jeff Davis County Museum** with a display of old post office artifacts, including the original post office window and scales from the time when first-class mail cost three cents an ounce. Period clothing and other regional memorabilia are on display. Closed Saturday, Sunday and mornings. ~ 61 East Coffee Street, Hazlehurst; 912-375-2557.

Drop by the **Hazlehurst–Jeff Davis County Visitors Bureau** to pick up maps and brochures for visitors who may have a hard time finding their way around the back roads. Closed Saturday and Sunday. ~ 95 East Jarman Street, Hazlehurst; 912-375-4543; www.hazlehurst-jeffdavis.com.

Luther Turner used to grind corn into grits for neighbor farmers who didn't have their own mills and now his son-in-law, Jack Harris Runnell, has taken over what he calls the **Frogbottom Grist Mill**. There's a cornfield right next to the "mill," which is about the size of a one-car garage (and which only recently got vinyl siding). You can watch corn being ground and buy some of the farm's exquisite cane syrup. ~ 65 Luther Turner Road, Hazlehurst; 912-375-4073.

From Hazlehurst, the simplest route to **Vidalia**, home of the famous Vidalia onions, is via Route 135. If you like these sweet-tasting vegetables, you can arrange for a **Farm Tour of Vidalia**, which visits onion farms in the spring and tobacco and cotton farms in the fall. To do that, drop by the **Vidalia Area Convention and Visitors Bureau** for information on these and other tours and local points of interest as well as maps and brochures on regional

AUTHOR FAVORITE

I could hardly believe my eyes when I saw the last general order from Robert E. Lee to the Army of North Virginia, dated April 10, 1865, on display in a glass case at the **Blue and Gray Museum**. This artifact is one of hundreds housed in this former train depot, which chronicles the unique history of this friendly town, living testimony that the Civil War is really over (at least in Fitzgerald). Also on display are a key from Andersonville Prison, a Congressional Medal of Honor for valor at Vicksburg, photographs of Fitzgerald's last four Union vets and more prosaic items such as historically interesting household goods donated by families. Closed Sunday and Monday. Admission. ~ 116 North Johnston Street, Fitzgerald; 229-426-5069, 800-386-4642; www.fitzgeraldga.org.

and state attractions. Closed Saturday and Sunday. ~ 100 Vidalia Sweet Onion Drive, Vidalia; 912-538-8687; www.vidaliaga.com.

Leaving Vidalia, follow Route 280 to **McRae**. Right in the middle of this tiny town is **Liberty Square**, which boasts a scaled-down replica of the Statue of Liberty, a 32-foot-tall work of art fashioned from cypress (the torch) and black gum (her head), with a coating of fiberglass, courtesy of a local boat maker. The town also has copies of the Declaration of Independence, its own Liberty Bell and a marble memorial to the soldiers of Telfair County who died in battle.

On the southern outskirts of town, you can look at (but not enter) the **Talmadge Home**, the residence of two Georgia governors, Eugene Talmadge and his son, Herman Eugene Talmadge. ~ Route 341S, McRae.

For more information about the area, visit the **Telfair County Chamber of Commerce**. Closed weekends. ~ 120 East Oak Street, McRae; 229-868-6365; www.telfairco.com.

There are several routes to **Fitzgerald** from McRae; to stay off Route 75, take Route 319 all the way to this unusual town. Nearly a century ago, long before *Money* magazine began its "Best Places to Live" series, a newspaper editor named P. H. Fitzgerald began promoting the idea of a place in the South where Union veterans could begin life anew. The town of Fitzgerald was founded in 1895, 30 years after the Civil War, with just such a concept in mind. For information on local attractions, visit the Welcome Center. ~ 115 South Main Street; 229-426-5033, 800-386-4642.

From Fitzgerald, Route 125 leads to the small town of **Irwinville**. When you reach the turnoff to tiny Route 32, turn left (south) and you will shortly arrive at the **Jefferson Davis Memorial Museum**. This is the site where the Confederate president was captured on May 10, 1865; in fact, one of the exhibits includes part of the tree where Davis was standing when the Union soldiers caught up with him. Other Civil War artifacts are handsomely presented in this small but stately museum. Closed Monday. Admission. ~ 338 Jeff Davis Park Road, Route 32, near Irwinville; 229-831-2335.

◄ *HIDDEN*

When you leave the museum, return to Route 125 and continue southwest to **Tifton**, which is just off Route 75. Tifton's historic downtown has been revitalized as part of Georgia's Main Street Program, but it still has a way to go before it becomes a tourist destination.

The thing to see in Tifton is the **Georgia Agrirama Living History Museum**, which is about the size of some actual small towns in Georgia. Families could spend half a day here, at least, inspecting structures like the blacksmith's shop, a one-room school, a water-powered grist mill and a print shop that still operates the

◄ *HIDDEN*

way it did in the 19th century—35 restored structures in all. You can take a ride on a logging train into the woods, come back and tour the saw mill and the turpentine still and then watch various farm activities such as blacksmithing. The possibilities are nearly endless. All the buildings are furnished in period style and staffed by costumed interpreters who manage to act as if they're hearing each question for the first time. Closed Sunday and Monday. Admission. ~ Off Exit 20 from Route 95, Tifton; 229-386-3344; ww.agrirama.com.

The streets on the west side of Fitzgerald are named for Confederate generals, while those on the east bear the names of Union generals.

When you have toured the sights of Tifton, get on Route 75 heading south to **Valdosta**. Home to Valdosta State College, this city is known for its historic buildings. The city prospered as an inland marketing center in the heyday of Sea Island Cotton.

From Route 75, take Exit 5 and drive past the Valdosta Mall to Norman Drive, a long block east of the interstate. To pick up a driving-tour map, a list of motels and the like, stop in at the **Valdosta-Lowndes County Convention and Visitors Bureau.** You can also find out how and when to tour the few mansions that are open to the public. Closed Sunday. ~ 1 Meeting Place, Valdosta; 229-245-0513, 800-569-8687, fax 229-245-5240; www.valdostatourism.com.

The **Historic Driving Tour** leads to some 56 houses and churches and even a cemetery, many of them in various National Register Historic districts. The visitors center will be able to point you in the right direction.

The **Lowndes County Courthouse** was assigned its location when the city was laid out in 1859. The present building is the third courthouse constructed on the square; it dates from the early 1900s. Designed by Frank P. Milburn, it has a massive portico on the south side, domes in the corners and a grand central dome. Closed Saturday and Sunday. ~ Between River Street and Central Avenue, Valdosta; 229-671-2620.

After viewing the courthouse square, return west to Toombs Avenue, head north for a couple of blocks and then turn right for one block, then left again on North Patterson Street. The downtown area's many one-way streets make this a challenging city to explore, but once you drive out to North Patterson Street you will be rewarded with the sight of many stately homes. Chief among them is **The Crescent.** Built in 1898, this neoclassical house is the former home of U.S. Senator William S. West. It got its name from the semicircular portico that is supported by 13 Doric columns. Saved from the wrecker's ball in 1951, it is now the Garden Center and on the National Register of Historic Places. It is open for tours. Closed Saturday, Sunday and mornings, except by appointment. Admission. ~ 904 North Patterson Street, Valdosta; 229-244-6747.

In Little Ocmulgee State Park is the **Pete Phillips Lodge**, named for a former member of the Georgia House of Representatives. The 60-room "lodge" is more of a motel, but the rooms are only a few steps from the very nice restaurant and not much farther from the golf course. Right on the lakeshore, close to the fishing dock, ten pleasant cottages are supplied with fully equipped kitchens as well as sheets and towels. ~ Route 319/441, McRae; 229-868-7474, 800-864-7275. MODERATE TO DELUXE.

Gracing a lovely tree-lined boulevard, the **Dorminy-Massee House** is the place to stay in Fitzgerald. This historic mansion's eight rooms have high ceilings and are lavishly decorated. Full breakfast is included. ~ 516 West Central Avenue, Fitzgerald; 229-423-3123. MODERATE.

Benton Lee's Steakhouse takes its beef seriously, serving heroic portions of T-bone, sirloin and the like. Non-beef selections include quail, chicken, 'gator nuggets and seafood. This riverfront outpost, a hit since the day it opened in 1960, seats up to 300 in an unpretentious dining hall, with tons of regional memorabilia. ~ 138 Benton Powell Road, Uvalda, off Route 221 about ten miles northeast of Hazlehurst; 912-594-6931, 912-594-6751. MODERATE TO DELUXE.

Seven miles west of Hazlehurst, just on the other side of the Altamaha River, **Stinson's Bar-B-Que** is a hole-in-the-wall that dishes out "Love at first bite!" Even if you order the shrimp plate, you'll be charged less than $9. They also have catfish, hamburger steak, cheeseburgers and barbecue by the pound. Eat here on red-and-white plastic tablecloths or order to go. It's right on the road. Closed Sunday. ~ Route 341, Lumber City; 912-363-4788. BUDGET.

The menu at the **Fairway Grill** at Pete Philips Lodge Restaurant in the Little Ocmulgee State Park features down-home treats along the lines of fried chicken and pork chops, all reasonably priced. The dining room, which serves three meals a day, overlooks the golf course at this extremely nice state park. ~ Route 319/441, McRae; 229-868-7474, 800-864-7275. BUDGET TO MODERATE.

For more than a quarter-century, **Charles Seafood Restaurant** has been dishing up more seafood than you could fit on a shrimp boat. It's entirely possible that the fading lamé—yes, l-a-m-é— wallpaper has been here all along, competing with fish nets and leatherette seating for your interior decorating envy. However, this is just a simple restaurant, very popular locally, a bit east of Route 75. There are virtually no adjectives on the menu, which lists flounder, catfish, perch, bream, mullet (and in season, roe, which is pretty addictive), quail, frogs' legs and hamburgers. They have side orders worth mentioning: hushpuppies, cheese grits and alligator tail. Wines by the glass and a homemade peach cobbler ought to keep you going for a couple of days. Closed Sunday. ~ 701 West 7th Street, Tifton; 229-382-9696. BUDGET TO MODERATE.

If Valdosta were blessed with half-a-dozen bistros, you might not give **Ming's Chinese Restaurant** a second glance. However, under the circumstances, you could do worse than to take a meal in this modest, family-run establishment just a block or so from the courthouse. There are lots of beef, pork, chicken and shrimp dishes, including curried versions and the unusual-sounding sizzling Kon-bar shrimp, which you don't see every day, even in San Francisco. Closed Sunday. ~ 508 North Patterson Street, Valdosta; 229-247-9868. BUDGET.

HIDDEN ► Sharing its roof with a Trax gas station, **Macadoo's Grille** is a local take on the big national franchises. It's no place to linger over a meal, but it's bright, clean and has burgers, sandwiches, slaw dogs and the like, as well as a pretty good breakfast menu, available until 10:30 a.m. They're only too happy to fix your order to go. Plus, it's near some of Valdosta's historic homes. Closed Sunday. ~ 1501 North Ashley Street, Valdosta; 229-241-2095. BUDGET.

SHOPPING There are some outlet stores around Valdosta, but you'll find few quaint shops in this section of Georgia. The best bet is in the downtown area.

HIDDEN ► The **Country Store** at the Georgia Agrirama is a fabulous source of small gifts that would make perfect stocking stuffers. There are also books on locomotion, history, flowers and other subjects like cooking, jams and jellies and odd things like Clark Gable paper dolls. ~ Off Exit 20 from Route 95, Tifton; 229-386-3344.

NIGHTLIFE People who live in farm country tend to go to bed early, but there are still a few things to do after dark in this part of the world.

The **Grande Theatre of Fitzgerald**, a restored 1930s movie house, is used frequently for the performing arts. It has 847 seats and an enlarged orchestra pit. ~ 119 South Main Street, Fitzgerald; 229-426-5090, 800-386-4642.

HIDDEN ► On a sporadic basis, the Wiregrass Opera performs some Saturday nights at the **Georgia Agrirama Living History Museum** complex. ~ Off Exit 20 from Route 95, Tifton; 229-386-3344.

PARKS **LITTLE OCMULGEE STATE PARK** 𝕏 ⛴ ⚓ ⚓ 🛥 🛶 The grounds of the Shamrock Springs Health Spa were absorbed into the land that residents donated back in the 1930s to create this 1277-acre park, named for the Hichiti Indian phrase for "bubbling water." The Civilian Conservation Corps helped here, as they did with other Georgia parks, building roads, structures and the dam. A 265-acre lake impounded on the Little Ocmulgee River, attracts waterfowl, alligators, gopher tortoises and terrestrial mammals like opossums, armadillos and deer. Its 60-room lodge has a full-service restaurant. There are two tennis courts and an 18-hole golf course in addition to seasonal miniature golf, plus picnic areas and canoe/pedal boat rentals. Day-use fee, $2. ~ Route 319/441, two miles north of McRae; 229-868-7474, 800-864-7275.

▲ There are 55 tent/RV sites; $17 to $19 per night. Ten cottages are also available; $70 to $95 per night. Reservations: 800-864-7275.

Outdoor Adventures

With so much open shoreline, marshland and saltwater, coastal Georgia beckons with almost endless opportunities for hikers, golfers, fishers and other outdoors fans.

FISHING

Fishing is a major sport in southeast Georgia—in fact, just about everywhere in the state. The possibilities range from the grand (sailfish and dolphin fish in deep-sea charter boats) to the modest (crabbing off a public dock using a piece of string tied to a chicken neck and a rock). In between, you can fish for sea trout and flounder in the ocean and rivers, and bass, bream and catfish in inland lakes. For information on fishing licenses, call 800-933-2627.

> A license is required for saltwater and freshwater fishing. You can buy a license just about any place that sells bait.

There are several fishing piers on the Golden Isles; you can also try surf fishing. Piers are located at the **Clam Creek Foot Bridge** (912-635-2119) at the north end of Jekyll Island; the **St. Simons Pier** on Mallery Street on St. Simons Island; and the **McKay River Fishing Pier** below the bridge on St. Simons Island Causeway.

Hardware stores and marinas sell bait and fishing tackle. A nice shop is **Orvis/The Bedford Sportsman South**. Closed Sunday and Monday. ~ 3405 Frederica Road, St. Simons Island; 912-638-5454.

Bait is also sold at **Gisco Seafood Market**, where you can pick up ice and other accessories for a day on the docks. Closed Sunday and Monday. ~ 2020 Demere Road, St. Simons Island; 912-638-7546.

If you're interested in offshore fishing, **Coastal Island Charter Fishing** can take you in search of tarpon, shark, king mackerel, Spanish mackerel, cobia amberjack and barracuda. For a shorter trip, consider fishing "inshore"—closer to the mainland—for trout. ~ 912-638-0241, 888-288-5030; www.charterfish.net.

Telfair County residents boast that the largest largemouth bass ever caught was fished out of **Montgomery Lake** off the Ocmulgee River on June 2, 1932. It weighed 22 pounds and 4 ounces. So get a license and grab a rod and reel and try your luck.

SAILING   The rivers, creeks and inlets are ideal for easy sailing in this part of Georgia. Small boats allow close inspection of wildlife, including egrets and dolphins, which frequent these waters. Even experienced sailors, however, know better than to head across sounds, much less into open water, without charts and emergency equipment. Sudden squalls are common, especially in late summer and early fall, which is hurricane season.

Charter boats are widely available in the Golden Isles and allow you to relax without having to worry about tides and charts. A number of captains are affiliated with various booking associations and marinas. You can arrange outings through the **Inland Charter Boat Service**. ~ Cloister Docks, Sea Island; 912-638-3611 ext. 5202. Another option is the **Golden Isles Charter Fishing Association**. ~ Golden Isles Marina, 206 Marine Drive off the St. Simons Island Causeway; 912-638-7673. Also on St. Simons Island, **Dunbar Sales, Inc.** will arrange charters. ~ Golden Isles Marina; 912-638-8573.

If you prefer to go it alone, local tide charts are widely available in coastal Georgia; many telephone books include them. **Barry's Beach Service** rents sailboats. ~ 420 Arnold Road, St. Simons Island; 912-638-8053, 800-669-5215.

CANOEING   The Golden Isles are the best-known places for canoeing and
& KAYAKING kayaking in southeast Georgia, but you can go canoeing in the Okefenokee as well. You definitely want to be experienced because the water is shallow and sometimes a breeze will turn into a strong wind, making it difficult to turn around.

Kayaks and canoes are a good means of getting into some narrow and often shallow tidal creeks, the small waterways that run between rivers, creeks and sounds and meander through the tall marsh grass, sometimes almost disappearing at low tide. One good source for vessels on St. Simons Island is **Ocean Motion Surf Shop**. ~ 1300 Ocean Boulevard; 912-638-5225, 800-669-5215. Another is **Southeast Adventure Outfitters**. You must call ahead to arrange the rental. ~ 313 Mallery Street; 912-638-6732.

For a quiet, even intimate, experience in the mostly warm coastal waters around the Golden Isles, sign up with **Up the Creek Kayak Tours**. ~ 111 Osborne Street, Brunswick; 912-882-0911.

BOATING   Boating is, for the most part, very easy in southeast Georgia. You
& WATER   can spend a lot of time on the water without ever venturing into
SKIING   open ocean. Which is a good idea, unless you're an experienced sailor and/or have a very large craft. Georgia law requires a distance of 1000 feet between power craft (including jet skis) and the shoreline.

The **Salt Marsh Nature Tour** follows the narrow tidal creeks between Sea Island and St. Simons Island, allowing passengers aboard the 24-foot pontoon boat the opportunity to identify herons, egrets, pelicans, occasional bottle-nosed dolphins and maybe even a river otter. The *Marsh Hen* also takes four to six passengers on dolphin quests, sunset cruises and other tours. They provide binoculars for their traveling guests. ~ St. Simons Island; 912-638-9354; www.marshtours.com.

If you want to try going out on your own, rent a boat and pick up all the related items you need at the **Jekyll Harbor Marina**. ~ South Riverview Drive, Jekyll Island; 912-635-3137.

SCUBA DIVING

Exploring the ocean depths is a popular sport off the coast of Georgia. There's no visibility to speak of close to shore, but farther out you can see schools of larger fish. You can get instruction and arrange charters through the **Island Dive Center**. Dives are weather-dependent; the season usually runs from the end of May to the end of September. ~ Golden Isles Marina, St. Simons Causeway; 912-638-6590, 800-940-3483; www.islanddivecenter.com.

GOLF

Palm trees, stands of pine and graceful live oaks, backed by marsh grass and blue water, make southeast Georgia a duffer's dream. If you don't score under par, at least you can expect glorious scenery.

In Shellman Bluff, between Midway and Darien, the **Sapelo Hammock Golf Club** has five sets of tees—enough to make almost anyone happy (to the extent that any golfer can be said to be truly happy). The 6900-yard course runs beside marshes and trees, one of the prettiest layouts in the area. ~ At Cooper's Point, 500 Marshview Drive, Shellman Bluff; 912-832-4653, 877-266-7376.

The Golden Isles are synonymous with fine golf and you can find something to challenge you at **Sea Palms Golf Club**'s three nine-hole courses. George Cobb designed the original 18 holes, which include the Tall Pines and Great Oaks nines (the latter is the longest). Tom Jackson designed the shorter and newer Sea Palms West. ~ 5445 Frederica Road, St. Simons Island; 912-638-9041, 800-841-6268.

The medium-length **Glynco Golf Course** has undulating greens and very generous fairways. Water comes into play on four of

AUTHOR FAVORITE

I find scenery one of the most important factors in picking a place to play a few holes, and **Waterford Landing Golf Course** fills the bill. Overlooking salt marsh and flanked by Georgia pines and great old oak trees, it offers 18 links-style holes, PGA instruction, a driving range and a snack bar. ~ 731 Waterford Landing Road, Richmond Hill; 912-727-4848.

the nine holes. There are 419 Bermuda fairways and 328 Bermuda greens. Snack bar, driving range and putting green are on site. ~ 1 Vogel Road, Brunswick; 912-264-9521.

Voted one of the best golf courses in the country by the readers of *Golf Digest* and *Golfweek*, **Osprey Cove** is a links-style, 18-hole course. Known for its manicured greens, the course is set among tidal inlets and salt marshes that virtually guarantee some wildlife sightings as you make the rounds. ~ 123 Osprey Drive, St. Marys; 912-882-5575, 800-352-5575.

Located between St. Marys and Route 95 (Exit 2), **Laurel Island Links** is one of the region's newer golf destinations. Carved out of forest land on the banks of the Crooked River, this 18-hole, par-72 course features a number of marshfront holes. ~ 233 Marsh Harbour Parkway, Kingsland; 912-729-7277.

Laura S. Walker State Park boasts an 18-hole, par-72, 6800-yard championship course, called The Lakes, with a driving range, pro shop, snack bar and clubhouse. ~ 5653 Laura Walker Road, Waycross; 912-285-6154.

TENNIS

You can find public courts at several parks in Brunswick, including two acrylic courts at **Selden Park**. ~ 4th and Newcastle streets.

Most tennis courts on Jekyll are at resorts, but anyone can play at the **Jekyll Island Tennis Center**, where 7 of the 13 courts are lighted. Reservations recommended. Fee. ~ Captain Wylly Road; 912-635-3154, 877-453-5955.

BIKING

Even without many paths specific for pedaling purposes, cyclists can find plenty of flat roads where traffic is light. It's a good idea to pay special attention to traffic, since most locals aren't accustomed to sharing the road with those on two wheels. You should also call ahead to make sure the road you're interested in hasn't been rained out.

Jekyll Island, seven and a half miles long and one and a half miles wide, is flat as a crab cake. Aside from the little streets around the Jekyll Island Club Hotel, there are bike paths along North Riverview Drive in the Historic District all the way to the north end of the island and back along North Beachview Drive. The path veers towards the beach along motel row, roughly from the Jekyll Estates Inn to just south of the Convention Center. The route then continues on South Beachview Drive and ends near Jekyll Point. There's also a path connecting South Beachview with North Riverview drives near the middle of the island along Captain Willy Road.

You can bicycle on the **nine-mile driving loop** at the Eastern Entrance to the Okefenokee Swamp in Okefenokee National Wildlife Refuge and Wilderness Area.

Bike Rentals You can rent bikes at the **Jekyll Island Club Hotel** (912-635-2600), **Villas by the Sea** (912-635-2521) or **Maxwell's**

Variety and True Value Hardware Store (912-635-2205). On St. Simons Island, try the **Ocean Motion Surf Co.** ~ 1300 Ocean Boulevard; 912-638-8053, 800-669-5215.

The flat landscape in this part of Georgia makes all hiking trails moderate ones, though if you set out at a brisk pace on a warm day you can get quite a workout. Call ahead to make sure the trail you're interested in hasn't been rained out. All distances listed for hiking trails are one way unless otherwise specified.

HIKING

A trail runs along the scenic riverfront at Fort McAllister State Historic Park. Called the **Savage Island Nature Trail** (1.3 miles), it is close to picnic areas, camp sites and the fort's earthwork fortifications.

You don't have to spend the night at Melon Bluff in Midway to enjoy hiking amid thousands of preserved acres. One option is the short **Butterfly Trail** (.2 mile) between the Nature Center and Old Ferry Road. The owners have plans to install a butterfly-friendly garden along this path. Across Old Ferry Road from the end of the Butterfly Trail, the **Cross Woods Trail** (.3 mile) ends at **Lost Bluff Trail** (.2 mile); when you get to that intersection, you can turn left to Lost Bluff for a view of the rice fields, or turn right and link with Mule Crossing. This leads .2 mile back to Old Ferry Road near the Butterfly Trail and the Nature Center. For a longer outing, the **Bluff Trail** (2 miles) leads from Old Ferry Road across a bridge where a stream runs below during rainy season. It runs above the vestiges of old rice channels; this plantation staple was grown throughout the Melon Bluff area in the lower places. Admission.

Crooked River State Park has a nature trail (1.5 miles) that covers four environmental ecosystems. Very hot in summer, the trail is cooled somewhat by the four-acre lake and occasional breezes off the river.

You can hike (or bike) on the **nine-mile driving loop** at the Eastern Entrance to the Okefenokee Swamp in the Okefenokee

◆◆◆

SHORELINE TRAIL RIDES

Forget dreams of riding in the surf, but you can get on a horse and take it onto the sand. The best times are early morning and late afternoon, since it's often too hot in the middle of the day to think about leather saddles. **Victoria's Carriages & Trail Rides** offers regularly scheduled beach trail rides most mornings. There's also a one-and-a-half-hour sunset beach ride. Excursions depart from the Clam Creek picnic area at the north end of Jekyll Island, but you should make reservations in advance to guarantee a ride. Closed Sunday. ~ Jekyll Island; 912-635-9500.

National Wildlife Refuge. The **Canal Digger's Trail** (.5 mile) winds around the Suwannee Canal, built in 1891 to drain the swamp. This trail takes you across footbridges, among upland pine forests and near the water. An interpretive guide is at the trailhead and at the visitors center. There's also the **wooden walkway** (.75 mile) into Chesser Prairie that crosses through cypress trees and by open prairie marshlands.

Depending on your luck and the time of day, you may see small wildlife like opossums and squirrels—sometimes even deer—on the **Big Creek Nature Trail** (1.1 miles) in Laura S. Walker State Park. It's a flat trail, partly covered in boardwalk, that leads deep into a pine and hardwood forest.

▼▼▼▼▼▼▼▼▼▼ Transportation

CAR

Route 17 runs south from Savannah into Florida and accesses most of the smaller towns near the coast. **Route 95** is the major north–south artery, which runs parallel to **Route 17** to the west. Most of the roads, even federal highways, in the interior are two lanes. Sections of **Route 1** in the Waycross area, a major hub, may expand to four lanes. The western boundary of the southeast region is the north–south **Route 75**.

AIR

The **Brunswick-Golden Isles Airport** is served by Atlantic Southeast Airlines. ~ www.glynncountyairports. Other airlines that serve the region fly into Savannah, a little more than an hour's drive to the north of Brunswick via Route 95. Please see Chapter Two for details.

BUS

Greyhound Bus Lines (800-231-2222; www.greyhound.com) has stations in Brunswick at 1101 Gloucester Street, 912-265-2800; in Waycross at 405 Tebeau Street, 912-283-7211; and in Valdosta at 200 North Oak Street; 229-242-8575.

CAR RENTALS

Hertz Rent A Car (800-654-3131) and **Avis Rent A Car** (800-230-4898) have outlets on St. Simons Island and in Brunswick at the Glynco Jetport. Local car-rental agencies include **Auto Rentals of Brunswick**. Closed Sunday. ~ 3576 Darien Highway; 912-264-0530. The closest source of other major automobile rentals is the Savannah airport. Please see Chapter Two for details.

TAXIS

City Cab serves all of Glynn County, including St. Simons and Jekyll islands, and provides transport between the airports in Savannah and Brunswick. ~ 912-264-3760. Other taxi services include **Courtesy Cab** (912-265-5002) and **St. Simons Cab Co.** (912-638-3790).

FOUR

Southwest and West Central Georgia

Plantations and presidents are the theme of this part of the state. While much is made of the historic plantations, there aren't very many open to the public, alas. A few of them do have tours, however, and you can even spend the night in one of the nicest ones. The very existence of plantations speaks volumes about the history of Southwest Georgia: the cotton and peanuts, the farmers and the slaves and, later, the wealthy who still come in from around the country to hunt quail and other game on private acreage.

The therapeutic waters around the Warm Springs area attracted President Franklin Delano Roosevelt to this neck of the woods to ease the pain in his crippled legs. For years, he made the pilgrimage to bask in the hot water provided courtesy of Pine Mountain. Eventually, he built a home here that was inevitably called the Little White House. The six-room cottage where he died in April 1945 looks the way it did more than half a century ago.

James Earl Carter turned 21 the year of FDR's death. It would be decades before he was elected governor of Georgia and then announce his candidacy for the presidency at the train depot in his hometown of Plains. The modest town now boasts the Jimmy Carter National Historic Site, a must for anyone interested in American history.

There were other lesser-known heroes in this region, from the soldiers who built Fort Gaines in 1814 to the group of citizens in Colquitt who rallied their town spirit and raised enough money to produce the excellent folk opera *Swamp Gravy*, which is still performed today.

Thomasville, close to the Florida border, has a handful of plantations, some of which still welcome quail hunters in season. In the late 19th century, the area became extremely popular with snowbirds eager to leave the harsh northern climate. Since this elegant city escaped major destruction during the Civil War, many historic structures still stand, including a number of beautiful Victorians, some of which have been converted into bed-and-breakfast inns.

The largest city in southwest Georgia is Columbus, on the Chattahoochee River that separates Georgia from Alabama. Once the site of a Creek Indian village, the area started as a trading post and developed into the last frontier town of the original 13 colonies. Its military history (this was where boats and gunpowder were produced during the Civil War) continues today in the form of Fort Benning, home of the National Infantry Museum. Like many other Georgia towns, it has developed riverfront walkways.

The most famous military site in Southwest Georgia, however, is Andersonville, the infamous Civil War prison and cemetery. In 1998, the multimillion-dollar Prisoner of War museum opened next door, a powerful testimony to the men and women who were captured in every U.S. war since the American Revolution.

This area of Georgia is defined by small towns, from Bainbridge to tiny Parrott, which may not have major attractions but nonetheless create a patchwork of rural culture with many quirky delights found on side streets and back roads.

▼▼▼▼▼▼▼▼▼▼▼▼▼
Southwest Corner

This section of Georgia is one of the most diverse —if not in landscape, at least in the way people live on the land. Thomasville is the proper dowager, her Victorian residences dressed to the nines. Bainbridge is a working-person's town, while Colquitt is a hub for farmers and a place where community spirit really means something. Down around Lake Seminole is the place for sports lovers, especially those who like to fish, whereas Fort Gaines still has a little touch of the pioneer town it once was, the kind of place where everybody knows everybody else.

SIGHTS

HIDDEN ▶

Located several miles south of Thomasville, **Pebble Hill Plantation** affords visitors a glimpse into a lifestyle that may not be entirely gone with the wind, but is certainly rare today. The 3000-acre estate can claim an antebellum heritage, but the 34 acres open to the public today are traced directly to 1896, the year the property, which was established in the 1820s, was acquired by Howard Melville Hanna. This Cleveland businessman and his family developed the estate and turned it into a quail-hunting retreat; the carriage house, stables, kennels, cow barn, dog hospital, dairy, log-cabin schoolhouse, swimming pool and other outbuildings tell stories about the lives of the well-to-do who once lived here. More fascinating is the Main House. Hanna's granddaughter, known affectionately as Miss Pansy, filled the mansion with a mind-blowing collection of artwork (an entire room is decorated in hound paintings), decorative pieces, fine furnishings, sporting trophies, books and personal mementos. The dazzle is in the detail—a closet stuffed with equestrian ribbons, a dining table set with Royal Worcester Audubon Birds of America, woodwork embellished by the resident carver. Upon her death in 1978, the Pebble Hill Plantation became a museum, which opened to the public in 1983. You can wander the grounds at will, but the main house

Southwest & West Central Georgia

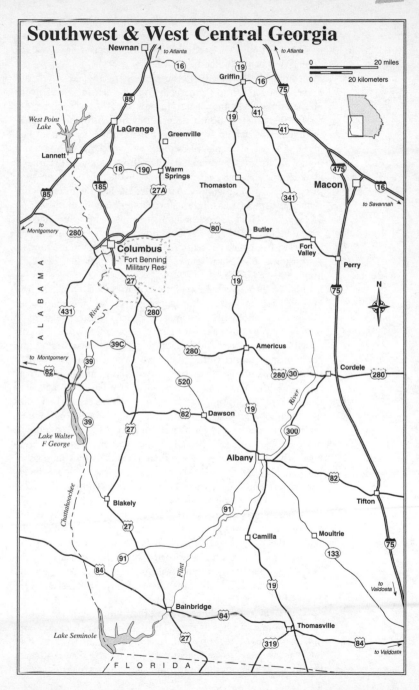

can be viewed only by guided tour, which typically lasts one and a half hours. Closed Monday and the month of September. Admission. ~ Route 319, five miles south of Thomasville; 229-226-2344; www.pebblehill.com.

It's quite a drive into the historic district, where a few old homes are open for tours; many are on the "Driving Tour" available from the Welcome Center. Except for its orange-sherbet exterior, oriental-style porch decorations and fish-scale shingles, the **Lapham-Patterson House State Historic Site** fits right into its low-key Thomasville neighborhood. No wonder it was named a National Historic Landmark in 1975. It was about 90 years old at that time, having been built by a prosperous Chicago shoe merchant, C. W. Lapham, who installed the latest in modern conveniences such as a gas lighting system and indoor plumbing. In 1905, James G. Patterson bought the house, and it remained in the family until 1970. Forty-five-minute tours of the house and its period furnishings are offered on the hour. Closed Monday. Admission. ~ 626 North Dawson Street, Thomasville; 229-225-4004, 800-864-7275.

Practically across the street, the **Thomas County Museum of History** looks innocuous but contains a veritable warehouse of photographs and artifacts depicting the city's history. The most fascinating portions of the tour involve the stories, tales, myths and gossip about the famed plantation life in these parts. As the guide usually points out, for instance, you couldn't really call your digs a plantation without plenty of slaves, and only ten percent of Southerners owned the requisite five slaves. In fact, only three percent of Southerners ever owned slaves at all. Time flies by as you look and listen to stories about, say, Millpond, which set the standard for proper plantation living by boasting a house nearly an acre in size, approached by a two-and-a-half-mile tree-lined driveway. Allow plenty of time to examine these and other buildings and exhibits. Closed Sunday and the last week in September. Admission. ~ 725 North Dawson Street, Thomasville; 229-226-7664; www.rose.net/~history.

A few blocks to the south, the neat-and-tidy **Hardy Bryan House** is the oldest two-story house in downtown Thomasville. Built in the 1830s by Hardy Bryan as the main house of a small farm complex long since absorbed into the historic district, the Greek Revival–style landmark is distinguished by a free-standing second-story porch. ~ 312 North Broad Street, Thomasville; 229-226-6016.

Oak trees are deeply revered in the southeastern U.S., so of course Thomasville has its own. **The Big Oak** dates back to about 1685, stretches 68 feet up and has a limb spread of 162 feet. Peer into its branches to see the resurrection fern, a benign growth that looks like a goner until the morning after a good rain, when it will have turned green practically overnight. Look for the tree and its accompanying gazebo on a nice piece of land, two-thirds of an acre near the Federal Courthouse. ~ Corner of North Crawford and East Monroe streets, Thomasville.

The biggest botanical attraction in Thomasville—which calls itself the City of Roses—is the **Thomasville Rose Garden**. To reach it, take Smith Street (Route 84) east towards Cherokee Lake. The half-acre garden starts blooming in April, if it is warm enough, and reaches its peak in early May. What began as a nursery in 1898 evolved into a site for an All-American Rose Selection trial garden by the mid-1950s. New roses were tested here for hardiness, resistance to disease and overall appeal to garden hobbyists until 1994, when the nursery closed and the city took it over as a municipal rose garden with more than 500 specimens. ~ Cherokee Lake at the corner of Smith and Covington avenues, Thomasville.

You can pick up self-guided tour maps at the **Thomasville Welcome Center**. Closed Sunday. ~ 401 South Broad Street, Thomasville; 229-228-7877, 866-577-3600; www.thomasvillega.com.

From downtown Thomasville, head west on Route 84 to Bainbridge, about 30 minutes away on the banks of the Flint River.

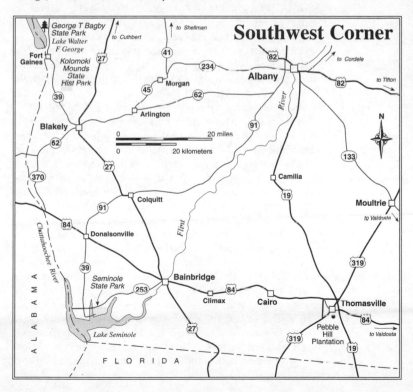

En route you will pass towns with wonderful names like Cairo and Climax.

On a hot day, a good choice (especially if you have kids in tow) is a cool tour of the **M&M Ice Company**, where block ice is still made the old-fashioned way. Visitors who've never seen a plant like this will likely be surprised to see 350-pound blocks of ice roll out. Colored ice is also made here. Closed Saturday afternoon and Sunday except by appointment. ~ 309 2nd Avenue Northeast, Cairo; 229-377-3422.

Also in town is the **Cairo Antique Auto Museum**. Auto aficionados can examine antique cars from every decade of the 20th century, plus antique bicycles and motorcycles. Open the first Saturday of every month. Admission. ~ 1125 Route 84E, Cairo; 229-377-3911.

> If you have trouble finding Fort Gaines Frontier Village or other area attractions, pick up a self-guided tour map and audio CD at George T. Bagby State Park. ~ 229-768-2571.

When you reach Bainbridge by continuing on Route 84 for another 15 minutes, you can pick up maps and other tourist information at the **Bainbridge-Decatur County Chamber of Commerce**. It's housed in the 1921 McKenzie-Reynolds House. Closed Saturday and Sunday. ~ 100 Basin Circle, Bainbridge; 229-246-4774, 800-243-4774, fax 229-243-7633; www.bain bridgegachamber.com.

The **Bainbridge Driving Tour** passes by 50 sites, including the old Indian village where the Battle of Fowlstown took place during the American Revolution. This and the Gator Line Stage Inn, where the stagecoach stopped in the mid-1800s, are both south on Route 97, as is La Loma Plantation, which derived its main income from pear trees in the early part of the 19th century.

After touring Bainbridge, take a side trip for about 16 miles on Route 253 to see one of the country's top bass-fishing lakes. **Lake Seminole**, wedged into the southwestern corner of the state, attracts sportspeople with 12,000 acres of shallow water (averaging 15 feet in depth), much of which is studded with tree stumps and lily pads as far as the eye can see. Fish camps, naturally, as well as the Seminole State Park, accommodate anglers.

From the lake, head north on Route 39 through Donalsonville. If you don't go to Seminole from Bainbridge, you can drive directly 15 miles northwest on Route 1 and Route 27 to **Colquitt**. This is a town to watch because it's got more civic spirit than cities ten times its size. Or 30 times its size. Its seasonal production of *Swamp Gravy* (see "Swamp Gravy" below) has attracted a lot of attention, but there's also a quaint little downtown that is gradually getting spiffed up.

On the main square is **Tarrer Inn**. Now a hotel and restaurant on the National Register of Historic Places, it was built in 1861 as a residence, burned down in 1902, and was resurrected in 1905 as a boardinghouse. ~ 155 South Cuthbert Street, Colquitt; 229-758-2888; www.tarrerinn.com.

You can find tourist information at the **Colquitt Miller County Chamber of Commerce**. Closed Saturday and Sunday. ~ 166 South 1st Street, Colquitt; 229-758-2400.

West of Colquitt, look for a continuation of Route 1/27 and continue northwest to the town of Blakely. In the northwest corner of Courthouse Square, the **Confederate Flagpole**, which was put up in 1861, is the last remaining wooden Confederate flagpole in existence. ~ Route 27, Blakely.

Near Blakely are two unusual attractions: a historic bridge and an older—much, much older—American Indian site. About eight miles southwest of Blakely along Route 62, look first for the Hilton School sign, then on the right for a small sign for the **Coheelee Creek Covered Bridge**. Since it is another mile from the   ◄ *HIDDEN* main road, you will have to make a few turns—two to the right and then one to the left—to see this 96-foot long, double-span bridge, constructed in 1891. ~ Off Route 62, Blakely.

From this site, head back to Blakely and turn left on Route 39 (a pretty drive beside some of the peanut farms for which this area is known) for roughly three miles until you see the signs for the **Kolomoki Mounds State Historic Park**, which is about midway   ◄ *HIDDEN* between Route 39 and Route 27. Seven Indian mounds, built by the Swift Creek and Weeden Island Indians, remain in this 1293-acre park, looking quite mysterious and imposing; the largest of them is 56 feet tall with a base measuring 325 by 200 feet, quite an accomplishment considering that each mound was constructed of earth basketful by basketful by some of the approximately 2000 Indians whose village life was centered here. An excellent museum at the west entrance details the region's American Indian cultures from as far back as 5000 B.C. up to the 13th century. To understand them better, look for the exhibit showing the interior of one just as the archaeologists left it. The museum is closed Sunday morning and Monday. Admission. ~ Route 27, Blakely; 229-724-2150, 800-864-7275.

Route 39 continues northwest, a pretty two-lane road that passes small farms but few houses. About 18 miles from Bainbridge, Fort Gaines came into existence as the westernmost point of the American frontier back in 1814. The town that grew up around it has all but obliterated the remains of the fort itself, but it's here, now known as the **Fort Gaines Frontier Village**. Despite   ◄ *HIDDEN* the name, there's nothing theme park–like about this open-air museum on a bluff above the Chattahoochee River. Most of the structures on display were moved here from elsewhere. The first house, for example, is a double-penned dog trot house, formerly the home of Newt Ingram over in Zetto; the Ingram House is a

Text continued on page 152.

Swamp
Gravy

In an old brick warehouse just a block off Colquitt's town square, magical things have been happening. The community, including people from nearby towns, have put together a show that is as professional as it is touching, and it's so good it was named the official folk play of the 1996 Summer Olympics.

No one could have predicted what a success this project would be. Back in 1990, Joy Jinks, a moving force in the newly formed Southwest Georgia/Colquitt Arts Council, traveled to New York City to attend a conference. There, she met with Richard Geer. A Ph.D. and artistic director who founded the Steamboat Repertory Theater, Geer had never been to Jinks' town, but he did know something about putting on performances in rural areas. Over lunch, she told him, "Our community has always wanted to do a play." Geer's response? "Let's do it!"

From that modest beginning came the story of the people who live in southwest Georgia, their hopes and dreams, their personal stories and their folk remedies.

The talent search and job of putting together a script involved the efforts of many people, but especially playwright Jo Carson, who has a background in oral history, and play coordinator Karen Kimbrel. As the play evolved—and would continue to change and grow—people came to tell their stories. These are what make up the backbone of every performance.

On October 10, 1992, *Swamp Gravy Sketches* opened in the Miller County Elementary School with work as the theme. By 1993, *Swamp Gravy* was performed more than 30 times all over the state to promote the 1994 performance. The 1995 spring season, *The Gospel Truth*, is still recalled as a powerful drama centered around a fiery Baptist preacher. All along, the people behind the scenes interviewed southwest Georgia people to infuse new life into the story lines while others busily restored the old Cotton Hall, which would become home to the production. As this went on, *Swamp Gravy* received arts grants that have helped sustain it to this day.

On a typical performance night at the hall, three platforms are arranged at odd angles in the center of the theater. Seating is stadium style, as if the audience is there to watch a football game. Part of the appeal of *Swamp Gravy* is that no one is forced to remain in their seats. You can get up and move closer as the cast members exhort everyone: "We want you to feel good."

One production, *Good Medicine*, technically had two acts but the scenes changed so often—sometimes just by music, mood and lighting—that it seemed like more. There were mini-dramas set in a cemetery, in a doctor's office with a reluctant nurse, in the woods, at a funeral. Every few minutes, somebody sang a song. The comedy and tragedy of daily existence came to life as events unfolded. By the end, after laughing out loud, many in the audience visibly wept during the moving closing number.

To find out the upcoming schedule of shows, contact the Colquitt/Miller County Arts Council, P.O. Box 567, Colquitt, GA 39837; 229-758-5450; www.swampgravy.com.

SWAMP GRAVY RECIPE

Swamp gravy is one of those dishes that help extend a meal when the pantry is a little bare or unexpected guests show up. There are infinite variations; some people add corn or beans while others prefer to spice up the basic recipe by adding a diced jalapeño pepper. Or two.

Fry some fish golden brown. Pour off the grease but leave some of the drippings. In the drippings, brown:

    4 or 5 finely diced potatoes
    2 or 3 finely diced onions
    1 chopped bell pepper (optional)

When these are tender, add a large can of tomatoes, salt and pepper to taste, and 1 or 2 teaspoons of Louisiana Hot Sauce. Pick some of the meat off one or two of the cooked fish and add to the mixture. Simmer for as long as you can resist the wonderful aroma.

single log house from Sutton's Cross Roads; the log corn crib came from a nearby farm. Also here are a grist mill, a cane mill and a smokehouse, which has a dirt floor where poles run horizontally mid-way up so that the meats could be hung for smoking. Nearby is a pioneer cemetery and a partial replica of the actual fort. ~ 100 Bluff Street, Fort Gaines.

A look-see at the ten-bedroom, three-parlor **John Dill House** will give you an idea of Fort Gaines' prosperity, at least at one point in time. Built in 1820, it has 15 fireplaces, many with special features. But since the bed and breakfast closed in 1998, you'll only be able to admire features like the Stage Coach Portico, added when the home was used as a stagecoach inn, and the fan-design wrought-iron fence. ~ 102 South Washington Street, Fort Gaines.

Heading north from Fort Gaines on Route 39, you will pass the entrance to the 300-acre **George T. Bagby State Park** on the banks of Lake Walter F. George; from here, you can see Alabama across the water. (See "Parks" below for more information.) ~ Route 39, three miles north of Fort Gaines.

LODGING

From funky fish camps to deluxe plantation homes, the range of lodging in Southwest Georgia just about runs the gamut. Most of them offer typical Southern hospitality, meaning they wouldn't dream of sending you on your way without a proper breakfast. On the downside, these places (when you can find them) are greatly outnumbered by chain motels. Thomasville and Columbus boast the lion's share of small inns.

HIDDEN ▶

Luxurious and refined without being stuffy, **Melhana Plantation** is the kind of place many travelers dream of resting their overstimulated heads. The setting is incomparable: 40 landscaped acres that contain an antebellum main house, a carriage house and several other historic buildings, an indoor pool and formal gardens. There's even a small theater where *Gone with the Wind* was first screened privately in the 1930s. Opened in 1997, the inn has four types of accommodations. There are nine rooms in the main house; other buildings include six cottages, five remodeled farm structures and one five-bedroom house. Many rooms have fireplaces and whirlpool tubs. One room in the main house, Melrose (named for one of the original plantations on the site), has ten-foot ceilings, peach-colored walls, contrasting ceiling moldings, hardwood floors and distinctive furnishings such as a four-poster bed so high it can be entered only with the aid of a bench step. The Hibernia Cottage is a suite in the former creamery with its own garden. Amenities include on-site tennis courts and access to skeet shooting and horseback riding nearby. The resort has a fine dining room and breakfast is included. ~ 301 Showboat Lane, Thomasville; 229-226-2290, 888-920-3030, fax 229-226-4585; www.melhana.com. ULTRA-DELUXE.

You can play Southern belle (or beau) to the hilt at the **Dawson Street Bed and Breakfast.** Listed on the National Register of Historic Places for good reason, the B&B has elegant staircases, 12-foot ceilings, ten fireplaces, and formal grounds to the manor. The six rooms are fairly large and feature private baths, lots of windows and good views of either the grounds or the surrounding historic neighborhood. There's a formal living room, a dining room and a pool. Full breakfast is included. ~ 324 North Dawson Street, Thomasville; 229-226-7515, fax 229-226-7570; www. dawsonstinn.com, e-mail rdmitch@dawsonstinn.com. DELUXE TO ULTRA-DELUXE.

At the next corner, white columns announce the **Evans House Bed and Breakfast,** a yellow clapboard Victorian with a porch swing and white wicker chairs that beg you to sit for a spell. Four rooms and suites are decorated with antiques appropriate to this 1898 structure. It's close enough to downtown to walk to historic attractions, unless it's raining or very hot. If it's dry and cool, borrow one of the inn's bicycles and pedal around the park across the street. Full breakfast and brandy and sweets at bedtime are included. ~ 725 South Hansell Street, Thomasville; 229-226-1343, 800-344-4717, fax 229-226-0653. MODERATE TO DELUXE.

Wingate's Lodge bills itself as a fish camp—"not a marina, not a resort." And it means what it says. These are bare-bones accommodations meant for serious anglers, not the kind who want room service or fresh flowers by the bedside. There are two-bedroom cabins with a kitchen (bring your own kitchen utensils) in between and even cable TV. There are a couple of two-bedroom modular homes and, for groups (usually a bunch

AUTHOR FAVORITE

I was amazed to see the collection of Lalique and Waterford crystal at the **Paxton House Inn,** where each of the nine rooms boasts its own display of decorative objects, including Hummel and Russian dolls. Along with an assortment of impressive antiques and ceilings that soar to 13 feet on the ground floor and 12 upstairs, these accommodations are truly unforgettable. If you visit in spring or summer, ask for a room with a view of the neighboring rose garden. Another option is a separate two-story garden cottage. Or maybe you like the idea of staying in a pool house. Paxton House won the Georgia Trust for Historic Preservation's Outstanding Restoration Award in 1997. Full breakfast is included. ~ 445 Remington Avenue, Thomasville; 229-226-5197; www.1884paxtonhouse inn.com. ULTRA-DELUXE.

of gung ho fishermen), the Stag Lodge, which has 18 single beds. It's all quite rustic—and not rustic as in quaint, either. But you can't beat the atmosphere or the location—if you love to fish. Be sure to hunt down Jack, by the way, who knows absolutely everything about the area. ~ 139 Wingate Road, Bainbridge; 229-246-0658, fax 229-246-5518; www.wingateslodge.com. BUDGET.

When somebody in southwest Georgia asks if you're going to "Tara," they probably aren't talking about Scarlett O'Hara's fictional home. It's just the way a lot of folks pronounce **Tarrer Inn**. This small hotel in Colquitt's town square doesn't need to steal thunder from anyone. The guest rooms are charming, intensely decorated with period antiques, textured wall coverings, richly embroidered bed clothes and handpainted panels, plus either light curtains or big plantation shutters that make the cozy spaces feel larger. In all, there are 12 rooms, one suite, a veranda, a dining room and a courtyard at this former 19th-century boardinghouse. Full breakfast is included. ~ 155 South Cuthbert Street, Colquitt; 229-758-2888, 888-282-7737, fax 229-758-2825; www.tarrer inn.com, e-mail info@tarrerinn.com. MODERATE TO DELUXE.

When the **Sutlive House** was converted into a B&B inn in 1995, the owners found so much space between the floors that there was room to install sunken tubs in both suites. Hardwood floors, bookshelves and antiques make this the loveliest inn in town. The Sutlive Suite has a canopy bed, painted floors and ceiling fans. The Magnolia Suite boasts white wall-to-wall carpet and a four-poster bed. Balconies front the facade on both levels. Full breakfast is included. ~ 204 South Washington Street, Fort Gaines; 229-768-3546, fax 229-768-3204. MODERATE TO DELUXE.

The Walter F. George Lodge at George T. Bagby State Park has 60 rooms in a structure that looks a lot like a chain establishment. Located practically on the lake, the accommodations are spacious, however, with two sinks (even a hairdryer), excellent lighting and bordered wallpaper but immovable windows. If you need more space, ask for a junior suite or one of the five cottages. There's an on-site restaurant and a pool. This is the best place to stay for miles around. ~ Route 39, four miles north of Fort Gaines; 229-768-2571. BUDGET TO MODERATE.

DINING

It's not all catfish and country-fried chicken in southwest Georgia. Proximity to the Gulf of Mexico means plenty of places import shrimp and other seafood; quail is a regional delicacy and in plentiful supply. Barbecue joints are not limited to big cities; in fact, some of the best places are to be found on the back roads.

HIDDEN ►

For an evening that will leave you feeling like a beneficent Old Southerner, make reservations for dinner at the **Chapin Rooms** at Melhana Plantation. The dining room in this exquisitely restored plantation house gives privileged guests a chance to relax in gracious surroundings, perhaps after a round of cocktails in the nearby parlor. Fresh seafood such as Gulf shrimp is delivered daily, accompanied by fresh herbs picked that morning in the estate gardens. Entrées are along the lines of stuffed quail, New Zealand lamb, braised pork loin and a grilled eggplant Napoleon. The wine list is the best in southwest Georgia and not overpriced, especially the California selections. Good luck resisting desserts like creamy buttermilk pie and marble cheesecake with amaretto sauce. All this is delivered by an attentive young waitstaff that keeps tables supplied with fine crystal, china and silver. Gentlemen must wear jackets. ~ 301 Showboat Lane, Thomasville; 229-226-2290, 888-920-3030; www.melhana.com. ULTRA-DELUXE.

What may be the biggest sign in Thomasville helps to locate **George & Louie's Fresh Seafood Restaurant**. Which helps when folks are in a hurry. And if you're really in a rush, you can call in your order and pick it up at the drive-through window. Whether you eat out or inside the single-story, off-white structure that looks suspiciously like a '50s drive-in burger joint, the menu is the same: shrimp, scallop, catfish, snapper and oyster plates (which come with salad, hushpuppies and fries or cheese grits). You don't come across fresh homemade deviled crab very often in southwest Georgia; this may be your only chance to try it. You can also get boiled seafoods, salads, chicken and seafood shish kebab as well as sandwiches, burgers and eight side dishes, including fried green tomatoes. Closed Sunday. ~ 216 Remington Avenue, Thomasville; 229-226-1218. BUDGET TO MODERATE.

At the **Neel House Restaurant** you'll find fairly sophisticated, upscale dining in an elegant setting. The 1907 building was badly damaged by fire in the '70s but has been renovated to its original neoclassical splendor. Stuffed pheasant, rack of lamb and filet

AUTHOR FAVORITE

I like the homey hustle and bustle of the **Market Diner**, a busy restaurant in the State Farmer's Market complex. Flanked by plain wood walls, a buffet table full of country-style fixin's sits in the middle of the room, under constant attack by hungry diners. You can also order seafood platters, quail and a choice of vegetables from butter beans to turnip greens as well as sweet potato soufflé. Chicken gizzards are the house specialty, which says a lot. Don't miss the homemade desserts. The nicest place to sit is in the brick-floored side room. Although the market is usually closed on Sunday, the diner is one of the few places in town that's open to the public every day of the week. ~ 502 Smith Avenue, Thomasville; 229-225-1777. BUDGET TO MODERATE.

mignon are among the offerings, along with a modest but satisfactory wine list. The less chi-chi bistro, located with the bar in the basement, features heartier entrées like fish and chips, quesadillas and pork chops. ~ 502 South Broad Street, Thomasville; 229-227-6300. MODERATE TO ULTRA-DELUXE.

The **Marketplace Café** is ideal for the shop-'til-you-droppers. You can peruse the 90-plus antique dealers at the Toscoga Marketplace until you get peckish, and then pick up a decent sandwich at the café. The place also offers dinner, if you're willing to eat before 6 p.m. ~ 209 South Broad Street, Thomasville; 229-227-6777, 888-949-2818. BUDGET.

Stuck behind a nondescript glass storefront in the heart of decidedly non-Latino downtown, **Old Mexico** may not look too authentic. However, when your thoughts turn away from gravy and toward taco sauce, this is the best game in town. A good choice of appetizers and à la carte items add up to a very inexpensive meal, or you can spend a few dollars more for a full dinner. Top of the line are the "super especialidades" such as pork chops, shrimp, chicken and T-bone, or green or chicken enchiladas. Don't even think of asking for substitutions. Closed Sunday. ~ 116 North Broad Street, Thomasville; 229-228-6767. BUDGET.

In all likelihood, some people in Bainbridge go to the early church service on Sunday morning just so they can beat the crowd to the **Decatur House**. It looks like a thousand other roadside restaurants and banks in the South—red brick with white columns even though it doesn't have a second story—but was a hit from day one. At lunch, you go through the buffet line; at dinner, it's à la carte. Expect to find many of the same classic Southern dishes at both meals. ~ 1697 Tallahassee Highway, Bainbridge; 229-243-8811. MODERATE.

HIDDEN ▶ The Wingate family has been serving food to guests since 1952, starting with a barbecue stand at a country store during the Truman administration. Today, the menu at **Wingate's Lodge and Restaurant** has expanded considerably. The specialty is barbecue but you can also get catfish and shrimp. The house salad dressing is a specialty and, as always, the restaurant will cook up any fish you catch and clean. This place is way beyond casual, with angling and other historical memorabilia cluttering every wall, and when they ran out of wall they started hanging stuff from the rafters. There's not a more laidback joint in the whole of south Georgia. No lunch on Sunday; no dinner Monday or Tuesday. ~ 139 Wingate Road, Bainbridge; 229-246-0658; www.wingate slodge.com. BUDGET TO MODERATE.

The **Tarrer Inn** was built in 1861 as a residence. In 1905 it became the Hunter House, where travelers could dine and spend the night. Now restored and listed on the National Register of Historic Places, the inn is open a few days a week for buffet lunch and/

or dinner. The menu is classically Southern—fried chicken and pecan pie, for instance—and the famed local fruit, mayhaw, is incorporated into several dishes. The three dining rooms are decorated somewhat differently, but all have patterned rugs and an unobtrusive ambience. No dinner Sunday or Wednesday. Closed Monday and Tuesday. ~ 155 South Cuthbert Street, Colquitt; 229-758-2888; www.tarrerinn.com. BUDGET TO MODERATE.

Helen's Pirate's Cove looks more like a residential care facility than a restaurant. A walkway leads from the parking lot across a creek to the one-story brick building. The interior is equally plain, with ceiling fans and some big photographs of Colquitt, including the old courthouse, now long gone. The menu lists catfish, mullet, shrimp, oysters and over 20 types of sandwiches and burgers; there's a buffet lunch. Closed Sunday. ~ 411 East Bush Street, Colquitt; 229-758-5058. BUDGET TO MODERATE.

The Pilothouse Restaurant at George T. Bagby State Park has a pretty view and a decent menu, with quality plastic tablecloths, artificial flowers and huge windows on two sides. Good buys include sautéed shrimp, grilled steak, kebabs and fried catfish. It's probably not the best spot if you're looking for something ultra-spicy, but they do offer barbecued beef. You can also pig out at the salad bar. No dinner on Sunday. ~ Four miles north of Fort Gaines on Route 39; 229-768-2571. BUDGET.

As in most of Georgia, antiques and collectibles provide retail high points.

SHOPPING

Broad Street is the retail mecca in Thomasville. A fine antique store, C. H. Whitney stocks century-old china platters and 18th- and 19th-century furniture. Closed Sunday and Monday and mornings. ~ 118 Remington Avenue, Thomasville; 229-227-1005.

For offbeat treasures to give or to keep, check out the merchandise at Firefly, where Russian rugs and lamps made out of unusual materials (say, an old toaster) make for a fun excursion. Closed Sunday. ~ 125 South Broad Street, Thomasville; 229-226-6363.

FARM-FRESH FUN

Even if you're not planning to cook dinner, you might want to peruse the produce at the **State Farmer's Market**. The second-largest such market in the southeastern U.S. (only Atlanta's is bigger), it is the place for the best and freshest of regional produce such as the sweet-as-apples Vidalia onions. You're also likely to find jars of mayhaw jelly, a specialty concocted from berries that grow on trees deep in the swamps. Closed Sunday. ~ 502 Smith Avenue, Thomasville; 229-225-4072.

Sirens carries vintage vinyl, CDs and cassettes, as well as an array of merchandise ranging from Japanese lanterns to jewelry. Closed Sunday. ~ 123 South Broad Street, Thomasville; 229-226-1081.

One of Georgia's better small bookstores, the **Bookshelf** has a great selection of regional tomes. Closed Sunday. ~ 108 East Jackson Street, Thomasville; 229-228-7767.

For its size, Bainbridge has an impressive number of antique emporiums, but bear in mind several are closed on Sunday. The prettiest is **Sharon House Antiques and Interiors**, known for fine furnishings and interior decorating items. Closed Sunday and Monday. ~ 113 East Water Street, Bainbridge; 229-246-8999.

You can also try **Country Treasures** (1314 Dothan Road; 229-246-5955) and **Jewels & Junk Antiques** (1204 Dothan Road; 229-246-2518).

There are some little shops clustered around Willis Park in the historic district. They're ideal for just poking around, looking through odd and unusual collectibles and consignment items augmented by estate-sale merchandise. ~ Bainbridge.

NIGHTLIFE   The residents of the small towns that comprise this section have early bedtimes or, at the most, visit with neighbors or head to the corner saloon come nightfall. It is close enough to Columbus and Atlanta to make the jaunt to either an easy one-hour drive each way.

The **Bainbridge Little Theater** puts on a number of musicals and dramas throughout the year. ~ P.O. Box 1245, Bainbridge, GA 31717; 229-246-8345; www.bainbridgelittletheater.com.

In the spring and fall, the town of Colquitt is the site of the wonderful musical comedy *Swamp Gravy*, based on family stories, folklore and tall tales of southwest Georgia. Performances are held in Cotton Hall, a renovated cotton warehouse. ~ P.O. Box 567, Colquitt, GA 39837; 229-758-5450; www.swampgravy.com.

PARKS   **CHENEY GRIFFIN PARK** 🚣 🚤 ⛵ Located right on the Flint River, this city park has scenic picnic areas and four tennis courts lit for night play, as well as a playground. Also here is Flint River Seafood (closed Sunday; 220 North Bruton Street; 229-246-3362), known for the best hamburgers in town. ~ Located near the intersection of Bruton, Broughton and Water streets, Bainbridge; 229-248-2010.

EARLE MAY BOAT BASIN 🏃 🚣 🚤 ⛵ Located on U.S. Army Corps of Engineers land, this 600-acre marina/park has something for almost everyone who likes the outdoors. There are four fields for baseball and softball, a football field, volleyball courts, a large playground area, docks, a fish pond and even a beach area on the Flint River. Nearby are parts of an old saw mill.

People love to pick up some day-old bread and feed the collection of emus, mules and goats through the fence. A narrow boardwalk runs half a mile down to the river. ~ Off West Shotwell Street at Route 27/84 Bypass; Bainbridge; 229-246-4774.

SEMINOLE STATE PARK 🚤 ⚓ Hunkered around the shore of Lake Seminole, the fifth-largest bass-fishing lake in the country, this 604-acre park has lots to offer the active family. The gopher tortoise, the only tortoise native to Georgia, makes itself at home in the wiregrass community habitat along the two-and-a-quarter-mile nature trail. Catfish, bream and crappie also inhabit the lake. Nature programs are offered in the summer; boat, canoe and bike rentals are available. There's even a miniature golf course. Day-use fee, $2. ~ 7870 State Park Drive off Route 39, 16 miles south of Donalsonville; 229-861-3137.

> At Earle May Boat Basin, you can view the No. 2132 Locomotive, a steam locomotive known as "Old Reliable" that was built in the early 1920s in Louisville, Kentucky, for the L&N Railroad (Louisville and Nashville) and was then retired in 1950.

▲ There are 50 tent/RV trailer sites; $17 to $21 per night. Fourteen cottages—one of them handicapped accessible—augment plentiful camping facilities; $85 to $100 per night. Reservations: 800-864-7275.

KOLOMOKI MOUNDS STATE HISTORIC PARK 🚶 ⚓ 🚤 ⚓ ◀ *HIDDEN*

Named for the seven ancient American Indian mounds on the premises—the subject of the interpretive museum (admission; see "Sights" above) on the grounds—this 1293-acre park might well be spooky at night. Within its boundaries are miles of hiking and nature trails; of course, the mounds lend to the atmosphere (the only way to see the inside of one is to gain admission to the museum during operating hours). Lakes Yahola and Kolomoki are open year-round for fishing; you can buy a license at the park office. There's also a miniature golf course in the park. Day-use fee, $2. ~ 205 Indian Mound Road off Route 27, six miles north of Blakely; 229-724-2150.

▲ There are 43 tent/RV sites; $17 to $19 per night. Reservations: 800-864-7275.

GEORGE T. BAGBY STATE PARK 🚶 ⚓ ⛵ ⚓ 🚤 ⚓ Situated at the southern end of the 48,000-acre Lake Walter F. George, this 700-acre park affords more of a wilderness experience than many parks, yet it has oodles of amenities. There are five moderate-priced cottages to rent, a 60-room lodge and a full-service restaurant (see "Lodging" and "Dining"). Ideal for birdwatching, the park is best known for fishing, particularly catfish, all kinds of bass and bream. Day-use fee, $2. ~ Off Route 39, three and a half miles north of Fort Gaines; 229-768-2571, 800-864-7275 (cottage reservations).

Albany to Columbus

It's a short drive from Fort Gaines up to the charming village of Lumpkin. Down the road is the up-and-coming hamlet of Parrott, where the locals are hard at work restoring what looks remarkably like a Wild West town.

After Parrott, Albany seems like a major metropolitan area. It is about a 16-mile drive from the little town to the big city via Route 520, which hooks up with Route 82 just south of Dawson. This section of Georgia includes part of what the state tourism people call Presidential Pathways, thanks to the presence of Plains (Jimmy Carter Country) and Warm Springs (where President Franklin D. Roosevelt built his winter retreat).

SIGHTS

From George T. Bagby State Park, continue north on Route 39 to Florence, which is about 35 miles north of Fort Gaines. Turn east onto Route 39 for roughly ten miles to visit **Providence Canyon State Park**, a spectacular 1003-acre parcel that is about halfway between Florence and Lumpkin. Known as Georgia's "Little Grand Canyon," this magical place was named for the 1832 Providence Methodist Church, an original log structure moved here in 1839. To learn how these 150-foot-wide gorges, clad in what looks like white powder, evolved over the past eight million years, stop first at the excellent visitors center and watch a 13-minute video explaining the formation of the surrounding scenery. According to the show, the Indian myths are almost as plausible as the geologic facts. The deep cuts were formed by water, true, but don't look around for any great river. Instead, the erosion was—and still is—caused by rainfall. Against the backdrop of so much white, the canyon's profusion of trees and wildflowers is especially stunning in the spring and fall. Some ten miles of hiking trails lead to breathtaking panoramas and a pioneer campsite. The tougher trails don't look hard going down, but only experienced hikers should travel far on them because getting back up is quite a challenge. Parking fee (except on Wednesday). ~ Route 39, seven miles west of Lumpkin; 229-838-6202, 800-864-7275.

Returning to Route 39 from the park, continue eastward to **Lumpkin**. When you reach the intersection of Route 39 and Route 27, you can probably find a parking place right in front of the **Bedingfield Inn Museum**. Built in 1836 by Dr. Bryan Bedingfield, the structure was both a family residence and a stop for stagecoach and other travelers. It has been fully restored; the rooms were painted in colors as close as possible to the original bright hues favored by this prosperous family. The Public Room, to the right as you enter, was a gathering place for the men to swap political views, share crop information and have a drink or a smoke. Other ground-floor rooms were normally reserved for the family but occasionally used for dining or as parlors for visitors. These and the upstairs family rooms have been furnished with period pieces, some made by local cabinet workers, intended to reflect the lifestyle of a well-heeled family in the mid-1800s. Closed Monday. Admission. ~ Route 27, Lumpkin; 229-838-6419; www. bedingfieldinn.org.

From this corner of the Square, you can walk to sights. To your right as you walk or drive from the Bedingfield Inn are two old stores worth a peek. **The Singer Company**, Georgia's oldest hardware store, has recently closed for business, after operating on this very corner since 1838. Established by Johann George Singer, a German immigrant, it was run by his great-great grandson. ~ On the Square, 201 Main Street, Lumpkin.

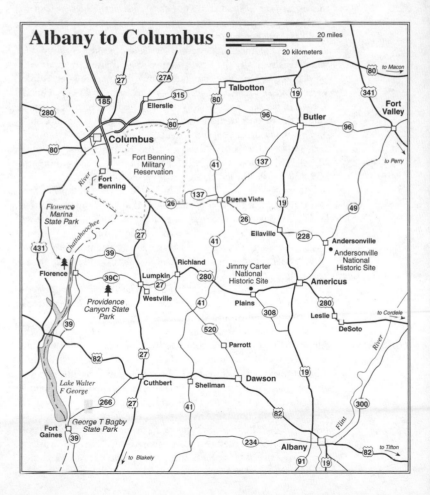

A couple of doors down, **Dr. Hatchett's Drug Store Museum** is housed in an early-1900s building. Patent medicines, medical equipment and classic old-time drugstore items are displayed much as they were 100 years ago. Closed Sunday and Monday. ~ On the Square, Lumpkin; 229-838-6419.

As you drive around this town, which was named for Wilson Lumpkin, governor of the state during the four years following Lumpkin's incorporation in 1830, you will see signs for the **Stage Coach Trail**. If you want to drive past a couple of dozen ante-bellum homes, just follow the signs.

HIDDEN ►

When you leave the town square, continue east half a mile until you see, on the right, signs for **Westville**. In this sprawling living-history village, they like to say, "It's always 1850." It's neither as large as Williamsburg nor as complete; the idea is to show a town as it would be evolving in the mid-19th century. That's why you'll see residences (from farmhouses to elegant homes complete with stately columns) and essential service shops like a blacksmith's, which was typically the first structure to go up in a town, as well as a church, a school and a cotton gin, which came later. Adults seem to like this reality-based fantasyland as much as kids. Guides dressed in period costumes are on hand to explain historical details while craftspeople demonstrate the art of shoemaking or candle dipping. Closed Sunday and Monday, the first week of January, and Sunday through Wednesday from mid-December to mid-March. Admission. ~ Martin Luther King Jr. Drive, Lumpkin; 229-838-6310, 888-733-1850; www.westville.org.

Return to Route 27/1 and continue east to Richland, where you will see the sign to Route 520. This is a fairly major road that leads all the way to Albany. En route, you will pass by a town with the wondrous name of **Parrott**. A one-street burg with the flavor of a frontier town, it has been gaining attention as old and new residents alike dust off and rehabilitate old buildings to house shops and cafés.

Enter Albany on Route 82 and stay on it as it veers directly south. In about 18 blocks, turn right onto Route 234. In a couple of miles turn right onto Meadowlark Drive.

HIDDEN ►

There's just one word for the collection of African art at the **Albany Museum of Art**: stunning. Recognized as one of the best of its kind in the southeastern U.S., the permanent collection is mined for various exhibits throughout the year. In addition to fine arts such as sculpture, displays include textiles, jewelry, religious implements such as crucifixion and fertility figures, ceremonial knives, masks and musical instruments. The spacious museum also houses its own holding of 19th- and 20th-century American and European art, but they pale in comparison. Lectures on various topics are offered by docents and other specialists; most are open to the public and are usually free of charge. Closed Sunday and

Monday. Admission. ~ 311 Meadowlark Drive, Albany; 229-439-8400; www.albanymuseum.com.

After viewing the museum's works, return to Route 234 and Route 82S; Route 82 will turn eastward in a few blocks; after eight long blocks, turn left on Route 91 for about four blocks, then right on Roosevelt Avenue, which comes to an end near the river. There is a parking lot here near the old railroad tracks.

Located in a 1913 Union Station depot, the **Thronateeska Heritage Museum** features both permanent and changing historical exhibits ranging from Indian artifacts to antique automobiles and carriages, with an emphasis on regional developments. The **Wetherbee Planetarium** is also part of this complex; it presents four to five shows annually. Closed Sunday through Wednesday. ~ 100 West Roosevelt Avenue, Albany; 229-432-6955; www.heritage center.org, e-mail info@heritagecenter.org.

> Parrott's Wild West look is so impressive that the town was used as the film set for the movie *The Long Riders.*

Nearby, the **Flood of 1994 Memorial** honors the volunteers who contributed time and effort to rebuild Albany after the Flint River leapt its banks and caused extensive damage. Close by is the **Vietnam Memorial**, which lists the names of 42 men from Lee and Dougherty counties who lost their lives during the war in Southeast Asia. The memorial is fashioned from a 12-ton block of Georgia marble. ~ Front and Oglethorpe streets, Albany.

For a peaceful interlude and a break from driving in traffic, head west on West Broad Street for four or five short blocks, turn right (north) on Martin Luther King Boulevard and continue roughly three miles to Route 19, where you will see signs to **The Parks at Chehaw**. Secluded among the Georgia pines, Chehaw Wild Animal Park was laid out by noted naturalist Jim Fowler (of *Wild Kingdom* fame); its 293 acres were set aside within the 779-acre tract to simulate as realistically as possible the habitats of cheetahs, bobcats, bison, elk, elephants and colobus monkeys. You can even get out of the automobile and board the Wiregrass Express for a 20-minute train ride through the park; tickets are sold at the zoo ticket booth. Or you can hike on six miles of trails that trace Muckalee Creek, bike or fish, or picnic in the Play Park. Admission. ~ 105 Chehaw Park Road, Route 91; 229-430-5275; www. parksatchehaw.org.

When you leave the park, turn right onto Route 19 and continue for 20 miles, then turn off to the northwest on Route 308. In another 11 miles, you will arrive in what used to be the unremarkable town of **Plains** (population about 716). This humble place is where James Earl Carter, the 39th U.S. presidency, was born. But what really changed things was the day he announced his candidacy for the presidency at the train depot in the heart of town. Mr. Carter and his wife Rosalynn are still active in the local church and visitors may spot them walking or biking around town.

In 1998, the National Park Service consolidated a great deal of Carter memorabilia and housed it in the old Plains High School, which educated Carter, his wife and their three sons. This modest building is now the **Jimmy Carter National Historic Site**. The story of the town's beloved and still-successful native son is told in photographs, documents and other displays in various former classrooms. They cover his rural childhood and his role in both national and international politics. There is an extensive bookstore in the lobby of the building. This is also the place to find out Mr. Carter's schedule for teaching Sunday school at Maranatha Baptist Church in town. ~ 300 North Bond Street, Plains; 229-824-4104; www.nps.gov/jica.

About a half mile from the Depot, you can pose for a photo with the 13-foot-tall Smiling Peanut, fashioned from wooden hoops, chicken wire, aluminum foil and polyurethane. ~ Route 45N, Plains.

The National Park Service also operates the **Jimmy Carter Boyhood Farm**, which is located on the Old Plains Highway two and a half miles from the center of town (the intersection of Route 280 and Route 45). You may even run into Jimmy himself: when he has visitors in town, he'll sometimes give them a personal tour. Otherwise, you're on your own with a self-guided tour of the property. ~ 229-824-4104.

Another site, right downtown on Main Street, is the historic **Depot** where Carter announced his candidacy in 1976. The oldest structure in Plains, it houses a collection of campaign buttons and other political memorabilia. Across Main Street from the Depot is the defunct filling station that belonged to Carter's late brother, Billy.

You can find a map of the area, as well as lodging suggestions and other advice, at the **Plains Visitor Information Center**. ~ 1763 Route 280, Plains; 229-824-7477; www.plainsgeorgia.com, e-mail plains@georgia.org.

From Plains, head east on Route 280 for eight miles to the city of **Americus**. As you enter the downtown area on Lamar Street, you will see the offices of **Habitat for Humanity International** on your right. This is the place to sign up for extended tours of the International Village, where you can see examples of housing from all over the world and an excursion to various local sites where the organization, of which Jimmy Carter is the most famous member, has constructed housing for the poor. Call in advance to sign up for regularly scheduled tours. Closed Saturday and Sunday. ~ 121 Habitat Street, Americus; 229-924-6935; www.habitat.org, e-mail publicinfo@hfhi.org.

A couple of blocks farther on Lamar Street, look for the castle-like facade of the **Windsor Hotel**, which will be on your left. It's easy to find if you keep your eye out for the tell-tale turret. This hotel was built in 1892 and was restored and reopened in 1991. Guest rooms occupy the tower, but you can tour the lobby or enjoy lunch or a drink on the second-floor porch. ~ 125 West Lamar Street, Americus; 229-924-1555, 888-297-9567; www. windsor-americus.com, e-mail windsor@sowega.net.

A side trip down Route 280 leads to a couple of unusual points of interest. In about ten miles, you'll come to the town of **Leslie**. Once you see the **Georgia Rural Telephone Museum**, chances are, cell phones will never look the same. The museum is housed in a 1911 cotton warehouse large enough to hold some 2000 pieces of telephone memorabilia, including those hand-cranked wooden voice boxes people used to wind up before asking the town operator to hook them up to someone else's house. There's a lot more here than old phones, such as a model of Alexander Graham Bell's workshop. Closed Saturday and Sunday. ~ 135 North Barley Avenue (Route 280W), Leslie; 229-874-4786; www.grtm.org.

Back on Route 49, continue until you see the exit for Andersonville. On the west side of the highway is the **Andersonville Civil War Village**, which is mostly a collection of shops and restaurants. In the village is the **Drummer Boy Museum** (open by appointment only; admission), inspired by two young drummer boys—one Union, one Confederate. Although the collection is packed into a small former store, it's considered one of the finest Civil War museums anywhere and tells the personal stories of the two boys. There's an excellent selection of photographs taken by Mathew Brady at the nearby prison camp, as well as other memorabilia such as an eight-by-ten-foot diorama of the Andersonville Prison Camp and the town (117 Church Street). Nearby is the **Wirz Monument**, named for the Commander of Andersonville Prison, Captain Henry Wirz, who was charged with the famously inhumane treatment of prisoners there and sentenced to death by hanging. (There are pictures of his execution on view at the Drummer Boy Museum.) ~ Route 49, Andersonville; 229-924-2558; www.andersonvillegeorgia.com.

On the other side of the highway, you will find signs indicating the **Andersonville National Historic Site and Cemetery**. Camp Sumter, as it was known officially, was built to house up to 10,000 prisoners during the Civil War. But the prison population swelled to some 32,000 at one time, creating disastrous conditions that killed an estimated 13,000 Union soldiers. Malnutrition, disease and starvation almost killed the rest, wasting away many of the soldiers to the point it was said that you would have to line up seven soldiers to create a shadow. Most of the prisoners who were incarcerated in September 1864 were moved out to coastal camps when General William T. Sherman occupied Atlanta. Clara Barton arrived after the war to find out what happened to the many missing Union soldiers. She located and marked all the graves of most of the dead, but nearly 500 remained unaccounted for. Eventually the cemetery became a memorial park and then, in 1970, a National Historic Site. ~ 496 Cemetery Road, Andersonville; 229-924-0343; www.nps.gov/ande.

A separate entrance just up Route 49 leads to the **National Prisoner of War Museum**, a 10,000-square-foot structure that honors the 800,000 Americans captured during armed conflicts, from the Revolutionary War to the Persian Gulf War. As soon as visitors step inside the first exhibit room, which is darkened, they hear the sound of footsteps going faster and faster. Then a searchlight comes on and they hear a voice shout, "Halt!" It's very unsettling, as it is meant to be. The National Park Service and untold numbers of workers, soldiers, survivors and their families contributed time, effort and mementos such as personal letters to create a museum they hope will do justice to the brave men and women who suffered for their country. From this, the Capture exhibit, the tour leads through Journey to Camp, Living Conditions, News and Communications, Privation, Morale and Relationships, and Escape and Freedom. Along the way, you'll find interactive displays and short video clips of former POWs relating their harrowing experiences (including one by Arizona Senator John McCain, who spent five years as a POW in Vietnam). Visitors may also sit inside a cell and try on the leg shackles used in one camp, and view the terrifying bamboo cages used by the North Vietnamese to restrain Americans captured in that country. In all, the POW museum houses over 430 photographs and graphics, plus several videos and another 200 artifacts. The commemorative courtyard out back leads to the Andersonville Prison site, which includes carefully reconstructed portions of the Civil War prison wall and gate. ~ 496 Cemetery Road, 13 miles north of Americus and half a mile north of the town of Andersonville; 229-924-0343; www.nps.gov/ande.

From Andersonville, the trip to **Buena Vista** is all back roads and will take as long as you want it to, somewhere between 30 and 45 minutes. The simplest option is to take Route 228 westward toward Columbus. Near Ellaville, jog right on Route 3 and then west on Route 26, which takes you into the town of Buena Vista. Find Route 41 and go north almost a mile, turning left on Route 137 and right onto Route 78. Continue for another half-mile to reach a real work of art.

HIDDEN ▶   **Pasaquan** is the mind-boggling legacy of one Eddie Owens Martin, a sixth-grade drop-out who ran away from his home in Buena Vista at the age of 14. The story is a bit murky—the way Martin would have wanted it—but through his adventures in New York, including a near-fatal period of illness and prison time on narcotics charges, he was reborn as Saint EOM. When he inherited his family's sharecropper farm in 1957, Martin returned to west Georgia and spent the rest of his life as an artist, painting mandalas, fashioning colorful sculpture and creating other artworks inspired by the visions in his head. Pasaquan, to Saint EOM, meant "where the past meets the future." Here in his own five-acre world, he felt as if he were living in a temple of his own design. Virtually every inch of several buildings are painted or encrusted with shapes borrowed from African, American Indian and Asian mythologies. Martin slept little, which explains the stupefying amount of work he produced here, which is a little bit like a Maya ruin, a little bit circus, and all wild. An author named Tom Patterson wrote a well-illustrated book, published by the Jargon Society, called *St. EOM in the Land of Pasaquan*, in which you can learn just about all there is to know about this remarkable artist who died in 1986. Tours available by appointment only. Admission. ~ Pasaquan Preservation Society, Eddie Martin Road, Buena Vista; 229-649-9444; www.pasaquan.com.

After touring Pasaquan, return to downtown Buena Vista. From here, Route 26 continues west to its intersection with Route 27/280, a combined highway that leads to Columbus. Just before you reach the city, you will see exit signs for the **Fort Benning Military Reservation**. Off the freeway, more signs will lead you to the **National Infantry Museum**. This imaginative, 30,000-square-foot museum has three floors of materials telling the story of the American foot soldier, with sections on particular wars, and the evolution of uniforms and weaponry such as the Flintlock musket. One especially good exhibit explains what music has meant to soldiers. Then there are little gems, such as Ulysses S. Grant's liquor cabinet, stocked with fancy little bottles of gin, whiskey and sherry. Since Fort Benning is the largest infantry training school in the world, there's more stashed away behind the scenes than could ever be displayed here at one time. ~ Baltzell Avenue, Fort Benning; 706-545-2958; www.benning mwr.com.

◀ HIDDEN

From Fort Benning, continue north on Route 27/280 for about ten minutes, roughly paralleling the Chattahoochee River, which serves as the state line with Alabama. Stay on Route 27

MILE HIGH

From Americus, taking Route 49 north toward Andersonville will lead past Souther Airfield. The **Lindbergh Memorial** here honors the 1923 visit of pilot Charles Lindbergh. He came here to buy and test the single-engine plane, *Jenny*, four years prior to his legendary solo flight across the Atlantic Ocean. ~ Route 49.

until you reach the Civic Center in the South Commons; turn left into the parking lot.

Entering Columbus proper via Victory Drive (Route 27), you'll find more military history. An 87-foot reconstruction of the iron-clad CSS *Albemarle* is the most expensive exhibit at the **Port Columbus National Civil War Naval Museum**, which opened in 2001. That's partly because, inside, visitors are treated to an audio-visual re-creation of the surprise Union attack in November 1864. But the most prized relic is probably a flag (a huge banner with a design based on the Confederate flag) that was purloined after the war and kept hidden for some 138 years in a cedar chest in Ohio. There's much more to see at the $8 million, 40,000-square-foot museum, which now claims the CSS *Jackson*, the CSS *Chatta-hoochee* and other artifacts that had been housed at the nearby James Woodruff Confederate Naval Museum, which didn't really have the space to do the ironclads justice. Guided tours available. Admission. ~ 1002 Victory Drive, Columbus; 706-327-9798; www.portcolumbus.org, e-mail cwnavy@portcolumbus.org.

> The list of illustrious soldiers who went through Fort Benning is long and includes Omar Bradley, Dwight D. Eisenhower and George C. Marshall.

From the naval museum, continue north on Route 27 to 7th Street; turn left and continue across 1st Avenue. Six historic homes are clustered near this intersection and are open only on Heritage Corner Tours, but anyone is welcome to drive by. One, the **Pemberton House**, is particularly interesting in terms of Georgia's Number One icon. Tall tales and conflicting claims abound regarding the origins of Coca-Cola, but there's no argument that it was Dr. John Pemberton who concocted the winning formula. His first home in Columbus, where he lived from 1855 to 1860, was relocated from another part of town and restored in the 1970s by the Coca-Cola Foundation. Ninety percent of the furniture inside is original and, because the good doctor's sisters-in-law saved like a packrat, the place (including a faux pharmacy out back) is filled with family mementos. It might be a fancier house had Pemberton not sold the formula for his "French wine of cocoa" for $1700 to Asa Candler. In 1902, Candler changed the name to Coca-Cola, started bottling it mixed with well water (later, soda water was substituted), took out the cocaine, and sold the formula to the Woodruffs 15 years later for $25 million. ~ 11 West 7th Street, Columbus. (To make an appointment, call the Historic Columbus Foundation. ~ 706-322-0756.)

Though geared mostly toward schoolchildren, the **Coca-Cola Space Science Center** has interesting lobby displays that should keep grown-ups from fidgeting. Affiliated with Columbus State University, the center displays moon rocks and offers a chance to sit in a replica of the Apollo 13 capsule (which may give you a bit of claustrophobia and renewed respect for actor Tom Hanks, whose movie *Apollo 13* showed us NASA behind the scenes). There's also a planetarium with regular shows and weekend laser concerts. Closed Monday. Admission. ~ 701 Front Avenue, Columbus; 706-649-1470; www.ccssc.org, e-mail info@ccssc.org.

From the center, head to 10th Street and turn left. In one block on your right will be the **Columbus Convention and Visitors Bureau.** Here you can pick up enough pamphlets and brochures to fill the back seat of your car, or simply watch a 12-minute video introduction to the city. Closed Sunday. ~ 900 Front Avenue, Columbus; 706-322-1613, 800-999-1613, fax 706-322-0701; www. visitcolumbusga.com.

The nearby **Columbus Riverwalk**, a gracefully landscaped promenade featuring red brick and ironwork, ambles along beside the Chattahoochee River for some 15 miles.

If the Columbus Riverwalk doesn't satisfy your yen for a waterborne adventure, sign on for a sightseeing or dinner cruise aboard the **Chattahoochee Princess Riverboat**. This authentic 1880s riverboat offers outings on the weekends and at other times by special arrangement. At press time the *Princess* was not operating due to a problem with the dock; make sure to call ahead. Admission. ~ Columbus Riverwalk; 706-322-5331.

After leaving the visitors bureau, head south on Bay Avenue and go left on 9th Street, continuing to 1st Avenue. The **Springer Opera House**, the official State Theater of Georgia, was restored in 1998 to its original red-and-gold glory. John Philip Sousa, Will Rogers, Irving Berlin, Oscar Wilde and Edwin Booth all made appearances in this historic edifice. In addition to regular performances, backstage tours (admission) are offered. Closed Saturday through Monday. ~ 103 10th Street, Columbus; 706-327-3688, 888-332-5200, fax 706-324-4461; www.springeroperahouse.org, e-mail info@springeroperahouse.org.

For a more in-depth look at regional history, leave the opera house and continue east on 9th Street to 10th Avenue; turn left for two blocks and turn right on Wynnton Road. In about a quarter-mile, prepare to turn left into a major driveway. Begin your visit to the **Columbus Museum** by viewing an 18-minute film tracing the history of the Chattahoochee Valley. Shown every two hours, it's a rudimentary introduction to the people, the land, the river and the culture, from major industries right down to local barbecue techniques. In the same building, the Chattahoochee Legacy gallery has full-scale replicas of period dwellings and one of an old schoolroom, exhibits from Rood Creek Indian mounds down near Florence, and old photos, such as one from the turn of the 20th century showing "dinner toters," children who ran lunches to their parents working in the mills. A children's discovery museum, American art and furniture, and changing exhibits fill out the three-story contemporary museum. Closed

Monday. ~ 1251 Wynnton Road, Columbus; 706-649-0713, fax 706-649-1070; www.columbusmuseum.com, e-mail information@ columbusmuseum.com.

HIDDEN ►   **Oxbow Meadows** is a nature discovery center on 1600 acres of hardwood wetland habitat on the east side of Columbus. Focusing on the natural and cultural history of the region, this hands-on interpretive facility has a small live animal collection of regional reptiles, insects, amphibians and fish. There are also mounted mammals, birds and reptiles. For a closer look, you can follow walking trails that lead away from the center. Closed Sunday morning and Monday. ~ 3535 South Lumpkin Road, Columbus; 706-687-4090; oxbow.colstate.edu.

LODGING   A good location for a motel doesn't necessarily mean proximity to attractions; access to thoroughfares, shopping centers and chain restaurants can also be important. That's one of the good things about the **Holiday Inn** near the Albany Mall and Liberty Parkway (Route 19). These are A-plus motel accommodations, typically with complementary white-on-green patterns in the carpeting and upholstered furniture. The two stories encircle a courtyard pool and hot tub. ~ 2701 Dawson Road, Albany; 229-883-8100, fax 229-883-5669. MODERATE.

HIDDEN ►   Known chiefly as a destination for sport hunters, **Wynfield Plantation** is also open during the off-season (April through September) for guests who couldn't shoot a quail even if they wanted to. Luxurious accommodations are in two-bedroom cabins set in the quiet of the deep pine woods a few miles west of Albany. Each cabin has a living room and a front porch set with chairs. The lodge is open for meals during the hunting season, but in the off-season, only a breakfast basket is available. ~ Route 82, Albany; mailing address: P.O. Box 71686, Albany, GA 31708; 229-889-0193; www.wynfieldplantation.com, e-mail experiences@ wynfieldplantation.com. MODERATE TO DELUXE.

A pretty brick house across from the Depot and practically next door to what used to be Billy Carter's gas station, the **Plains Bed & Breakfast Inn** is centrally located for touring the town. Ceiling fans and beadboard ceilings give these four rooms and suites a comfortable feel. But what's remarkable is that this is where Miss Lillian, former President Jimmy Carter's mother, used to live. The innkeeper may regale you with tidbits (such as that the town was originally known as The Plains of Dura before it was shortened, or the fact that Carter was the first president to be born in a hospital), so if you don't like Carter-abilia, stay somewhere else. Full breakfast is included. ~ 100 West Church Street, Plains; 229-824-7252. MODERATE.

The **Plains Historic Inn** is also full of Carter-abilia, but with a twist: each room is decorated from a different decade, beginning in the 1920s and ending in that tasteful decade of the '80s. (The 1970s room, of course, is the "Presidential Suite.") The Carters were actually involved in the development of the inn: Mrs. Carter shopped for many of the rooms' period pieces and the former president himself refinished the staircase steps. The place also has a 25-dealer antique mall downstairs for easy-access shopping. ~ 106 Main Street, Plains; 229-824-4517. MODERATE TO DELUXE.

When you walk into the **Windsor Hotel**, your first thought may be that its best days are behind it. You may be right. Still, the clean, sizable guest rooms and nice reproduction furniture, plus its downtown location two blocks from the headquarters of Habitat for Humanity International, make it worth a second look. In addition, there's a spa. The restaurant is beautiful but not recommended except for light meals or drinks, which guests may take out onto the porch. ~ 125 West Lamar Street, Americus; 229-924-1555, 888-297-9567; www.windsor-americus.com, e-mail windsor@sowega.net. DELUXE.

A few blocks west of downtown Americus, **The 1906 Pathway Inn** provides the poshest accommodations in town. Five guest rooms on the first and second floors of this 1906 mansion are luxuriously furnished in high-end antiques, and all bear the names of famous people like Lindbergh and Roosevelt. The inn boasts a "withdrawing" room, where guests may relax, as opposed to the more formal dining room. Full breakfast is included. ~ 501 South Lee Street, Americus; 229-928-2078, 800-889-1466; www.1906pathwayinn.com, e-mail info@1906pathwayinn.com. MODERATE TO DELUXE.

The **Americus Garden Inn** occupies an 1848 mansion less than a mile from downtown. Trimmed with a white balcony on the ground floor and gingerbread woodwork on the second, the inn

AUTHOR FAVORITE

I felt right at home in the Painter's Cottage at the **1870 Rothschild-Pound House** because it combined privacy with the convenience of the main house right next door. My room, one of six cottages, was large, with moss-green walls and a small dressing room. The ten guest rooms in the main house have 14-foot ceilings, mahogany mantels and antique beds—mostly four-posters fashioned from mahogany or pine. The inn also rents out 14 fully furnished small houses. Full breakfast is always included. ~ 201 7th Street, Columbus; 706-322-4075, 800-585-4075, fax 706-322-3772; www.thepoundhouseinn.com, e-mail info@the poundhouseinn.com. DELUXE TO ULTRA-DELUXE.

has eight accommodations (each with private telephone, TV and VCR, a rare combination in a bed and breakfast), most on the large side. Full breakfast is included. ~ 504 Rees Park, Americus; 229-931-0122, 888-758-4749, fax 229-924-3186; www.americus gardeninn.com, e-mail info@americusgardeninn.com. DELUXE.

HIDDEN ►

There are few places to spend the night around Andersonville, so it's the lucky guest who checks in with the Sheppard family, who live across the road from **A Place Away Cottage Bed and Breakfast**. This unusual arrangement adds an extra element of privacy to this semi-B&B experience. The cozy cottage is actually a duplex, with a shared kitchen and rear deck facing a woodsy meadow. One room has a queen-size bed, the other a double and a single. Both have minimal decor beyond plaid bedspreads, ruffled curtains atop Venetian blinds and bookcases. When you call for reservations, you'll be given directions to the nearby house where guests check in and pick up keys. ~ 110 North Oglethorpe Street, Andersonville; 229-924-1044. BUDGET.

The **Sign of the Dove** is a combination restaurant and B&B unlike any other in the area. This beautifully decorated inn is a neoclassical Georgian cottage circa 1908 that's listed on the National Register of Historic Places. There are three rooms upstairs in the main house and another four in the guest cottage. Full breakfast is included. Dinner is available Fridays, and lunch is served on Sundays. ~ 108 Church Street, Buena Vista; 229-649-3663, 888-690-3663, fax 912-649-5940; www.sign-of-the-dove.com, e-mail dkarmer@sign-of-the-dove.com. BUDGET TO MODERATE.

The room where Miss Lillian (Jimmy Carter's mother) lived is available for a night's stay at the Plains Bed & Breakfast Inn.

The **Wyndham Columbus** has two major attributes that distinguish it from its stable mates: its historic district location near the Riverwalk and the fact that it's built around a century-old landmark, the Empire Woodruff Grist Mill, at one time the largest flour mill in the South. Beyond the old brick facade, concrete, steel and glass encase 177 guest rooms, all nicely done, anonymous hotel accommodations. ~ 800 Front Avenue, Columbus; 706-324-1800, fax 706-576-4413; www.wyndhamga.com. MODERATE TO DELUXE.

The **Gates House Bed and Breakfast** should be called the Gates Houses, since a second structure was opened in 2001. The original, Gates West, is a two-story Colonial revival–style house dating to 1880 and has three rooms; Gates East, circa 1873, has six lavishly decorated rooms. All the accommodations have custom silk bedspreads, designer window treatments and oriental carpets; many have jacuzzis, VCRs, DVDs and internet access. Bikes and helmets can be borrowed for touring the nearby riverfront. The inn also has a separate cottage available for weekly rental. ~ 802 Broadway, Columbus; 706-324-6464, 800-891-

3187, fax 706-324-2070; www.gateshouse.com. DELUXE TO
ULTRA-DELUXE.

Southwest Georgia is blessed with a number of tea houses.
Julianna's fancy tea-parlor-and-gift shop is in Cuthbert, a town
located 20 miles south of Lumpkin on Route 27SR1. Here, ladies
(and some gentlemen) sit down to elegant repasts of finger sandwiches, scones, fresh fruit, pastries and other dainty food, served
on lacy, floral-patterned mats and china. Guests may sit in the
parlor or on an enclosed "Secret Garden"–type courtyard. The
parlor room in this converted bank building has a fireplace, making it even cozier. But the greatest thing about this place—aside
from more than a dozen teas—is the amazing collection of hats.
Customers are free to pick out a pink-brimmed sunhat or a fur-
lined beret or a grand garden chapeau from among dozens displayed for this purpose. It may sound like too much, but it's fun
to play dress-up. No dinner. Closed Sunday and Monday. ~ 109
South Peachtree Street, Cuthbert; 229-732-5523. MODERATE.

DINING

Off-duty cops and other local regulars keep **Michelle's Res-**
taurant going . . . and going. Every day from dawn 'til after dark,
this down-home place serves breakfast, cafeteria-style lunch and
à la carte dinners. The exception is Sunday, when there's a midday buffet. From chicken, meatloaf and sandwiches to more exotic
fare like oysters and gizzards, you can't get much more down-to-
earth than this simple two-room standby. ~ Main Street, Lumpkin; 229-838-9991. BUDGET TO MODERATE.

◄ *HIDDEN*

Half café, half shop, the bright, white-walled **Chinaberry Café**
has red-and-white tabletops and lots of sweets, including cara-
mel cake baked by the town beautician. There is also a list of
salad plates, burgers, grilled chicken and BLTs, and homemade
soups. Lunch daily; dinner on Friday and Saturday only. Closed
Monday. ~ 118 Main Street, Parrott; 229-623-2233. BUDGET TO
MODERATE.

The Plantation Grille upgrades the Westover Crossings Shopping Center with white columns and plantation shutters. Inside,
white tablecloths and arched room dividers may not evoke a plantation, but it's one of the most elegant settings in Albany, with a
Continental/Southern menu to match. Closed Sunday and Monday. ~ 621 North Westover Boulevard, Albany; 229-439-1138,
fax 229-439-4156. DELUXE TO ULTRA-DELUXE.

◄ *HIDDEN*

Taupe rules at **Merry Acres Restaurant,** where the interior design is your basic generic contemporary chic. Here you can find a
dozen seafood dishes, including grouper in parchment and snapper
Dijon, as well as prime rib and filet mignon. They all come with
salad and potatoes or rice. A couple of pastas and appetizers round
out the menu. No dinner Sunday through Wednesday. ~ 1504
Dawson Road, Albany; 229-439-2261. DELUXE TO ULTRA-DELUXE.

HIDDEN ► In addition to the requisite sombreros, panchos and piñatas, **El Vaquero Mexican Restaurant** also has colorful embroidered dresses hanging on the wall, which may be a first. Similarly, the 60-item menu hews the standard line with a few distinguishing touches such as *chiles poblanas* with shrimp. The restaurant is tucked into the rear of a small shopping complex not far from the Albany Mall. ~ 2700 Dawson Road, Albany; 229-435-8448. BUDGET TO MODERATE.

Cajun shrimp salad, baby back ribs and nightly specials at **Dingus Magee's** offer some of the spiciest eating you will find in Americus or anywhere near it. There's a lively bar and light fare such as sandwiches at this popular hangout, which has siblings in Statesboro and Vidalia. Closed Sunday. ~ 120 North Lee Street, Albany; 229-924-6333. MODERATE.

The best deal in town is the big Southern-style buffet served at **Mom's Kitchen**. This is the place to chow down on fried chicken and other meats (sometimes including quail) and all the vegetables you can fit on the plate. No dinner on Sunday. Closed Monday. ~ 203 Church Street, Plains; 229-824-5458. BUDGET.

President Jimmy Carter signed the guestbook at **Granny's Kitchen,** which has a reputation for serving meals that will keep everybody working on the peanut farm all day. Fried chicken, meatloaf, vegetables and pie for dessert ought to do the trick. Closed Sunday. ~ Route 19S and Route 280W, Americus; 229-924-0028. BUDGET.

HIDDEN ► They've been running a lunch counter at the **Dinglewood Pharmacy** since the 1920s, so by now they know how to make a burger, a grilled cheese sandwich and some local delicacies. This is an institution, plain and simple, and a low-key alternative to fast-food outlets. Closed Sunday. ~ 1939 Wynnton Road, Columbus; 706-322-0616. BUDGET.

The **Goetchius House** might be hard to pronounce, but it is the most elegant restaurant in Columbus. New Orleans–style wrought iron and floor-to-ceiling windows imbue the facade of this 1840s house with Deep South atmosphere. Guests are ushered into one of two gracious parlors or, on balmy evenings, to back-porch tables overlooking a lawn with a formal fountain. The only disappointment is that out back is the sound of nearby highway traffic. However, the cuisine is entertainment enough: frogs legs Bourguignon, veal Oscar, chateaubriand, tournedos, *coq au vin* and, with a nod to the locale, onion and she-crab soup. Closed Sunday. ~ 405 Broadway, Columbus; 706-324-4863; www. goetchiushouse.com, e-mail wbludau@earthlink.net. DELUXE TO ULTRA-DELUXE.

HIDDEN ► **Minnie's Uptown Restaurant**'s success can be easily measured. It began as a squat, pale-green building named Minnie's, then expanded next door to incorporate a bakery before annexing the cor-

ner of the building so that the full restaurant name runs the length
of the building. At 12:05 p.m. the line is out the door; patrons
wait their turn for black-eyed peas, rutabagas, turnip greens, beef
tips, fried chicken and other veggies and meats that change from
day to day. Even with a gallon of sweet tea, you'd be hard pressed
to spend more than $7 for lunch in this cafeteria-style favorite.
Closed Saturday and Sunday. ~ 104 8th Street, Columbus; 706-
322-2766. BUDGET.

Country's B.B.Q. occupies a totally overhauled old bus station,
so don't worry about dressing up. This is the spot to learn about
Chattahoochee Valley barbecue, which some say gets its special
flavors from being grilled over green saplings (instead of aged
wood). Order pork, ribs, beef or chicken and judge for yourself,
or stick to baked sweet potatoes, grilled chicken salad or a vegetable plate. With the exception of Coca-Cola, which is served in
a bottle, drinks arrive at your table in jars. ~ 1329 Broadway,
Columbus; 706-596-8910. (There are two other locations at 3137
Mercury Drive, 706-563-7604; and 6298 Veterans Parkway, 706-
660-1415.) BUDGET TO MODERATE.

Tavern on the Square is the place for hearty sandwiches, soups
and soup-salad-sandwich combinations. All the workers in the
neighborhood seems to go to this pubby spot on their lunch hour
at least once a week. Closed Sunday. ~ 14 11th Street, Columbus;
706-324-2238. BUDGET TO ULTRA-DELUXE.

The Cannon Brewpub is easy to find: look for the Civil War
cannon installed in front of a pair of vintage downtown store-
fronts. Inside, you can pair the house-made beers and ales with
pizza, pasta, steaks and hamburgers. Your best bet: pizza with a
white sauce instead of the same old tomato mix. ~ 1041 Broadway, Columbus; 706-653-2337; www.cannonbrew.com. BUDGET
TO DELUXE.

AUTHOR FAVORITE

    I found the blend of classic bistro and cutting-edge restaurant at
The Olive Branch a satisfactory arrangement. You can order something
simple like ribeye steak on creamy potatoes or a more complex dish along
the lines of sautéed shrimp in a cylinder of flaky phyllo topped with pesto.
No matter where you sit or what you order, you get a view of the open
kitchen, where a frantically busy crew works hard at providing something for just about everyone, with an emphasis on Mediterranean food.
I also appreciated the restaurant's solid list of wines served by the
glass, always a boon to the solo diner. Closed Sunday. ~ 1032
Broadway, Columbus; 706-322-7410. MODERATE TO ULTRA-DELUXE.

Light dishes such as a Thai salad, spicy coconut milk soup and crisp spring rolls with bean threads and vegetables make an ideal lunch break at **Chili Thai.** At night, the curries (best washed down with a Singha beer) get rave reviews, as does a dessert of mango and sticky rice. This is the kind of authentic, family-run ethnic restaurant you rarely encounter in Georgia outside of Atlanta. Closed Saturday and Sunday. ~ 5870 Veterans Parkway, Columbus; 706-494-0850. BUDGET.

SHOPPING   **Julianna's** is jam-packed with antiques and collectibles. If you like hats, you'll love shopping whether or not you stay for tea. ~ 109 South Peachtree Street, Cuthbert; 229-732-5523.

On Parrott's burgeoning street, **Maridean's Marketplace** houses 16 or so stalls with dealers from all over the state proffering high-end antiques and porcelain from the U.S. and Europe. Closed Sunday and Monday. ~ 110 East Main Street, Parrott; 229-623-4123.

Hidden inside **Robert Alan's Salon** is a chic little shop with high-fashion, low-price costume jewelry (including clip-on earrings) and a few colorful dresses in natural fibers. It also carries a limited selection of gift items such as small decorative pillows. Closed Saturday through Monday. ~ 1217 Dawson Road, Albany; 229-439-4007.

MB Estate Sales offers easy pickings for antiques, from furniture to jewelry. Closed Sunday. ~ 115 North Jackson Street, Americus; 229-924-4409.

The shop on the ground floor of **Habitat for Humanity International** is delightful, with, of course, books by and about Jimmy Carter. You can buy caps, T-shirts and very useful windbreakers emblazoned with the organization's name or logo, as well as educational toys. ~ 121 Habitat Street, Americus; 229-924-6935.

HIDDEN ▶   The **Quartermaster's Sale Store** in the National Infantry Museum at Fort Benning stocks military-related books, toys, army bears and other paraphernalia. ~ Baltzell Avenue, Fort Benning; 706-687-3297; www.benningmuseumgift.com.

◆◆

ANTIQUES IN ANDERSONVILLE

Several small stores are clustered around the main intersection in tiny Andersonville and, as you would suspect, most of them carry tons of Civil War-a-bilia. One is the **Andersonville Antiques**, where the owner finds it just about impossible to keep any authentic relics in stock, but does sell old pistols, Coca-Cola signs and a hodgepodge of cheaper stuff. Closed mornings. ~ 109 Oglethorpe Street, Andersonville; 229-924-1044.

Antiques vie with more contemporary interior decorative pieces at the fine shops of Columbus (not counting the malls, of course). From fine crystal to heirloom carpet to old silver, the hunting is good at **Charles and Di Antiques and Collectibles**. Closed Sunday. ~ 7805 Veterans Parkway, Columbus; 706-324-3314.

European and American antiques, architectural accessories for the garden (actually, they would look good in some houses), fine linens for bed and bath, and smaller things like potpourri and candles make **1617 Wynnton** look more residential than commercial. Closed Monday. ~ 1617 Wynnton Road, Columbus; 706-324-4121.

If you must choose a mall, make it the **Peachtree Mall**. The interior is a take on Tara, with white columns, courtyards, fountains and even park-like benches placed beneath palm trees. Anchored by five major department stores (Parisian and Dillard's, among them), this is a good place to window-shop on hot or rainy days. Also here is Rich's, the South's most famous department store. ~ 3131 Manchester Expressway, Columbus; 706-327-1578.

A residential setting makes the merchandise at **Joni's Antiques** particularly appealing. Glass, china and furniture, along with specialty decorator items, are their calling card. Closed Sunday. ~ 4021 Macon Road, Columbus; 706-562-9802.

The **Columbus State Farmers Market** provides a convenient outlet for regional farmers to display and sell their fresh fruits, vegetables, flowers and other products to regular customers as well as the wholesale market, from 7 a.m. to 9:30 p.m. daily. ~ 318 10th Street, Columbus; 706-649-7448, 706-649-7449.

Aside from nightclubs, there is not a lot to do after dark in these parts, except for films, symphony and theater productions. But here are a few suggestions.   **NIGHTLIFE**

Theatre Albany presents six productions—comedies, musicals and dramas—every season in a restored antebellum home. ~ 514 Pine Avenue, Albany; 229-439-7193; www.theatrealbany.com.

The pub and game room at **Pat's Place** is open most nights, with live music on Tuesday and karaoke on Saturday. ~ 1526 South Lee Street, Americus; 229-924-0033.

The **Rylander Theater** is a neat old restored vaudeville house that shows an eclectic range of movies. Think *Willy Wonka and the Chocolate Factory*, *Carrie* and *Citizen Kane*. There are traveling musical acts as well. ~ 310 West Lamar Street, Americus; 229-931-0001; www.rylander.org.

Dramatic productions and musical shows are presented on the stage of the 300-seat **Liberty Theatre Cultural Center**. Opened in 1924 as an entertainment facility for the city's African-American population, it closed in 1974 and then, thanks to community involvement, reopened in 1996. ~ 823 8th Avenue, Columbus; 706-653-7566.

The **RiverCenter for the Performing Arts** opened in 2001, giving downtown Columbus a cultural boost. National touring concert and theatrical companies and local music and dance organizations perform in the Heard Theater, one of three stages in the complex of five interconnected buildings that takes up an entire city block. ~ 900 Broadway, Columbus; 706-653-7993; www.river center.org, e-mail information@rivercenter.org.

The historic **Springer Opera House** offers more culture—this time straight from the diaphragm—from September through May. Musicals like *Grease* and *The Sound of Music* number among the performances. ~ 103 10th Street, Columbus; 706-324-5714; www.springeroperahouse.org.

If you like laser light shows and other interactive media performances, check out the **Omnisphere Theater** at the Coca-Cola Space Science Center. In addition to these high-tech treats, the theater is also a venue for various live theater productions, musical concerts and other special events. Admission. ~ 701 Front Avenue, Columbus; 706-649-1470; www.ccssc.org, e-mail info@ccssc.org.

Rock music alternates with jazz and blues Friday and Saturday nights at the **Uptown Tap**. Cover. ~ 1024 Broadway, Columbus; 706-653-8277.

The Loft is a cavernous brick-walled space atop the busy Olive Branch restaurant. A bandstand and cocktail tables occupy the front half of the space, the bar the middle third and pool tables the rear portion. This place jumps with live local music, usually starting about 10 p.m. To keep up your strength, you can order light fare like chicken wings and burgers. Closed Sunday through Tuesday. ~ 1032 Broadway, Columbus; 706-322-7410.

Benjamin's Fine Foods & Spirits offers deejay dancing Tuesday through Saturday (when it's open until 3 a.m.). ~ 3396 Buena Vista Road, Columbus; 706-682-0002.

The **Columbus Symphony Orchestra** performs at the RiverCenter. The season runs from October into early May. ~ 13 East 10th Street, Columbus; 706-323-5059; www.csoga.org.

PARKS

FLORENCE MARINA STATE PARK 🛶 ⎇ 🚤 🛥 ⌐ The northern end of Lake Walter F. George, where the waters of the Chattahoochee River form the state line with Alabama, is an ideal place for a public marina. This 173-acre piece of land was a private recreation area before it became a state park in 1986. Harking back to more ancient history, the Kirbo Interpretive Center here has artifacts dating from the prehistoric Paleo-Indian period as well as exhibits on the more recent past. A clubhouse, a pool and a miniature golf course are among the amenities here, along with a bathhouse and laundromat. The fishing pier is lit for nighttime angling. Day-use fee, $2. ~ Route 39, Florence; 229-838-4244.

▲ There are 43 tent/RV sites; $18 to $20 per night. In addition, the park has six two-bedroom cottages and eight one-room efficiencies at moderate rates; all have kitchen facilities. Reservations: 800-864-7275.

The walls of Providence Canyon, an 1108-acre natural geographical wonder, reveal colorful strata of iron, manganese, mica and other minerals.

PROVIDENCE CANYON STATE PARK 🏃 This is the most unusual park in all of Georgia, thanks to the 16 150-foot-wide gorges, formed over millennia by rainfall, that gleam with white powder. Excellent hiking trails pass by white pines, rhododendrons, azaleas and wildflowers galore; keep an eye out for armadillos, white-tailed deer, foxes, turkeys and woodpeckers. In addition, a visitors center offers interpretive displays. Day-use fee, $2. ~ Route 39, seven miles west of Lumpkin; 229-838-6202.

▲ There are six backcountry sites; $4 per night. Reservations: 800-864-7275.

North of Columbus travelers enter a diverse region, where mountain parks and huge lakes give way to country towns that are now beginning to become bedroom communities for Atlanta. The historic Warm Springs area where President Franklin Delano Roosevelt had a retreat that gave the nearby town a historic cachet is less than half-an-hour's drive from the fabled gardens of Callaway at Pine Mountain.

Columbus to Newnan

From Columbus, head north on Route 85/27; at Ellerslie, turn east on Route 315 to **Talbotton** (pronounced TALL-b'tun). Now a quaint country village, Talbotton had its heyday in the middle of the 19th century. But it counts as its native sons and daughters two governors, six U.S. Congressmen, two chief justices of the Georgia Supreme Court, two generals and five college presidents.

SIGHTS

The historic **Zion Episcopal Church** dates to 1848 and looks the part. No one knows the name of the master builder who constructed this Gothic Revival church that looks to be right out of the English countryside. It's made of native heart pine and walnut and still has its original 1850 Pilcher organ, which still plays. ~ Intersection of Routes 80 and 208, Talbotton.

◀ HIDDEN

When you exit the church, look across the way and to the right. The tall white antebellum columns of the **Straus-LeVert Memorial Hall** may make you think of Tara, but the hall was built in 1853 as the centerpiece of LeVert College, an all-female academy named for Madame Octavia Walton LeVert. An accomplished linguist specializing in American Native languages, she was asked by President Andrew Jackson to come up with a name for the newly established capital of Florida. She chose Tallahassee, a Seminole word meaning "beautiful land." ~ One block east of Zion Episcopal Church, Talbotton.

For a driving tour map of these and 13 other historic sites in town, visit the **Talbot County Chamber of Commerce.** Closed Saturday and Sunday. ~ At the corner of Monroe and Adams streets; 706-665-8079; www.talbotgeorgia.com, e-mail talbotco@gnat.net.

HIDDEN ▶

From Talbotton, take Route 41 north six miles to **Woodland.** Continue two blocks past the intersection with Route 36 to find the **Old South Farm Museum.** This is a real treasure, an old industrial building near the railroad tracks that is jam-packed with machinery, equipment and gadgets gleaned from the countryside over a period of years by a retired county extension agency employee. From plantation days to the early part of the 20th century, the history of the rural South is told in this collection. Shoe lasts, fly sprayers, ice cream churners, thrashers, tractors, wagons, hay balers and more—including a peach-packing shed housing the equipment used to grow Georgia's most famous crop—will fascinate visitors for as long as they feel like poking around. Call before you visit. Admission. ~ Woodland; 706-674-2894.

Leave Woodland on the road you came in on, heading north on Route 41. In six more miles, turn west on Route 190 for five miles, then north on Route 85 for four miles to the town of **Warm Springs.** This is a quiet town where a lively tourist trade has sprung up because of President Franklin D. Roosevelt's legacy. Springs still burble here as they did when the president made this area his hideaway.

In the downtown area is the old **Hotel Warm Springs Bed & Breakfast Inn,** where visiting dignitaries stayed back in the '30s and '40s and where visitors still spend the night. The story of how Roosevelt came to choose Warm Springs and how few people at the time knew of his polio is told at an amazingly well-preserved place just south of town via Route 85. ~ 47 Broad Street, Warm Springs; 706-655-2114.

In 2004, the state of Georgia opened the **Franklin D. Roosevelt Museum in the Little White House State Historic Site.** Roosevelt's life, his role in America's recovery from the Great Depression, his leadership during World War II and his personal struggle with polio are chronicled in the 11,000-square-foot structure, which also houses the legendary president's hand-controlled 1938 Ford convertible and his personal stagecoach. Visitors can also listen to some of FDR's "Fireside Chats" playing on a 1930s radio. Admission. ~ 401 Little White House Road, Route 85, Warm Springs; 706-655-5870; www.fdr-littlewhitehouse.org.

The **Roosevelt Warm Springs Institute for Rehabilitation** was founded by FDR in 1927 for polio patients. There is a small historic exhibition as well as the quadrangle and the pools where the president took therapy and visited with other patients. ~ 6351 Roosevelt Highway, east of Warm Springs on Route 27A; 706-655-5000; www.roosevelttrehab.org.

One of several similar facilities in Georgia, the **Warm Springs** HIDDEN
Regional Fisheries Center and Aquarium was established in 1990 as a field station incorporating a centralized Fish Health Center, a National Fish Hatchery, a Fish Technology Center and an environmental education unit into a single complex. A warm-water hatchery, it does best with species of fish, such as sturgeon, paddlefish and striped bass, that propagate in summer water temperatures ranging from 75° to 85°. Once they reach adequate size, they are released into the wild. Visitors are welcome to visit the aquarium, where one tank is used to house reptiles during the summer. ~ South of Warm Springs on Route 27A; 706-655-3382.

From Warm Springs, take Route 27A south then Route 190 west. In 12 miles, you'll be in the **Franklin D. Roosevelt State Park**; at 9047 acres, it's the largest state park in Georgia. The president's Civilian Conservation Corps built many of the log cabins, bridges, trails, picnic areas and the swimming pool that thousands enjoy today. **Dowdell's Knob** was FDR's favorite spot to HIDDEN

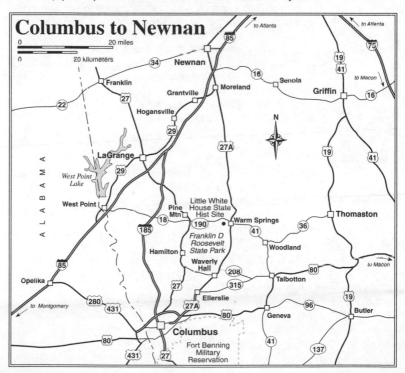

picnic and contemplate matters of state. And judging by the photographs, he did it in style, with picnic tables draped in linens, hot foods served from silver platters, and blankets spread out on chairs or automobile seats borrowed from the car and placed on the ground. This scenic spot with marvelous views is where he mulled over the upcoming founding of the United Nations, according to historians. Located at 1395 feet, it's at its best near sunset. ~ Route 190, Pine Mountain in Franklin D. Roosevelt State Park; 707-663-4858.

From the park, continue northwest toward the town of Pine Mountain. When you reach Route 18, turn left for about a mile until you see the entrance to **Callaway Gardens**. A combination of gardens, paths, golf courses, tennis courts, hotels and restaurants, the entire complex is larger than Franklin D. Roosevelt State Park up the road. It's all the vision of Cason Callaway, who believed "every child should see something beautiful before the age of six." There's a Disney-esque quality to the resort, but you simply can't fake flowers. And they are beautiful, particularly the plunifora azalea that Callaway made the resort's emblem.

You will need a map to find your way around. The absolute best way is on a bicycle (they are rented here, but don't expect recent models); secondly, you can walk, though you may spend all day doing it; lastly, you can drive, but you would miss the really good stuff that is not auto-accessible. High points include the recently renovated **Cecil B. Day Butterfly Center**, which claims to be the largest glass-enclosed butterfly conservatory in North America. The little creatures will indeed land on your shoulder if you stand still, though on a spring or fall weekend standing still is out of the question; the crowds are so large someone will be pushing you from behind. Seasonal flowers are displayed in the

sights

AUTHOR FAVORITE

Although no guided tours are offered, the **Little White House State Historic Site** is a must-see. You can really get a feel for how quiet Roosevelt's life was in this woodsy retreat—it's so quiet, in fact, that you'd hardly be surprised to see the president come in. His dog's leash hangs in a closet; Fala's scratches are still visible on the back door. The 1938 Ford convertible sits in the garage. There are dishes in the kitchen of this six-room cottage he built in 1933, before he was president. Over the years, from 1924 to 1945, FDR made 41 trips—at first to bathe his polio-crippled legs in the mineral spring and later just to escape Washington. And this is where he died, in a chair here in the living room, on April 12, 1945. You can see a short film, view his effects and in general take it all in. Admission. ~ 401 Little White House Road, Route 85, Warm Springs; 706-655-5870; www.fdr-littlewhitehouse.org.

five-acre **John A. Sibley Horticultural Center**, both in and out of doors. Tucked away is the **Ida Cason Callaway Memorial Chapel**, where organ concerts are held—a great place to meditate. Other points of interest include Mr. Cason's Vegetable Garden, which sounds very Mr. Greenjeans but is a monstrous seven-and-a-half-acre sloped mini-farm packed with demonstration flower, herb and vegetable plantings. The Pioneer Log Cabin, hand-hewn in the 1830s, is furnished in period style. There's a fishing dock in addition to Robin Lake Beach, where white sand stretches to the water's edge. Admission. ~ Route 27, Pine Mountain; 706-663-2281, 800-225-5292; www.callawaygardens.com, e-mail info@callawaygardens.com.

The llamas, giraffes, deer, camels and even the zebras walk right up to the cars that creep through **Pine Mountain Wild Animal Park**. You can drive through the 500-acre preserve or take a guided bus tour (in season) to see hundreds of exotic animals in an almost unbelievable setting. Take your camera or you may think you weren't ever really all that close to these animals. In fact, you are encouraged to buy some alfalfa pellets and hold out your hand to the wild animals. For something tamer, stroll through Old MacDonald's Petting Farm, where you can pet and feed nice little rabbits and pigs. There are protected areas for monkeys, alligators, black bears and snakes. Admission. ~ 1300 Oak Grove Road, off Route 27, Pine Mountain; 706-663-8744, 800-367-2751; www.animalsafari.com, e-mail info@animalsafari.com.

◄ HIDDEN

From Pine Mountain, take scenic Route 27, which enters LaGrange from the south. Exit on Morgan Street, go left on Greenville Street, left on Main Street and then left on Hines Street, since several one-way streets cross the downtown area. There is street parking near the **Chattahoochee Valley Art Museum**, a grand building dating from 1892 and restored by the Callaway Foundation. It houses an outstanding art collection displayed in four galleries and a shop for arts and crafts. Closed Sunday and Monday. Admission. ~ 112 LaFayette Parkway, LaGrange; 706-882-3267; www.cvam-online.org, e-mail info@cvam-online.org.

Once you have viewed the collection, return to Greenville Street and go west on Broad Street (Route 29) until you reach Evers-Hill Street; turn right and go two blocks. Although it's in a nice enough neighborhood, the appearance of **Bellevue Historical House** is startling in its stateliness. The mansion was built for Benjamin Harvey Hill, an attorney and Georgia and U.S. congressman, over the course of two years in the early 1850s. With its Ionic columns marching across wide porticos, it is considered one of the finest examples of Greek Revival architecture in Georgia. Inside, the home is partly furnished in period style, including the rosewood piano that has been in the parlor since the 1800s, and portraits of the Hills. Massive carved cornices atop

◄ HIDDEN

doors and windows, plaster ceiling medallions and black Carrara marble mantles reflect the taste and prominence of the family who lived in what is now a National Historic Landmark. Closed Sunday and Monday. Admission. ~ 204 Ben Hill Street, LaGrange; 706-884-1832.

When you leave the mansion, return to Broad Street/Route 29 and drive westward for another type of art experience. Turning left on Forrest Avenue leads you to the **Lamar Dodd Art Center.** Known mostly for its instruction in the arts, the center also has a permanent collection of works by international artists, including, naturally, Lamar Dodd. What's dazzling about the place, though, is the high-quality student exhibits shown here from time to time. Closed Saturday and Sunday, and when school's not in session. ~ 302 Forrest Avenue, on the campus of LaGrange College, LaGrange; 706-812-7211; www.lagrange.edu.

Return north on Forrest Avenue, cross Route 29, jog right on Broad Street and then left on Country Club Road, bound for West Point Lake if you're in the mood for a water view. Otherwise, turn right when you get back to Route 29 and head north. You'll pass through cute towns like Hogansville and Grantville.

The big attraction in Grantville is a most unusual structure, formerly a bed-and-breakfast inn. **Bonnie Castle** was built in 1896 and embellished with a turret, stained glass and other indicators of its Victorian heritage. ~ 2 Post Street, Grantville; 770-583-3090, 800-261-3090; www.bonnie-castle.com.

Continue on Route 29 from Grantville northeast, crossing Route 85, to reach **Moreland**. It's hard to imagine there are towns similarly small that boast three museums. Granted, none of them is open regular hours, but still. . . .

Right on Route 29 is the **Lewis Grizzard Museum**. For what seems like forever, Grizzard was a humor columnist and author who more or less celebrated the good ol' boy life. After his untimely death in 1994 at the age of 47, friends and family gathered his typewriters, family photographs, mementos and manuscripts and put them in a 19th-century country-store building in the heart of his hometown. ~ 27 Main Street, Moreland; 770-304-1490, 800-826-9382; www.coweta.ga.us.

The **Erskine Caldwell Birthplace & Museum**, also known as the Little Manse, has been restored to its 1903 appearance. With one big change: it's been relocated to the town square. Caldwell, who wrote *Tobacco Road* and more than 50 other books, is still loved and hated for his ruthlessly frank depiction of the rural South in the 1930s and '40s. His works can be read in 27 languages, and many of them—the English ones—can be bought here. It's a modest home but contains a very moving display of memorabilia and photographs. Closed Monday through Friday. Admission. ~ Moreland; 770-251-4438; www.coweta.ga.us.

It's a short trip from Moreland to **Senoia**, which isn't much bigger. (Continue north on Route 27A to Route 85 and look for Route 16 heading east.) In about 15 miles, you will enter this charming village.

In downtown Senoia, you can get a glimpse into another aspect of the town's past. A local family collected Model-A Fords along with elegant late-19th- and early-20th-century carriages and opened the **Buggy Shop Museum** in an early 1900s building that holds a lot more, including an antique psychoanalyst's couch and handmade sunglasses from the late 1800s, plus some Coca-Cola memorabilia. Closed Monday though Friday. ~ Main Street, Senoia; 770-253-1018; e-mail buggyshopsenoia@aol.com.

From Senoia, head back west along Route 16, cross Route 85, and turn north on Route 27A, which enters **Newnan** from the south. After the last few stops, this qualifies as a big city, but it's the small-town hospitality that you will remember.

Court Square is where most things in town happen. The **Coweta County Courthouse**, originally built in 1823 from logs on the square, was in use for only a year before a new courthouse was ordered; the neo-Greek-designed structure was completed in 1904. It's been modified many times over the years. ~ Court Square, Newnan.

From the square, head west on Washington Street, turn right on College Street and continue three blocks to Temple Street. During the Civil War, Newnan gained a reputation as the "hospital city of the Confederacy." Six field hospitals were located in churches, homes and other buildings throughout the city. An authentic Confederate battle flag, period photographs, many weapons and other artifacts have been assembled from that era and are on display at the **Male Academy Museum**. An exhibit of period non-military clothing from the 1860s to the 1950s is accompanied by storyboards detailing the origin, fabric and style of the pieces. The building, by the way, was an all-boy academy focusing on   ◀ *HIDDEN*

SPINNING YARN

Although it hasn't been a working mill in ages, the **Old Mill Museum** manages to evoke the workplace of knitting mills in the early part of the 1900s. Be sure to ask to see the dips in the floor, which tell a story. The structure was built in 1894 as a store; in the 1920s, it became the Moreland Knitting Mill and in 1983 was donated by Bressler Industries to the town. It houses antique farming equipment and World War II–era memorabilia relating to life in rural Georgia. At press time, the museum was undergoing some renovations, so be sure to call before you visit. ~ Main Street, Moreland; 770-251-3428.

college preparatory courses. Back in the 1880s, 60 students paid $100 a year for the privilege and, at that, had to bring not only their lunches but also their own chairs. Closed Monday and Friday, and weekend mornings. Admission. ~ 30 Temple Avenue, Newnan; 770-251-0207; www.nchistoricalsociety.org.

Available at the academy are maps for a driving tour of Newnan's antebellum homes, most of which are in and around the downtown area. The brochure lists 23 sights, though there are plenty of wannabes around. The **Parrott-Camp-Soucy House** is an acclaimed Victorian that was enlarged in 1855 to look more Stick-Eastlake and French Mansard. ~ 155 Greenville Street, Newnan. Built in 1852, the Greek Revival **North-Young-Rosenzweig House** is one-and-a-half stories high with an impressive demeanor despite the additions of Victoriana such as a bay window. ~ 141 Greenville Street, Newnan. Grandest of all is the **Ware House**, which began life in LaGrange in 1850 and was moved here and restored in 1951 by a relative of the original owner. ~ 70 Woodbine Circle, Newnan.

> The media, Secret Service agents and even foreign dignitaries lodged at Hotel Warm Springs Bed and Breakfast when Roosevelt was staying nearby at the Little White House.

LODGING   A pretty, white two-story clapboard, **Raintree Farms** bed and breakfast was built in 1833—but over in Talbot County. It was moved to its present location, board by board, around 1898. And it looks great, with a columned front porch spanning the width of the structure. Inside, five guest accommodations offer a lively variety. Family photographs, a beadboard ceiling and a carved mahogany four-poster from New Orleans distinguish the Moore Room. Off the kitchen, a cute room is done in yellow-and-white-striped wallpaper. The Provençal color scheme is continued upstairs in another room, while two others have red and peach walls. Family furnishings and oriental rugs are arranged throughout the large house. Full breakfast is included. ~ 8060 Route 208, near Route 95, Waverly Hall about 15 miles east of Talbotton; 706-582-3227, 800-433-0627. DELUXE.

The biggest building in town, the **Hotel Warm Springs Bed and Breakfast Inn** has several large rooms that may seem a little drafty but are truly comfortable. In addition, no two are exactly alike, or even much alike at all. This 1907 stalwart, originally called the Tuscawilla Hotel, was rehabbed to look as much like it did in 1941 as possible. The 16-foot ceilings in the lobby and the massive old reception desk certainly hark back to simpler times, as do the oak and other antiques in the ten rooms and three suites arranged in the two upper floors. Full breakfast is included. ~ 47 Broad Street, Warm Springs; 706-655-2114, 800-366-7616; www.hotelwarmspringsbb.org. MODERATE TO ULTRA-DELUXE.

You can visit Callaway Gardens without having to pay resort prices for accommodations. One alternative to the hotels is the 11-room **Fireside Inn,** with its assortment of units, including family rooms with three double beds. The decor is cute in a modest way, and there is a pool open in the summer. ~ 355 North Main Street, Pine Mountain; 706-663-4141 or 706-663-4488; www.firesideinn-ga.com. MODERATE.

Pine Mountain's most Victorian B&B is the **Chipley Murrah**   ◄ HIDDEN
Bed and Breakfast. Built in the late 1890s, it was restored and opened as an inn in 1991. There are three rooms (one with two double beds) and one suite in the main house. Most rooms have four-posters and other antiques. All accommodations have 12-foot ceilings and extensive molding. Also on the grounds are three attractive cottages that will accommodate up to eight people. Full breakfast is included (except for cottage guests). Two-night minimum on weekends for rooms. Closed in January. ~ 207 West Harris Street, Pine Mountain; 706-663-9801, 888-782-0797; www.chipley-murrah.com. DELUXE TO ULTRA-DELUXE.

Callaway Gardens offers three tiers of accommodations, none of them cheap. The least expensive are the spacious 349 rooms and suites at the two-story **Mountain Creek Inn,** a souped-up motel in a lovely landscaped setting. Pricier are the one- and two-bedroom **Southern Pine Cottages,** each of which has a full kitchen, fireplace, screened porch and deck among the pines. Top-of-the-line are the **Mountain Creek Villas,** which come in one- to four-bedroom sizes. ~ Route 27, Pine Mountain; 706-663-2281, 800-225-5292, fax 706-663-5090; www.callawaygardens.com, e-mail info@callawaygardens.com. ULTRA-DELUXE.

Magnolia Hall, despite its name, is more tropical than antebellum. Built by a relative of the Callaway (of Gardens fame) clan, it was a rental property before getting an overhaul in 1994. Of the three ground-floor rooms, the Walton Room has a big bed and two huge reading chairs; Green Street is sort of a great-aunt's room with angel paintings hanging on striped walls; and Carey's Corner has floral everything. The attic has been converted into a suite featuring the tiger-maple bedroom set that once belonged to Miss Louise. Another upstairs room, Miss Virginia's, has a small sitting room with two Queen Anne–style recliners. Located behind the courthouse in a picturesque town about ten miles south of Pine Mountain, the gracious Victorian sits on a full acre landscaped with century-old hollies and, of course, a huge magnolia tree. ~ 127 Barnes Mill Road, Hamilton; 706-628-4566, 877-813-4394; www.magnoliahallbb.com. DELUXE.

For classic antebellum ambience, it's hard to beat the **Grand**   ◄ HIDDEN
Wisteria Plantation, a neoclassical manor built around 1832 and listed on the National Register of Historic Places. The stately white columns alone are enough to give one the vapors. Five dis-

tinctive rooms are richly painted and furnished in period pieces. Continental breakfasts weekdays and full breakfasts on weekends are included. ~ 15380 Route 27A, Greenville; 706-672-0072; www.grandwisteria.com, e-mail grandwisteria@bellsouth.net. DELUXE TO ULTRA-DELUXE.

The **Culpepper House** looks—but wasn't—born for the role. What looks like a very nice family home was built in 1871 and is now a butter-yellow bed and breakfast with three upstairs guest rooms, the largest of which is the eight-sided Lamb Room. Family pieces collected over the years add a warm feeling to the inn, which has nifty features like 12-foot ceilings on the ground floor, pocket doors, stained glass and rocking chairs. Breakfast is included. ~ 35 Broad Street, Senoia; 770-599-8182; www.culpepperhouse.com, e-mail reservations@culpepperhouse.com. DELUXE.

DINING

HIDDEN ►

The **Farmhouse** sounds like some fancy place out in the country, but when you finally find it and see the rusty tin roof, you may decide it's just a dive. In fact, it is neither. It's an old caretaker's house that's been fixed up and serves the best food you can find for miles around. Opened in 1981 as a crafts shop–cum–snack bar by five partners with $100 and absolutely no idea what they were getting into, The Farmhouse soon had lines backed up past the well out front. The porch has windows overlooking a lake and a grassy meadow, and that's where you'll want to sit. Order at the counter and feast on chicken and dumplings and tasty veggies like candied yams, steamed cabbage, butter peas and a bang-up squash casserole that makes most folks ask for the recipe. Reservations are required for Friday-night dinner. No dinner Saturday. Closed Sunday through Thursday. ~ 469 Farmhouse Road, off Route 85, Ellerslie; 706-561-3435. BUDGET TO MODERATE.

Mac's Barbecue isn't quite big enough to qualify as a hole-in-the-wall, but you can wiggle in for barbecued pork or chicken and homemade desserts. ~ Main Street at Route 27, Warm Springs; 706-655-2472. BUDGET.

Next door to the Q joint but much larger is **Mac's Steak House,** where all kinds of steaks, as well as grilled shrimp and other dishes, are served. Closed Sunday through Thursday. ~ Main Street at Route 27, Warm Springs; 706-655-2472. MODERATE.

On warm days, a crowd gathers on the patio to cool off with a cold one at the **Sportman's Grill**. It's a big pub-style place with seating out front for enjoying the passing parade as well as inside. Burgers, sandwiches, salads, steaks and chicken and a full bar are offered. Closed Sunday. ~ Chipley Village, Route 354 and Route 27, Pine Mountain; 706-663-8064. MODERATE.

The place for barbecue in Pine Mountain is the **Whistling Pig Café**. You can also opt for hamburgers, hot dogs, fried green tomatoes or homemade fries. No dinner Monday through Thursday.

Closed Sunday. ~ Route 27, Pine Mountain; 706-663-4647.
BUDGET.

Inside the Callaway Gardens' Mountain Creek Inn, the
Plantation Room has, as you might expect, a carpet of flower
blossoms. Decorated with trellising and plantation shutters, the
restaurant is an extremely good value, with a choice of buffet or
à la carte. The cold breakfast is an especially good deal, since it
serves you more than most people can eat at one time for around
$10. Special meals include a Friday-night seafood buffet and a
Saturday-night Italian buffet, both of which are half-price for
children. ~ Callaway Gardens, Route 27, Pine Mountain; 706-
663-5182. DELUXE TO ULTRA-DELUXE.

The **Callaway Country Kitchen** is so old-fashioned that it
takes no reservations. Rustic decor and a piney mountain view
set the tone for down-home breakfasts and simple lunches and
dinners. A children's menu is available. ~ Callaway Gardens,
Route 27, Pine Mountain; 706-663-5182. BUDGET TO MODERATE.

Taste of Lemon is an out-of-the-way delight with seating in   ◄ HIDDEN
different small ground-floor rooms fringed in white lace curtains.
There's no standing printed menu; it's written new each day on
a blackboard and the servers recite it. It may include salmon croquettes, a chicken dish and always a wonderful vegetable plate
as well as a fresh salad. No dinner. Closed Saturday and Sunday.
~ 208 South Morgan Street, LaGrange; 706-882-5382. BUDGET.

In a bright white clapboard building with deep yellow walls
is the **Chapultepec Mexican Restaurant**. The menu doesn't sound
exciting unless you love Mexican food and are spending any time
in this part of the world. Aside from enchiladas, flautas, fajitas
and rellenos, the most interesting things at this friendly spot are
the chimichanga dinner and the chorizo burrito. Closed Sunday.
~ 7285 Route 16E, Senoia; 770-599-9717. MODERATE.

AUTHOR FAVORITE

Chances are you'll have to wait in line for lunch or dinner at
The Bulloch House Restaurant, but it's certainly worth it. Originally a
residence built in 1892, the mansion was restored as a restaurant in 1990.
The meals are served in the former residential rooms on the main floor
or in a slightly more formal addition done in teal with white windows.
Diners have their choice of a buffet (including fried green tomatoes)
or a few à la carte items like chicken and various salads, and lots of
desserts along the lines of apple cobbler. No dinner Sunday through
Thursday. ~ Bulloch Street, Route 27A, Warm Springs; 706-655-9068.
BUDGET TO MODERATE.

The "new" location for **Sprayberry's Barbecue** is almost as significant as the original eatery downtown. The latter opened on Jackson Street in 1926; the new one, in 1995 way out near Route 85. At both places, when they say 'cue, they mean beef or pork; very few chicken dishes are on the menu. Most plates come with Brunswick stew and/or onion rings, fries, pickles and slaw. You can get fried catfish, shrimp or chicken, but you'd be missing a major Newnan tradition. Closed Sunday. ~ 1060 Bullsboro Drive (Route 34E), at Route 85, Exit 9, Newnan; 770-253-5080 (original location, 229 Jackson Street, Newnan; 770-253-4421). BUDGET TO MODERATE.

A vivid red neon sign directs travelers along Route 34E to the **Dynasty Restaurant and Bakery**, an upscale, stand-alone Chinese restaurant despite the red Spanish tile roof and white columns out front. Inside, the emphasis is solidly Chinese, of course. Dainty parasols hang over the bar and the elegant dining room is romantically lit. Among the ubiquitous dishes here are some less widely encountered, such as Hunan calamari and Cantonese lobster. The staff is very eager to please, and if that means whipping up steak and fries Western-style, all you have to do is ask. This is a good place to remember if you're looking for a decent meal on a Sunday night, when most other places are closed. ~ 34 Bullsboro Drive (Route 34E), Newnan; 770-251-5418; www.dynasty-chinese.com. BUDGET TO DELUXE.

Ten East Washington, located less than a block off the town square, offers a pleasant melange of European and Deep South dishes. Diners can begin, for instance, with crab cakes or portobello mushroom ravioli, then proceed to Mediterranean chicken, fish, filet mignon or one of the chef's specials, which tend to be the most European dishes. Dinner is served on the porch or inside on the ground floor of a converted residence. Instead of having decorative plates actually mounted on the walls, as is common in many European *auberges*, here the plates are only stenciled onto the wall. A nice touch. Closed Sunday. ~ 10 East Washington Street, Newnan; 770-502-9100. DELUXE.

MADE WITH LOVE

Character dolls, re-creations of old-timey playthings, are the specialty at **Loveleigh Novelties**. Made with black walnut heads, these old dolls were unusual even early in the 20th century when Mrs. Itura Rosalein Colley Leigh made them. They show African Americans in dignified demeanor and are considered collector's items since each is handmade, signed, dated and numbered in editions of 500. You can view the dolls by appointment only. ~ 2 Post Street in Bonnie Castle, Grantville; 770-583-2080, 800-261-3090.

The **Redneck Gourmet** grabbed one of the best restaurant names in Georgia. It's about as relaxed as you can get and still expect to be served. Burgers—including a "chickin" burger and a "hawg" burger—dominate the menu, but putting a grilled shrimp salad on a "redneck" menu seems kind of questionable. Daily specials range from jambalaya to Brunswick stew. No dinner. Closed Saturday and Sunday. ~ 11 North Court Square, Newnan; 770-251-0092. BUDGET TO MODERATE.

On the National Register of Historic Places, **Golden's on the Square Restaurant** serves country-style buffets daily in a great big room flanked by sandblasted brick walls. A low wooden wall planted with greenery serves as a room divider. Service is cafeteria style; food choices include grouper, fried shrimp, prime rib, sweet potatoes and Jello. Closed Monday. ~ 9 East Court Square, Newnan; 770-251-4300. BUDGET.

More than 100 shops are cheek by jowl in the **Antiques & Crafts Unlimited Mall**. Regional artists Arthur Riggs and Roberta Geter sell here, but there are also many collectibles. ~ 7679 Route 27A, Warm Springs; 706-655-2468.

SHOPPING

Warm Springs Village Mall is full of kitsch, little cutesy collectibles, candles, dolls, etc. It may not be the place for that dream antique, but if you collect anything along the lines of Beanie Babies, this may be your idea of nirvana. ~ 69 Broad Street, Warm Springs; 706-655-2166.

On the outskirts of Senoia, **Carriage House Country Antiques & Gifts** carries antiques, primitives, collectibles, quilts and more. Closed Monday through Thursday. ~ 7412 East Route 16, Senoia; 770-599-6321.

Scott's Book Store is a large shop that carries many of Lewis Grizzard's works as well as the usual bookstore merchandise. Closed Sunday. ~ 28 South Court Square, Newnan; 770-253-2960.

For all manner of regional condiments, visit **Redneck Gourmet Market**. Closed Saturday and Sunday. ~ 11 North Court Square, Newnan; 770-251-0092.

Just off Court Square, **Guy's Book Nook** specializes in rare, antique, collectible and out-of-print works, as well as less-obscure used books. Closed Saturday and Sunday. ~ 32 Perry Street, Newnan; 770-253-1769.

The small towns north of Columbus are not known for their nightlife. With the big city so close, top entertainers usually prefer to appear at a venue in Atlanta (see Chapter Five for more information). It's only about an hour's drive from Newnan to downtown Atlanta and just a little farther to Midtown and Buckhead, the busiest neighborhoods after dark. By taking Route 75 through town to the Route 85 split, you can get from Newnan

NIGHTLIFE

to the Woodruff Center for the Arts or a Buckhead nightclub in short order, as long as you don't try to do it during rush hour.

Otherwise, for hardcore gospel and bluegrass shows, try **Hoofers**. The shows take place in a quaint red barn known, appropriately, as the "Gospel Barn." ~ 3472 Hogansville Road, LaGrange; 706-885-9300.

PARKS

FRANKLIN D. ROOSEVELT STATE PARK
Claiming some 9000 acres atop Pine Mountain, this heavily forested park is a highly desirable refuge in the heat of summer. But it's lovely year-round, with countless views of the surrounding landscape. Even on a casual walk, you are likely to see hickory, blackjack oak, chestnut oak and, on the top of the ridge, black oaks, undergrown with huckleberry and paw paw shrubs; rhododendrons and waterfalls are common spring sights on the mountain. A sturdy stone visitors center, built by Roosevelt's Civilian Conservation Corps, has exhibits and an information desk where you can pick up hiking maps. The Corps also built the pool (hours vary). Nearby is an overlook, but the best one is at Dowdell's Knob, where FDR used to picnic frequently. Day-use fee, $2. ~ Route 190, Pine Mountain; 706-663-4858, 800-864-7275.

▲ There are 140 tent/RV sites; $18 to $20 per night. There are 22 fully equipped cottages hidden away but within sight of the lake; $65 to $135 per night. Reservations: 800-864-7275. You must register with the rangers to camp.

CALLAWAY GARDENS
This privately owned attraction thrives on visitors, who can come for the day or spend the night in an inn or villa. The gardens are not just one garden but an array, including a butterfly habitat, a 20,000-square-foot greenhouse, and a Victory Garden, where a wide range of vegetables are tended. In all, Callaway Gardens encompasses some 2500 acres of gardens, woodlands, golf courses and pathways shared by walkers and cyclists alike—even the occasional baby carriage. Admission. ~ Route 27, Pine Mountain; 706-663-2281, 800-225-5292; www.callawaygardens.com.

WEST POINT LAKE DAM AND VISITOR CENTER
So far west it's practically in Alabama, what's known as West Point Lake includes a 52,000-acre public recreation area, a 26,000-acre lake brimming with largemouth and hybrid striped bass, crappie and channel catfish, and some 10,000 acres of game preserve that appeal to birdwatchers. In all, there are 525 miles of shoreline just a few miles west of LaGrange. ~ 7500 Resource Management Drive, West Point; 706-645-2937; www.westpt.sam.usace.army.mil.

▲ There is camping at the nearby **R. Shaefer Heard Campground**, which has 117 tent/RV sites during the summer (fewer in winter); $20 per night. ~ 101 Shaefer Heard Campground Road, West Point; 706-645-2404.

The Flint and Chattahoochee are the major rivers in southwest and central Georgia. Central Georgia's lakes have been called an angler's paradise because of the variety of fish, including bass, bream and crappie.

Outdoor Adventures

FISHING

The nice thing about fishing in **Walter F. George Lake** is that Georgia and Alabama fishing licenses (required for freshwater fishing) are honored in both states. But the great thing about fishing here is the largemouth bass, white bass, hybrids, crappie, channel catfish and bream. Bank fishing is recommended at public docks and near bridges at the mouths of tributary creeks. You can get a current generation schedule for the Walter F. George and George W. Andrews dams by calling 229-768-2424.

You can fish to your heart's content at the 25,900-acre **West Point Lake**. It's the centerpiece of an even larger public recreation area on the Georgia–Alabama state line that includes a 10,000-acre wildlife management area. Featuring a wide array of fish, the lake is known primarily as a largemouth bass fishery but also has good populations of crappie and channel catfish. The state stocks hybrid striped bass in the lake. ~ The visitors center is three miles north of West Point, off Route 29; 706-645-2937.

Highland Marina offers guide services if you want to explore West Point Lake. ~ 1000 Seminole Lane, LaGrange; 706-882-3437; www.highlandmarina.com.

Lake Seminole is one of the best bass-fishing lakes in the southeastern U.S., but you can also have good luck with bream and giant catfish. Boat and canoe rentals are available to maneuver the 12,000 acres of shallow water. ~ Route 39, 16 miles south of Donalsonville; 229-861-3137.

AUTHOR FAVORITE

I was happy to find a moderate trail that let me see some of the most dramatic sights at Providence Canyon State Park. The **Canyon Loop Trail** (3 miles) that begins and ends at the visitors center is mostly easy, though there are some elevation changes. Best enjoyed in dry weather, the walk, blazed with white markings to keep hikers on the right trail and loaded with switchbacks, affords spectacular views of the eroded canyon walls.

BOATING   One of the best ways to see the Chattahoochee River is from the comfort of **Dragonfly River Tours'** 42-foot trimaran. Equipped for up to 47 passengers, the river cruise can take you on a guided tour of hidden Indian mounds, or just to a catered sandbar event. You can choose a day excursion or an overnight trip. ~ 1233 Munro Avenue, Columbus; 888-464-3378.

GOLF   While Augusta and the Metro Atlanta area get most of the attention, this part of Georgia offers a good deal of variety for golfers.

The par-72 **Country Oaks Golf Course** has three lakes surrounded by pines, magnolias and other trees. ~ 6841 Route 122, Thomasville; 229-225-4333.

On the shores of Lake Walter F. George, the **George T. Bagby State Park & Lodge** has an 18-hole golf course; it has 64 bunkers and lush fairways set off with a golden long Bahia rough. The hill behind the green on No. 10 has two large pecan trees and a great view. ~ Route 39, Fort Gaines; 229-768-3714.

The 18-hole layout at **Flint River Municipal Golf Course** was once the domain of Air Force officers. Now it includes lots of water hazards, a par-five number 10 hole, a putting green, practice bunker, pro shop and snack bar. ~ 2000 McAdams Road, Albany; 229-430-5267.

Located close to Route 75 about half an hour from Americus, the **Georgia Veterans Golf Course** is considered one of the best values in the state. It was designed by architect Denis Griffiths, who managed to make a challenging, 7059-yard course with 105 bunkers out of a flat bottomland. ~ Georgia Veterans State Park, 2315 Route 280W, Cordele; 229-276-2377, 800-434-0982; www.golfgeorgia.org.

Callaway Gardens has three outstanding courses: the Mountain View Golf Course, which is the most expensive, and the Lake View and Gardens View courses. All offer summer twilight rates after 5 p.m. The executive nine-hole course, the Sky View Course, is the bargain of the lot. Golf clubs, range balls, club storage and personal instruction are all available. ~ Route 27, Pine Mountain; 800-225-5292.

The **Godwin Creek Golf Course** is a First Tee course, meaning it's devoted to introducing children to the sport—although adults are welcome to play these nine holes anytime. Families will find three par-fours and six par-threes on the links-style course. ~ 403 42nd Street, Columbus; 706-324-0583.

Natural grass and gently rolling fairways evoke a Scottish Links course at the 18-hole **Orchard Hills Golf Club,** but the Antebellum Clubhouse reads more like the Old South. ~ 600 East Route 16, Newnan; 770-251-5683; www.orchardhills.com.

Guided horseback rides on 20 miles of trails in the Franklin D. **RIDING**
Roosevelt State Park are offered by the hour, half-day, full-day **STABLES**
or overnight through **Roosevelt Riding Stables**. The one-hour
Bridle Trail ride follows a creek along the base of the mountain and
is recommended for children and rank novices. The two-hour
Thoroughbred Trail excursion climbs to the top of Pine Mountain for lake and valley views. More experienced riders should
enjoy the Buffalo Trail, which meanders all over the mountains,
mostly away from the more-congested standard trails. Reservations are required. ~ Route 354, Franklin D. Roosevelt State Park;
706-628-7463, 877-696-4613.

There's also horseback riding available at **Butts Mill Farm**,
where kids can also get hayrides and visit the petting zoo. ~ 2280
Butts Mill Road, Pine Mountain; 706-663-7400; www.buttsmill
farm.com.

Callaway Gardens has trails (including the ten-mile Discovery **BIKING**
Bicycle Trail) that wend through pine forests and skirt past gardens. The trails are slightly banked in places and sometimes make
sharp turns and cross little bridges. You can rent low-tech bikes
at the beach center if you didn't bring your own. You won't want
to take them out on the highway but if you do have your own 10-
or 15-speed wheels, you can use them here or farther afield. Admission. ~ Route 27, Pine Mountain; 706-663-2281, 800-225-
5292; www.callawaygardens.com.

There is also good riding along Route 27 between Pine
Mountain and beyond.

All distances listed for hiking trails are one way unless otherwise **HIKING**
noted.

At George T. Bagby State Park, you can pick up a decent map
(including descriptions of various plants) to the **Chattahoochee
Trail** (3 miles). It's a few feet above the lake, which is at an elevation of 180 feet. Made of hard-packed sand and a boardwalk—
which makes portions wheelchair accessible with assistance—
this trail has four loops and connecting paths. In warm weather,
you're likely to see alligators; a gazebo provides a place to sit and
watch the wildlife.

For unusual surroundings, few places can match—let alone
beat—Providence Canyon State Park. Known as The Little Grand
Canyon, this 1108-acre park boasts 150-foot canyons, rolling
hills and plenty of azaleas, rhododendrons and other shrubs and
trees. The **Backpacking Trail** (7 miles) is blazed with red markings and coincides with the canyon trail for a bit as you head in
a clockwise direction around the canyon rim. You are bound to
see woodpeckers having a field day amid the dead pine trees that

litter the ground; there are also turkeys, owls and other birds that like to nest in tree cavities. Keep an eye out for armadillos, raccoons, gray foxes and white-tailed deer as well as the less-exciting squirrels. Despite the changes in elevation, this is a moderate trail and open year-round.

The **Pine Mountain Trail** (40 miles) runs from the Callaway Country Store on Route 27 to the WJSP TV tower on Route 85W. For a trail map and camping information, stop at the Franklin D. Roosevelt State Park Office. ~ 2970 Route 190, Pine Mountain; 706-663-4858.

Miles of trails at **Callaway Gardens** loop through the pine forests and past gardens en route to various attractions. Walkers, cyclists and the occasional baby stroller share the wide paths, which are mostly shaded and offer shelter even during a drizzle. Everyone seems to walk from the butterfly exhibit to the chapel and elsewhere, but if you arrive early or late you should find room to get an aerobic workout of several miles.

Franklin D. Roosevelt State Park on Pine Mountain has two recommended trails. The **Mountain Creek Loop Trail** (3.2 miles) passes through several plant habitats as it runs around the campground. **Dowdell's Knob Loop** (4.3 miles) leads to FDR's favorite picnic spot.

Transportation

CAR

Route 75 forms the eastern backbone of Southwest Georgia; the Alabama state line, where the Chattahoochee River runs, is the western boundary. In between are few major highways other than Route 75 that extend from LaGrange to Atlanta and **Route 85** between Columbus and LaGrange, but rather a maze of two-lane roads. **Route 84** skirts the southern boundary of the state between Thomasville and the Alabama state line; **Route 19** runs north from Thomasville all the way to Atlanta.

AIR

Columbus Metropolitan Airport (706-324-2449; www.flycolum busga.com) is the only airport with regular service in this travel region. It is served by ASA/Delta Connections.

Hartsfield-Jackson Atlanta International Airport in southwest Atlanta is only a couple of hours from Columbus but nearly six hours from Thomasville. It is served by Air Canada, Air France, Air Tran, America West, American Airlines, British Airways, Continental, Delta Air Lines, Frontier, KLM, Korean Air, Midwest, Lufthansa, Northwest, United Airlines, US Airways and VARIG. ~ www.atlanta-airport.com.

BUS

Several towns are served by **Greyhound Bus Lines** (800-231-2222; www.greyhound.com). In Thomasville, the station is at 1123 West Jackson Street; in Albany at 300 West Oglethorpe

Boulevard; in Americus at 510 West Forsyth Street; and in Columbus at 818 Veterans Parkway.

Most major rental agencies have franchises at Columbus Metropolitan Airport. These include **Budget Rent A Car** (800-527-0700); **National Car Rental** (800-227-7368), which also offers minivans, 15-passenger vans and one-way rentals; **Avis Rent A Car** (800-230-4898), **Enterprise Rent A Car** (800-261-7331) and **Hertz Rent A Car** (800-230-4898).

CAR RENTALS

Columbus may have more independent cab companies per capita than any other city in Georgia. From **Airborne Taxi Co.** (706-689-1556) to **Yellow Cab** (706-322-1616), there are more than a dozen, although some listed in the local Yellow Pages are actually based across the river in Phenix City, Alabama.

TAXIS

FIVE

Atlanta

For decades, drivers have noticed the electronic sign displayed beside the road on the 2000 block of Peachtree Street. It provides an up-to-the-hour figure that reflects Atlanta's current population. It's unlikely that in all this time the numbers have ever gone down. In Atlanta, the number of citizens, like just about everything else, seems to go only in one direction. Up. And up and up.

No one who took a look at the real estate in the northwest Georgia woods in the late 1700s would have predicted a great city would come of it—no commercially navigable waterway, not much in the way of agricultural promise. The fact that it's 1000 feet above sea level . . . well, it could work. Or not work.

What the site did have was a convenient location for a railroad terminus. Lodged amidst three high granite ridges, it was a natural nexus for rail transport. The Georgia Legislature decided to build the Western & Atlantic railroad south from Tennessee to improve the transport link to the lucrative Northern markets. So what the hey, they must have thought, let's call the place Terminus.

By the mid-1800s, the town that started in 1837 as Terminus became Marthasville, and then ultimately Atlanta was thriving as people and goods from Augusta, Macon and Mobile were moved to Tennessee and beyond.

Naturally, this made the city a sitting duck when General Sherman decided to burn the state of Georgia. Actually, contrary to images from *Gone with the Wind*, the city was already mostly in ruins by the time Sherman began his infamous "March to the Sea," having taken over Atlanta on September 2, 1864. Yet, phoenix-like, the city revived itself. It's been said that Scarlett O'Hara is the patron saint of the city, and in many ways it is true.

Atlanta is pushy in the same way Scarlett was. Just after the Civil War, when the state was considering relocating the capital to Atlanta (despite the fact that Macon was more central and Milledgeville had invested a fortune in laying out a governor's mansion and other state facilities), Atlantans pushed and pressed for the honor. As a Milledgeville editorial of the time opined, "If Atlanta could suck as hard as it could blow, the Chattahoochee River would run north instead of south."

If any English-speaking people on Planet Earth hadn't heard of Atlanta before the 1996 Summer Olympics, odds are, they have now. For all its boosterism, Atlantans sometimes worry how they come across. As one prominent businessman said just before everybody came to town for the Games, "What if they get here and find out we're all hat and no cattle?"

He needn't have worried. Atlanta's legacy from the summer of 1996 is lasting in terms of infrastructure, at the very least. Still a major commercial hub, Atlanta lists among the companies with world headquarters here such firms as BellSouth, the Coca-Cola Company, Cox Communications, Delta Air Lines, United Parcel Service, Turner Broadcasting, Georgia Pacific, Equifax, Home Depot and Ritz-Carlton Hotels. To name a few.

Today, although Atlanta proper has just about a half-million people, the greater (20-county) metropolitan population has topped four million. Hailed for its quality of life, its green-ness, and its hospitality to business as well as to visitors, Atlanta shows no signs of slowing down.

It's telling that the top attraction in terms of visitors to Atlanta is CNN Headquarters, with Stone Mountain Park a distant second.

Peachtree is the name most often associated with Atlanta. No wonder. There are 32 different roadways with that name in the title. And you can bet there's traffic on all of them.

Actually, it's the interstates, Perimeter Road (Route 285) and Route 400, that are really bumper-to-bumper. In the city itself, there's always another way to get where you're going. Yet traffic defines this city as much as the Southern drawl most of its residents have, by nature or by design. Like Los Angeles, it's a city on wheels.

Unlike L.A., though, Atlanta has a wonderful transit system known as MARTA (Metro Atlanta Rapid Transit Authority) that can get you within a few blocks of almost anywhere. Mastering this system should be your first priority when visiting this boomtown.

Downtown Atlanta

Downtown Atlanta, once the city's undisputed business hub, is now the province of conventions, professional sports and higher education. It's a warren of boulevards and side streets that lead to open expanses yet to be filled in. The 1996 Summer Olympics gave the area an economic shot in the arm but Atlanta's incessant boosterism claims that growth would have happened anyway. For the purposes of guiding you through the area, the term Downtown extends past the traditional borders to include neighborhoods south of Ralph David Abernathy Boulevard. The northern border remains North Avenue, which is the demarcation with Midtown. Also included in this section is the nexus for the younger crowd, Little Five Points, which is roughly Atlanta's contemporary version of San Francisco's Haight-Ashbury district in the '60s and '70s—only without the actual hippies. North of Little Five Points is the Virginia-Highland neighborhood, one of the hip places to live thanks to a plethora of restaurants, shops and bungalows inhabited by, of course, hip people.

SIGHTS   A handful of attractions are grouped near the Capitol, but several others, such as the zoo, will require a car or MARTA to reach.

The Victorian lifestyle is on display at **The Wren's Nest** in southwest Atlanta. Author-journalist Joel Chandler Harris lived here with his family from 1881 to 1908. The curry-yellow Queen Anne Victorian was extensively restored in 1996, though the decor has remained the same since Mrs. Harris moved out in 1913, after decreeing that Mr. Harris' room be left the way it was the day he died. The furnishings, the elaborate wallpaper and other details are telling, but nothing compares to learning more about the complex man whose folksy characters (Br'er Rabbit and Br'er Fox among them) became internationally known through Chandler's *Uncle Remus Tales*. Kids of all ages will enjoy the storytelling on selected weekends. Closed Sunday and Monday. Admission. ~ 1050 Ralph David Abernathy Boulevard Southwest; 404-753-7735.

HIDDEN ►

From The Wren's Nest, it's a short drive to Atlanta's—and maybe Georgia's and possibly the Southeast U.S.'s—only fine-arts museum dedicated to African-American art, **Hammonds House**. Before his death in 1985, Dr. Otis Thrash Hammonds, a prominent local physician, collected more than 250 pieces ranging from Harlem Renaissance works to black memorabilia to Haitian art. In 1988, his residence, an 1870 Eastlake-style Victorian in the city's oldest neighborhood, West End, was converted into a museum, which acquired his collection. Hammonds House also hosts traveling exhibitions and serves as a cultural resource center. Closed Monday and weekend mornings. ~ 503 Peeples Street Southwest; 404-752-8730; www.hammonds house.org, e-mail mail@hammondshouse.org.

To the west of Route 75, off the Turner Field/Olympic Stadium exit, is **Turner Field**. Many of Atlanta's attractions have behind-the-scenes programs for visitors; baseball fans won't want to miss the tours given here. You won't get to swing a bat but you do start the tour in the Braves Museum then visit a Braves luxury suite, the press box and the broadcast booth, the clubhouse and the Braves' dugout. Closed on home-game days. Admission. ~ 755 Hank Aaron Drive Southeast; 404-614-2311, 404-614-2310; www.bravesmuseum.com.

East of Turner Field, signs point to **Grant Park**, which has two major points of interest. Highlights of **Zoo Atlanta** include the Sumatran Tiger Forest (where these rare tigers prowl, sip from a stream or rinse off under a waterfall), the Ford African Rain Forest (with 23 gorillas and growing), the Masai Mara habitat replicating the Kenyan plains (where giraffes and zebras roam freely together on open land), and a wide range of conservation, research, recreational and educational programs. Admission. ~ Cherokee and Atlanta avenues; 404-624-5600, 888-945-5432; www.zooatlanta.com.

In the same park, the **Atlanta Cyclorama** is famed for its mammoth work, "The Battle of Atlanta." It's hard to exaggerate the impact of a painting in the round that is 42 feet high and 358 in circumference, with more than 16,000 square feet of canvas. A diorama in front of it has a 3-D landscape animated with war

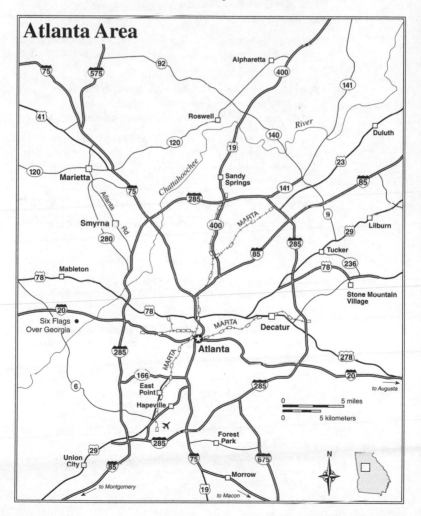

Text continued on page 204.

Three-day Weekend

Atlanta

Day 1
- Drop your luggage off at the **Georgian Terrace** (page 222), where the stars of *Gone with the Wind* stayed during the movie premiere, and prepare for an active day.

- First stop is the **Fox Theatre** (page 220), across the street from the hotel, for a colorful tour.

- Join locals for lunch at **Cha Gio** (page 225), a Vietnamese restaurant that's been a popular favorite since it opened in 1977. Best of all, it serves lunch all afternoon.

- A MARTA train will zip you to the nearby **High Museum of Art** (page 218), where blockbuster shows, a sterling permanent exhibit and the impressive architecture offer a mini-course in art history.

- Take another MARTA train over to **Little Five Points** (page 211) to see what the young and hip are up to. Check out the merchandise at the **Junkman's Daughter** (page 214) and return to the hotel via MARTA.

- Splurge on Southern-tinged gourmet fare at **City Grill** (page 213).

- Catch a show—perhaps a ballet or concert—at the historic Fox Theatre before calling it a day.

Day 2
- Enjoy breakfast at the inn, then explore the outdoor and indoor exhibitions in the **Atlanta Botanical Garden** (page 220) before embarking on a walk around Piedmont Park.

- The cul-de-sac known as **Miami Circle** (page 228) boasts dozens of shops, most of them specializing in antiques and other home decor. Window shop until lunchtime.

- Experiment with different small plates (called *tapas*) at **Eclipse di Luna** (page 224), an atmospheric Mediterranean restaurant tucked away at the far end of Miami Circle.

- Spend a couple of hours meandering through the adjacent shopping malls **Lenox Square** (page 229) and **Phipps Plaza** (page 229), home to major national chains as well as specialty stores and restaurants.

- Forget returning to the hotel. Instead, drive a few blocks for a delightfully different kind of dinner at **Fogo de Chao** (page 225), a South American restaurant where the specialty is meats served by costumed waiters.

- Chill out to cool jazz at **Dante's Down the Hatch** (page 215), where you can also have a nightcap before turning in for the day.

Day 3

- Order a second cup of coffee and finish the *Atlanta Journal-Constitution* during a leisurely breakfast at the Georgian Terrace before driving out to **Stone Mountain** (page 235), where the leaders of the Confederacy are carved into the side of the mountain. Take the tram to the top of the world's largest granite outcropping, then get out for a hike.

- Drive to the nearby town of Stone Mountain for lunch at the **Sycamore Grill** (page 240), a pretty restaurant across the road from the village shops.

- Bone up on ancient history at the **Michael C. Carlos Museum** (page 234) on the campus of Emory University.

- Spend the afternoon getting to know the charming neighborhood known as **Virginia-Highland** (page 210), home to innumerable shops and restaurants of all kinds. People-watch from the vantage point of a café along the main drag.

- Scoop up some cutting-edge seafood at **BluePointe** (page 226). After dinner, hang out at **Blind Willie's** (page 216) and groove to some R&B.

figures—soldiers, horses, etc.—and when the lights go down and the action starts, visitors sometimes start to flinch from the visual effects, enhanced by a narration by James Earl Jones. Admission. ~ 800 Cherokee Avenue Southeast; 404-658-7625; www.beatatlanta.com.

HIDDEN ►

On the east side of Grant Park is a street named Boulevard; take it several blocks north to Memorial Drive. The historic **Oakland Cemetery**, which began in 1850 when the city obtained six acres for burial use, is the final resting place of many interesting people. For the next 34 years, almost every person who died in Atlanta was buried in this cemetery. But no grave is more famous than that of Margaret Mitchell, whose *Gone with the Wind* has sold countless copies in virtually every language. Also here are Victorian and religious sculptures and symbols, various mausolea in Gothic Revival and neoclassical styles, and other points of interest in what is now an 88-acre site, the third-largest green space (after Piedmont and Grant parks) in the city. The visitors center is closed weekends but the cemetery remains open. You can take a guided or self-guided tour of the grounds. Admission. ~ 248 Oakland Avenue Southeast; 404-688-2107; www.oaklandcemetery.com.

Leaving Oakland Cemetery, head toward the heart of downtown Atlanta on Memorial Drive (Route 154); when you reach Capitol Avenue, turn right to visit one of the Georgia's most important buildings.

The stately rotunda of the **Georgia State Capitol** soars 237 feet to a dome covered in 23-karat gold mined in nearby Dahlonega. In the rotunda are portraits of presidents George Washington and Andrew Jackson as well as famous Georgians including Benjamin Harvey Hill and Robert Toombs, and figures from the state's earliest days such as General James Oglethorpe and the French general Marquis de Lafayette. Marble busts of George Walton, Button Gwinnett and Dr. Lyman Hall—Georgia's signers of the Declaration of the Independence—are also on display. Also in the capitol building is the aptly named **Georgia Capitol Museum**. The rather modest collection includes memorabilia along the lines of historical battle flags. Tours are given four times a day during the week. Closed Saturday and Sunday. ~ 200 Washington Street; 404-656-2844, 404-651-6996 (museum); www.sos.state.ga.us/museum.

When you leave the Capitol, follow Martin Luther King Jr. Drive to the west for one block to visit a local shrine. The world's most-recognized trademark got its corporate start in Atlanta long before CNN came into U.S. households. So naturally the Coca-Cola Company is not only headquartered here, it has **The World of Coca-Cola**. A self-guided tour begins on the third floor with a look at bottling mechanisms that would put most California

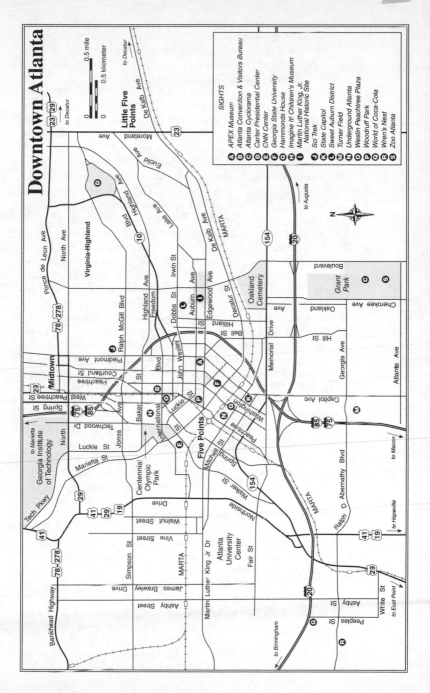

Downtown Atlanta

Little Five Points

SIGHTS

- **A** APEX Museum
- **B** Atlanta Convention & Visitors Bureau
- **C** Atlanta Cyclorama
- **D** Carter Presidential Center
- **E** CNN Center
- **F** Georgia State University
- **G** Hammonds House
- **H** Imagine It! Children's Museum
- **I** Martin Luther King, Jr. National Historic Site
- **J** Sci Trek
- **K** State Capitol
- **L** Sweet Auburn District
- **M** Turner Field
- **N** Underground Atlanta
- **O** Westin Peachtree Plaza
- **P** Woodruff Park
- **Q** World of Coca-Cola
- **R** Wren's Nest
- **S** Zoo Atlanta

wineries to shame. A video tells the story of the invention of the famously secret formula and how the elixir was eventually introduced in soda fountains, beginning here. A pair of entrepreneurs came up with the magic idea: bottle it. Other floors of exhibits cover international advertising and promotion, production and the like. Most visitors will inevitably get very thirsty for The Real Thing. No problem. Just put your plastic cup into a dispensing gizmo and stand back. Way back. Admission. ~ 55 Martin Luther King Jr. Drive; 404-676-5151, 800-676-2653; www.woccat lanta.com.

Until you've seen it, it's hard to grasp the meaning of **Underground Atlanta**. Its history dates to the late 19th century, when Atlanta emerged as a busy railroad hub. The area around Alabama Street in downtown Atlanta was a natural for commercial development, what with inbound and outbound passengers crowding in on a daily basis. To ease the congestion of the crisscrossing railway tracks, which forced traffic—even then, emerging as a thorn in the city's side—to a crawl or complete halt. The solution was to raise the east–west streets so that they connected with viaducts; today Upper Alabama Street remains elevated above Lower Alabama Street. The merchants wanted to be up where their doors could open to foot traffic so they abandoned their lower levels to storage or complete neglect. Today it's filled with shops, many of them national chain outlets, along with vending carts. It's a far cry from Lenox Square but does have interesting features from a civic history standpoint. As you go through it, look for markers explaining various historic sites. You can get an information sheet at the Underground Atlanta Information Booth on Lower Alabama Street near the escalators. ~ 50 Upper Alabama Street; 404-523-2311; www.underground-atlanta.com.

Atlanta University Center is a collection of six different schools dating to the late 1860s, when a school for ex-slaves was founded. With Clark Atlanta University, Morehouse College, the Morehouse School of Medicine, Spelman College, Morris Brown College and the Interdenominational Theological Center, AUC is the country's largest African-American academic center. Throughout the year the colleges present a number of films, exhibits and other public events related to African-American culture. ~ Off Martin Luther King Jr. Drive between Sunset Street and James Brawley Drive; 404-522-8980.

If you go back along Martin Luther King Jr. Drive to Washington Street and turn left for two blocks you will come to the **Georgia State University** complex comprising six colleges. It's the second-largest state university in Georgia, enrolling about 25,000 students.

Afterwards, head north across Edgewood Avenue to Auburn Avenue and turn right for a block. Just past Courtland Street you will see, on your right, a museum building. The APEX **Museum** (the acronym stands for African American Panoramic Experience) demonstrates—through exhibits, videos and memorabilia—the cultural heritage of African Americans and its impact on the development of the country. Inside the stately brick building at Auburn Avenue near Courtland Street, a 15-minute video tells the story of the neighborhood of Sweet Auburn, narrated by actress Cicely Tyson and political leader Julian Bond; there are exhibits of West African sculpture and other artworks, as well as a replica of a vintage trolley. Closed Monday. Admission. ~ 135 Auburn Avenue Northeast; 404-523-2739; www.apexmuseum.org.

Continue east on Auburn Avenue, a route that will take you through the **Sweet Auburn** district rich in African-American heritage. When you cross Jackson, you will be in the midst of a major complex devoted to Martin Luther King, Jr., and the Civil Rights movement. It includes the Martin Luther King, Jr., Center for Non-Violent Social Change (usually referred to as The King Center), where the intertwined stories of Dr. King and the movement are chronicled. Begin at the Welcome Center on Auburn Avenue between Jackson Street and Boulevard before continuing to the Martin Luther King, Jr., Birth Home two blocks down, the King Center and then back to Ebenezer Baptist Church.

The tapes of some of the late reverend's impassioned speeches are so riveting that some visitors spend hours at the **Martin Luther King, Jr. National Historic Site**. Born in 1909 at 501 Auburn Avenue to a Baptist minister and a musician, King graduated at the age of 19 from Atlanta's Morehouse College, earning an additional two degrees by the age of 27—one from Crozer Theological Seminary and another, in systematic theology, from

AUTHOR FAVORITE

I grew up near the real "Moon River," which inspired the famous theme song for *Breakfast at Tiffany's*, and so I was especially entranced with the **Johnny Mercer Collection** at Georgia State University. Mercer, born in Savannah in 1909, penned more than 1000 song lyrics between 1930 and his death in 1976, as well as the music for 55 of them, although he could neither read music nor play an instrument. Sheet music, correspondence, handwritten manuscripts, recordings and tapes of televised appearances are on display here, honoring the man who wrote songs as diverse as "The Days of Wine and Roses" and "I'm an Old Cow Hand." Closed Saturday and Sunday except by appointment. ~ Library South Building, Georgia State University, 103 Decatur Street; 404-651-2477.

Boston University. His impact not only on the African-American community but on the entire Civil Rights movement is unparalleled. Some of his story is told here, in poignant exhibits that include one of his pastoral robes and personal items from the family, such as a dress worn by his widow, Coretta Scott King. Viewing the collections here and in nearby buildings, many visitors learn new details or may be reminded of King's innumerable achievements such as his 1970 Grammy Award, on view here, for the Best Spoken Word Recording (for "Why I Oppose the War in Viet Nam"). The self-guided tour starts at the National Park Service Visitor Center, near his **gravesite**, a large marble tomb embossed with a plaque quoting his "Free at Last" speech. The tomb rests on a platform surrounded by water. A free brochure details other sights in the Martin Luther King, Jr., Historic District (a.k.a. Sweet Auburn), including his **birth home** (501 Auburn Avenue), which is open for 30-minute tours of 15 people or less. ~ 450 Auburn Avenue Northeast; 404-331-5190, 404-331-6922; www.nps.gov/malu.

Three generations of the King family have presided over the **Ebenezer Baptist Church**. It was here, in the basement of this 1922 Gothic Revival–style building, that Martin Luther King, Jr., organized the Southern Christian Leadership Conference (SCLC) in 1957. And it was here that mourners gathered by the thousands for Dr. King's funeral following his 1968 assassination. Almost unbelievably, it was also here, in 1974, that Dr. King's mother was killed by an assassin's bullet as she sat in front of the church organ. It remains a powerful centerpiece of the Civil Rights movement in Atlanta. Closed Sunday except for services. ~ 407 Auburn Avenue Northeast; 404-688-7263.

For a walking tour of Sweet Auburn, contact the Atlanta Preservation Center. (See "Ambling through Atlanta" sidebar.)

When you leave the Martin Luther King, Jr., site, head north on Boulevard and right on Freedom Parkway for about three blocks. It's one mile to the exit you want to take.

What's called the **Carter Presidential Center** is equal parts Carter and presidency. An introductory 30-minute video, for example,

AMBLING THROUGH ATLANTA

The **Atlanta Preservation Center** offers numerous guided walks in different city areas at regularly scheduled times. The West End, Druid Hills, Sweet Auburn, Ansley Park, Grant Park and Historic Downtown can be explored with a knowledgeable guide for one to two hours for a nominal fee. ~ 327 Saint Paul Avenue, Atlanta; 404-876-2041; www. preserveatlanta.com.

is devoted to all the U.S. presidents of the 20th century. But there's plenty for Carter fans to enjoy, especially the life-size replica of his Oval Office, where, via recording, he explains why he chose to use John Kennedy's desk. Also on display are various gifts of state (from India, Ireland, Thailand, etc.), family photos and memorabilia from Carter's presidential campaign, interactive consoles detailing the success of the Carter Center's efforts at conflict resolution, souvenirs from the White House years and part of the Carter Presidential Library. The former President's Nobel Peace Prize is also on display. The library holds some 27 million pages of documents and more than 1.5 million photographs. Located two miles from downtown on a 37-acre hillock, the center consists of several buildings embracing a Japanese garden and landscaped ponds. Admission. ~ 453 Freedom Parkway; 404-420-5100; www.cartercenter.org, e-mail carterweb@emory.edu.

Return to central downtown via Freedom Parkway, cross the interstate and head west on John Wesley Dobbs Avenue. You can park just before you reach Peachtree Street.

Downtown office workers have an alternative to yet another boring lunch hour: they can visit the **High Museum of Art's Folk Art & Photography Galleries** on the lower floors of the Georgia-Pacific Center. Shows are displayed on various levels in this pocket museum that also features lectures and other special events. Folk art is definitely a growth industry, nowhere more so than in the Deep South, and as photography continues its rise in both popularity and respect, this museum is bound to become better known. Closed Sunday. Admission. ~ 30 John Wesley Dobbs Avenue; 404-577-6940; www.high.org.

◄ HIDDEN

A few blocks north on Peachtree Street is the Westin Peachtree Plaza hotel. It's not the hotel you've come to see, but what you can see *from* the hotel. Take a two-minute elevator ride up 72 stories to the **Sun Dial Restaurant, Bar & View** for the best view you'll ever get of Atlanta without being airborne. (You won't be airborne here but you will be moving if you visit the rotating restaurant or bar.) Visitors can take a self-guided walking tour around the rim and begin to figure out the lay of the land; close-up views of the major sites are afforded by telescope. Admission. ~ 210 Peachtree Street Northwest; 404-589-7506.

◄ HIDDEN

When you depart the hotel go left (west) on International Boulevard for a couple of blocks to **Centennial Olympic Park**. Flanked by the giant towers of CNN and other corporate offices, this wide open space replaces much of a rundown neighborhood. Within its 20 acres is Centennial Plaza, commemorating the 100th anniversary of the modern Olympic Games, which contains 23 flags honoring the host countries. There's also a fountain shaped like the five Olympic rings. Landscaped with trees, shrubs, statuary, pools and lawn, the park is one of the loveliest legacies of the 1996 Summer Olympic Games. ~ 265 West Park Avenue; 404-223-4412.

Another block out International Boulevard will take you to your next destination. Squatting on an entire block between the heart of downtown and the Centennial Olympic Park, the world headquarters of CNN (**Cable News Network**) provides a visual reminder of founder Ted Turner's impact on the city. In the vast lobby, amid shops hawking Braves' caps and CNN logo-abilia, an open-air studio lets members of the public participate in a week-day afternoon broadcast of *Talkback Live*. More interesting by far are the 45-minute tours of the whole building, starting with a ride up the escalator to the eighth floor. Ever wondered how teleprompters work? How does the TV meteorologist know where Memphis is when his back is always to the U.S. map? These and a gazillion other questions are answered in a rapid-fire tour that takes you into most of the network newsrooms, telling the story of CNN's revolutionary, unrehearsed, on-the-spot, 24-hour world-news coverage. Admission for tours. ~ CNN Center; 404-827-2300, 877-426-6868; www.cnn.com/studiotour.

While you're downtown, drop by the **Atlanta Convention & Visitors Bureau**, where you can find brochures, maps and all manner of information for Atlanta and farther afield. It's located above the Peachtree Center Mall. Closed Saturday and Sunday. ~ 233 Peachtree Street Northeast, Suite 100; 404-521-6600, 800-285-2682, fax 404-577-3293; www.atlanta.com.

Head north on Peachtree and turn left on Baker Street. At the **Imagine It! Children's Museum**, families can enjoy activities such as exploring the sources of food and translating information about nutrition into recipe ideas, or even loading a delivery truck with a "forklift." Kids on their own can paint walls, make music, create sand sculptures or join an international dance troupe for a while. The exhibits and interactive programs are all about creativity, learning and stimulating the imagination. Admission. ~ 275 Olympic Centennial Park Drive; 404-659-5437; www.imagineit-cma.org.

Atlanta's hands-on, interactive science museum for all ages is **Sci Trek**, and it garners top marks for many of its 150 permanent exhibits. The idea is to explain scientific principles using games, toys and models so that learning is painless. What the heck, it's fun even if you don't learn anything. One hall is devoted to simple machines like levers; the Hall of Light and Perception is better than the hall of mirrors at a county fair. The KidSpace has smaller, kinder exhibits. Admission. ~ 395 Piedmont Avenue Northeast; 404-522-5500; www.scitrek.org.

Virginia-Highland is popular with young marrieds who have moved beyond funk but aren't ready, willing or able to try for a spot in, say, Buckhead; it's a loosely defined area that extends well into Midtown. It's chockablock with cottages and small houses, but the scene is on Highland Avenue, particularly. There are almost as many restaurants of all stripes as there are shops— nearly all of them one of a kind. If you want nationally known stores, head to the malls.

Little Five Points—as distinguished from Five Points—emanates from the intersection of Moreland, Euclid and McLendon avenues. You can find counterparts to this neighborhood in Manhattan's East Village and San Francisco's Haight-Ashbury district. People live around here but the street action draws people from all over, especially teenagers and their older siblings looking for hip and funky clothes and a sense of community.

If you want to stay overnight in the downtown area, choices are limited. The **Westin Peachtree Plaza** is right in the heart of things: a wonderful five-story atrium, pool, exercise equipment, the Sun Dial restaurant on the 73rd floor, and over 1000 rooms make it one of the best choices. Decor is typically hotel pastel, though the premier suites on floors 41-50 and 48 offer top-flight accommodations. ~ 210 West Peachtree Street Northwest; 888-447-8159, fax 404-589-7424; www.westin.com. DELUXE TO ULTRA-DELUXE.

LODGING

The fanciest digs can be found (as they can be all over the world) at the **Ritz-Carlton Atlanta** (there's another Ritz-Carlton in Buckhead). The fabulous lobby is decked out with fine art and the rooms are pure Ritz: top-notch residential furnishings, carpeted floors, luxurious amenities and not a whole lot of space. If you're not up for a five-diamond hotel, you can go for afternoon tea and be waited on hand and foot by the legendarily hospitable staff at this 25-story, 444-room hotel. ~ 181 Peachtree Street Northeast; 404-659-0400, 800-241-3333, fax 404-688-0400; www.ritz-carlton.com. ULTRA-DELUXE.

Until a few years ago, there was one non-chain hotel in the neighborhood, the Barclay, which is now the **Quality Hotel**. It has 79 rooms, done in a combination of mauve and floral prints; all

TWISTING AND TURNING

When the kids need to blow off some steam, take them out to **Six Flags Over Georgia**, west of downtown off Route 20. The massive amusement park boasts more than 100 rides, including artificial whitewater rapids, for both the timid and the fearless. The 60-m.p.h. Viper ride should prepare everyone in the family for driving on Atlanta's freeways. On October weekends, it all turns into a giant goblins' hollow. Hours and days of operation vary by season; call ahead. Admission. ~ 275 Riverside Parkway, Austell; 770-948-9290; www.sixflags.com/georgia.

have a downtown view and a few of them even have balconies. ~ 89 Luckie Street; 404-524-7991, 800-228-5151, fax 404-525-0672; www.qualityinnatlanta.com, e-mail info@qualityinnatlanta.com. MODERATE.

HIDDEN ►   Within walking distance of the shops and restaurants that give Little Five Points its character is the **Inman Park Inn Bed & Breakfast/Woodruff House**. It overlooks Springvale Park in a National Register of Historic Places neighborhood that reflects the influence of Frederick Law Olmsted, who designed New York City's Central Park as well as other parks and neighborhoods in Atlanta. The brick Tudor-style inn was built in 1912 as a "honeymoon residence" for Robert W. Woodruff, the Coca-Cola magnate, and has 12-foot ceilings, heart-of-pine floors, fireplaces and a walled garden. Three modest accommodations (one upstairs) are furnished with 18th- and 19th-century antiques and oriental rugs. Continental breakfast is included. ~ 100 Waverly Way Northeast; 404-668-9498, 404-668-6792 (mobile), fax 404-524-9939; www.inmanparkbandb.com, e-mail info@inmanparkbandb.com. MODERATE TO DELUXE.

DINING   Restaurants in this area are geared either to the worker bees who need a place for lunch or executives and conventioneers who meet in the finer spots to continue business over dinner. There is a smattering of wonderfully inventive places, too, if you keep an eye out. While Virginia-Highland is the trendy spot, the best bet in town for ethnic dining is around Little Five Points.

With its stone floors painted maroon, its Dijon-yellow stone walls stamped with fleurs-de-lis and an antique wooden banquette, **Les Fleurs de Lis Café** would do justice to the Left Bank of HIDDEN ►   the Seine. House-made pâté, *croque monsieur* and other French bistro-style dishes are available at lunch; crêpes and other delicacies are served at breakfast; and more substantial fare on Thursday nights. You can find this little piece of Paris tucked inside the Healey Building. No dinner Friday through Wednesday. ~ 57 Forsyth Street, Suite R-8; 404-230-9151. BUDGET TO MODERATE.

Even if you're from Manhattan, you will find little fault with the pastrami sandwich at **111 MLK**. This and other New York–style sandwiches (most have names, such as the "Oy Vay" with chopped chicken liver, corned beef and pastrami stuffed between slices of rye bread) and various salads keep Atlantans coming back for more. No dinner. Closed Saturday and Sunday. ~ 111 Martin Luther King Jr. Drive; 404-523-0109. BUDGET.

If you feel like your head is spinning, not to worry. The **Sun Dial Restaurant, Bar & View** atop the Westin Peachtree Plaza slowly rotates, giving diners a wonderful view. The menu is Continental and not distinguished by much except a knock-out bourbon-shrimp salad that's extra spicy—a nice surprise. For a 360-degree view, head up to the Sun Dial View at the tippy top of the hotel. ~ 210 Peachtree Street Northwest; 404-589-7506. ULTRA-DELUXE.

From sushi to wasabi steak to Malaysian curry chicken, the menu lives up to the name at the **Pacific Rim Bistro**. Glass walls front the street while the casual interior is an upbeat mix of red walls, lacquered furniture and halogen lighting. No lunch on weekends. ~ 303 Peachtree Center Avenue; 404-893-0018. MODERATE TO DELUXE.

VIRGINIA-HIGHLAND Exposed brick walls and well-trod hardwood floors infuse **Noche** with a romantic ambience suited to its semi-exotic tapas, little plates of (mostly) Spanish appetizers. If you're not familiar with manchego cheese or *huitlacoche* (an aromatic Mexican corn fungus), this would be the place to try it, paired with wine, an aged tequila (*anejo*) or a specialty cocktail. The margaritas are a big draw for the young crowd that congregates in this lively residential district. No lunch Saturday or Sunday. ~ 1000 Virginia Avenue; 404-815-9155. MODERATE.

LITTLE FIVE POINTS Tantalizing aromas immediately entice as soon as you open the door to **The Olive Bistro**, a modest counter-plus-tables. It's easy to make a meal from "meze," or a Middle Eastern first course like hummus dip, baked eggplant and similar small, pungent plates. Salads and sandwiches run along the same lines, only not quite as ethnic. Bigger entrées are grilled rosemary chicken, Mediterranean lasagne and a Mediterranean quiche. Try a Turkish coffee or sweet baklava and you are still likely to spend less than $9 a person. Closed Monday. ~ 1099-A Euclid Avenue Northeast; phone/fax 404-582-0029. BUDGET.

AUTHOR FAVORITE

In a setting more suited to a bank than a restaurant, **City Grill** claims the most elegant ambiance in downtown Atlanta. Of course, when you get your bill—even though dinners are prix-fixe—you may wish it were a bank, but when all is said and done, the prices are appropriate for the food and the decor, which includes murals and marble. Lamb, veal and seafood all receive the deluxe treatment, with an accent on Southern and Southwestern specialties. If you want to see the city's movers and shakers, drop in here at lunch or at cocktail time. Few locals go downtown for dinner, unless it's to a private club. No lunch Saturday. Closed Sunday. ~ 50 Hurt Plaza; 404-524-2489; www.citygrillatlanta.com, e-mail info@citygrillatlanta.com. ULTRA-DELUXE.

Even if you decide not to eat at the **Euclid Avenue Yacht Club,** you ought to at least stick your head in. The place looks like your average neighborhood bar but it's mostly a restaurant, at least until later in the evening. They offer a variety of sandwiches, a Yacht Dog (kosher beef on a poppy-seed bun), a veggie burger, a cheese steak and the like. There are usually Blue Plate specials and popcorn, "microwaved to perfection." ~ 1136 Euclid Avenue Northeast; 404-688-2582. BUDGET.

The **Vortex Bar & Grill** may have the best burgers in town, but you'll never get around to ordering one if you read the long list of etiquette rules on the back of the menu, including an Idiot Policy designed to refuse service to jerks. That settled, feel free to enter the huge skull that serves as a doorway and work your way past the motorcycle into the vortex. The menu features fun dishes like Mexican heart attacks, omelets, sandwiches and an awesome array of burgers. Oh, and there are several Great Big Weenies to choose from. ~ 438 Moreland Avenue Northeast; 404-688-1828. BUDGET.

SHOPPING   Major-league shopping in the downtown neighborhood is indeed gone with the wind, especially since Rich's pulled out its flagship store and, like everyone else, withdrew to the malls. But there are some choices, especially in novelty items, vintage and new clothing, books, ethnic art, furniture and home accents, in the Little Five Points area. Virginia-Highland is dominated by clothing and interior-design boutiques with price tags ranging from moderate to expensive.

If you're pressed for time, need souvenirs and don't want to pay airport prices, drop in to **Just A Dollar** and similar stores in **Underground Atlanta.** Besides the little shops that sell this and that, you will find many vending-cart merchants, sort of a county-fair atmosphere, minus the natural light. Essentially, Underground Atlanta sounds a lot more interesting than it is and you wouldn't miss much by skipping it. ~ Martin Luther King Jr. Drive and other access points; 404-523-2311; www.underground-atlanta.com.

FASHION FETISH

Junkman's Daughter in Little Five Points looks like a bad acid trip but is pretty harmless, selling doodads, earrings, clothing (including Hawaiian shirts) and those black five-pound boots that look more heavy than comfortable. The most interesting part of this very big store is the fetish room, where leather masks and other S&M paraphernalia are sold—along with how-to books!—to anyone who can prove they're over. 18 years of age. ~ 464 Moreland Avenue Northeast; 404-577-3188.

The **World of Coca-Cola** sells more than Coke, but you'll have a hard time finding a mug, sweatshirt, jacket, cap or T-shirt without the familiar logo. Some of the merchandise is very nice quality, so if you're caught in a rainstorm or a suddenly chilly day, remember to look in here. You don't have to gain admission to the exhibits if you just want to shop. ~ 55 Martin Luther King Jr. Drive; 404-676-5151; www.woccatlanta.com.

LITTLE FIVE POINTS   **Sevananda** claims to be the oldest and biggest natural foods store in the southeastern U.S. so it's the place to find healthful snacks and potions. ~ 467 Moreland Avenue; 404-681-2831.

New, rare and even weird books are the stock in trade at **A Cappella Books**. ~ 1133 Euclid Avenue Northeast; 404-681-5128.

For alternative merchandise like fetish wear, vinyl, latex and various leather items, check out **Lucky Devil**. ~ 1158 Euclid Avenue Northeast; 404-522-0351.

If you want your ears (or anything else) tattooed or pierced, the Little Five Points area is the place to go. Ditto if you want crystals or clothes for a 12-year-old going on 22. But there are some places worth a stop either for the merchandise or just for the experience.

NIGHTLIFE

Newly refurbished with many antiques, including a Steinway piano, **Dante's Down the Hatch** offers live jazz and folk singing nightly (except Monday). For an extra $6, you can be seated on the 17th-century Spanish galleon installed close to the music. You can also order dinner—as long as you like fondue. ~ 3380 Peachtree Road; 404-266-1600.

Blues in the Alley is just the thing if you're up for a glass of wine and some live blues. There's an open jam session every Sunday afternoon. Occasional cover. ~ Underground Atlanta, 50 Upper Alabama Street Southwest; 404-584-7557; www.bluesin thealley.net.

Okay, it's touristy, but it's always fun to have a cocktail (or dinner) in a revolving restaurant such as **Polaris** on top of the Hyatt Regency Atlanta. Designed by John Portman, the hotel and its spinning rooftop aerie were positively cutting-edge back on opening day some 30 years ago. ~ 265 Peachtree Street Northeast; 404-577-1234.

Housed in a former church, **The Tabernacle** has five funky floors with two performance stages where you can see the likes of Willie Brown or even James Brown, but most likely not major rock acts. ~ 152 Luckie Street; 404-659-9022; www.atlantacon certs.com (for performance schedule).

The **Atlanta Ballet** dates back to the opening of the Fox Theatre in 1929. These days, the dancers tread these old boards only for the seasonal *Nutcracker* performances; otherwise, they are most likely to be at the Atlanta Civic Center performing both classical and contemporary productions. ~ 1400 Peachtree Street Northwest; 404-873-5811, 404-892-3303 (box office); www.at lantaballet.com.

The **Atlanta Civic Center** is the venue for a variety of productions, including pop concerts, dance performances and Broadway musicals. ~ 395 Piedmont Avenue Northeast; 404-523-6275; www.atlanticiviccenter.com.

VIRGINIA-HIGHLAND The place for blues is **Blind Willie's**, a storefront club that packs 'em in for some of the country's top R&B entertainers. Cover. ~ 828 North Highland Avenue Northeast; 404-873-2583.

In the heart of the neighborhood is local favorite **Moe's and Joe's**. Check it out if you're 20-something or feel like revisiting your college days, only with a better jukebox sound system. ~ 1033 North Highland Avenue Northeast; 404-873-6090.

In the middle of the 20th century, the dark, abandoned Lower Alabama Street was developed as a commercial enterprise dubbed Underground Atlanta—despite the fact that none of it is technically below ground.

LITTLE FIVE POINTS Dad's Garage Theatre Company offers cutting-edge performances, especially of the improv variety. ~ 280 Elizabeth Street Northeast; 404-523-3141; www.dads garage.com.

The **Horizon Theatre Company** produces new works by contemporary playwrights from late January to mid-August. ~ Euclid and Austin avenues; 404-584-7450; www.horizontheatre.com.

The **Variety Playhouse** attracts big names—after all, it has 1000 seats to fill in a former movie theater that has dancing room in front of the stage. Cover. ~ 1099 Euclid Avenue Northeast; 404-521-1786; www.variety-playhouse.com.

College, rockabilly and alternative bands play most nights at the **Star Community Bar** (call it the Star Bar if you value your reputation). The jukebox in the basement, boasting 5000 selections, will paralyze you with indecision. Cover depends on the band's popularity. ~ 437 Moreland Avenue Northeast; 404-681-9018; www.starbar.net.

PARKS   **CARTER PRESIDENTIAL CENTER GARDENS** Best visited in the spring, when hundreds of roses bloom, this park is accessible via the Freedom Parkway; look for the circle of flags at the entrance to the center, where various flowers blossom at different times of the year. In this complex is the 2500-square-foot rose garden, featuring some 80 varieties as well as a meadow filled with wildflowers, acres of native oak forests and, across the lake, Japanese gardens designed by master gardener Kinsaku Nakane. The larger waterfall represents President Carter; the smaller, his wife,

Rosalynn. The cherry trees here blossom from late March into early May. It makes for a delightful respite from downtown's hustle and bustle. ~ 453 Freedom Parkway; 404-331-3900, www.cartercenter.org.

CENTENNIAL OLYMPIC PARK Located downtown next to the Georgia World Congress Center are 21 acres of green space. The privately funded but state-owned park served as the main gathering place during the Summer Olympic Games in 1996. Light towers, fountains, commemorative brick pavers and the Fountain of Rings make it an elegant addition to the neighborhood. There is precious little landscaping in this urban park, whose appeal lies in its open vistas and commemorative value. ~ 265 West Park Avenue; 404-223-4412; www.centennialpark.com.

WOODRUFF PARK Named for the late Coca-Cola executive Robert W. Woodruff, this oasis in an urban jungle offers a waterfall, a 30-foot fountain, benches and a music pavilion. In the western corner is a bronze statue of a woman and a bird known as "Phoenix Rising from the Ashes," a reference to the city's re-emergence after the devastation of the Civil War. ~ 65 Park Place; 404-817-6815.

▼▼▼▼▼▼▼▼▼▼▼▼
Greater Midtown and Buckhead

Midtown is designated as the middle part of the city, starting north of North Avenue up to the Route 85/75 split, bordered by Monroe Drive on the east and Route 85/75 on the west; Peachtree Street is the main north–south axis. It's defined almost as much by attitude as by geographical boundaries. Buckhead, still the most desirable residential address in Atlanta (it's the area code for the governor's mansion), was aptly described in Tom Wolfe's 1998 novel, *A Man in Full*. Beautiful homes sit on enormous lots that sweep up from the street; lawns, azaleas, oaks, pines, dogwoods and other trees make many private homes look like English parks. The main route, at least for gawking, is West Paces Ferry; many side streets wander through this handsome, hilly district where any really striking residence could fetch at least $1 million on the market. The Buckhead part of town begins at the Route 75/85 split and is bordered by the perimeter road, Route 400 on the east and Route 75 on the west. Peachtree Road, as it's called here (also Route 9 and Route 19) runs up and down the center; it's lined with shops and excellent restaurants, of which Buckhead has a preponderance. The area around Lenox Plaza is also a booming business mecca, with highrise offices flanking the main intersections.

Attractions are far-flung in this area, but you can use MARTA to reach most of them. Be sure to allow time for a leisurely stroll in Piedmont Park.

SIGHTS

Just a few blocks north of the Fox Theatre, where the movie version made its premiere, is the apartment where the author of *Gone with the Wind* wrote most of that Pulitzer Prize–winning opus. The place Margaret Mitchell affectionately called "the Dump," one of ten units carved out of a two-story single-family home, is actually rather nice. It's part of the **Margaret Mitchell House & Museum**, a must-stop on any visit to Atlanta. Mitchell's typewriter is on view here, along with a 17-minute video shown in the adjacent visitors center. Photographs also illustrate Mitchell's generosity; she was active in charity work and set up a school for African-American doctors. It was only through the dedication of local volunteers and an infusion of corporate funds that the museum came into existence at all, then survived two mysterious arson fires. The house, which was something of a bohemian gathering place when Mitchell and her husband, John Marsh, lived here from 1925 to 1932, was declared a National Historic Landmark in 1996. Admission. ~ 999 Peachtree Street Northeast; 404-249-7015; www.gwtw.org.

From the Mitchell complex, head west on 10th Street to find an unusual museum on the Georgia Tech campus. Anyone who's ever wondered who invented Kleenex and why, how come we use rectangular paper instead of square, or anything else about the 2200-year history of papermaking need wonder no longer.

HIDDEN ►

The **Robert C. Williams American Museum of Papermaking** can explain these things and much more. An internationally renowned resource on the history of paper and paper technology, it has exhibits as well as more than 2000 books and a remarkable collection of over 10,000 watermarks, papers, tools, machines and manuscripts. Located in the Institute of Paper Science and Technology on the Georgia Tech campus. ~ 500 10th Street; 404-894-7840, fax 404-894-4778; www.ipst.gatech.edu/amp.

Return to Peachtree Street and turn left. When the stunningly white **High Museum of Art** opened to a rapt audience in 1983, it was a slam-dunk entry into the American Institute of Architects' list of the top ten buildings of the 1980s. Inside, spiraling walkways encircle a light-filled atrium, giving visitors fresh perspectives on exhibits of both traveling shows and the museum's rotating collection. The High's holdings are concentrated in contemporary art, a decorative-arts collection with an emphasis on 19th- and 20th-century American furniture, American landscape paintings, European painting and sculpture from the 14th through the 19th centuries, photography and ceremonial figures from Africa. Admission. ~ 1280 Peachtree Street Northeast; 404-733-4400; www.high.org.

North of the High, the **Museum of Contemporary Art of Georgia** (MOCA GA) has a permanent collection of 250 pieces dating to the mid-1940s that represents the work of some 110

Greater Midtown and Buckhead

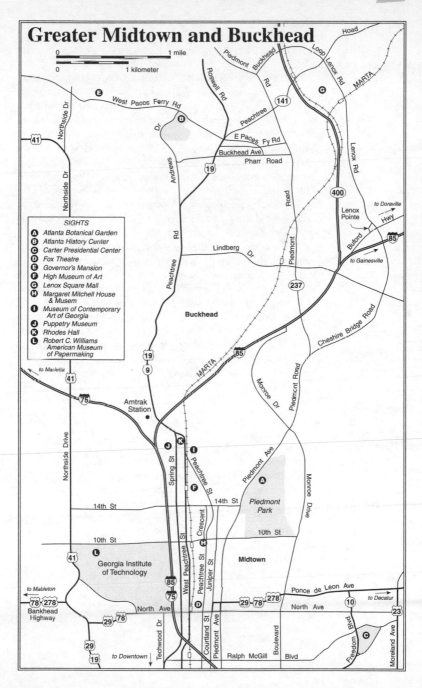

0 _____ 1 mile
0 _____ 1 kilometer

SIGHTS
Ⓐ Atlanta Botanical Garden
Ⓑ Atlanta History Center
Ⓒ Carter Presidential Center
Ⓓ Fox Theatre
Ⓔ Governor's Mansion
Ⓕ High Museum of Art
Ⓖ Lenox Square Mall
Ⓗ Margaret Mitchell House
   & Musem
Ⓘ Museum of Contemporary
   Art of Georgia
Ⓙ Puppetry Museum
Ⓚ Rhodes Hall
Ⓛ Robert C. Williams
   American Museum
   of Papermaking

Georgia artists in virtually all media. Works include paintings, prints, sculpture, computer-generated pieces, photographs and installations. Closed Sunday and Monday. ~ 1447 Peachtree Street; 404-881-1109; www.mocaga.org.

Nearby, fans of elaborate Victorian architectural details including stained-glass windows, fancy plasterwork and the like are likely to ooh and aah at **Rhodes Hall**. Unless you're invited to one of the social events here (it's a prime location for weddings and other parties), you'll have to pay to get in and poke around. Closed Saturday. Admission. ~ 1516 Peachtree Street Northeast; 404-885-7800; www.rhodeshall.org.

Upon leaving Rhodes Hall, continue south on Peachtree Street to 14th Street, and turn left, which will take you through one of the city's prettiest neighborhoods to Piedmont Avenue. Across the street to the north is the **Piedmont Driving Club**, the private club that Tom Wolfe sliced and diced in *A Man in Full*.

On the same side of the street is **Piedmont Park**; look for the entrance to the **Atlanta Botanical Garden**, which is often called the city's living museum. The more crowded the city gets, the more the garden, located in the northwest corner of Piedmont Park, reminds people of Manhattan's great Central Park. Arranged on 15 landscaped acres with another 15 acres of woodlands, this urban haven is mostly outdoors, with special areas for Japanese plants, roses and perennials. In spring, look for flowering vines such as a lavender wisteria, which is the most photographed plant at the gardens. The Fuqua Conservatory harbors tropical, desert and rare specimens from all over the world, thousands of them threatened in the wild with extinction. Of special interest

AUTHOR FAVORITE

sights   I consider the legendary **Fox Theatre** itself just as dramatic as many of the shows performed here. From the eye-popping lobby to the jaw-dropping "sky" ceiling (with stars twinkling and clouds drifting above Moorish minarets), this 1929 gem from the days of classic movie palaces is a treat. Throughout—and I mean right down to the restrooms—the Fox is replete with Moorish and Egyptian details, all of which would have been obliterated by the wrecking ball had it not been for the passions of local preservationists. Whether or not there is a dance, film or concert scheduled, you can still take a tour of this National Historic Landmark. They're offered Monday, Wednesday, Thursday and Saturday mornings. Do it. Admission. ~ 660 Peachtree Street Northeast; 404-881-2100; www.foxtheatre.org, e-mail information@foxtheatre.org.

are indoor and outdoor exhibits of carnivorous plants, and, in the conservatory lobby, a display of brightly colored poison-dart frogs. Closed Monday. Admission. ~ 1345 Piedmont Avenue Northeast; 404-876-5859; www.atlantabotanicalgarden.org, e-mail info@atlantabotanicalgarden.org.

From the garden, you'll be heading west towards Spring Street to find something the whole family can enjoy. Whether the kids are in tow or not, the **Puppetry Museum** can be a real pick-me-up. Both grown-ups and little ones will recognize some of the characters from the *Muppet Show* but the collection here reaches far beyond the States and England to include Colombian clay figures, Javanese shadow puppets and even Chinese hand puppets. Call ahead to see if there are any performances offered while you're in town. Closed Monday. Admission. ~ The Center for Puppetry Arts, 1404 Spring Street Northwest; 404-873-3391; www.puppet.org.

BUCKHEAD   From the puppet show, return to Peachtree Street and take it all the way north until it's time to turn left onto West Paces Ferry Road. In a few pretty blocks, you will come upon the **Atlanta History Center**. Here, amid 33 acres of gardens and woodland acres that bloom in the spring with native flowers and rare plants, this painstakingly maintained complex includes the 1928 **Swan House** mansion, which was originally the servants' quarters and now shelters a luncheon restaurant, gift shop and art gallery. The 1840s **Tullie Smith farmhouse** was moved here from nearby DeKalb County in the late 1960s. It's considered a classic "plantation plain" farmhouse circa 1835. There are also outbuildings such as a log barn, double corncrib and slave cabin as well as a museum with both standing and changing exhibits on topics such as the Civil War and/or Atlanta's African-American heritage. Tours of the house are led by costumed docents. This is the kind of place locals visit over and over again. Admission. ~ 130 West Paces Ferry Road Northwest; 404-814-4000; www.atl hist.org, e-mail information@atlantahistorycenter.com.

In the beautiful West Paces Ferry district of Buckhead—so accurately described in Tom Wolfe's novel *A Man in Full*—is the **Georgia Governor's Mansion**. The 24,000-square-foot property belongs to the people of Georgia, although they, and you, may visit only on Tuesday, Wednesday and Thursday mornings. Like the early governor's mansion down in Milledgeville, this one is done in the Greek Revival style; it is furnished with 19th-century paintings and other pieces. Don't ask to visit the second floor, which contains the private family quarters. Closed Friday through Monday and afternoons. ~ 391 West Paces Ferry Road Northwest; 404-261-1776.

◄ HIDDEN

The **Atlanta Convention & Visitors Bureau** has a drop-in welcome center in Lenox Square. Closed Sunday morning and Monday. ~ 3393 Peachtree Road Northeast.

LODGING   Aside from a couple of major hotels that belong to chains, this area has several bed and breakfasts. Most are convenient to the High Museum and Piedmont Park.

You could easily mistake the **Sheraton Midtown Colony Square** for an executive office building, what with its grand lobby and all the foot traffic in the ground-floor plaza. In fact it is part of a complex that does include offices. Conveniently located near a MARTA station and within walking distance of the High Museum of Art, the Colony Square has 467 rooms. Those on the upper floors offer views, but all the accommodations are decorated, as you would expect from this address, in subtle, muted colors. Travelers who like to stay in shape on the road can make use of a health club and pool. ~ 188 14th Street; 404-892-6000, 800-422-7895, fax 404-872-9192; www.sheratoncolony square.com. ULTRA-DELUXE.

Between Peachtree Street and Piedmont Park, the **Ansley Inn** occupies a three-story brick Tudor-style mansion that fits right into the high-toned residential neighborhood. Built at the turn of the 20th century, it has a sizable living room outfitted with a marble fireplace. There are 12 rooms in the main house and more in an annex, all decorated like the finest Buckhead homes; some of the furnishings are even original to the house. Ask about midweek discounts. Full breakfast is included. Gay-friendly. ~ 253 15th Street Northeast; 404-872-9000, 800-446-5416, fax 404-892-2318; www.ansleyinn.com, e-mail reservations@ansley inn.com. ULTRA-DELUXE.

AUTHOR FAVORITE

I tried to imagine which room at the **Georgian Terrace** Clark Gable stayed in during the premiere festivities surrounding the opening of *Gone with the Wind* in 1937. Across the street from the Fox Theatre, the handsome hotel is fittingly dramatic, with a spacious marble lobby and a circular ten-story atrium. Oversized art—bronze-framed prints of old Europe—fake ficus plants, tables and chairs make the accommodations suitable for entertaining or meeting with clients. Nine stories were added to the original ten, making room for 325 large suites. Room colors are in muted, earthy tones like pale mustard and light rust. ~ 659 Peachtree Street Northeast; 404-897-1991, 800-651-2316, fax 404-724-9116; www.thegeorgian terrace.com. ULTRA-DELUXE.

The **Shellmont Bed & Breakfast Inn** is the kind of place repeat guests book even before making their airline reservations. An 1891 residence on the National Register, it has a beautiful two-story stained-glass window to greet you. There are four rooms (a two-room suite upstairs) and a separate two-room cottage (where they stash visitors under 12); all have private baths. The gardens are studded with statues, fishponds and stone pathways. The antiques are nice but not intimidating; the service helpful but not intrusive. Full breakfast is included. ~ 821 Piedmont Avenue Northeast; 404-872-9290, fax 404-872-5379; www.shellmont. com, e-mail innkeeper@shellmont.com. DELUXE TO ULTRA-DELUXE.

Built in 1929, the stately **Beverly Hills Inn** was an apartment house for elderly women before being converted into Atlanta's first bed-and-breakfast inn in 1982. Its 18 rooms on three floors are exceptionally large for a B&B and are furnished in a subdued residential style, with hardwood floors and a small kitchen; each has a small balcony. The inn has a conservatory and a garden room decorated to resemble a French bistro. It is located near some of Buckhead's best shopping areas. ~ 65 Sheridan Drive Northeast; 404-233-8520, 800-331-8520, fax 404-233-8659; www.beverlyhillsinn.com, e-mail res@beverlyhillsinn.com. DELUXE TO ULTRA-DELUXE.

◄ HIDDEN

The neighborhood of Midtown has wonderful restaurants, but Buckhead is the place to be for cutting-edge dining.

DINING

Atlanta, notorious as a tough restaurant town, has a soft spot for **Mary Mac's Tea Room**. It's been here for half a century because it's got good food and a hammer lock—if that's the right phrase—on Southern hospitality. Fried chicken and turnip greens, sweet potato soufflé and meatloaf are good here, but the cream cheese pound cake and peach cobbler are dishes only Mama used to make, and all the haute cuisine in the world will never replace them for born-and-bred Southerners. There are daily entrées, everyday side dishes, and all sorts of combinations. You can't go wrong, and you'll have a hard time spending $15 unless you really pig out. ~ 224 Ponce de León Avenue Northeast; 404-876-1800; www.marymacs.com. BUDGET TO DELUXE.

◄ HIDDEN

For a taste of Low Country cooking—think Charleston—head to the innovative **South City Kitchen**. Hey, it's where all the hip people go for everything from grits to fried catfish (with stops for she-crab soup, crab hash and pulled pork sandwiches along the way), all served out of an open kitchen in a minimalist space carved out of an old bungalow in the shadow of some highrises. ~ 1144 Crescent Avenue Northeast; 404-873-7358. MODERATE TO ULTRA-DELUXE.

◄ HIDDEN

Joe's on Juniper occupies an old cottage on a small side street between Peachtree and Piedmont streets near the Margaret Mitch-

◄ HIDDEN

ell House. In good weather, patrons opt for relaxing on the big porch and patio. No-nonsense dining choices include hamburgers, chili, soup and fancy hot dogs. The beer list is much longer than the menu, so it's no surprise that towards the end of the evening, everyone tends to congregate in the increasingly loud inside room, with several neon signs and pulsating music. It's a good-time joint and very friendly. ~ 1049 Juniper Street Northeast; 404-875-6634. BUDGET TO MODERATE.

HIDDEN ►

You don't have to be a genius to recognize the potential of the menu at **Einstein's**. There are a lot of inspired choices like grilled tamari chicken and soba noodles, Cajun chicken linguini, sage-crusted pork tenderloin and coconut-coated shrimp, as well as vegetarian options such as a root-vegetable burger and goat-cheese-and-black-bean enchiladas. This Mexi-Italian influence is seen throughout, though there are some regional items like trout with pecans. Right after work, people start claiming the red chairs set at black tables on the brick-lined patio in front of this most unusual structure—three cream-colored bungalows linked together, with eating in two and a bar in the middle. ~ 1077 Juniper Street Northeast; 404-876-7925; www.einsteinsatlanta. com. BUDGET TO DELUXE.

Bacchanalia, one of Atlanta's top restaurants, prepares a prix-fixe four-course menu that attracts a hip young crowd as well as well-heeled, high-heeled matrons. Exposed brick and dim lighting contribute to the calm, upscale atmosphere. The choices change daily but you can expect dishes along the lines of crab fritters or squab with gnocchi. No lunch Monday and Tuesday. Closed Sunday. ~ 1198 Howell Mill Road; 404-365-0410. ULTRA-DELUXE.

Incense and sitar music set the stage at **Touch of India**, which prides itself on authentic tandoori and curries in a room festooned with sparkling Indian fabrics and other cheery crafts. The best deal is the ultra-deep four-course lunch special (meat or vegetarian) with a different option each weekday. À la carte dinner choices include kabobs, plus lamb, chicken, shrimp and vegetarian fare. Or you can put together your own banquet with samosas, mulligatawny soup, *pappadum* and a variety of Indian accompaniments. No lunch Sunday. ~ 1037 Peachtree Street Northeast; 404-876-7777. BUDGET TO MODERATE.

HIDDEN ►

BUCKHEAD Eclipse di Luna claims a funky warehouse setting at the deep end of Miami Circle. Serving mainly tapas, the little dishes of Spain, it has the perfect menu for shoppers looking for fuel between forays, though the selection is better in the evening. The small plates cost only $3 to $5 apiece, but the tab can run up if you can't resist grilled pork chop with spring peas, spiced potatoes with romesco sauce, grilled octopus with chickpeas and

tomatoes, grilled broccoli with sweet onion, or lightly fried calamari with tomato salsa, to name a few choices. There's live jazz
and Latin music Wednesday through Saturday. No lunch Sunday.
Closed Monday. ~ 764 Miami Circle; 404-846-0449; www.
eclipsediluna.com. BUDGET TO MODERATE.

Nava has been hot for years because of its first-rate food and
because the decor is attractive and seats—mostly tiered banquettes—are arranged so you can see who else is there (and what
they're eating). Hands-down the best Southwestern cuisine in
Atlanta, and probably the southeastern U.S., Nava offers many
small dishes that can be ordered in a series so you can sample a
variety of items. Among the most interesting ones are crawfish
enchiladas, barbecued rabbit tostada, fire-roasted quail, shrimp
with mango glaze, grilled sea bass, and Key lime chicken, not to
mention raspberry crème brûlée and a banana quesadilla for
dessert. No lunch Saturday and Sunday. ~ 3060 Peachtree Road
Northwest; 404-240-1984. MODERATE TO ULTRA-DELUXE.

For something entirely different—even for Atlanta—**Fogo de
Chao** offers a taste of Brazil: specifically, the *churrasco* of the
southern part of that country, known for tableside service of meat
cut right before your eyes. As in a Brazilian *churrascaria*, waiters
dressed gaucho-style roam the room carrying swords filled with
one of 15 different cuts of beef, pork, lamb and poultry. Guests
control the rate of service with a small circular chip; green side
up means "I want more" while red side up means "I can't eat any
more right now." Meals are rounded out with an extravagant
buffet of salads, vegetables, South American rice and beans, and
various relishes and condiments. The only odd note is the decor
of the room, which looks more like a banker's club than a typical *churrascaria*, but at least you'll never have to ask, "Where's

AUTHOR FAVORITE

It's too bad more restaurants don't stay open between lunch and
dinner. When I'm traveling, I often like to eat at odd hours—just one more
reason to love **Cha Gio**. A dish of spring rolls or summer rolls will tide
you over. It would be a shame not to stay on for classic Vietnamese dishes
with stir-fried snow peas and other vegetables, chicken with curry, sweet
and sour shrimp, red snapper marinated with lemongrass and other delicacies from an extensive menu. Cha Gio was founded in 1977 by members of a Vietnamese family who escaped Saigon on one of the last
planes out. Closed Sunday. ~ 132 10th Street Northeast; 404-885-
9387. BUDGET.

the beef?" No lunch Saturday and Sunday. ~ 3101 Piedmont Road; 404-266-9988. ULTRA-DELUXE.

The **Atlanta Fish Market** is easy to find. Look for a fish head roughly the size of the Titanic jutting out over Pharr Road. This cavernous space is well-known for getting twice-daily deliveries of fresh seafood; they even update the menu two times a day to reflect changes. On a scale of one to ten, the menu is a ten. The sheer range of choice is impossible to beat: Dungeness crab, Chilean sea bass, Gulf red snapper, Florida pompano, Atlantic halibut, Maryland soft-shell crab and other selections just begin to tell the story. And there are almost as many wine selections as there are fish. No lunch Sunday. ~ 265 Pharr Road Northeast; 404-262-3165. MODERATE TO ULTRA-DELUXE.

The **Cheesecake Factory** tries to be all things to all people—in both decor and cuisine. If you go there after 5 p.m., expect a lot of noise and long lines. The piped-in music would be too loud as well, if you could hear it over the din. The monstrous laminated menu jumps all over the globe—Vietnamese spring rolls, Mexican quesadillas, steak, Cajun food, pasta, pizza. You can dine outdoors or in the huge main room partly divided by booths, with alabaster light fixtures the size of turtle shells suspended over the action. The big bar upstairs is much quieter, a good place to wait for a table. ~ 3024 Peachtree Street Northeast; 404-816-2555; www.thecheesecakefactory.com. MODERATE TO ULTRA-DELUXE.

When you want seafood and you want it cutting-edge, set sail for **BluePointe**. The bar here, especially on Friday evenings, is a scene itself, but so is the dramatic architecture that, like the food, manages to connect the Deep South with the Far East. An ex-

◆◆◆

THE HILLS ARE ALIVE

Frederick Law Olmsted, famous for designing Manhattan's Central Park, is also responsible for Atlanta's green landscape. Although Inman, Morningside and Ansley parks were all inspired by his visionary work, he was directly responsible only for **Druid Hills**. Original developer Joel Hurt commissioned a preliminary design from Olmsted, who delivered it in 1892 but died before the work was completed. His successors implemented and refined the master plan for the neighborhood that includes Emory University and Fernbank. Rolling, forested hills are interspersed with a tremendous variety of architectural styles, including Georgian, Gothic, Mediterranean, Tudor and neoclassical. In spring, a drive through this residential jewel is a must. ~ Bounded by Fairview Road, LaVista Road, Scott Boulevard and Briarcliff Road.

tensive oyster bar and sushi list will get you in the swim before you go deeper with dishes like ginger-roasted codfish with pork cracklin' and wok-seared mustard greens. No lunch Saturday and Sunday. ~ 3455 Peachtree Road; 404-237-9070. DELUXE TO ULTRA-DELUXE.

The **Buckhead Diner** was an instant hit and led the way for many other restaurants that realized you could serve first-rate food without an overly formal setting. Neon, marble, leather and wood set a chic tone that seems timeless. You may find a meatloaf (perhaps made from veal, not hamburger) and dishes more associated with California cuisine on the innovative menu. The list of wines by the glass is exceptionally long for Atlanta. ~ 3073 Piedmont Road Northeast; 404-262-3336. BUDGET TO DELUXE.

There's a definite nightclubby vibe to **Pricci**: you can almost imagine Kim Basinger (she's actually a Georgia native) slinking in wearing something with a neckline down to there. You don't really have to wear something glamorous to dine here, but jeans would definitely be uncool. The menu is elegant, extensive and Italian. After a choice of ten pastas, the main courses include lamb shank, veal scallopini, lobster tails and sea bass with kalamata olives and fresh basil. ~ 500 Pharr Road Northeast; 404-237-2941. MODERATE TO ULTRA-DELUXE.

Atlanta is extremely unusual in that many if not most of its great restaurants are part of a shopping center, office building or hotel. **Brasserie La Coze** is on the ground level at Lenox Square, where it attracts a steady stream of Buckhead diners. Specialties include a perfect mussels *mariniere, coq au vin,* duck *cassoulet* and other French bistro fare. Closed Sunday. ~ 3393 Peachtree Road Northeast; 404-266-1440. MODERATE TO ULTRA-DELUXE.

◄ HIDDEN

Not all of Buckhead's French restaurants are expensive. A pleasant exception is the **Anis Café & Bistro**, which serves Mediterranean cuisine in a converted cottage off Pharr Road. In good weather, lucky patrons can dine on the brick patio in the shade of a tree or an umbrella. Good choices at this romantic retreat include a classic bouillabaisse, roast chicken and salad or ravioli Niçoise. ~ 2974 Grandview Avenue; 404-233-9889. MODERATE.

◄ HIDDEN

In business since the early 1980s, the **Grand China Restaurant** is a sizable cut above generic Chinese restaurants. Soft lighting and fresh flowers, with easy-listening music in the background, create a serene setting for a menu incorporating Cantonese, Hunan, Mandarin and Szechwan dishes. There's also a children's menu. ~ 2975 Peachtree Road; 404-231-8690. BUDGET TO MODERATE.

One of the most exciting restaurants in town is the **Horseradish Grill**. Along with dishes you think you've seen before like fried chicken with cream gravy, the changing menu offers an array of contemporary Southern dishes. Some are fantastic, some are over-ambitious, but everything is regional. The wine list is tops and the bar—quite a scene. No lunch Saturday. ~ 4320 Powers Ferry Road Northwest in Chastain Park; 404-255-7277; www.horse radishgrill.com, e-mail info@horseradishgrill.com. DELUXE TO ULTRA-DELUXE.

If you have three or four hours at the end of the day, and deep pockets, it may be the night to dine at **Seeger's** (but only if you've made reservations). The restaurant, owned by the chef who made the Ritz-Carlton's Dining Room a household name (at least in Buckhead), opened in 1997 in a Craftsman-style bungalow. The decor is intentionally minimalist so diners can concentrate on dishes like rabbit piccata, squab with hazelnuts and tuna tart. There's a choice of two multicourse prix-fixe menus. Wine is extra. Closed Sunday. ~ 111 West Paces Ferry Road Northwest; 404-846-9779; www.seegers.com, e-mail manager@seegers.com. ULTRA-DELUXE.

SHOPPING   Except for the malls, stores in this part of town vary from block to block. Some are bunched together while others stand alone so that you see the signs just as you're driving by—and if you're on Peachtree, good luck finding a place to hang a U-turn. The neighborhood northwest of Georgia Tech near Howell Mill Road (west of Route 41) is known to savvy shoppers as a wonderful source of retailers offering major discounts on shoes, clothing and home accessories. Even if you're not buying, it's worth a look-see.

The **Robert C. Williams American Museum of Papermaking gift shop** stocks paper gifts and other items of interest to the papermaker and the paper historian, including handmade cards and ornaments, paper jewelry, arts and crafts items and museum logo apparel. ~ 500 10th Street; 404-894-7840.

Forsyth Fabric is a warehouse-size emporium of heavily discounted fabrics. Every kind of fabric you can think of—from handkerchief linens to heavy woolens and even burlap—is here. Buy it when you see it because the store is crawling with the city's top interior decorators and if they see it first, you're out of luck. For truly unbelievable bargains, ask to see the even lower-priced

AUTHOR FAVORITE

In my imagination I redecorated my house several times over while visiting the shops in a Buckhead cul-de-sac called **Miami Circle**. Dozens of dealers in home furnishings, art and accessories are grouped within walking distance of one another and parking's a breeze. The **Miami Circle Design Market** has several dealers in accent pieces under one roof. ~ 730 Miami Circle; 404-841-9777; www.buckhead.net/ miamicircle.

selection around the corner at Forsyth Closeouts on Howell Mill Road. ~ 1190 Foster Street Northwest; 404-351-6050.

No Mas! Productions imports hand-forged furniture and hand crafted home accessories, mostly from Central and South America. Chairs, lanterns, bowls, pillows, items for the garden are just samples of what's in stock. Closed Sunday. ~ 790 Huff Road Northwest; 404-350-0907.

BUCKHEAD The merchandise at Buckhead's big malls is legendary—lots of it in lots of price ranges. You'll find three floors of upscale chain stores at **Lenox Square**, including Neiman Marcus and Macy's as well as Kate Spade and 240 other specialty retailers, a food court and movie theater. ~ Peachtree and Lenox roads; 404-233-6767.

Phipps Plaza, catticorner from Lenox, houses just about everything that Lenox doesn't, most importantly **Barney's, Giorgio Armani, Niketown, Saks 5th Avenue** and **Lord & Taylor.** ~ Peachtree and Lenox roads; 404-261-7910.

Need something chic yet casual to wear to brunch? Cocktails? Shopping? A Braves game? **Luna** is the one-stop source for trendy, young-thinking women. ~ 3167 Peachtree Road Northeast; 404-233-5344.

The name **Kangaroo Pouch** gives the game away; you know this is the place for dressing and accessorizing infants, toddlers and young kids. Closed Sunday. ~ 56 East Andrews Drive Northwest; 404-231-1616.

Boxwood's Gardens and Gifts is an unfailing source of tasteful decorative items for the home, from china and other tabletop items to little knickknacks as well as garden accessories. Closed Sunday. ~ 100 East Andrews Drive Northwest; 404-233-3400.

French and English antiques can be found at **Deering Antiques.** ~ 670 Miami Circle; 404-233-6333.

The **Atlanta Opera**, founded in 1985, performs at the Fox Theatre. ~ 728 West Peachtree Street Northwest; 404-881-8801, 800-356-6372 (tickets); www.atlantaopera.org.   **NIGHTLIFE**

In the 1970s, the stretch of Peachtree Street between 10th and 14th was the closest thing in Atlanta to San Francisco's legendarily hippie Haight-Ashbury District. Before and after, The Strip was and is a popular singles spot, conveniently located for people on their way home to North Metro from an office job downtown. (The area also has some top gay bars; see "Atlanta Gay Scene" below.)

The **Woodruff Arts Center** in Midtown houses the city's major fine-arts organizations, including the symphony and a major theater company. The **Alliance Theatre Company** (www.alliancetheatre.org) presents contemporary plays and world and regional premieres along with classic dramas in the 800-seat Alliance

Theatre and the 200-seat Hertz Stage. It is the leading professional resident theater, attracting some 320,000 people annually. ~ 1280 Peachtree Street Northeast; 404-733-4600; www.woodruff center.org.

The **Atlanta Symphony Orchestra** (ASO), which opened more than half a century ago, performs more than 200 times every year. In addition to the 72-concert Master Season in Symphony Hall from September to May, the ASO offers concerts of light classics and popular favorites as well as family and holiday concerts. The outdoor performances in Chastain Park are so unstuffy that they are apt to include appearances by well-known country singers. ~ 1280 Peachtree Street Northeast; 404-733-4949; www.atlantasymphony.org.

John Philip Sousa wrote "King Cotton" for the 1895 States and International Exposition and performed it for the first time at Piedmont Park.

Housed in a former restaurant, **Smith's Olde Bar** often has live entertainment until 4 a.m. weekdays and 3 a.m. Saturday (the legal limit in both cases). The showroom upstairs charges a cover for medium- to well-known bands, local and out-of-towners. ~ 1578 Piedmont Avenue Northeast; 404-875-1522; www.smithsoldebar.com.

The Blue Light Company at the Red Light Café has live music and a different form of entertainment each night. Wednesday is open-mic night, where you might hear singers and poets. Closed Sunday. Cover. ~ 553 Amsterdam Avenue; 404-874-7828.

BUCKHEAD   The **Uptown Comedy Corner** is known for showcasing black comedians in its 300-seat showroom, where performers appear three times on Friday and Saturday and once on Tuesday, Wednesday and Thursday. In addition, the Corner hosts live hip-hop and R&B music. Closed Monday. Cover. ~ 2140 Peachtree Road Northwest; 404-350-6990.

The **Capitol City Opera**, which employs an average of 60 classically trained singers, performs two opera theater shows per year, a quarterly recital series (Sunday of Songs), a monthly restaurant series (Dinner and a Diva), a vocal competition, a summer workshop, touring madrigals, touring gala singers, *Così Fan Tutte* on tour, a summer pops concert, and an astonishing 150 to 200 performances solely for children every year. Its offices are in Buckhead, but performances are held at various locations throughout Atlanta. ~ 1266 West Paces Ferry Road #451; 404-454-6213; www.cityopera.com.

PARKS   **PIEDMONT PARK** 🚲 ♨ This 180-acre park is extensively landscaped, with a playground, bike paths, promenade and visitors center. As the largest park in the city, it is a major venue for strollers and for informal football and baseball games; softball leagues use the athletic fields for spring and summer games. Back in 1895, when the Cotton States and International Exposition took place, the landscape design firm of the Olmsted Brothers was commissioned to design the park, which still has the same design. The park became public in 1904 when the city bought the land. Today it's so popular that parking is often nonexistent; however, the park is easily accessible from the MARTA Arts Center station at 15th Street. ~ Piedmont Avenue and 14th Street; 404-817-6744.

Atlanta Gay Scene

Atlanta, particularly the Midtown neighborhood, offers more for gay and lesbian travelers than anyplace else in Georgia. A good place to get a grip on the scene is to pick up a copy of the *Southern Voice*, a weekly newspaper that covers world, national and local news as well as arts and entertainment and features on the home and community. In business since 1988, this is the premier publication covering gay and lesbian issues; it's available free at newsstands and newspaper racks around the city. Its sibling, the newer *Eclipse*, is geared towards gay men's entertainment. It is not as widely available but you can find it at gay bookstores and at clubs and adult stores where the *Southern Voice* is carried. If you're looking for news and events listings, you can find the latter on the web at www.sovo.com. Or you can call the paper directly at 404-876-0789. Another website to check in advance of your visit is www.gayatlanta.com.

SHOPPING

Outwrite Bookstore & Coffeehouse is an excellent source of information as well as books on every conceivable subject, with, of course, a special section relating to gay and lesbian topics. ~ 991 Piedmont Avenue Northeast; 404-607-0082; www.outwrite books.com.

Brushstrokes claims to be the largest "variety" store in town. They're big on dance music CDs and tapes and gay videos as well as souvenirs. ~ 1510-J Piedmont Road Northeast; 404-876-6567.

Charis Books & More says it's the oldest independent feminist bookstore in the South. This is the place not only to buy books but to meet and mingle at the store's frequent events, which are described on its website. ~ 1189 Euclid Avenue; 404-524-0304; www.charis.booksense.com.

NIGHTLIFE

Nightlife is headquartered in Midtown, though you can find gay- and lesbian-friendly bars virtually anywhere in the city.

Atlanta's biggest gay bar is **Backstreet**, one of several spots in town that requires membership (usually $10 for three months or so) in order to stay open past the 4 a.m. curfew. This one actually stays open 24/7. There's lots of dance energy or, if you prefer to watch others perform, you can check out Charlie Brown's

Cabaret, a drag show performed Thursday through Sunday. Cover. ~ 845 Peachtree Street Northeast; 404-873-1986; www.back streetatlanta.com.

Leather chaps and bare chests are the scene at a couple of Atlanta hotspots, including **Hoedowns**. Sunday afternoon is a major event, with similar action Friday and Saturday. Dance lessons are offered Tuesday through Thursday and Sunday. The deejay gets rave reviews. Closed Monday. ~ 931 Monroe Drive Northeast; 404-876-0001; www.hoedownsatlanta.com.

The Heretic is known as a leather bar; in fact, consider the dress code to be strictly cowboy. ~ 2069 Cheshire Bridge Road Northeast; 404-325-3061.

There are two Buddies, but you want the one called **Buddies Cheshire Square**. (The Midtown sibling doesn't have as nice a reputation.) Closed Sunday. ~ 2345 Cheshire Bridge Road Northeast; 404-634-5895.

Maybe **Woof's** is not Atlanta's only gay sports bar, as it advertises, but it definitely offers sports on 22 TVs, plus darts, pool, drinks and some food. ~ 2415 Piedmont Avenue; 404-869-9422; www.woofsatlanta.com.

My Sister's Room occasionally has live music, but mostly this lesbian bar is set up for hanging around, with a couple of air hockey tables. Wednesday is karaoke night, while Thursday is trivia night. Closed Monday and Tuesday. ~ 222 East Howard Avenue, Decatur; 404-370-1990.

▼▼▼▼▼▼▼▼▼▼▼
Eastside Atlanta

The eastern part of Atlanta is less defined than the other areas in this chapter, but for touring purposes includes the area around Emory University, the city of Decatur, Stone Mountain and a couple of attractions off the beaten path. The funky neighborhood actually called East Atlanta is fun to visit, but only for the shops and restaurants; there are no cultural institutions here unless you count the lifestyles of the locals.

SIGHTS

Fine art, wild animals and a giant granite rock are part of the myriad draws to this loosely linked area of town. You will need a car or the energy to take a series of buses to tour this section.

The name of Asa Candler may not be famous outside Georgia, but here the name means a lot. The former home of the son of Coca-Cola, Asa G. Candler, the **Callanwolde Fine Arts Center** serves as the fine-arts center for DeKalb County, with classes, performances and concerts. It's also open for self-guided tours. Callanwolde was designed by Henry Hornbostle, the same architect behind Emory University. Only 12 of the original 27 acres of the estate are intact today, and they can only hint at the grandeur of the full holdings. The palatial grounds and buildings were established in 1920 here in the Druid Hills neighborhood, itself laid out by Frederick Law Olmsted. Closed Sunday. ~ 980 Briarcliff Road Northeast, Atlanta; 404-872-5338; www.callanwolde.org.

Atlanta is home to several major research centers, including the headquarters of the American Cancer Society, Georgia Institute of Technology Research, and Emory University. None gets more attention worldwide, however, than the **Centers for Disease Control and Prevention** (CDC). It has been operating since the mid-1950s and now has 12 separate divisions focusing on virtually every aspect of human health. ~ 1600 Clifton Road Northeast, Atlanta; 404-639-0830, 800-311-3435; www.cdc.gov.

Emory University is one of the most acclaimed centers of higher education in the country, with a high faculty-to-student ratio, seven libraries and graduate schools of medicine, nursing, theology, law, business, arts and sciences, and public health. Emory University Hospital is one of the finest in the nation. More than 10,000

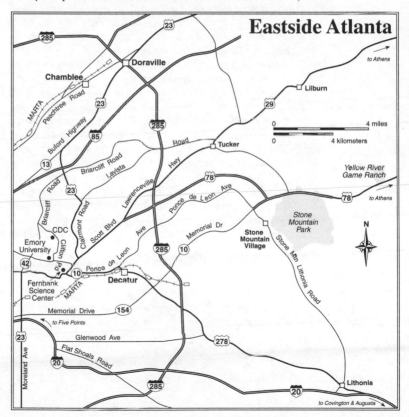

Eastside Atlanta

students attend the various schools, quite a jump from the original 15 who comprised the first student body back in 1836.

HIDDEN ▶

In the heart of the campus is an outstanding art museum, the likes of which you won't find anywhere else in the southeastern U.S. The **Michael C. Carlos Museum** is a fascinating trove of some 16,000 objects, including art from almost all over the world and artworks on paper dating to the Middle Ages. Housed in a 45,000-square-foot building whose interior space was designed by Michael Graves, the exhibits are works of art in and of themselves. Until you've seen Papagoyo ceramics from Greater Nicoya (Nicaragua and Costa Rica today), you can't imagine how many exciting ceramic styles have existed over the centuries. Also from the ancient Americas are burial urns from Colombia, Greek amphora from 460 B.C., glass and bracelets from the Roman Empire, and ancient cuneiform tablets. One can't hope to take it all in. Closed Monday. ~ 571 South Kilgo Street, Atlanta; 404-727-4282; www.carlos.emory.edu.south, e-mail carlos@emory.edu.

Leaving the Emory campus, return to Briarcliff Road, head south and turn left, east, onto Ponce de León Avenue, which will take you almost all the way to an interesting pair of attractions. The **Fernbank Science Center** came into existence in 1967 with the idea of supplementing the education of local students with interpretive science programs; it claims to be the only center of its kind owned by a public school system. It houses exhibits on space exploration, ecology and geology, covered in basic terms that may underwhelm kids who've graduated from grade school; otherwise, it's so wonderful that you can expect to find many students on field trips here. The center is part of a complex that incorporates the Fernbank Forest and the Fernbank Museum of Natural History. Behind the science center, the 65-acre **Fernbank Forest** has two miles of paved trails that lead into a variety of habitats, including hardwood trees and wildflower plantings, among other things such as an underground window and a greenhouse. The planetarium is closed on Monday. Admission to the planetarium

HEALTH ODYSSEY

The **Global Health Odyssey Museum** (GHO) is a small exhibit area with an attached theater in the Centers for Disease Control and Prevention (CDC). It serves as both a visitors center and an interactive educational facility. Besides the cafeteria and a souvenir store, the museum is the only part of CDC that is open to the public. Reservations to tour the GHO must be made in advance by telephone or online. ~ 1600 Clifton Road Northeast, Atlanta; 404-639-0830, 800-311-3435; www.cdc.gov.

only. ~ 156 Heaton Park Drive Northeast, Atlanta; 678-874-7102; www.fsc.fernbank.edu.

Only a mile away is the **Fernbank Museum of Natural History**, where you can experience "A Walk through Time in Georgia," a series of 15 exhibits. If this sounds big, it is: Fernbank boasts the world's largest dinosaur skeleton exhibit and the largest natural-history collection in the country south of Washington's Smithsonian. In addition, you can learn about multicultural design and the physical properties of light and sound; kids will get a kick out of the interactive Fantasy Forest. Films are shown here on an IMAX screen; on Friday nights you can pair it with a martini. Admission. ~ 767 Clifton Road Northeast, Atlanta; 404-370-0960; www.fernbank.edu/museum.

Return to Ponce de León Avenue and turn left, heading for Decatur. In the heart of this small city, take a look at the **Old Courthouse on the Square**. This 1898 beauty, well-restored, contains an archive of 1500 volumes plus a three-room museum of regional interest, including some Civil War displays. Closed Saturday and Sunday. ~ 101 East Court House Square, Decatur; 404-373-1088; www.dekalbhistory.org, e-mail dhs@dekalbhistory.org.

When you depart Decatur, follow Ponce de León Avenue to Route 285, go north to Route 78 and proceed east to "the eighth wonder of the world."

A stone's throw from Stone Mountain, **Stone Mountain Village** is a folksy adjunct to the wonderful park. It developed into a busy little burg after the rail line reached here in 1900 to ferry daytrippers from the big city en route to the massive granite dome nearby. Most of the shops and restaurants are located along Main Street; at the end of the street is the Stone Mountain Village Welcome Center (closed Sunday; 891 Main Street), where you can pick up a guide to some 250 historical sites within the hamlet. ~ Main and Poole streets, Stone Mountain Village; 770-879-4971; www.stonemountainvillage.com.

Stone Mountain Park is one of those things you just have to see to understand. Of course, you could see it from an airplane from many miles away, but it's not the same. If you have time for just one activity, make it the Skylift, which gives you a breathtaking ride in a Swiss cable car up the side of the granite outcropping, the largest exposed one on the face of the planet. You can hike around here, but better you should hike down. At the base, a steam locomotive loops around the five-mile diameter, giving you a view from all sides. The first white man to set his eyes on this sight is believed to have been the Spanish captain Juan Pardo, who set about encircling present-day Georgia with a series of forts. He called it Crystal Mountain because it shone in the sun and was surrounded by precious stones, but he and his men had little time for rockhounding, given the presence of the native Indians. Within this 32,000-acre park are an antebellum plantation, two golf courses, a waterslide complex, a tennis center, a scenic railroad, two hotels, a restaurant, a resort and conference center, a paddlewheel steamboat and a Civil War museum, plus a petting zoo. The zoo is in a sort of glade, with raised boardwalks where you can look out and spot otters and other wildlife.

The park's most stunning attraction is perhaps the **Confederate Memorial**, the world's largest piece of sculpture. It's 90 feet tall and 190 feet across, poking more than 11 feet out from the mountain. It took 55 years (with a hiatus from 1928 to 1964) to complete this work in 1970. Confederate President Jefferson Davis and generals Robert E. Lee and Stonewall Jackson ride their steeds across the three-acre frame. Wow. In summer, nightly **laser shows**, choreographed to popular music, are projected onto the mountain's natural north face. Admission. ~ Route 78, Stone Mountain; 770-498-5600, 800-317-2006; www.stonemountainpark.org.

After spending some time at Stone Mountain, return to Route 78 and drive east to the outskirts of Lilburn to see some animals. The 25-acre **Yellow River Game Ranch** is not your most upbeat animal attraction but there's a lot of it. Deer, squirrels, pigs, goats, skunks and a groundhog named Robert E. Lee (or "Beau," as he's affectionately known) frolic freely in this commercial park. "Scary" animals like wolves, foxes, black bears and bobcats are secured in open-air enclosures. Children who want to get up close can visit "Bunnie Burrows," a rabbit warren where the inmates nibble crackers and carrots proffered by little hands (the visitors center sells animal crackers). The park is forested, pleasant to walk because of the shade and very popular with school groups, but the animals don't seem all that spirited. Admission. ~ 4525 Route 78, Lilburn; 770-972-6643, 877-972-6643; www.yellowrivergameranch.com, e-mail gameranch@mindspring.com.

HIDDEN ►

LODGING The **Cheshire Motor Inn**, side by side with The Colonnade restaurant, could scarcely be more convenient for falling asleep after a big meal. This is standard motel fare, except for nice trees around the place, with standard amenities (meaning color cable TV). ~ 1865 Cheshire Bridge Road, Atlanta; 404-872-9628, 800-827-9628. MODERATE.

There are a couple of places to spend the night in Decatur. The **Sycamore House** is in a very nice historic district, convenient to shops, restaurants and MARTA. Two upstairs rooms have queen bed and twins; the first-floor suite also has a private bath. If you've been traveling, unwind in the heated pool and hot tub in the garden. There's a resident cat and dog on the premises and small pets are accepted. Full breakfast is included. ~ 9624 Sycamore Street, Decatur; 404-378-0685, fax 404-373-7123. DELUXE.

In the vicinity of Stone Mountain, the **Village Inn Bed & Breakfast** is located in an 1820s home large enough for six guest rooms, all with two-person spa tubs, private baths and individually selected antique furnishings. This is a good location for touring the village as well as for visiting the park. Full breakfast is included. ~ 992 Ridge Avenue, Stone Mountain Village; 770-469-3459, 800-214-8385, fax 770-469-1051; www.villageinn bb.com, e-mail villageb@villageinnbb.com. ULTRA-DELUXE.

Within the park itself, the brick, two-story **Stone Mountain Park Inn** makes no pretense about being antebellum, despite the white columns marching across the portico. Beneath the columns, wooden rocking chairs are set out in a row to take in the view. The 92 rooms are decorated in pastels and floral wainscoting and wallpaper. There's a restaurant downstairs. ~ Stone Mountain Park; 770-469-3311, fax 770-498-5691; www.stonemountainpark.com. ULTRA-DELUXE.

DINING

There are some classic restaurants in this part of town, including at least one soul place and another old-timey Southern spot where you'll want to steal the homemade breads. The best array of inexpensive ethnic restaurants can be found in DeKalb County in northeast Atlanta beyond the perimeter road.

◀ *HIDDEN*

The Colonnade has been an Atlanta standby for decades and looks like the kind of place families drive to on a Sunday evening. After waiting your turn, you can order grilled amberjack or sea bass, veal parmesan or specials like frogs' legs, plus all manner of Southern classics like sweet potato soufflé and fried catfish filet. There's a low ceiling, patterned carpeting and leatherette banquettes. If you come here twice, you'll probably see many of the same people. Just try not to fill up on the piping-hot home-

AUTHOR FAVORITE

There's a lot to do around Emory University, which is why I recommend the **Emory Inn**. Linked to the 198-room Emory Conference Center Hotel, it has 107 rooms in a rather odd configuration. The rooms are handsome in a standard kind of way; nothing particularly special but comfortable and clean. Due to its location, this is a good place to seek bargain rates on the weekends. ~ 1615 Clifton Road, Atlanta; 404-712-6000, fax 404-712-6025. ULTRA-DELUXE.

made breads and rolls, which are divine. No lunch Monday or Tuesday. No credit cards. ~ 1879 Cheshire Bridge Road, Atlanta; 404-874-5642. BUDGET TO DELUXE.

It's not recommended as a true dining experience, but you can get something quickly and conveniently at **Dusty's Barbecue** near Emory. It's hog heaven for students who need lots of food at cheap prices: pork, beef and chicken 'cue, combo plates, veggie sides and sandwiches, plus beer, wine, pies and cakes. ~ 1815 Briarcliff Road, Atlanta; 404-320-6264; www.dustys.com, e-mail dustys@ mindspring.com. BUDGET.

Located in a multi-ethnic shopping center, **Café Bombay** is a simple bastion of Indian cuisine and a real bargain at lunchtime. The Formica tables and steaming steel buffet speak volumes about the modest prices here for chicken and other goodies right out of the tandoori oven, curries and—good news for vegetarians—lots of choices such as spinach and potatoes cooked with ginger and fried mixed-vegetable fritters. Fancier dishes are served only at dinner. No lunch on Sunday. ~ 2615 Briarcliff Road, Atlanta; 404-320-0229. BUDGET TO MODERATE.

Down in East Atlanta are a bunch of truly interesting places to eat, some of them quite special. (These places are also close to the Atlanta Zoo.)

The **Flatiron Restaurant & Bar** has black leather, glass walls and a neat barewood floor. To meet some locals, grab a stool at the bar and order a cold drink to start, then a lentil burger or one of various hamburgers. There are roasted vegetables, parmesan chicken and pasta. ~ 520 Flat Shoals Avenue, Atlanta; 404-688-8864. BUDGET.

Locals favor the stuffed pan-seared filet mignon and the charbroiled salmon steak (garnished with mango-dried cherry salsa and served in a phyllo cup), but **Café Lily** offers many other entrées just as interesting, including what the chef calls shrimp beignets, which is actually an imaginative pasta dish. The room is striking, with lilac walls, white trim and one wall that's all glass. ~ 308 West Ponce de León Avenue, Decatur; 404-371-9119; www.cafelily.com. MODERATE TO DELUXE.

In the busy blocks around the downtown square, **Siam Thai Restaurant** is an oasis of serenity, with clean lines, low lights and stylized green shutters on the interior walls. It's a good spot for grazing through the appetizer list before moving on, or opting to stay seated for hot dishes such as chicken and shrimp sautéed in tamarind sauce or a whole snapper topped with chili sauce. ~ 123 Sycamore Street, Decatur; 404-371-4333. BUDGET TO MODERATE.

Sage serves contemporary American cuisine in a bistro setting complete with a full-service bar specializing in 9.5-ounce martinis. Like its neighbors on restaurant row, Sage pulls diners in with appetizers and abundant outdoor seating (usually from mid-April well into October, when evenings are usually balmy). The menu has a small collection of pasta, meat, seafood and vegetarian selections. Closed Monday. ~ 121 Sycamore Street, Decatur; 404-373-5574; e-mail sageonsycamore@earthlink.net. BUDGET.

Sometimes a simple bowl of soup is all that's needed to restore vitality. That's the philosophy at **Pho 96**, where the specialties are Vietnamese beef and chicken noodle soups. Not all the offerings are so simple, however. Several fortifying combos, for example, include various cuts of beef (eye round, well-done flank). Rice plates, incorporating pork chops or grilled chicken, are also served in this simple room, with minimal decor and a nice aquamarine light courtesy of vertically slatted blinds. ~ 500 Buford Highway, Chamblee; 770-452-9644. BUDGET.

Located in front of the Flea Market, **La Kermes Mexican Restaurant** is dressed up in primary colors almost as loud as the music that pulsates through the room. But it's worth putting up with if you're in the mood for *chiles rellenos*, various enchiladas and other south-of-the-border standbys. ~ 5000 Buford Highway, Chamblee; 770-454-9964. BUDGET TO MODERATE.

The **Oriental Pearl Seafood Restaurant** anchors one end of a   ◄ HIDDEN
complex that includes a Chinese cultural center and various small shops and service establishments. Patrons are greeted by a rushing wall of water in the entryway, which leads to a great big room with a rectangle of bright green neon glowing on the rim of the ceiling. While the five-page menu lists a lot of dishes available elsewhere, there are some exceptions, such as eggplant stuffed with shrimp, duck meat with mustard greens soup, Dungeness crab with

AUTHOR FAVORITE

If you've never seen a good ol' boy manipulating chopsticks to get the last of his kim chee, you have a treat in store: it's one of those cultural anomalies you never forget. And the kim chee is very good at **Seoul Garden Restaurant**. The best of many bargains is the daily weekday lunch box, a nice compartmentalized meal with chicken or seafood teriyaki, along with tempura veggies, salad, rice and five or six condiments. Korean barbecue, spicy stews, some Japanese dishes (including sushi) and house specialties such as stir-fried octopus, spicy raw blue crab and sliced boiled beef feet are among the main courses. The waitstaff is very patient in explaining items to non-Korean-speaking customers. (An added bonus: it's open all afternoon.) ~ 5938 Buford Highway, Doraville; 770-452-0123. MODERATE TO DELUXE.

curry sauce (Malaysian style) and fried shredded beef. It's also known as one of the better spots for dim sum. ~ 5399 New Peachtree Road, Chamblee; 770-986-9330. MODERATE.

In Stone Mountain Village, the pretty **Sycamore Grill** specializes in innovative Southern cuisine. Located in what was the old Alexander Hotel (circa 1836) on the edge of the village, the Grill is known for its fresh Georgia mountain trout, pan-seared duck breast, Cajun-spiced chicken breast and marinated flank steak as well as its deep-dish Key lime pie. This chic spot has bright art hanging on cheery yellow walls. Closed Sunday and Monday. ~ 5329 Mimosa Drive, Stone Mountain Village; 770-465-6789; www.thesycamoregrill.com. DELUXE TO ULTRA-DELUXE.

SHOPPING   Though there's a truly funky flea market in the area, I don't recommend it. I do, however, recommend the **Dekalb Farmer's Market**, which specializes in produce. You'll also find fish, deli items and regional snacks. ~ 3000 East Ponce de León Avenue, Decatur; 404-377-6400; www.dekalbfarmersmarket.com.

There are dozens of small shops—many of them devoted to Civil War memorabilia and crafts—huddled on the covered sidewalks of Stone Mountain Village.

NIGHTLIFE   The **Punch Line** is the state's premier comedy location; alumni include Jerry Seinfeld, Tim Allen and Ellen Degeneres. There's a one-drink minimum; weekend tickets go fast. Cover. ~ 280 Hilderbrand Drive Northeast, Atlanta; 404-252-0394; www.punch line.com.

A mixed crowd is drawn to **City Lights Dance Club**, which offers deejay and live music with different themes (swing, Latin, etc.) on different nights. This is a place you go purely to dance: lessons are included in the cover charge, and alcohol is not served. Cover. ~ 4001 Presidential Parkway, Atlanta; 770-451-5461; www.citylightsdanceclub.com.

AUTHOR FAVORITE

My jaw dropped when I took my first gander at **Great Gatsby's Auction Gallery**—and that was just from the outside. The garden ornaments, fountains and statuary alone are worth a trip, but for a real blast, head inside to explore gallery after gallery of furnishings and paintings, many of them museum-quality and many of them staggeringly ornate. Offbeat items along the lines of old slot machines, classic jukeboxes, even a cigar store Indian and more await your popping eyes. Closed Sunday. ~ 5070 Peachtree Industrial Boulevard, Atlanta; 770-457-1903; www.gatsbys.com, e-mail internet@gatsbys.com.

There aren't many places to hear country music in Atlanta, but you can count on **Mama's Country Showcase**. Thousands of fans can scoot their boots around a humongous dance floor to deejayed tunes. Don't know how to Texas Two-Step? Free dance lessons are offered Saturday. Closed Sunday through Thursday. Cover. ~ 3952 Covington Highway, Decatur; 404-288-6262; www.mamascountryshowcase.com.

STONE MOUNTAIN PARK 🏃 Stone Mountain is a world unto itself. Its name was derived from the world's largest chunk of exposed granite, an 825-foot-tall landmark easily visible from airplanes and much of north Georgia. On it is the world's largest bas-relief sculpture, a carving of Confederate President Jefferson Davis and generals Robert E. Lee and Stonewall Jackson, all on horseback. The emphasis is on the commercial attractions but this is a wonderful place to get some exercise as well. Rowing events were held at the lake here during the 1996 Summer Olympic Games. You can also hike up the mountain (or ride the sky-tram), take a mini-train tour past all the sights, stroll the wildlife trails, fish in the stocked lake (with a valid Georgia license that is sold here in season), ice skate, shoot miniature golf or the real thing on 27 holes. Admission. ~ Route 78, Stone Mountain; 770-498-5690, 800-317-2006; www.stonemountainpark.org.

PARKS

North Metro Atlanta

Pastoral landscapes alternate with shopping malls and forested residential neighborhoods from Duluth west to Marietta. A detailed street map will prove to be your best friend as you explore the region. The best way to go from east to west or vice versa is via Route 285; the major south–north artery is Route 400, which frequently comes to a standstill at rush hour. Duluth is a major source of the commuters who clog the interstates; Dunwoody is an upscale suburban area; Alpharetta is known for horse farms and antiques; Roswell, for shops, antiques and some restaurants. Marietta is one of the up-and-coming towns, with a burgeoning historical and cultural scene.

History is a big draw, from the Civil War battlefields at Kennesaw to the antique shops in Roswell. Several fine old homes have been well preserved, particularly in Roswell and Marietta, and are open for touring. There are also a number of attractions for kids.

SIGHTS

One needn't be a history buff to have a good time at the **Southeastern Railway Museum**. True, without the advent of the railroad, Atlanta would never have become the first landlocked American city to evolve into a major urban force. But there's just something fun about trains. One of the most historic cars here is the 1911 "Superb," the wonderfully restored Pullman car that

◀ *HIDDEN*

President Warren Harding rode in 1923 across the country. After he died in San Francisco, that same car transported his body back to Washington and then to Marion, Ohio, for burial. Other cars tell stories of the town that was called "Terminus" until 1843, when it was renamed "Marthasville" and then "Atlanta" in 1845, the year the first train arrived via the Georgia Railroad. When visitors hear, "All aboard," they can climb up for a short ride around the site in either restored cabooses or converted open-air freight cars. Closed Sunday through Wednesday and additional days in winter; call ahead. Admission. ~ 3595 South Old Peachtree Road, Duluth; 770-476-2013; www.srmduluth.org.

When you've finished your train ride, take Route 23 (Buford Highway) south through Norcross, turning right onto Jimmy Carter Boulevard, which merges with Holcomb Bridge Road (both are known as Route 140). This route leads you into Roswell.

Historic **Roswell** was founded in 1839 as a New England–style village that grew up around the wool and cotton mills. As a result, it has several antebellum homes, two of which are open to the public. Both Roswell and the much-larger Marietta were strategic targets during the Civil War, but most of their historic districts are still standing. Nearby is Kennesaw Mountain and its battlefields.

From Martin Road, turn south on Route 9/120 (Alpharetta Highway, which becomes Alpharetta Street) toward the heart of town. Invisible to traffic only a block away, the **Smith Plantation House** crowns a forested hillock just a stone's throw from City Hall. The house, with its pristine white columns glistening through the oak trees, was built in 1845 by Archibald Smith, who moved here to escape the sometimes suffocating heat and humidity of coastal Georgia. He and his family settled on some 300 acres of farmland less than a mile north of Roswell's town square. The home and its 13 outbuildings, as well as their contents, have been preserved by the Smith descendants. The original walnut plantation desk still stands in the downstairs library, and in the four upstairs bedrooms are marble-topped chests and washstands, antique armoires and even a canopy bed from the mid-19th century. Though many old homes have been restored and refurnished with period antiques, this is a rare opportunity to see exactly how Southern planters lived in the mid-19th century. Closed Sunday. Admission. ~ 935 Alpharetta Street, Roswell; 770-641-3978, 800-776-7935.

When you leave the plantation, continue south on Alpharetta Street to downtown Roswell. The **Historic Roswell Convention and Visitors Bureau**, near the **Historic Roswell Square**, has maps of the area and brochures on regional attractions. The center also offers a variety of walking tours of the town. ~ 617 Atlanta Street, Roswell; 770-640-3253, 800-776-7935; www.cvb.roswell.ga.us.

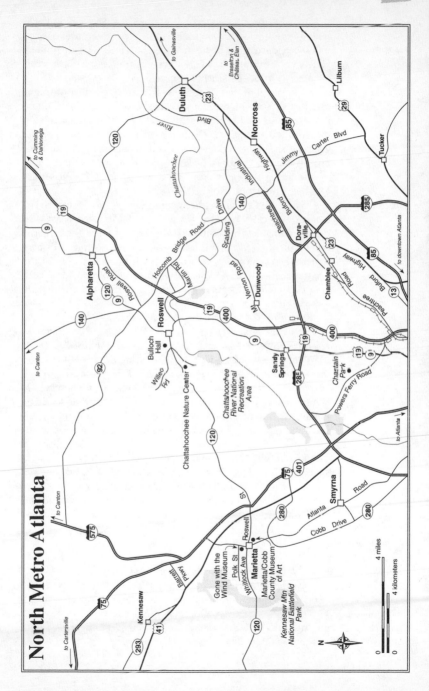

North Metro Atlanta

to Cartersville

to Canton

to Canton

to Cumming & Dahlonega

to Gainesville

to Braselton & Château, Elan

to downtown Atlanta

to Atlanta

Kennesaw

Barrett Pkwy

75

575

293

41

Gone with the Wind Museum

Polk St

Whitlock Ave

Marietta

Marietta/Cobb County Museum of Art

Kennesaw Mtn National Battlefield Park

120

Roswell St

Atlanta Road

Cobb Drive

280

280

Smyrna

75

401

Roswell Road

Alpharetta

Roswell Road

120

9

9

140

19

9

120

92

Bulloch Hall

Willeo Fwy

Chattahoochee Nature Center

Roswell

Holcomb Bridge Road

Martin Rd

Chattahoochee River

Scalding Drive

Vernon Rd

140

120

Chattahoochee River National Recreation Area

19

400

9

19

400

Dunwoody

Sandy Springs

285

Chastain Park

Powers Ferry Road

13

9

Duluth

23

Norcross

Peachtree Industrial Highway

Buford Highway

85

Doraville

23

Chamblee

Buford Highway

Peachtree Road

285

85

13

Jimmy Carter Blvd

Tucker

Lilburn

29

N

0   4 miles

0   4 kilometers

HIDDEN ▶

One of Roswell's first settlers, Major James Stephens Bulloch, built a grand mansion one block west of the town square back in 1840. Constructed of heart pine, the Greek Revival **Bulloch Hall** is a rare example of what's known as true temple-form architecture, with full pedimented portico. The floor plan is four-square—typical of that period—with an equal number of rooms on either side of a high-ceilinged entry hall. Not only is the house impressive, so are the grounds: Bulloch Hall claims 142 trees on the Historic Tree Register. The house has another historic footnote: it was the site of the wedding of Bulloch's daughter, Mittie, to Theodore Roosevelt. Visitors who sign up for tours may want to allow time to linger in the gift shop of this special house. Admission. ~ 180 Bulloch Avenue, Roswell; 770-992-1731.

HIDDEN ▶

To find the **Chattahoochee Nature Center**, head south on Atlanta Street (which becomes Roswell Road) to Azalea Drive, turn right and then left on Willeo Road for half a mile. The center is known for its bird rehabilitation clinic, but also runs a display center where visitors can learn about the natural history of the Chattahoochee River in this area. No pets allowed. Admission. ~ 9135 Willeo Road, Roswell; 770-992-2055; www.chattnature center.com.

Return to Roswell Road and travel north to Route 120, also known as the Marietta Highway. It takes about 20 minutes to reach the town of **Marietta** on a good day. Established in 1824, Marietta occupied a critical position during the Civil War when the railroad that ran through town was destroyed by Sherman's March. Despite the destruction, approximately 100 antebellum homes remain; you can pick up a guided tour map at the Welcome Center, but don't expect to be admitted into what are mostly private homes. Despite its proximity to Atlanta, Marietta is politically conservative, as you might expect when you remember that Cobb County is Newt Gingrich country.

From the highway, turn south on Church Street and continue several blocks to **Marietta Square**, bordered on the north by Lawrence Street. The square is ground zero for a number of food and other fun festivals when bands often play here in Glover Park.

AUTHOR FAVORITE

If, like me, you are fond of history and/or trains, check out the **Southern Museum of Civil War and Locomotive History**. At this sub-suburban attraction, wooden freight cars, vintage steam locomotives, Pullmans—some 70 pieces of rolling stock altogether—comprise a sizable collection that is operated by the Atlanta Chapter of the National Railway Historical Society. See page 246 for more information.

Around this landscaped plaza is a plethora of shops and restaurants, as well as a couple of major attractions.

A block west of the square is the **Marietta Welcome Center and Visitors Bureau,** one of the best-stocked information centers in the state. They give out maps for self-guided tours of the five National Register Historic Districts in town. Closed Sunday morning. ~ 4 Depot Street, Marietta; 770-429-1115, 800-835-0445; www.mariettasquare.com.

In a restored brick 1880s warehouse, you can see the gown Scarlett wore on her honeymoon with Rhett and a raft of other movie memorabilia at the **Gone with the Wind Museum, Scarlett on the Square.** One section is devoted to the African-American cast members, including Hattie McDaniel, who played Mammy. Closed Sunday. Admission. ~ 18 Whitlock Avenue, Marietta; 770-794-5576; www.gwtwmarietta.com.

Nearby is the **Marietta Museum of History,** on the second and third floors of Kennesaw House, itself of historic importance. Part of the museum is arranged a bit like a residence, with an antique quilt hung above an old brick fireplace, mannequins in period dress standing near or sitting on antique furnishings, and portraits of prominent citizens hung on the walls as in some grand manse. There is an exhibit on the sewing arts, including samples of crochet, needle lace, tatting and other techniques considered essential to the repertoire of a proper young Cobb County lady circa 1880 (especially in an area with so many mills). The War Room tells the story of Union soldiers who stayed here in 1862 and tried to steal a Confederate locomotive (see "Southern Museum of Civil War and Locomotive History" below). Closed Sunday morning. Admission. ~ 1 Depot Street, Suite 200, Marietta; 770-528-0431; www.mariettahistory.org.

On the southeast rim of the square, near the corner of Anderson Street, the **Marietta/Cobb County Museum of Art** focuses on visual art of the 19th and 20th centuries. Closed Sunday morning and Monday. Admission. ~ 30 Atlanta Street, Marietta; 770-528-1444; www.mariettasquare.com/mcma, e-mail mcma@ mariettasquare.com.

After seeing the art shows, head north on Cherokee Street to Polk Street, turn left and cross the railroad tracks to view the **Root House Museum.** In 1844, William Root, a local pharmacist, paid $200 for a half-acre lot here and built a plain frame house, which was later moved out of the way for construction of a library. Various remodelings were done to the home before the Cobb Landmarks and Historical Society took it over and moved it to the corner of Powder Springs Road and Polk Street, just two blocks from where it was built. One of the oldest frame houses in town, it can be toured with docents who explain the period furnishings and details of construction. It's surrounded by flower

◄ HIDDEN

beds and vegetable plots planted with greenery in the style of the mid-19th century. Closed Sunday and Monday. Admission. ~ 145 Denmead Street, Marietta; 770-426-4982; www.cobbland marks.com.

The Root House is en route to Kennesaw, although the route gets a little tricky and you have to keep an eagle eye out for sign-posts.

The largest waterpark in the southeastern U.S., **White Water and American Adventures Atlanta** is the number-one place to be during a heat wave. Millions of gallons of water are pumped to create waterfalls, pools and even waves. Closed after Labor Day until Memorial Day. Admission. ~ 250 North Cobb Parkway (Route 41), Marietta; 770-424-9283; www.sixflags.com.

HIDDEN ▶ Take Kennesaw Avenue northwest until you see the turnoff for **Kennesaw Mountain National Battlefield Park**. Between the famous Civil War battles of Chattanooga and Chickamauga to the north and Atlanta to the south, Kennesaw was the site of ferocious fighting in 1864. You can walk around on your own or take a bus (sometimes the bus ride is required because of crowds) and visit 11 miles of earthwork fortifications where the Confederates entrenched along the ridgetops of Big and Little Kennesaw Mountain (the peaks) south to the Powder Springs Road, hoping to block Union invasion. Sherman, who did ad-mire the beauty of the region, obviously overcame his reluctance to engage his troops but an unsuccessful attack produced heavy casualties that inspired the Union soldiers to call their approach the "Dead Angle." Sherman resumed his proven flanking ma-neuvers, though, pressing on to Atlanta, which fell on September 2, 1864. The 2884-acre park preserves the battleground where General Joseph E. Johnston's troops temporarily halted the Union advance. The visitors center has exhibits, books and maps. ~ 900 Kennesaw Moun-tain Drive, Kennesaw; 770-427-4686; www.nps. gov/kemo.

The attempted theft of "The General" was dram-atized in the Walt Disney movie *The Great Loco-motive Chase*, with Fess Parker.

When you leave the park, continue north to the town of Kennesaw via Old Route 41, which crosses Route 41 and becomes Main Street. The total distance from the park's exit to the **Southern Museum of Civil War and Locomotive History** is three and a half miles. The story that began at the Kennesaw House with the soldiers who tried to steal a locomotive continues here, with the piece of iron rooster they call "The General." Inside a former cotton gin the size of a han-gar, "The General" glistens, its polished red-and-black exterior showing the result of care and attention. The old locomotive still draws admirers who know the story of its glory days. On April 12, 1862, a bunch of Union soldiers stole a train with the intention of destroying Confederate supply lines between Chattanooga and Atlanta. Confederate soldiers gave chase, finally recapturing their train about 86 miles away in what some regard as the most dramatic incident of the entire war. It was enshrined here, only 100 yards from where "she" was stolen, exactly 110 years from the date known as the Andrews Raid. Other Civil War artifacts and related exhibits round out the museum's collection. The museum also hosts traveling Smithsonian exhibits and sponsors a lecture series. (The red caboose is on display in front of this museum, along with a historical plaque; there is no charge to view them.) Admission. ~ 2829 Cherokee Street, Kennesaw; 770-427-2117; www.southernmuseum.org.

Not to worry, there are tons of chain motels and hotels in north Atlanta. However, the few small inns available tend to be in the heart of small cities convenient to attractions.

LODGING

    Buford Highway is full of restaurants, stores and, farther out, automobile repair shops. Practically the only halfway decent accommodations are at the **Atlanta Inn**, located one mile inside Route 285, the perimeter road. Thirty-seven rooms in a pair of two-story buildings face each other across a barren country road. They're clean enough and outfitted with the same floral bedcovers seen in roadside motels coast to coast. ~ 5114 Buford Highway, Doraville; 770-452-8500. MODERATE.

    If you want to stay at **Ten-Fifty Canton Street**, you'd better call far in advance. The converted white clapboard bed and breakfast has only three accommodations and, given its location only a couple of blocks north of Canton Street's shopping mecca, rooms are much in demand. Quilts and turn-of-the-20th-century-style furnishings give rooms a period flair, but it's really a contemporary inn. No children allowed. ~ 1050 Canton Street, Roswell; 770-998-1050; www.canton1050.com, e-mail canton 1050@aol.com. DELUXE TO ULTRA-DELUXE.

    Most of the chain lodging in this area can be found along Holcomb Bridge Road. However, the **Brookwood Inn Atlanta-Roswell** is conveniently located for travelers on Old Dogwood Road, which is right off Route 400. There's a pool. All the corridors and elevators are exterior at this three-story, 129-room motel. Travelers get a complimentary continental breakfast and free local calls, which makes it a good deal. ~ 9995 Old Dogwood Road, Roswell; 770-587-5161. BUDGET.

    The five guest rooms at **The Stanley House** bed-and-breakfast inn are decorated in Victorian fashion, from the period-style wallpaper to the antiques and reproductions. The three-story, turreted Queen Anne home was built in 1895 for Woodrow Wilson's aunt, Felie Woodrow, and has a landscaped courtyard

Text continued on page 250.

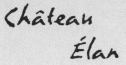

Château Élan

Move over, California, and get ready to toast Georgia's wineries. Just outside of Atlanta is a 2600-acre winery and vineyard that dwarfs even the big guys in the Napa Valley.

The centerpiece of Château Élan is a stunning replica of a 16th-century chateau that looks like one you might see in the French countryside, though this is not a duplicate of any particular structure but an amalgamation of architectural features. The entrance of the chateau is tiled with quarry stones, set off with wrought-iron fences, Parisian-style street lamps and other homages to France.

Situated about half an hour outside Metro Atlanta and 55 miles from Hartsfield-Jackson International Airport, Château Élan is practically a town in itself, with everything but its own zip code. Amid gently rolling hills you'll find several restaurants, an inn, art galleries, an equestrian center, golf courses and a full-service spa. While it is best known for its award-winning wines, it is also a destination to which people return again and again, perhaps to have lunch, shop or just stroll around. It doesn't hurt that Road Atlanta, a site for major auto-racing events and a driving school, is just four miles away. The excursion is ideal for a Sunday afternoon diversion. And admission is free.

Established in 1982, the winery has been producing wines employing modern techniques since 1984. The idea evolved when the founders sampled wine made from the Muscadine grapes that grow wild along country roads throughout the southeastern U.S.; the rich, fertile land of the north Georgia foothills seemed ideal for raising vinifera grapes. Most of the grapes used are grown within the state and the list, including Georgia Merlot, American Merlot, Georgia Chardonnay, a Founder's Reserve Cabernet Sauvignon, American Riesling, Georgia Riesling, Pinot Noir, White Zinfandel and proprietary wines as well as a port, has garnered more than 250 national and international awards.

The wine can be sampled and purchased in the **Wine Market**, which also carries a supply of wine-related items as well as kitchenware and ready-to-eat foods. However, you needn't go with store-bought when there are so many choices on the Chateau's restaurant menus—seven in all.

Le Clos has a formal atmosphere befitting its multicourse classic French meals, expertly paired with Château Élan's wines. Jackets are required for gentlemen. Reservations required. Closed Monday through Wednesday. ~ ULTRA-DELUXE.

For something lighter, **Fleur-de-Lis** has a heart-healthy menu. Nutritious gourmet cuisine is offered at breakfast, lunch and dinner, and all the dishes are analyzed by the spa chef for fat, cholesterol, sodium and calorie content. No dinner Sunday through Thursday. ~ DELUXE.

The South of France takes center stage in the **Versailles Room**, which, despite its name, has a relaxed patio-style ambiance. Located in the Inn's enormous glass atrium, it features beef, poultry and seafood entrées prepared à la Provence. Breakfast and lunch are served buffet-style; dinner is à la carte. ~ MODERATE TO ULTRA-DELUXE.

Café Elan is the best choice for the casual daytripper. Housed in the château, this bistro concentrates on light entrées such as quiches, salads, sandwiches and soups at lunch and dinner. ~ MODERATE TO ULTRA-DELUXE.

Overlooking the atrium, the casual **L'Auberge** has a big-screen TV, billiard tables, a dart board and a little putting green. This is a good place to drop in for snacks Monday through Friday after 5 p.m. and earlier on the weekend. A more upscale meal is served after 6 p.m. ~ BUDGET TO ULTRA-DELUXE.

Paddy's Irish Pub is devoted to traditional Irish fare and spirits and has live entertainment Friday and Saturday nights. No lunch Monday through Friday. ~ BUDGET TO MODERATE.

The Spa at Château Élan is a full-fledged health environment, with programs like fitness assessment, stress management and personal training. The emphasis on well-being is evidenced in the work of a highly trained staff of therapists who are expert in various massages, aromatherapy and reflexology. There's even a library of books, video tapes and CDs selected for their relaxing impact. Aerobics classes, steam rooms, facials, water aerobics, and body sculpting are also available daily. In addition, the spa has 14 overnight accommodations located upstairs from the spa facilities. ~ ULTRA-DELUXE.

The main hotel on the premises, however, is the **Inn at Château Élan**. Here, the 277 guest rooms and suites all have oversized tubs and a separate shower, and large desks and big closets. The style is luxury-end residential, with window shutters, pastel colors and country French furnishings. ~ 100 Rue Charlemagne, Braselton; 678-425-0900, 800-233-9463, fax 770-271-6915; www.chateauelan.com, e-mail chateau@chateau elan.com. ULTRA-DELUXE.

To reach Château Élan from Atlanta, head northeast on Route 85 past Route 285 to Exit 48 (Route 211); the complex is left of the interstate.

where guests gather in the evenings. ~ 236 Church Street, Marietta; 770-426-1881; www.thestanleyhouse.com. MODERATE TO DELUXE.

As soon as you set eyes on **The Whitlock Inn**, you can see why brides and grooms frequently choose it for their nuptial site. Located at one end of a National Register Historic District, the inn has a ballroom that seats over 100, as well as smaller function rooms. Built as a residence in 1900, this white Victorian boasts several porches, four chimneys and classic touches like green shutters. Gleaming wood and floral wallpaper that fit in beautifully with the period antiques in all five guest rooms put this B&B in the upper crust of hostelries. All the rooms are distinct with private baths: the Magnolia Room has a red-and-green color scheme with a canopy bed; the Bridal Room is outfitted with a queen-size high poster bed; the Marietta Room features a queen-size sleigh bed and a view of old Marietta and the trains (the sounds of which may have interrupted more than one honeymoon). Continental breakfast is included. ~ 57 Whitlock Avenue, Marietta; 770-428-1495; www.whitlockinn.com, e-mail alexis@whitlockinn.com. DELUXE.

The **Marietta Conference Center & Resort**, decorated with crystal chandeliers and wall murals, specializes in large groups, with extensive meeting space and all kinds of support services. However, you can rent one of the 199 rooms here, where weekend getaway packages are available. There's a restaurant and lodge, tennis courts, a spa and a championship golf course on the premises. ~ 500 Powder Springs Street, Marietta; 770-427-2500, 888-685-2500; www.mariettaresort.com, e-mail info@marietta resort.com. DELUXE TO ULTRA-DELUXE.

AUTHOR FAVORITE

Sixty Polk Street—a.k.a. the Edmunston/Law/Ladd/Mertes House, in honor of the succeeding families who have lived here since about 1872—is a beautifully maintained example of Victorian French Regency architecture. That sounds fussy, but it really isn't. Four upstairs guest rooms have private baths, though one is next door to the room and has an original clawfoot tub. One features Victorian furniture; another, pieces from the later Empire period. Another room, the Grand Woode Suite, has original built-in furniture. Throughout the house, keep an eye out for the owners' collections, which range from the sublime (elegant chandeliers) to the not-so-sublime (antique commodes). ~ 60 Polk Street, Marietta; 770-419-1688, 800-845-7266; www.sixtypolkstreet.com, e-mail jmertes@aol.com. DELUXE TO ULTRA-DELUXE.

From dining in old homes to quick-and-cheap barbecue, you can indulge in a variety of meals in this region.

DINING

You never really know where you'll find outstanding Northern Italian cuisine. Certainly you might not think to look in a strip mall on the cusp of Alpharetta north of the perimeter at a place called **Cucina di Paulo**. Antipastos look familiar here, with the exception of *melanzane bruschetta*, grilled Italian bread with eggplant and cannellini beans along with other things. Gnocchi, farfalle, rigatoni and other pastas get different kinds of sauces. House specialties include veal scaloppine (prepared two ways) and daily delights, perhaps grilled fish with garlic mashed potatoes. Cucina di Paulo is contained in one large room with an open kitchen and questionable acoustics. Reservations advised. Closed Monday. ~ 8560 Holcomb Bridge Road, Alpharetta; 770-587-1051. MODERATE TO DELUXE.

◀ *HIDDEN*

As you approach Roswell, you'll pass right by **Slope's BBQ**. Hickory-smoked and hand-pulled, the chicken and pork in this modest one-room spot come in plates, as salads, in large portions, in combos, kid's sizes, whatever. Look for a tiny brick building that just happens to be up a small slope. Closed Sunday. ~ 34 Crossville Road, Roswell; 770-518-7000; www.slopesbbq.com, e-mail info@slopesbbq.com. BUDGET TO MODERATE.

◀ *HIDDEN*

Near Roswell Square, **Chaplins** is a bar/restaurant in a small shopping complex. Named for actor Charlie Chaplin, Chaplins used to screen silent movies for its guests. This is a good option for lunch if you arrive in town famished, though the lunch menu is more limited than the dinner version, which lists ribeye. Burgers, grilled chicken, calzones, gyros, lots of munchies to tide you over, and salads for the health-conscious supply a range that should work for everyone. ~ 555 South Atlanta Street, Roswell; 770-642-6981; www.chaplinsroswell.com. BUDGET TO MODERATE.

Greenwood's is so hard to find that even the restaurant's menu explains that the street it's on is next to the Fire Department off Route 9. Works for me. Before the place even opens for dinner, people are milling around outside this cottage, knowing they can expect perfect Southern food elevated to special heights: chicken pot pie, trout fillet, rotisserie duck with plum sauce, black-eyed peas, honey-glazed duck, sweet potatoes, and pies and homemade ice cream for dessert. All this and wine and beer, too. Closed Monday and Tuesday. ~ 1087 Green Street, Roswell; 770-992-5383. MODERATE.

◀ *HIDDEN*

Shrimp and scallop satay, roast duck, basil catfish, steamed snapper with ginger, and mango ice cream are among the unusual choices at the **Thai Emerald Restaurant**, where you can dine indoors or out. You can also order more traditional entrées, including curries and noodles, at this family-owned spot tucked behind Kohl's department store in the Crossville Commons

◀ *HIDDEN*

Shopping Center. No lunch Friday or Saturday. ~ 540 Route 92 West, Roswell; 770-552-6700, fax 770-552-6718; www.thai emeraldrestaurant.com. MODERATE TO DELUXE.

From the get-go, **Dick & Harry's** has been pulling in suburbanites who like the combination of urban cuisine and shopping-center parking-lot accessibility. The place is justifiably renowned for its meaty baked crab cakes and other seafood, but you shouldn't neglect options like veal scaloppine or lamb chops. No lunch on weekends. Closed Sunday. ~ 1570 Holcomb Bridge Road, Suite 810, Roswell; 770-641-8757, fax 770-641-8884; www.dickandharrys.com. MODERATE TO ULTRA-DELUXE.

When locals want to give you directions to anything in Marietta, they nearly always mention The Big Chicken. If you're heading from downtown, you'll be told to go out past The Big Chicken and **Williamson Bros. Bar-B-Q** will be on your left. Otherwise, you'd probably never find it. No matter what time of day it is, by the time you arrive the parking lot will probably be full, aromatic smoke will be curling toward heaven and all the outside seats will be taken. That's okay; it's great to eat inside in one of the oh-so-cozy nooks or settle down at a table in a larger room. Once settled, tuck into all kinds of barbecue, most of it available as platters (i.e., accompanied by two sides of your choice: onion rings, corn on the cob, Brunswick stew). They also sell sandwiches, but unless it's off the rotisserie, why bother? Unbelievably, there's also "Bros. Lite," a list of items that may not be as fattening as the regular stuff. Again, why bother? ~ 1425 Roswell Road, Marietta; 770-971-3201, fax 770-971-3694; www.williamsonbros.com. BUDGET TO DELUXE.

HIDDEN ▶

On the Square, **Le Peep** serves Le Breakfast and Le Lunch, but not Le Dinner. In a roomy corner spot with lattice accents, fake plants and lots of windows, diners consider whether to stick with mundane items like soup, salads and sandwiches, or to cut loose

AUTHOR FAVORITE

It was a pleasant surprise to find one of metro Atlanta's best restaurants tucked into a cul-de-sac next to a shopping center. **Van Gogh's Restaurant and Bar** is a large bungalow with several rooms, including one with lots of brick. It's a delightful setting for entrées like blackened mahimahi, prosciutto-wrapped salmon over couscous, lump crab cakes and chipotle-marinated pork tenderloin. Main courses at lunch feature some of these same dishes at about half the cost. No lunch Saturday. ~ 70 West Crossville Road, Alpharetta; 770-993-1156; www.knowwhere togogh.com. DELUXE TO ULTRA-DELUXE.

with Highway in a skillet or a luncheon crêpe with chicken, seafood or spinach. This spot definitely has the best Highway menu
in town. No dinner. ~ 70 South Park Square, Marietta; 770-426-
5161. BUDGET.

You can find Mexican food a couple of blocks off Marietta
Square at **La Parrilla Mexican Restaurant,** a bright orange eatery
with blue accents. Inside, it's quieter than it looks, with diners
seated around a large room under the light of red-and-white
Tiffany-style fixtures. They offer a mammoth menu, including
everyday items plus Mexican pizza, Mexi-pork chops (grilled,
with rice-beans-sauce) and *picadillo*, chunks of sirloin cooked in
red chile sauce. Almost everything is $9. ~ 29 South Marietta
Parkway, Marietta; 770-427-0055. BUDGET.

At the intersection of Hansel and Cherokee streets a half-
block north of Marietta Square, the **House of Lu** is the town's   ◄ HIDDEN
upscale Asian eatery. Green leatherette booths face granite tabletops along the window-lined street side; a decorative mirror anchors the far end of the pretty room. Here, patrons feast on
Walnut Shrimp in Bird's Nest, stir-fried scallops and shrimp with
asparagus, and Ku Lu (sweet and sour) chicken. Aside from these
specialties, treats include Szechwan eggplant, Mongolian beef,
and the vegetarian Peking Buddha's Delight. Otherwise, it's a
fairly short menu for a Chinese restaurant. ~ 89 Cherokee Street,
Marietta; 770-794-8831. MODERATE TO DELUXE.

You can wear your shorts to **Hemingway's Tropical Bar &
Grill,** and you may even be overdressed if it's a hot day. This is
the local island-inspired hangout, with lots of Jimmy Buffett–
type music and not-quite-full-meal offerings like barbecue pork
sandwiches, fried or jerk shrimp, fajita wraps, empanadas, po'
boy sandwiches, Cuban cheese steaks and a slew of salads, including slaw. On nice days, patrons spill out onto tables in the
side alley to drink beer in the shade of Budweiser umbrellas. No
dinner Sunday. ~ 29 West Park Square, Marietta; 770-427-5445;
www.hemingwaysmarietta.com, e-mail mike@hemingwaysmari
etta.com. BUDGET TO DELUXE.

There are a few big discount places in and around Duluth. For   **SHOPPING**
boutiques and high-quality antiques, head west to Roswell and
Alpharetta.

Alpharetta, just a few miles from Roswell, has many good antique stores. Among them are **Laura Ramsey Antiques, Inc.,** where
English and French antiques are the drawing card. Closed Sunday
and Monday. ~ 220 South Main Street, Alpharetta; 770-475-2085.

In a town full of antique shops, the **Roswell Antique Mall** is
a convenient stop where you can view the wares of more than 200
dealers. A lot of Atlanta estates end up here, usually in parcels, but

there are innumerable small pieces (mirrors, etc.) in addition to furnishings. ~ 700 Holcomb Bridge Road, Roswell; 770-993-7200.

In the heart of town, **Mulberry House Antiques** is located in a multiroom cottage exquisitely decorated with 18th- and 19th-century furniture, both country and formal in style. Fine and folk art, quilts and rugs are part of the high-quality merchandise. Closed Sunday through Wednesday, except by appointment. ~ 1028 Canton Street, Roswell; 770-998-6851.

The collection at the Gone with the Wind Museum has been displayed at Walt Disney World's MGM Studios.

The Board of Trade, located in a brown shack, specializes in porcelain, silver, lamps, prints and other decorative items. Closed Sunday. ~ 964 Atlanta Street, Roswell; 770-640-7615.

Toys, games, and Civil War–related books are among the stock at the **Marietta Museum Gift Shop**. ~ 1 Depot Street, Marietta; 770-528-0430.

The **Historic Marietta Square Farmers Market** proffers locally grown fruits, vegetables, herbs, plants and flowers as well as jams, jellies, breads and other baked goods, on Saturday mornings from May to October. ~ In the First Baptist Church parking lot on the corner of Church and Hansell streets, Marietta; 770-499-9393.

Local gourmet food products, home and kitchen accessories, yard art, birdhouses, herb baskets, cut flowers and more are displayed at the **Church Street Market**, located in a circa-1910 service station. Closed Sunday. ~131 Church Street, Marietta; 770-499-9393.

Books on *Gone with the Wind* and other merchandise related to the legendary movie can be found at the **Gone with the Wind Museum gift shop**. ~ 18 Whitlock Avenue, Marietta; 770-794-5576.

NIGHTLIFE With the exception of some of your rowdier restaurants, the north side of Atlanta beyond the perimeter is pretty quiet—no doubt because so many people who live here get up early for work most days. Despite this, an impressive cultural life hums north of the big city.

Grammy Award–winning songwriters perform at 10 p.m. Fridays and Saturdays at **The Swallow at the Hollow**, which serves barbecue except during shows. Closed Monday and Tuesday. Cover. ~ 1072 Green Street, Roswell; 678-352-1975; www.theswallowatthehollow.com.

Comedies, musicals and dramas are the stock at **Kudzu Playhouse**, which represents a full season of family theater. ~ 608 Holcomb Bridge Road, Roswell; 770-594-1020; www.kudzu playhouse.com.

The **Georgia Ensemble Theatre** produces professional shows in Roswell's 600-seat Municipal Auditorium.. ~ 950 Forrest Street, Roswell; 770-641-1260; www.get.org.

Hemingway's has live rock bands on Friday and Saturday nights, a changing lineup that has included groups that cover Jimmy Buffett songs—the perfect soundtrack for this bar/café. ~ 29 West Park Square, Marietta; 770-427-5445.

The **Theatre in the Square** has won awards for its top-notch performances, six productions from August to July. There are generally no performances on Monday, but two shows on Sunday. Previous bills included *The Night of the Iguana, The Front Page* and a satire on *Wuthering Heights*. ~ 11 Whitlock Avenue, Marietta; 770-422-8369; www.theatreinthesquare.com.

Dave & Buster's is to adults what Disneyland is to kids. Video games, virtual-reality simulators, bars, a dinner theater, shuffleboard courts and other recreational facilities draw tons of people at night. Kids can come with adults, but anyone under 21 must leave by 10 p.m. Open until 2 a.m. Friday and Saturday. ~ 2215 Dave & Busters Drive Southeast, Marietta; 770-951-5554; www.daveandbusters.com.

Cowboy's Concert Hall gives new meaning to country club. Its 4000-square-foot dancefloor is practically big enough for all the country fans in Georgia. Sunday is "family night." Closed Monday and Tuesday. Cover. ~ 1750 North Roberts Road Northwest, Kennesaw; 770-426-5006.

CHASTAIN PARK 🐴 Bounded by West Wieuca Road, Powers Ferry Road and Lake Forest Drive, Chastain is a destination in itself for lovers of the outdoors. There are athletic fields for baseball, football and soccer as well as a gym. The Atlanta Lawn Tennis Association uses the Chastain courts for their tournaments. For less focused activity, there is a playground and a three-and-a-half-mile jogging trail that you can, of course, walk or jog. The 6000-seat amphitheater is a popular venue for entertainment such as concerts by the Atlanta Symphony. ~ Four miles south of Route 285 off the Powers Ferry Exit; 404-817-6785.

PARKS

KENNESAW MOUNTAIN NATIONAL BATTLEFIELD PARK 🚶 ◀ *HIDDEN*
🐴 A visitors center displays exhibits on the Atlanta Campaign, one of the Civil War battles where the Confederate troops prevailed. The park is dedicated to preserving relics of the war but even if you're not interested in that aspect, you can meander on 16 miles of wooded hiking trails that zig and zag throughout this 2884-acre park. There are restrooms at the visitors center. ~ 900 Kennesaw Mountain Drive, Kennesaw; 770-427-4686; www.nps.gov/kemo.

Outdoor Adventures

**RIVER
RAFTING**

Chattahoochee Outfitters rents rafts, canoes, kayaks and tubes so you can float on the Chattahoochee River as it flows through Roswell. ~ 203 Azalea Drive, Roswell; 770-641-3705.

The **Nantahala Outdoor Center** offers whitewater trips on the Ocoee and Chattooga rivers in Georgia as well as the Nantahala, French Broad and Nolichucky in Tennessee and North Carolina. ~ 13077 Route 19 West, Bryson City, NC; 800-232-7238; www.noc.com.

GOLF

Atlanta's famed greenery makes playing golf in and around the city a great pleasure. Many clubs are semiprivate, meaning non-members are welcome to pay and play.

The closest course to downtown Atlanta is the 18-hole **Bobby Jones Golf Course**, named after the famous native golfer. It's situated on part of the Battle of Peachtree Creek site and seems to always be crowded. ~ 384 Woodward Way, Atlanta; 404-355-1009.

For municipal courses, the prize goes to **Browns Mill Golf Course**, 18 holes and well within the perimeter. ~ 480 Cleveland Avenue, Atlanta; 404-366-3573.

Good and bad news about the **North Fulton Golf Course**, which dates to the 1940s. Golfers give it high marks for a great layout, but they also have to cope with small greens. ~ 216 West Wieuca Road, Atlanta; 404-255-0723.

The **Alfred "Tup" Holmes Club** has 18 holes with plenty of dog legs configured on a former Confederate breastworks. Bermuda greens cover mildly hilly terrain; it's a good choice for intermediates. ~ 2300 Wilson Drive, Atlanta; 404-753-6158.

The **Stone Mountain Golf Club** includes 36 holes designed by Robert Trent Jones. Nine of the holes are lakeside at this course, which is among the best-rated in the U.S. If you hope to play on a weekend or holiday, you should call for reservations at least a week in advance. ~ 1145 Stonewall Jackson Drive, Stone Mountain; 770-465-3278; www.stonemountaingolf.com.

The par-71 **Château Course** at Château Élan has contoured fairways, thick Bermuda roughs and lakes and pools strategically placed around 170 acres. It's best enjoyed by walking along three

GIDDY UP

It's unusual to find riding stables right in the city; most of the horsey set is centered up around Alpharetta, and few provide rental horses. But in Chastain Park you will find the **Chastain Horse Park**, right in the fashionable north side of the city. ~ 4371 Powers Ferry Road, Atlanta; 404-252-4244.

lakes and two creeks, adding up to 10 water holes out of 18. Seventeen bunkers shape the fairways and give definition to the smooth bent-grass greens. The par-72 **Woodlands Course** has nine holes out and nine holes in on an overseeded course that provides green fairways year-round. Natural features, including lots of trees and a number of elevation changes, add to the feeling of being out in the country. In addition, Château Élan offers par-3 golf, in which the holes are marked with lighted flagsticks, glow markers and tiki torches. Each golfer gets glow balls, clubs and flashlights. So if you knock a ball into the rough, you'll at least be able to find it. ~ Château Élan, 6060 Golf Club Drive, Braselton; 678-425-6050; www.chateauelan.com.

TENNIS

Named for a legendary local star of the 1940s, the **Bitsy Grant Tennis Center** has 10 hard courts and 13 clay ones (wonderful for hot weather) at the city's top public facility. ~ 2125 Northside Drive; 404-609-7193.

There are 12 outdoor hard courts lit for night play during the week at the **Piedmont Park Tennis Center**. There are also showers and lockers. Fee. ~ Piedmont Avenue at 14th Street; 404-853-3461.

Chastain Park has nine hard courts that fill up quickly. Make reservations. ~ 110 West Wieuca Road; 404-255-3210.

ICE SKATING

You can bet the **Parkaire Ice Arena** is packed when the temperatures outside hit 95 degrees. It's open year-round, with limited hours of free skating due to scheduled classes and special events. Fee. ~ 4880 Lower Roswell Road, Marietta; 770-973-0753.

BIKING

Freedom Park, a 45-acre park with jogging and biking paths, is located near the Carter Center. The bicycle trail, called Freedom Trail, provides access to every point in the park and leads into downtown Atlanta; it also forms a segment of the Atlanta/Stone Mountain Trail. ~ Accessible at Boulevard and Jackson Street and on North Avenue from Moreland to Candler Park.

Bike Rentals To cruise around Atlanta, the full-service **Skate Escape Bike Shop** offers single-speed cruisers. Mountain bikes can be rented to ride the 15 miles to Stone Mountain. Helmets cost extra. ~ 1086 Piedmont Avenue Northeast, Atlanta; 404-892-1292.

HIKING

The **Atlanta-DeKalb Greenway Trail System** offers miles of trails and streets for biking, hiking and walking; at points, biking doesn't work and you'll need a trail map if you're on wheels. You can get a map from many bicycle vendors and from the PATH Foundation. ~ 4200 Northside Parkway Northwest, Building 12, Atlanta; 404-355-6438; www.pathfoundation.org.

In Atlanta, the **Trolley Line Trail** (6.7 miles) connects downtown all the way to Agnes Scott College in Decatur, by way of Georgia State University, the Martin Luther King Jr. Historic Site and historic Cabbagetown, East Lake and Reynoldstown neighborhoods.

The **Westside Trail** (10.6 miles) links Greenbriar Mall in the southwest part of town to downtown via the Hightower MARTA station. This trail connects all the MARTA stations on the west line, and passes the Atlanta University complex as well as the Georgia Dome area.

The **Stone Mountain/Atlanta Greenway Trail** (18 miles) extends from Georgia Tech, along the Freedom Parkway and east to Stone Mountain Park.

The **nature trail** at the Chattahoochee Nature Center rambles over 127 acres of woodlands and wetlands. Here you will likely see, depending on the season, joe pyeweed, jewelweed and tulip poplar in bloom. A canopy of oaks and hickory trees soars above the smaller dogwood. Along the river, look closely among the moss-clad rocks for skinks, moles and mice. If you're not afraid to get your feet wet, you might come across frogs and salamanders; in and above the marsh are belted kingfishers and great blue herons.

In fact, there are eight trails in the Chattahoochee River National Recreation Area. The **Cochran Shoals Unit** (2.5-mile loop) has a fitness trail that is accessible to the disabled. Cochran Shoals Park extends over some 968 acres, making it the largest park along the Chattahoochee, covering fields, woodlands and wetlands where you can have excellent luck birding and sighting wildlife. While most are nearly level, two 1.5-mile trails run up about 50 feet into forested areas. The **Sope Creek Trail** (1.5 miles) is especially nice in spring as it goes through the ruins of the Marietta Paper Mill. En route, you can hike around Sibly Pond, a popular winter waterfowl hangout frequented by belted kingfishers and wood

AUTHOR FAVORITE

I never made it to the top of the 1000-foot ridge at the **Kennesaw Mountain National Battlefield Park**, but you can enjoy some good hikes even if you don't go that far. Trails here lead through hardwood forests to grand views of the mountains, a plateau and a valley to the north. You will find various starting points for the 16 miles of walkable trails; the main one is at the visitors center, where you should pick up a good map. There is plenty of ascent to deal with but the descent, especially to Pigeon Hill and Burnt Hickory Road, is steep, rocky and, in places, washed away.

ducks. The **Gundy Creek Trail** (1.5 miles) departs from the fitness trail and passes through a wet area—keep an eye out for raccoon and opossum pawprints—up past an old barn to a shaded ridge, where hardwood trees change colors in the autumn. In the Gundy Creek ravine in early spring you're likely to see trilliums and wild ginger, among other spring wildflowers.

Transportation

CAR

Encircled by the perimeter road, **Route 285**, Atlanta is bisected by **Route 75** and **Route 85**, which diverge, as they head north, at the southern edge of Buckhead. Peachtree Street and Piedmont Avenue are the major non-interstate south–north arteries. Atlanta's only toll road is **Route 400**; drivers pay a 50-cent toll between Lenox Road and the Glenridge exit. High Occupancy Vehicle (HOV) lanes on the far left (set off by a broken white line) are intended for cars with two or more people.

AIR

Hartsfield-Jackson Atlanta International Airport, 20 miles south of the city, is served by more than 30 major carriers, including numerous international airlines. One of the world's busiest airports, it handles some 2000 flights a day. The domestic concourses alone have nearly 150 passenger gates, so allow plenty of time if you are flying out. An underground train system whisks passengers between concourses, which saves a great deal of time. The major airlines at Hartsfield include Air Canada, Air France, American Airlines, British Airways, Continental, Delta Air Lines, Japan Air Lines, KLM, Lufthansa, Northwest, United and US Airways. ~ www.atlanta-airport.com.

BUS

Greyhound Bus Lines connects Atlanta with major cities all over the country, as well as numerous towns around Georgia. ~ 232 Forsyth Street, Atlanta; 404-584-1728, 800-231-2222; www.greyhound.com.

TRAIN

Amtrak trains stop at the Brookwood station in Midtown. ~ 1688 Peachtree Street Northwest, Atlanta; 404-881-3060, 800-872-7245; www.amtrak.com.

PUBLIC TRANSIT

MARTA runs Atlanta's bus and rapid rail transit system, with nearly 700 buses that cover 150 routes. Far more convenient to most points in the greater metropolitan area is the rail system, which runs from 4:45 a.m. (5:15 a.m. Saturday, 6 a.m. Sunday) to 1 a.m. (12:45 a.m. Saturday, Sunday and holidays). MARTA has a line all the way to Hartsfield International Airport; the ride to the city is about 20 minutes, but 50 minutes if you are going all the way north beyond the perimeter road to Sandy Springs. ~ 2424 Piedmont Road Northeast, Atlanta; 404-848-4711; www.itsmarta.com.

CAR RENTALS

All the major automobile rental agencies have outlets at Hartsfield-Jackson International Airport or near it. They are **Alamo Rent A Car** (800-462-5266), **Avis Rent A Car** (800-230-4898), **Budget Rent A Car** (404-530-3000, 800-527-0700), **Dollar Rent A Car** (800-800-3665) and **Hertz Rent A Car** (800-654-3131). **Enterprise Rent A Car** (800-736-8222) has many satellite offices in north and south Atlanta as well as at the airport.

TAXIS

In Atlanta proper, the major taxi companies are **Atlanta Yellow Cab Co.** (404-521-0200), **Buckhead Safety Cab Co.** (404-233-1152) and **Checker Cab Company Inc.** (404-351-1111), specializing in Downtown and Northside. **Su-Taxi** (404-255-6333) provides Spanish-speaking service.

Airport-licensed wheelchair-accessible (lift) van service is offered through **Around Town Tours** (770-909-9091) or **North Express** (404-354-9746). Reservations required.

For travel to, from and near Marietta, you can try **Eastside Taxi Service** (770-421-9285) or **Victory Cab** (770-428-2626).

SIX

The Mountains

The high country in north Georgia is the wildest part of the state. Statuesque mountains, tumbling waterfalls, deep gorges, pristine streams and other preserved patches of nature are its hallmarks. It stands apart from the rest of Georgia; relics of plantations are few and far between and modest in comparison to some of the Tara-like remains found to the south. Although much of the area is a short drive from the megalopolis of Atlanta, you won't be finding much in the way of interstates, traffic jams or avant-garde restaurants. This is where people go to get away from it all, to follow scenic roads that cut through the mountains and lead to unexpected treasures.

For all their romance, "The Mountains" have seen their share of tragedy. From the persecution of the native Cherokee nation—inarguably the most advanced American Indian tribe in the history of the country—to the fierce and fatal conflicts on the battlefield at Chickamauga—the region is metaphorically stained with blood and tears. Much is made of what became of American Indians in the Wild West, but what happened to the Cherokees here makes an equally sad chapter in American history. The trouble is often traced to the discovery of gold in Dahlonega in the early 19th century, which led to what was essentially a land grab, but it is likely the results—most poignantly, the tragic removal of the natives on the Trail of Tears—would have come to pass with or without the frenzy that attends the prospects of a fast road to riches.

Today, you will not see traces of this episode, at least on the surface, in the charming hill towns of Dahlonega and Blue Ridge. No secret is made of the facts, but they're not exactly tourist fare, either. The land that was taken from the natives turned out to be riddled with gold, treasures that rightfully belonged to the original owners. Instead, it was white men who made their fortunes in these hills. Visitors can go into the very mines where laborers toiled to bring the ore up from the bowels of the earth. These on-site excursions can be thrilling and teach more about history by walking in the footsteps of the past than any written account.

You can follow the history of the Cherokees on well-marked routes such as the Chieftains Trail just as you can get a grasp of the rigors of the Civil War on the Blue & Gray Trail. The Lookout Mountain Parkway and the Southern High-roads Driving Tour lead visitors through the mountains, forests and canyons where hikers sometimes seem to outnumber automobiles.

There is far more here than natural history and lessons in human nature, however. It is a place of outstanding people such as Martha Berry, who was born with a silver spoon but used her position to help the children of Appalachia by founding the college in Rome that bears her name. In the northeastern corner, the Dillard family is a household name, thanks to their hospitality complex not far from the North Carolina state line. Nearby, the Foxfire Museum relates the story of another pioneering educator who, though not really an ambitious man, helped the cause of Appalachia by recording the stories of its people and honoring their heritage. Women have made their marks in many ways. Dalton alone claims a number of interesting natives, including Catherine Evans, the carpet industry pioneer, and newswoman Deborah Norville, as well as erstwhile celebrity Marla Maples. Adairsville was the first city in Georgia to be listed in its entirety on the National Register of Historic Places, thanks to efforts made by its women's club.

Toward the east are numerous sources for folk art, which has finally been recognized as a legitimate American art form. A number of rustic lodges have become living art in themselves; like a picture in an old family photograph album, the scene of people rocking and talking on the front porch after a day of fishing on a mountain lake is nostalgia in living color.

Adventure outfitters offer visitors from all over the world a chance to raft the same river that hosted the whitewater events during the 1996 Summer Olympics, which were headquartered in Atlanta. Less-strenuous delights abound as well, from strolls around old town squares to bicycling on country roads to maybe even finding a rocking chair of your own.

Northwest Mountains

North of Atlanta, the rise is gradual until you get to the seven hills of Rome and, not far beyond, part of the Cumberland Plateau. This northwest corner of the state is anchored by Lookout Mountain, a 100-mile-long pedestal that straddles Georgia's boundaries with Tennessee and Alabama. In its shadow are the ghostly reminders of Civil War battles. This is an area of towns and small cities, many with their own quiet delights.

SIGHTS

HIDDEN ►

From Route 75, take Exit 288; turn left at the end of the ramp and look for the brown signs that indicate Georgia historical sites. No legacy of the American Indians who once populated this region is more impressive than the **Etowah Indian Mounds**. The largest and most important Indian settlement in the Etowah Valley, the mounds and the village site were used between A.D. 1000 and 1500. The flat-topped earthen knolls served as a platform for the home of the chief, or priest, temples and mortuary houses. As far as is known, the name was derived from the English word

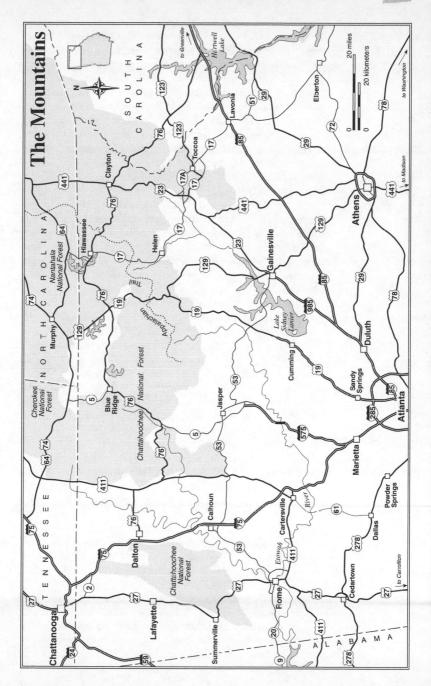

"hightower"; the first published description of it was found in a journal kept by a 19th-century reverend who investigated the underbrush beside the Etowah River and was agape at what he discovered. Visitors to the site can pick up a self-guided tour map that explains the significance of the religious ceremonies and other rituals practiced here; it takes quite awhile to cover the half-mile trail. The best part for some will be the section along the riverbank where hickory and persimmon trees once grew, providing food for the inhabitants, and where river cane furnished the shafts for arrows. A small museum houses some 400 specimens collected from the area and a theater where a short video is screened. Closed Monday. Admission. ~ 813 Indian Mounds Road Southwest, Cartersville; 770-387-3747.

Head north from the mounds into central **Cartersville**, less than a ten-minute drive through residential areas. The town was named not for a local but for a frequent and wealthy visitor, Colonel Farrish Carter, who proposed the idea in jest sometime in the 1850s. When the railroad tracks were re-routed in the wake of the Civil War, Cartersville stole business from the original county seat (Cassville) and shops, churches and residences sprouted around the downtown core. You won't see much in the way of antebellum homes, though a notable exception is Roselawn, the former home of evangelist Samuel Porter Jones that is now a museum. This is not the most scenic of mountain towns, but there are a couple of points of interest downtown, including a 1910 theater that opens occasionally for performances. (Please see "Nightlife" below.) For a map of the area, drop by the **Cartersville-Bartow County Convention and Visitors Bureau**. Closed Sunday morning. ~ 1 Friendship Plaza, Cartersville; 770-387-1357, 800-733-2280, fax 770-386-1220; www.notatlanta.org, e-mail cvb@notatlanta.org.

At the **Bartow History Center**, displays of workshops, farmsteads and general stores from the 1840s through World War II show visitors how the pioneers and their descendants lived in the northwest Georgia mountain country over the decades. Closed Monday. Admission. ~ 13 North Wall Street, Cartersville; 770-382-3818.

Also downtown is the **Young Brothers Pharmacy**, whose claim to fame is the site of the world's first Coca-Cola painted wall advertisement, dating to 1894 and restored in 1989. ~ 2 West Main Street, Cartersville; 770-382-4010.

Located a few blocks to the west, **Roselawn** is now a county-owned museum. To reach it, head west on Main Street to the second traffic signal (Bartow Street), turn right for one block then left onto Cherokee Avenue before turning left again onto Fite Street. The Roselawn driveway will be the first one on the left. Samuel Porter Jones (1847–1906) was a well-known evangelist hailed for having converted Captain Tom Ryman, for whom Nashville's historic Ryman Auditorium, original home of the Grand Ole Opry, is named. He did many a good deed, particularly for orphans down in Decatur. This brick Victorian mansion shares the grounds with the original smokehouse, the carriage house, and the schoolhouse where the Jones children were educated. The second and third floors house museums dedicated to Jones as well as to the Daughters of the Confederacy and the first female U.S. senator, Rebecca Felton, who was once a teacher of Jones. Closed from noon to 1 p.m. and on Monday. Admission. ~ 224 West Cherokee Avenue, Cartersville; 770-387-5162.

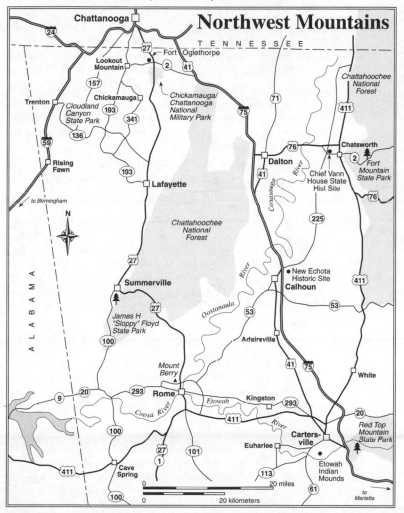

Northwest Mountains

American Indian Driving Tour

American Indians had a strong presence in the Georgia mountains as early as A.D. 950 and continuing until the Cherokee, an advanced civilization with its own alphabet and government, were forcibly removed from the area beginning in 1838, following the discovery of gold in the region's hills. This tour traces some notable locations relating to Indian history.

ETOWAH INDIAN MOUNDS   Begin this 125-mile excursion in the ancient grounds of the Etowah Indian Mounds (page 262) south of Cartersville, one of several sites in Georgia that have educated archaeologists and others on the culture and history of the native Americans.

EUHARLEE COVERED BRIDGE   Travel a short distance west on Route 61/113 to see the Euharlee Covered Bridge (page 266), one of several built by architect Horace King. King, who was of Indian, Caucasian and African-American descent, was born a slave in South Carolina and set free before the Civil War.

INSTITUTIONS OF LEARNING   Northwest of Cartersville via Route 293, keep an eye out for historical markers south of Kingston that mark

---

Rockhounds who know that geologic history reveals a lot about an area won't want to miss the **William Weinman Mineral Museum**. To reach it from Main Street, take Route 75N to Exit 293 and turn left, to the west, and follow the signs. Kids will enjoy handling some of the exhibits, looking at fossils and walking into a replica of a limestone cave with its own waterfall. Closed Sunday. Admission. ~ 51 Mineral Museum Drive Northeast, White; 770-386-0576.

Some travelers "collect" covered bridges and if you're one of them, detour west from Cartersville via Route 61/113 and head west on Euharlee Road for 5.5 miles. You'll come upon the

HIDDEN ►

Euharlee Covered Bridge, one of the oldest in Georgia. Built in 1886 by master bridge builder Washington W. King to span the Etowah River, it is on the National Register. ~ Euharlee Road, Cartersville.

After moseying around Cartersville, detour a few miles north to Adairsville for a garden tour. The public is welcome to explore **Barnsley Gardens**, part of a sprawling estate that encompasses English village–style accommodations, a golf course, a spa and several restaurants. The gardens were originally laid out in the

the locations of the **Cherokee Baptist College** and **Cassville Female College** on the right. These were the first institutions of higher learning in Cherokee Georgia. The college was built in 1854 for boys; it burned down in 1856 and was rebuilt the following year—only to be destroyed by the Union Army in 1864—as was the female college.

NEW ECHOTA   Visit one of the most compelling American Indian sites, New Echota (page 274), by continuing north and east on Firetower Road across Route 75 to Route 411. Head north to Pine Log, west on Route 140 and the north on Shopes Lake Road across Dews Pond Road to find the place that was established in 1825 as the capital of the Cherokee Nation. A print shop here published the first issue of a national Cherokee newspaper. When the Cherokee were forced out in the late 1830s along the infamous Trail of Tears, New Echota almost disappeared. It has now been restored and visitors can tour the courthouse, the council house and the print shop, among other structures.

CHIEF VANN HOUSE STATE HISTORIC SITE   Follow Route 225 north to Chatsworth to visit "the showplace of the Cherokee nation," as **Chief Joseph Vann's home** was known. The home has been extensively restored and is open for tours as part of the Chief Vann House State Historic Site (page 282).

late 1800s by cotton baron Godfrey Barnsley, who also had an Italianate manor house constructed for his wife, Julia. The layout was inspired by Andrew Jackson Downing, a 19th-century architect famous for designing the White House grounds as well as the Washington Mall. When German Prince Hubertus Fugger bought the run-down estate in 1988, he looked to Downing's book for guidance in rebuilding the formal gardens, which were opened to the public in 1992, and feature blooms throughout the year as well as 88 species of pine dating to the mid-19th century. (A museum in the kitchen wing contains artifacts from the Civil War and other memorabilia concerning the Barnsley family history.) Admission. ~ 597 Barnsley Gardens Road, Adairsville; 770-773-7480, 877-773-2447; www.barnsleyresort.com.

Return south on Route 41 and head to **Rome** on Route 411. Built on, yes, seven hills, Rome grew up where two rivers, the Oostanaula and the Etowah, meet to form the Coosa River. The ups and downs make the city seem larger than it is; the population is only a little over 30,000.

Familiarize yourself further with the region's background at the **Rome Area History Museum**. In this unpretentious setting, exhibits are arranged as a walk through time, beginning in 1540, long before the white men arrived, to the present day. Special are the displays on the Civil War, the Girl Scouts and Coca-Cola. Closed Sunday and Monday. Admission. ~ 305 Broad Street, Rome; 706-235-8051; www.romehistorymuseum.com.

Also on Broad Street, in front of City Hall, is the **Capitoline Wolf**, given to the city in 1929 by Benito Mussolini. As you might expect, the statue relates the short but dramatic lives of the twin brothers Romulus and Remus. It was Romulus, you may remember from Ancient Civ class, who slew Remus and went on to build Rome. A little more exciting than this Rome's history, but then again, the local version is less bloody. ~ 601 Broad Street, Rome; 706-295-5576.

If you have time on your hands—or mind—head up Broad Street and take a left on East 5th Avenue to mount the 107-step spiral staircase of the 1871 **Clocktower Museum**. Originally built to house a water tank, its exhibits—restored clock works—and city murals must compete for the visitor's attention with near-panoramic views of the outside rivers and hills from the observation deck. At 104 feet, the tower was used as an observation post during World War II blackouts. Closed Monday through Friday and from December through March. ~ 2nd Street at East 5th Avenue, Rome; 706-236-4430.

Return to Broad Street and head left across the Etowah River (the covered bridge is long gone but try to imagine it) to visit an impressive cemetery. Turn right on Branham Avenue, continue for one-third of a mile, then left onto Pennington Avenue, left again **HIDDEN ▶** on Myrtle Street and soon you will see the gates to the **Myrtle Hill Cemetery**. Ellen Axson Wilson, President Woodrow Wilson's first wife (whom he met in the Rome church where her father was pastor), is buried here. To see her gravesite, veer right after you enter the gates; the 377 Civil War soldiers' graves are on the left side. ~ Myrtle Street, Rome; 800-444-1834.

After walking around the cemetery and admiring its many monuments, take Broad Street back to the City Hall area and turn left to drive out Riverside Parkway.

Just before you come to the Civic Center, make an information stop at a 1901 train depot complete with caboose. The **Greater Rome Convention & Visitors Bureau** not only has brochures and maps, but even a cassette tape to guide you as you tour the city. Closed Sunday. ~ 402 Civic Center Drive, Rome; 706-295-5576, 800-444-1834, fax 706-236-5029; www.romegeorgia.org.

HIDDEN ▶ Continue on Riverside Parkway for a short distance. The **Chieftains Museum/Major Ridge Home**, housed in a white clapboard plantation house that began life in the 1790s as a modest log cabin, tells the story of the Coosa River Valley with special em-

From
Riches
to Rags

If the executives at Disney studios haven't made a movie about Martha Berry, they ought to think about it. It's a riches to rags story—Miss Berry having the riches and sharing them with the people in rags. There is a movie of sorts about Berry and her good works: it's 28 minutes long and is shown at the Martha Berry Museum on the campus of Rome's Berry College. It's unlikely anyone who sees the film is unmoved by it.

Born in 1866 as the second child (of eight) of a wealthy couple, Berry enjoyed comforts not even imagined by her less fortunate neighbors (not that too many of them were found on the grounds of the family estate, Oak Hill). Berry used to study in a small cabin near the main house. One day, the story goes, she looked out the window to see several young children peering back at her. She invited them in to read Bible stories and then began conducting regular Sunday school classes.

Her parents, Thomas and Frances, taught her a cardinal rule of philanthropy: It's better to help someone learn and work than it is to drown them in charity. Berry's dream was to establish a college for the rural poor of Appalachia, and from the Sunday school she went on to establish an industrial and agricultural boarding school on the 83 acres donated by her father in 1902. In the 1920s, Mr. and Mrs. Henry Ford helped to expand the campus.

Oak Hill, the house where Berry was born and lived for most of her 76 years, is decorated as it was back in 1942; in fact, the log cabin in which Berry's legacy began still stands. She is buried beneath a tree beside a nearby chapel on the property.

phasis on the region's American Indian heritage; this was the original home of Cherokee leader, Major Ridge. The ground-floor hallway has exposed hand-hewn logs of the original structure and exhibits of 18th-century Cherokee attire. Upstairs is the self-explanatory Rome Room and an entire room devoted to the Chieftains' collections, including hats and other clothing. On the porch are various household items pertinent to the Coosa Valley. Closed Sunday and Monday. Admission. ~ 501 Riverside Parkway, Rome; 706-291-9494; www.chieftainsmuseum.org.

When you leave the museum, drive north to visit the largest contiguous college campus in the country. Turn left onto Georgia Loop 1 and look for signs to **Berry College**. Before you reach Route 27, Oak Hill and the Martha Berry Museum will be on your left. You could spend half a day meandering around this vast campus, which, at last count, topped 28,000 acres. The first five students were all male; Berry opened a girls' school in 1909. All the students worked their way through school, attending classes for nine months and working off their tuition the other three. To this day, students must work on campus in some capacity, be it landscaping or milking the cows. The religious convictions of Berry are evidenced in many ways, but most obviously in the numerous spires and steeples that punctuate the campus landscape. She thought that seeing them would remind the students—as well as the faculty—of God's beneficence. Also on campus are hills, lakes, woods and handsome buildings, most notably the **Ford Buildings**, a group of imposing English Gothic structures donated by Henry Ford between 1925 and 1932 that surround a reflecting pool. They would look more at home in Sussex, but they are a graceful addition to a truly beautiful college campus. Visitors are welcome to visit the **Carriage House**, which contains vintage vehicles such as Martha Berry's buggy and some antique Fords; the **Formal Garden**, the **Sundial Garden**, the **Sunken**

NATURE AT WORK

The odd formations at Rock City Gardens started at the beginning of the Paleozoic era some 600 million years ago. Streams transported layers of sand, silt and clay into basins of water that in turn created limestone. As earthquakes toppled large rock boulders, passageways were formed in the spaces between two or more rocks that fell at angles. These upheavals were followed by the faulting and folding that created the Appalachian Mountain chain. The coup de grâce was the Ice Age of about a million years ago, when below-freezing temperatures split the chunks of sandstone. It is these sandstone layers that support the broken and crooked cliffs that enthrall visitors.

Garden and the **Goldfish Garden**. The **Greenhouse Growing Area** (706-232-5374), with three greenhouses that have enough room for 25,000 plants used annually in the Oak Hill gardens, is open by appointment.

The true-life story of the amazing Ms. Berry is told at the **Martha Berry Museum and Art Gallery** and at the **Oak Hill** plantation nearby. A 28-minute video paints the picture of an inspiring woman who was born to privilege and used it to help impoverished youth from all over Appalachia. The idea was to provide them with an education, which began in a log cabin now dwarfed by the contemporary structures of the main part of the campus. The museum is more of a reception area for a visit to the 1847 white-columned Oak Hill, where the family lived. Many of their antiques and art works are on display. Admission. ~ 24 Veterans Memorial Highway, Berry College, Mount Berry; 706-291-1860, 800-220-5504; www.berry.edu/oakhill.

If you'd like to visit a quaint old town that is as yet not over-run with tourists (at least not during the week), head southwest from Rome for about half an hour on Route 27 and Route 411 to **Cave Spring**. There are no hot little restaurants here, but you'll find a couple of places to eat, a few spots to spend a lazy night and at least one attraction in addition to some 90 historic buildings and sites. For details, call the city of Cave Spring at 706-777-3382.

◄ HIDDEN

A couple of long blocks from the main intersection, take a left when you see the sign for **Rolater Park**. The historic town of Cave Spring is off this road. The spring water that flows from this revered cave is so fresh that locals bring empty bottles to fill; you can find some for sale at stores around town. The sparkling water trickles into a shallow pool and then into a 1.5-acre swimming pool built in the shape of the state of Georgia. Dozens of historic homes surround the leafy, 29-acre park. Closed Monday through Thursday. Admission to cave. ~ Georgia Avenue, Cave Spring; 706-777-8439.

When you've gotten your fill at the spring, head just west of town to hook up with Route 100, which runs north about 20 miles, bordering on James H. Floyd State Park (see "Parks" below) before arriving in Summerville.

From Summerville, take Route 27 north just past Lafayette and turn west onto **Route 136**, which leads up to **Lookout Mountain**. Part of the Cumberland Plateau that runs parallel to the Appalachian chain, this mountain is so big—100 miles in length—that it stretches into both Tennessee and Alabama; in fact, 21 miles are in Georgia. One of the prettiest places on Lookout is **Cloudland Canyon State Park**. The 3485-acre parcel clings to a precipitous gorge, and therein lies the pretty part. There are hiking trails and even if you don't have time for a long stroll, it's worth going a few yards from the picnic area to take in the views, which face two different angles into the scenic canyon. Trees are anchored to the steep slopes and, in the late summer and early fall, are a colorful sight. ~ Route 136, Lookout Mountain; 706-657-4050, 800-864-7275.

You have to go almost into Tennessee to see some of the most amazing views of all. Most Southerners have heard of **Rock City**, but for some it sounds like just a tourist trap, probably gaudy and expensive. Well, it may trap some tourists, briefly, but it is a blast to visit this unbelievable warren of pathways with many a treasure lurking within. To reach this attraction, return to Route 136 and head back east to the intersection of Route 157; go north until you reach the turnoff to Rock City. Rock City was developed by Garnet and Frieda Carter back during the Depression. What began as a modest attempt at rock gardening expanded to include swinging bridges, tons of wildflowers and statues of gnomes. Rock City Gardens is now a complex with a restaurant, a gift shop and a café out on the trail near a spectacular waterfall. When visitors begin wending through the warren of formations, they inevitably doubt this could all have come about naturally. But the eerie outcroppings of the igneous and metamorphic base rock are authentic. From this basic landscape, however, mankind took the place to the limit. Whimsical bridges were built, fairytale creatures were lit up in the grottoes, and trails were fashioned and landscaped. It takes about 90 minutes to make your way full circle but despite some hokey parts, it is an absolutely delightful experience. You can buy birdseed (along with lots of other things) at the entrance but there is so much to see—walls of flowers, swinging bridges, artfully grown lichen, the path beneath the waterfall and then the stupendous view from atop—that you may not want to waste your time feeding feathered friends. Some folks say you can see seven states from up here, but would you settle for five (Georgia, Alabama, North Carolina, South Carolina and Tennessee)? Admission. ~ 1400 Patten Road, Lookout Mountain; 706-820-2531, 800-854-0675; www.seerockcity.com.

Rock City is near the Georgia state line with Tennessee. When you leave Lookout Mountain, look for Route 2 that leads to Fort Oglethorpe. It's not the city itself that's so intriguing, but the Civil War history that draws thousands of visitors every year. Turn right onto Route 27 and continue south to the outskirts of town.

You really cannot miss the **Chickamauga/Chattanooga National Military Park**. Not only is it the largest and oldest U.S. military park, it is the site of the Civil War's second-bloodiest battle. Looking at the undulating hills, the bucolic wide-open spaces and the forested slopes beyond, especially on a sunny spring day, it is hard to imagine the horrors that took place here in the fall of 1863. At stake was Chattanooga, a key rail center for the Confederacy. As the Union army moved down from Tennessee, 43,000 Confederate troops ducked in to defend the road to Chattanooga. Eventually, the Confederates, though outnumbered, prevailed. The battles continued up to Chattanooga and nearby Missionary Ridge, where the Confederates were outmaneuvered by the Union soldiers, who ultimately took over Chattanooga and used it as the base for General Sherman's march to Atlanta and the sea. Start your visit with a 26-minute multimedia program, the "Battle of Chickamauga," before driving around, following the excellent map provided by the visitors center that describes the events that took place at exact points within the park. ~ 3370 Lafayette Road, Fort Oglethorpe; 706-866-9241; www.nps.gov/chch.

The town of New Echota was the capital of the Cherokee Indian nation from 1825 to 1838.

After touring the battlefield park, return to Fort Oglethorpe and take Route 2 east to Route 75, which leads south roughly ten miles to the city of **Dalton**. Known as the Carpet Capital of the World, it is home to several mills.

Visitors can take **carpet mill tours** at several companies in and around Dalton. First, you see a video about the process, then it's off to the mill, equipped with headsets for further information. You don't actually get to see the yarn but do see the tufting process, the dyeing, the drying and the latex put on as well as the carpets trimmed and packaged. Another tour focuses on rugs. The tours last from 90 minutes to two hours, door to door, and are free and available by appointment only Monday through Friday. Call or visit the **Dalton Convention and Visitors Bureau** to make arrangements. Closed Saturday and Sunday. ~ 2211 Dug Gap Battle Road, Dalton; 706-272-7676, 800-331-3258, fax 706-278-5811; www.daltoncvb.com.

The visitors bureau is located near the interstate. It's a couple of miles to the heart of the city via Route 76 (locally, West Walnut Avenue) to Route 41 (Thornton Avenue). Turn north for a few blocks to the central business district.

This route leads past the **Blunt House,** the home of Dalton's first mayor, which is open by appointment only. If you're interested in only a look-see, you can always drive by this 1848 mansion on the cusp of downtown. Admission. ~ 506 South Thornton Avenue, Dalton; 706-278-0217.

Continuing on Thornton Avenue, cross Cuyler Street, fork right onto Selvidge Street two blocks to Crawford Street, turn right and you're almost at the train tracks.

Now occupied by a restaurant on a tiny street not even marked on most city maps, the **Dalton Depot** was built in 1852 and used as a terminal (known as the W & A Depot) until 1978.

◄ HIDDEN

It marks the original center of Dalton; the surveying of the city began here, at a spot designated in the lobby, and extended for one mile in all directions. Closed Sunday. ~ 110 Depot Street, Dalton; 706-226-3160.

From the Depot, walk west on Crawford Street past Pentz and you will find the **Wink Theatre**. Now used for civic events, it was built in 1938 by one J.C.M. Wink. It opened in 1941 as the first air-conditioned building downtown and remained a movie house until 1972. ~ 115 East Crawford Street, Dalton; 706-226-9465; www.winktheatre.com.

This theater and many other points of interest are pointed out on walking tours. The Downtown Development department offers **Dalton Downtown Development Walking Tours** in this Main Street city, pointing out the architectural features that tell the story of the town's past. You can pick up a self-guided walking tour map or arrange for a guide. Closed Saturday and Sunday. ~ 210 North Pentz Street, Dalton; 706-278-3332.

Head north on Selvidge Street and bear left on Chattanooga Avenue (not Road) to reach one of the oldest buildings in town. **Hamilton House at Crown Gardens and Archives** contains exhibits on the city's textile industry, paying special attention to the chenille bedspread niche that precipitated the boom in carpet making. There are also displays on Cherokee history and other genealogy. Closed Saturday through Monday. Admission. ~ 715 Chattanooga Avenue, Dalton; 706-278-0217.

HIDDEN ▶ If you take Route 41 north (Glenwood Avenue) and bear right on Route 71 for a few miles, you'll find the historic **Prater's Mill**. This water-powered grist mill was constructed in 1855 with slave labor. It's open during daylight hours. Except for the County Fair (on Mother's Day weekend) and Columbus Day, admission is free. ~ 500 Prater's Mill Road, Dalton; 706-272-7676.

After touring Dalton, it's time for a trip on country roads. To visit an interesting Cherokee sight, detour down Route 71 towards Calhoun and turn onto Route 225. Once you're close to it, signs will led you to the **New Echota Historic Site**, just half a mile east of Route 75. What was once part of a town called New Echota, this site has only one remaining original building, the **Worcester House**, where a white missionary lived. Closer to the highway is a re-creation of the village that includes a newspaper office where the *Cherokee Phoenix* was printed and a two-story building where the Cherokee Supreme Court (the nation was structured after the form of the U.S. government, oddly enough) once sat. The welcome center here has exhibits and a short film telling the tragic tale of the Cherokees' forcible removal from the region in 1838 and their Trail of Tears journey to the West. Closed Monday. Admission. ~ 1211 Chatsworth Highway, Calhoun; 706-624-1321, 800-864-7275.

Barnsley Inn and Golf Resort has a long history, dating to the **LODGING**
forced removal in 1838 of the Cherokee. One Godfrey Barnsley,
a cotton broker from England, purchased 10,000 acres of former
Cherokee land and built an Italian-style manor house and English
gardens for his wife and their six children in the 1840s. Barnsley
et al. are long gone, but in the 1980s, a German prince bought
1300 acres of the badly deteriorated estate and set to work restoring the gardens, which were opened to the public in 1992.
Inspired by the original English style, Prince Hubertus Fugger designed an inn to resemble a 19th-century pedestrian village, including 33 guest cottages. The stylishly and comfortably decorated one-, two- and four-bedroom units have private porches,
historic colors, wood-burning fireplaces, antique armoires, ceiling
fans and a wet bar and refrigerator, along with accessories such
as antique gardening tools and chenille throws. The resort has
a spa, three restaurants and a golf course. Plan to stay at least
two nights or you'll be sorry. ~ 597 Barnsley Gardens Road,
Adairsville; 770-773-7480, 877-773-2447, fax 770-773-1779;
www.barnsleyresort.com, e-mail barnsley@mindspring.com.
ULTRA-DELUXE.

A few blocks from downtown Rome in a fine residential
neighborhood, the **Claremont House Bed & Breakfast** is at the
top of a long rise. It's a dazzler, built by Colonel Hamilton Yancey
in 1882. "The Colonel"—a wealthy cotton farmer—and his wife
had seven children and they all lived in the small house in back
while the mansion was under construction. It took two years to
build the 8000-square-foot Second Empire Gothic Victorian, instantly recognizable by its elaborate gingerbread trim. Mrs.
Yancey named the place in honor of her cousin Clare; three generations of Yanceys lived here until it was sold in an auction in
the early 1960s. Today six large guest rooms, outfitted for comfort as well as convenience, have private baths, fireplaces and period antiques such as the four-poster in the Magnolia Room, accessible by a step stool. If you stay here, ask about the huge safe,
framed with walnut, built into the main stairwell. Full breakfast

AUTHOR FAVORITE

When I want to get away from it all, I think of a mountaintop hideaway like
Cloudland Canyon State Park. In addition to camping sites, the park
has 16 cottages that are close to trailheads; both two- and three-bedroom models are available. Prices are slightly higher on the weekends
and there is a seven-night minimum for the comfortable cottages. ~
Route 136, Lookout Mountain; 706-657-4050. MODERATE TO DELUXE.

is included. ~ 906 East 2nd Avenue, Rome; 706-291-0900, 800-254-4797, fax 706-802-0551; www.theclaremonthouse.net. DE-LUXE TO ULTRA-DELUXE.

Rome has an adequate supply of chain lodging but one place stands head and shoulders—quite literally—above the rest: the **Hampton Inn.** Located about two and a half miles east of downtown, this two-story motel has 65 comfortable rooms nicely laid out, a workout room, a small pool and free in-room movies, plus a continental breakfast in the lobby. All the corridors are interior, so you never feel exposed. Plus, it's close to one of the best restaurants in Rome. Full breakfast included. ~ 21 Chateau Drive, Rome; 706-232-9551. MODERATE.

A short walk from the intersection (Cave Spring has just one), **The Tumlin House Bed & Breakfast** has four second-story accommodations (two share a bath) in an 1842 Victorian. It's not a fancy house—although there are some lovely period lighting fixtures—but it's rambling and comfortable. The names reflect the decor (the Oriental Room has an oriental rug, for instance). Full breakfast is included. ~ 38 Alabama Street, Cave Spring; 706-777-0066, 800-939-3880. MODERATE.

Right in Rolater Park, the **Hearn Academy Inn** began life as a dormitory for the Hearn Manual Labor School. Don't let that put you off; it's quite elegant, with antiques like rocking chairs and pretty dried vine wreaths for decor. Bare wood floors and portraits of somebody's ancestors add a little class to this two-story inn with five accommodations. Closed for renovations; call ahead. ~ 13 Cedar Town Street Southwest, Rolater Park, Cave Spring; 706-777-8865. MODERATE.

The 28 accommodations at the red brick motel called **Creekside Inn** offer a couple of pleasant, if modest, surprises. They all sport fresh bright colors—none of that pathetic motel wallpaper—and some of them are extra-large. Beyond those features, however, the two-story motel is like a million others, except that it's within walking distance of shops, restaurants and Rolater Park.

SURVIVAL OF THE FITTEST

The **Gordon-Lee Mansion,** a circa-1847 Greek Revival home, was the only structure in Chickamauga to survive the Battle of Chickamauga. In fact, it served as General Rosecrans' headquarters, then as his main hospital, during the bloodiest two days in U.S. history. After the Union retreat into Chattanooga, 25 Confederate physicians stayed here with their patients, preferring to be captured rather than abandon them. The house is now a National Historic Site.

Efficiencies are available. ~ 1 Georgia Avenue, Cave Spring; 706-777-3887. BUDGET.

The cottage-in-the-woods **Chanticleer Inn** may have passed its   ◀ HIDDEN
prime, but the complex as a whole hangs on to a certain alpine
charm. For example, some rooms have the type of pale blue striped-
and-floral wallpaper usually associated with adolescent girls' bedrooms, but when combined with some well-worn antiques and
country prints—hey, it kinda works. One-story stone-clad duplexes
rub shoulders on a shady side of Lookout Mountain, practically
at the gates to Rock City and not far from the Chattanooga,
Tennessee, city limits. Suites are available. Amenities include a
pool and a cholesterol-laden continental breakfast. ~ 1300 Mock-
ingbird Lane, Lookout Mountain; 706-820-2015. BUDGET TO
MODERATE.

Century-old pines, the tinkling of a waterfall and whimsical
garden art set the tone for romance and relaxation at the **Garden**   ◀ HIDDEN
Walk Inn on Lookout Mountain. Thirteen accommodations in
an assortment of cottages are decorated mostly with floral patterns. All the rooms and suites have coffeemakers and mini-
fridges, and some have fireplaces and/or jacuzzis. Amenities include an outdoor pool and hot tub. Full breakfast in the main
house is included. ~ 1206 Lula Lake Road, Lookout Mountain;
706-820-4127, 800-617-0503; www.gardenwalkinn.com. MOD-
ERATE TO ULTRA-DELUXE.

The magnificent **Gordon-Lee Mansion** is the reigning grande   ◀ HIDDEN
dame of a cute but admittedly minute hamlet that seems all the
more humble for the inn's presence. The only building in town
that wasn't destroyed during the Battle of Chickamauga, this
grand inn has but four rooms (one is a suite) plus a nearby log
cabin; all have private baths. Formal English gardens as well as
plantings of herbs and vegetables grace the landscaping; inside,
ornate chandeliers, collections of crystal and glass, and oriental
carpets more than hold their own against a palpable backdrop
of Southern gentility. Full breakfast included except for log cabin
guests. ~ 217 Cove Road, Chickamauga, six miles from Lookout
Mountain; 706-375-4728, 800-487-4728; www.gordon-leeman
sion.com, e-mail glmbh1@aol.com. MODERATE TO DELUXE.

The carpet industry has been good to the **Holly Tree House**,
which offers a homey alternative to the chain hotels and motels that
clog Dalton's major arteries. Business travelers from all over the
world, the majority of the inn's guests, must enjoy the fine accommodations in this late 1924 home built by a bigwig with the
American thread company. The four upstairs rooms are individually decorated with a mix of antiques and a TV/VCR for screening the inn's collection of more than 100 films on video. Hardwood floors and other original architectural features make this

one of the more memorable places to stay in the region. Full breakfast is included. ~ 217 West Cuyler Street, Dalton; 706-278-6620. MODERATE.

DINING

You'll find some excellent restaurants in the larger towns in this section of Georgia, but per square mile, there are fewer places for barbecue than anywhere else in the state. As is true elsewhere, the farther you get from the main drags, the fewer the chain outlets.

One of several businesses operating "Under the Bridge"—a nook of downtown called that because of the bridge above it that's crossed by 45 trains each day—the **Appalachian Grill** occupies one of the buildings dating to at least the early 1900s. Lump crab cakes, pan-seared tilapia (a light white fish), Smoky Mountain trout and shrimp florentine are popular items on a menu that also features daily specials. No lunch Saturday. Closed Sunday. ~ 14 East Church Street, Cartersville; 770-607-5357. MODERATE TO DELUXE.

Ethnic eating is a rare pleasure in these hills, so don't miss **Patcharee Thai Restaurant**. The Thai owners are happy to accommodate diners unaccustomed to hot Asian spices by lowering the heat factor upon request. Recommended entrées include chicken satay, garlic pepper shrimp and *larb* beef, a traditionally spicy dish that also works well with milder seasonings. Closed Sunday. ~ 19 South Public Square, Cartersville; 770-386-3388. BUDGET TO MODERATE.

HIDDEN ►

The **Rice House Restaurant**, the formal dining spot at Barnsley Gardens, is in a restored 1854 farmhouse that still bears bullet holes dating from the Civil War. The truly upscale cuisine includes dishes such as prosciutto-wrapped pork tenderloin with truffle sauce, pan-seared skate, herb-roasted wild sturgeon and grilled Black Angus filet with *foie gras*–stuffed morels. Closed Sunday through Thursday. ~ 597 Barnsley Gardens Road, Adairsville; 770-773-7480, 877-773-2447. ULTRA-DELUXE.

HIDDEN ►

The **Country Gentleman** graces a tiny back road between two chain motels on the road between Cartersville and Rome. The menu is more Continental than country, however: steak, shrimp, oysters, rainbow trout, veal and seafood, including a fettuccini seafood sampler and blackened chicken alfredo. The Country Gentleman is actually a Greek who migrated here from San Francisco and opened this large restaurant in 1978. ~ 26 Chateau Drive, Rome; 706-232-7000. MODERATE TO DELUXE.

For a cheap breakfast (a side of grits is 85 cents), barbecue (ribs, beef, turkey, pork), burger or hot dog, get thee to **Ole Tymer BBQ** for a meal on the fly. ~ 1000 North Broad Street, Rome; 706-234-8000. BUDGET.

Nobody drives from Atlanta, or even Rome, simply to have dinner in Cave Spring because there are no outstanding restaurants. But the homestyle cooking at **The Gray Horse** will definitely fill you up and make you feel right at home. ~ On the Square, Cave Spring; 706-777-3766. BUDGET.

The most you can hope for in most shopping-mall restaurants is passable food and inoffensive decor. The **Emperor Garden Chinese Restaurant** is the exception, with wall-to-wall jade-green and black lacquer accents plus beautiful silk screening. The menu, while not expensive for the most part, is slightly upscale, with scallops, shrimp and duck dishes along with the usual beef, chicken and pork. No lunch Saturday. ~ 1347 West Walnut Avenue, Dalton; 706-226-8380. MODERATE.

The **Cornerstone Grill** doesn't look like much—but then, if you judged every book by its cover, you'd never learn anything. Inside, the big attraction (other than the private booths) is the list of wood-grilled entrées like duck breast, chicken breast, fresh fish and steaks. The menu also has grilled meats and pastas. The appetizers are worth a look if you like crisp frogs' legs or roasted poblano pepper. ~ 2311 Chattanooga Road, Dalton; 706-529-2500. DELUXE.

◄ HIDDEN

The top dining spot in Dalton is **The Depot**, housed in—you guessed it—an old train depot. Conveniently located, it's surprisingly spacious. The center of the main room is raised and wrapped with a brass railing dividing it from the banquettes that line the walls, interspersed with arched windows that admit natural light; the brick walls are painted green, the open-beam ceiling is hung with fans and semi-industrial lighting, and framed photos abound. Portions are substantial, whether you're ordering the certified Angus beef (one version comes smothered in mushrooms, provolone and beer), seafood (Alaskan crab, pecan trout), or monstrous salads like an excellent one with shrimp and spinach. Closed Sunday. ~ 110 Depot Street, Dalton; 706-226-3160. MODERATE.

Though a bit north of downtown, **The Spiced Apple** is one of the most popular places in town. Low-lit and intimate—but not exactly romantic—stylized posters hang on the brick wall beside

◆◆◆

A BIT OF ITALY IN ROME

La Scala, with its second-floor dining room, reminded me of restaurants in Italy—and not just because of the murals. The cooking here is first-rate and I would recommend either the fettuccini La Scala (with crushed peppers and walnuts) or the pasta Emilia (with white beans and grilled Italian sausages). Heartier are various chicken and veal dishes and the tomato based cioppino, filled with mussels, shrimp, calamari and bay scallops yet still manages to be low in fat and cholesterol. Closed Sunday. ~ 413 Broad Street, Rome; 706-238-9000. MODERATE TO DELUXE.

each cozy booth. It's big on soups, salads and sandwiches in all kinds of combinations; some, like pastrami, barbecued pork and roast beef, are on the hefty side; the restaurant is especially known for its extensive dessert list. In short, if you're looking to pack on some pounds, this would be a good place to start. Closed Saturday and Sunday. ~ 908 Glenwood Square, Dalton; 706-278-6009. BUDGET.

There's no handout menu at **John's** BBQ, just a board behind the counter listing what's available. You can pick and choose among beef, chicken, pork and shrimp, accompanied by beans, coleslaw and the like. For dessert, icebox lemon pie and homemade chocolate pie make a tough choice if ever there was one. Red-and-white-checked plastic tablecloths dress up this squat brown building at the back of a large gravel parking lot. Closed Saturday and Sunday. ~ 411 North Glenwood Avenue, Dalton; 706-226-1769. BUDGET.

SHOPPING For your own little one or someone else's, you can find infants' clothing at **Baby's Own Designs**. ~ 22 East Church Street, Cartersville; 770-607-0081.

Hemingway might have felt at ease among the Peacock Alley bed linens, imported chests, Rowe sofas and other tasteful home accessories at **Rush Home**. We can't imagine what he'd have thought of the wedding and baby gifts. ~ 18 West Main Street, Cartersville; 770-607-5009.

For fine attire and accessories, try **J. Brandon Clothier**, the nicest place in town. ~ 4 Public Square, Cartersville; 770-607-5400.

Sixty dealers are grouped under one roof at **Liz's Antiques**, which specializes in collectibles and gifts. ~ 1277 Joe Frank Harris Parkway (Route 41), Cartersville; 770-606-0035.

Mel and Mimi's is a boutique with women's specialty clothing, accessories and gifts. Closed Sunday. ~ 203 East 8th Street, Rome; 706-295-4203.

NEAT NICKNAME

How did James H. "Sloppy" Floyd get his name? James Floyd was on the high school football team, only 5'5" and very "robust." Despite his height, he required a large-size jersey. It hung so far down that his coach declared him "Sloppy." James liked the nickname and it stuck, even throughout his long career in the Georgia State Legislature. After his death in 1974, his memory remained strong in the community, where he was highly regarded as a decent and caring politician. (Many local sites now bear the "Sloppy" moniker.)

The **Little Goose 'N Gander** is just what you'd guess: a boutique for clothing and accessories sized for children and pre-teens. ~ 213 Broad Street, Rome; 706-295-7521.

Wisteria Lane is the perfect name for a place that specializes in collectibles and home accessories. ~ 227 Broad Street, Rome; 706-234-1619.

The **Tanger Outlet Center of Dalton** has dozens of shops and major stores, almost every last one of them part of a national chain, but all offering bargains. ~ 1001 Market Street, Dalton; 706-277-2688, 800-409-7029.

Since the 1960s, the **Pumphouse Players** have been performing musicals, radio theater and one-act plays. You can catch them at the Legion Theater and the Grand Theater. ~ 114-C West Main Street, Cartersville; 770-387-2610.   **NIGHTLIFE**

The **Grand Theater of Cartersville** is a restored 1910 structure that presents comedy, drama, musicals, opera and ballet. ~ 7 North Wall Street, Cartersville; 770-386-7343.

The **Rome Little Theatre** presents plays, musicals, dramas and youth programs in the historic 1929 DeSoto Theatre. ~ 530 Broad Street, Rome; 706-295-7171.

Founded in 1921 as the first symphony in the South, the **Rome Symphony** performs about one concert every other month. The schedule is available on its website. ~ 21 John Maddox Drive, Rome; 706-291-7967; www.romesymphony.org.

JAMES H. "SLOPPY" FLOYD STATE PARK 🏃 🚤 🛶 ⚓ Nestled at the foot of the Chattahoochee River and surrounded by the Chattahoochee National Forest, Floyd Park is considered both a mountain and a valley park, noted for great camping and fishing. Two scenic lakes provide bass, catfish and brim for anglers. Many native trees abound on this 561-acre parcel, including chestnut oak and buckeye, both rare for this part of the state. Peaceful, clean and pretty campsites bring visitors back again and again. Pedal boat rentals are available. Day-use fee, $2. ~ Off Route 27, three miles southeast of Summerville; 706-857-0826.   **PARKS**

▲ There are 25 tent/RV sites; $20 to $22 per night. Two pioneer sites are available for primitive group camping; $50 per night. Four cottages rent for $95 to $105 per night. Reservations: 800-864-7275.

MARSHALL FOREST PRESERVE 🏃 Part of an old farm that was purchased and inherited in pieces from the family that had owned it since the late 1800s, this 315-acre preserve harbors rare species such as the large-flowered skullcap, as well as red trillium, dwarf iris and toothworts that blossom in the spring; in all, more than 300 species flourish here. Trails cut through old-growth pine and   ◀ HIDDEN hardwood forest. ~ Off Route 20S, Horseleg Creek Road, Rome; 404-873-6946.

CLOUDLAND CANYON STATE PARK 🏃 🏊 With ridges rising to nearly 2000 feet in elevation and sliced with deep gorges and valleys, this is the largest public park in the Lookout Mountain area. It is indeed up among the clouds, having been created atop one of the typically flat-topped mountains of the Cumberland Plateau. This 3485-acre park crosses Sitton Gulch Creek, a small river hidden most of the year beneath leafy trees. The creek runs over two waterfalls, one of them 100 feet tall, ending in a photogenic natural pool. There are also tennis courts and picnic areas. Day-use fee, $2. ~ Route 136, Lookout Mountain; 706-657-4050.

▲ There are 73 tent/RV sites, $19 to $22 per night; and 30 primitive sites are $10 per night. Sixteen two- and three-bedroom cabins cost $85 to $115 per night, with a seven-night minimum stay. Reservations: 800-864-7275.

▼▼▼▼▼▼▼▼▼▼▼▼▼
Middle Mountains

This is the region that saw the first gold rush in the United States—decades before they cried "Eureka!" in the Sierra out in California. Majestic mountains, scenic byways and some offbeat attractions make this part of Georgia extremely popular, especially on weekends.

SIGHTS

HIDDEN ►

After visiting the New Echota site in Calhoun, drive to Chatsworth via Route 225 and turn right to follow Route 52/76. Turn north on Route 411 and look for the brown markers indicating **Chief Vann House State Historic Site**. The red-brick, three-story 1804 house reveals the richness of Cherokee life in the late 1700s and early 1800s. James Vann was half-Scot but as a half-Cherokee he helped create a Moravian mission for the education of young Cherokees. Vann, who had a reputation as a mean drunk, was shot in a tavern in 1809, at the age of 41; his son Joseph managed to acquire the showplace family home despite opposition from the Council of Chiefs. The argument over title didn't end there and the house, despite near-constant occupation by a dozen or more residents, slowly deteriorated over a century and a half before being restored and dedicated in 1958. By this time, some of the family's heirlooms were returned and are on display in this intriguing house that was architecturally ahead of its time; one look at the floating staircase is quite convincing (its cantilevered position seems to defy the laws of physics). Closed Monday. Admission. ~ Intersection of Route 225 and Route 52A, Chatsworth; 706-695-2598.

When you leave the chief's house, it's time for a drive in the country; head south on Route 411 and east on Route 76. It's a scenic drive to the town of **Ellijay**, where you'll really start to feel you're in the mountains. In apple season, this place is jumping; in fact, the Georgia Apple Festival is held the second and third weekends of October after an estimated 600,000 apples are harvested each year. Otherwise, it's a cute mountain town that's fun to explore for a couple of hours. You can pick up maps for hiking the Appalachian Trail, which has access points nearby, and other places of interest at the **Gilmer County Chamber of Commerce**. ~ 368 Craig Street, Ellijay; 706-635-7400, fax 706-635-7410; www.gilmerchamber.com.

For a side trip before continuing to the gold mining town of Dahlonega, head north on Route 76 through the Chattahoochee National Forest to the towns of **Blue Ridge** and **McCaysville**, which share the state line with Copperhill, Tennessee. Downtown Blue Ridge, though tiny, serves as the headquarters of the Blue Ridge Scenic Railway and has shops on the streets near the railroad tracks. McCaysville is, if anything, even quieter. The clean air and mountain views are the main attractions and they are quite sufficient. It's through this area that the Ocoee River (called the Toccoa River on the Georgia side), site of the 1996 Summer Olympics whitewater rafting competition, flows.

There are lots of RV parks and wilderness access points around Blue Ridge. But you can also leave the driving to some-

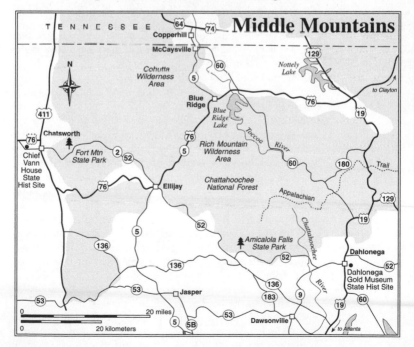

one else and take a ride in either enclosed coaches or an open-air car on the **Blue Ridge Scenic Railway**. The rail trip is 26 miles round-trip to McCaysville, where there's a 45-minute stopover. Closed November through May. Fee. ~ 241 Depot Street, Blue Ridge; 706-632-9833, 800-934-1898; www.brscenic.com.

After your drive around these mountain towns, return to Ellijay and continue east on Route 52 toward one of Georgia's prettiest state parks, a distance of some 15 miles. **Amicalola Falls State Park** (see "Parks" below) has a spectacu-lar 729-foot-high waterfall and some pretty great views, though you have to cruise a wide winding road to reach them. To get to the park from Blue Ridge, take Route 76 south and then Route 52 south for another 20 miles. ~ Route 52, Dawsonville; 706-265-4703.

Some of the pathways in the Consolidated Gold Mines are a little steep but this is a fabulous place to be on hot summer days, as it's always cool under-ground.

When you finish gazing at the waterfall, resume traveling east on Route 52 to the charming town of Dahlonega. If you like automobiles, especially automo-bile racing, however, you might want to turn right when you exit the park and follow Route 52 a mile or so—you'll pass a pump-kin store that's only open in the fall—to where it meets Route 183 and Route 136. Turn left and when you reach a fork in a few miles, bear right and stay on Route 183, which leads to **Dawsonville**.

Dawsonville's tiny downtown is centered by an antebellum courthouse. The red brick **Dawson County Courthouse** is the only working courthouse in the state dating to the late 1850s. ~ 1 Courthouse Square, Dawsonville; 706-265-6278.

On the far side of the courthouse—which functions as a square—you can pick up Route 9, which will take you north into **Dahlonega**. This is one of those postcard towns, beautiful at any time of year, framed by hills and centered by a town square. For additional information and brochures on activities in the area, stop by the **Dahlonega Chamber of Commerce and Regional Welcome Center**, open daily on the square. ~ 13 South Park Street, Dahlonega; 706-864-3711, 800-231-5543; www.dahlonega.org.

In the middle of that square is the **Dahlonega Gold Museum State Historic Site**. In this former courthouse, visitors can go up-stairs into the old courtroom and watch a multimedia show about mining and Georgia's role in gold production. It's information-packed, but for more excitement, visit one of the gold mines near town. Admission. ~ Public Square, Dahlonega; 706-864-2257.

HIDDEN ▶

One of the best tours in the state is offered at the **Consolidated Gold Mines**, in its heyday the biggest mine in north Georgia. Visitors trek down, down, down into the caves, led by a gold miner who knows every nook and cranny, the meaning of every protruding broken-off drill bit and the history of his trade in all detail—and he knows how to scare the wits out of you by turning off his flashlight about halfway through the 40-minute tour. You'll also be treated to the deafening sounds the miners had to put up with as they worked their fingers to the bone and risked their lives to haul gold from more than 250 feet below the earth's surface. Admission. ~ 185 Consolidated Road, Dahlonega; 706-864-8473; www.consolidatedgoldmine.com.

You can pan for gold at Consolidated, but for a homey touch, head out to the **Crisson Gold Mine**. This is more a kid-sized place where you can take your time and get plenty of instruction dipping and shaking the pan, looking for those elusive sparkling rocks. Admission. ~ 2736 Morrison Moore Parkway East, Dahlonega; 706-864-6363; www.crissongoldmine.com.

◀ HIDDEN

For all its scenery, it's surprising there are so few inns in the central Georgia mountains, but the ones here are distinctive and friendly.

LODGING

The **Budget Host Inn** has two stories and 30 rooms that are comfortable and large for an inexpensive motel. The corridors are exterior but at least they have mountain views. ~ 34 Jeff Drive, Ellijay; 706-635-5311, fax 706-635-5313. BUDGET TO MODERATE.

The **Blue Ridge Inn** is an eight-bedroom clapboard house a couple of blocks from downtown and the Blue Ridge Railway depot. The accommodations look like someone lives there—in other words, not extraordinary but comfortable. Closed December through April. ~ 477 West 1st Street, Blue Ridge; 706-632-0222; www.blueridgeinnbandb.com. MODERATE.

The three-story **Lodge at Amicalola Falls State Park** has 57 glorified motel rooms in a setting worthy of a five-star hotel. Decor is simple, running to pastels and prints. There are also 14 two-bedroom cabins available, and though they are not exactly gorgeous, some do come with fireplaces and screened porches. ~ Route 52, 15 miles northwest of Dawsonville; 800-864-7275. MODERATE TO ULTRA-DELUXE.

Amicalola Falls State Park also has accommodations accessible only by foot. The **Len Foote Hike Inn** offers the comforts of a hostel—soft bed, hot showers, cold and hot drinks in the dining room and woodburning stoves in the common areas—with the experience of the wilderness. It's a moderate, five-mile hike from the top of the falls to the inn. It takes from two to four hours, so you must check in at the visitors center by 2 p.m. to arrive before dinner. You only need to take your personal items, including water for the trail, a first-aid kit and a flashlight—but excluding cell phones, beepers and radios. Dinner and breakfast are served family style. ~ Route 52, 15 miles northwest of Dawsonville; 800-864-7275; www.hikeinn.com. MODERATE.

If you like to stay off the beaten path, you'll enjoy tracking down **Forrest Hills Mountain Resort & Conference Center**. It's

◀ HIDDEN

unlikely this hideaway gets a lot of walk-in business. What it does get is a lot of honeymooners who plan well in advance and dominate the complex in pairs like few other places. Its 140 acres encompass groups of accommodations with names like Victorian Cottages, LoveBird Cabins, Wildernest, and Mountain Laurel Cupid Cabins. The 30 rooms are quite nice but standard issue, with good reproduction furniture, fireplaces and/or whirl-pools, romantic nooks, private porches and the like. Some are huge—the cabins approximate 1000 square feet and some suites are even larger than that. These nests are arranged up the hill from the couples-only dining room. (There is also a second restaurant.) You may be able to horseback ride alone; on the other hand, there may be rules against it. ~ 135 Forrest Hills Road, Dahlonega; 706-864-6456, 800-654-6313, fax 706-864-0757; www.forresthillsresort.com, e-mail info@foresths.com. DELUXE TO ULTRA-DELUXE.

> Although California's Sierra foothills got most of the attention, the first Ameri-can gold rush took place in Dahlonega in 1828, more than 40 years before Sutter struck gold in the West.

For a cozy, old-fashioned B&B experience, the **Worley Homestead Inn** is hard to beat. Seven guest rooms in this mid-19th-century home (named for Confederate Captain William J. Worley) are decorated to the nines with lace, dolls, knickknacks and old photographs (an antique wedding dress even hangs in one room). Typical of very old houses in Georgia's gold country, the Worley Homestead's rooms are small compared to newer inns and the clutter makes them seem smaller still. However, a nice second-story veranda, a large patio and a gazebo afford guests ample elbow room. Full breakfast is included. ~ 168 West Main Street, Dahlonega; 706-864-7002, 800-348-8094, fax 706-867-9872. MODERATE TO DELUXE.

With its crisp cream-and-green exterior and neat landscaping, the **Smith House Inn** looks like it must be the latest addition to Dahlonega's lodging scene, but in fact it's probably the oldest. Its origins are rooted in local lore, dating to 1884 when one Captain Hall bought an acre of land east of the town square and discov-ered a rich vein of gold ore on the site. Thwarted from mining it by city fathers concerned about a community mining operation so close to the square, Hall built his house smack on top of the vein. The property evolved into an inn in the 1920s. Today, the 18 guest rooms have been updated and given a variety of treat-ments, some with two-tone color schemes, others with pale sponge-painted walls and still others with a distinctly masculine aspect. Continental breakfast is included. ~ 84 South Chestatee Street, Dahlonega; 706-867-7000, 800-852-9577; www.smith house.com, e-mail info@smithhouse.com. MODERATE TO DELUXE.

The owners of the **Royal Guard Inn** don't carry the Scandi-navian theme too far. There's just a hint of the Norwegian in the names of the rooms and the decor, which is mostly what you'd find in any nice North Georgia hills home. Four accommodations on the second floor are typified by the Princess Room, which boasts a white bed, floral patterns and plantation shutters; all have private bath. Everything is fresh and pretty and you even get a full breakfast. ~ 65 Park Street South, Dahlonega; 706-864-1713, 877-659-0739; e-mail royalguardbnb@yahoo.com. DELUXE TO ULTRA-DELUXE.

There are some surprising finds in the ethnic food department in this neck of the woods, but fine dining is the exception. Still, you'll find value for your restaurant dollar in most places.   **DINING**

Piazza is open daily and serves inexpensive Italian fare, including veal dishes as well as lasagna and other pastas. ~ 24 East Main Street, Dahlonega; 706-864-5978. BUDGET.

The **Smith House Restaurant** occupies a largely subterranean space that the original property owners used as a basement. Far from cozy, it can accommodate 250 diners. Everyone is seated family style, 12 to a table, so as to meet, greet, eat . . . and pass the dumplings, please. And fried chicken, ham, okra, sweet potatoes, beef stew or whatever is on that day's huge platters. ~ 84 South Chestatee Street, Dahlonega; 706-867-7000. BUDGET TO MODERATE.   ◄ HIDDEN

Miniature serapes and ceiling fans hardly turn **El Maguey Mexican Restaurant** into something that looks authentic, but despite all the oak and other country touches, it looks nice. More importantly, it's one of the few places in the region to get fresh flautas, enchiladas rancheras, Texas fajitas and the usual taco-burrito-chimichanga spectrum. Closed Sunday. ~ 61 West Main Street, Dahlonega; 706-864-9152. MODERATE.

Rick's occupies a 19th-century white clapboard house a couple of blocks from the town square. A great deal of refurbishing fashioned this old home into several dining rooms where diners feast on fancy salads, regional appetizers and main courses like house-smoked ham, steak, pasta and seafood. A wine list rounds out the offerings. There's also dining upstairs and on the veranda. Pale green walls and painted floors create a breezy contemporary ambiance. Closed Tuesday. ~ 47 South Park Street, Dahlonega; 706-864-9422. DELUXE.

Dahlonega has the best shopping in this region, thanks to the stores that flank its downtown square. **Quigley's Rare Books and Antiques** has a reputation that extends beyond state lines, with an outstanding selection of first editions in numerous fields. Specialties include the Civil War, poetry and children's books. Also here in the historic **Hall Building** (built in 1882–1883 for gold miners) are old maps, sheet music, comics and a raft of antiques. Closed Monday. ~ 104 North Public Square, Dahlonega; 706-864-0161.   **SHOPPING**

Jones and Company stocks elegant gifts and home accessories, such as lamps and mirrors, linens, afghans, throws and paperware. ~ 35 North Chestatee Street, Dahlonega; 706-864-6282.

The **Dahlonega Tasting Room** is great for sampling Cherokee Rose, Chardonnay, White Riesling and other wines from this prolific producer. ~ 16 North Park Street, Dahlonega; 706-864-8275.

Hometown Book Store is the place for regional maps from all kinds of sources, including geologic and mineral maps and guides to lakes and rivers and even Indian maps. The book selection is likewise diverse, with a section on American Indian history, trail guides, Georgia history, nature and more. Closed Wednesday. ~ 114 North Park Street, Dahlonega; 706-864-7225.

The original Rockhouse Country Store was built in 1936; the "rock" is actually amber quartz crystal from a nearby vein.

Near the town square, **Vintage Music** specializes in vintage guitars, fiddles, banjoes and mandolins. For dulcimers and other hard-to-find instruments, you can peruse the catalog. ~ 37 Park Street South, Dahlonega; 706-864-2682, 800-326-9188.

On the Dawsonville side of town (five and a half miles from the square), **Sackett's Knoll Antique Clocks** has a wide assortment of American antique clocks, possibly the largest in the state. Closed Sunday; open Saturday by appointment. ~ 3934 Route 9, Dahlonega; 706-864-7581.

HIDDEN ►

A few miles from town is perhaps the most amazing store in the Georgia Mountains. The **Rockhouse Country Store** is a local landmark, located approximately in the middle of nowhere (but just two miles from town), that stocks a stupefying range of folk art. Some of the works are excellent, some are less so, and many are signed. There are more primitive paintings, sculptures and found objects here than you'll see anywhere else. ~ 1127-A Route 52E at Rockhouse Road, Dahlonega; 706-864-0305, 888-541-3799.

The Middle Mountains are a far cry from Macy's, with most of the best retailers huddled around Dahlonega's square. An exception is the marvelous roadside **Cherokee Music Company** (a stone's throw from Route 19 on the east side of the highway). This single-story warehouse is filled with restored jukeboxes—Seeburgs, Wurlitzers from the '40s and '50s, and even a rare Rock-Ola. While not exactly a museum, this store has so much variety that it can give visitors a grasp of the development of American pop music. Also on the showroom floor are vintage soda fountain seats and pinball machines. ~ 5515 Setting Down Road, Cumming; 770-887-7580.

NIGHTLIFE From Dahlonega or elsewhere in the Middle Mountains, it's a short drive to the live performances in Cartersville and less than two hours from Atlanta. One of the few places open at night in the area is the **Dawsonville Pool Room**, where you can grab a hamburger, shoot some pool and buy Bill Elliott racing souvenirs. It's open until at least 10 p.m. every night. ~ East 1st Street, Dawsonville; 706-265-2792.

Live musical and theatrical performances are offered at the **Holly Theater**. The facility was named for one Holly Brannon, who actually built three theaters in Dahlonega after he was transferred up from his job as a projectionist at the Fox Theatre in Atlanta. ~ 69 West Main Street, Dahlonega; 706-864-3759; www. hollytheater.org.

AMICALOLA FALLS STATE PARK 🏃 ⛴ Among the most stunning in the Georgia park system, these 1021 acres are rightly named for the 729-foot waterfall, said to be the highest one east of the Rockies. The Cherokee Indians called it "Ama Kalola," or Tumbling Waters, and you can get a good view of it from the overlook bridge at the top. The park is a major starting-out point for hiking the Appalachian Trail; the 8.1-mile approach trail leading to the southern terminus of the Appalachian Trail starts right at the visitors center. There's a pretty lodge with a restaurant way up the mountain. Other facilities include playgrounds and picnic shelters. Day-use fee, $2. ~ 240 Amicalola Falls State Park Road, 15 miles west of Dahlonega off Route 52; 706-265-4703, 800-573-9656.

▲ There are 24 tent/RV sites, $17 to $19 per night; and 14 cottages, $79 to $159 per night. Reservations: 800-864-7275.

PARKS

Northeast Mountains & the Piedmont

The northeast corner of Georgia is the most rugged, with the high peaks of the Appalachian and Blue Ridge mountain chains soaring above gentle valleys, while big rolling hills and green pastures characterize the Piedmont region. Lakes, rivers, streams and dozens of waterfalls in various configurations lure nature lovers year-round. Within and around the Chattahoochee National Forest, much of which is in northeast Georgia, is a vast playground for hiking, fishing, boating, golfing, camping, whitewater rafting, horseback riding, bird-watching, canoeing, tubing, bicycling, kayaking and canoeing. You'll find country lodges, home-cooked meals and shopping opportunities (especially for folk art) as well as museums, which tend to be small and focused on regional heritage.

From Dahlonega, continue north on Route 19, bear right on Route 11 and turn north until the intersection with Route 180. Head east for seven miles, then left on the 180 spur. Go up the mountain for three miles to the parking lot. From there you can pick

SIGHTS

up a bus or walk the very steep paved half-mile path to the highest point in the state.

Brasstown Bald got its name from a bastardization of the Cherokee phrase for "new green place." From its 4784-foot summit (the highest point in the state), you can see forever, or at least all over North Georgia. When it's clear—some summer days are too hazy—you can see all the way to Atlanta. Little wonder the forest service has a fire tower up here. You can see a video about the mountain and learn more about the Trail of Tears at the **mountaintop museum**. Like the gold mines in Dahlonega, this is a good place to retreat on hot summer days because no temperature over 84° has ever been recorded here. It's a very steep paved half-mile path to the top. You may also take a bus. Admission. ~ Route 180 Spur, Blairsville, 706-896-2556; or Brasstown Ranger District, Blairsville, 706-745-6928.

After taking in the view, return to Route 180 to the intersection with Route 11 and turn towards Blairsville. **Young Harris** is, with the exception of a major resort and a few restaurants, largely a wide space on a pretty road. **Blairsville** is more of a classic mountain town, with an old courthouse as well as cottages for rent out in the woods.

Leaving Blairsville on Route 76, you will skirt **Chatuge Lake**, which straddles the state line with North Carolina. Just before you reach the town of Hiawassee, you'll drive by the entrance to HIDDEN ▶ the **Fred Hamilton Rhododendron Gardens**, tucked behind the Georgia Mountain Fairgrounds. Drive up to the top of the parking lot and walk to the entrance. It's best to visit in the spring, when more than 3000 rhododendrons and azaleas, including the only known domestic yellow azalea, blossom between mid-April and mid-June; the wildflowers have a longer season. ~ Route 76W, Hiawassee; 706-896-4191; www.georgia-mountain-fair.com.

Scenic Route 76 continues on its scenic route east to Clayton. About halfway there, look for the turnoff on the right to Route 197, which leads to Moccasin Creek State Park (see "Parks" below) and **Clarkesville**, which is basically a lovely intersection with HIDDEN ▶ a terrific place to eat. In a few miles you'll arrive at the **Lake Burton State Fish Hatchery**, a good stop for stretching your legs and taking a gander at the fish. Several concrete raceways froth with trout in various sizes. You can learn how the Georgia hatchery system works to replenish streams with these fish, and there's a fishing pool (for kids only). ~ 3695 Route 197, Clarkesville; 706-947-3112; www.burtongallery.net.

South of the fish hatchery are two landmarks. One is the HIDDEN ▶ **Burton Gallery & Emporium**, which you can reach by turning left onto Burton Dam Road. Famous for its folk art, wood carvings, sculptures, antique fishing tackle and bird carvings, this gallery is worth a look even if you are not a shopper or collector. ~ 295 Cherokee Ridge Drive, Clarkesville; 706-947-1351, 877-947-1351; www.burtongallery.net.

A few miles south, the **Batesville General Store** is a blast from the past (though the food is contemporary) with old-time products and a hospitable country atmosphere you may have thought no longer existed in America. Don't miss the biscuits and cinnamon rolls. ~ 11801 Route 197N, Clarkesville; 706-947-3434.

After touring these hidden attractions and maybe having lunch at the Batesville General Store, return to Route 76 and continue to Clayton, where it intersects with Route 23/441. Turn

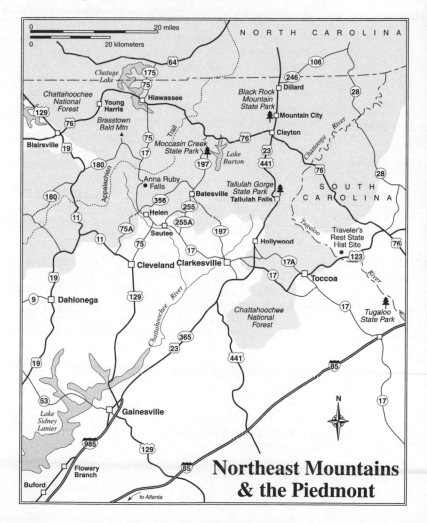

Northeast Mountains & the Piedmont

north for the short drive to **Mountain City**. Anyone familiar with the books, videos and general theory of Foxfire will want to visit the **Foxfire Museum**. The whole thing got started back in the late 1960s when a local English class hit upon an inspired approach for occupying its fidgety students. It started a magazine, which evolved into a series of articles on tales of actual mountain people whose words and wisdom kept the project afloat. In 1972, some of the articles were assembled into the *Foxfire Book*; the first printing of 30,000 sold quickly and the proceeds underwrote a recording studio, publishing house, television studio and meeting hall. The story is told at this museum, which exhibits toys, egg baskets and other simple tools for Appalachian living in the late-19th and early-20th century and has a small store where you can buy books, tapes and folk art. The museum—actually a log cabin built by students—houses an old wagon built by a local blacksmith, complete with wagon jack. Also on the grounds is a 19th-century grist mill moved here from Dahlonega. Closed Saturday and Sunday. Admission. ~ 2837 Route 441S, Mountain City; 706-746-5828, fax 706-746-5829; www.foxfire.org.

When you've finished at Foxfire, continue north on Route 441 practically to the state line to a town called **Dillard**. There

HIDDEN ▶

you can turn left on Betty's Creek Road to see the **Hambidge Center & Gallery**. By now you'll have noticed that you're deep in Folk Crafts Country, so to speak. And this is a prime center of it, a place to see quality work housed in a historic building amid 600 bucolic acres. The center was founded by Mary Hambidge, an artist intent on preserving the arts and crafts aspects of Appalachian culture. In addition to an artist-in-residence program, the center offers occasional educational programs to the public. Closed Saturday and Sunday. ~ Located six miles northwest of Route 441 on Betty's Creek Road, Dillard; 706-746-5718; www.hambridge.org.

By turning around and heading south on Route 441 past central Clayton, you'll see some animals. **Tut's Game Preserve** has a collection of Georgia black bears—better to see them here than in the wild—and less formidable wildlife such as deer, peacocks, hawks, eagles and llamas. Admission. ~ Route 441 and Seed Tick Road, Clayton; 706-782-6218, 800-621-1768; www.tutsmountain.com.

Route 441 continues south to Tallulah Falls, the nearest town to the spectacular **Tallulah Gorge State Park**. In the late 19th and early 20th centuries, this area became a prime attraction for honeymooners and other vacationers drawn, as many are to Niagara Falls today, by spectacular waterfalls. Tallulah Falls are, in fact, not one but several falls. Thanks to unusual geologic factors, the 600-foot gorge is unlike any other. The flora and fauna that thrive here are almost as unusual, including the rare crevice-dwelling green salamander, Carolina hemlock and a rare trillium, one of winter's most spectacular blossoms; rare fringed polygala are found here along with Carolina rhododendron. Though the gorge has been here since the Cherokee Indians lived around here, only a handful of white hunters and traders ventured into the gorge. The latter told stories about a race of "little people" they believed inhabited the crevices in the cliffs; the Cherokee were just as suspicious, fearing that one of the cave entrances led directly to the "Happy Hunting Grounds." The "terrible" Tallulah River once narrowed at the top of the gorge, creating a series of falls that attracted swarms of tourists, who settled in at a variety of hotels (one of them big enough for 300 guests). Refreshing summer temperatures, views and all that water created a major tourist attraction during hot Southern summers. Eventually, a forerunner of the Georgia Power Company bought the land at the head of the gorge—the first step towards taming the Tallulah. By 1913, geologists finished a dam and ultimately used the harnessed electricity to run Atlanta's trolley cars. Today, a trickle is all that remains of the once-mighty river but it's a breathtaking landscape nonetheless.

Tallulah Falls are carved in resistant quartzite instead of the gneisses and schists of nearby mountains.

From the gorge, remain on Route 441 until just past Hollywood, and take Route 17 east toward the town of Toccoa. Before you arrive in town, you will see signs on your left for Toccoa Falls College, a private school affiliated with the Southern Baptist church. Drive onto the semi-rural setting and follow signs to the amazing Toccoa Falls. After you've seen the falls to the north, the 186-foot drop may appear underwhelming, but the area has a tragic history that lends a definite poignancy. Long a tourist attraction, the falls were the scene of a devastating occurrence when, on November 6, 1977, the water pushed through the dam above and killed 39 people as it flooded the interdenominational bible-college campus. You'd never know it to look at the place today. The walk and scenery are as tranquil as can be, but the story is a reminder of the ultimate power of natural forces. Admission. ~ Toccoa Falls College campus, Route 17, Toccoa; 706-886-6831, 800-868-3257.

◄ HIDDEN

If you continue east after viewing these falls, stop by the Toccoa–Stephens County Chamber of Commerce, which has information about other local sites, accommodations and recreational opportunities. Closed Saturday and Sunday. ~ 901 East Currahee Street, Toccoa; 706-886-2132, fax 706-886-2133; www.toccoagachamber.com.

On the far side of town, take Route 123 east toward South Carolina; just before the state line is the Traveler's Rest State Historic Site. The place really was a resting place for weary travelers in the early 1800s. The southern portion of the house was built around 1815 and later expanded before owner James Wylly sold it to Devereaux Jarrett, who operated a number of businesses. It was under his ownership that the place was doubled in size and became known as Traveler's Rest. Had he lived today, he probably would have owned a string of Hiltons. The property was sold to the state in 1955 and is now a National Historic Landmark. You can take a guided tour of the architecturally distinct plantation home and surrounding site, which includes the original dairy house and a couple of reconstructed buildings. It's a good idea to call ahead to make sure a ranger is on duty. Closed Monday (except on legal holidays) through Wednesday. Admission. ~ 8162 Riverdale Road, Toccoa; 706-886-2256.

Return to Toccoa and Route 17 and follow the signs to **Clarkesville**. It's not that there is a great deal to see in the hill town, but it makes a good headquarters for touring the area.

Continue northwest from Clarkesville on Route 17 and stop in the crossroads town of **Sautee**. Just before you come to the Route 255 turnoff, you can see, on the right, the **Old Sautee Store**, also a makeshift museum. The front half is the old part, complete with a wooden Indian guarding the door. Inside, there's an antique dentist chair and a motley assortment of other relics such as antique signs along the lines of "American Biscuits." The back, or newer half, of the building, is, unexpectedly, a Scandinavian gift shop. ~ Route 17 and 255, Sautee; 706-878-2281; www.sauteestore.com.

From Sautee, you can drive a short distance west on Route 17 to what is inevitably described as the Alpine town of **Helen**. This is definitely the kind of place you either love or hate. It's doubtful that things get this relentlessly Alpine even in Switzerland, but you be the judge: Is it a village or an open-air shopping mall? Helen is naturally a mountain town, with a rich gold-mining his-

AUTHOR FAVORITE

I've seen a lot of waterfalls, but never a twin set until **Anna Ruby Falls**. You can reach them by taking a sidetrip from Helen up Route 356. This scenic duo flows from Curtis Creek and York Creek, tumbling side by side to form Smith Creek, a tributary of the Chattahoochee River. There's a visitors center with exhibits on the area and touch-me animal furs. The back porch overlooks a creek brimming with trout (food pellets for sale). It's a little less than half a mile via paved trail to the falls. Admission. ~ Route 356, Helen; 706-878-3574.

tory, but unadulterated tourism has taken over. When you arrive, find one of the parking lots off to the side and ramble around Main Street.

Kids might like to visit the model railroad **Charlemagne's Kingdom,** which has 400 feet of track, computerized trains, an autobahn and little towns and villages depicting German scenes "from the North Sea to the Alps" in miniature. Admission. ~ 8808 North Main Street, Helen; 706-878-2200; www.georgiamodelrailroad.com.

From the falls, return to Helen and take Route 75A south to **Cleveland** for one reason only. If you think the Cabbage Patch doll craze is over, there's a place not far from the center of town that will convince you otherwise. At **Babyland General Hospital,** you may be surprised to hear "doctors" being paged over the intercom to "deliver" babies, which, thankfully, you learn come not from big dolls but from cabbage leaves. I am not making this up. Of course there's a major market for Xavier Roberts' creations—signed, rare and otherwise—going on here, but part of the fun is watching grownups as well as kids ooh and ahh over the little ones. ~ 73 West Underwood Street, Cleveland; 706-865-2171; www.cabbagepatchkids.com.

From Cleveland, Route 129 leads south to **Gainesville,** the big city at the north end of Lake Sidney Lanier that abounds with trees and many 19th-century homes converted into low-key commercial properties. Route 129 passes through the **Green Street Historic District,** where broad boulevards are flanked with Victorian and Neoclassical Revival homes from the late 19th and early 20th centuries. ~ 770-297-1141; www.gainesville.org.

In one of these grand residences, the **Quinlan Visual Arts Center** houses regional art and touring exhibits in pretty galleries. It specializes in folk art, contemporary crafts, paintings and sculpture. Admission. ~ 514 Green Street, Gainesville; 770-536-2575; www.quinlanartscenter.org.

Just after Route 129 (also Green Street and E. E. Butler Parkway) crosses Academy Street, you'll find the **Greater Hall County Chamber of Commerce,** which has information about the nearby islands of Lake Lanier and the highlands to the north as well as directions to the Green Street Historic District and other parts of town. Closed Saturday and Sunday. ~ 230 E. E. Butler Parkway, Gainesville; 770-532-6206, fax 770-535-8419; www.ghcc.com.

Between Academy Street and Brenau Avenue, just off Route 129, look for signs to **Chief Whitepath's Cabin.** Cherokee Chief   ◄ HIDDEN
Whitepath led a rebellion against the erosion of Cherokee culture and his cabin is now a museum showcasing Cherokee and early American artifacts; one room is furnished as it might have been

when it was occupied by the chief, who died on the Trail of Tears. Admission. ~ 403 Brenau Avenue, Gainesville; 770-536-0889.

The historic cabin is now part of the **Georgia Mountains History Museum**, where the permanent exhibit details regional history and includes a gallery devoted to Ed Dodd, who created the "Mark Trail" comic strip. The complex also includes the Northeast Georgia Sports Hall of Fame. Closed Monday. Admission. ~ 322 Academy Street, Gainesville; 770-297-5900.

The **Carousel** in the Lakeshore Mall is an 18-foot-tall Venetian model outfitted with handcrafted animals to ride. Closed Sunday morning. Admission. ~ 150 Pearl Nix Parkway, Gainesville; 770-535-8877.

For a respite from what passes for urban stress, head out the Jesse Jewell Parkway from downtown and bear left on the Atlanta Highway (Route 13). Go about two and a half miles, crossing a bridge and some railroad tracks until you see a white water tower on your right. Turn left, towards Chicopee Woods, then **HIDDEN ►** take a quick right. You'll see a sign that points to the **Elachee Nature Science Center**. In this truly sylvan setting is a contemporary natural-history museum with live animals on displays, a native plant garden and fabulous hiking trails. Closed Sunday. Admission. ~ 2125 Elachee Drive, Gainesville; 770-535-1976; www.elachee.org.

Down the road a bit are the towns of semi-bucolic **Flowery Branch** and the neo-gentrified **Buford**. The latter is in danger of being co-opted as the latest Saturday afternoon escape destination for Atlantans, which isn't all bad since it's giving the town an economic shot in the arm. Main Street is enjoying a rebirth as people escaping both the urban and the suburban lifestyle find a bit of country here without having to sacrifice nice stores and good food. Flowery Branch is the perfect name for this hamlet, with only a main crossroads to serve as downtown.

LODGING   Pretty it ain't, but the **Seasons Inn** is clean and practically in Blairsville's town square. Actually, it's in an odd little shopping cul-de-sac a stone's throw from the Union County Courthouse. Some of the two dozen rooms on two floors have furniture painted "country blue," a welcome break from the same old wood veneer furnishings in other motels. Best of all, every room has a view. ~ On the Square, Blairsville; 706-745-1631, 800-901-4422, fax 706-745-1334. BUDGET TO MODERATE.

Manicured greens, perfect landscaping (dogwoods, sycamores, hardwood oaks) and a generally shipshape appearance distinguish the grounds of the 503-acre **Brasstown Valley Resort**. The three-story, green-and-white main lodge has the look of an old-fashioned summer resort hotel, which in fact the owners have

HIDDEN ►

largely re-created. The 102 rooms here are on the large side, if not huge, and have white wallpaper with green details, big French windows and lots of light. They are reached by a glass walkway that leads from the Great Room, which is dominated by a 72-foot-tall stone fireplace (although one's attention is easily diverted by the sight of very large, naturally shed antler chandeliers). There are also another 32 accommodations in nearby cottages. ~ 6321 Route 76, Young Harris; 706-379-9900, 800-201-3205; www.brasstownvalley.com, e-mail info@brasstown valley.com. ULTRA-DELUXE.

The three-story, 105-room **Lake Chatuge Lodge** was built on a knoll on the shores of this tree-lined lake. The lobby boasts a big stone fireplace, comfy club chairs and oversized hunting prints hither and yon. But the truth is, the place, though quite warm and pleasant, is not so much a hunting lodge as an upscale chain hotel. The typical spiffy room has hunter-green venetian blinds, sturdy blond wood furniture, and a postage stamp–size patio or balcony. From here, you can walk down to the adjacent Georgia Mountain Fairgrounds or tour the Hamilton Rhododendron Gardens. ~ 653 Route 76, Hiawassee; 706-896-5253, 800-613-4349, fax 706-896-2876; www.lakechatugelodge.com. DELUXE.

◄ HIDDEN

Guests at **Mountain Memories** will regret it if they arrive too late to enjoy the spectacular sunset over Lake Chatuge. The hillside country inn claims panoramic views from decks and a communal gazebo. The B&B, an older home that's been completely remodeled, clings to a gentle hillside above the town of Hiawassee. Four of the six guest rooms face the lake, with the mountains of Georgia, North Carolina and Tennessee ringing the horizon. Each accommodation has its own in-room hot tub and private entrance. "Sunset" has a separate sitting room; "Lovers" has a king-size white-clad bed and a satiny chair for reading, watching TV or whatever. The innkeepers offer a number of thoughtful amenities, from terrycloth robes to a 24-hour cappuccino machine in the lower-level game room to a lending library of 400 VCR tapes. ~ 385 Chancey Drive, Hiawassee; 706-896-8439, 800-335-8439; www.mountain-memories-inn.com, e-mail mail@mountainmemoriesbandb.com. ULTRA-DELUXE.

◄ HIDDEN

The refined York House has been host to such notable guests as Joel Chandler Harris and Walt Disney.

The **York House**, secluded on a side road a quarter-mile off Route 441/23 on the north edge of Mountain City, is a vision of white and green at the foot of the Blue Ridge Mountains. Its wide railed porches and veritable forest of evergreen trees urge visitors to slow down and appreciate their surroundings. Built in 1896 to accommodate railroad passengers, it claims to be the oldest continuously operating inn in Georgia. What began as a two-story

◄ HIDDEN

cabin is now a sizable inn with 13 accommodations on two floors, including a suite that is part of the original structure (and has the working fireplace to prove it). Wall-to-wall carpeting throughout is a luxury, especially in wintertime. Guests find rocking chairs in front of almost every room; they also have use of a small kitchen and picnic tables in the shade of a five-acre forest in the back of the property. Full breakfast is included. ~ York House Road off Route 441, Mountain City; 706-746-2068, 800-231-9675; www.gamountains.com/yorkhouse, e-mail yorkhouse@all tell.net. MODERATE TO DELUXE.

Behind Dillard's Family Restaurant is the **Dillard House**, a complex of one- and two-story motel-like buildings that look about as bland as possible. The rooms are no surprise: think Holiday Inn with exterior corridors. However, the rural setting is nice and the views are lovely. There are three two-bedroom units and five efficiencies, and this 66-room motel does have a pool and tennis courts (and, for a fee, horseback riding). Dillard House also rents several cottages, which are more expensive. The restaurant serves three meals a day. ~ 768 Franklin Street (Route 441), Dillard; 706-746-5348, 800-541-0671, fax 706-746-3344; www.dillard house.com. MODERATE TO ULTRA-DELUXE.

The **Stonebrook Inn** is an above-average motel with 30 rooms on two floors. Accommodations run to floral bedspreads and easy chairs perfect for watching HBO, CNN and ESPN on the 20-channel cable TV. Refrigerator and microwave available, and there's a pool next door. ~ 698 Route 441 South, Clayton; 706-782-4702, 877-779-4702; www.stonebrookinn.com, e-mail info@ stonebrookinn.com. MODERATE.

AUTHOR FAVORITE

When it comes to wake-up calls, I prefer chirping birds to alarm clocks. That's what you'll hear around **Glen-Ella Springs Inn and Conference Center**. Surrounded by woodlands about eight miles north of Clarkesville, this 16-room hideaway is rustic without being primitive. Bare wood or lightly painted walls, floors and ceilings are warmed up with four-poster beds and country-print upholstery and bed linens. Glen-Ella claims 17 acres, part of a 600-acre tract awarded in the 1830s to Glen and Ella Davidson as part of the great Cherokee land giveaway. It was built in 1875 as a family home and upgraded and expanded over time to accommodate paying guests. There's a pool and hiking just up the road. Full breakfast. ~ 1789 Bear Gap Road, Clarkesville; 706-754-7295, 877-456-7527, fax 706-754-1560; www.glenella.com, e-mail info@glenella.com. ULTRA-DELUXE.

Located many blocks south of downtown Clarkesville, **The Burns-Sutton Inn** has the imposing mien of a grande dame. Built in the early 1900s by a pair of master carpenters, it has numerous Victorian embellishments—balustrades, hand-carved fireplace mantels and stained-glass windows. Its seven guest accommodations, most with private bath, include two suites large enough for families; four are on the second floor, three on the attic level. The furniture varies from room to room: sometimes massive, sometimes more delicate, with accents like lace tablecloths tucked under glass circles cut to fit a tabletop precisely. The occasional odd touches, such as one bureau mirror frame festooned with postcards of Elvis Presley, make the inn really memorable. ~ 855 Washington Street, Clarkesville; 706-754-5565. MODERATE TO DELUXE.

Hidden in plain sight, the 1920 **Nacoochee Valley Guest House** exudes charm, perhaps because despite its small size it has a rambling kind of feel. The three rooms are as different as can be. The Cherub Room is cozy enough for honeymooners, with a king-size bed, fireplace and its own entrance. The sunken Oak Room has a sitting area and can actually sleep four. Irresistible, though, is the upstairs Meadow Room, where the headboard is made from the old barn sidings and the view through French windows takes in much of the valley. A full breakfast rounds out the amenities. No credit cards. ~ 2220 Route 17, Sautee; 706-878-3830; www.letsgotobernies.com. MODERATE TO DELUXE.

To really get into the spirit of the town of Helen, check into **The Helendorf River Inn & Conference Center**. Right on the Chattahoochee riverbank, this two- and three-story hotel has 99 rooms and suites, some of them quite large with private balconies overlooking the rushing waters. Best of all, six of the rooms have kitchens and some are okay for pets. Like other hotels in this area, this one offers real deals in the off-season (i.e., December until late June). ~ 33 Muniche Strass, Helen; phone/fax 706-878-2271, 800-445-2271; www.helendorf.com. MODERATE TO DELUXE.

Also on the Chattahoochee and crowned with a turret, **The Castle Inn** is essentially a two-story motel with 12 rooms. Accommodations are a comfortable size but despite balconies, some of them can be a bit dark so be sure to inquire ahead. There's an unrelated restaurant on the ground floor, which can be convenient but noisy on weekend nights during summer and fall. ~ 8287 North Main Street, Helen; 706-878-3140, 877-878-3140, fax 706-878-2470; www.castleinn-helen.com. DELUXE TO ULTRA-DELUXE.

The **Dunlap House** is bigger than it looks from the gracious boulevard it faces. Old homes that can incorporate ten guest rooms are rare, but this 1910 residence does it without strain. Accommodations are medium to large in size, with pleasant enough furniture and totally forgettable art on the walls. It's one of the best places to stay in Gainesville—it was certainly good enough for Jody Foster, Charles Kuralt and other celebrities, including Tom Cruise and Paul Newman, who have stayed here while racing cars at nearby Road Atlanta. The Dunlap House is in the historic Green Street neighborhood, close to restaurants and other historic structures. ~ 635 Green Street, Gainesville; 770-536-0200, 800-276-2935, fax 770-503-7857; www.dunlaphouse.com. MODERATE TO ULTRA-DELUXE.

HIDDEN ► While subdivisions sprout on surrounding highways and byways, the **Whitworth Inn** seems to hang on to yesteryear. That is only an illusion, however, for despite a facade that could pass as neo-semi-Revival-esque, the place was actually built in the mid-1980s. The decor in the ten second-story guest accommodations is not much to look at—think of it as a sleep incentive—but the place has a beautiful garden, a serenity consistent with the countryside, and it's close to all the activities Lake Lanier has to offer. Full breakfast is included. ~ 6593 McEver Road, Flowery Branch; 770-967-2386, fax 770-967-2649; www.whitworthinn.com, e-mail visit@whitworthinn.com. MODERATE.

DINING Mountain streams provide plenty of trout in this part of the state. Some of the rustic resorts can be counted on for very good home cooking, though fast foods are more common the farther south you travel.

HIDDEN ► Just a couple of blocks off the town square, **Cook's Country Kitchen** is one of those standbys, the kind of place you end up going to again and again because it's so easy and inexpensive. The big blue clapboard cottage has just one big room in which you can order from the menu or a grease board that lists daily specials like fried squash. Lunch is meat-and-threes (a Tennessean term for one meat dish and three vegetables) or à la carte; dinner is à la carte and lists chicken breast, pork chops, country ham, shrimp, deep fried flounder and barbecue. Closed Sunday. ~ 105 Pat Haralson Memorial Drive, Blairsville; 706-745-1332. BUDGET TO MODERATE.

HIDDEN ► The lodge-like **Brasstown Valley Resort Dining Room** is a big, beautiful, woodsy room, although its location makes it feel more bustling than relaxing at times. Specialties range from delicate pan-fried trout to good old (but upscaled) Georgia chicken pot pie to a variety of seasonal selections. ~ 6321 Route 76, Young Harris; 706-379-9900. MODERATE TO ULTRA-DELUXE.

Enrico's Lakeview Restaurant focuses on veal (five preparations), chicken, beef, seafood and pasta. And of course there's pizza and calzone. The house caesar salad is a good way to begin what will probably be a filling meal. This and one of the chef's special mussels appetizers might be enough, especially if you succumb to the piping hot Italian bread that comes with the meal. ~ 3295 Dogwood Lane, Hiawassee; 706-896-1990, fax 706-896-2357. MODERATE.

Gleaming woods, plenty of windows and a lakeside locale add a lot of oomph to dining at **Watercrest at Fieldstone**. You can snack on some pecan-crusted trout or shrimp and grits while considering your main course for the evening. Pork chop? New York strip? *Coq au vin*? Lamb chops? Veal Oscar? This spacious restaurant, part of the Fieldstone Inn complex, even has a vegetarian casserole. ~ 3499 Route 76, Hiawassee; 706-896-2262. MODERATE TO DELUXE.

The highway signs proclaiming **Dillard's Family Restaurant** make it sound like a funky old roadside establishment, but in fact the place, part of a complex incorporating a store and a motel, is almost stately. Family-style food (pork chops, chicken, vegetables) is served in a huge part of the building that seats a whopping 250 diners for three meals a day. ~ 768 Franklin Street (Route 441), Dillard; 706-746-5348. MODERATE.

It was in Flowery Branch that the term "Porterville" steak was coined, in honor of a local family of restaurateurs.

Granny's Kuntry Kitchen may sound forbidding to gourmets, but this simple, homey spot goes beyond "kuntry" with some Southwestern-style cooking: grilled fish, quesadillas and spicy dishes. You'll also find sandwiches, salads, beer and wine and daily chef's specials. No dinner on Sunday. Closed Saturday. ~ Depot Center, Route 441S, Clayton; 706-782-3914. BUDGET.

If you approach Clayton from the south, you'll pass **Julia's Steak & Seafood**. But you really shouldn't. This is a surprisingly sophisticated restaurant, with grilled meats, chicken and seafood and specialties like rainbow trout and homemade crab cakes. Family-owned and -operated since 1989, Julia's also has an extensive wine list and all desserts are made on the premises. Closed Sunday and Monday. ~ Lofty Branch Lane, Lofty Branch (about five miles south of Clayton); 706-782-2052. MODERATE TO DELUXE.

Bell's Drive-In, which is the big local favorite for quick country-style food, is almost indistinguishable from the fast-food places that line the highway. It's not the world's friendliest place but the fried chicken and catfish are good. Closed Sunday and Monday. ~ 1013 Route 17S, Toccoa; 706-886-5933. BUDGET.

Beautiful wood plank floors (and walls and ceilings) make the cool, dark **Batesville General Store** an especially welcome reprieve from driving. Red-and-white checked tablecloths and handmade straightback chairs share the interior with a modern version of a general store. Food is fresh and non-greasy: barbecue chicken and other sandwiches, with fries or chips, BLT and other sandwiches, omelets, pancakes, Key lime pie. All this plus friendly

service and nice vibes make this a treasure worth stopping for. ~
11801 Route 197N, Clarkesville; 706-947-3434. BUDGET.

HIDDEN ► 　　One of the top-rated restaurants in Georgia is the **Glen-Ella Springs Inn**'s dining room. It's cozy and a little bit country, so some folks are probably surprised, if not stunned, to find specials such as a boneless filet of mountain trout with herbs and pecans, jumbo shrimp served over fried Parmesan grits, rack of lamb with sweet potatoes and a jalapeño-mint sauce, and sinful desserts like molten chocolate cake. Those who enjoy wine with dinner are welcome to bring a bottle, as this part of Georgia is "dry." ~ 1789 Bear Gap Road, Clarkesville; 706-754-7295. DELUXE TO ULTRA-DELUXE.

HIDDEN ► 　　**Bernie's**, tucked into the 1920 Nacoochee Valley Guest House, consists of three charming dining areas on the ground floor. Diners have a choice of veal piccata, grilled quail, filet mignon, *fruits de mer* (a creamy seafood medley) and other upscale French country-style dishes you might not expect at a crossroads in Sautee. The restaurant can also accommodate vegetarians. Closed Sunday through Tuesday. ~ 2220 Route 17, Sautee; 706-878-3830. DELUXE TO ULTRA-DELUXE.

HIDDEN ► 　　Two miles beyond Anna Ruby Falls on Route 356, the **Tanglewood Restaurant** is a woodsy place with natural pine walls, a fireplace and mountain views through large windows. If you have to wait for supper, rock on the porch. The theme here is "mountain country cooking," as in big breakfasts, fried catfish (available as all-you-can-eat), farm-raised rainbow trout, T-bones, grilled ham and various chicken dishes. Closed Monday. ~ 3359 Route 356, four miles east of Helen, Sautee; 706-878-1044. BUDGET TO MODERATE.

HIDDEN ► 　　**The Troll Tavern** is, of course, located beneath the bridge. A nice deck overlooks the water; there are seats inside as well. The fare is a mix of Mexican, German and vegetarian, strong on sand-

◆◆◆

DINNER WITH A SPLASH OF DRAMA

The dramatic scenery around Tallulah Falls deserves a restaurant like **Isabelle's**, which occupies a striking site above the highway with views of the surrounding hillsides. It was built in 1880 as Pine Terrace, a Victorian home in the then-popular mountain resort of Tallulah Falls. (Those boom times ended in 1913, with the damming of the falls by Georgia Power.) An appealing and extensive menu includes, if not something for everyone, enough choices to keep hunger at bay. Chicken, filet mignon, seafood, salads, side dishes and desserts like Key lime pie are served in three dining rooms and a porch that's been enclosed and decorated with rolling shades and ceiling fans. No dinner Sunday, Monday or Wednesday. ~ Route 441N, Tallulah Falls; 706-754-5614. MODERATE.

wiches and wurst platters, with chicken, fish, beef and pasta dishes rounding out the menu along with a full bar. It's a local institution but if you can't find it, look for The Castle Inn. ~ Under the bridge, Main Street, Helen; 706-878-3117. BUDGET TO MODERATE.

Luna's is the prettiest restaurant in Gainesville. It occupies part of the ground floor of Hunt Tower, a downtown office building, and offers diners the pleasant aspect of a fine residence, with upholstered furniture and sophisticated colors. The cuisine is, of course, Continental. This is the place to save for a night when you want elegant candlelight and steak or chicken dishes accompanied by wines from what is probably the best list in Gainesville. Paella, filet mignon and Cajun shrimp are the main fare. No lunch Saturday. Closed Sunday. ~ 200 Main Street, Gainesville; 770-531-0848. DELUXE TO ULTRA-DELUXE.

◄ HIDDEN

Basically a beer and pizza joint—with a big smoking section and a large beer selection—**The Monkey Barrel** is for really kicking back. Nothing's too fancy, just wooden tables and chairs in a square room. Snack on some garlic pizza dough rolls while deciding which salads, pizzas, pastas, hamburgers or specialty whole-wheat crust pies to have. Choices of the latter are quite extensive, including ingredients like jalapeños, barbecue sauce, pineapple and bacon. Closed Sunday. ~ 115 Washington Street Northeast, Gainesville; 770-287-0970. BUDGET TO MODERATE.

The **Aqua Terra Bistro** opened in 1999, bringing a touch of Atlanta's hip Virginia-Highland neighborhood vibe to this little town. The menu of duck breast, diver scallops, sea bass and the like leans toward European fusion. ~ 55 Main Street, Buford; 770-271-3000. DELUXE TO ULTRA-DELUXE.

Until **Third Coast Grille** came along, the odds of finding jerk chicken near Lake Sidney Lanier were pretty slim. But just off a big highway, amid fiberglass repair shops and dock lockers, this Caribbeanesque restaurant is an island of semi-urban chic. Painted palm trees sway on stucco walls behind brightly painted furniture, creating nonstop cheer. The dinner menu includes fried or grilled shrimp, beef kabobs, baby back ribs, lobster and trout. The Coast Salad features chicken rubbed with a spicy jerk concoction and mixed with mandarin oranges and tomatoes. ~ 5713 Holiday Road, Buford; 770-614-9508. MODERATE TO DELUXE.

◄ HIDDEN

Helen has the upper hand in terms of merchants, but for quality, travelers are better off in the countryside or at arts-and-crafts galleries.

SHOPPING

The **Mark of the Potter** is a serious destination for many area shoppers and return visitors impressed with the high-quality contemporary crafts sold in a converted grist mill. The shop has handmade pieces in wood, metal, ceramic and glass as well as jewelry and woven pieces. ~ 9982 Route 197, Clarkesville; 706-947-3440.

Unicoi Outfitters sells fly-fishing equipment by Orvis, Bauer, Cortland and other top names. It claims to have the largest selection of flies in the Georgia mountains. ~ 7280 South Main Street, Helen; 706-878-3083.

If you want to buy a fancy beer stein and have it engraved, stop in at **Damron's Alpine Glass Engraving and Damron's Gifts** in the heart of town. ~ 8600 Main Street, Helen; 706-878-2087, 800-572-2892.

Unless you love crowds, don't go near the town of Helen in October, especially around Oktoberfest on the middle two weekends.

Jewelry, clocks, wooden shoes, dolls, curtain lace and Delft tiles should tip off even the most obtuse shopper who wanders into **Windmill Dutch Imports**. Everything here is imported from Holland. ~ White Horse Square, Helen; 706-878-3444.

Candlesticks is the retail outlet for the nearby North Georgia Candle Factory. You can watch candles being carved before picking out the ones you want. ~ 8685 North Main Street, Helen; 706-878-3214.

Big chain stores like Sears and JC Penney as well as more than 70 specialty shops and services (plus a four-screen theater and the Venetian Carousel) can be found at the **Colonial Mall Lakeshore**. ~ 150 Pearl Nix Parkway, Gainesville; 770-535-8877.

The Gallery Shop located at the Quinlan Visual Arts Center has original fine art and crafts for sale along with books, puzzles and museum notecards. ~ 514 Green Street, Gainesville; 770-536-2575.

Gifts and books relating to natural history comprise the charming assortment of merchandise in the **Gift Shop** at the Elachee Nature Science Center. ~ 2125 Elachee Drive, Gainesville; 770-535-1976.

NIGHTLIFE The ultracasual **Monkey Barrel** has live rock-and-roll Wednesday, Friday and Saturday nights. Closed Sunday. Cover except on Wednesday. ~ 115 Washington Street Northeast, Gainesville; 770-287-0970.

If you just can't take any more mountain peace and quiet, the big city is close enough to make a reasonable outing.

PARKS **MOCCASIN CREEK STATE PARK** Named for the creek that flows through it (which in turn probably got its name in the late 1800s when pioneers found Cherokee or Creek moccasin prints on the sandy bank), this 32-acre park is popular for trout fishing from late March through October. There's a catch, though: only those aged 11 and younger or 65 and older are allowed to fish in this part of Moccasin Creek. Lake Burton, a 2800-acre body of water that sustains largemouth bass, smallmouth bass, spotted bass and white bass, sits at the southwestern boundary; licenses and trout stamp can be purchased at the park office. Because of its elevation of 2000 feet, the park enjoys moderate summer temperatures in addition to 80 inches of rain each year that nourish the forests and wildflowers. There is a playground and canoe rentals are available seasonally. You can request a campsite with either a lake or creek view. Day-use fee, $2. ~ 3655 Route 197, Clarkesville; 706-947-3194, 800-864-7275.

▲ There are 54 tent/RV sites; $14 to $24 per night. Reservations: 800-864-7275.

TALLULAH GORGE STATE PARK 🏃 🚲 🏊 ⛷ 🛶 With a two-mile-long gorge as its centerpiece, this is arguably the most dramatic Georgia state park. It is also one of the newest and includes 2689 acres surrounding the gorge. Scenes from the movie *Deliverance* were filmed here, while *The Great Locomotive Chase* was shot here in the 1950s as the old Tallulah Falls Railroad was being demolished. Though the Tallulah River was dammed in 1912, the Department of Natural Resources, along with the Georgia Power Company and various environmental organizations, has instituted a series of regular releases several weekends each year; the ranger station has information on the dates. The views are just as spectacular now as then, and it doesn't take much imagination to envision one of the marvelous stunts of all time. In 1886, thousands of onlookers gathered to watch Professor Leon walk a tightrope across the canyon; although one of his lines snapped and caused him to fall, he righted himself and completed the walk. You can experience Leon's view firsthand from a suspension bridge that spans the gorge at a height of 80 feet. The gorge has hiking trails on which you can see various waterfalls, wildflowers like trillium and creatures such as green salamanders. Facilities include restrooms, showers, a picnic area, tennis courts and a 63-acre lake with a beach. Day-use fee, $4. ~ On Route 441 between Clarkesville and Clayton; turn east on South Rock Mountain Road and proceed one mile and then follow the signs; Tallulah Falls; 706-754-7970.

▲ There are 50 tent/RV sites; $20 per night. Reservations: 800-864-7275.

Outdoor Adventures

The Georgia mountains offer year-round recreation, including occasional snow in the winter. Hiking is most popular in the spring, which brings on thousands of acres of wildflowers and blooming shrubs. The changing leaves of autumn make this another favorite time to be outdoors.

FISHING

Lakes—both natural and manmade—and a plethora of rivers and streams make the Georgia Mountains a major angling destination. Though trout fishing is regulated by season, there are plenty of other fish, including catfish, bream and several types of bass.

You'll find places where you can fish in streams or creeks, from a boat or off a pier.

At **James H. "Sloppy" Floyd State Park,** two scenic lakes— one 17 acres and the other more than twice that size—brim with bass, catfish and bream for anglers. Boats are available for rent and there's a boat ramp at each lake. ~ Three miles southeast of Summerville off Route 27; 706-857-0826, 800-864-7275.

> Whether you fish or not, you can go home with trout from Andy's Trout Farm. They rent equipment and sell fish by the pound. ~ Betty's Creek Road, Dillard; 706-746-2550.

Moccasin Creek State Park, tantalizingly next door to a state fish hatchery, has legit fishing off a pier—though only for those under 11 or over 65 years old. You can take a boat out on Lake Burton to catch several species of bass. ~ 3655 Route 197, Clarkesville; 706-947-3194, 800-864-7275.

Lake Sidney Lanier, in the foothills of the Blue Ridge Mountains, features day-use areas, a number of parks and more than 100 islands where boaters can retreat in privacy. Game fish include striped bass, largemouth bass, smallmouth bass, crappie and other species. Brook, rainbow and brown trout can be found below the Buford Dam (at the southwest corner of the lake). More details are available from the Resource Manager's Office on the southeast side of the lake. ~ Buford; 770-945-9531.

CANOEING & KAYAKING Spring runoff allows excellent rafting and canoeing opportunities throughout the Georgia Mountains. The Chattooga, Chestatee and other rivers are best in the spring but lakes Tugalo and Tallulah allow leisurely paddling.

For a quick trip on a river but not necessarily in a hard-framed craft, there's always tubing. **Appalachian Outfitters** offers outings on the Etowah River as well as on the Chestatee River about an hour north of Atlanta. ~ Route 60 at Yahola Creek Bridge, Dahlonega; 706-864-7117, 800-426-7117; www.canoegeorgia.com.

Wildwater Ltd. Rafting offers full-service whitewater rafting trips for families and other groups. They lead half-day to two-day outings on the National Wild and Scenic Chattooga River. ~ 1254 Academy Road, Clayton; 800-451-9972; www.wildwater-rafting.com.

Tallulah Adventures rents canoes for paddling around Tugaloo and Tallulah lakes. They'll be happy to act as guides but you probably won't require any assistance in still water. Closed Tuesday and Wednesday except by appointment. ~ 940 Scenic Loop 15, Tallulah Falls; 706-754-4318; www.tallulahpoint.com.

SKIING The place to get in some downhill action in Georgia is at **Sky Valley Golf and Ski Resort,** the southernmost resort in the eastern U.S.

HIDDEN ► Like many Southern ski resorts, it indeed resorts to blowing in snow to cover the slopes during dry winters. During the warmer months, Sky Valley offers 18 holes of golf along with tennis. ~ East of Dillard via Route 246, Sky Valley; 800-437-2716.

Most horseback riding in the mountains is on forested land so there won't be a lot of wild galloping. On the other hand, there's no more perfect way to explore the woods than on the back of a horse.

RIDING STABLES

Gold City Corral & Carriage Company offers guided rides in the mountains surrounding Amicalola Falls State Park. You can also arrange carriage and wagon hay rides and even campouts, including riding, camping and cowboy-style meals. ~ Forrest Hills Mountain Resort, 49 Forrest Hills Road, Dahlonega; 706-867-9395; www.goldcitycorral.com.

One- and two-hour rides are offered on 250 densely forested acres next to the Chattahoochee National Forest. Instruction and group rates are available at **Trackrock Stables**. ~ 4890 Trackrock Campground Road, Blairsville; 706-745-5252, 800-826-0073; www.trackrock.com.

You can arrange farm, river, trail or children's ring rides or even an all-day outing into the Chattooga Wilderness through **Dillard House Stables**. ~ Old Dillard Road, Dillard; 706-746-2038; www.dillardhousestables.com.

Tanagers, vireos, orioles and warblers—as well as ravens—are especially prominent on spring mornings in the **Chattahoochee National Forest**, which, at 700,000 acres, is the state's largest Important Bird Area (IBA). The other IBAs in north Georgia are Ivylog Mountains (Blairsville), Dawson Forest (Dawsonville) and the Chicopee Woods Nature Preserve at the Elachee Nature Center (Gainesville).

BIRDING

The climate in the Georgia mountains from early spring through late fall is ideal for outdoor activities such as golf. You won't be charged an arm and a leg, either, and the courses aren't as crowded as they are in other parts of the state where golf is king.

GOLF

The 18-hole, Tom Fazio–designed course at **Barnsley Gardens Resort** has 70 bunkers and a par of 72. The resort offers a putting green, practice range, lessons, golf shop, carts and a teaching pro. Only spikeless shoes are allowed. ~ 597 Barnsley Gardens Road, Adairsville; 770-773-7480, 877-773-2447.

The **Royal Oaks Golf Club** has extremely reasonable rates for its 18-hole course. Don't know much about golf? You can rent clubs here and take PGA lessons from the pro. ~ 256 Summit Ridge Drive Southeast, Cartersville; 770-382-3999.

The **Stonebridge Golf Club**, at the base of Lavender Mountain in the Appalachian foothills, is owned and operated by the

Text continued on page 310.

Cascading
Waters

There's no such thing as an ugly waterfall; the sight of cascading water satisfies some basic human yearning. Is it the negative ions? The purity of the water? The fact that you often have to hike for miles to see one? Whatever the reason, the Georgia Mountains are the place to slake that thirst for nature at her most beautiful.

An abundance of rivers and creeks creates waterfalls nearly year-round. The Tallulah River once provided one of the most spectacular falls before it was dammed. A few times a year, however, the water is allowed to run off into the Tallulah Gorge. But even modest waterways are capable of producing wonderful waterfalls such as Anna Ruby Falls, a double waterfall created when the Curist and York creeks join Smith Creek in the Chattooga Ranger District. (This one, by the way, was named for Anna Ruby Nichols by her father, a colonel who purchased the falls and nearby land after the Civil War, allowing father and daughter to spend endless days on horseback exploring the forests.)

Some waterfalls are visible from the road or nearby so you don't have to be a hiker to see them. Others, as described below, are accessible only by trails. As pretty as these falls are, remember to be careful and obey any posted warnings. The following, all located in the Northeast Mountains, are a smattering of cascades to explore.

BLAIRSVILLE–CLEVELAND AREA   DeSoto Falls, named for explorer Hernando DeSoto, comprises five waterfalls on a three-mile section of the DeSoto Falls Trail located in the 650-acre Chestatee Ranger District. The lower falls cascade 20 feet; the middle, the prettiest part, drops 80 feet; the upper falls crash down a granite facade for nearly 200 feet and are visible from a flat formation overlooking the water. Parts of the upper and lower falls can be viewed from Route 129. ~ To get there, head north from Cleveland on Route 129 for 15 miles.

Helton Creek Falls Trail (.3 mile) follows Helton Creek to **Helton Creek Falls**. These two waterfalls, with a total vertical drop of over 100 feet, are in the Brasstown Ranger District. ~ Take Route 129 south from Blairsville for 11 miles; turn left on the first gravel road past the entrance to Vogel State Park and continue 2.2 miles to a parking area near the trailhead.

CLARKESVILLE AREA **Panther Creek Falls** can be reached by hiking along Panther Creek Falls Trail (5.5 miles) through hemlock and white pine. The trail, decorated with wildflowers and ferns, passes a series of cascades—and the falls—and terminates where Panther Creek is joined by Davidson Creek. It's a popular area for trout fishing. Hikers toting large packs need to keep an eye out for rocky overhangs. ~ Take Route 23/441 north from Clarkesville for ten miles to the Panther Creek Recreation Area, which is in the Chattooga Ranger District.

CLAYTON AREA This part of the mountains has more waterfalls than any other except for the region between Helen and Hiawassee. Some of them are relatively small.

Only five minutes from downtown Clayton, **Becky Branch Falls** is only a 20-foot cascade but is blessed with a bridge at the base of the falls. ~ Head east on Warwoman Road for 2.8 miles, park and walk up the right branch of the trail for about 200 yards to the bridge.

Minnehaha Falls can be reached by the Minnehaha Trail (.4 mile). With falling and shoaling, the waterfall is about as wide as it is high, roughly 100 feet. ~ Go north from Tallulah Falls for three miles to the Rabun Beach Recreation Area sign. Turn left onto Old Route 441 for 2.5 miles, then left on Lake Rabun Road, continuing one mile past the recreation area. Turn left onto Low Gap Road and follow it as it forks left, going for 1.5 miles to the trailhead on the right side of the road.

Anna Ruby Falls is really two falls in one. Curtis and York creeks join on the slopes of Tray Mountain in twin falls, with the Curtis side falling 153 feet and the York 50 feet. You can reach it on the paved Anna Ruby Falls Trail (.4 mile). It's steep but benches give people a chance to rest and contemplate. There's an observation deck at the base of the falls. Admission. ~ Take Route 75 north from Helen for one mile, turn right on Route 356 for 1.5 miles and then left at the entrance road to the falls.

Raven Cliff Falls is one of the most intriguing because its water flows through a split in a solid rock outcropping cascading 100 feet. It's a three-parter, and another three waterfalls are located on Dodd Creek, the largest of which is downstream from Raven Cliff Falls. It's in an undeveloped area of the Chattooga Ranger District, so remember, you're on your own. ~ Drive north from Helen on Route 75 for 1.5 miles, go left on Route 356 (Route 75A) and continue 2.3 miles to the Russell-Brasstown Scenic Byway. Turn right for 2.5 miles to the trailhead.

city of Rome. It's a championship 18-hole course regarded as one of the top 20 facilities in the state. ~ 6585 Stonebridge Drive, Rome; 706-236-5046, 800-336-5046.

Laid out by golf great Gary Player, the 18-hole, 183-acre **Nob North Golf Course** features seven lakes and 59 bunkers. ~ 298 Nob North Drive, Cohutta, ten miles north of Dalton via Route 71; 706-694-8505.

Rabun County Golf Club is an inexpensive alternative to major-league 18-hole courses with nine holes open every day. It's challenging and mountainous nonetheless, with a pro shop on site. ~ 1322 Old Route 441, Clayton; 706-782-5500.

Open year-round, **Eagle Greens at Skitt Mountain** offers a fun 18-hole course for quality play for all levels. The course, which opened in 1965, is set on 125 acres of rolling terrain. ~ 7883 Route 254, Cleveland; 706-865-2277.

If you don't like water hazards, you should be happy at one Clarkesville course. Very little water impedes your progress through the natural terrain at **Apple Mountain,** where golfers of all levels can find challenges amid the 18 holes. ~ 901 Rockford Creek Road, Clarkesville; 706-754-2255.

TENNIS

The **Rome/Floyd Tennis Center** won a USTA (United States Tennis Association) award for outstanding design. It has 16 lighted courts and offers individual and group lessons from USTA professionals. ~ 300 West 3rd Street, Rome; 706-290-0072.

Tallulah Gorge State Park has two lighted courts. ~ Route 441, Tallulah Falls; 706-754-7970.

BIKING

You'll see University of Georgia students on bicycles, but given that most of the mountain region is, well, kind of hilly, there are relatively few trails. The Tallulah Falls area has a few places to ride on and off the trail.

Both the intermediate and advanced segments of the six-mile **Ridgeway Mountain Bike Trail** can provide a challenge to riders of all skill levels. Fee. ~ Route 282, Ellijay; 706-334-2248; www.carters.sam.usace.army.mil.

AUTHOR FAVORITE

I could forget all about pars and bogeys at a place like the **Nicklaus Golf Club at Birch River,** which opened in 2000 in a scenic mountain valley. Players cross the river five times during 18 holes on this Jack Nicklaus–designed, par-72 course. ~ 639 Birch River Drive, Dahlonega; 706-867-7900, 866-271-5700; www.nicklausgolfbirchriver.com.

Bike Rentals There are mountain bike trails at Gainesville College and in Chicopee Woods. For maps, contact **Adventure Cycle**. ~ 770-534-1190; www.adventurecycles.com.

This being a mountainous region, hikers can expect major changes in elevation, particularly on the more remote trails (such as at the bottom of Cloudland Canyon State Park). But there is something for hikers of just about any level, including those who might better be described as strollers. All distances listed for hiking trails are one way unless otherwise noted.

The easiest trails in the Georgia mountains can be found at the **Marshall Forest Preserve**. The two trails are only about a quarter-mile each, running through an old-growth forest of mixed pine and hardwood. The best part is the **Big Pine Braille Trail** for the visually impaired, which includes oak trees as well as long-leaf pine trees that are much more common the flatlands of the coast.

In addition to the quarter-mile trail that follows the rim over-looking the canyon, **Cloudland Canyon State Park** has two major trails. The **West Rim Loop Trail** (4.5 miles) is moderate, except in a handful of steep and rocky places; the part that leads down to the falls is tough but short. More strenuous is the **Back Country Trail** (6.2 miles). Its highest point is nearly 2000 feet (slightly higher than the West Rim's zenith). Waterfalls and wildlife make both of these popular choices.

The trails in **Chickamauga/Chattanooga Battlefield National Military Park** have the bonus of an education in Civil War history. The **Perimeter Trail**, marked in blue, departs the visitor center along Route 27 to the Florida Monument and heads south on the western side of the park through woods and fields. Pick up the Glenn-Kelly Road and follow it to Glenn-Viniard Road to Route 27 (Lafayette Road). On this, the west side, the **Historical Trail** (pink), the **Cannon Trail** (yellow) and the **Memorial Trail** (white) join the Perimeter Trail. Stick to the blue markers and you will eventually return to the visitors center. The park has seven trails in all and you can get a well-marked map at the center.

There is a steep paved trail to the **Brasstown Bald**, but beyond the parking area you'll find the trail head to the **Arkaquah Trail** (5.5 miles). This moderate route leads through laurel groves and other woodlands where the ground is blanketed with wild-flowers in early spring. This trail is popular with birders who often spot raptors, warblers, thrush and tanagers, among other species. You can get more information from the Brasstown Ranger District in Blairsville or from the Brasstown Bald Visitor Center. ~ Route 180, Blairsville; 706-896-2556.

You can pick up the **Bartram Trail** in Clayton and access some 40 miles that are marked with black and yellow signs. It's

HIKING

◀ HIDDEN

named for Quaker naturalist William Bartram, who blazed it more than two centuries ago. Pick up maps at the Georgia Welcome Center. ~ 232 North Route 441, Clayton; 706-782-5113.

For a simple leg-stretcher, join the crowd on the **Lion's Eye Nature Trail** (1 mile) at Anna Ruby Falls. It follows Smith Creek to the twin falls. ~ Route 256, Helen; 706-878-2201.

The most famous trail in this part of the world is, of course, the **Appalachian Trail**, which begins at Springer Mountain just north of Amicalola Falls State Park and ends in Maine, about 2100 miles to the north. In all that distance, you will find only 11 primitive shelters, spaced roughly a day's hike apart. You may hike it in all seasons, but if you plan to go the whole way, it's best to begin in March or April. For more details, contact the Georgia Appalachian Trail Club (404-634-6495) or the U.S. Forest Service supervisor. ~ Gainesville; 706-532-6366.

▼▼▼▼▼▼▼▼▼▼
Transportation

CAR

On the west side of the Georgia mountains, **Route 75** slices from Atlanta all the way to the Tennessee state line. On the east side, it has no counterpart but instead a maze of mountain roads. The major north–south arteries in the eastern mountains are **Route 23/441** and, to a much lesser extent, **Route 19**. **Route 53** is the most convenient and direct link from west to east in the southern portion of the mountains, while **Route 76** skims the northern part.

AIR

The nearest major airport is **Hartsfield-Jackson Atlanta International Airport**. Please see Chapter Five for information on regularly scheduled air transportation. Most of the mountain section is within a two-hour drive from Atlanta.

In Rome, several companies offer transportation service to the Atlanta airport, including **Best Journey Tours** (706-234-7337) and **Shuttle Tran** (706-235-5466).

BUS

Greyhound Bus Lines makes stops in Rome at 868 Spider Webb Drive, in Dalton at 448 North Thorton, and in Gainesville at 1780 Martin Luther King Boulevard. ~ 800-231-2222; www.greyhound.com.

CAR RENTALS

There are two major auto-rental companies in Rome, including **Enterprise Rent A Car** (706-290-1093) and **Florida Rent A Car** (706-291-0723). There are numerous car-rental agencies at Hartsfield-Jackson International Airport. (See Chapter Five.)

SEVEN

East Central Georgia

The deep-loamed and naturally watered hills of northeast Georgia were ripe for settlement even before General Oglethorpe arrived from England to found the state and establish Savannah in 1733. The confluence of the Savannah and Broad rivers, near what is now the town of Washington, lured many families from western Europe; they established the first forts in the area and gave the region a jumpstart on what would one day become an outstanding collection of historic homes. Heard's Fort, a frontier haven, was designated as the temporary capital of Georgia in 1780. That same year, a charter was issued to establish the town of Washington, named for George Washington, who, when he came to Georgia, confirmed it as the first city in the country chartered in his name. By the close of the Civil War, the Whitehall section of the town was opened for settlement by a white entrepreneur named Nicholas Wylie, and affordable housing was, at last, available for freed slaves.

Partially in the Piedmont, partially in the flatlands of the middle of the state, East Central Georgia is a mixed bag. In this region, the Bulldog rules. It's the University of Georgia mascot and an icon to the thousands of UGA graduates who regularly make the pilgrimage from all over the state—and beyond—for the college football games that turn Athens into a feverish madhouse every fall. Compared to these fans, the golf aficionados who descend on Augusta for the Masters Tournament each spring are the picture of decorum. And it's a fitting comparison because Athens is defined by students, and Augusta by a more sedate, if not quite antebellum, mentality. The other major town hereabouts is Washington, a trove of historic architecture that attracts visitors who want to see examples of Federal, Greek Revival, Victorian and contemporary houses. Washington is located in the county of Wilkes, one of the eight original Georgia counties and the only one that never fell under British control during the American Revolution.

From Washington down to Statesboro, which is close to Savannah, there are no big cities. Several interesting towns, some no bigger than villages, line the back roads; Louisville, for instance, was the state's first permanent capital. Crawfordville is a one-street wonder blessed with a terrific state park and museum. One of the best towns, Wrightsboro, doesn't technically exist anymore but is still worth visiting. Statesboro is a college town not known for its cultural attributes, but the campus boasts a terrific raptor center.

Augusta, which was the second city (after Savannah) to be laid out by General James Oglethorpe, sits on the state line with South Carolina. The Savannah River, freshwater at this point, rolls by the downtown area. In the early 1800s, following Eli Whitney's invention of an experimental cotton gin near Washington in 1793, the cotton industry put Augusta on the map. When the Augusta Canal was installed in the 1840s, the city had the water power necessary to run its textile mills, attracting more than 100 mercantile firms in the middle of the century.

Augusta's mild winters and scores of antebellum homes—spared during Sherman's march to the sea during the Civil War—contributed to the development of the city as a capital of golf, a sport that has made the city famous for The Masters tournament, held in the spring as the dogwoods and azaleas are at their dazzling peak. At the same time golf was rising to prominence, aristocratic families, their fortunes ruined by the war, opened their doors to Northerners eager to escape the rigors of a Yankee winter. By the 1890s, the area had become a major winter resort destination. These same Northerners helped establish what remains the city's most enviable address: the neighborhood of Summerhill. Often called The Hill, it is populated full-time by Southerners today (though who knows how many of their ancestors were born north of the Mason-Dixon line).

▼▼▼▼▼▼▼▼▼▼
Athens Area

To many Georgians, Athens is synonymous with the University of Georgia. Athens is, of course, much more than the UGA. Calling itself the "Classic City" because so much of its architecture is inspired by Greek models that give the area around the campus a sedate appearance, Athens is also the site of the first garden club in the United States. It's a fitting locale for the stunning State Botanical Gardens, one of the region's loveliest attractions, a 293-acre enclave on the banks of the Oconee River.

SIGHTS

Athens and Augusta are the major cities in this section but before you reach Athens from the mountains, you'll pass through at least one town well worth a stop. Tiny **Jefferson**, sitting patiently by the roadside like a passenger whom the bus has long passed, has reason to be proud. It's the birthplace of anesthesia.

When you have finished exploring Jefferson, drive a few miles north and take Route 85 toward South Carolina. Georgia shares a watery border with South Carolina, meaning there are numerous lakes and tributaries for fishing, boating and just plain relaxing. One of these is **Hartwell Lake**, which, though mostly on the South Carolina side, has plenty of Georgia access as well. A total of 56,000 acres, the lake was named for the nearby town that, in turn, was named for Nancy Hart, a Revolutionary War heroine. If you get a map of the lake, you're bound to notice that most of the creeks are named after distances—Six-Mile Creek and so forth. Perhaps they were really named, as legend has it, by Issaqueena, a Cherokee maiden who kept track of the mileage as she rode to Forty Ninety-Six to warn settlers of an imminent attack. With 962 miles of shoreline, Hartwell Lake is among the state's most popular. ~ Off Route 29, Hartwell; 706-856-0300, 888-893-0678.

The **Hart County Historical Museum** is more of a historical resource than a museum, though you will find displays of re-

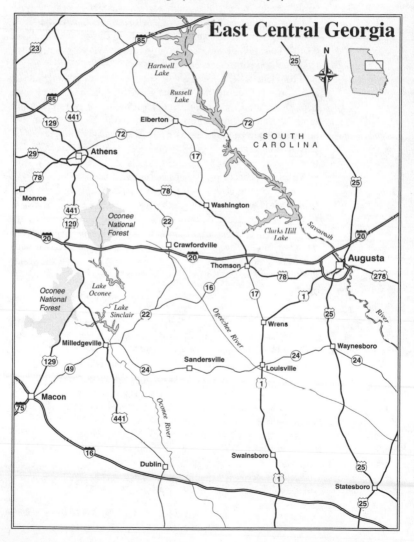

East Central Georgia

gional interest. More compelling is the structure itself: the Teasley-Holland House is the one-story frame house that, though it looks somewhat Victorian, actually dates back to 1800. It is home to the local **chamber of commerce** (706-376-8590). Closed Saturday and Sunday. ~ 31 East Howell Street, Hartwell; 706-376-6330; www.hart-chamber.org, e-mail hartchamber@hart com.net.

The **Center of the World Monument** honors the site where the Cherokee Indians met to hold their tribal council on an assembly ground until 1783, when a treaty was signed with the government. A huge chunk of granite with a marker tells the story of how the American Indians came to hold this place in such esteem. ~ Four miles from downtown Hartwell via Royston-bound Route 29 (on south side of road); 706-376-8590.

From Hartwell, the straightest route to **Athens** is via Route 29 and Route 106. Enter the Classic City from the north on Route 106. Dominated by the University of Georgia's ever-expanding campus, Athens (population 101,489) is the largest city in the northeast Piedmont area, situated at an elevation of 800 feet. The university was chartered in 1785 and opened in 1801, five years before the city was incorporated. Nicknamed the Classic City after its Grecian predecessor, Athens is known for its impressive collection of columned mansions. It boasts a couple of firsts, one being that it was the home of the first garden club in the country; in fact, there are dozens of gardens and clubs in this leafy green city. The University of Georgia was the first state-chartered university in the country. Today, its name is more associated with top rock bands such as R.E.M. and the B-52's—both of whom got their start with "Bulldog" audiences.

sights

AUTHOR FAVORITE
Some of my favorite museums focus on just one person, and the **Crawford W. Long Museum** is a prime example. Dr. Long was the first physician to use ether for surgical anesthesia, as the exhibits here explain in fascinating detail. Born in Danielsville in 1815, Long graduated from the University of Pennsylvania Medical School and had just begun his practice in this town when he figured out how to make surgery pain-free. Perhaps there should be an adjacent museum honoring James Venable, the first patient to undergo surgery with anesthesia (in 1842, to remove a neck cyst). Personal items, supporting documents, a detailed diorama showing the first operation and other exhibits make this a fascinating stop for people who take modern medicine for granted. Closed Sunday and Monday. Admission. ~ 28 College Street, Jefferson; 706-367-5307; www.crawfordlong.org.

For an overview of what to do and see in Athens (and how to get there), stop by the **Athens Welcome Center**, which is housed in the **Church-Waddel-Brumby House**. Built around 1820, this Federal-style structure was home to University of Georgia president Moses Waddel and is now also a museum with period furnishings and decorative arts. Along with free maps and brochures and helpful directions, the center also offers a bookshop with many titles of regional interest. City tours ($15) depart at 2 p.m. ~ 280 East Dougherty Street, Athens; 706-353-1820, fax 706-353-1770; www.visitathensga.com.

Armed with information, head down Dougherty Street (which becomes Prince Street) a couple of blocks to see an intriguing building. If you think, "Seen one fire station, seen 'em all," you haven't seen **Fire Station Number Two** in downtown Athens. It's a two-story brick Victorian number, built in a triangular shape. This is where the **Athens-Clarke Heritage Foundation** is headquartered along with an art gallery. ~ 489 Prince Avenue, Athens; 706-353-1801.

Nearby is one of the Classic City's quirkier sights, the **Tree That Owns Itself**. Yep, it's legal. In the late 1800s, one professor W. H. Jackson so enjoyed the shade of this tree that he deeded to it the surrounding plot of land, 16 feet in diameter. ~ Corner of Dearing and Finley streets, Athens.

A few blocks down the street, the **Taylor-Grady House** is a Greek Revival mansion built in 1844. Henry W. Grady, who went on to become a legendary editor at the *Atlanta Journal-Constitution*, lived here while attending journalism school at the university in the late 1860s. Today, the Junior League operates it as a house museum, furnished with period pieces and claiming status as a National Historic Landmark due to Grady's residency. Closed Saturday and Sunday. Guided tours available by reservation through the Athens Welcome Center. Admission. ~ 634 Prince Avenue, Athens; 706-549-8688; www.achfonline.com.

The **Upson House** (1847) is a stately Greek Revival mansion whose brick walls have been stuccoed to make them look like smooth stone. Now on the National Register of Historic Places, the house features silver doorknobs and covered keyholes, herringbone parquet floors or quarter-sawed oak bordered with inlaid mahogany and rosewood, solid mahogany doors and stairways, and foot-and-a-half-thick brick walls. Closed Saturday and Sunday. ~ 1022 Prince Avenue, Athens; 706-354-5380.

The **U.S. Navy Supply Corps School and Museum** displays ship models, uniforms, equipment, photographs and other items of historical interest. One of only 11 official U.S. Navy museums, it is housed in a 1910 Carnegie Library on the National Register of Historic Places. Its archives are available for research by appointment only. Closed Saturday and Sunday. ~ 1425 Prince Avenue, Athens; 706-354-7349.

In front of City Hall, the **Double Barreled Cannon** dates from 1863, manufactured in time to defend the city from Sherman's army. Sadly, the cannon failed to fire two balls simultaneously when it really counted. However, one shot did fell a cow in a nearby field. ~ City Hall, College and Hancock streets, Athens.

After you have admired the cannon, head east on Hancock Street to Hull Street and go left for a block and a half to see an important piece of the city's African-American heritage.

The **Morton Theatre,** a modest four-story structure in the heart of town, is one of Athens' nifty success stories. Whereas most Georgia theaters for African Americans were not black-owned, Monroe Bowers "Pink" Morton organized and raised a building that from the very beginning was part of the black community. In its heyday, the theater hosted entertainers as varied as classical pianists, vaudeville acts, revues and singers like Bessie Smith and Cab Calloway. When it started showing movies, the big-name acts faded away. After a period of neglect, the building, now on the National Register of Historic Places, was restored and is once again the site of live performances. Free tours available with reservations. Office closed Saturday and Sunday. (See "Athens' African-American Heritage" for more information.) ~ 195 West Washington Street, Athens; 706-613-3770, fax 706-613-3772; www.mortontheatre.com.

Nearby is the **First African Methodist Episcopal Church,** built in 1916 in the Romanesque Revival style. It was organized in 1866 by Reverend Henry McNeal Turner, the first black chaplain in the U.S. Army. (See "Athens' African-American Heritage" for more information.) ~ 521 North Hull Street, Athens; 706-548-3878.

Headquartered in the middle of the city, the **University of Georgia** seems to emanate from the campus. The Arch, considered the gateway to the main campus, is downtown on Broad Street near Herty Drive. You can pick up a map of UGA at the Athens Welcome Center or on campus if you would like to explore it in detail. Two of UGA's major attractions can be found on the east campus. The location of the **University of Georgia Visitors Center,** on the edge of UGA's east campus, tells a story in itself. It's housed in a spruced-up dairy barn; that's how fast the university is expanding into the rural countryside. Here guests can get information about not only the school but the city as well. There are also exhibits on campus life, distinguished alumni and university history. ~ Four Towers Building, College Station Road, Athens; 706-542-0842.

Many delights abound on university grounds, but none more wonderful than the **Georgia Museum of Art.** In addition to some

20 exhibits a year, the museum owns more than 7000 pieces of art that, of course, cannot all be displayed at once. This institution got its start in 1945 with Alfred H. Holbrook's donation of 100 American paintings, an area in which the collection continues to be strong. Over the years, the holdings have expanded to include Italian Renaissance works as well as prints and drawings by European and Asian artists. All these are housed in a contemporary structure with all the benefits of state-of-the-art lighting and outstanding docent tours. Available by reservation only. ~ 90 Carlton Street, East Campus Triangle, Athens; 706-542-4662, fax 706-542-1051; www.uga.edu/gamuseum.

After leaving the east campus, head south on South Milledge Avenue and continue past the Athens perimeter road (Loop 10) for a walk in the woods. Don't pick the daisies—or the azaleas, roses, dahlias, rhododendrons or other flowering plants—at the **State Botanical Garden of Georgia**, though you will certainly be

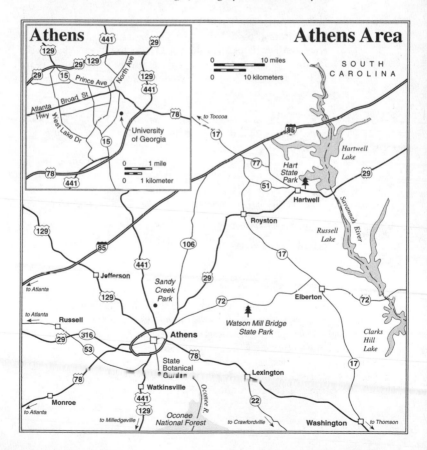

tempted in this 313-acre horticultural wonderland. Part of the university system, it's also the official State Theme Garden. You'll see ornamental, beneficial plants, vines and more; inside the atrium is a rainforest with bromeliads and orchids almost constantly in bloom. Of several outdoor plantings beside brick-lined walkways (such as Shade Tolerant, Annual/Perennial and Native Flora), one of the most intriguing is the garden of plants from which medicines have been developed, such as belladonna, digitalis and codeine, an ideal garden for what the tour guide jokingly called "root diggers and wandering quacks." ~ 2450 South Milledge Avenue, Athens; 706-524-1244; www.uga.edu/botgarden.

After admiring the plantings, head over to Route 129/441, which leads in the direction of Watkinsville and Macon. The **Antebellum Trail** that starts in Athens and leads to Macon runs through **Watkinsville**, a village just south of the Classic City. For its size, it must have more artists per capita than anywhere this side of the Seine. Your first stop in town should be the oldest stage stop in these parts. **The Eagle Tavern** doubles as the **Oconee County Visitor Bureau & Welcome Center.** It was a stage stop and tavern in the late 1700s and is furnished in period style. Sadly, the bar is closed, but you can get your fill of tourist information. ~ 3rd and Main streets, Route 441, Watkinsville; 706-769-5197; www.visitoconee.com.

LODGING

HIDDEN ►

With a tad less architectural ornamentation, **The Skelton House** could have belonged to Ozzie and Harriet. This crisp white clapboard house was built in the late 1800s by Hartwell attorney Jim Skelton and his wife, Jessie. The huge front porch and a smaller matching second-floor gallery still look like grandma's going to come out in her apron at any second. When you walk in the front door, freshly baked cookies and breads send an aromatic greet-

AUTHOR FAVORITE

Everyone's idea of romance is a little different, but for me, the gorgeous setting and offbeat rooms at **Ashford Manor** fill the bill. Within walking distance of "downtown" Watkinsville yet close to Athens dining and nightlife, this 1893 Victorian mansion opened as a B&B in 1997. Its six guest rooms on two floors are memorable and imaginatively decorated; all have private baths and private phone lines. The five acres of landscaped grounds are so beautiful they are popular for receptions and other social gatherings. The inn accepts pets for an additional charge. Full breakfast is included. ~ 5 Harden Hill Road, Watkinsville; 706-769-2633; www.ambedandbreakfast.com. DELUXE.

ing. It's not at all surprising to find that the room with a four-poster bed and deep-green walls displaying family photos is called "Mama and Papa." The other rooms are named after various family members: "Wilma," for instance, is English garden style with Battenburg lace curtains; "Carey" has the tailored touches that would befit the young man who grew up to be a judge. And so it goes with the other four accommodations, all in good taste and great condition (unlike some family homes we could name) and with private baths. A full breakfast is included. ~ 97 Benson Street, Hartwell; 706-376-7969, 877-556-3790, fax 706-856-3139; www.theskeltonhouse.com, e-mail skeltonhouse@hart com.net. MODERATE TO DELUXE.

Two woodsy A-plus cabins are available for rent at **Hart State Park**. With two bedrooms sporting four double beds, central heat, air conditioning and fully equipped kitchens, these share a boat dock. Both are lakeside, with screened porches to appreciate the view. There's a $2 parking fee for access to the park and some advance reservations require a two-night minimum. ~ 330 Hart State Park Road, Hartwell; 706-376-8756, 800-864-7275. BUDGET TO MODERATE.

◄ HIDDEN

The Nicholson House Inn is not far from the highway, but it feels like it's far out in the country and a little bit out of time. The property was a land grant back in 1779 and became known as Gum Springs, thanks to a hollow gum tree that was used to cap off a spring on the property and make it work like a fountain. Exquisitely decorated, the seven guest rooms in this Colonial Revival–style structure are furnished with American period antiques. Additional accommodations are in the nearby carriage house. Cotton farmers en route to Athens used to camp out here. Today the property consists of six wooded acres and is the ideal place to get away from it all without driving miles and miles from town. If you rock on the veranda long enough, you'll inevitably spot a deer grazing in the grassy field. ~ 6295 Jefferson Road, Athens; 706-353-2200, fax 706-353-7799; www.nichol sonhouseinn.com, e-mail chneely@aol.com. DELUXE TO ULTRA-DELUXE.

◄ HIDDEN

Soaring ceilings in all guest rooms add extra graciousness to the **Magnolia Terrace Guest House**. Fireplace mantles, hardwood floors, simple antiques and cool Martha Stewart–type colors like pale green and light blue add up to a pleasing blend of historic and contemporary accents. There are also myriad details many guests will be tempted to re-create at home, such as the tables covered in starchy linens and then topped with rounds of glass cut to fit perfectly. Each of the eight rooms (four downstairs, four on the second floor) is named after a notable historical figure, such as the Hiram Room, named for the first black female den-

Text continued on page 324.

Athens' African-American Heritage

All of Georgia's major cities can boast at least something in the way of African-American culture, but there are also several points of interest in and around Athens.

Chief among them is the **Morton Theatre**. Macon has its Douglass Theater and Savannah the Star Theater, but what made the Morton stand out from the beginning is that it alone was conceived and owned by an African American. Monroe "Pink" Morton knew that to be truly successful, the theater he started would have to be more than an entertainment venue, so he made it into a center for business, social and cultural activities. Here, on what is now a modest but highly visible downtown corner, he counted among his tenants a dentist's office, a pharmacy, a bakery and a medical clinic. Politicians of the early 20th century knew that they would have to get to know the people here if they had any hope of capturing the local black voting power. The theater opened in May 1910 with a concert by classical pianist Alice Carter Simmons of the Oberlin Ohio Conservatory, who was followed by vaudeville acts, Bessie Smith, Louis Armstrong, Cab Calloway and other entertainers, including revues from New York's Cotton Club. Eventually it was transformed into a movie theater; later, groups like the B-52's and R.E.M. conducted rehearsals and filmed videos here. But the building was neglected, and the 1000-seat Morton was saved only through a joint arrangement between municipal government and the nonprofit Morton Theatre Corporation. Now on the National Register of Historic Places, it functions as a community performing-arts space. ~ 195 West Washington Street; 706-613-3770.

Another downtown site on the tour is the **First African Methodist Episcopal Church**, organized in 1866 (the year after the Civil War ended) by Reverend Henry McNeal Turner, the first black chaplain in the U.S. Army. A short time later, Turner was one of the 33 African Americans who served in the Georgia General Assembly between 1868 and 1870. He and the others were expelled "because of their color," after which Turner moved to Savannah and headed the St. Phillip Monumental AME Church there. The red-brick Romanesque Revival–style church standing today was built in 1916. ~ 521 North Hull Street; 706-548-3878.

Numerous prominent African-American Athenians have lived in the **West Hancock Historic District**. Originally established just west of the city, this residential neighborhood—also home to several churches and businesses—was annexed and is now on the National Register of Historic Places. The first African-American female dentist in the state, Ida Mae Hiram lived on Hancock Avenue. She practiced in Athens for 55 years; her office, by the way, was located in the Morton Theatre building. ~ Bounded by West Hancock and Glenhaven avenues and Reese, Billups, Indale and Spring streets.

A short drive west of Athens, the **Chestnut Grove Baptist Church** was built in 1885. In 1896, the congregation added a one-room schoolhouse that functioned as the focal point of the community's educational and social life, a critical service in the confusing years following emancipation. One of the few remaining one-room schoolhouses in the state, it and the church (which was rebuilt in 1970) are located about 15 minutes from downtown Athens. To reach the church, head out Broad Street from downtown Athens and follow Route 316 west for about ten minutes to the intersection of Timothy and Epps Bridge roads. Sunday morning services are held at 8 a.m. and 11 a.m. ~ 610 Epps Bridge Road.

A couple of sites important to many African-American Athenians are literally nourishing places. **Weaver D's Fine Foods** gained some fame back when the Athens-born rock group R.E.M. adopted the restaurant's motto, "Automatic! Automatic for the People," as the title of one of its best-selling albums. ~ 1016 Broad Street; 706-353-7797.

In the same neighborhood as the Morton Theatre, **Wilson's Soul Food** has dished out pork chops the size of a dinner plate—among other things—for countless diners looking for a home cooked meal. See "Dining" for more information. ~ 351 North Hull Street; 706-353-7289.

tist registered in Georgia; all have private bath. Built in 1912 by cotton broker James M. Rogers, this Colonial Revival house was home to the Chi Psi fraternity for some 20 years; from the late 1940s to the late '70s, it was a restaurant. It was remodeled and modernized in 1994 by new owners. Full breakfast is included on weekends. ~ 277 Hill Street, Athens; 706-548-3860, fax 706-369-3469; www.bbonline.com/ga/magnoliaterrace. DELUXE TO ULTRA-DELUXE.

DINING

HIDDEN ►

Once I saw the menu (and the wine list) at **Vickery Parke**, I understood why people routinely drive from as far away as Atlanta to dine here. The historic Horton-Vickery House (circa 1875), one of the oldest dwellings in town, is not a fancy Victorian but a spare, attractive bungalow with pastel walls and a friendly staff that takes advantage of local ingredients to keep things fresh. Wild-mushroom tart, crab-stuffed shrimp and a mixed grill of venison, beef tenderloin and Hartwell emu show the kitchen at its best. Closed Sunday and Monday. ~ 21 Vickery Street, Hartwell; phone/fax 706-376-2006. MODERATE TO ULTRA-DELUXE.

Fletcher's is the place to go for big, hearty dinners in Hartwell. Salmon filet, fried shrimp, brook trout, Delmonica steaks and prime rib, along with baby back ribs and pastas, are served in a big room with lots of greenery and windows. ~ 329 East Franklin Street, Hartwell; 706-376-7070. BUDGET TO MODERATE.

The **East-West Bistro** is an odd duck, essentially two restaurants in one. The less formal and "east"-ern part of the place is on the ground floor, a spacious room with a lively bar scene and a relatively inexpensive, rather eclectic menu (*panang* curry, tempura, fried eggplant, salmon in rice paper). Booths float in the middle of a long, high-ceilinged room. The vibe upstairs at **Uptown** is more sedate as befits a pricier menu, with white linen tablecloths and formally dressed arched windows through which diners have a lovely treetop view. The food is a mix of Italian and Southern. Grilled yellowfin tuna with pesto, chicken saltimbocca and pasta dishes can be accompanied by selections from an acclaimed wine list. ~ 351 East Broad Street, Athens; 706-546-9378, fax 706-546-9935. MODERATE TO ULTRA-DELUXE.

Harry Bissett's New Orleans Café is a legend in these parts. It's about the only place for Cajun and Creole cuisine—including lots of oysters—but you can also get steak, veal and fish. It looks a little like a Louisiana bar and it jumps at night. If you prefer dining in relative quiet, try the weekend brunch. ~ 279 East Broad Street, Athens; 706-353-7065, fax 706-549-7802. MODERATE TO DELUXE.

Just thinking about **The Grit** probably transports many a UGA alumnus back to Athens. It's not gritty, and grits aren't even a big part of the menu at this vegetarian standby cuddled on the corner of a triangular block not far from campus. The food is good, healthful and even a bit fun, served in a diner atmosphere. Though Michael Stipe of R.E.M. owns the building, don't expect to see him at the next table. ~ 199 Prince Avenue, Athens; 706-543-6592. BUDGET TO MODERATE.

Mia Madonna is a European-style bistro in a historic Cotton Exchange building. A blend of French and Italian cuisines, the menu features a mixed grill (lamb chop, house-made sausage and ribs), steak *frites* (sliced steak on a bed of homemade fries), salmon sautéed with lemon and thyme and served with thumb-print potatoes, and sautéed grouper crusted in finely grated potatoes. ~ 269 North Hull Street, Athens; 706-548-1804. MODERATE.

It's wall-to-wall Italy at **Bischero Specialita' Italiane,** from the china to the chairs to the flatware, all imported from the mother country. Housed in a recently renovated Coca-Cola bottling plant, this is the best place in town for classic dishes such as tenderloin in *porcini* mushroom sauce, a Livornese-style seafood stew, and grilled New York strip with aged balsamic vinegar and arugula. The rustic dining room has a brick-towered wood-burning oven that turns out roast chicken and authentic Neapolitan pizza. Naturally, there's an all-Italian wine list, and for dessert, expect traditional fare such as *panna cotta* and *tiramisu.* ~ 237 Prince Avenue, Athens; 706-316-1006. DELUXE.

A restaurant that lives up to its billing, **Wilson's Soul Food** is conveniently located near the university. Students can get an approximation of home cooking via a menu that changes a little every day but generally includes meatloaf, barbecued pork chops and fried chicken; collard greens and lima beans are among the many vegetables. Some things are so good they're made daily, like macaroni and cheese, homemade pies, cakes and cobblers, and sweet potato custard. You can eat at one of about 20 tables or order take-out. No dinner. Closed Sunday. ~ 351 North Hull Street, Athens; 706-353-7289. BUDGET.

AUTHOR FAVORITE

Five and Ten is head and shoulders above the rest of the Athens dining scene and in fact could be a success even if transplanted to sophisticated Atlanta. Don't judge it by its concrete floors and blackboard specials. Let your palate make the call: cinnamon-braised lamb shank and fried catfish spiced with fenugreek and fennel are typical fare from owner/chef Hugh Acheson, who's claimed his own fan club since being declared "Best New Chef" by *Food & Wine Magazine.* Five and Ten serves high tea on Saturday afternoons and brunch on Sundays. ~ 1653 South Lumpkin Street, Athens; 706-546-7300. DELUXE TO ULTRA-DELUXE.

The clientele is as eclectic as the menu at **The Last Resort Grill**. Crab cakes, shrimp quesadillas, *adobo* salmon and chicken enchiladas are among the choices; you can get shrimp and grits at brunch. The wine list is extensive and there is patio seating year-round at the place locals call simply "The Grill." ~ 184 West Clayton Street, Athens; 706-549-0810. MODERATE TO DELUXE.

SHOPPING   Furniture, fine art and home accessories are the kinds of "essential comforts" carried at **The Wooden Shoe** on the square in downtown Hartwell. ~ 24 North Forest Avenue, Hartwell; 706-376-6006.

American crafts, locally crafted pottery, jewelry, stuffed animals, children's books and toiletries make up most of the merchandise at **Homeplace**. ~ 1676 South Lumpkin Street, Athens; 706-549-0829.

The **Junkman's Daughter's Brother**—who may or may not really be related to the quirky Junkman's Daughter in Atlanta—sells clothing and gifts. ~ 458 East Clayton Street, Athens; 706-543-4454.

For leather clothing and other goods, the place to go is **Masada Leather**. From belts (hand-dyed, waxed, polished, with a variety of solid brass buckles) to footwear (Birkenstock and NAOTs, among others) to bags, wallets and more, this store stocks an unusual assortment. ~ 238 East Clayton Street, Athens; 706-546-5014.

The **Beechwood Shopping Center** harbors a number of stores including **Rolling Pin** (706-354-8080), a gourmet kitchen shop. ~ Corner of Alps and Baxter streets, Athens.

For model enthusiasts, the **Athens Hobby Center** is a mecca. ~ 10 Huntington Road, Athens; 706-549-1413.

Watkinsville has more shops per inch than anyplace south of 5th Avenue. At least it seems that way. **Ruggiere**, a gallery, showcases fine regional art by well-known names as well as antiques and accessories for the home. ~ 12 South Main Street, Watkinsville; 706-769-7247.

DIM BULBS, BRIGHT STARS

The **40 Watt Club**, famous to rock fans as the old haunt of R.E.M. who got their start here (and at other local clubs) as well as the B-52's, may still be the place to see the megastars of the millennium. Although it's best known for rock, it also books some R&B acts. Closed Sunday. Cover. ~ 285 West Washington Street, Athens; 706-549-7871; www.40watt.com.

About Nostalgia carries a hodgepodge of collectibles, odd antiques and other quirky items. They are also willing to track down something for you. ~ 8 North Main Street, Watkinsville; 706-769-1215.

A good shop for browsing or gift-buying is **Details**, which has furniture and smaller items, such as lamps and oil paintings. ~ 2411 Hog Mountain Road, Watkinsville; 706-769-8464.

Given the number of musicians who've made it big after starting in Athens—R.E.M., the B-52's and Widespread Panic come to mind—this is a good town for seeing tomorrow's headliners tonight, while there's only a modest cover charge. **NIGHTLIFE**

The **Classic Center** is the venue of choice for touring Broadway shows, classical concerts, and country, blues and gospel performances as well as community events. There's also a brief children's season in March and April. ~ 300 North Thomas Street, Athens; 706-357-4444; www.classiccenter.com.

Cheap movies and regional band performances draw crowds to the **Georgia Theater**. Built it 1889, the theater was renovated in 1935, which has left it with an art-deco facade. ~ 215 North Lumpkin Street, Athens; 706-549-9918.

Occasional touring groups and local bands of all stripes play the former African-American vaudeville venue, the **Morton Theatre**. ~ 195 West Washington Street, Athens; 706-613-3770.

HART STATE PARK 🚲 ⛵ ⛱ 🚤 🛥 This secluded yet popular park is mostly water (or so it seems), with 56,000-acre Hartwell Lake as its centerpiece and reason for existence. Largemouth bass, striped bass, catfish, black crappie, bluegill, bream, walleye pike and other fish populate the lake. The 147 acres of parkland, hosting rolling hillsides lightly forested with hardwoods and pine, was built by the Corps of Engineers and opened in 1968 about one and a half miles north of the Hartwell city limits. With cabins (see "Lodging" above) and campsites, Hart makes a good place to hole up for a while. There's a sandy beach, picnic area and bathhouse, all of which are free. The lake's playgrounds are in a shaded area in the day-use section; there are also volleyball and horseshoe pit areas. Day-use fee, $2. ~ 330 Hart State Park Road, Hartwell; 706-376-8756. **PARKS**

▲ There are 78 tent/RV sites, $15 to $17 per night; and 16 walk-in sites, $11 to $13 per night. Reservations: 800-864-7275.

MEMORIAL PARK With 72 acres of rolling hills, this popular park has a lake, picnic shelters, walking trails, playground area and a small zoo. ~ 293 Gran Ellen Drive, Athens; 706-613-3580.

SANDY CREEK PARK 🏃 ⛱ 🚤 🛥 With 760 acres to play in, this park on the north side of town offers a great deal for your nominal recreation dollar. Within it is the 260-acre Chapman Lake; you can rent boats at the boat house and go fishing for bass, catfish, bream and crappie. There are even tournaments in the spring. The lake is open for swimming (allowed in the roped-in area only) from Memorial Day weekend to Labor Day weekend. There are also a couple of tennis courts, a basketball court, all kinds of ball fields and several large pavilions as well as less formal picnic sites. The trails within the park aren't named except for one that leads all the way to a nature center just over four miles away. A three-mile trail runs beside the lake but can't go around it completely because of a swampy area. Very unusual, too, are the conveniences for dogs: Fido will find three private dog runs ($1 an hour) as well as a free group play area. There are several camping options, including primitive sites, tent shelters (with roof and decks) and "crow's nests." The last are accessible by a ladder, have a double deck and a roof and are, understandably, very popular with Boy Scouts. Nearby are a grill, picnic tables and a fire pit. There are no concessions within the park, so come prepared. Entrance fee, $20. ~ 400 Bob Holman Road (off Route 441, about three miles north of The Loop), Athens; 706-613-3631.

▲ There are 23 primitive sites, $10 per night; 8 tent shelters, $10 per night; and 2 crow's nests, $50 per night.

BISHOP PARK 🚲 This popular community park has 11 tennis courts (all of them lit and two covered), a basketball court, a pool, a softball diamond and a playground. There's a .7-mile blacktop road through the park on which you can walk or ride a bike. ~ 705 Sunset Drive, Athens; 706-613-3589.

Washington to Statesboro

Following the Civil War, about $1.5 million in gold—the remainder of the Confederate treasury—was moved from Richmond, Virginia, in boxes and chests to towns throughout the South in an attempt to elude seizure by the Union army. The last known town to hide the fortune was Washington; some of the gold was captured with Jefferson Davis in Irwinville but since $100,000 was known to be stored in a Washington bank, the legend persists that the rest of the gold is buried somewhere in the county. Which explains why you may see fortune hunters digging in the vicinity of the old stagecoach road. Most of the towns between here and Statesboro are small, but historic Louisville, briefly a capital, is a nice place to stroll around. Statesboro is not really a tourist town; the most interesting attractions are on the campus of Georgia Southern University.

SIGHTS   Most of the things to see in the precious town of Washington are within walking distance of the main square. Unlike many small towns, this one has been spared the onslaught of fast-food rows, light industry and other forms of urban blight, except for the outskirts. Washington has become well-known in the last couple of decades for its well-preserved downtown, leading to crowding on pretty spring and fall weekends.

A block away from the square, the **Washington-Wilkes Chamber of Commerce** is the place to make your first call in this intense town. You can find out about walking tours, historical sights and other points of interest. In any event, pick up a copy of the *Visitors Guide*, which will explain in brief detail some of the his-

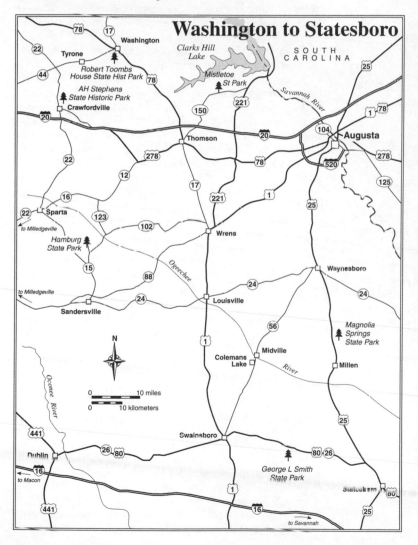

Washington to Statesboro

toric houses. Though most of the 83 sites on the list are not open to the public, they are so intriguing that it's nice to have a reference in hand to tell you more about a structure that strikes your fancy. The chamber is housed in the Greek Revival **Zirbes-Ledbetter House** that dates to about 1905. ~ 104 East Liberty Street, Washington; 706-678-2013; www.washingtonwilkes.com.

At the corner of Liberty and Jefferson streets, less than a block from the Chamber of Commerce, is the **Mary Willis Library**. Established in 1888, it was the first free public library in Georgia and is the oldest one still used as a library. Note the Tiffany windows. Closed Sunday. ~ 204 East Liberty Street, Washington; 706-678-7736.

From the library, head toward Courthouse Square on Jefferson Street and turn right onto Robert Toombs Avenue.

In a couple of blocks you will come to the **Robert Toombs House State Historic Site**. Toombs was born in this county in 1810, the son of Revolutionary War soldier Major James Toombs. A man who definitely marched to his own drum, he rebelled against the discipline imposed at the University of Georgia to the point that he was not allowed to graduate. After a legal career in Washington and election to service in the Georgia legislature, he served in both the U.S. House of Representatives and the Senate before being appointed Secretary of State for the Confederacy, thanks no doubt to his strong opinions about secession. After distinguishing himself for bravery at the Battle of Antietam, Toombs rebelled again, refusing to swear allegiance to the Union after the war. Exiled from his home in Washington, he continued his life as an outspoken statesman, albeit an unelected one, and after his death in 1885 his home remained in the family for another century. It is now owned by the state. Here you will find furnishings and other items that belonged to the Toombses, though most of the furniture is not original. Don't miss the riveting film portraying an elderly Toombs being interviewed by a young reporter. Closed Monday. Admission. ~ 216 East Robert Toombs Avenue, Washington; 706-678-2226, fax 706-678-7515.

The first vacation Bible school in Georgia was offered at the First Baptist Church in Washington.

When you leave the Toombs museum, continue to the corner and turn right on Grove Street. The **Washington Historical Museum** will be on your right. Dating to approximately 1835, the museum houses such Confederate relics as Jefferson Davis' camp chest. A gift from British sympathizers, it was used by him up until the very last cabinet meeting. There's something very moving about seeing such a personal item that helps bring the period to life. Closed Monday. Admission. ~ 308 East Robert Toombs Avenue, Washington; 706-678-2105.

Near the town square is the **First Baptist Church**. Organized in 1827, the church is known for its stained-glass windows. Nancy

Mercer, daughter of first pastor Jesse Mercer, is buried here in the basement. It's easy to see the church on weekdays; you have a choice of four services on Sunday. ~ 105 West Robert Toombs Avenue, Washington; 706-678-2912.

If you continue west on Robert Toombs Avenue, the street becomes Route 78/Lexington Avenue as it approaches **Callaway Plantation**. The site comprises five historic buildings, including an 18th-century hewn long house, a smokehouse and, most interesting, two stately homes. One is a 1790s Federal Plains–style structure furnished in period style. The other is an 1869 red-brick Greek Revival house. Together, they illustrate the upwardly mobile lifestyle of families from the pioneer days to the turn of the 20th century. To add to the time warp, the surrounding fields are planted with crops that would have been raised here in the 19th century. Closed Monday. Admission. ~ Route 78, five miles west of Washington; 706-678-7060.

◄ HIDDEN

When you leave the plantation, head west for Route 44, driving southwest to Tyrone, where you will turn south onto Route 22, which leads to Crawfordville. En route you will come to the signs for the 1161-acre **A. H. Stephens State Historic Park**. Here you can tour **Liberty Hall**, once the home of U.S. congressman Alexander Stephens, whose love for the Union did not keep him from accepting the vice presidency of the Confederacy. Later he served as the governor of Georgia. He is buried here in a grave marked by a monument in front of the 1830s house. Inside, a museum illustrates his life through both military and civilian artifacts. Closed Monday. Admission. ~ Two miles north of Route 20 via Route 22 exit, Crawfordville; 706-456-2602 (park), 706-456-2221 (museum).

With its old homes and wide main street where little has changed in decades, **Crawfordville** not only looks like a movie set—it has been one. This is where *Paris Trout* and *Home Fires Burning* were filmed and, more recently, *Sweet Home Alabama* with Reese Witherspoon.

From Crawfordville, take Route 20 east about 20 miles to Thomson and then turn north onto Route 78. In about five miles you will come to the turnoff that leads to the remains of **Wrightsboro**. Settled in 1768 by Quakers, this was the last of the planned Colonial towns. The 1810 Wrightsboro Church is still here, as is, of course, the pine-shaded cemetery where historical markers tell the story. (For more details, contact the Thomson-McDuffie Tourism Bureau at the address below.) ~ Wrightsboro Road, Wrightsboro.

◄ HIDDEN

When you leave the cemetery, return south and cross Route 20, heading for the town of **Thomson**. The old **Thomson Depot**, built in 1860, now houses the Chamber of Commerce and the **Thomson-McDuffie Tourism Bureau**. The helpful staff will give you directions to Wrightsboro if you need them. Closed Saturday and Sunday. ~ 111 Railroad Street, Thomson; 706-597-1000; www.thomson-mcduffie.org.

Leave Thomson and head south on Route 17 to Route 221; a pretty drive leads to the quirky town of **Louisville**. The town was the state capital from 1795 to 1805, Georgia's first permanent capital. But Louisville is the only town in the world, someone said, that can strut standing still. These are the folks who didn't even wince when a comparison of the census of 1820 with that of 1920 showed that the city had gained but a single citizen in all that time, swelling the rolls to 1039. It's an interesting place to wander around, considering it was an early example of a pre-fab town, laid out with streets and buildings—including a governor's mansion and a state capitol—before anyone moved in. Named for Louis XVI of France, it follows a grid pattern, with the east–west streets numbered and the north–south ones named for trees.

Stop in at the **Jefferson County Chamber of Commerce** downtown to inquire about tours of this Cotton Belt town. Closed Saturday and Sunday. ~ 302 East Broad Street, Louisville; 478-625-8134; www.jeffersoncounty.org.

About a block away, the **Old Market House** dates to the mid-1790s, predating even the city's layout. In this great oak timber structure, slaves were once traded. A bell cast in France in 1772 hangs in the tower; it was intended for a New Orleans convent until pirates off the coast near Savannah sacked the French ship carrying it. The bell wound up here in the capital, where it was rung to celebrate the independence of the original 13 colonies. It is rarely rung today. ~ Broad and Mulberry streets, Louisville; 478-625-3166.

After moseying around Louisville, take Route 1 south to Swainsboro, proceeding east on Route 26 and then Route 80 into **Statesboro**. This drive should take roughly an hour. Continue through town on the same highway (known as Main Street in town) to the campus of **Georgia Southern University** on the southwest edge of the city.

The university was founded in 1906, at a time when Statesboro was flourishing as a cotton-shipping center (shipping one-eighth of the world's supply of cotton). Today some 14,000 students seek traditional four-year and graduate degrees at this 634-acre campus of pine trees and gently rolling hills.

On campus is GSU **Museum**, known for its collection of fossilized sea creatures, including a 26-foot monosaur, and two large aquariums depicting sea life on what are now the coastal plains. As is the case with so many museums, this one has a quirky side attraction: a two-pound fragment of a meteorite that fell on a nearby town. ~ Rosenwald Building on Southern Drive, a half mile south of Route 301/25, Statesboro; 912-681-5444.

Tucked into a wooded area of the campus is the **Lamar Q.** ◀ *HIDDEN*
Ball, Jr. Raptor Center. Visitors can get fairly close to eagles, ospreys, owls, vultures and falcons, close enough to see the curved
talons and sharp curved beaks that help the birds capture and kill
their prey—usually rodents but sometimes larger mammals and
even medium-to-large birds—before tearing the carcass into yummy
bite-sized pieces. Wooden walkways lead around to the different
habitats. There are regularly scheduled reptile shows and bird
shows featuring trained falcons. Closed Sunday from June
though August. Admission. ~ Georgia Southern University,
Statesboro; 912-681-0831.

When you have visited with the eagles, continue south on
Route 301/25 a mile or so to Veteran's Memorial Parkway; turn
left and head for the intersection with Route 67; turn left again
and continue to Georgia Avenue, turn onto Bland Avenue and
you are almost at the **Georgia Southern Botanical Garden.** It was ◀ *HIDDEN*
amateur naturalist Dan Bland who envisioned a garden of plants
native to the Georgia coastal plain, including ornamental favorites such as magnolias, bayberries and azaleas now embedded
in Southern tradition. These are among the delights at this botanical wonderland, which also features a Butterfly Border of plants
that attract the lovely winged insects, a children's vegetable garden, an arboretum, barns and other farm buildings. Closed Sunday morning and Saturday. ~ 1505 Bland Avenue, Statesboro;
912-871-1149.

For maps and brochures about the area, stop by the **Statesboro Convention & Visitors Bureau.** Closed Saturday and
Sunday. ~ 332 South Main Street, Statesboro; 912-489-1869,
800-568-3301, fax 912-489-2688; www.visit-statesboro.com.

You might wonder why the **Laurel & Hardy Museum** is located in tiny little Harlem. Oliver Hardy was born here in 1892.
One of only two museums in the United States dedicated to one
of the all-time greatest movie comedy teams—Stan Laurel and
Oliver Hardy—it is filled with memorabilia from all over the
world including toys, figurines, posters and a lot more. Movies

◆◆◆

MORE THAN GOLF

Although it's host to the Masters Tournament, golf isn't the only game in
Augusta. The annual Cutting Horse Futurity and Festival is the largest
equestrian event of its kind east of the Mississippi, with popular competitions and a Western-style festival to boot. The river attracts three major
water-sports events every year: River Race Augusta, the Augusta Invi-
tational Rowing Regatta and the Augusta Southern Nationals (which
features drag-boat races—too Southern for words).

are shown daily here in Babe's Bijou. ~ 250 North Louisville Street, Harlem; 706-556-0401, 888-288-9108; www.laureland hardymuseum.org.

LODGING

HIDDEN ►

Washington has a number of inns in old homes featuring Federal, Greek-Revival and other architectural styles. One place in particular, **The Cottage at Poplar Corner,** offers an exceptional level of privacy. This remodeled mid-19th-century cottage behind an antebellum manor has a living room with a queen-size sofa bed, a separate bedroom and a small kitchen. The unit is decorated in a blend of family pieces and American antiques. Guests are treated to breakfast and, in warm weather, access to the swimming pool. ~ 210 West Liberty Street, Washington; 706-678-2453. MODERATE TO DELUXE.

HIDDEN ►

The **1810 Country Inn and Winery** is centered around the main house, a classic example of Piedmont Plains architecture. The 13-acre property, which includes a heated pool and hot tub, has been restored to show off a house built entirely of Georgia heart pine, the finest part of the wood known for its resistance to bad weather. Seeming acres of the wood and detailed moldings surprisingly ornate for an early 1800s Georgia plantation structure distinguish the rooms. A total of eight rooms and three suites are divided among this and three outbuildings, furnished largely with antiques and Civil War memorabilia. Full breakfast is included. ~ 254 North Seymour Drive, Thomson; 706-595-3156, fax 706-595-3155; www.1810westinn.com. MODERATE TO ULTRA-DELUXE.

HIDDEN ►

Old Town Plantation and Retreat is the perfect name for a property that sits in the middle of nowhere. Actually, it's closer to Wadley and Midville than it is to Louisville, all part of a 4000-acre parcel that traces its origins to the 1760s when it included a Colonial trading post. The Comer family built the 26 buildings, including a smokehouse, grist mill, library, water tower, church

AUTHOR FAVORITE

The most memorable accommodations I enjoyed in this part of Georgia were at **Colemans Lake Resort** on the banks of the Ogeechee River. Simple cabins and campsites encourage complete relaxation at this 100-acre family-owned retreat. Guests can gaze out through a canopy of cypress trees drenched in moss or sit on docks for a better look at the wildlife (waterfowl as well as alligators). A pool, restaurant and canoes are at your fingertips. ~ Off Route 58 south of Midville, Colemans Lake; 478-589-7726. MODERATE TO DELUXE.

and main house, sometime between 1898 and 1910; you can see ruins around the property. The accommodations here are the most elegant in the entire region, but they are not stuffy. Guest cottages offer four rooms furnished with antiques and lovely views of the rest of the place. Breakfast is served in the main house, a 1910 yellow stucco number with heart pine floors. There are gardens, a pool house and tennis courts as well, and the innkeeper can arrange for river excursions, fishing trips and other outdoor adventures. ~ 8910 Route 17 South, Louisville; 478-589-7419, 888-754-2717. MODERATE TO ULTRA-DELUXE.

The simplest inn would suffice for a traveler weary of roadside lodging, but sometimes you get lucky. The 16-room **Statesboro Inn** has a beautiful wide veranda studded with Tuscan columns, bay windows, and numerous wood and brass finishes. The deluxe rooms in the main house are appointed with Victoriana while those in the adjacent 1880s Craftsman-style Brannen House are more contemporary. Some of the six accommodations in the main house have odd-shaped ceilings because they are essentially carved out of the attic, but they are all spacious. One has a screened porch, another a skylight, others jet tubs. If you don't like patterned wallpaper, ask for the cheery yellow number. Built for the William Guy Raines family, this 1904 inn is on the National Register of Historic Places. It's also one of the best places to eat for miles around. Full breakfast is included. Closed last week of December. ~ 106 South Main Street, Statesboro; 912-489-8628, 800-846-9466, fax 912-489-4785; www.statesboroinn.com, e-mail frontdesk@statesboroinn.com. MODERATE TO ULTRA-DELUXE.

What looks like a cross between a motel and a two-story condominium is the **Trellis Garden Inn**. Intersected by covered crosswalks, gardens and a big swimming pool, the inn has 40 comfortable rooms (including one king suite with kitchen) that have balconies, recliners, sofa sleepers and ceiling fans as well as dataports. A souped-up continental breakfast is included in the room rate. As with other lodging in the area, this one books up during football season when there's a home game at GSU. ~ 107 South Main Street, Statesboro; 912-489-8781, 800-475-1380, fax 912-764-5461; www.trellisgardeninn.com, e-mail trellis@frontiernet. net. MODERATE.

DINING

There are pitifully few places to eat around Louisville, but just when you least expect it, up pops a Chinese restaurant. **Loon Wah Restaurant** serves Szechuan and Cantonese dishes in a modest room with floral carpeting and what appear to be Chinese light fixtures. Sweet-and-sour pork, curry chicken and shrimp with garlic sauce might be a nice change from grits and barbecue, but don't expect the moon. Closed Sunday. ~ 124 Broad Street, Louisville; 478-625-9133. BUDGET TO MODERATE.

HIDDEN ▶

On busy Saturday nights, more than 300 people from miles around converge on the **Colemans Lake Resort and Seafood Restaurant**. They come for the food and the setting—both unequalled in this corner of the world. As the resort evolved over the past 74 years, the eatery sprouted more and more rooms until they constituted a maze. Try for a water-view table in the glassed-in dining room (perhaps after cocktails on the deck), and then order up scallops, flounder, shrimp, duckling, frogs' legs, quail, steak or, in the right season, wild alligator. There's a full bar and an impressive wine list of more than 60 choices. Buffet dinner on Friday and Saturday. ~ Off Route 58, south of Midville, Colemans Lake; 478-589-7726. MODERATE TO DELUXE.

The parlors of the Victorian **Statesboro Inn & Restaurant** have been converted to accommodate a cozy restaurant that serves only Sunday buffet. You can find Southern country classics, including a knockout squab casserole. ~ 106 South Main Street, Statesboro; 912-489-8628, fax 912-489-4785. MODERATE TO DELUXE.

Sunday dinner in these parts, by the way, is the midday meal (and the serious one of the day). Later on, people may have what's called supper.

If you've never been treated to a classic Southern Sunday dinner, you may be very confused when you walk into the historic **Beaver House Restaurant**. As soon as you sit down, the dishes start coming to the table: steaming platters of fried chicken, country ham, pole beans (more or less green beans), mashed potatoes, and on and on and on. Biscuits, of course, and diet-busting desserts are a given. À la carte items—crab legs, fettuccini, fried shrimp, prime rib, pork loin and many other dishes along with some substantial dinner salads—are other options. Though most people drink iced tea (sweet), they may order wine and beer. Friends and family have gathered in this old mansion for nearly a century; it's a big white house in need of a fresh face but the stately columns and wide veranda compensate for the occasional spots of chipped paint. ~ 121 South Main Street, Statesboro; 912-764-2821. BUDGET TO MODERATE.

Vandy's Barbecue has earned a reputation as the best place in the state to get pork and chicken grilled over an open pit. You'll find homestyle side dishes to take out or sit down and enjoy on the spot. Best of all, it's open from 6 a.m. to 5 p.m. Closed Sunday. ~ 22 West Vine Street, Statesboro; 912-764-2444. Second location in the Statesboro Mall is open daily with later hours: 38B Statesboro Mall, Route 80 and Brannan Road; 912-764-3033. BUDGET.

SHOPPING

Shopping in this region is best in Washington, a town known for antiques and collectibles.

For traditional antiques, **Carl's Antiques** specializes in fine furniture. ~ 722 East Robert Toombs Avenue, Washington; 706-678-2043.

Statesboro has quite a few antique stores—some right in town and some on the outskirts. The **British Tea Room & Antiques** sells antiques and collectibles, including tea cups, as well as scones. ~ 210 South Zetterower Avenue, Statesboro; 912-489-4821.

You can find a gift for just about anyone at the **Wild Petunia**, which carries artwork, home accessories, fancy foods and personal items such as jewelry and pocketbooks. Closed Sunday through Tuesday. ~ 413 South Main Street, Statesboro; 912-764-6558.

The shop at the **Lamar Q. Ball, Jr. Raptor Center** has all kinds of neat natural-history stuff, from books to toys to stuffed animals. ~ Georgia Southern University, Statesboro; 912-681-0831.

NIGHTLIFE

In this part of rural Georgia, nightlife by and large consists of counting lightning bugs, which are strictly a summer phenomenon. However, the **Georgia Southern University Symphony** offers year-round performances. For a schedule, call the GSU Information Line. ~ 912-681-5611; www.gasou.edu.

PARKS

A. H. STEPHENS STATE HISTORIC PARK Located just a hop, skip and jump—okay, a whole mile—from Crawfordville's main street, this 1161-acre park is a blend of natural and historical attractions. The extensive gardens add to the beauty of the woods, but most of the park is open land. Named for the Vice President of the Confederacy and one-time Georgia governor, A. H. Stephens is known for its extensive collection of Confederate artifacts and memorabilia, housed in the museum here and in Liberty Hall, the home Stephens built around 1875. The Historic Site (admission) is closed Monday. There are picnic areas and a fishing lake; private boats are available for rent. Day-use fee, $2. ~ Located north of Crawfordville one mile on Route 278; 706-456-2602.

▲ There are 25 tent/RV sites, $16 to $18 per night; and 4 cottages, $60 to $85 per night. Reservations: 800-864-7275.

MISTLETOE STATE PARK The 72,000-acre Clarks Hill Lake, with a 1200-mile shoreline, dominates this 1972-acre park as it curves its way through the vicinity; forests and a creek complete the picture. The park was named after Mistletoe Junction, an area where mistletoe was gathered in the early 20th century. Perhaps one of the best bass-fishing spots in the U.S., the lake has no limits on boats and has three boat ramps; John boats and canoes are available for rent. Swimming is allowed at designated beaches by picnic grounds. Fifteen miles of trails for hikers are maintained, and though bikes are allowed on these trails, hikers have the right of way. Keep an eye out for wild turkey and Canada geese. Ranger programs are occasionally offered. Day-use fee, $2. ~ Located off Route 150, eight miles north of Route 20 at Exit 175; 706-541-0321.

▲ There are 92 lakefront tent/RV sites, $17 to $20 per night; 1 pioneer site for up to 75 campers, $25 and up; and 4 walk-in sites, $8 per night. There are also 10 fully equipped cottages; $100 per night. Reservations: 800-864-7275.

HAMBURG STATE PARK 🚶 🚣 🛥 🛶 Fishing and boating are the major attractions of this park, whose 741 acres are located around 225-acre Hamburg Lake. A one-and-a-half-mile hiking trail wends around the lake. Since a wide variety of freshwater fish (bass, bream, crappie, catfish) thrive in this area, the fish are usually biting. Boats, canoes and paddleboats are available for rent. The park center is open year-round and offers summer ranger programs. Especially popular is the tour of the 1921 Old Grist Mill, originally operated as both a cotton gin and grist mill; cornmeal can be purchased there. Reptile programs focus on snakes, and there is a canoeing program on the Ogeechee River in the spring led by rangers. There are restrooms, showers and a laundry area. Day-use fee, $2. ~ Located on Hamburg Road off Route 102, about 20 miles southwest of Thomson; 478-552-2393, 800-864-7275.

▲ There are 30 lakefront tent/RV sites; $17 to $19 per night.

MAGNOLIA SPRINGS STATE PARK 🚶 🚴 🚣 🎣 🛥 🛶 Crystal-clear springs pump seven million gallons of water per day into this pretty, shady park, providing habitats for alligator and other wildlife. These 1071 acres were known as Camp Lawton during the Civil War; used as a prison camp, remnants of its past can still be seen here. A small aquarium has a pathetic but compelling collection of fish and reptiles. Amenities include playgrounds, a pool, picnic areas and an interpretive boardwalk. Day-use fee, $2. ~ 1053 Magnolia Springs Drive, five miles north of Millen on Route 25; 478-982-1660.

▲ There are 26 tent/RV sites, $15 to $17 per night; 3 walk-in sites, $13 per night; and 5 two- and three-bedroom cabins, $60 to $95 per night. Reservations: 800-864-7275.

▼▼▼▼▼▼▼▼▼▼

Augusta

The second-oldest city in the state, Augusta was founded in 1736, when General Oglethorpe carried his penchant for laying out cities up from Savannah to the area often considered "uplands" by coastal residents. It was named for the Princess of Wales (the mother of King George III), and was first an Indian fur-trading post before serving as a military outpost for coastal Savannah. Although the British occupation during the American Revolution and the siege by Colonial forces afterwards laid waste to the city, it was rebuilt and even designated state capital in 1786 until the capital was moved again in 1795. Despite its powderworks, Augusta survived Sherman's bloody March to the Sea. As a result, the town has many antebellum homes, set on wide boulevards shaded by magnolias.

Augusta's population has swelled to about 200,000. If it seems busier, it's probably because so many people live in North Augusta in South Carolina on the other side of the Savannah River. The downtown area is picking up steam, especially since the construction of a walkway along the riverfront. The city, like Savannah, sits on the river bluff but it took a long time for Augustans to begin to capitalize on that fact. And no matter what the city fathers do, it seems Augusta is still viewed, first and foremost, as the locale of the legendary Masters golf tournament that takes place every spring.

Unlike Savannah, however, Augusta is hardly compact. Thanks to the mid-1990s development of Riverwalk, which links the Morris Museum of Art, Fort Discovery and the Cotton Exchange, downtown has a certain definition. The rest of the city, though, is so spread out that a car is necessary to see most of the other points of interest. If it weren't for Riverwalk, in fact, many visitors would be hard-pressed to know the Savannah River is there. Summerhill, the nicest place to live, is off to one side while West Augusta feels like one long commercial strip. Finally, North Augusta and Aiken across the South Carolina line sometimes overwhelm the identity of the Georgia city.

Nonetheless, its location and temperate climate seduced 19th-century Northerners eager to escape the harshness of winter; the prospect of paying guests, on the other hand, tempted many a homeowner to rent rooms to augment incomes stunted by the economic devastation of the war. Many visitors liked the place so much they settled, usually in the Summerhill neighborhood known as "The Hill." By the 1890s, Augusta was a proper resort town. One hotel owner, in an effort to beguile the tedium of long—

AUTHOR FAVORITE

History came alive for me at the **Morris Museum of Art**, where my favorite exhibit included works by itinerant artists who traveled the region painting portraits of the gentry in the 19th century. The focus here is on a brilliantly exhibited collection covering these and other works representing two centuries of regional art. On a more contemporary note, the museum's permanent collection includes works by Robert Rauschenberg and Augusta native Jasper Johns. Also housed here is the Center for the Study of Southern Painting (open Monday through Friday), a reference library and archives. Closed Monday. Admission (except on Sunday). ~ Riverfront Center, 1 10th Street; 706-724-7501, fax 706 724-7612; www.themorris.org.

if mild—winters, installed a nine-hole golf course on his property. The Yankee guests cottoned to the game so quickly that the following year a full 18-hole course was built. That course, in time, became the Augusta Country Club, only slightly less regarded than its world-famous neighbor, the Augusta National, home of the legendary Masters Tournament each spring.

The **Augusta Metropolitan Convention & Visitors Bureau** is a good place to start a tour of Augusta. It is an excellent source of information on the environs. Closed Saturday and Sunday. ~ Enterprise Mill at 1450 Greene Street; 706-823-6600, 800-726-0243; www.augustaga.org, e-mail amcvb@augustaga.org.

HIDDEN ►

The country's only industrial power canal still in use for its original purposes, the Augusta Canal was built in 1845 to exploit the water power of the Savannah River. The **Augusta Canal National Heritage Area** offers guided tours, in replica canal cargo boat, of working 19th-century textile mills, the Confederate Powder Works, a rare 18th-century residence and more. Petersburg boat tours make regularly scheduled trips from the interpretive center. Admission. ~ 1450 Greene Street; 706-823-7089, 888-659-8926; www.augustacanal.com.

The bureau has a welcome center in the historic **Cotton Exchange**, where visitors can get a close look at what was long known as Georgia's "white gold." Yet the biggest thrill is seeing the old 45-foot-long blackboard that listed the details of the market, posting daily prices from as far away as England. Exhibits explain the various grades; you'll learn that this is where the phrase "fair to middling" was derived. Also on display are tools like cotton hooks and a tester, a heavy iron stick that was stuck in cotton bales to make sure they were firmly packed with the same quality of cotton throughout, as well as a big blow-up of the evil boll weevil, the bane of the cotton farmer and merchant. An active cotton exchange until 1964, this place was the second-largest inland market in the world (after Memphis), and it may be the top attraction in town. ~ 32 8th Street; 706-724-4067.

After ogling the boll weevil, head toward the river on 7th Street. **The National Science Center's Fort Discovery** is not all fun and games. It just looks that way, what with children firing off laser guns, people walking on the moon and others maneuvering robots, and all sorts of fascinating and hyperactive stuff going on. In all, this combination science museum/fun house has some 250 interactive exhibits. It's two stories and 128,000 square feet of what you might call barely managed chaos. Admission. ~ 7th Street at Riverwalk; 706-821-0200, 800-325-5445; www. nscdiscovery.org.

For a look back in time following the futuristic fun of Fort Discovery, take a stroll down the bricklined **Riverwalk Augusta**. It runs on several levels atop the old river levee. There are plenty

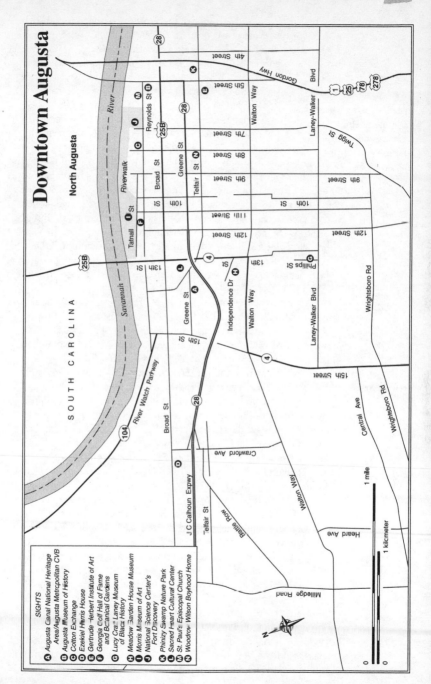

Downtown Augusta

North Augusta

SOUTH CAROLINA

Savannah

River

Riverwalk

SIGHTS
A Augusta Canal National Heritage
  Area/Augusta Metropolitan CVB
B Augusta Museum of History
C Cotton Exchange
D Ezekiel Harris House
E Gertrude Herbert Institute of Art
F Georgia Golf Hall of Fame
  and Botanical Gardens
G Lucy Craft Laney Museum
  of Black History
H Meadow Garden House Museum
I Morris Museum of Art
J National Science Center's
  Fort Discovery
K Phinizy Swamp Nature Park
L Sacred Heart Cultural Center
M St. Paul's Episcopal Church
N Woodrow Wilson Boyhood Home

of places to rest and just take in the scenery, to linger and absorb outdoor historical displays, or to relax and picnic. Within yards of the walkway are restaurants, shops and hotels.

The **Georgia Golf Hall of Fame and Botanical Gardens** opened in 2001 on 17 acres beside the Savannah River. More than 800 varieties of bright, miniature roses lie beyond the arbor at the entrance to the Rose Garden, while the Formal Garden is filled with plants and flowers in a tidy palette of green and white. The Asian Garden features a koi pond, a moon gate and plants from the Orient. The Tropical Garden is adorned with palm and banana trees and multicolored birds of paradise. The Pergola Garden has two 30-foot brick towers with a clock and a temperature gauge. When that gauge heats up, an automatic misting system cools things off, flowers and visitors alike. Throughout these gardens, life-size bronze sculptures honor golf's greatest players, including Atlanta native Bobby Jones as well as Arnold Palmer, Ben Hogan and Jack Nicklaus. Closed Monday. Admission. ~ 1 11th Street; 706-724-4443, 888-874-4443; www.gghf.org.

At the Sacred Heart Cultural Center, see if you can detect the 15 styles of exterior brickwork.

After visiting the gardens, head out Broad Street past Route 25. Just off Broad are all that remains of the **Confederate Powder Works:** a 176-foot-tall obelisk chimney in front of Sibley Mill. During the Civil War, the facility manufactured more than two million pounds of gunpowder. ~ 1717 Goodrich Street; 706-724-0436.

HIDDEN ▶

Farther down Broad on the left, just past Crawford Avenue, is the 1797 **Ezekiel Harris House**, the second-oldest structure in Augusta. This excellent example of post-Revolutionary architecture sports twin chimneys at either end and a double porch, as well as some New England architectural features such as a gambrel roof and vaulted hallway. Harris migrated here from South Carolina and built a tobacco warehouse, in addition to the house, to attract planters to the area. Closed Sunday. Admission. ~ 1830 Broad Street; 706-724-0436.

Return to the city core and turn left onto Greene Street just before Route 25 to see one of the city's architectural masterpieces. When a wedding is held at this historic Augusta church, folding chairs have to be set up since the pews were all sold (or stolen) from what is now the **Sacred Heart Cultural Center**. Happily, the red brick, double-spired Romanesque church, whose cornerstone was laid in 1898 and deconsecrated by the Catholic church in the early 1970s, was spared the wrecking ball and remains one of the prettiest structures in town. Extensive renovations, conducted in 1987 with donations largely from a local corporate executive savior, resuscitated the building so that today you can see the stained-glass windows designed by a German craftsman, the elaborate high altar, the Italian marble columns and other architectural details. Guided tours are offered in the afternoons, or you can guide yourself weekdays. The old rectory houses the administrative offices of the Augusta Ballet, the Augusta Opera, the Augusta Symphony and other nonprofit cultural organizations. Closed Saturday and Sunday. ~ 1301 Greene Street; 706-826-4700; www.sacredheartaugusta.org.

The **Boyhood Home of President Woodrow Wilson** has 14 rooms furnished in mid-19th-century Victorian style, including 13 original pieces of furniture and other family mementoes. Wilson, who once said, "The only place in the country, the only place in the world, where nothing has to be explained to me, is the South," lived here longer than anywhere else, from 1860 to 1870. This Presbyterian manse is on the National Register of Historic Places. Closed Sunday and Monday. Admission. ~ 419 7th Street; 706-722-9828.

Next, head to 13th Street and turn right on Walton Way to visit the home of George Walton, one of Georgia's signers of the Declaration of Independence and the youngest signer of all. **Meadow Garden House Museum**, now on the National Register   ◀ HIDDEN
of Historic Places, is the city's oldest structure, six years older than Ezekiel Harris' house. Furnished in period style, the house is managed by the Daughters of the American Revolution. Among its interesting features is the ladder that leads to the upper floor. Closed Saturday and Sunday except by appointment. Admission. ~ 1320 Independence Drive; 706-724-4174.

Nearby is the Lucy **Craft Laney Museum of Black History**.   ◀ HIDDEN
To reach it, return to 13th Street and continue to Laney Walker Boulevard, turn right and look for Philip Street. This modest bungalow was once the home of one of the country's most influential black educators. Laney founded the Haines Normal Institute in 1883 and her home contains many period pieces. Her gravesite is around the corner on Laney Walker Boulevard. Open only by appointment. ~ 1116 Philips Street; 706-724-3526; www.lucy craftlaneymuseum.com.

When you depart the museum, head back down Laney Walker Boulevard to 5th Street, turn left and drive to Telfair Street. On your left will be the **Gertrude Herbert Institute of Art**. The building is a work of art unto itself, boasting a graceful double exterior stairway leading to a three-story Federalist-style house; Georgia legislator Nicholas Ware had it built in 1818 for $40,000 in 19th-century dollars. With its elliptical front facade and ornate interior accents, no wonder this was also referred to as "Ware's Folly." At any rate, its galleries exhibit work by regional and national artists; some of the best pieces are by up-and-coming talent. Closed Sunday, Monday and Saturday except by appointment. Admission. ~ 506 Telfair Street; 706-724-5495; www.ghia.org.

When you leave the mansion, continue heading toward the river on 5th Street. At the corner of Reynolds and 6th streets is the **Augusta Museum of History**. In this 48,000-square-foot contemporary building, permanent galleries contain Revolutionary and Civil War weapons and uniforms, natural-history exhibits, American Indian cultural collections, and photographs and artifacts illustrating the city's history. It even houses "Old No. 302," the Georgia Railroad's last working steam engine. Closed Monday. Admission. ~ 560 Reynolds Street; 706-722-8454; www.augustamuseum.org.

Head back toward the Morris Museum and check out some of the sites along the way. Near the fort is **St. Paul's Episcopal Church**, where the city was founded as Fort Augusta. The original church was built on this site in 1739. The second church followed in 1750 and the structure you see today is the fourth to be built here. Notable Americans such as William Few, a signer of the U.S. Constitution, are buried in the church graveyard. Tours are available by appointment except on Sunday. ~ 6th and Reynolds streets; 706-724-2485.

On the next block, the **Eighth Street Plaza**, the main entrance to Riverwalk, features antique lighting fixtures and a fountain constructed from century-old bricks. Between 9th and 10th streets on the lower level is a miniature garden with a waterfall known as **Takurazuka**, a gift to the city from Japan. At 11th Street is an informative display, the **National Weather Service Reporting Station**. It's both a data-gathering and reporting center where visitors can get immediate information about current weather conditions.

LODGING The city's non-chain offerings are few and far between, but the ones that exist tend to be outstanding and their numbers will

AUTHOR FAVORITE

I remember **The Partridge Inn** from my childhood, when it seemed to be the hub of adult activity. In fact, guests here have included debutantes and presidents. The hotel was established in the late 19th century when Morris Partridge realized that winter-time tourists needed more places to stay. Over the years, he kept adding on to the original two-story residence, and you can trace the hotel's history through the lobby exhibition of photographs, postcards, newspapers, letters and other artifacts. The 155-room hotel has been recently completely renovated and a new club floor added. Some rooms have kitchens, but there's also a restaurant. Full breakfast. ~ 2110 Walton Way; 706-737-8888, 800-476-6888, fax 706-731-0826; www.partridgeinn.com, e-mail info@partridgeinn.com. DELUXE TO ULTRA-DELUXE.

doubtless increase with the burgeoning popularity of the shops and restaurants near Riverwalk.

If you want to stay near the riverfront, your best bet is the **Radisson Riverfront Hotel**, an 11-story, 234-room hostelry with river views. The decor is an upscale assortment of subdued colors and well-made contemporary furniture. A typical room is spacious with a writing desk, a straightback chair and a wingback chair that create the feeling of a very nice home office. The hotel accepts small pets and has a pool as well as a restaurant, a gym, covered parking and conference facilities. ~ 2 10th Street; 706-722-8900, fax 706-823-6513. ULTRA-DELUXE.

For a real dose of good old Southern living, check into **The Azalea Inn**, located in what is called Olde Town. The magically expanding inn currently claims three Victorians comprising 21 guest rooms. With variety like this, accommodations are bound to be a little different depending on which room you have. Some suites have kitchenettes and/or glassed-in sunporches; all have private whirlpool baths, fireplaces and 11-foot ceilings. Number 316, for instance, has a sunporch with discreet pull-up shades for privacy, a king-size four-poster bed, teal green walls and carpeting. Period furnishings and rockers on the porch round out the landed gentry ambiance. A full breakfast is served in your room. ~ 312–334 Greene Street; 706-724-3454; www.theazaleainn. com. DELUXE.

The **West Bank Inn** stands out on chain-motel row with clean standard rooms—some quite large—that are equipped with a microwaves, mini-fridges and VCRs. Two stories contain 47 rooms with exterior corridors. Continental breakfast is included. ~ 2904 Washington Road; phone/fax 706-733-1724. BUDGET TO MODERATE.

DINING

Augusta restaurant choices range from elegant eateries in the oldest sections of town to pubs to ethnic spots. Of late, there are more and more places offering contemporary cuisine, particularly out on Washington Road.

◀ *HIDDEN*

Gorin's Café & Grill, on the ground floor inside Fort Discovery, is a lively place, perfect for kids or folks too busy for a regular restaurant meal. It serves cheesesteaks, hamburgers, grilled chicken, deli sandwiches, melts, salads and kids' meals, as well as the full spectrum of soda shop treats. ~ One 7th Street; 706-774-1388. BUDGET.

Some 30 desserts await diners at **The Boll Weevil Café & Sweetery**, but first you have to eat your vegetables. Or chicken. Or tuna, ham, cheese, crêpes, casseroles, jambalaya or whatever. Soups, salads, sandwiches and pizzas come in myriad guises, many of them offbeat like the Jose (corned beef, cabbage slaw, jalapeños and Swiss cheese). Only then can you think about ordering bourbon pecan pie, *tiramisu*, brownie fudge cheesecake or Georgia peach tart. Dining is in two main rooms—one white, one red— and the dozy brick-lined bar at this riverfront favorite. ~ 10 9th Street; 706-722-7772. BUDGET.

Beamies at the River (well, almost at the river) is the place young professionals gather to take the edge off the workday, order some seafood or maybe steak, chicken or gumbo. It's one big room decorated with ceiling fans and colorful parrots; there's a nice covered patio out back. Closed Monday. ~ 9th Street at Reynolds Street; 706-724-6593. BUDGET TO MODERATE.

Even Augustans who swear they "never eat in a hotel restaurant" can't stay away from **Augustino's** at the Radisson on Riverwalk. Glossy woods and Roman shades make a handsomely elegant setting for chicken Anton (roma and sun-dried tomatoes and portobello mushrooms), stuffed salmon, New York steak and other Italian selections. ~ 2 10th Street; 706-823-6521. DELUXE.

The **Whistlestop Café** is a corner spot close to the railroad tracks, obviously a neighborhood hangout where the same people have breakfast every day. With a handful of booths, a few stools and some red lace café curtains, the café is nothing remotely fancy but it does have burgers, salads, regular sandwiches (and non-regular ones, such as fried bologna) as well as full plates and side orders. No dinner. ~ 573 Greene Street; 706-724-8224. BUDGET.

La Maison on Telfair is the city's most elegant dining room, a vision in pink on the corner of 4th and Telfair. The restored 1853 mansion has gorgeous chandeliers, polished wood floors and a menu to match: pecan wood–smoked salmon wrapped in potato crust, Dover sole, sweetbreads with lobster medallions, lamb and game such as pheasant and venison. Closed Sunday. ~ 404 Telfair Street; 706-722-4805. DELUXE TO ULTRA-DELUXE.

Every city in America has a **Luigi's**—or at least an approximation of it. Italian murals of Venice and other places, a nod to classicism with arches and other continental touches tell you before you see the menu that you can expect Mediterranean food, heavy on Italian and Greek. Toasted ravioli, seafood fettuccine, chopped steak provolone, moussaka and desserts like baklava are typical choices at dinner and Friday lunch in this informal hideaway, in business since 1949. Closed Sunday. ~ 590 Broad Street; 706-722-4056. BUDGET TO MODERATE.

The **Pizza Joint** is a rarity, a pizza joint that actually serves sandwiches and other foods as well as a wild assortment of toppings, including a vegetarian version dubbed "Tree-huggers." The room is long and shiny with chrome, eclectic art, high stools and booths. Very popular, it's also open late Friday and Saturday (until 2 a.m.), a godsend to hungry travelers. ~ 1283 Broad Street; 706-774-0037. BUDGET TO MODERATE.

Faux mountains, real cascading water and a forest of tropical plants transport patrons to a fantasy world at **Bambu**. In addition to sushi, the restaurant inside the Partridge Inn serves entrées such as mustard- and wasabi-crusted filet mignon, crab-stuffed Idaho rainbow trout with pesto couscous and teriyaki cream, and sesame-crusted tuna loin in a balsamic-soy glaze. Presentations are playful and the scene is as sophisticated as you'll find in Augusta. Closed Sunday and Monday. ~ 2110 Walton Way; 706-312-7777. ULTRA-DELUXE.

Café du Teau is the closest thing in Augusta to a bistro. Most dishes get a twist from the traditional, however. For instance, the escargot is served with a shiitake ragoût; the scallops come with couscous and pesto. The elegant menu covers the duck-pasta-chicken-seafood-steak-veal front with several dishes in each category. All entrées include soup or salad. This is the place to come when you get a craving for an elaborate dish like a fettuccini *fruit de la mer*, veal Oscar or steak *au poivre*. Closed Monday. ~ 1855 Central Avenue; 706-733-3505. DELUXE TO ULTRA-DELUXE.

Augustans have been grabbing lunch at the **Fat Man's Café** since 1951, and the staff is as familiar to them as their own family members. This old diner is a great place to bring the kids for hamburgers, barbecue, and fried ham and other sandwiches. Anyone worried about a balanced meal can order from a sizable list of side dishes like squash casserole and cole slaw. No dinner. Closed Saturday and Sunday. ~ 1717 Laney Walker Boulevard; 706-733-1740. BUDGET.

The gargantuan parking lot is the first hint that **Sconyers Bar-B-Q** is one of Augusta's best-loved restaurants. Secluded on the far side of a knoll beyond a shopping center yet within earshot of Route 520, the rambling wood-frame capital of 'cue is accessible via a wooden footbridge over little springs and waterfalls. Wheelbarrows and other farm-like items adorn the front; inside, it's hog heaven. And those who want to dine "high on the hog" will

---

WAITING FOR SUNSHINE

An Augusta institution since the 1950s, the **Sunshine Bakery** serves lunch all day. But if you go at noon, you'll probably have to stand in a long line of locals who know the sandwich specials by heart: Reuben, Dutch Rhubun (turkey and muenster cheese on a dark roll, no sauerkraut), hot pastrami and other cheese-and-meat combos. All are best enjoyed with the house drink, Sunshine Tea, a thirst-quenching blend of lemon and tea. You can sit at small tables or in booths set against exposed brick walls. The bakery side sells German breads and fancy pastries. ~ 1209 Broad Street; 706-724-2302. BUDGET.

find themselves in luck. Closed Sunday and Monday. ~ 2250 Sconyers Way; 706-790-5411. BUDGET TO MODERATE.

The **French Market Grille** is so jammed that the establishment doesn't deign to take reservations. Patrons clearly crave specialties such as Creole filé gumbo (crammed with fish, crab, shrimp, chicken, vegetables, sausage and rice in an over-the-top combination); Cajun-style catfish; jambalaya with andouille, ham *and* shrimp; shrimp or crawfish étouffée and more mainstream fare like pasta, soft-shell crab (in season) and trout amandine. A cross between a fern bar and a French Quarter tourist trap, it's consistently rated as one of Augusta's best restaurants. Closed Sunday. ~ 425 Highland Avenue in the Surrey Center; 706-737-4865. (There's another branch at 368 Fury's Ferry Road; 706-855-5111.) MODERATE TO DELUXE.

SHOPPING   The **Museum Shop** in the Morris Museum of Art has notecards, reproductions, books on art, golf and architecture, picture frames and more. ~ Riverfront Center, 1 20th Street; 706-828-3807.

Artists' Row, centered in the 1000 block of Broad Street, is the place to find works by visual artists, ten of whom hold open studios midday Thursday, Friday and Saturday. **Artistic Perceptions**, for example, specializes in oil paintings and stained glass. ~ 551 Broad Street; 706-724-8739.

Just off Broad Street, **The Raven's Hoard** has jewelry and unusual collectibles such as vases, jewelry and figurines. Closed during early July. ~ 131 12th Street; 706-724-3830.

NIGHTLIFE   The **Augusta Ballet** performs at the Imperial Theatre from October through May, for an annual total of four productions presented several times each. ~ 745 Broad Street; 706-261-0555.

The **Augusta Symphony Orchestra** presents a full season of classical music from late September to late April at the Augusta State University Performing Arts Theatre. In addition, it offers a series of casual classics in the same venue, a chamber series at the Unitarian Church, and Pops at the Bell, three productions at Bell

AUTHOR FAVORITE

I'm always looking for a store where I can lose myself in browsing and where, even if I do succumb to temptation, the damage won't be too bad. That's one reason I like **Fat Man's**, where the emphasis is on Christmas and other holiday merchandise but not to the exclusion of toys, baskets, flowers and cake kits. Plus, if I ever need to rent a costume while I'm in town, I know where to go. ~ 1545 Laney-Walker Boulevard, Augusta; 706-722-0796.

Auditorium. ~ P.O. Box 579, Augusta, GA 30903; 706-826-4705;
www.augustasymphony.org.

The **Cotton Patch** has live music until midnight on Friday
and Saturday and until 10 p.m. Sunday. ~ 816 Cotton Lane; 706-
724-4511.

OGLETHORPE PARK At the east end of Riverwalk on the lower
level, off 6th Street, this park is adjacent to the Southern Railroad
Bridge. It has teeter-totters, jungle gyms and a picnic area.
Mostly hidden by the bridge, the small plot of ground is in shadows much of the time but makes a nice refuge from the city
streets only a block away. ~ Below Reynolds Street east of 7th
Street.

PARKS

PHINIZY SWAMP NATURE PARK 🏃 Augusta's first urban nature
park sits on 1110 acres near downtown. It is still being developed by EcoSystems Institute, but red-shouldered owls, blue
herons, otters, alligators and the rarely seen bobcat can be ob-
served in their natural setting against a background chorus of kingfishers and tree frogs. The Swamp has served as a conduit for waste
and storm water since 1880 and only recently has it been recovered. Wetlands, streams, swamps, a lake and access to the Savannah River will one day be enhanced by raised wooden boardwalks. ~ EcoSystems Institute, 435 Telfair Street; 706-828-2109.

All the fishing in this section of Georgia is in
fresh water so you will need a license, easily purchased near most large bodies of water.

Outdoor Adventures

Some of the best bass-fishing spots in Georgia, maybe even the
whole country, can be found at **Mistletoe State Park**. The 76,000-
acre lake here has largemouth and smallmouth bass as well as bluegill, catfish and crappie. ~ Off Route 150; 706-541-0321.

FISHING

If you're thinking of playing a couple of rounds where Tiger Woods
and Bobby Jones—and nearly every great player in between—
made their mark, think again. The Augusta National Golf Club
and the Augusta Country Club are both private. However, you
can at least participate in the great sporting tradition that put
Augusta on the map.

GOLF

Bentgrass greens, rolling Bermuda fairways and rough layout
by Mike Young make for challenging play at the scenic **Cateechee
Golf Club**. ~ 140 Cateechee Trail, Hartwell; 706-986-4653;
www.cateechee.com.

If you like water, tee off at the **Hartwell Golf Club**. The tees
are midsize, the greens are small and the water is interspersed
with hills. ~ 755 Golf Course Road, Hartwell; 706-376-8161.

The semiprivate, 18-hole **Green Hills Country Club** allows the
public in at some very reasonable rates. If you're playing on a

holiday or weekend, tee times must be reserved. ~ 4090 Barnett Shoals Road, Athens; 706-548-6032.

The **Jones Creek Course** is sometimes called the "poor man's Augusta National." Designed by Rees Jones, it is an 18-hole public course considered to have an excellent practice facility and professional instruction. ~ 4101 Hammonds Ferry Road, Augusta; 706-860-4228.

BIKING

Without real bicycle routes, this section of Georgia is not exactly a cyclist's dream. Unless you know local conditions, it's hard to tell what traffic will be like on even the country roads at various times of day. But there are a couple of places to consider.

In Athens, there is no real bike path but a couple of roads (e.g., Epps Bridge Road and Baxter Avenue) have added the start of bicycle lanes. If you head out Prince Avenue north (it becomes Route 129) to the Athens Country Club, you can get onto Jefferson River Road, which runs three or four miles as a fairly safe thoroughfare before becoming a rural road where the riding is considered pleasant by local cyclists.

Mistletoe State Park has four nature trails, three of which are two miles long. The park's management allows mountain biking on the fourth one, **Rock Dam Trail** (8 miles). Expect some hills, though that's not the tough part. The trail crosses two creeks without benefit of bridges and passes a natural rock dam.

A scenic ride along the Savannah River can be had via the **Augusta Canal Trail**, which runs from Martinez to downtown Augusta.

Bike Rentals You can rent a single road bike and get some advice on cycling routes at **Dixon's Bicycle Shop**. Within a few miles of Athens are plenty of country roads of varying length. The staffers here seem to know their stuff. ~ 257 West Broad Street, Athens; 706-549-2453.

AUTHOR FAVORITE

I can't imagine a gardener who wouldn't love strolling around the **State Botanical Garden of Georgia**. There are five miles of easy trails on mostly flat land, with a few gentle slopes for good measure. All are marked with color coding but experienced hikers will want to mix and match for a longer excursion. If you see blazes of color you didn't expect, you've probably taken someone's shortcut. The orange and white trails run mainly around the perimeter (total about three miles) and will give you the best workout with the fewest companions.

In Augusta, you can rent bikes from **Outspoken Bicylces** (1904 Walton Way; 706-736-2486) or the **Martinez Bicycle Company** (138 Davis Road, Martinez; 706-863-6862); 24 hours' notice is advised.

This part of Georgia is mostly flat, but there are some exceptions to the general rule: though the trails are flat, Clarks Hill Lake, for example, is at an elevation of 330 feet.

HIKING

All distances listed for hiking trails are one way unless otherwise noted.

Accessed by one of two roads, the nature trail (.5 mile) at **Hart State Park** loops through gentle slopes near the middle of the peninsula; you can reach the lake from either side.

At Sandy Creek Park, the **Cook's Trail** (4.1 miles) starts at the nature center. It's gentle enough to take the kids along for a leg-stretcher, crossing over bridges and a swamp.

At **Mistletoe State Park**, located on the banks of Clarks Hill Lake, there are two trailheads near the park entrance. The **Clatt Creek Trail** (1.3 miles) leads through mixed hardwood and pine forest and through terraces built on what used to be farmland. In the abandoned fields, you'll see loblolly pine and persimmon trees near the trail, which leads to Clatt Creek just before it empties into the lake. Keep an eye out for a sizable flock of Canada geese that likes the bay and the grassy areas of the park. Spring and fall are best for spotting wildflowers. **Turkey Trot** (1.2 miles) is the other trailhead at the entrance to Mistletoe. This loop runs with scenery almost identical (except for the creek) to that of Clatt Creek. **Twin Oaks Trail** (1.9 miles) sweeps between the campground, the park office and the beach area. Like the others in this park, it is an easy hike.

For an easy walk, the **Augusta Canal Trail** (8.5 miles) runs along the Savannah River from Martinez all the way to the Old Cotton Exchange Visitors Center on the banks of the river downtown. Seven miles of it are on the canal and river; the remaining mile and a half are urban. There is no discernible change in elevation, which leaves hikers free to enjoy the scenery and wildlife, including bald eagles, wood storks, deer, muskrats, beavers, wild turkeys and, if you're lucky, an alligator or two. The trail follows an old mule towpath; the mules were harnessed to barges and towed them down the canal back in the days when there were no trees in the way. En route are sights such as George Walton's Meadow Garden (circa 1790) and an old textile mill. ~ Contact the Augusta Canal Authority, 1450 Green Street, Augusta; 706-823-7089, 888-659-8926.

▼▼▼▼▼▼▼▼▼▼▼   Athens is about one and a half hours from Atlanta via
Transportation   any number of routes, but the recent expansion of **Route 29** makes that one an easy choice. From the mountains,
CAR   it is accessible by crossing **Route 85** and heading south on **Route 106**. The main route between Athens and Augusta, **Route 78**, leads through the charming town of Washington. Augusta is at the eastern Georgia end of **Route 20**; the city is also connected to the south via **Route 25**. To drive Augusta from Savannah takes nearly two hours via Route 25 and **Route 80**.

AIR   Atlantic Southeast Airlines, Delta's subsidiary, and US Airways fly in and out of the **Augusta Regional Airport**. ~ www.augusta regionalairport.com.

   E-Z Ride of Augusta runs a shuttle between Augusta and Hartsfield-Jackson International Airport in Atlanta. ~ 4268 Frontage Road, Augusta; 706-860-4900.

   Bulldog Limousine serves Atlanta's Hartsfield-Jackson International Airport with door-to-door service for Athens customers. ~ 706-613-5206. **William Murrell & Associates** is another airport shuttle service. ~ 706-722-2616.

BUS   **Greyhound** (800-231-2222; www.greyhound.com) stops in Athens at 220 West Broad Street and in Augusta at 1128 Greene Street.

TRAIN   **Amtrak** serves metropolitan Augusta; inconveniently, the station is in Denmark, S.C., about 48 miles away. The closest stop to Athens is 50 miles away in Gainesville at 116 Industrial Boulevard. ~ 800-872-7245; www.amtrak.com.

TAXIS   In Athens, **Your Cab Company** runs 24 hours a day and makes frequent trips to Atlanta's Hartsfield-Jackson International Airport at $100 for two people one-way. ~ 706-546-5844.

   Metropolitan Augusta has several taxi-cab services, including **Augusta Limousine and Cab Co.** (706-724-3543) and **Yellow Cab** (706-722-8811).

CAR RENTALS   **Hertz Rent A Car** (800-654-3131) and **Avis Rent A Car** (888-897-8448) both have outlets at Athens Municipal Airport (706-543-5984). **Hertz** also has a branch at Augusta Regional Airport, as do **Avis**, **Budget** (800-527-0700), **Enterprise** (800-736-8222) and **National** (800-227-7368).

EIGHT

Middle Georgia

The middle of the state can be characterized as a romantic blend of antebellum homes and peach orchards, with mostly sleepy towns packed with restored buildings and historic downtowns. Madison, with some 3500 residents, is the loveliest of them all since its beauty was spared the devastating effects of General Sherman's March to the Sea. Toward the end of 1864, when Sherman was fresh from bringing Atlanta to its knees and cutting a swath that would culminate at Savannah, he approached the outskirts of town, where he was met by former Senator Joshua Hill. It is Hill, who knew Sherman in Washington, who is credited with arranging a peaceful surrender and avoiding the pillaging that decimated nearby towns like Clinton.

Watkinsville, near Athens, was on the short list for Georgia's capital at the end of the 18th century, but it was deemed inappropriate because of the feared effects of the presence of the Eagle Tavern. Instead, Milledgeville won the honor; it remained the capital until the capital was relocated to Atlanta in 1868. Its downtown was laid out with squares and a grand governor's mansion; the grid pattern makes the simple town easy to tour. Milledgeville largely escaped Civil War damage, except for a state penitentiary, and its mansions are numerous. The city, which rose on the former site of Fort Defiance, claims several unique aspects, such as being the only town in the world to require a train to stop at a traffic light. It was also the first in Georgia to develop an industry around pecans.

The governor briefly lived at a house on Greene Street, the same one writer Flannery O'Connor occupied much later when she moved to Milledgeville from Savannah in 1938. Enrolling at the nearby Georgia State College for Women, she began her first novel, *Wise Blood*, in New England, where she lived until 1950, when she was diagnosed with lupus and returned to Milledgeville. She was a daring writer who used her stories and novels to depict Christian fundamentalism as the worst kind of fanaticism, a point of view that won her as many enemies as fans. Her works and other memorabilia are exhibited at the Georgia College library.

Macon, though only a short drive from Milledgeville and even Madison, is by comparison a bustling metropolitan hub. Situated on the Ocmulgee River at a juncture of interstates, it is graced with thousands of cherry trees, estimated at 275,000, that bloom in the spring in a profusion that rivals cherry blossoms in Japan (which is, by the way, where the trees came from). Situated close to the center of the state, it would have been a logical choice for the capital but never had a chance against Atlanta. Its historic downtown is being developed at a fast pace, making the most of its location.

▼▼▼▼▼▼▼▼▼▼▼▼▼▼▼▼▼
Madison to Milledgeville

Every town has a story. In the South, that goes double or triple. This is the land of brave Confederate soldiers and daring deeds, the tales of Uncle Remus and Br'er Rabbit, and a bevy of antebellum mansions where the hostess may seem to be living in a time warp. Visitors absorb details of the Civil War as if by osmosis, at least in the smaller towns. No matter which side of the War Between the States wins your sympathy, though, you'll be made to feel welcome.

SIGHTS

It's a straightforward drive from Augusta via Route 20 to the delightful town of **Madison**. Here you'll find many restored homes and several inns that predate the Civil War.

The reason so many structures are intact is because General Sherman was prevailed upon by an old family friend. Joshua Hill, a native son who became a U.S. senator, had befriended Sherman's brother when they were cadets at West Point. Hill's uniform coat is among the sizable collection of Civil War and other regional artifacts displayed at the **Madison-Morgan Cultural Center**. The museum shares the magnificent 1895 Romanesque Revival building with an auditorium used for community events. Wandering around the building, it's easy to envision it in the days when it served as one of the South's first grade schools made of brick. Closed Monday. Admission. ~ 434 South Main Street, Madison; 706-342-4743; www.madisonmorgancultural.org.

Catticorner is **Heritage Hall**, a museum in a Greek Revival house built for Dr. Elijah Evans Jones in 1833. If you look closely you can see scrawled messages on the windowpanes, where Jones family members wrote notes like "I Love Will." Though not original, the furnishings are appropriate to the period. Admission. ~ 227 South Main Street, Madison; 706-342-9627, 800-545-8771; www.friendsoftheheritagehall.com.

Continue up Main Street to the town square and drop into the **Madison-Morgan Chamber of Commerce Welcome Center**, which is in a two-story brick building that was once both City Hall and fire station. The city offices moved out in the 1930s and the original fire bell has been returned to the building's cupola. Here you can get brochures and a walking-tour map of Madison's large

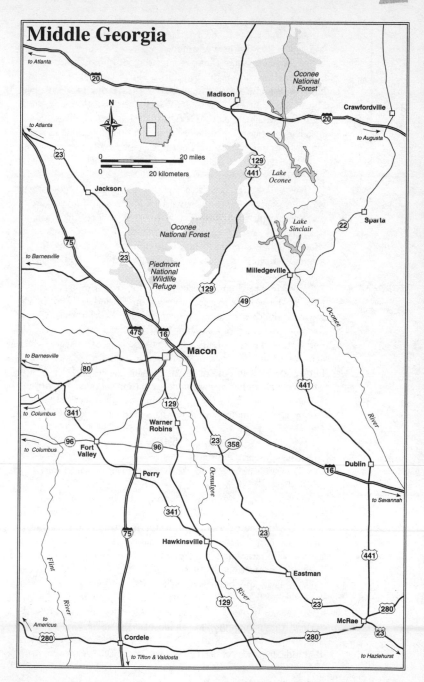

Middle Georgia

to Atlanta

20

Madison

Oconee
National
Forest

Crawfordville

20

to Augusta

N

129
441

Lake
Oconee

to Atlanta

23

0   20 miles
0   20 kilometers

Jackson

Lake
Sinclair

22

Sparta

Oconee
National
Forest

75

23

Piedmont
National
Wildlife
Refuge

Milledgeville

129

49

to Barnesville

Oconee

River

475   16

Macon

441

to Barnesville

80

129

to Columbus   341

Warner
Robins

23   358

96

96   Fort
Valley

16   Dublin

to Columbus

Perry

to Savannah

Ocmulgee

River

75

341

23

Hawkinsville

441

23

Eastman

Flint

River

129

River

280

23

441

to
Americus

McRae

23

280

Cordele

280

to Hazlehurst

to Tifton & Valdosta

National Historic District, which lists more than 100 buildings. Closed Sunday. ~ 115 East Jefferson Street, Madison; 706-342-4454, 800-709-7406; www.madisonga.org.

Nearby is a home that predates the Morgan County Courthouse by nearly a century. An outstanding example of Piedmont Plain–style architecture widely used in rural America, the **Rogers House** was built in 1810 by Reuben Rogers. On the same site is the **Rose Cottage**, which was built in 1891 by Adeline Rose. Rose, who had been born into slavery, earned money by taking in washing and ironing, mostly for boarders at the Hardy House (which was owned by comedian Oliver Hardy's mother). ~ 179 East Jefferson Street, Madison; 706-343-0190.

The walking tour leads to several historic sites. Among them is the photogenic Classic Revival **Oak House**, built on the site of an earlier home that burned in the late 1800s. The current structure, erected just before the turn of the 20th century, was renovated in 1994, tripling its size although the oak carvings in the original stairway banisters remain in the home. ~ 617 Dixie Avenue, Madison.

HIDDEN ►   The **Morgan County African-American Museum** is headquartered in the Horace Moore House. Constructed in 1895, it was moved to its present location in the Round Bowl Spring Area of the downtown historic district in 1993. The museum is not very old and it still collects artifacts relating to the lives of African Americans in the county, seeking to preserve the heritage and contributions of African Americans to the culture of the Deep South. The living room has appropriate period furnishings; the Morgan County Room relates the people and their history; the African Room has African artwork and other exhibits. Closed Sunday and Monday. ~ 156 Academy Street, Madison; 706-342-9191.

See the "Walking Tour" below for more information on Madison's historic buildings.

When you have toured the wonderful homes and museums of Madison, it is time to move south on the Antebellum Trail. Route 441 travels down to Eatonton and beyond. But first it runs past a fascinating site about five miles north of Eatonton. The HIDDEN ►   **Rock Eagle Mound** lies in a protected roadside field now part of the Rock Eagle 4-H Center. It is shaped like a prone bird—an eagle—with outstretched wings and its head facing eastward, rising about ten feet above the surrounding surface. Constructed of milky quartz and boulders of all shapes and sizes, the effigy is best viewed from a slim granite observation tower the government put up in 1937. C. C. Jones, a Georgia historian, first described the intriguing eagle shape back in 1877 for the Smithsonian Institute. Needless to say, further studies have been done that indicate it was constructed more than 5000 years ago, probably as a structure significant in the religious life of an ancient people who apparently predated the Egyptians. Talk about antebellum. ~ 350 Rock Eagle Road Northwest off Route 441, five miles north of Eatonton; 706-484-2831.

Continue to **Eatonton** and head for Courthouse Square, which hosts what is perhaps the world's one and only **Br'er Rabbit Statue** (see page 360 for more details.). Joel Chandler Harris, who wrote the *Uncle Remus Tales*, was born and raised around here.

Down the street from Courthouse Square is the museum dedicated to Joel Chandler Harris and his alter ego, Uncle Remus. In a log cabin fashioned from two local slave cabins that look very much as if the old storyteller might have lived there, the **Uncle Remus Museum** exudes a rustic charm. The biggest exhibit is a sizable portrait of Uncle Remus and the little boy to whom he told his tales. But the most endearing displays are the shadow boxes that hold elaborate wood carvings of Br'er Rabbit and the other "critters" that populate the folksy stories spun by Harris. In the windows are pictures of antebellum plantations. First editions of Harris' works and related articles fill a counter in the main room of this small, lovable old homeplace in Turner Park. Closed Tuesday from September to May. Admission. ~ 214 South Oak Street, Eatonton; 706-485-6856.

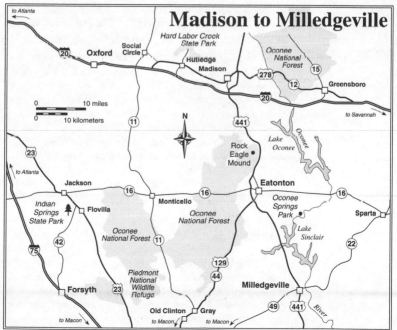

Madison to Milledgeville

WALKING TOUR
Madison

Find out for yourself why preservationists are so thrilled that General Sherman spared Madison's historic buildings during the Civil War. Begin with a visit to the **Madison-Morgan Chamber of Commerce Welcome Center** (page 343), a two-story brick building dating to the late 1880s. Pick up a map of the town and make arrangements for any tours that interest you at designated residences along this 1.4-mile walk.

MADISONIAN Next door to the chamber is the Madisonian (circa 1875), an excellent example of Federal architecture. Here also is an elaborate garden named "Editors Walk" in honor of editors who have served Morgan County, including the present occupants the *Madisonian* and the *Lake Oconee Free Press*. ~ 131 East Jefferson Street.

MORGAN COUNTY COURTHOUSE Cross Hancock Street and you'll be at the beaux arts–style Morgan County Courthouse, which is now listed on the National Register of Historic Places. ~ Hancock Street.

ROGERS HOUSE On the far side of the Morgan County Courthouse is the Rogers House (circa 1810), a Plantation Plain–style structure that was common in the early days of settlement. It's open daily for tours, as is the adjacent **Rose Cottage**. ~ 179 East Jefferson Street.

MAIN STREET Turn around, walk up Jefferson Street the way you came to South Main, and turn left for three blocks to Jones Alley. Here is the circa-1835 **Heritage Hall** (page 354), built in a sophisticated Greek Revival style by a doctor who served with the Confederacy and decorated in authentic period antiques. ~ 277 South Main Street. Continue along South Main and cross Central Avenue. On your left is the **Baptist Church**, which was constructed with bricks made by slaves from a nearby plantation. ~ 328 South Main Street. Walk to the end of the block and look left at the Old English–style **Presbyterian Church** (circa 1842). Admire the Tiffany stained-glass windows here and note that the

Eatonton's other famous native is remembered with the **Alice Walker Driving Trail**, which takes in some of the sites relating to the Pulitzer Prize–winning author of *The Color Purple* and other works. A self-guided tour map is available at the **Eatonton/Putnam County Chamber of Commerce**. ~ 105 Sumter Street, Eatonton; 706-485-7701; www.eatonton.com.

HIDDEN ► The old **Adelle Theatre** in downtown Eatonton opened on November 6, 1914, featuring silent movies, traveling shows and 20-piece orchestras. It's gone now, built over and hidden inside pastor's daughter grew up to marry President Woodrow Wilson. ~ 382 South Main Street. Keep going down the street. Just before you reach Foster Street is a good spot to stop. You can spend some time touring the **Madison-Morgan Cultural Center** (page 354), a Romanesque Revival–style building that is now a center for performing and visual arts. ~ 434 South Main Street. Walk another long block and cross Hunter Street. On your left is the **Hunter House** (circa 1883). Take out your camera (just like the hordes before you) when you get to the Queen Anne–style residence, whose Madison-made millwork and elaborate spindlework porch make it the most photographed building in town. ~ 498 South Main Street.

STAGE COACH INN/CORNELIUS VASON HOUSE   Continue on South Main and turn right onto Walton. In one block make a right on Old Post Road. At the next corner is one of the oldest structures in town, the Stage Coach Inn/Cornelius Vason House (circa 1800). Back when the Old Post Road was on the stage route between Charleston and New Orleans, this was an inn with wings on either side that were later moved to the side property for use as guesthouses. ~ 549 Old Post Road.

FREDERICK FOSTER HOUSE   Turn left at the corner, go one block on Walker Street, then head right on Academy Street for four blocks. Just past Kolb Street, on your left, is a puzzler. Try to figure out which parts are original and which were later added to the two-room cabin now known as the Frederick Foster House (circa 1818). ~ 292 Academy Street.

MORGAN COUNTY AFRICAN-AMERICAN MUSEUM   Continue along Academy Street for three more blocks to Burnett Street. At the corner of Burnett and Academy is the Morgan County African-American Museum (page 356), which was moved in 1993 to its present site. ~ 156 Academy Street.

TUELL TOWNHOUSE   Turn right on Burnett, walk one block, then make a left to find Tuell Court. Wrap up your tour at the Tuell Townhouse, a former mule barn, cotton warehouse, paint shop and auto dealership that was converted into a residence and is considered an excellent adaptation of an historic building. ~ 110 Tuell Court.

the Blackwell Furniture Company. But wait. When you look more closely, except for the leveling of the main floor in the 1950s, there have been no significant alterations to the original theater. You can still see the slanting floor of the balcony and the metal-lined projection room, which, along with the ticket window, are still intact. It ceased operation as a theater in 1923. ~ 107 North Madison Avenue, Eatonton; 706-485-2261.

After visiting Eatonton, press on south toward the city of **Milledgeville**, roughly 20 miles farther on Route 441. When you get to town, turn onto Wilkinson Street and go to the corner of Hancock Street. On your left is **Milledgeville & Baldwin County Welcome Center/Convention & Visitors Bureau** (closed Sunday). Here you can pick up maps and information on trolley tours. Most of what you'll want to see in town is within easy walking distance of the center. You can also sign up here for the two-hour **Milledgeville Trolley Tour**, which costs $10 ($5 for children) and hits the major points of interest. These tours are very informative, especially if you're interested in the numerous historic homes. The guides aren't just along for the ride; they are some of the best in the business, throwing in tidbits, witticisms and local lore along with the basic facts. The trolleys run on regular schedules Monday through Saturday mornings. ~ 200 West Hancock Street, Milledgeville; 478-482-4687, 800-653-1804; www.milledgevillecvb.com.

Milledgeville's **Historic District** is bounded by Thomas, Franklin, Elbert and Tattnall streets, including the houses on the border streets. Most are either private homes or offices. There are more than 200 architectural landmarks, several of them on the National Register of Historic Places.

One of the most stunning old homes, on the same block as the Welcome Center, is the **Stovall-Conn-Gardner House**, also known as "Thirteen Columns." Each of these stately cylinders, topped with Ionic capitals, honors one of the original 13 colonies. It was built around 1825 in the Federal Transitional style with late additions of Greek Revival features. John Marlor, believed to be the imaginative architect behind the design, apparently disregarded true symmetry and the result is impressive. The two-story clapboard building now houses private offices. ~ 141 South Wilkinson Street, Milledgeville.

Across the street is the **McComb-Hollomon-Waddell House**, which remained in the original family from 1879 to 1982. Made of brick with wood trim, the house looks like it's made of stone

AUTHOR FAVORITE

One of my favorite fictional characters is immortalized on the Courthouse Square in Eatonton. The **Br'er Rabbit Statue** is probably the only one in the world. The reason it exists is because author Joel Chandler Harris, who introduced this and other characters in his *Uncle Remus Tales* was born and raised around Eatonton. The statue, about the size of a human, is fully dressed and painted in bright colors. It doesn't look formal enough to share the square with the courthouse, but once you've read Uncle Remus, you can appreciate the humor. ~ Courthouse Square, Eatonton; 706-485-7701.

because sand was mixed with the original paint. It, too, is asymmetrical in design and also a law office. ~ 130 South Wilkinson Street, Milledgeville.

Directly across Hancock Street is the **Baldwin County Courthouse**, a two-story brick Victorian dating from the 1880s that has a Second Empire Clock Tower. The original courthouse, built in 1814, was destroyed, then replaced in 1847 by another one that burned down in 1861. ~ 201 West Hancock Street, Milledgeville.

Two blocks away, the **Old State Capitol** is a Gothic structure of national importance because it is probably the oldest public building in the country. Built to serve as the seat of Georgia state government from 1807 to 1868, the building was partially destroyed by fire. Restored in 1943, its exterior is a replica of the original. Gates that stand at both north and south entrances to the square were erected in the 1860s after the Civil War, fashioned from bricks recovered from an arsenal destroyed by General Sherman's troops. The capitol has been restored and is open for tours. The **Old Capitol Museum** here houses exhibits on local history and culture. ~ 201 East Greene Street, Milledgeville; 478-453-1803; www.oldcapitolmuseum.com.

After looking over the old capitol, head up Greene Street back to Clarke Street and turn right. You will come upon the **Old Governor's Mansion** on your right. Dating to 1838 and now a National Historic Landmark, it was built explicitly as the executive mansion and was home to state governors from 1839 to 1868. A less-welcome guest was General Sherman, who occupied it during the Civil War. Pale pink stucco, a bit worn away, covers Georgia brick, yet it is still considered one of the most perfect and imposing examples of Greek Revival architecture in the county. Closed Monday. Admission. ~ 120 South Clarke Street, Milledgeville; 478-445-4545.

Teachers and other people interested in the history of education might like to examine the **Museum and Archives of Georgia Education**. Located in a 1900 Classical Revival building with Corinthian columns and a Palladian window, the museum houses records, artifacts and memorabilia documenting the development of education in the state. It is an adjunct of the Georgia College of Education. Closed Saturday and Sunday. ~ 131 South Clarke Street, Milledgeville; 478-445-4391.

On the **Georgia College** campus near the corner of Clarke and Montgomery streets is the **Ina Dillard Russell Library**, where the staff has organized the **Flannery O'Connor Memorial Room**   ◄ HIDDEN
on the second floor. Although she was born in Savannah, O'Connor moved to Milledgeville at the age of 13 when her father was diagnosed with lupus; she lived here, off and on, until she died in 1964. Archived here are articles and reviews from her high school years. After her first short story, "The Geranium,"

was published, the library began the collection in earnest. Eventually, it grew to more than 6000 pages of manuscripts, including a draft of *Wise Blood,* her first novel; almost everything is kept under glass and accessible only to scholars with advance clearance. However there is a short video that helps tell the story of her life and her untimely death from lupus. Books with O'Connor's notations in the margins and several of her paintings, including a self-portrait, help round out the mini-museum that honors one of the leading literary lights of her day and, to some, one of the finest writers of any time. Closed when school is not in session. ~ Georgia College, Clarke and Montgomery streets, Milledgeville; 478-445-0988.

Milledgeville claims to be the only city in the country that was originally laid out as a state capital.

When you leave the Georgia College campus, take Montgomery Street two blocks to Wayne Street and turn right to visit the **John Marlor Arts Center**. The combination Federal–early Greek Revival house was built by English master builder John Marlor circa 1830 as a wedding present for his second wife. The house is certainly worth a visit on its own, but it is also one of three historic structures that comprise the **Milledgeville–Baldwin County Allied Arts Center**. Visitors are given guided tours of the current exhibitions. Closed Sunday. Admission. ~ 200 North Wayne Street, Milledgeville; 478-452-3950.

Flannery O'Connor is buried not far from the college at **Memory Hill Cemetery**, the oldest burial ground in the city. The parcel was originally designated as one of four 20-acre public squares in the 1803 town plan; later it became known as Cemetery Square. O'Connor's grave is to the left of the main entry gates, adjacent to that of her father; the family plot is surrounded by a low stone wall. Also in memorial are slave plots and the graves of Revolutionary War dead as well as Georgia politicians. ~ Franklin and Liberty streets, Milledgeville; 800-653-1804.

After visiting the cemetery, you can take a drive south of town to see some outstanding examples of Georgia flora and fauna. *HIDDEN* ► Head south on Route 441 (a.k.a. Irwinton Road) to **Lockerly Arboretum**. Here, the typical Piedmont topography—rolling and uneven—supports a wide variety of shrubs and trees all carefully labeled and catalogued at this private, non-profit facility. Lockerly is more horticultural laboratory than showplace garden, but you'd have to split hairs to agree with that. The 47-acre arboretum is open to groups interested in horticulture, ecology, gardening and botany; they may arrange to be met by a guide. Closed Sunday. ~ 1534 Irwinton Road, Milledgeville; 912-452-2112; www.lockerlyarboretum.org.

HIDDEN ► Between Milledgeville and Macon is a historic property now known as **Andalusia: Flannery O'Connor's Farm**. Readers who have read the author's descriptions in *The Habit of Being*, a collection of her letters, may find themselves in familiar territory. The oldest structures here date back to the early 1800s, though the property was probably occupied earlier. The author and her mother moved to Andalusia after she began to exhibit symptoms of lupus, the disease that killed her father. It was here that she completed *Wise Blood*, which was published in 1952. She spent the mornings writing and the afternoons tending to her peafowl. She remained here until her death in 1964. Part of a larger tract, the 325-acre farm was acquired in 1931 by O'Connor's uncle, Dr. Bernard Cline. Andalusia is open for self-guided tours and screenings of PBS video production of O'Connor's story "The Displaced Person," which was filmed on location at Andalusia in 1976. Closed Wednesday through Friday and Sunday. ~ Route 441, Milledgeville; 478-454-4029; www.andalusiafarm.org.

Three museums in Greensboro are open by appointment only. The **1807 Old Gaol** (East Greene Street) is one of the oldest jails in the state. It is patterned after the Bastille with castellated battlements. The second floor has a trap door that was once used for hangings.

The **L. L. Wyatt Law Enforcement Museum** (Main and Broad streets) once served as both the county jail and the home of noted Sheriff L. L. Wyatt. When he was away, his wife served as the jailer.

The **Historical Museum of Greene County** (201 East Greene Street) exhibits photographs, manuscripts and other artifacts that afford a look at the people and events that shaped the county's early days.

To arrange a visit to any of these sites, contact Greene County Tourism at 706-453-0380 or 866-341-4466.

LODGING

The **Brady Inn** offers a dollop of 1800s Victorian charm in contrast to the town's many Federal- and Greek Revival–style structures. In two adjacent Victorians, heartpine floors and mantels, period furnishings and functioning fireplaces enhance the historic atmosphere. All seven guest accommodations are big and comfy as are the rocking chairs on the porch. Closed in January, February, July and August. Full breakfast is included. ~ 250 North 2nd Street, Madison; 706-342-4400, fax 706-342-9287; www.bradyinn.com. MODERATE.

The **Madison Oaks Inn & Gardens** is a bed and breakfast with a lot of extras. After a hot day of touring downtown, guests can take a dip in the pool or a nap in the hammock, explore the gardens, read on the veranda, take a bike ride, or play horseshoes, croquet or bocce ball. Other amenities rare for a country inn include bathrobes, hairdryers, irons and satellite TV. The four well-appointed accommodations have a mix of antiques and

Text continued on page 366.

A Tale
of One City

It's barely a town anymore, a ghost of its former bustling self. Once the county seat, the town of Old Clinton is little more than a crossroads today, but you can find it by traveling two miles southwest of Gray and one block west of Route 129. While cities such as Savannah, Atlanta and Macon have a trade based on their having survived the Civil War, boasting an array of antebellum this and that, Old Clinton's history is more poignant. The fighting destroyed almost everything.

Clinton was settled after the Creek cession in 1805 and the establishment of Jones County in 1807. Many of the people who settled here were New Englanders; they laid out the town in a grid and built houses close to the street—elements more often associated with the North than with the South. From 1810, when the citizenry numbered 85, to 1820, Clinton had grown to become the fourth largest town in Georgia. By 1829, the town counted 56 homes, 10 stores, 4 taverns, 5 law offices, 3 doctors, 8 mechanic shops, several hotels, a cotton gin factory, a tannery, a blacksmith shop and Clinton Academy.

When news of Georgia's secession reached the town in January 1861, the reaction was jubilation, accompanied by the firing of rifles and the ringing of church bells. Clintonians departed in droves to join the fighting in Virginia. Those who didn't join the war effort directly contributed leather from the tannery and food and fodder from nearby plantations and farms.

The fighting came to Clinton's doorstep in 1864, when 2000 Federal raiders galloped into town on their way to Macon and Andersonville. They stole, plundered and pillaged an estimated half-a-million dollars' worth of property in Jones County, with Clinton bearing the brunt. The worst was yet to come, however. When the Union forces were beaten back from Macon, they returned to Clinton, skirmishing through the town's streets with what was left of the Confederate cavalry. The Federals emptied the jail of their compatriots and then burned it to the ground. Eventually, the Confederate brigade led by Clinton native Alfred Iverson fought back and captured 500 prisoners.

The elation was shortlived. In November 1864, a 5000-strong Federal cavalry force occupied the town and in its wake arrived an entire army corps of more than 15,000 troops, hundreds of wagons and 4000 head of cattle—all bound for a rendezvous with Sherman in Savannah. Like a herd of mad locusts, they demolished about a third of the town that was left, burning residences, the schoolhouse, churches, the tannery—even fences and outbuildings. As Clintonians reeled, having seen their town decimated, nearby Gray prospered and soon took over the mantle of county seat.

In 1974, the Old Clinton Historical Society was formed to restore and preserve Clinton, starting with the oldest structure in the town, the McCarthy-Pope House, circa 1809. Each May, the Society and the descendants of Confederate veterans present "Clinton's War Days," re-enacting local battles complete with authentic uniforms and weapons. It is possible to tour Old Clinton with a guide from the Society, often accompanied by a "Confederate soldier" looking and acting the part. On your own you can look at the old homes, the Clinton Methodist Church and the nearby Clinton Cemetery. To arrange a formal tour, contact Earline at 478-986-5300.

contemporary furnishings; most have a garden view[...]
fast is included. ~ 766 East Avenue, Madison; 70[...]
www.madisonoaksinn.com. ULTRA-DELUXE.

HIDDEN ▶   Outside town, **The Farmhouse Inn at Hundred Acr[...]**
alas, not an old plantation house but a contemporary c[...]
pretty house, though, set amid meadows, gardens and, yes[...]
acreage. In addition to five private rooms decorated in c[...]
motifs, more modern accommodations are available in the[...]
room Hillside Cottage; the four-room Ellis Lane Farmhou[...]
which is suitable for a family reunion; and a pair of lofts. [...]
stocked fish pond and roaming flocks of geese, wild turkey and[...]
deer make this the kind of place you might like to stay at for a
week. ~ 1051 Meadow Lane, Madison; 706-342-7933, 866-253-
0023; www.thefarmhouseinn.com, e-mail thefarmhouseinn@
bellsouth.net. ULTRA-DELUXE.

Horseback riding, swimming, volleyball and a hot tub set the
HIDDEN ▶   **Southern Cross Guest Ranch** apart from most Antebellum Trail
inns. A cross between a dude ranch and a plantation, Southern
Cross is a red-brick, white-columned, 12,000-square-foot mansion
with 16 guest rooms decorated in various motifs—some rustic with
a Western theme, some in a more conservative Southern/Victorian
style. Breakfast and/or dinner plans are also available. ~ 1670
Bethany Church Road, Madison; 706-342-8027, fax 706-342-
8114; www.southcross.com, e-mail mail@southcross.com. DELUXE
TO ULTRA-DELUXE.

HIDDEN ▶   **Harbor Club** is a residential community on the shores of Lake
Oconee, but overnight guests are welcome in its fully equipped
posh villas. Overnight stays of up to three nights include a round
of golf, access to the swim and tennis center and the restaurants
as well as a continental breakfast. There is one catch: you have
to take a tour, just as you would in a Mexican resort, but it's a

---

VIVID ORIGINAL

Painted in the same colors as it was originally in the 1830s, **Burnett Place**
is so vivid that some people think the indigo blue and goldenrod yellow can't
be authentic. But it's true. It was built by a hardware store owner so you
don't see the elaborate moldings and other fancy architectural details
prevalent in neighboring houses built mostly by cotton plantation owners
of the day. The restoration job is so thorough that the inn is listed on the
National Register of Historic Places. Upstairs, the James Madison, one of
the three rooms, has a four-poster bed and stenciled wallpaper; this is
where Clint Eastwood stayed once while filming *Midnight in the Garden
of Good and Evil*. ~ 317 Old Post Road, Madison; 706-342-4034;
www.burnettplace.com, e-mail info@burnettplace.com. MODERATE.

pleasant spot and the low price makes it a steal. ~ One Club Drive, Greensboro; 706-453-9690, 800-505-4653. MODERATE.

The Ritz-Carlton Lodge at Reynolds Plantation has 251 guest accommodations, all with private verandas and most over-looking Lake Oconee. All of them are huge—460-square-foot rooms and 892-square-foot suites—and are furnished in the deluxe-residential style typical of Ritz-Carlton properties. The main attraction here is the golf course at Reynolds Plantation, so golf packages are available. ~ 1 Lake Oconee Trail, Greensboro; 706-467-0600; www.ritzcarlton.com. ULTRA-DELUXE.

Down the street from the Old Governor's Mansion, the **Antebellum Inn** is a Greek Revival home dating from the late 1800s. Amenities are ultra-modern, though: there are private phone lines with answering machines and computer modem hookups in all five guest rooms. Wrapped with porches, graced with extensive landscaping and claiming a full-size swimming pool, the inn includes a full breakfast in its rates. ~ 200 North Columbia Street, Milledgeville; 478-454-5400; www.antebelluminn.com, e-mail ante bell@antebelluminn.com. DELUXE.

Ye Olde Colonial Restaurant, on the Square since 1954, is a corner café that looks like it's been there a lot longer than that. But forget the name. This former bank building is the happening spot for cafeteria-style breakfast, lunch and dinner. They do a North Carolina–style barbecue pork, as well as barbecue beef, country-fried steak, fried chicken and roast beef, though the offerings can vary slightly from day to day. If you haven't tried Georgia's squash casserole, the version here should make you a believer. And if that doesn't work, console yourself with the blackberry cobbler available in season. Closed Sunday. ~ 108 East Washington Street, Madison; 706-342-2211. BUDGET TO MODERATE.

DINING

Located right on the Square, the **Madison Drug Co.** has an old-fashioned soda fountain and grill in addition to all the regular pharmacy stuff. This is where to go when an egg-salad sandwich would hit the spot. You can get the usual grilled stuff—burgers, hot dogs, onion rings and fish fillets—as well as ice cream cones, sundaes, sodas and floats. In fall and winter, several piping-hot homemade soups are available. No dinner. ~ 213 North Main Street, Madison; 706-342-1722. BUDGET.

Amici Italian Café, fairly simple with huge murals depicting Italian lake towns, is Madison's nod to the Mediterranean, albeit with some downhome touches like the Big Kahuna calzone stuffed with ham, pineapple, jalapeños and mozzarella cheese. Main courses can be as light as a pesto cappellini or a ricotta-stuffed ravioli or as hearty as a Beefeater gourmet pizza. It's one of the few restaurants in town with a wine and beer list and espresso drinks. ~ 113 South Main Street, Madison; 706-342-0000. BUDGET TO MODERATE.

The place for soul food on the Antebellum Trail is **Adrian's Place**. Barbecued ribs and three vegetables is a popular choice, but you can get steak and other meats as well. If you just want a mess o' veggies, expect to fork over a grand total of about $5. ~ 342 West Washington Street, Madison; 706-342-1600. BUDGET.

In a building just off the town square, **Madison Chop House Grille** is a good choice for hearty fare without a lot of sauces and gravy. It offers more salads than anywhere else in town, along with several steak, burger and sandwich choices. House specialties include chicken stir-fry, teriyaki pork chops, grilled salmon and barbecued baby back ribs as well as a vegetable platter (you can even ask them to hold the bacon from the baked potato). It also has a wine list, regional microbrews and espresso drinks. And it's open on Friday and Saturday until 10 p.m. ~ 202 South Main Street, Madison; 706-342-9009. MODERATE.

HIDDEN ►

About 15 miles east of Madison, the wonderfully named town of Social Circle is practically world-famous as the home of the **Blue Willow Inn**. This revamped mansion is the ideal place to get a taste of what Southern dining is all about, especially at midday on Sunday. Not only is the food excellent, you can't make reservations. You absolutely cannot rush and unless you arrive before they open for business, you'll wait. But even this is pleasant because everyone socializes on the front lawn or in the parlor. (As for big days like Mother's Day, a word of caution: don't bother. You virtually have to park in the next county.) The changing menu is so extensive that the restaurant has published a 240-page cookbook highlighting its specialties: stuffed zucchini squash, chicken tettrazini, fried oysters, seafood gumbo, peach cobbler. Closed Monday. ~ 294 North Cherokee Road, Social Circle; 770-464-2131. MODERATE.

HIDDEN ►

In 1997, a retired Coca-Cola Company executive opened the **Magnolia House** on the banks of Lake Oconee. He had painstakingly restored the 1820s red farmhouse, part of a working dairy farm until Georgia Power dammed the river. This lakeside retreat

AUTHOR FAVORITE

Like many Southerners, I never knew what vegetables tasted like until I grew up. **Café South** is a dream come true, offering home-style foods prepared by trained cooks who know better than to overcook turnip and collard greens. In petal-pink parlors, diners feast on fried chicken, cornbread, sweet potato soufflé and the best squash casserole I've ever tasted. Save room for peach cobbler, lemon squares, pecan pie or bread pudding. No dinner. Closed Saturday. ~ 132 Hardwick Street, Milledgeville; 478-452-3164. BUDGET TO MODERATE.

is a place to linger over dishes like fresh trout cakes, almond-crusted catfish, marinated flank steak or a rather elegant meat loaf and, for dessert, perhaps crème brûlée or the restaurant's legendary fried peach pie, available in peach season (summer). No lunch. Closed Sunday. ~ 1130 Greensboro Road, Eatonton; 706-484-1833, fax 706-453-1088; www.themagnoliahouse.net. MODERATE TO DELUXE.

Columbia Street boasts a variety of restaurants. In addition to delis and cafés, there's a popular Mexican eatery. **El Amigo** is a friendly place—as well it should be, given its name—where you can get standard fare. But you can also get some fun things like shrimp fajitas and other seafood that gets the south-of-the-border treatment. Best of all, it's open every day. ~ 2465 North Columbia Street, Milledgeville; 478-453-0027. BUDGET TO MODERATE.

In 2005, a spin-off of Café South opened downtown. The **Downtown Café South** serves the same country-style buffet lunch as the original, but it also serves breakfast and dinner. There is sit-down service at night, when the menu is more formal, including steaks, seafood and pastas. A specialty is the top-of-the-line Café's Trio, which includes a 6-ounce ribeye, a boneless chicken breast, salad and two side dishes for about $23. ~ 138-40 Hancock Street, Milledgeville; 478-804-9988. BUDGET TO MODERATE.

SHOPPING

Madison's town square is chockablock with boutiques, including **Saffold House Antiques**, showcasing a trove of antiques, estate pieces and collectibles. ~ 179 South Main Street, Madison; 706-342-3536.

223 South Main, located in a Queen Anne Victorian cottage, is a good shop for picking out a gift or finding something to decorate your home or garden. ~ 223 South Main Street, Madison; 706-342-9671.

NIGHTLIFE

Most of the towns in this area, especially the small ones along what's called the Antebellum Trail, roll up their sidewalks early. If they have sidewalks. There are a few places in Macon that stay open after dark and the clubs of Athens aren't far away, either.

BEACHES & PARKS

HARD LABOR CREEK STATE PARK 🏃 🏇 🚤 🛶 ⛵ Known for one of the best 18-hole golf courses in the state park system, this park got its name, the story goes, from either the slaves who worked in the area or by the American Indians who had trouble fording the creek. With 5804 acres, Hard Labor has two lakes, one (Lake Rutledge) with a swimming beach, and stables where you can keep your own horses billeted overnight; there's also golf. During the day, the park offers 22 miles of horseback-riding trails. There's a camp store as well as a restaurant within the park. Since 1989, Georgia State University has manned a research observatory housed in a 1000-square-foot building with several telescopes; one is believed to be the largest in the southeastern U.S. The observatory is open on occasional evenings from May to October, with viewing starting about 45 minutes after sunset on clear nights. Boat and canoe rentals are available. Day-use fee, $2. ~ Two miles north of Rutledge; 706-557-3001, 706-557-3006 (golf course).

▲ There are 51 tent/RV sites, $22 to $24 per night. In addition, 20 two-bedroom cottages rent for $85 to $95 per night. Reservations: 800-864-7275.

INDIAN SPRINGS STATE PARK 🏃 🏊 🚤 🛥 ⛵ Located north of the town of Forsyth, this is one of the oldest state parks in the country. The Creek Indians knew about the spring water here, which they used the same way we use spas today—for rejuvenation and purported health cures. William McIntosh, a Coweta Indian chief, built a hotel nearby in 1819; still standing, it is where he signed over all Creek lands in Georgia to the U.S. Not surprisingly, the so-called White Warrior was murdered by the Creeks that same year. By the late 1800s, Indian Springs had become a resort area; the 528-acre state park was installed in 1927. The original mineral springs cut a wide swath on a gentle hillside; they, as well as a 105-acre lake, allow for cooling off on hot summer days. A small museum, open seasonally, tells the history of the area with exhibits on American Indians and settlers alike. There are picnic areas, boat rentals, a miniature golf course and a nature trail connected by narrow roads that go up, down and around the low hills. Day-use fee, $2. ~ On Route 42, 678 Lake Clark Road, Flovilla; 770-504-2277.

▲ There are 88 tent/RV sites, $18 to $20 per night; and 10 cottages, $80 to $85 per night. Reservations: 800-864-7275.

OCONEE SPRINGS PARK 🏃 🚤 ⛵ On the shores of Lake Sinclair, this 12-acre park is carved out of a wooded area some 15 miles from Eatonton and 30 miles from Milledgeville. The 15,000-acre lake is popular for boating, fishing and other water sports. Facilities include a camp store, bathhouses, picnic tables, barbecue grills, pure tap water, electricity and garbage pickup. There is a small charge ($3) for use of the beach and swimming area and for picnicking. Closed Tuesday. ~ 109 South Spring Road, Eatonton; 706-485-8423.

▼▼▼▼▼▼▼▼▼▼

Macon

The biggest city in the middle of the state, Macon anchors one end of the Antebellum Trail. Remarkably, the town sustained minimal damage during the Civil War. In fact, the one cannonball that hit dead on smashed through a column of a beautiful Greek Revival residence that has since been known to residents and tourists alike by the moniker, "The Cannonball House."

When the powers that be decided to move the state capital from Milledgeville in the mid-19th century, it seems Macon would have been a logical choice: it is the most centrally located big city, easily accessible even then from all corners of Georgia. But the city fathers were no match for their peers in Atlanta, who were the precursors of today's civic boosters in what has since become the state's largest and most densely populated metropolitan area. At any rate, while the debate over the new capital's location raged on, one regional editorial harrumphed: "If Atlanta could suck as hard as it could blow, the Chattahoochee River would run north!"

SIGHTS

Spared major damage from the Civil War, dozens if not hundreds of antebellum homes still grace Macon's hills and even the flatter parts of the city. Most of its attractions are within walking distance of each other, ranging from the birthplace of Macon's best-known poet to museums devoted to the state's musical and sports heritages.

The shortest route from Milledgeville to Macon is Route 49; turn south when it runs into Route 129, which connects with Route 16. Take Route 16 south (towards Savannah) to the second exit and

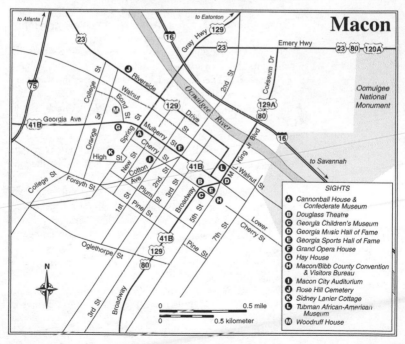

Macon

SIGHTS

- Ⓐ Cannonball House & Confederate Museum
- Ⓑ Douglass Theatre
- Ⓒ Georgia Children's Museum
- Ⓓ Georgia Music Hall of Fame
- Ⓔ Georgia Sports Hall of Fame
- Ⓕ Grand Opera House
- Ⓖ Hay House
- Ⓗ Macon/Bibb County Convention & Visitors Bureau
- Ⓘ Macon City Auditorium
- Ⓙ Rose Hill Cemetery
- Ⓚ Sidney Lanier Cottage
- Ⓛ Tubman African-American Museum
- Ⓜ Woodruff House

0   0.5 mile
0   0.5 kilometer

get off at Martin Luther King Jr. Boulevard. In about two blocks, continue straight on 5th Street. On your left will be the **Macon/ Bibb County Convention & Visitors Bureau and Welcome Center**. The helpful staff has loads of maps, brochures and information, including a Black Heritage Tour. ~ 200 Cherry Street; 478-743-3401, 800-768-3401; www.maconga.org.

The top stop on the Black Heritage Tour map (available from the Welcome Center) is the **Tubman African-American Museum**, which has a lot to take in. Local artist Wilfred Stroud's stylized mural of prominent African Americans dominates one wall with representations of African tribal princes as well as inventors, educators and political leaders from this country. Local legends Otis Redding and Little Richard are among other entertainment figures. Interestingly, it was a white Catholic priest who instigated the creation of the cultural center, which exhibits works by regional artists on a regular basis in the museum's 14 galleries. Closed Sunday morning. Admission. ~ 340 Walnut Street; 478-743-8544; www.tubmanmuseum.com.

Nearby is the **Douglass Theatre**, where entertainers including Ma Rainey, Cab Calloway, Little Richard and Otis Redding performed. After welcoming audiences from the 1920s to the 1970s, the Douglass closed for 20 years before it was restored and reopened in 1997 to present films and performances. Closed Saturday and Sunday. ~ 355 Martin Luther King Jr. Boulevard; 478-742-2000; www.douglasstheatre.org.

Crossing the Ocmulgee River, the **Otis Redding Memorial Bridge** honors the native son who made a name for himself as a singer, composer and performer. The year after Redding was killed in a plane crash in 1967, his "(Sittin' on) The Dock of the Bay" hit number one on the charts. ~ Martin Luther King Jr. Boulevard; 478-751-9280.

In the park on Riverside Drive near the bridge is a life-size **bronze sculpture of Otis Redding** depicted sitting on dock pilings, strumming a guitar with his song lyrics on a notepad beside him.

The **Grand Opera House** was known as the Academy of Music when it opened in 1884. Its seven-story-high stage was impressive then and it remains one of the largest in the country even now. On its boards trod stars including Sarah Bernhardt, Will Rogers, the Gish sisters and comedians like Bob Hope and George Burns and Gracie Allen. A guided tour highlights the trap doors in the floor that were installed for the performance of Houdini as well as performers' dressing rooms. Tours only by appointment. Admission. ~ 400 Poplar Street (office), 639 Mulberry Street (theater); 478-301-5460 (box office); www.mercer.edu/thegrand.com.

When you leave the opera house, take a left on 1st Street to the next corner, where you will see the **Macon City Auditorium**.

It claims the world's largest copper dome and a proscenium with a mural depicting Macon leaders throughout history. ~ 415 1st Street; 478-752-8400.

From the auditorium, head to Cherry Street to visit the **Georgia Sports Hall of Fame.** Opened in 1999, the facility features educational and interactive exhibits focusing on athletes—Georgia high school, college and professional as well as amateur sports. Even if you're not from around here, you've probably heard of such honorees as golfing great Bobby Jones, baseball legends Ty Cobb and Hank Aaron, "Mr. NASCAR" Bill Elliott, Olympic hurdler Edwin Moses and Wyomia Tyus, the first athlete (male or female) to win back-to-back Olympic gold medals in the 100-meter dash. Admission. ~ 301 Cherry Street; 478-752-1585; www.gshf.org.

At the five-floor **Georgia Children's Museum,** kids can explore the mysteries of the human body, try their hand at acting, pretend to be a lawyer and otherwise expand their little minds. They can also get creative with art or express themselves in television, radio or newspaper. ~ 382 Cherry Street; 478-755-9539; www.kidsboro.org.

Continue out Cherry Street to the corner, take a right on New Street, then a left on Mulberry Street. The **Cannonball House & Confederate Museum** is a good descriptor for a house museum where, almost unbelievably, the only cannonball to strike a Macon building in the 1864 Union Army attack came to rest in the parlor. To get there, it crashed through a column of this Greek Revival home, which otherwise looks pretty normal. Some of the rooms here are furnished to look like the chambers at old Wesleyan College (the first women's college in the country). The collection of Confederate artifacts is housed in the detached brick kitchen and servants' quarters in the rear. Admission. ~ 856 Mulberry Street; 478-745-5982; www.cannonballhouse.org.

Another block out Mulberry Street brings you to the fabulous **Hay House.** If you're going to visit only one of the city's ar-

sights

AUTHOR FAVORITE

Those of us who grew up on the music of Ray Charles and James Brown can find heaven at the **Georgia Music Hall of Fame.** It's not just about rock-and-roll, though you'll find tributes to Otis Redding and the Allman Brothers. Other greats, including Lena Horne, Jessye Norman, Johnny Mercer and bandleader Harry James are also honored in this paean to homegrown talent. Admission. ~ 200 Martin Luther King, Jr. Boulevard; 478-750-8555, 888-427-6257; www.gamusichall.com.

chitecturally important homes, it should probably be this one. From the 500-pound front doors to the 30-foot ceilings, this extensively restored Italian Renaissance–style villa is a knockout. In its day—the mid-19th century—it was also known for innovations such as indoor plumbing and walk-in closets, both rarities at the time. Fans of stained glass will be delighted to behold the elaborate "Four Seasons of a Vineyard" window in the dining room, which is topped by a stained-glass rosette. Admission. ~ 934 Georgia Avenue; 478-742-8155; www.hayhouse.org.

The **First Baptist Church** was established prior to emancipation; its original congregation worshipped in a nearby location until land and a building were deeded to them in 1845. ~ 595 New Street; 478-745-8368.

You needn't have read the Macon native's lyrical poem, "The Marshes of Glynn," inspired by the beauty of the Georgia coast, to appreciate the memorabilia displayed in the **Sidney Lanier Cottage**, an 1840 Victorian. There's something poignant about Lanier, who achieved a great deal in his 39 years; he was a mathematician, a lawyer, a linguist and a gifted musician acclaimed for his innate ability to play any instrument. After being captured by the Union Army, he fell sick and died a few years later. Closed Sunday. Admission. ~ 935 High Street; 478-743-3851.

From the cottage, head over to Orange Street and turn right onto it. A left on Washington, a right onto College and another right onto Bond Street will bring you to the **Woodruff House**. Of the various occupants since it was built in 1836 by master architect/builder Elam Alexander, the most interesting was Colonel Joseph Bond, hailed for making a record-setting cotton sale in 1857. The Robert Woodruff Foundation restored the mansion along with the city; it is owned and operated by Mercer University and open for tours by appointment only. Admission. ~ 988 Bond Street; 478-301-2715.

When you depart the Woodruff House, turn right onto Georgia Avenue and follow it until the name changes to Vineville Avenue, which leads to the **Museum of Arts & Sciences** and **Mark Smith Planetarium**. The museum is laid out to attract children with a scientist's workshop, an artist's garret, a simulated fossil dig and live animals in habitats, among other exhibits. The planetarium is one of the largest in Georgia. On Friday evening, weather permitting, the observatory is open at no charge. Admission. ~ 4182 Forsyth Road; 478-477-3232; www.masmacon.com, e-mail info@ masmacon.com.

Just up the road is the 200 wooded acres of **Wesleyan College**. In 1836, it was the first college in the world chartered to grant degrees to women. A four-year liberal arts college affiliated with the United Methodist Church, Wesleyan grants bachelor's degrees in more than 20 majors, plus the Master of Arts degree. The student body numbers about 500 students from 11 foreign countries and 18 states. A walk through the campus will take you past a lake and attractive Georgian brick buildings. ~ 4760 Forsyth Road; 478-477-1110; www.wesleyancollege.edu.

The **Washington Memorial Library** is known for having one of the best collections of African-American genealogical, archival and biographical information in the southeastern U.S. ~ 1180 Washington Avenue; 478-744-0800.

North of the historic downtown area, the **Pleasant Hill Historic District** was established around the 1860s. It was one of the first black neighborhoods to be listed on the National Register of Historic Places. ~ Bound by College, Rogers, Neal and Vineville streets.

Macon has more churches, per capita, than any other U.S. city.

One of Macon's most arresting sights is invisible during the day. Macon boasts more than 5000 structures on the National Register of Historic Places. **Lights on Macon** features 34 of these beauties illuminated nightly all year long. You can pick up a souvenir guidebook at the Welcome Center and other places. Or you can just drive around the downtown district and figure it out yourself. After dark, of course. ~ 478-743-3401.

If you retrace your steps to College Street and head toward Riverside Drive, you'll find **Rose Hill Cemetery**, the final resting place of such disparate citizens as Confederate and Union soldiers (enclosed in Confederate Square) and two members of the Allman Brothers Band (Duane Allman and Berry Oakley). Established in 1839, Rose Hill is one of the oldest cemetery parks in the U.S. and is listed on the National Register of Historic Places. ~ 1071 Riverside Drive; 478-751-9119.

◄ HIDDEN

From the cemetery, take Spring Street across the Ocmulgee River, past Route 16 and turn right onto Emery Highway. After you pass Broadway you will come to signs pointing to **Ocmulgee National Monument**. Here, in a huge park-like setting, is the largest archaeological development east of the Mississippi River. Established some 12,000 years ago, Ocmulgee encompasses a reconstructed prehistoric earthlodge and artifacts from the six different Indian groups who occupied the site, though not all at once. The tallest burial mound is just shy of 45 feet and dates from only about 1000 years ago. It was created by the Mississippian Indians; the Creeks followed, staying here until the 1830s. Prepare to do some walking if you hope to see it all, though you can see a lot from the comfort of a car. ~ 1207 Emery Highway; 478-752-8257, fax 478-752-8259; www.nps.gov/ocmu.

◄ HIDDEN

For a town with so much to see, Macon is very light on first-rate accommodations. While the Yellow Pages lists numerous chain motels, check with the visitors bureau before you make reserva-

LODGING

tions because some of them—particularly those in the budget category—are in questionable locations.

Macon's location at the center of the state makes it a busy crossroads for travelers bound in all directions. To serve them, several chain outfits operate motels convenient to freeway exits. With so many highways, it's easy to get from one of them to the restaurants and attractions in the middle of the city.

At Exit 1 of Route 475, **Best Western Inn and Suites** has 56 rooms and 20 suites on two floors. All the corridors are exterior, but the pool and whirlpool are indoors. Some rooms have their own whirlpools and there's a restaurant nearby. Breakfast and local phone calls are free. ~ 4681 Chambers Road; 478-781-5300, fax 478-784-8111. MODERATE.

Off Route 75, the **Holiday Inn Conference Center** is one of the few motels where small pets are accepted. It has 201 rooms in two stories, linked by exterior corridors. Amenities include a restaurant with full bar service, a swimming pool, a whirlpool, free local phone calls and free room upgrade subject to availability (with advance reservations). ~ 3590 Riverside Drive; 478-474-2610, fax 478-471-0712. MODERATE.

It's hard to exaggerate the delights of the **1842 Inn**, which is one of the best places to stay in all of Georgia. Arriving guests cannot believe their good fortune when they first lay eyes on this imposing Greek Revival mansion, its formal porch sporting 18 columns. It's set in one of the city's loveliest neighborhoods. Between the main house and a "cottage" beyond the central courtyard, 19 accommodations each have their charm. The furnishings are luxurious—antiques and beautifully framed artworks, elaborate beds, writing tables. It's a wonder anyone shows up for happy hour or even breakfast (which is included). If you stay here, book one more night than you planned to or you'll just kick yourself when you have to leave. ~ 353 College Street; phone/fax 478-741-1842, 800-336-1842; www.the1842inn.com, e-mail info@1842inn.com. ULTRA-DELUXE.

The best place to stay right in downtown Macon is the **Crowne Plaza**. The 300 rooms are large and comfortably appointed in subdued shades like gray and mauve; some have downtown views. Amenities include a health club and a pool as well as a ground-floor restaurant and concierge and babysitting services. ~ 108 1st Street; 478-746-1461, 800-227-6963, fax 478-746-1416. BUDGET TO DELUXE.

DINING

Not so long ago, looking for a good restaurant in Macon was hard duty, but the scene has improved in the last couple of years. You can still find simple food in unpretentious surroundings, but, especially downtown, finer fare is easier to find.

Sleeping
with Scarlett

Whether you're a fanatic about—or just a fan of—*Gone with the Wind*, you won't want to miss **Inn Scarlett's Footsteps**, about 50 miles northwest of Macon. Few inns can accommodate bus tours, let alone groups of up to 350, but Inn Scarlett's Footsteps is like no other. As the owners might say, it's a few oak trees short of a plantation, but the red-brick, white-columned mansion is definitely in the style of Ashley Wilkes' "Twelve Oaks." Inside this 8000-square-foot inn is enough *Gone with the Wind* memorabilia (one of the largest private *GWTW* collections in the country) to make Miss Melanie faint dead away.

With a minimum of 15 people (and maybe by making private arrangements), your touring party can be welcomed by "Scarlett" and "Rhett" or have afternoon tea with "Miss Melanie." At least one visitor has asked to see the final resting place of some of these fictional characters from one of the best-read and best-loved stories in American history.

If you decide to spend the night here, you may enjoy breakfast while gazing out at horses rambling in the side pasture; you may even choose to take a horse-and-carriage ride just like in the old days. Rooms are named and decorated for characters out of Margaret Mitchell's famous book: Scarlett's Room has a four-poster bed and an old-fashioned soaking tub, while Rhett's Room is furnished in English antiques to evoke his many trips to England; Melanie's Room is pastel and feminine, as readers of the book would expect, while Ashley's Suite displays an authentic Civil War uniform and other military mementos.

In all, there are four accommodations in the main house and five separate cottages. One is a duplex with a delightful porch—a wonderful spot to relax with a morning cup of coffee and watch the grass grow or the rain fall in perfect peace and quiet. There are less ornate rooms (one of which has wicker and pastels and the other a four-poster cherry wood bed), but they will appeal to travelers desperate for privacy. All guests are welcome to tour the Museum Room. Full breakfast is included. ~ 40 Old Flat Shoals Road, Concord; 770-884-9012, 800-886-7355; www.gwtw.com, e-mail gwtw@gwtw.com. MODERATE TO DELUXE.

HIDDEN ▶ Take the **Downtown Grill,** for instance. Hearty fare is given an upscale twist in favorites like mixed grill (filet, lamb and quail) and filet mignon stuffed with bleu cheese or cranberries and cheese; the menu also lists seafood such as salmon rolls with cream cheese and capers. Closed Sunday. ~ 562 Mulberry Street Lane; 478-742-5999. MODERATE TO ULTRA-DELUXE.

HIDDEN ▶ Of course, all the good places aren't new. **Nu-Way Wieners** has been here since 1916, making it, along with famous Nathan's, one of the two oldest hot dog stands in the country, and it serves hamburgers, too. It's open from early morning until early evening. Closed Sunday. ~ 430 Cotton Avenue; 478-743-1368; www.nu-wayweiners.com. BUDGET.

Located in a downtown alley, **Len Berg's** is a Macon landmark made of cinderblock where fans range from the city's movers and shakers to families looking for home cooking (without heating up the stove). In Georgia, salmon croquettes are a perennial favorite, as are macaroni and cheese, fried catfish, turkey with dressing and side dishes of vegetables, biscuits and cornbread. Mid-summer is the time to sample the fresh peach ice cream. Small rooms and booths give diners a choice of mingling or enjoying a more intimate meal. Closed Sunday. ~ 240 Post Office Alley; 478-742-9255. BUDGET.

The **Willow on Fifth,** city sister of the Blue Willow Inn in Social Circle, offers a classic Southern buffet daily. The food is so good you may want to buy their cookbook. No dinner Sunday. ~ 325 5th Street; 478-745-9007. BUDGET TO MODERATE.

For classic Italian fare with flair (forget the meatballs), the place to dine is **Natalia's.** This has been the town's top dress-up spot since 1984, appropriate for grilled veal chops, ribs and specialty pastas. It also has a full bar. Closed Sunday. ~ 2720 Riverside Drive; 478-741-1380. DELUXE TO ULTRA-DELUXE.

If you like Southern food—be it Southwesten, Southeastern, Cajun, Thai or French—check out **Magnolia's New South Grill.** It's a casual spot known for using fresh ingredients from the local farmers market to create sophisticated dishes. Whatever you try,

MUSICAL MAIN STREET

Cotton Avenue was one of the earliest roads in the area. Built on an Indian trail, it has long been an African-American "main street," where many black-owned businesses have prospered. **H&H Restaurant** is a home-cookin' restaurant just down Cotton Avenue from the offices of Capricorn Records, which brought Otis Redding as well as the Allman Brothers Band and other Southern musicians to the attention of national audiences. Closed Sunday. ~ 807 Forsyth Street; 478-742-9810. BUDGET.

save room for dessert, such as the peaches and ginger *brûlée*, which is the house specialty. No dinner Sunday and Monday. ~ 5580 Thomaston Road; 478-405-9494, fax 478-405-9497. DELUXE.

SHOPPING

There are a smattering of boutiques and galleries downtown. The **Macon Arts Gallery** sells ceramics, pottery, sculpture and fine paintings by regional artists and craftspeople. Closed Saturday (except by appointment) and Sunday. ~ 414 Cherry Street; 478-743-6940.

When Georgians say they're in tall or high cotton, they mean life is going well. That's why the owners of **High Cotton** picked that name for their specialty shop, which sells clothing, jewelry, "trash treasures" and an eclectic assortment of antiques. Closed Sunday and Monday. ~ 456 1st Street, Macon; 478-745-1886.

Most of the retail action, however, is found further afield. Macon's oldest shopping center is **Ingleside Village**, which has shops specializing in gifts, books, clothing and home decorations. Ingleside Village is an antique district with nine shops along or near Ingleside Avenue between Corbin and Rogers avenues just north of Route 41. Your best one-stop shopping is probably at the **Payne Village Antique Mall**. ~ 2390 Ingleside Avenue; 478-755-0075.

Dillard's, Rich's and JC Penney anchor the **Colonial Mall Macon**, the largest enclosed mall in the state. Eddie Bauer, Old Navy, Abercrombie & Fitch, the Bombay Company and more than 200 other shops offer apparel, jewelry, books, personal care items, toys and home accessories. The mall also has a two-story food court. Closed Sunday morning. ~ 3661 Eisenhower Parkway; 478-477-8840; www.colonialmallmacon.com.

In nearby Byron, about 16 miles from downtown, bargains can be found at more than two dozen retailers, including Dress Barn, Corningware, Hanes, Samsonite, Fieldcrest, Hushpuppies and other outlets, at **Peach Festival Outlet Center**. ~ 311 Route 49 at Exit 149, Byron; 478-956-1855.

NIGHTLIFE

The **Macon City Auditorium**, with its great big stage, is an excellent venue for rock bands and other entertainers. ~ 451 College Street; 478-752-8400.

The season at the **Grand Opera House** features local and national touring companies that perform major Broadway musicals and dramas from October until May. ~ 639 Mulberry Street; 478-301-5470.

Theatre Macon presents seven productions each year. Stage Two Season has weekend productions such as one-act plays, poetry readings and cabaret acts throughout the year. ~ 438 Cherry Street; 478-746-9485; www.theatremacon.com.

Dramas and musical performances are presented at the historic **Douglass Theatre** in the downtown historic district. ~ 355 Martin Luther King Jr. Boulevard; 478-742-2000.

Each year the **Macon Concert Association** organizes four productions of international artists and ensembles on the campus of Wesleyan College in Porter Auditorium. ~ P.O. Box 5694, Macon, GA 31208; 478-743-4625, 478-477-3741.

Peach County, just south of Macon, processes 90 percent of the peaches from the Peach State.

The **Macon Little Theatre's** season runs from July to June and always includes at least one musical. Other plays are mostly recognizable works that made it big on Broadway, but one special project—the annual Patsy Cline tribute—is an original that comes back in a different guise each year. ~ 4220 Forsyth Road; 478-477-3342, 478-471-7529; www.maconlittletheatre.org.

Founded in 1976, the 80-member **Macon Symphony Orchestra** presents three pops concerts a year along with six youth concerts and six subscription concerts. ~ 4760 Forsyth Road; 478-301-5300.

The music department at **Mercer University** puts on 40 to 50 concerts (classical and jazz performances along with faculty and visiting artist recitals) at Newton Recital Hall and Willingham Auditorium on campus. ~ 1400 Coleman Avenue; 478-301-2700.

The **Mercer University Theater Series** takes place at either the Grand Opera House or on campus at the Back Door Theater. ~ 1400 Coleman Avenue; 478-301-2700, box office 478-301-2958.

Whiskey River offers live country music and other entertainment Wednesday through Saturday. Cover. ~ 4570 Pio Nono Avenue; 478-788-3000

Live bands and other entertainment are presented Wednesday through Sunday at **550 Blues**. Cover. ~ 550 Riverside Drive; 478-750-0005.

Deejays play dance music most nights at **Chasen Lounge** in the Holiday Inn at the Conference Center. ~ 3590 Riverside Drive; 478-474-2610.

If the spirit moves you Thursday through Saturday, you can hear gospel music at **Buckner's Music Hall and Restaurant** up in Jackson. ~ 1168 Bucksnort Road (Route 75N, Exit 66), Jackson (about 45 minutes northwest of Macon); 770-775-6150.

BEACHES & PARKS

FREEDOM PARK This 27-acre park gives municipal government a good name. With a swimming pool, three softball diamonds, five baseball diamonds, picnic shelters, a playground and a game room, this tree-lined parcel is a gem. A seven-acre lake is stocked with bass, bream, crappie, channel catfish and other species and is open to licensed fishers from April to October, when it's closed for restocking. Canada geese, hawks, cranes and several kinds of ducks are frequent visitors, depending on the season. Closed Sunday. Swimming pool fee, $1. ~ 3301 Roff Avenue; 478-751-9280; www.macon.ga.us.

LAKE TOBESOFKEE RECREATION AREA ≈ ⚓ ⛵ Sandy Beach and Claystone parks offer picnic pavilions, restrooms and access to Lake Tobesofkee, which is fed by Tobesofkee Creek and stocked with a variety of fish (crappie, bream, catfish and several kinds of bass). There is a full marina and a lake-view restaurant at Claystone Park, and campsites there as well as at Arrowwood. White-sand beaches, the nicest ones west of the ocean, are replenished annually and staffed with lifeguards in summer. Sandy Beach has lighted tennis courts and a softball field. Pets are allowed. Day-use fee, $3. ~ 6600 Mosely-Dixon Road, three miles from Route 475 west of Macon; 478-474-8770; www.co.bibb.ga.us/laketobesofkee.

▲ There are 100 sites, some with water and electricity; $15 to $18 per night.

South of Macon

Small cities and country towns define the flat landscape south of Macon. The area is known for camellias, peaches and cotton, and, among people with a long memory, the tumultuous trial of Tom Woolfolk, charged with killing his family in a saga that preceded, and was later compared to, the ax-swinging antics of Lizzie Borden some three years later. Most of the drama—at least that part of it subsequent to the murders—took place in the Houston (pronounced HOW-stun) County Courthouse in Perry in 1887. "Bloody Tom" was hanged in 1890 after the case failed in its appeal to the Georgia Supreme Court. Ten years later, another murderer confessed to the crime.

Other towns in this area have more in the way of bonafide attractions, but mostly this is good meandering country, where the delights of out-of-the-way sights reward the leisurely visitor. From late November through March, the camellias provide a riot of color, followed by the billowing petals of peach blossoms later in the year.

SIGHTS

From Macon, the easiest route south is on the oh-so-boring interstate. If you are interested in aviation, however, head instead for Route 129, which runs down to **Warner Robins**, a trip that should take less than half an hour.

If you don't know a B-25 from a B-52, make a beeline to the **Museum of Aviation**, where nearly 100 aircraft and missiles are collected on Warner Robins Air Force Base. Smithsonian movies are shown on the hour and there are exhibits on World War I, Desert Storm, the Flying Tigers and the Tuskegee Airmen, among other displays. Admission. ~ 1942 Heritage Boulevard, Warner Robins; 478-926-6870; www.museumofaviation.org.

From Warner Robins, drive west on Route 247, cross Route 75 and head south on Route 49 for less than five miles. You are approaching one of the most fantastic camellia collections in Georgia, if not the country. **Massee Lane Gardens** has nine acres with some 2000 plants blooming in the winter and early spring in the shade of soaring pine trees. On the grounds are a greenhouse, a Japanese garden—stocked with *koi* for a meditative inspiration—a gazebo and, in a carefully tended gallery, what is considered the most complete collection of Edward Marshall Boehm porcelains in the world. There are also other porcelain figurines in the Stevens-Taylor Gallery and in the Fetterman Museum. If you're not acquainted with camellias, start your visit with a 15-minute slide presentation; afterward, you can buy camellia plants to take home. The Annual Camellia Festival is held the second week of each February. Admission. ~ 100 Massee Lane, Fort Valley; 478-967-2358, 478-967-2722; www.camellias-acs.com.

HIDDEN ►

The **Lane Packing Company**, which grows 30 varieties of peaches and 10 of pecans, is open for free, self-guided, cat-walk tours of their peach-packing facility from May through August. The seasonal tours are available daily from 8 a.m. to 8 p.m., depending on the harvest. Visitors are also welcome to pick strawberries from March through May. Also on site are a café (open for lunch), and a roadside market selling peaches, pecans and strawberries as well as seasonal fruits, and packaged peach and onion products such as jams and salad dressings. ~ 50 Lane Road, Fort Valley; 800-277-3224, 478-825-3592; www.lane packing.com.

When you leave the land of camellias, take Route 341 southeast and cross Route 75 to visit the town of **Perry**. Make your first pullover at Exit 42 and head east following signs to the **Perry Area Welcome Center**. You can get maps of the downtown historic district and information about antique shopping, a favorite Perry pastime. ~ 101 General Courtney Hodges Boulevard, Perry; 478-988-8000; www.perryga.com.

The point of a visit to Perry is the sweet little **historic downtown**, which should be the envy of towns five times its size. The restored buildings are mostly offices and shops but wandering around the four-square-block area is a delightful distraction, especially for people who like to shop in individually owned stores. You can pick up a walking-tour map at the Welcome Center.

There are a couple of points of interest in downtown Perry and they're across the street from each other. The **Houston County**

Courthouse you see today was built in 1850; the 1824 original was constructed the same year that the town of Wattsville was renamed in honor of Commodore Oliver Hazard Perry, who led his troops to a naval victory at Lake Erie in the War of 1812. It was Perry who is credited with saying, "We have met the enemy and they are ours," later paraphrased in the comic strip "Pogo" as "We have met the enemy and they is us." The old courthouse was the site of the trial of "Bloody Tom" Woolfolk (as journalists nicknamed him), a man charged with the brutal murder of nine members of his family in 1887. He was convicted in Bibb County that same year, but the state Supreme Court ordered a new trial. According to a recounting of the tale in *Touring the Backroads of North*

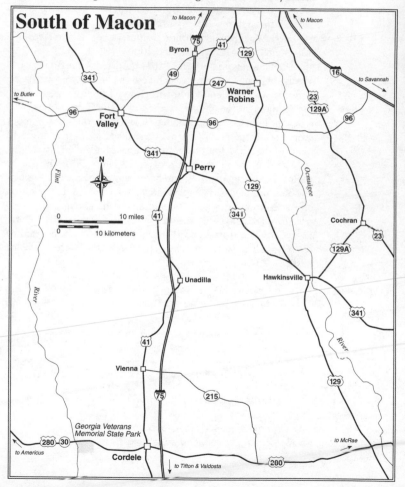

and South Georgia, Woolfolk was a day laborer on a plantation and none too happy to be living in poverty amidst such wealth. His Perry trial attracted a mob of onlookers, who probably had a field day with the rural names in the case—Georgia Bird, who married Tom in the corridor of a moving train and left him three weeks later, and Temperance West, one of the relatives Woolfolk murdered. It took a jury 12 minutes to declare him guilty—again—and he was hanged. ~ At the corner of Main and Jernigan streets.

No doubt many of the observers and newspaper reporters who flocked to Perry for the Tom Woolfolk murder trial booked into the **Perry Hotel**, across Main Street from the courthouse. The hotel began life as Cox's Inn, a stagecoach stop in the 1850s. It then became the Perry in the 1870s, and when automobile traffic started flowing through the area, visitors en route to Florida to escape the bitter Yankee winters found the hotel a convenient layover. ~ 800 Main Street, Perry; 478-987-1000.

After meandering around Perry, head south on Route 75 to **Vienna**, which is a town just a mile or so west of the interstate. Between Route 75 and the town, you will need to keep a lookout on the right (north) side of the road. The **Cotton Museum** is a delightful place to learn about Georgia's second-most famous crop. Local farmers and other interested citizens have contributed many of the items, but this museum, housed in an old farmhouse, is more than a collection of artifacts. A short video and all the tools for plowing, planting and harvesting make the other exhibits come alive. Displays explain how the farmers sold their cotton and even how slaves were bought and sold. The museum is especially interesting since the cotton consumption in this country nearly doubled from 1985 to 1995 and seems to be continuing on an upswing. Closed Sunday. ~ 1321 East Union Street, Vienna; 229-268-2045.

HIDDEN ►

LODGING   Located six miles east of Route 75 near Warner Robins Air Force Base, the **Holiday Inn of Warner Robins** has 152 meticulous rooms

AUTHOR FAVORITE

I liked the old-timey pace of things at the **New Perry Hotel/Motel**. The three-story inn opened in 1925 (on the site of the old Perry Hotel) and reached its heyday in the 1970s. There are 26 comfy rooms in the hotel and 17 motel accommodations around the pool. Pets are allowed with a fee. ~ 800 Main Street, Perry; 478-987-1000, 800-877-3779; www.new perryhotel.com, e-mail reservations@newperryhotel.com. BUDGET TO MODERATE.

arranged in three two-story buildings. It is pleasantly landscaped and has some deluxe poolside units as well as a restaurant. ~ 2024 Watson Boulevard, Warner Robins; 478-923-8871, fax 478-923-1930. MODERATE.

The **Comfort Inn**, right across the street from the Warner Robins Air Force Base Museum of Aviation, has 77 large, nicely furnished rooms, some with fireplaces and whirlpool baths. Also special, it has a good selection of suites, interior corridors on both stories, and a policy of accepting pets for a $25 fee. ~ Route 129 at Route 247, Warner Robins; 478-922-7555, fax 478-929-3404. BUDGET TO DELUXE.

In a neighborhood of very fine homes (what's called the Everett Square Historic District), a standout is the creamy brick Italian Renaissance Revival number known as the **Evans-Cantrell House**. Built in 1916 by A. J. "The Peach King" Evans, it was regarded as ahead of its time. Like the mansions built by other agricultural and mercantile kingpins in the past, this one was a showplace, with light switches in the closets, a double-headed shower in the master bath and a central vacuum system—advances that were high-tech in the old days. Four rooms with private baths carry out architectural details like hardwood floors, mahogany paneling and high ceilings that grace the ground-floor parlor, library and formal dining room. The guest rooms are decorated in antiques, including a convenient desk. A full breakfast is included. ~ 300 College Street, Fort Valley; 478-825-0611, 888-923-0611, fax 478-822-9925; www.evans-cantrellhouse.com. MODERATE TO DELUXE.

A collection of expertly preserved houses and cottages comprises **Henderson Village**, which welcomes overnight guests into what, at first glance, looks like an upscale retirement community. In all, some 24 rooms and suites are scattered among nine 19th-century homes and tenant cottages amid 18 acres. Each has a gas log fireplace, fine art and framed pressed regional plants. Game hunting excursions available. Full breakfast included. ~ 125 South Langston Circle, Perry; 478-988-8696, 888-615-9722, fax 478-988-9009; www.hendersonvillage.com, e-mail info@hendersonvillage.com. ULTRA-DELUXE.

DINING

The **New Perry Hotel Restaurant Dining Room** on the ground floor of the eponymous hotel is the kind of establishment where the local Kiwanis and Lions meet regularly. Classic Southern fare with all the trimmings is served in a green-and-white dining room with paintings of camellias on every wall. Expect dishes like grilled Georgia rainbow trout, Angus sirloin and teriyaki chicken with sides like cheese grits soufflé, turnip greens and broccoli cheese casserole. Closed Sunday. ~ 800 Main Street, Perry; 478-987-1000, 800-877-3779. MODERATE.

You don't have to be a guest of the inn to enjoy a meal at the **Langston House Restaurant** at Henderson Village. In this elegant, three-room dining room in a 19th-century house, three meals are served most days. Typical dinner entrées include Southern-fried sea bass, roast rack of lamb, barbecued salmon and asparagus tempura. No dinner Sunday. Closed Monday. ~ 125 South Langston Circle, Perry; 478-988-8696, 888-615-9722, fax 478-988-9009. DELUXE TO ULTRA-DELUXE.

SHOPPING While the big antique centers sprawl out on the interstate and the shopping centers fringe the old town, downtown Perry has one little restored street—Carroll—where window-shopping will almost inevitably lead to conversations with the owners and salespeople. If you'd like to read a bit deeper into Southern culture, pick up a novel or find something for the kids to look at, check out **The Perry Book Store**. It has both new and used fiction and nonfiction. Closed Sunday. ~ 907 Carroll Street, Perry; 478-987-0600.

> If you're traveling with a model airplane, Georgia Veterans Memorial State Park is the place to fly it; there's a model-airplane strip in the field behind the aircraft displays.

Also on this street, **Carlton Interiors** specializes in elegant home attire. Best of all, some of the gift items and accessories are small enough to tote or ship home. ~ 903 Carroll Street, Perry; 478-987-4511.

If you're traveling with small ones who seem to outgrow their outfits every week, take them to the **Sugarplum Tree**, which is jam-packed with clothes and gifts for infants, toddlers and older children. ~ 917 Carroll Street, Perry; 478-987-0970.

NIGHTLIFE Country, gospel and bluegrass music are performed at the **Powersville Opry** early every Saturday evening from 5 to 9:30 p.m. Admission is free but donations are welcome. ~ Powersville Road (off Route 49 and the 247 connector) between Byron and Fort Valley; 478-956-4983.

The **Perry Players Community Theatre** stages popular contemporary plays. ~ 813 Forrest Hill Road, Perry; 478-987-5354.

BEACHES & PARKS **GEORGIA VETERANS MEMORIAL STATE PARK** 🏃 🚣 ⛱ 🚤 ⛵
This park, with its 1308 acres of woodland and landscaped gardens on Lake Blackshear, is one of the state's top parks. It's not all that easy to find, and most people cruising at the maximum m.p.h. on nearby Route 75 probably aren't in the mood to explore. Established in 1946 in memory of Georgia veterans, it was formed by the backwater of the Crisp County hydroelectric dam, the first county-owned project of its kind in the U.S. The museum here boasts a B-29 bomber that flew in the South Pacific during World War II, as well as an F-84F, a powerful atomic bomb

carrier. There are also artillery pieces and both Sherman and Patton tanks, as befits a museum focused on the history of U.S. wars from the Revolution through Vietnam. Boaters have access to 8700 acres on Lake Blackshear; waterskiing is permitted. Swimming is allowed in the lake as well as in a swimming pool, both open between Memorial Day and Labor Day; there are bathhouses at both. Additional amenities include picnic areas. Day-use fee, $2. ~ Route 280, Cordele, about ten miles southwest of Vienna; 229-276-2371.

▲ There are 77 tent/RV sites, $17 to $22 per night. Reservations: 800-864-7275.

Outdoor Adventures

FISHING

The seven-acre lake at Macon's **Freedom Park** is stocked with bass, bream, crappie, channel catfish and other species. It's open from April to October but closed the rest of the year to allow the lake to be restocked.

From a boat or from the pier, you can angle for crappie, bream and several kinds of bass at **Lake Tobesofkee**. If you're camping at the lake and have any luck, you can cook up your catch on any of the permanent charcoal grills scattered around the campsites.

BOATING

Several lakes in this region allow boats but have none for rent, although there are exceptions. **Hard Labor Creek State Park** has boats and canoes. ~ Two miles north of Rutledge; 706-557-3001. **Indian Springs State Park** also has boats for rent. ~ 678 Lake Clark Road, Flovilla; 770-504-2277.

GOLF

Lakes and easy-going hills add a picturesque element to the golf courses in this region. There's a mix, from nine-hole municipal courses to the kind of resort courses that land on Top-10 lists.

In summer 2005, **The Creek at Hard Labor** got a major facelift with new ultra-dwarf Bermuda grass planted and expected to create one of the best playing surfaces in the area. The 18-hole, par-72 course has 39 bunkers plus a pro shop. ~ Hard Labor State Park, two miles north of Rutledge; 706-557-3006, 800-434-0982 (tee times).

The **Uncle Remus Golf Course** has only nine holes, but since it also has five sets of tees you can make it as challenging as you want. We're pretty sure you won't find any briar patches among the hazards. ~ 120 Hambone Holle Drive, Eatonton; 706-485-6850.

Great Waters, an 18-hole, par-72 course designed by Jack Nicklaus, is on the shores of Lake Oconee (at least, the back nine are). It's been voted second only to Augusta National as the top golf course in Georgia. ~ 130 Woodcrest Drive Northeast, Eatonton; 706-467-0600.

Tom Wieskopf and international course designer Jay Morrish designed the 18-hole course at **The Harbor Club**. Among the larger water hazards is Lake Oconee. ~ Route 44, Greensboro; 706-453-9690.

The **Barrington Hall Golf Club** has 18 holes as well as a pro shop and a full-service restaurant on the premises. Rare for a semiprivate course, Barrington has bent-grass greens and an exceptional layout rated three and a half stars by *Golf Digest*. Closed to the public Saturday and Sunday after 1 p.m., and Monday. ~ 104 Stoney Creek Drive, Macon; 478-757-8358.

Macon's municipal golf course is the **Bowden Golf Course**, which hosts the Cherry Blossom Four Ball Tournament every year during the Cherry Blossom Festival. The 18-hole course has a driving range, pro shop and snack bar. ~ 3111 Millerfield Road, Macon; 478-742-1610.

Located along Lake Blackshear and dotted with loblolly pines, the 18-hole **Georgia Veterans Memorial Golf Course** offers a challenging assortment of water, mounds and sand. There's a full-service pro shop as well as cart rentals. ~ Georgia Veterans Memorial State Park, Route 280, Cordele, about 10 miles southwest of Vienna; 229-276-2377.

TENNIS

Twelve lighted courts are located at the **Tattnall Square Tennis Center** in Tattnall Square Park. Lessons are available. Fee. ~ Oglethorpe and College streets, Macon; 478-751-9196.

The **John Drew Smith Tennis Center**, operated by the Macon Parks and Recreation Department, has 24 lit courts. Fee. ~ 3280 North Ingle Place, Macon; 478-474-5075.

HIKING

Hiking trails in this region are few and far between but regional parks offer ample opportunities for a stroll. All distances listed for hiking trails are one way unless otherwise noted.

The trails at **Ocmulgee National Monument** are interconnected, adding up to about six easy miles on the east side of Macon. You can pick up detailed maps and brochures at the visitors center. Expect only a few noticeable changes in elevation, all at various mounds such as the 45-foot-high Temple Mound. This is the best way to tour the historic site and observe wildlife (such as deer and other small mammals like squirrels and the flora) and mostly wildflowers and woodland habitats, stunning in spring and fall. The **Human Cultural Trails** (4 miles) focus on the mounds. The lowland **River Trail** (.9 mile) leads to the Ocmulgee River; it is easily navigable only during dry weather as it is occasionally flooded. Raccoons, beavers and muskrats are common sights along with ducks, kingfishers and other water birds. The **Opelofa Trail** (.25 mile) circles a swampy lowland and joins the **Loop Trail** (.3 mile) that's separate from the mounds.

The **Wildflower Trail** (.4 mile) is another good route for spotting birds and deer.

Madison, Milledgeville and Macon create a triangle marked by **Route 20** on the north and **Route 75** on the south. The major north–south highway is **Route 441** between Madison and Milledgeville, and **Route 49**, which runs most of the way between Milledgeville and Macon. South of Macon, Route 75 continues all the way to Florida.

Transportation

CAR

AIR

Macon's **Lewis B. Wilson Municipal Airport** is served by Atlantic Southeast Airlines (part of Delta), but larger aircraft are routed to Atlanta's Hartsfield-Jackson International Airport. It is simple to get shuttle service from Macon to Hartsfield. Allow about 90 minutes to two hours for the trip, depending on the time of day and the day of the week. ~ 1000 Terminal Drive, Macon; 478-788-3760.

In Macon, **Groome Transportation** offers transportation to and from the Atlanta airport (from both Macon and Warner Robins Air Force Base) every hour after about 4 a.m., with the last run south from the airport at around 9 p.m. ~ 4540 Sheraton Drive, Macon; 478-471-1616, 800-537-7903.

TRAIN

The nearest **Amtrak** (800-872-7245; www.amtrak.com) station is in Atlanta. See Chapter Five for more information.

BUS

Greyhound Bus Lines (800-231-2222; www.greyhound.com) has a station in Macon. ~ 65 Spring Street; 912-743-5411.

Georgia Trailways links Macon with other regional destinations at its station at 448 Pine Street; 912-743-8489.

CAR RENTALS

The drive from Atlanta's Hartsfield-Jackson International Airport to Macon is roughly one and a half hours. Please see Chapter Five for more information.

Hertz Rent A Car (800-654-3131) has cars in Macon at the Middle Georgia Regional Airport.

PUBLIC TRANSIT

The **Macon-Bibb County Transit Authority** provides intra-city bus service Monday through Saturday from 6 a.m. to 7:45 p.m via the Cherry Blossom Express for 75 cents one way. ~ 815 Riverside Drive, Macon; 478-746-1318, 478-746-1387; www. mta-mac.com.

TAXIS

There is no taxi service in the really small towns of middle Georgia but **Macon City Cab** (478-746-1121, 478-825-0422) serves Macon and Fort Valley. **Yellow Cab Co.** operates in both Macon (478-742-6464) and Milledgeville (478-453-7414). Serving Milledgeville are ABC **Taxi Cab Co.** (478-451-3281), **G&M Cab** (478-452-7727) and **Sugar Shack Taxicabs** (478-452-2841).

Index

Lodging Index

Dining Index

HIDDEN GUIDES

Adventure travel or a relaxing vacation?—"Hidden" guidebooks are the only travel books in the business to provide detailed information on both. Aimed at environmentally aware travelers, our motto is "Where Vacations Meet Adventures." These books combine details on unique hotels, restaurants and sightseeing with information on camping, sports and hiking for the outdoor enthusiast.

PARADISE FAMILY GUIDES

Ideal for families traveling with kids of any age—toddlers to teenagers—Paradise Family Guides offer a blend of travel information unlike any other guides to the Hawaiian islands. With vacation ideas and tropical adventures that are sure to satisfy both action-hungry youngsters and relaxation-seeking parents, these guides meet the specific needs of each and every family member.

Ulysses Press books are available at bookstores everywhere. If any of the following titles are unavailable at your local bookstore, ask the bookseller to order them.

You can also order books directly from Ulysses Press
P.O. Box 3440, Berkeley, CA 94703
800-377-2542 or 510-601-8301
fax: 510-601-8307
www.ulyssespress.com
e-mail: ulysses@ulyssespress.com

ABOUT THE AUTHOR

MARTY OLMSTEAD, a Savannah native, is a freelance writer based in Sonoma, California, where she specializes in articles on wine and food. She is author of *Hidden Tennessee* (Ulysses Press) and *The California Directory of Fine Wineries* (Ten Speed Press), and co-author of *Hidden Florida* (Ulysses Press) and *Hidden Wine Country* (Ulysses Press). Her articles have appeared in numerous national and regional publications, including *Travel & Leisure*, *Wine Adventure*, the *Los Angeles Times*, *America West*, *Odyssey* and the *San Francisco Chronicle*.

ABOUT THE ILLUSTRATOR

DOUG MᶜCARTHY, a native New Yorker, lives in the San Francisco Bay area with his family. His illustrations appear in a number of Ulysses Press guides, including *Hidden Kauai*, *Hidden British Columbia*, *Hidden Utah*, *Hidden Tennessee*, *Hidden Bahamas* and *The New Key to Ecuador and the Galápagos*.

HIDDEN GUIDEBOOKS

____ Hidden Arizona, $16.95
____ Hidden Bahamas, $14.95
____ Hidden Baja, $14.95
____ Hidden Belize, $15.95
____ Hidden Big Island of Hawaii, $13.95
____ Hidden Boston & Cape Cod, $14.95
____ Hidden British Columbia, $18.95
____ Hidden Cancún & the Yucatán, $16.95
____ Hidden Carolinas, $17.95
____ Hidden Coast of California, $18.95
____ Hidden Colorado, $15.95
____ Hidden Disneyland, $13.95
____ Hidden Florida, $18.95
____ Hidden Florida Keys & Everglades, $13.95
____ Hidden Georgia, $16.95
____ Hidden Guatemala, $16.95
____ Hidden Hawaii, $18.95
____ Hidden Idaho, $14.95
____ Hidden Kauai, $13.95
____ Hidden Los Angeles, $14.95
____ Hidden Maine, $15.95

____ Hidden Maui, $13.95
____ Hidden Miami, $14.95
____ Hidden Montana, $15.95
____ Hidden New England, $18.95
____ Hidden New Mexico, $15.95
____ Hidden New Orleans, $14.95
____ Hidden Oahu, $13.95
____ Hidden Oregon, $15.95
____ Hidden Pacific Northwest, $18.95
____ Hidden San Diego, $14.95
____ Hidden Salt Lake City, $14.95
____ Hidden San Francisco & Northern California, $18.95
____ Hidden Seattle, $13.95
____ Hidden Southern California, $18.95
____ Hidden Southwest, $19.95
____ Hidden Tahiti, $17.95
____ Hidden Tennessee, $16.95
____ Hidden Utah, $16.95
____ Hidden Walt Disney World, $13.95
____ Hidden Washington, $15.95
____ Hidden Wine Country, $13.95
____ Hidden Wyoming, $15.95

PARADISE FAMILY GUIDES

____ Paradise Family Guides: Kaua'i, $16.95
____ Paradise Family Guides: Maui, $16.95
____ Paradise Family Guides: Big Island of Hawai'i, $16.95

Mark the book(s) you're ordering and enter the total cost here ⟹ [   ]

California residents add 8.75% sales tax here ⟹ [   ]

Shipping, check box for your preferred method and enter cost here ⟹ [   ]

❑ BOOK RATE   FREE! FREE! FREE!

❑ PRIORITY MAIL/UPS GROUND   cost of postage

❑ UPS OVERNIGHT OR 2-DAY AIR   cost of postage

[   ]

Billing, enter total amount due here and check method of payment ⟹

❑ CHECK   ❑ MONEY ORDER

❑ VISA/MASTERCARD _____EXP. DATE_____

NAME _____PHONE_____

ADDRESS _____

CITY_____ STATE _____ ZIP _____

MONEY-BACK GUARANTEE ON DIRECT ORDERS PLACED THROUGH ULYSSES PRESS.